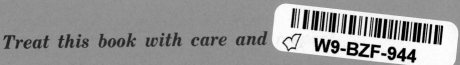

Treat this book with care and

It should become part of your personal
and professional library. It will
serve you well at any number
of points during your
professional career.

C. VAN EATON

Intermediate Microeconomic Theory

DAVID R. KAMERSCHEN

Professor and Head
Department of Economics
University of Georgia

LLOYD M. VALENTINE

Professor of Economics
Department of Economics
University of Cincinnati

Published by

SOUTH-WESTERN PUBLISHING CO.

H71

CINCINNATI   WEST CHICAGO, III.   DALLAS   PELHAM MANOR, N.Y.
PALO ALTO, CALIF.   BRIGHTON, ENGLAND

PREFACE

Our major goal in writing this text has been the clear presentation of the most important concepts of price theory. Although use of the theory and its applications are interspersed throughout the text narrative, the emphasis of the text is on the theory itself. However, we have tried to explain some theory within the context of significant contemporary economic problems and issues — letting the theoretical principles emerge as living and socially relevant explanations of economic reality.

The word "intermediate" in the title of this book is meant to signify that it is written expressly for students in courses in intermediate price theory typically at the junior-senior level, for students in microeconomics courses in first-year MBA and MA programs, and for students of managerial economics (if supplemented with some additional applications).

All the standard price theory topics are covered. The subject matter is decidedly specific, traditional, and theoretical. We tried to approach, in unique, often graphic, and hopefully lucid ways, areas which often remain foggy in students' minds. Much attention has been given to the wording of the narrative so that what is said is exactly what we meant to say. There are over 150 numbered graphs in the text designed to enhance understanding of the narrative. We hope that these will minimize ambiguities in students' minds; but beyond this, such graphs are a part of the language of economists without which many of us are tongue-tied.

Care has been taken to give a balanced treatment of the more conservative "Chicago School" theories about information, advertising, monopolistic competition, etc. Controversial issues have not been avoided, although we have tried to be careful in distinguishing conclusions based on objective, positive economics from those depending upon subjective value judgements and normative analysis.

The first three chapters contain most of what one needs to move from a beginning course in economics to the intermediate course. Chapter 1 contains an introduction into the nature, methodology, and techniques of microeconomics. In Chapter 2, an extended discussion of stock-dominated markets (as opposed to flow-dominated markets) is undertaken which, as far as we know, is unique among current texts. Chapter 3 is devoted entirely to the elasticities of demand and supply — another feature unique to this text.

Part 2: Demand — The Analysis of Consumer Behavior, includes the derivation of the demand schedule described in an intuitive manner and by the approaches of Marshall and Walras. Classical cardinal utility theory as well as ordinal utility theory is presented. The two alternative approaches to measuring the substitution and income effects — the Hicksian method and the Slutsky method — are described. Also included in this section are graphic presentations of indifference curves derived from utility functions and a demonstration of the logic of revealed preference theory.

In the following section, Part 3: Supply—The Analysis of Production and Cost, total variable cost, average variable cost, and marginal cost are derived graphically from the appropriate productivity schedules to help show the relationship between input expense and output cost. Both the production function and isoquantic approaches are explored as prerequisites in deriving supply curves.

Part 4: Market Organization and the Theory of the Firm, includes a discussion of the distinction between quasi and virtual (or shadow) supply curves, the delineation of six common misconceptions concerning monopoly, a detailed account of price discrimination, and an extended discussion of alternative oligopoly theories. Unique to this text is an entire chapter devoted to summarizing the economic effects of monopoly. This chapter fuses the economic theories and empirical findings of numerous economists which previously had been scattered in articles in professional journals, microeconomic theory textbooks, industrial organization textbooks, etc.

The last section, Part 5: Distribution Theory, devotes more space to factor pricing under alternative market combinations, including monopsony, and to the theory of distribution than do most intermediate price theory texts. After developing the general principles of functional distribution, we applied them to wages, rents, interest, and profits. A graphic presentation of the labor supply with a guaranteed minimum income is included.

The basic text requires no knowledge of mathematics beyond algebra and plane geometry. However, sections called "Mathematical Notes" have been appended to 12 of the 19 chapters. These appendices include economic concepts and phenomena that can be explained best through the use of formal mathematics. However, these appendices can be skipped easily without loss of continuity from one chapter to the next, although even those students who are not prepared to understand the mathematics should be aware of its importance for more advanced economics study.

Each chapter concludes with a series of questions and exercises. The Instructor's Manual answers the end-of-chapter questions and also details a carefully selected supplementary readings list for each chapter.

Since a textbook by its very nature represents a distillation of the ideas and concepts of numerous researchers in a field, we are heavily indebted to past and present economists. In addition, the text has been improved from questions, discussions, and comprehensive reviews by both students and faculty too numerous to name over the last ten years. However, we do wish to extend a particular expression of gratitude for the suggestions, corrections, and patience of successive classes of students at the University of Missouri, the University of Georgia, and the University of Cincinnati as the manuscript was going through various preparatory stages. Many of our faculty colleagues have been extremely generous in giving of their time and knowledge which contributed importantly. To them we are thankful.

It would be gratifying if we could claim that after studying this textbook one would know all the answers. Unfortunately, it is not that simple. Capable, competent, and experienced economists are not always in agreement with each other. However, an essential characteristic of any dynamic field of knowledge is that there are disagreements. These differences merely underscore the continuing importance of the field of microeconomic theory. Without any dispute, there would be neither challenge nor progress. Humanity emerged from the Dark Ages only when and because people began to question the traditional truths.

However, we do think that a mastery of the contents of this text will provide students with a tool box—complete with analytical knives, saws, pliers, and hammers—with which they can predict and explain economic behavior as well as analyze many contemporary problems, both large and small. Because the particular nature of these problems changes year to year, month to month, and even day to day, we have emphasized the theory itself in this text. Because microeconomics is problem-oriented, a microeconomic tool kit will allow students and their instructors, jointly or separately, to address some of the most significant and complicated problems faced by our society today. If students do not acquire these microeconomic tools or find microeconomics challenging, exciting, and useful after studying this text, the authors have failed in their basic purpose in writing the text. If we have failed, we are confident that the market, as usual, will mete out the appropriate punishment for producers who do not satisfy their consumers.

David R. Kamerschen
Athens, Georgia

Lloyd M. Valentine
Cincinnati, Ohio

CONTENTS

PART

1 INTRODUCTION AND METHODOLOGY

Chapter

1 Introduction   1

MICROECONOMIC THEORY. MANAGING SCARCE RESOURCES. PRODUCTION POSSIBILITY CURVE. METHODOLOGY. CHARACTERISTICS OF ECONOMIC THEORIES. Theory as Generalization. Theory as Abstraction. Mathematical and Graphical Techniques. THE PLAN OF STUDY.

Chapter

2 Fundamentals of Demand and Supply   13

THE BASIC NATURE OF A MARKET. THE DEMAND SIDE OF THE MARKET. Stock-Dominated Markets. Flow-Dominated Markets. Time and the Demand Curve. Other Determinants of Demand. LAW OF DEMAND. THE SUPPLY SIDE OF THE MARKET. Determinants of Supply. Importance of Costs of Production. Market Supply Curve. Joint Supply. LAW OF SUPPLY. SUPPLY AND DEMAND ANALYSIS.

Chapter

3 Elasticity of Demand and Supply   37

ELASTICITY. Price Elasticity of Demand Formulas. The Total Spending Test of Elasticity. Graphical Representation of Elasticity. REVENUE AND ELASTICITY. DETERMINANTS OF PRICE ELASTICITY OF DEMAND. OTHER ELASTICITIES. Cross Price Elasticity of Demand. Income Elasticity of Demand. Elasticity of Expectations. PRICE ELASTICITY OF SUPPLY. Arc Elasticity. Graphic Demonstration of Supply Elasticity. Proof of Linear Supply Elasticities. APPENDIX A: MATHEMATICAL NOTES ON DEMAND ELASTICITIES. Note 1: "Own" Price Elasticity of Demand. Note 2: Income Elasticity of Demand. Note 3: Cross Elasticity of Demand. Note 4: General Formulation. APPENDIX B: MATHEMATICAL NOTES ON SUPPLY ELASTICITIES. Note 1: Linear Supply Elasticities. Note 2: Linear Supply Curves, Elasticity, and Total Revenue.

PART

2 DEMAND—THE ANALYSIS OF CONSUMER BEHAVIOR

Chapter

4 Cardinal Utility Approach to Consumer Behavior 67

THE CONCEPT OF UTILITY. Objectives, Limitations, Problems. Cardinal and Ordinal Utility. TOTAL AND MARGINAL UTILITY. LAW OF DIMINISHING MARGINAL UTILITY. CONSUMER BEHAVIOR. Equimarginal Principle. Maximization of Utility Rules. Algebraic Solution of Optimum Conditions. DERIVATION OF THE DOWN-SLOPING DEMAND SCHEDULE FROM THE MARGINAL UTILITY SCHEDULE. Intuitive Approach. Marshallian Approach. Walrasian Approach. INCOME AND SUBSTITUTION EFFECTS SEPARATED. APPLICATIONS OF CARDINAL UTILITY THEORY. Consumer Surplus. Interpersonal Comparisons of Utility. Exchange. Economics of Search. Diamond-Water Paradox. APPENDIX: MATHEMATICAL NOTES. Note 1: Consumer Optimality. Method 1: Substitution Approach. Method 2: LaGrange Multipliers. Note 2: Consumer Surplus (*CS*). Note 3: Homogeneous Functions.

Chapter

5 Ordinal Utility or Indifference Curve Approach To Consumer Behavior 96

NATURE OF INDIFFERENCE RELATIONSHIPS. Completeness or Complete Ordering. Nonsatiation, or More is Preferred to Less. Consistency or Transitivity. Continuity or Substitutability. Optimality. Indifference Schedule. INDIFFERENCE CURVES FROM INDIFFERENCE SCHEDULE. Quadrant *A*. Quadrant *B*. Quadrant *C*. Quadrant *D*. CHARACTERISTICS OF INDIFFERENCE CURVES. COMPLEMENTS AND SUBSTITUTES. BUDGET LINE. UTILITY MAXIMIZATION WITH INDIFFERENCE CURVES. RELATION BETWEEN CARDINAL AND ORDINAL UTILITY APPROACHES. OTHER SIMILARITIES.

Chapter

6 Further Development and Application of Indifference Curve Analysis 121

SUMMARY OF OPTIMALITY WITH NORMAL INDIFFERENCE CURVES. CONSUMPTION DETERMINATION WITH NONNORMAL INDIFFERENCE CURVES. PRICE-CONSUMPTION CURVE AND DERIVATION OF DEMAND CURVE FROM AN INDIFFERENCE

CURVE. DERIVING PRICE ELASTICITY OF DEMAND (η) FROM THE PRICE-CONSUMPTION CURVE (*PCC*). INCOME-CONSUMPTION CURVE AND THE DERIVATION OF ENGEL CURVES. ENGEL CURVES AND INCOME ELASTICITY. THE INCOME EFFECT AND THE SUBSTITUTION EFFECT. Compensated Demand Functions: Hicksian Method. Compensated Demand Functions: Slutsky Method. Ordinary vs. Compensated Demand Functions. Giffen Good vs. Inferior Good. APPLICATIONS OF ORDINAL UTILITY THEORY. Consumer Surplus. Exchange. Supply of Labor Services. Additional Applications. REVEALED PREFERENCE THEORY. Constructing the Superior Boundary. Constructing the Inferior Boundary.

Chapter

7   Market Structure and the Firm's Demand Curve   149

FOUR BASIC MARKET MODELS. PURE COMPETITION. Other Competitive Dimensions. Characteristics of Competitive Markets. PURE MONOPOLY. MONOPOLISTIC COMPETITION. OLIGOPOLY. FURTHER STRUCTURAL CHARACTERISTICS. Proximity. Interproduct and Interindustry Competition. Technological Change. FIRM DEMAND CURVES AND MARKET ORGANIZATION. Perfect Competition. Imperfect Competition. Oligopoly.

PART

3   SUPPLY—THE ANALYSIS OF PRODUCTION AND COST

Chapter

8   Theory of Production   161

THE PRODUCTION FUNCTION. Technical and Economic Efficiency. Principle of Substitution. Importance of Technology. The Time Element. Cobb-Douglas Production Function. SHORT-RUN PRODUCTION FUNCTIONS. Variable Proportions and the Law of Proportionality. Qualifications of the Law of Proportionality. Three Ways of Looking at Variable Proportions. Profit-Maximizing Conduct. Factor Symmetry of Stages 1 and 3. Least-Cost or Maximum Output. Three Possible Interrelationships Among Factors. VARYING THE "FIXED" FACTOR. Algebraic Formulation of Returns to Scale. Causes of Returns to Scale. APPENDIX: MATHEMATICAL NOTES. Note 1: Production Functions. Note 2: Optimality Conditions.

Chapter

9   Isoquant Approach to Production Theory   189

ISOQUANTS. Graphic Illustration. Slope of an Isoquant. Characteristics of Isoquants. Elasticity of Substitution. Additional Characteristics. Short-Run and Long-Run Relations. Isoclines and Ridge

Lines. ISOCOSTS AND THE OPTIMUM COMBINATION OF INPUTS.
Factor-Cost or Isocost Equation. The Optimum Combination of
Factors. Substitution and Output Effect. TECHNICAL PROGRESS.
APPENDIX: MATHEMATICAL NOTES. Note 1: Factor Optimum.
Note 2: Proof that Factor Demand Curves Are Downsloping. Note 3:
Homogeneous Functions. Note 4: Expansion Path. Note 5: A Sum-
mary of the Mathematical Properties of a Homogeneous Production
Function of Degree One (i.e., Linear Homogeneous), $q = f(a,b)$.
Note 6: A Summary of the Mathematical Properties of Homogeneous
Production Functions of Degree n, $q = f(a,b)$.

Chapter

10   Costs of Production   213

DECISION-MAKING BY THE FIRM IN DIFFERENT TIME HORIZONS.
Equimarginal Principle. Meaning of Costs and Profits. Time Con-
siderations. Costs, Profits, and Supply. SHORT-RUN COST FUNC-
TIONS. Importance of the Law of Proportionality. Total Cost Curves.
Per-Unit Cost Curves. THE LONG RUN. LONG-RUN COST FUNC-
TIONS. INTERNAL VS. EXTERNAL ECONOMIES OF SCALE. AP-
PENDIX: MATHEMATICAL NOTES. Note 1: Short-Run Cost Func-
tions. Note 2: Long-Run Cost Functions. Note 3: Normal Cost
Conditions. Note 4: Derivation of Cost Functions.

PART

4   MARKET ORGANIZATION AND THE THEORY OF THE FIRM

Chapter

11   Short-Run Pricing and Production under Pure Competition   241

RULES FOR SHORT-RUN PROFIT MAXIMIZATION. Three Possible
Outcomes. Restatement and Proof of the Basic Profit-Maximizing
Algorithm. ILLUSTRATION OF THE THREE POSSIBLE OUTCOMES.
Tabular Analysis. Graphic Analysis. COMPETITIVE FIRM'S SHORT-
RUN SUPPLY CURVE. SHIFTS IN SUPPLY CURVES. COMPETITIVE
INDUSTRY'S SHORT-RUN SUPPLY CURVE. SHORT-RUN EQUILIB-
RIA: FIRM AND INDUSTRY. APPENDIX: MATHEMATICAL NOTES.
Note 1: Industry Supply and Demand Curves. Note 2: Optimality
Conditions. Note 3: Derivation of Elasticity of Demand for a Firm.

Chapter

12   Long-Run Pricing and Production under Pure Competition   265

LONG-RUN SUPPLY CURVE. CAPITALIZATION OF RETURNS TO
FIXED FACTORS. LONG-RUN INDUSTRY SUPPLY CURVES. The
Triple Equality $P = MC =$ (minimum) AC. Quasi and Virtual Supply

Curves. ECONOMIC EFFECTS OF PURE COMPETITION. Society's Use of Its Scarce Means of Production. Competitive Market Results. Allocative Efficiency: The Triple Equality. LIMITATIONS IN A PERFECTLY FUNCTIONING COMPETITIVE ENVIRONMENT. Collective Commodities. Static and Dynamic Considerations. SHORTCOMINGS AS A RESULT OF MARKET IMPERFECTIONS. Consumers' Side. Producers' Side. APPENDIX: MATHEMATICAL NOTES. Note 1: Long-Run Cost Functions and Competition.

Chapter

13   Pricing and Production under Pure Monopoly   283

WHAT IS PURE MONOPOLY? ATTAINING AND MAINTAINING MONOPOLY POSITIONS. Natural Monopoly. Efficiency through Economies of Large-Scale Production. Research and Technological Progress. Differentiated Products. Ownership of Essential Raw Materials. The Investment Banker. The Established Firm Advantage. Collusive Action or Anticompetitive Practices. "Legal" Monopolies. COST OF PRODUCTION AND SALES REVENUE UNDER MONOPOLY. Cost of Production. Sales Revenue. MONOPOLY PRICING IN THE IMMEDIATE PERIOD. MONOPOLY PRICING AND PRODUCTION IN THE SHORT RUN. MONOPOLY PRICING AND PRODUCTION IN THE LONG RUN. MULTIPLANT MONOPOLIST. SIX COMMON MISCONCEPTIONS CONCERNING MONOPOLY. The Monopolist Charges the Highest Possible Price. The Monopolist Tries to Maximize Per-Unit Profits. The Monopolist Tries to Maximize Total Revenue. The Monopolist Necessarily Makes "Excess" Profits. The Monopolist Has an Inelastic Demand Curve. The Monopolist Has a Supply Curve. APPENDIX: MATHEMATICAL NOTES. Note 1: $MR < P$ Under Monopoly. Note 2: Multiplant Monopolist.

Chapter

14   Pricing and Production under Monopolistic Competition   308

PRICE POLICY. ASSUMPTIONS OF THE MODEL OF MONOPOLISTIC COMPETITION. SHORT-RUN ANALYSIS. LONG-RUN ANALYSIS. Blocked Entry. Open Entry. EXCESS CAPACITY. NONUNIFORM COST AND DEMAND FUNCTIONS. NONPRICE COMPETITION. SELLING COSTS AND THE SELLING COST CURVE. Equimarginal Principle. The Alleged Wastes of Monopolistic Competition. Stigler's Position. Overview of the Controversy. APPENDIX: MATHEMATICAL NOTES. Note 1: Chamberlin's Monopolistic Competition and Long-Run Equilibrium.

Chapter

15   Pricing and Production under Oligopoly   325

QUALIFIED JOINT PROFIT-MAXIMIZATION HYPOTHESIS. CLASS 1 OLIGOPOLIES: INDEPENDENCE, UNORGANIZED NONCOLLUSION.

Cournot's Model. Bertrand's Model. Edgeworth's Model. Hotelling's Model. Chamberlin's Model. Sweezy's Kinked Demand Curve Model. CLASS 2 OLIGOPOLIES: ORGANIZED, FORMAL COLLUSION. Centralized Cartel. Market-Sharing Cartel. CLASS 3 OLIGOPOLIES: INFORMAL, TACIT COLLUSION. Price Leadership Models. Effective Price Leadership. APPENDIX: MATHEMATICAL NOTES. Note 1: Cournot Model. Note 2: The Market Shares Model. Note 3: Cournot's Cost Theorem.

Chapter

16   More on Imperfect Markets   349

RESULTS ASSUMING THE MONOPOLIST HAS LOWER COSTS. SUMMARY OF THE ECONOMIC EFFECTS OF IMPERFECT COMPETITION. The Monopolist Has a Price Policy. Higher Prices and Lower Output Under Monopoly Conditions. Criticisms of Profit Maximization Assumption. The Monopolist Can Earn Profits Even in the Long Run. Monopoly Has More Nonprice Competition. Monopoly May Reduce the Macroeconomic Flexibility and Stability of the Economy. The Monopolist's Response to a Change in Demand. Monopoly Prices and Quantities Relative to a Change in Costs. Monopoly May or May Not Be Conducive to Technological Advance and Innovation. Monopoly Prevents the Optimal Allocation of Resources. Monopoly Tends To Redistribute Income. Monopoly May Be More Discriminatory in Employment. Miscellaneous Effects of Monopoly. PUBLIC POLICIES TOWARD MONOPOLY. Economically Unjustifiable Monopolies and Monopolistic Practices. Social Objections to Monopolies. U.S. Policies to Promote Competition and Control Monopoly. REGULATING MONOPOLIES. Controlling Price. Controlling Monopoly Through Taxation. PRICE DISCRIMINATION. Control Over Supply. Elasticities Differ. Market Segmentation. PERFECT OR FIRST-DEGREE PRICE DISCRIMINATION. IMPERFECT PRICE DISCRIMINATION. APPENDIX: MATHEMATICAL NOTES. Note 1: Baumol's Constrained Sales Maximization (*CSM*) Model. Note 2: Form of Taxation and Monopoly Output. Note 3: Price Discrimination.

PART

5   DISTRIBUTION THEORY

Chapter

17   Short-Run Factor Pricing and Employment   387

ESSENTIALS OF INCOME DISTRIBUTION. The Law of Supply and Demand in the Resource Market. A Terse Outline of the Marginal Productivity Theory. Optimum Factor Proportions and Absolute Factor Amounts. DEMAND FOR A PRODUCTIVE SERVICE. Factor Demand as a Derived Demand. The Marginal Revenue Product. Shape of the Marginal Revenue Product Curve. FACTOR EQUILIBRIUM ANALYSIS. The Equimarginal Principle for Hiring Factors.

Summary of Factor Market Equilibrium Conditions. Total Analysis and Marginal Analysis. *MRP* Curve as the Firm's Short-Run Demand Curve. MARKET IMPERFECTIONS: MONOPOLY AND MONOPSONY. Monopoly. Monopsony. Bilateral Monopoly. A Summary of the Effects of Monopoly on Income Distribution. Monopoly-Monopsony Exploitation. DETERMINANTS OF SHORT-RUN FACTOR DEMAND. The Factor's Physical Productivity. Demand for the Commodities that the Factor Produces. The Prices of Other Factors. FIVE PRINCIPLES REGULATING THE ELASTICITY OF FACTOR DEMAND. APPENDIX: MATHEMATICAL NOTES. Note 1: Profit Maximization with Monopsony.

Chapter

18   Long-Run Factor Pricing and Employment   414

LONG-RUN FACTOR DEMAND CURVES: THE CASE OF SEVERAL VARIABLE RESOURCES. MARKET DEMAND CURVE. THE SUPPLY OF PRODUCTIVE SERVICES. The Total Supply of Factors. Supply of Human Effort. Land, Natural Resources, and the Nonhuman Capital Stock. Supply of Factors in Particular Uses. Factor Mobility and Factor Supply Elasticity. Dynamic Disequilibrium vs. Static Equilibrium Differentials. SUMMARY OF FIVE POSSIBLE FACTOR SUPPLY CONDITIONS. CRITICISMS OF THE MARGINAL PRODUCTIVITY THEORY. EULER'S THEOREM.

Chapter

19   Wages, Rent, Interest, and Profit   434

WAGE DETERMINATION. Real Wages, Money Wages, and Productivity. Specific Wages and Market Structure. THE GROWTH OF UNIONS. BASIC WAYS UNIONS TRY TO RAISE WAGES. Decrease the Supply of Labor. Increase the Demand for Labor. Increase Standard Wages Through Collective Bargaining. Monopsony and the Economic Effect of Unions. Effect of Wage Changes on Employment. Minimum Wages. HAVE UNIONS RAISED REAL WAGES? RENT. Transfer Earnings and Economic Rent Contrasted. Quasi-Rent. General Concept of Surplus. Henry George and the Single-Tax Movement. INTEREST. PROFIT. The Function of Natural Scarcity Profits. The Significance of Profits.

Author Index   457

Subject Index   460

1 INTRODUCTION AND METHODOLOGY

1 Introduction

While it is an unfortunate fact that there seems to be no completely satisfactory definition of economics, we all have some inkling of at least some of the important issues it examines: inflation, economic growth, unemployment, poverty, discrimination, etc. Although we cannot suggest a definition that may satisfactorily distinguish economics from several related disciplines, one reasonably descriptive definition of economics would be: *Economics is the science of how societies manage their scarce resources in accomplishing the goals of the society.*

The notion of "scarcity"—meaning at a zero price, demand exceeds supply—is crucial and is included explicitly or implicitly in all of the definitions that have been proposed of economics. Because resources (and hence final goods and services) are scarce, all societies must decide how they should allocate or assign their scarce supplies among competing ends so as to obtain the maximum possible social welfare.

An economic problem is said to exist whenever scarce means are pitted against alternative ends. That is, all economic problems originate in the scarcity of means. No society since the Garden of Eden has been known to achieve the state in which all people have unlimited income or, which amounts to the same thing, where all goods are free. However, scarcity is a necessary but not a sufficient condition for an economic problem to exist. No economic problem would exist if scarce means were used to satisfy a single, unambiguous end. This would be a technological problem. For instance, to produce a machine of maximum durability would be a purely technical problem involving no value judgments. However, if the objective changes to the "optimal" machine, where additional factors such as cost, efficiency, etc., are involved, an economic problem is present since choices and judgments must be made.

MICROECONOMIC THEORY

The whole of economics is customarily divided into two sections to facilitate learning: microeconomics and macroeconomics. In truth, the economic universe is composed of a spectrum of problems with microeconomics falling on one end and macroeconomics on the other end of this continuum. Any actual or real world problems always involve some admixture of microeconomic and macroeconomic elements. However, for didactic purposes it is often useful to assume that economic problems fall entirely into one or the other category. Since serious errors can be made in using micro tools to analyze macro problems and vice versa, care is cautioned. And in this book, of course, the overwhelming emphasis will be on those tools and problems falling into the microeconomic category.

Microeconomics or "price theory" is primarily concerned with individual economic units—a consumer, a producer, a speculator, a commodity, etc. Special situations—e.g., a market demand or supply curve—involve a degree of aggregation. In contrast, macroeconomics is primarily concerned with national aggregates or total values—aggregate consumption, investment, saving, etc. Put differently, microeconomics basically deals with the value or price of individual commodities and resources and with the distribution of income, whereas macroeconomics involves the level of income and employment in an entire society. That is, price theory investigates how resources are allocated so as to produce the present *composition* of total output and its distribution among the people, whereas macroeconomics tries to explain the *level* of total production and total income. Microeconomics deals with relative prices, macroeconomics with absolute prices. For example, to know that the absolute price of an apple is twenty-five cents is to know nothing of significance; but if we also know that the absolute price of an orange is fifty cents, then the relative price of an apple is one half of an orange, or the price of an orange is two apples. In other words, the relative price of two to one, or one to two, is of some significance. A problem in macroeconomics might involve the forecast that the prices of oranges, apples, and all other commodities are to double and thus change the value of the unit of money; but in microeconomics we would observe that since the relative price of oranges to apples did not change, no change in economic behavior would be expected.

Microeconomics is fundamental. In an important sense, microeconomics *is* economics. It is both a prerequisite and the cornerstone of all other branches of the field of economics. Anytime we ask the question, So what? the answer must be in microeconomic terms because we are interested in the individual, the person, or the family. If we are interested in the question, Is inflation good or bad? it takes microeconomic analysis to evaluate the question. We might know all there is to know about tax laws; but to understand their import, we need microeconomic analysis. We might know everything about air pollution, but determining what to do about it requires microeconomic analysis.

The authors of this text believe that it is virtually impossible to exaggerate the importance of the study of microeconomics. This is not to say that we think we have all the answers or that the received doctrine as presented here is the best theory possible, but in the absence of any superior approach we must use what we have and give it up only when improvements take place. In any case, we can think of only two alternatives to using microeconomic theory if we want to know the impact, say, of a new type of tax. They are divine revelation, about which we have nothing to say, and historical experience or experiment, of which there may not be any.

MANAGING SCARCE RESOURCES

There are at least three possible "pure" solutions as to how a society may elect to manage its scarce resources. These three solutions or forms of economic organization are tradition, command, and market. None of these polar cases exist in any actual societies.

For distinguishing among these types, it is useful to further subdivide microeconomics and macroeconomics into two parts each. That is, it is possible to argue that four universal problems are inherent in any type of economic organization: allocation, distribution, growth, and stability. The first two of these comprise microeconomics, the latter two macroeconomics. The allocation problem involves determining "what" and "how much" of each commodity shall be produced and choosing the technological method, the "how" by which this output is to emanate. Since no society can fully satisfy the desires of all its members, some method of priority in production must be established to maximize the social welfare with the available resources. Each society must also decide exactly how to divide total output among its constituent members. This is the "for whom" or distribution problem. The growth problem refers to the fact that societies are interested in achieving long-run or secular increases in per capita income over time and must make provisions—i.e., savings and capital formation—to do so. Finally, societies are interested in mitigating cyclical fluctuations in employment, etc., over shorter periods of time. This is the stability problem of macroeconomics.

Underdeveloped (or developing) countries usually solve these problems by tradition, using customary methods. Production takes place in much the same way as it did years ago. Since technology has advanced over time, these methods are generally less efficient than those of advanced nations.

Advanced nations generally use a market system—letting the price system solve these problems, such as in the U.S.—or a command system—letting authoritarian central rulers plan economic activities, as in China, Eastern Europe, and Russia. For instance, in the U.S. the prices and quantities of productive services owned by individuals primarily determine their share of the social pie; the price of capital—i.e., the interest rate—determines the proportion of society's resources that goes into economic growth (future consumption) vs. the proportion used for present consumption; consumer sovereignty along with business costs and supply decisions determines what is to be produced, etc.

We know that the production results achieved in our society over, say, the last 50 years have been dramatic. However, another society may wish to emphasize a different universal problem and would thus prefer a different economic organization. For example, if a society wishes to emphasize economic stability, it may prefer a command type rather than a market type of economic organization. Remember, though, that these two economic organizations are part of a continuum, with a pure 100 percent market society at one pole and a pure 100 percent command society at the other. All real world economies are "mixed" in that they lie somewhere between these two extremes. Economies are therefore always becoming more command oriented or more market oriented while never really reaching either pole.

Numerous writers have suggested criteria for choosing among these three basic solutions and all the possible hybrids formed by combining them. Bronfenbrenner suggests six criteria, four "purely" economic and two "quasi-economic" considerations.[1]

The four economic criteria are primarily the so-called universal problems discussed above. The first criterion is the standard of living, usually measured by the level of per capita income. Our justification for using this measure is based on the unverified probability that changes in economic welfare usually lead to changes in social welfare, though not necessarily of the same magnitude. Without such an assumption most economic analyses would lack relevance. A second criterion is the growth rate of this standard of living. Another is the equity of distribution of both the flow of income and the stock of wealth in the society. Since both of these are relevant in determining one's standard of living, they must be taken into account. In the Western World two philosophical principles regulating distribution have prevailed, productivity and equality. That is, we have thought people are entitled to the "fruits of their own labor" — the productivity precept — and yet we have felt a more equal distribution of income is desirable — the equality belief. Although people may be equal in some philosophical or legal sense, they certainly are not in an economic sense — e.g., persons who are less endowed mentally and physically have a lower "value" productivity than others. Hence, the principles are often in conflict. Throughout most of our history the productivity principle has predominated, but in recent times it appears that the equity precept has grown in acceptance. A fourth criterion is the stability of the standard of living, especially against downward pressures. This includes both short-run oscillations in economic activity, usually referred to as "business cycles," as well as longer run shifts concomitant with adjustments to technological change, especially automation.

A quasi-economic criterion is the treatment of civil liberties in the system. A highly efficient economic machine that utilizes forced labor, for example, would be downgraded for infringing on civil liberties. Finally, the mental and physical health of the members of the society should be considered. An economic organization which is careless about safety standards or breeds extreme mental pressures suffers by this criterion.

PRODUCTION POSSIBILITY CURVE

One useful device for illustrating the general problem of economic scarcity or the specific "purely" economic criteria illustrated above is a *production possibility curve*. A production possibility or product transformation curve shows that for any given period of time a society has a certain maximum productive capacity, determined by the quantity and quality of its working population and of its other natural resources, capital equipment, and technological

---

[1] Martin Bronfenbrenner, "A Middlebrow Introduction to Economic Methodology," *The Structure of Economic Science, Essays on Methodology,* edited by Sherman Roy Krupp (Englewood Cliffs: Prentice-Hall, 1966), pp. 5–24. A number of our remarks on methodology are indebted to this excellent essay. The interested reader should find a number of the articles in this volume rewarding.

knowledge. These give the society its menu of alternative production possibilities for that period. At the same time, the law of scarcity tells us that society's total wants exceed its production possibilities. Assuming that total productive capacity is utilized, the problem is to choose the pattern of utilization among the various alternatives available. Thus, the production of more x goods requires the sacrifice of some y goods. The x goods are transformed into y goods by diverting resources from one use to the other. Figure 1–1 depicts an illustrative production possibility curve.

FIGURE 1–1 Production Possibility Curve

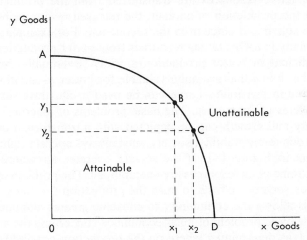

The boundary line $ABCD$ separates the areas of choice that are attainable in the period in question from those that are unattainable. The economy cannot be outside the curve and will not be inside if there is full employment. For example, the society could be at point A, consuming only y goods ($0A$ units of them). However, since society rarely, if ever, prefers to devote all its productive resources to the output of just one commodity but rather prefers some combined output of many different commodities and services, the practical problem is one of choosing among alternatives at the margin—a little more of this, a little less of that. For example, the typical question is, Should society be at point B, consuming $0y_1$ units of y and $0x_1$ units of x, or should it be at point C, associated with $0y_2$ units of y and $0x_2$ units of x? Society can move from point B to point C at the cost of sacrificing y_1y_2 units of y to acquire the additional x_1x_2 units of x.

The fundamental law of scarcity is illustrated by the fact that the production possibility curve falls from left to right. This means that with given productive resources fully employed, the production of any one or group of particular goods and services necessarily means that less of some other can be produced. In short, there is always some positive opportunity cost involved in acquiring more of x (or y) with the economy operating at full capacity. This is of course the essence of the numerous discussions of "guns vs. butter."

In addition to being downward sloping, the typical transformation curve is thought to be concave (bloated outward). Thus, while the curve's downward slope shows that the opportunity costs are positive and substitution is necessary in a full employment economy, the concavity shows that the opportunity costs are increasing as more and more x (or y) is acquired, and the substitution must take place on an ever-increasing basis. More and more units of y must be given up to produce an additional unit of x as the production of x gets larger, i.e., as the society moves downward along its transformation curve from A to D.

The explanation for this concavity is straightforward. In commonsense terms, as productive resources are transferred from the production of one commodity to the production of another, the released resources become progressively less suited and efficient in the second use. For example, to produce more guns initially involves taking resources from butter production that were relatively inefficient in butter production anyway. Eventually, however, resources must be drawn that are quite valuable for butter production.[2]

The production possibility curve can be used to illustrate several of the universal problems of economics. The basic problems of macroeconomics involving stability and growth can be depicted with a transformation curve. In brief, to attain economic stability, society must always operate right on boundary line $ABCD$ in Figure 1–1. If the society operates anywhere inside the boundary line, some of its resources are unemployed. The problem of economic growth involves society's efforts to push the production frontier outward and rightward. This allows the community to consume greater amounts of both x and y. Also, the basic problem of microeconomics concerning the allocation of resources involves determining where on the production possibility curve the society should be. This assumes that the stability question has been solved and that society is on the frontier line. The precise point at which the society's social welfare is maximized can only be resolved if that society's tastes and preferences are known. As will be illustrated later, the subjective concept of a community consumption indifference curve must be superimposed on the objective concept of a transformation curve to determine this. The tangency point between the two curves turns out to be the socially optimal position. Finally, in a market economy, once the allocative decision is made on the composition of output, it is perforce made on the distribution of income. In general, the more x that is produced relative to y, the greater the distributive share of the output that will accrue to resource owners more skilled in producing x than y.

METHODOLOGY

In arriving at useful economic principles two general methods may be employed: (1) a theoretical or deductive method and (2) an empirical or inductive method. In the first case conclusions are reached solely by building logically tight theoretical models, whereas in the second case observations on real world

---

[2] There is a more important but less straightforward reason for the concavity, assuming homogeneous productive factors; but this argument shall be deferred to a later chapter.

data are used to help arrive at conclusions. Most economists today would say that these two methods are complementary; one should supplement rather than supplant the other.

However, there is still controversy over the emphasis to be placed on each. There are three main methodological positions prevailing among economists today.[3]

Extreme Apriorism. This theoretical group emphasizes deductive reasoning, believing no theory can be proved or refuted by empirical testing. Logic and introspection are all the extreme apriorists use to develop their theories. Perhaps the most famous work of this School belongs to Lionel Robbins.[4]

Ultraempiricism. An empirical group that thinks theory must be empirically tested at every step represents another extreme. These people prefer only deductive methods, starting the analysis with facts instead of axioms. Probably the most quoted authority on this position is T. W. Hutchison.[5]

Logical Positivism. A middle group embraces the positive economists who place primary emphasis on a model's ability to predict. Models that predict better are considered superior. They feel the conclusions can be tested but not the basic assumptions or axioms. The assumptions need not be "realistic" if the model "predicts" accurately. Probably the most famous of the positivism proponents is Milton Friedman.[6]

We are interested in microeconomics as a positive ("what is") science rather than as a normative ("what ought to be") discipline. As a positive science, economics is interested in examining the alternative means to given ends without praising or denigrating any of them. For example, without attempting to evaluate the goal, we can analyze through price theory the ramifications of the government's attempt to set minimum wages in the economy.

Of course, economic theories are also useful as explanations of what has in fact occurred. But economic theory as a predictive device is emphasized here. For purposes of social control, prediction is vital. But even if control is not possible, forecasting is vital. Even though we cannot control the weather, we can prepare for it by carrying an umbrella.

---

[3] This distinction is based on Fritz Machlup, "The Problem of Verification in Economics," *Southern Economic Journal,* Vol. XXII (July, 1955), pp. 1–21 and is reviewed in Charles E. Ferguson, *Microeconomic Theory* (3d ed.; Homewood: Richard D. Irwin, 1972), pp. 6–8.

[4] Lionel Robbins, *An Essay on the Nature and Significance of Economic Science* (2d ed.; London: Macmillan & Co., 1935). Also in this School would be John Stuart Mill, Ludwig von Mises, and Frank H. Knight.

[5] T. W. Hutchison, *The Significance and Basic Postulates of Economic Theory* (London: Macmillan & Co., 1938). The so-called Institutionalist School, especially Wesley C. Mitchell, and the German Historical School would also fit into this category.

[6] Milton Friedman, "The Methodology of Positive Economics," *Essays in Positive Economics* (Chicago: University of Chicago Press, 1954), pp. 3–43. Also prominent in this group is Paul A. Samuelson, *Foundations of Economic Analysis* (Cambridge: Harvard University Press, 1947), although there are also important differences between Friedman and Samuelson on some methodological points.

Prediction in this text does not mean prophesy. A prediction is merely a conditional statement; if so and so happens, the following will result. For example, if in a competitive market the desire for olives increases, economists can predict that the quantity of olives demanded and the price of olives will increase. On the other hand, if they forecasted that in three years people's preferences for olives will change and hence the demand and price of olives will increase, that is a prophesy. Unfortunately, economists are not able to gaze into a crystal ball and with great acuity give infallible prophesies about future events. In fact, economists have not been notably successful on long-run forecasts. Someone once remarked that: "Economic prophesies are to reality as astrology is to the stars." However, with even a little training in elementary economics, one is able to at least make some general conditional statements or predictions that are likely to hold in the great majority of cases.

It is generally easier to make valid predictions for groups, particularly large groups, than for individuals or small groups. The profitability of insurance companies attests to the validity of the famous "law of large numbers" that underlies this conclusion. This celebrated maxim predicts that chance or random aberrations tend to cancel out for large samples. Thus, while an insurance company cannot predict whose home will burn up, it can predict how many will do so in a large area. Similarly, while a few sleepy firms might charge lower prices and some aggressive ones inflated prices for olives as the demand increases, on the average higher prices can be predicted for competitive firms.

CHARACTERISTICS OF ECONOMIC THEORIES

At this point, it might be well to discuss the concept of a theory as the term is used in economics. Put simply, a theory contains two or more relations, which are statements relating two or more things. For example, we have a theory of individual consumption behavior. In it we postulate that an individual's preferences between two goods varies as the consumption rate of these two goods changes. That is one relation. We also postulate that the consumer faces a price relation between the two goods. If we now say that the consumer wishes to maximize his or her well-being, subject to the limitations imposed by the individual's purchasing power, we can determine the relative amounts of the two goods the consumer will consume.

For a set of relations to be a theory, it must be possible to make statements which can be tested to determine if they are false. For example, from consumer theory we can make the statement that if the price of one good increases while the other remains the same, our consumer will decrease purchases of the commodity whose price increased and increase purchases of the other. This statement can be subjected to empirical (that is, real-world or statistical) testing.

With a theory of individual consumer behavior, a new relation, relating the price of the good to the amounts that can be sold, can be constructed by aggregating all individuals in the market. This, of course, is the familiar demand curve. If we vary the consumers' income or purchasing power instead of the price of the goods, we get a relation between quantity of sales and income.

When this relation is aggregated, we get the consumption-income relation, which, when aggregated over all households and all consumer commodities, becomes the consumption function of macroeconomics.

The procedure is analogous on the supply side, where we start with the relations involved in the individual producing firm's decision processes and generate aggregate supply-price relationships. Combining the demand and the supply relations, we determine price and quantity, at which point we can hypothesize that if certain variables change, for instance new uses are found for a product, or wage rates change, price and quantity will change in a specified way. Again this statement can be tested statistically.

Notice that, in what we have just done, one theory may contain other theories. A national income determination theory would have to contain a multitude of subtheories. Reiterating, a theory is a set of relations from which we can derive testable hypotheses. A theory's usefulness depends upon how well we can predict from it and how important the hypotheses are to us.

Economic theories have three important characteristics. They are (1) general, (2) abstract, and (3) amenable to graphical and mathematical analysis.

Theory as Generalization

Economic theories are generalizations because their conclusions are subject to exceptions and are often only tolerably accurate. They are useful in predicting the proper direction of a given shift in the economic environment, but not the precise magnitude of the shift to, say, four decimal places. For instance, an important economic principle is that, other things being equal, people will not buy less and usually will buy more of a given commodity as its price falls. Exceptions can and do occur. Furthermore, no one is able to predict the precise change in consumption with a high degree of accuracy. Economics is always making predictions that involve a certain degree of likelihood. An economist is not unlike Sherlock Holmes who always sought solutions in which "the probability lies in that direction."

The fundamental reason for the inexactness of economics or indeed of any social science is that controlled laboratory experiments cannot be conducted as in the natural or physical sciences. An economist's laboratory is the real world. He or she must therefore *assume* other things are equal—the so-called *ceteris paribus* proviso—in analyzing certain problems. To illustrate: Suppose that we predict, *ceteris paribus,* that the Fred Jorgenson family will buy less steak over the next month if the price of steak goes up. Suppose, however, that the Jorgensons in fact bought more steak as its price went up. Does this mean the law on which the above prediction was based is invalid or faulty? No! What might have happened is that "other things" may not actually have been equal; Fred may have received an unexpected pay raise or the price of pork chops, hamburgers, or other substitute meats in general may have gone up even more than steak. Our prediction assumed that variables such as the family's income and the price of other closely related and substitutable products did not change. Of course, if other things seldom remained equal in the actual world, the above principle would be rather useless as a predictive device. However, although

economics is admittedly an inexact science, there are certain timeless principles that stand up quite well as useful predictive devices.

Theory as Abstraction

The second feature worth noting about theories is that they are necessarily
abstractions. To abstract means to simplify a problem to manageable proportions. Just as a map is manageable because it does not present each and every
surface in the area mapped — or the map would be as large as the area itself — a
theory is useful because it tries to eliminate some of the secondary features of
reality so as to highlight the essential characteristics. We abstract because we
usually cannot encompass all of the welter of detail in the real world. In economics the noneconomic aspects of a problem, in addition to some of its economic characteristics, are deleted, suppressed, or minimized to make a useful
theory.

Because realism exacts a price, a more complex theory is not inexorably
superior to a simpler one. A leading economist puts it this way:

> Of course, I am not opposed to realism *per se.* To oppose greater realism
> when it can be achieved without cost is like being against virtue. What I am
> arguing is that *increased realism, like greater generality, usually involves a
> cost in decreased manipulability and insight into the workings of our models.*
> For one thing, when models are too complex we often find that the mathe-
> matician has not as yet supplied us with tools that are both appropriate and
> adequate. It often becomes necessary, therefore, to economize on the intro-
> duction of realism into our analysis.[7]

The process of abstraction is not unique to economics. Physical and natural sciences also employ abstraction. The study of mechanics invariably starts
out by assuming there is no friction, when, in fact, there always is friction.
Furthermore, just as many of us have been "speaking prose" all our lives without knowing it, so too have we been abstracting all our lives. Whenever we
say, for example, that we saw a "man" walking down the street, we are abstracting. If we were not abstracting, we would say we saw a man six feet two
inches tall, weighing $185\frac{1}{2}$ pounds, with blue eyes, brown hair, and a ruddy
complexion, dressed in a brown pinstriped suit, walking east on Main Street,
etc! Clearly, there is a genuine need for abstraction in our everyday lives as
well as in the study of economics.

Mathematical and Graphical Techniques

Finally, it is often possible to express many economic theories graphically,
using coordinate geometry. In all, economists use three languages: ordinary
prose, pictorial geometry, and formal mathematics. It is important to realize
that no one method is best for all problems and all people. To reason otherwise

---

[7] William J. Baumol, *Business Behavior, Value and Growth* (rev. ed.; New York: Harcourt,
Brace & World, 1967), p. 4. (Italics supplied.)

is analogous to asking whether a penknife is a better tool than a hatchet. The answer depends upon the task and the user. Obviously, for sharpening a pencil a penknife would be preferred to a hatchet; whereas for cutting down a tree, a hatchet would be preferred. By the same token the capabilities of the person using the tool are important. It is conceivable, for instance, to take an extreme example, that a lumberjack might be more proficient with a hatchet even for relatively small jobs that most of us would prefer to perform with a penknife.

For the most part these three methods — verbal, mathematical, and pictorial — are interchangeable. However, this text emphasizes and normally fuses all three approaches, but with the main stress on the verbal and graphic. Almost all key concepts in intermediate price theory can be explained without the use of mathematics. However, there are some economic phenomena and some concepts for which formal mathematics is the preferred tool. We take up some of these in the chapter appendices labeled "Mathematical Notes."

THE PLAN OF STUDY

One of the most profound statements about economics is that everything depends on everything else. This interdependence means that there is no logical starting and ending point in the study. We could start at any part of the operation of an economy and include all of the subjects in the field. Microeconomics as an instructional area has been taught long enough to overcome most of the pedagogical bugs, and most instructors and authors now have pretty well standardized the instructional outline. In this text we follow the steps normally traveled.

The apparent goal of the study is to determine the relative prices and quantities of goods and services produced and traded in the economy. While this is of significance in itself, the processes and the forces involved are of even greater importance. We hope this becomes evident as we proceed through the text.

The first substantive chapter deals with the general topic of supply and demand. Both of these together determine the equilibrium prices and quantities of commodities. We follow tradition in concentrating first on the demand side. The several chapters on demand can be the first subject only because we assume the consumer's income or wealth is given. In fact the consumer's ability to purchase things depends on that individual's contribution to the production of other goods and services, the value of which depends on other individuals' evaluation of what the first person produces and the productivity of other contributing productive services. Thus, demand and supply conditions elsewhere are fundamental to any given demand for any particular product.

With the individual's ability to buy and the prices of goods and services taken as given, the amounts the individual is willing to buy depend on the relative utilities or satisfaction expected from the specific commodities. The two major approaches to demand analysis are presented in Chapters 4–6, that is, the marginal utility approach and the indifference curve method. Chapter 7 looks at demand from the point of view of the firm or industry which produces the product.

In the demand chapters we establish that the quantities consumers wish to buy increase as the relative price of the product falls, and vice versa; that normally more will be bought as income or wealth increases; and that demand depends on a number of other factors. It is then natural to move on to the study of the availability of the goods for which there is a demand, that is, the supply side. This requires an understanding of production, or how resources and the services of the factors of production are transformed into commodities which people want. The theory of production is covered in two complementary ways: the classical theory and the more recently developed isoquant approach. Production theory leads to the conversion into costs of production, and costs of production are the major determinant of the supply curve.

After building the underlying structure of demand and supply, the text considers the significance of different market structures. We start with the purely competitive circumstance, then the opposite extreme of monopoly, and then the intermediate cases of monopolistic competition and oligopoly.

The last portion of the text is important to the study of income distribution and resource allocation since it deals with the pricing and employment of the services of the factors of production. In a general way we describe wages as the payment for labor service, rent as the price of the use of land or natural resources, interest as the return on capital, and profit as a residual return to the risk-taker of enterprise. With this discussion we come full circle, since the returns to the factors establish the ability of factor owners to demand goods and services.

QUESTIONS

1. The definition of "scarcity" on page 1 uses the phrase "at zero price." Can you explain why that phrase is necessary?
2. This chapter makes a distinction between absolute prices and relative prices. Explain the difference and discuss the significance of the two concepts.
3. In what respect is microeconomics more "fundamental" than macroeconomics? Does this mean that microeconomics is more "important" than macroeconomics?
4. Compare the ways in which the universal economic problems are solved in a market-directed economy with how they are solved in a command economy.
5. A production possibility curve is always drawn as concave to the origin. Draw one which is convex to the origin and explain what this would mean. Evaluate the plausibility of the existence of such a curve.
6. Do you think it is possible to have a deductive approach to economics with no induction, or a purely inductive method with absolutely no deduction involved? Explain your answer.
7. Discuss these statements:
   (a) The simplest theory is the most abstract.
   (b) A theory which includes everything that is relevant would be useless.
   (c) Economists predict well, but are not particularly good forecasters.
8. A famous economist once said, "In order to know anything, it is necessary to know everything; but in order to talk about anything, it is necessary to neglect a great deal." Explain.

2   Fundamentals of Demand and Supply

The universal problems are solved in our economy with the aid of competition and market-directed or -influenced prices. There is a *market* whenever the possibility exists for sellers and buyers to agree to exchange. An essential element of a market is communication among the potential parties to an exchange. This communication may be face to face, but can be by any other medium — print, telephone, telegraph, drums, etc. A market has no geographical requirements in the economic sense, though communications and costs of effecting transactions often vary with distance and geography.

THE BASIC NATURE OF A MARKET

If money is not one element in an exchange, that market is referred to as *barter.* Barter is usually so costly or, to put it the other way around, money is so efficient that most markets do involve money. The reason is that only the party wishing to buy something for money needs to search for or investigate the attributes of what is being purchased. Also, money costs less to handle than do commodities.

A particular market cannot be specified very rigorously primarily because of the difficulty of defining the commodity or commodities involved. We can speak of the market for automobiles, and in some vague sense such a market exists, but is there really such a thing as an automobile? Or are there only Chevrolets, Rolls Royces, Volkswagens, etc? Or are there only blue, two-door, 1977 Chevrolet Impalas with an automatic transmission, etc., etc., in the same place at the same time? All markets seem to merge at one end of the spectrum, but diverge at the other. Clearly the degree of substitutability is important in deciding whether two commodities are in the same market or not. A starting point, at least, is the definition that two commodities are the same commodity if they are perfect substitutes for each other. As we include goods in the market which are less and less substitutable for each other, the concept of the market becomes less precise. But as the definition of the commodity, and hence the market, becomes narrower (i.e., more precise), it gets less interesting. Generally we are more interested in a class of commodities than in specific, narrowly defined ones.

The concept of markets is so general that it virtually encompasses an economist's spectrum of interests. The economic system is usually divided into four all-encompassing markets: the *commodity market,* which includes goods and services of all descriptions, whether final or to be used in further production; the *labor market,* which is the market for the services of people in production; the *money market,* which is the demand for and supply of the medium of exchange; and the *bond market,* which includes all debt instruments except money. There are, of course, a very large number of markets within these large categories; and while macroeconomics usually deals with the broad classes, microeconomics relates to the interrelationships among the more finely defined smaller markets.

THE DEMAND SIDE OF THE MARKET

A market always contains a supply side and a demand side. Several chapters immediately following this one will intensively analyze demand and supply. At this stage we will discuss the very important fundamentals, including the interactions between the two sides which determine the price and the quantities produced and sold.

We start the study of demand with an analysis of a *stock-dominated market,* that is, a market in which the demand is for a commodity to own or hold a fixed amount of. Our example uses the commodity pianos, but such a market is more or less characteristic of the market for paintings of a deceased artist, the real estate market, and the stock, bond, and money markets.

We then proceed to discuss flow-dominated markets, which traditionally have been the main concern of most microeconomics textbooks. A *flow-dominated market* is one in which the buyer purchases and consumes at some rate per unit of time, and output is more or less continuous over time. Most grocery items, fuel, electricity, and services of all kinds fall into this category. Many markets are mixtures of both flows and stocks, automobiles and household appliances being rather obvious cases.

Stock-Dominated Markets

In the development of the concept of demand, we normally start by studying the smallest unit, the individual or the household as the decision-making entity. For some problems we will view demand as perceived (imperfectly) by the seller or producer of the product.

There are a number of other issues about which we need to be clear when speaking of demand. First, considering the individual demander facing a given commodity, we ask what is being demanded. If we start at the very beginning, the individual desires some innate values—elimination of hunger or thirst, prestige, recognition, status, power, wisdom, peace of mind, love, compassion, and on through a list we could never complete—things that economists are frequently accused of ignoring. Economists usually neglect these things because we feel we are not equipped to contribute anything to their analysis, and we leave them to the psychologist, sociologist, theologian, and anyone else who is interested. We do not deny their fundamental importance.

To satisfy those basic desires, consumers wish to have services. They want certain qualities such as flavor, nutrition, some kind of transportation, music or other entertainment, etc. They can buy some of these directly in the form of services from sellers of these services. They can acquire others through the purchase of goods whose services are released over time. One can't buy the services of an apple without buying the apple, but one can get some of the services of an automobile without buying the automobile. The decision to buy services directly or to acquire services by owning the good which provides the service depends on the relative costs of the two options, which in turn depends partly on the consumer's own circumstances and desired pattern of consumption. We presume the household's goal is to maximize the utility derivable from its purchasing power.

These desires become economically significant when placed in the context of *effective demand;* that is, the desire to acquire goods and services must be backed by the ability and willingness to pay. People's appetites affect no economic variable unless the people translate their wishes into credible offers to buy or actually make purchases. At an auction it is not just the actual buyer who determines the price; all of the bidders influence the final price.

There is a difference between the desire to own something and the desire to buy something. I own a piano, but I have no desire to buy one. I wish to continue to derive the services of that piano; therefore, I wish to continue to possess it as long as my circumstances and the price of pianos remain roughly unchanged. What we are getting at here is something called *stock demand,* that is, the demand to own a good at all conceivable market prices, given that other independent variables are held constant.

There is some price at which I would be willing to sell my piano, and of course I would be willing to sell at any higher price. The price at which I am just willing to sell is called my *reservation price.* Am I a demander or a supplier? The answer is that I am both. As long as the price is below my reservation price, I have a stock demand for one piano. When the price is above my reservation price, I am willing to sell one piano. Presumably, some individuals in the community do not now own a piano but would be willing to buy one at some given price or at any price below that price. Such an individual would only be on the demand side, and the given price referred to would be that person's reservation price. There might also be people who own a piano who would be willing to sell it at some high price; and if the price got low enough, they would be willing to buy a second piano.

Suppose we envision a closed community of 1,000 people in which there are 100 pianos.[1] They are all owned by someone, and there is no way to manufacture or import any more. Figure 2–1 shows a *stock supply (S)* of 100 pianos. At a price of $10,000, all who own pianos would be willing to sell them; that is, they would prefer the other goods and services that $10,000 would buy to owning a piano. Thus, at the $10,000 price the demand for pianos would be zero. If the price drops to $9,400, 10 families would wish to keep their

---

[1] The analysis of stock demand is developed from the classic article by Philip H. Wicksteed, "The Scope and Method of Political Economy," *The Economic Journal,* Vol. XXIV (1914), pp. 1–23; reprinted in *AEA Readings in Price Theory,* Vol. VI, edited by George Stigler and Kenneth Boulding (Homewood: Richard D. Irwin, 1952), pp. 3–26.

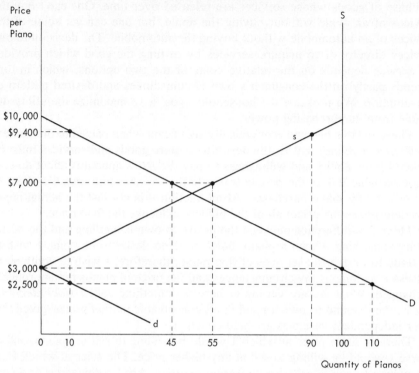

FIGURE 2-1 Stock Supply and Demand, and Willingness to Buy or Sell

pianos and 90 owners would be willing to sell. The demand to own or hold would be 10; the supply in the sense of willingness to sell at this price would be 90. As we go down the scale of prices, fewer piano owners would be willing to sell and (saying the same thing) more would be willing to continue to hold. On the graph, *s* is the willingness-to-sell curve interpreted as a schedule of reservation prices at or above which owners of the specified number would be willing to sell. The curve *D* is the *stock demand curve* and is derived from subtracting *s* from the stock supply of 100. For example, when the price is $7,000, *s* is 55, so the demand to own is 45 (since the stock supply is 100).

When the price is $3,000, no one who owns a piano would be willing to sell it. Therefore, the stock demand for pianos at that price is exactly 100— equal to the stock supply. This is an equilibrium situation. The market is "cleared" in that the commodity is held by those who wish to hold it, and those who do not hold any are unwilling to pay as much as the equilibrium price for one.

An interesting aspect of this case is that the equilibrium price exists even though no transactions take place. There are buyers and sellers waiting to make transactions if anything happens to change the price.

It is frequently argued that when a market is "thin," meaning that sales are few relative to the size of the existing stock, the price established is somehow not very meaningful. Such comments, which are most often made about the stock market (that is, the organized securities exchanges), the bond market, or the real estate market, reflect a lack of understanding of the point being made here. When a market for stocks is in equilibrium—when the forces of demand and supply are exactly offsetting—there will be no exchanges.

If for some reason the price were to fall, there are potential buyers as shown by the *d* curve, which is the demand-to-buy curve of those who do not currently own a piano. This curve is derived from the *D* curve at prices below the equilibrium price. For example, at a price of $2,500, 10 nonowners would be willing to buy a piano. On the other hand, if the price were above the equilibrium, there are potential sellers willing to sell.

Exchange will take place in our piano market, or in any other stock-dominated market, if those who make up the market change their attitudes toward the commodity (even if total demand remains unchanged) or if the total demand or total stock changes. If one owner (the numbers involved are irrelevant) who had been unwilling to sell at the equilibrium price ($3,000) now decides to sell and at the same time a nonowner becomes willing to buy at the current price, both the *d* curve and the *s* curve shift to the right by one unit to *d'* and *s'* respectively in Figure 2–2. A single transaction takes place, but the price remains unchanged. Following the sale, the original *s* and *d* curves will be reestablished.

If a warehouse were discovered with 10 additional pianos in it, the owner would offer these for sale. The stock supply would shift to 110, as shown in Figure 2–3. The willingness-to-sell curve (*s*) shifts to the right by 10 units to

FIGURE 2–2 Offsetting Changes in Willingness to Buy and Sell— Exchange Takes Place

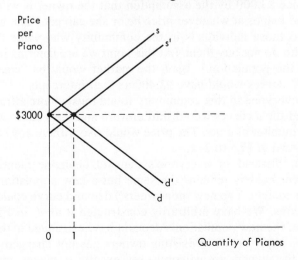

FIGURE 2-3   Addition to the Stock Supply

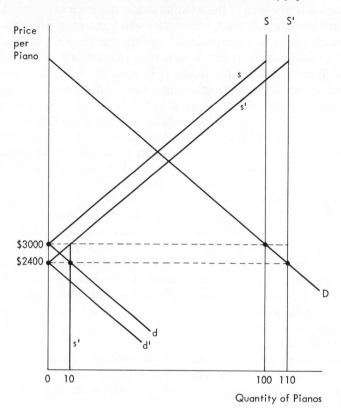

s', indicating 10 more pianos offered for sale at all prices. (The *s'* curve is vertical up to price $3,000 by the assumption that the owner is willing to sell the 10 new-found pianos at whatever price he or she can get.) The new pianos would be sold to those individuals in the community who value them more than do those who do not buy them. (At this point we are ignoring income differences among the population.) Again the market would be "cleared," and the new *s'* and *d'* curves would have $2,400 as their intercepts.

If suddenly everyone in this community found music more attractive than before, the *D* and the *d* curves would shift upward and the *s* curve would shift left by the same number of units. The price would rise without any sales taking place. This is shown in Figure 2-4.

Suppose that, instead of everyone's demand changing identically, the demand by current holders remains the same but a new population of music lovers enters the society. The new (nonowners') demand curve could take any number of positions. We have arbitrarily constructed it as d_n in Figure 2-5, and the amount of the new population's demand has been added to the *D* curve to form *D'*. The supply curve of existing owners has not changed; so at the higher price P_1, the owners are willing to sell exactly q_s pianos and the new

FIGURE 2-4   Increase in the Demand for Pianos

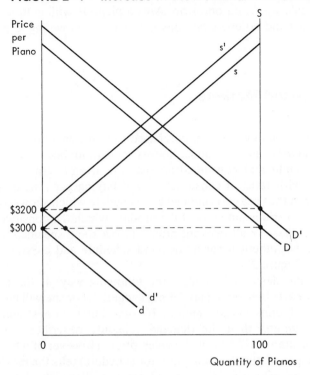

FIGURE 2-5   Increase in Demand by Population Increase

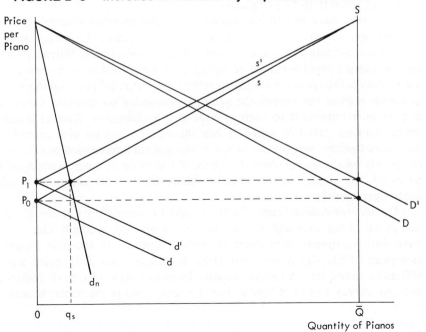

people are willing to buy exactly that number. Again the market is cleared; and after the sale at P_1, no one who owns a piano is willing to sell (reflected in the shift to s') and no one who does not own one is willing to pay as much as P_1 to get one.

Flow-Dominated Markets

While many commodities are purchased only infrequently and consumed almost continuously, as are pianos, houses, or automobiles, some goods and services are bought and consumed almost concurrently. In these cases the analysis deals with rates of consumption and buying per time unit. Demand by a consumer in these cases is defined as a schedule which shows, other things being equal, the various amounts of the product which the consumer is willing and able to purchase at all relevant prices during some specified time period. An illustrative hypothetical partial demand schedule and curve are shown in Table 2–1 and Figure 2–6.

Normally the demand is read in the following way: If the consumer is faced with any particular price (say $3 per gadget), he or she will buy the designated number of units (4) per month. If some outside constraint limits the purchasable amounts, then the demand schedule describes the maximum number the consumer will buy at the given price. However, if a fixed quantity constraint is imposed, the demand curve (or schedule) tells the maximum price the buyer will be willing to pay for that amount. Thus, if allowed to buy a maximum of six gadgets per month, this consumer would be willing to pay up to but not more than $2 per gadget.

It is very easy to run into semantic difficulties when discussing demand and supply, so economists have adopted a particular language agreement which we must follow if we are to communicate effectively. Whenever we use the unqualified word *demand* (or *supply*), we are referring to the entire schedule or curve. Whenever we want to refer to a particular point on the schedule or curve, we use the expression *quantity demanded* (or *quantity supplied*). It is especially important to keep in mind that *a change in demand* means the whole demand curve or schedule has shifted or taken on new quantities for the various prices, and that *a change in the quantity demanded* refers to different points on the same schedule. Thus, if the price of gadgets changed from $4 to $3, the change in the quantity demanded by this consumer would be 2 units per month.

The *market demand curve* for the product is simply the horizontal summation of all of the individuals' demand curves for that product. Thus, if there were 100 consumers with demand curves identical to those in Figure 2–6 at a price of $3, 400 gadgets would be demanded; and if the price were $2, 600 units would be bought per month. In most cases, of course, individuals' demand curves will be different, but the procedure is the same; however, in

TABLE 2-1   A Hypothetical Partial Demand Schedule for Gadgets

Unit Price of Gadgets	Quantity of Gadgets Demanded Per Month
0	10
$1	8
$2	6
$3	4
$4	2
$5	0

Note: This demand schedule is derived from the following equation: Letting Q_d = quantity demanded and P = price, $Q_d = 10 - 2P$.

FIGURE 2-6   Flow Demand Curve

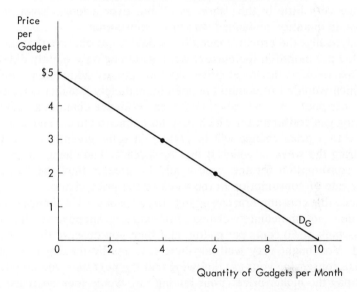

Quantity of Gadgets per Month

this case when the price falls, not only do buyers purchase more units, but people who were not buyers before may enter the market.

The *firm's demand curve* is the quantity per unit of time the firm would expect to sell at all feasible prices. If the firm is a monopoly seller of the commodity, the market demand curve and the firm's demand curve are identical. However, if a large number of firms are selling the same product, the demand curve of a single firm will be a horizontal line at the going price. This demand curve reflects the fact that if the firm set a price above the going price, its sales would be zero; if the firm set a price below the market price, it would be behaving "unwisely"; and if the firm set a price at the market price, it could sell any quantity it wished to sell. This is generally descriptive of a firm engaged in a perfectly competitive market.

Time and the Demand Curve

In the hypothetical demand curve just discussed, the time dimension was specified as one month. That unit has to remain fixed, but the demand curve may refer to the quantity (at a monthly rate) that will be bought today, the coming week, or the current year, depending upon the purpose of the analysis or on the available data. Rigorously, we should deal only with demand curves for some extremely short period of time—one for today, a new one tomorrow, etc.; but as a practical matter we often use longer periods. To give an example of the relevance of this issue, consider the question which was of such great concern during the early 1970s when petroleum prices started to rise dramatically and threatened to continue to rise. Gas and oil consumption was expected to change very little in the "short run," but over a longer span of time the reduction in quantity demanded was to be substantial.

Analytically, the proper conception would be to observe that the quantity demanded per month in the current week would be only slightly different than it was last week at the lower price. As time passes, adjustments will be possible which wouldn't or couldn't happen immediately. Smaller cars, gas saving options, car pools, bus ridership, and even residence changes are all means of decreasing gas consumption which may take time to effect. Thus, the quantity response to a price change will be greater in some given week in the future than during the week in which it first took place. The change in the monthly rate of consumption for the year would be greater than the change in the monthly rate of consumption in the week of the price change.

Notice that consumption can change because of a price change even though buying does not immediately change. For example, suppose you had just filled your gas tank at 60 cents per gallon, and then you observe that the price has doubled. You might very well consume less gas by making fewer trips and otherwise conserving your gas, knowing that the next time you buy it, you will have to pay the higher price. Your buying rate would then decrease to reflect your lower rate of consumption.

Other Determinants of Demand

Economists stress the price-quantity demanded relation because of its fundamental role in the resource allocation problem, but this does not imply that price is the only or even the most important determinant of the quantity demanded. Nevertheless, when we refer to "the demand curve," we mean quantity demanded as a function of price, other things remaining constant. In other words, quantity demanded is also a function of other things.

For an individual's demand schedule, the most important of these other determinants are: (1) the income or wealth of the individual (including access to credit); (2) the prices of other commodities — in particular those of goods and services closely related in consumption; (3) the consumer's tastes and preferences, influenced by information and advertising; (4) consumer expectations concerning future prices and income;[2] and (5) the consumer's goal, which in this text is always assumed to be maximization of utility. For a market demand curve, in addition to these five determinants, a sixth must also be held constant: (6) the number and characteristics (with respect to the consumption preferences) of the population.

The demand relationship for a commodity is usually condensed in functional notation to:

$$QD_x = f(P_x, I, P_y, T) \tag{2.1}$$

where QD_x = the quantity of commodity x demanded per unit of time
P_x = the price per unit of commodity x
I = income or other measure of purchasing power
P_y = the prices of other commodities (y)
T = tastes or preferences

The demand curve for commodity x as a function of the price of commodity x is then written:

$$QD_x = f(P_x | \overline{I}, \overline{P}_y, \overline{T}) \tag{2.2}$$

which means that all variables other than its own price have been held constant, that is, *ceteris paribus*.

LAW OF DEMAND

The most important characteristic of a typical or "normal" demand curve is that it falls from left to right (i.e., has a *negative slope*), indicating that, other things being equal, larger quantities of a good or service will be purchased at lower market prices. This property of a demand curve is so important that it is referred to as the *law of demand*. This piece of economic doctrine is one of the two essential ingredients of the law of demand and supply, which in turn explains the formulation of competitive prices. More precisely, the law of demand states that given the determinants (or "other things held equal"), there generally is an inverse relationship between the price of a commodity and its quantity demanded. That is, as the price of a product falls, the corresponding quantity demanded rises; or, alternatively, as price increases, the corresponding quantity demanded falls. The downslope of the demand curve reflects the fact that a consumer will ordinarily buy more of a product per any

---

[2] Strictly speaking, this one is already included in (2) since future commodities are "other commodities."

time unit at a lower price than at a higher price. (The precise explanation for this downslope is developed in detail later.) Similarly, total or market demand follows the same law of demand.

A change in demand for a commodity occurs whenever any of the determinants of demand, other than its own price, change. For example, if income increases, the whole demand curve or schedule shifts, indicating the willingness of consumers to buy a larger quantity of x at all prices. Such a shift in demand is shown in Figure 2–7.

FIGURE 2–7   Change in Demand due to Change in Income

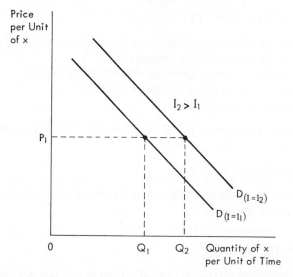

Figure 2–7 assumes a positive relation between the quantity of x demanded and income. There must be a relation like that drawn in Figure 2–8, where, incidentally, price and all other variables except income are held constant.

When the price is P_1 (in Figure 2–7) and income is I_1 (in Figure 2–8), the quantity demanded of this commodity is $0Q_1$ (on both graphs). An increase in income from I_1 to I_2 shifts the demand curve (as a function of price) from $D_{(I=I_1)}$ to $D_{(I=I_2)}$. The amount of that shift can be read from Figure 2–8, because $D_{(P=P_1)}$ indicates the amount demanded at different income levels, given that the price is P_1. Assuming that the slope of the income-demand curve would remain the same at all prices, the price-demand curve would shift in a parallel fashion, as done in Figure 2–7 by the amount Q_1Q_2.

The assumption made in this example of a positive relationship between the amount demanded and income is the usual one. We refer to such commodities as *normal* or *superior goods*. Where the relationship is negative, that is, where an increase in income leads to a reduction in quantity demanded, the commodity is called an *inferior good*.

**FIGURE 2–8   Quantity Demanded as a
Function of Income**

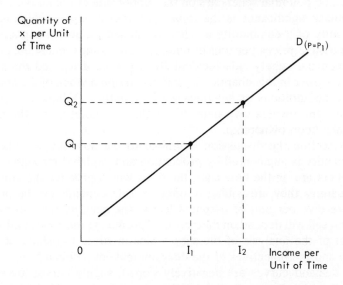

Since the market demand curve is the sum of individual demand schedules, if the latter fall from left to right, so must the former.[3] The negatively sloping market demand curve should not therefore be very surprising.

Economists generally explain the downsloping individual demand curve in one of the following ways: (1) the marginal utility approach; (2) the indifference curve approach; (3) the revealed preference approach; and (4) modern axiomatic choice theory. Each of these approaches to demand theory leads to the conclusion that the demand curve for the individual is downward sloping in conformity with the law of demand. We will cover the mentioned approaches (except number 4) in some detail in later chapters, so we will not pursue them here.

One observation, though, seems pertinent. All of the theoretical explanations of the law of demand treat the individual as behaving in some logical or systematic fashion. It has been noted, however, that as long as the income constraint is binding, any rules of behavior, including purely random selection of goods, result in downward sloping demand curves.[4] The point is that given any set of consumer-willingness-to-buy rules and given any income distribution, the higher the price of the product, the smaller the number of people with the ability to buy; and at lower prices, more buyers will be able to buy more of the commodity.

---

[3] Technically, it is possible for the market demand curve not to be downsloping, even if all the individual curves were downsloping; but it requires such unusual conditions regarding the redistribution of income that we rule it out on pragmatic grounds. See Edward J. Mishan, "Theories of Consumer Behavior: A Cynical View," *Economica*, N.S. (February, 1961).

[4] Gary S. Becker, "Irrational Behavior and Economic Theory," *Journal of Political Economy*, Vol. LXX (February, 1962), pp. 1–13.

THE SUPPLY SIDE OF THE MARKET

Sellers and potential sellers are on the supply side of the market. The relation of primary significance is the *supply schedule* or *curve,* which is defined as the quantity of a commodity a seller, or all sellers, are willing and able to sell at all possible prices per unit of time, all other things remaining equal. We touched upon the supply side incidentally when we discussed the stock demand curve earlier in this chapter. In that discussion a stock of the commodity existed and no additions or deletions were permitted. Willingness to sell depended upon the owners own demand for the commodity, and the ability to sell depended upon ownership.

In this section the discussion is limited to the flow supply, wherein the existing quantity is augmented by production and depleted through consumption. Suppliers are, in the flow case, the firms which produce the commodity, and the quantity they are willing to offer for sale depends on the price they expect to receive per unit of output. Clearly, the quantity they are willing to produce and sell will depend on their costs of producing the goods and services. Thus, most of the analysis of the supply side involves the study of costs of production and the objectives of the decision makers within a firm.

While demand curves are negatively sloped, supply curves are normally positively sloped, meaning that the higher the price per unit of a commodity, the greater the quantity the producers are willing and able to sell. Table 2–2 and Figure 2–9 show a simple example of a possible supply curve for a particular firm. While a supply curve or schedule is supposed to represent the rate at which the firm is willing to sell, it really shows the rate at which the firm will produce. These two, the sales rate and the production rate, will be the same if the firm's stock of inventory remains constant in physical size. However, firms will sometimes find it advantageous to produce and sell at different rates, allowing the inventory stock to vary. This is a dynamic consideration which, unfortunately, we cannot handle in a very rigorous way until we have completed the static analysis. So, in general, the supply curves we will be discussing will assume that sales and production are concurrent.

TABLE 2–2   A Hypothetical Partial Supply Schedule for Gadgets

Unit Price of Gadgets	Quantity of Gadgets Supplied Per Month
$5	21
$4	16
$3	11
$2	6
$1	1

Note: This supply schedule is derived from the following equation: Letting Q_s = quantity supplied and P = price, $Q_s = 5P - 4$.

FIGURE 2-9   Supply Curve

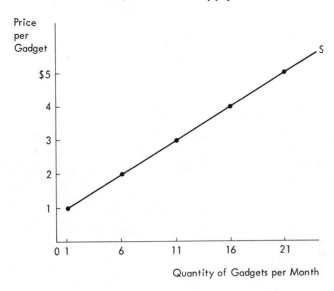

The supply curve of Figure 2–9 implicitly assumes that the firm is a "price taker." That is, given the price of $4, the firm will supply at the rate of 16 gadgets per month. If the firm had the power to effectively set the price itself, it would not have a supply curve. It would choose the price and quantity pair which would maximize the objectives of the firm.

A change in supply means a shift in the entire supply schedule or curve, an increase indicating that at any given price a larger quantity would be forthcoming, or alternatively producers would be willing to produce and sell any given quantity at a lower price. *A change in the quantity supplied* refers to movements along a given supply curve, the quantity increasing as the price increases.

Determinants of Supply

The "other things being equal" proviso in the definition of supply means that the basic determinants of supply must be held constant to correctly determine the influence of price changes — and price changes alone — on the quantity supplied of a commodity. For the supply schedule of an individual firm for a particular commodity, the most important determinants are: (1) the state of technology or the productivity of productive factors; (2) resource prices (or more generally the supply of resources to the specific group of suppliers in question); (3) prices of other commodities closely related to the commodity in production; (4) business people's expectations about future prospects for prices, costs, sales, and the state of the economy in general; (5) the firm's goals;

and (6) the weather, strikes, and other short-run forces.[5] Doubtless, other factors influence the quantities offered for sale by an individual firm, but these are probably the most important. To obtain a *market* or *industry supply curve,* you would need to hold these six things constant for all the individual firms in addition to holding constant: (7) the number and character of the firms in the industry.

Importance of Costs of Production

The first two determinants are the two components of production costs. There is a very close relationship between production costs and supply. As a matter of fact, we will later demonstrate that cost and supply data are synonymous in that behind every flow supply curve is a cost curve. Anything which lowers production costs, such as a technological improvement or a decline in resource prices, will increase supply. With lower costs, businesses will find it profitable to offer a larger amount of the commodity at each possible price. In addition, profits in this industry will attract new firms, which will also expand supply. Since knowledge is seldom lost, technological change almost invariably causes the supply of commodities to increase.

Of course, a change in the price of a particular factor of production will affect various industries differently. A decrease in the price of a factor will cause a larger decrease in the costs and hence a larger increase in the production rate for those commodities that employ relatively large amounts of this factor than for those goods that utilize little of the factor. For instance, a decline in the price of steel should have a larger effect on the costs of production of automobiles than of swimming suits.

The prices of commodities that require roughly the same production facilities as the commodity in question can affect its entire supply curve. Suppose, for example, that the production of black-and-white television sets uses much of the same equipment and labor as does the production of color television sets. Therefore, if the price of color television sets increases, black-and-white set prices remaining the same, black-and-white manufacturers will likely hasten to shift to the production of color sets. As another example, if the price of pork increases significantly, the supply of pigskin will increase.

A firm's goals are crucial in explaining supply relationships. If a firm has altruistic motives, it may choose to supply unprofitable items for the good of society. If a firm chooses to maximize its sales revenue, this too may call for supplying some quantity of output such that the last few units may be unprofitable. If a firm wants to maximize its status in the community, it may prefer to produce a less profitable but more prestigious line of products. And there are

---

[5] All of these determinants, along with the elasticity of expectations as to future prices, would constitute short-run supply determinants. The long-run determinants include technology, money income, and variations in taste altering the demand schedule of resources (not final goods). For an excellent discussion of some of the problems involving formulating these *ceteris paribus* conditions, see Richard E. Brumberg, "Ceteris Paribus for Supply Curves," *The Economic Journal* (June, 1953), pp. 462–467; reprinted in *Readings in Microeconomics,* edited by David R. Kamerschen (New York: John Wiley & Sons, 1969), Ch. 14, pp. 229–234.

numerous other possible goals. Despite the abundance of possible objectives, most economists assume the goal of the typical firm is profit or net worth maximization. The typical big-business executive and the entrepreneur of economic theory are still blood relatives. As a hypothesis, profit maximization is subject to all the usual tests and may be rejected in favor of an alternative hypothesis that makes more accurate predictions about a firm's behavior regarding the quantities it offers for sale. The empirical evidence has not yet demonstrated convincingly that any of these alternative hypotheses yield better, or even as good, predictions as those of the profit maximization theory. And many of the non-profit-maximization theories have been shown to be palpably false. The one objective which seems clearly to have the strongest logical case is maximization of the firm's present value.

The weather is, of course, an important influence in the output of agricultural crops. Expectations as to future prices on the supply side are more ambiguous than on the demand side. Higher expected future prices for a commodity would always lead to an increase in the present demand for a commodity. However, higher expected future prices might either increase or decrease the amount currently offered for sale. However, in most manufactures, the expectation of high future prices causes firms to "tool up," expand capacity, and increase production immediately—all of which spell an increase in supply. Some groups, however, such as farmers, might withhold some of their current harvest, anticipating higher prices, such as during the Nixon administration's price freeze programs. On balance, the expansionary effects of increased expected future prices will probably prevail over industry as a whole.

Market Supply Curve

Once again the market (industry) curve is a horizontal summation of the individual (firm) curves.[6] This is illustrated in Figure 2–10.

This figure assumes, for simplicity, that there are only three firms, Alpha, Beta, and Gamma, in this competitive industry. The industry supply curve is generated by horizontally summing the quantities each firm offers for sale at all the various prices. For instance, at $0P_1$, the industry output of $0Q_1$ is composed of $0b_1 + 0g_1$ since Alpha supplied none at this price. At price $0P_2$, the total quantity supplied, $0Q_2$, is the sum of $0a_1 + 0b_2 + 0g_2$. At price $0P_3$, the quantity supplied of $0Q_3$ is composed of $0a_2 + 0b_3 + 0g_3$.

Joint Supply

Joint supply has to do with joint products or items which cannot easily be produced separately. They are joined in a common origin. Examples of jointly

---

[6] As on the demand side, to accomplish the transition from an individual to a market schedule by simply summing the quantities by each individual at the various possible prices, there must be no external effects. On the supply side these external production effects are referred to as external economies and diseconomies of scale. For instance, if factor prices rise because all firms in a given industry have expanded, the market supply curve will be less responsive (elastic) than a simple summation curve.

FIGURE 2–10 Market Supply as the Summation of Individual Supplies

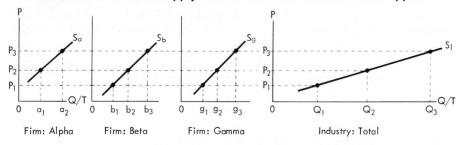

Firm: Alpha   Firm: Beta   Firm: Gamma   Industry: Total

Note: Q/T refers to the quantity supplied per unit of time.

produced items include beef and hides, coke and gas, gasoline and kerosene, wheat and straw, etc.

LAW OF SUPPLY

In Figure 2–10 illustrating market supply, upward sloping curves for the firm and the industry were assumed. In fact, the most important characteristic of a typical or normal supply curve is that it rises from left to right (i.e., has a *positive slope*), indicating that, other things being equal, sellers will supply larger quantities of commodities at higher market prices. More formally, the *law of supply* states that given the other determinants, there generally is a positive relationship between price and quantity supplied—both on the firm and industry level.

The supply curve of an individual producer in a competitive market is upsloping because of the *law of diminishing returns,* which after all kinds of testing has always emerged essentially uncontradicted. This principle states that, given the state of technology and the resource base, when the quantity of one input factor (for example labor) increases relative to other factors, the first factor's increment of output will, after some point, diminish. Translated into cost terms, this law means that the addition to total costs of producing a commodity rises as total output expands. Since the cost of producing additional units of output increases, a higher price will be needed to induce the firm to produce the larger output. Thus, the firm's supply curve is positively sloped.

The law of diminishing returns is so fundamental to the economics of the supply side that several chapters are needed to discuss its principle ramifications and implications. So if you feel that the above paragraph is an inadequate explanation, you are right.

The upslope of market supply curves may be more easily explained than the individual curve. At higher product prices, larger profits are made, which makes entry into this industry more attractive. And since the number of firms affects the industry supply curve, the entry of new firms would increase the industry quantity supplied even if no existing firms increased their output at all. The price is an incentive for a supplier to produce and sell a product. The higher the price, the stronger the incentive for existing suppliers to expand their output and for new firms to shift to the production of this product.

For the output of a particular product to increase (in response to a higher price), resources will have to be drawn from other uses. In general, we would expect that to induce these factors of production to move to the new occupation, a higher wage or other resource price would have to be offered. In addition to this argument, less suitable or less efficient resources will sometimes have to be employed, resulting in higher costs as output expands.

The exceptions to this law of supply are thought to be slightly more common than the exceptions to the law of demand. Exceptions may be found only in firms and industries that have decreasing or constant cost curves. However, decreasing-cost industries due to economies of scale are quite rare over prolonged periods of time in the U.S. economy.

SUPPLY AND DEMAND ANALYSIS

The *law of supply and demand* starts with the proposition that there exists something called the *equilibrium price*. This is the price at which supply is equal to demand; or, spelled out, it is the price at which the quantity sellers wish to sell is exactly equal to the quantity buyers wish to buy. It is equilibrium in that both buyers and sellers are able to engage in what they judge to be their optimum behavior. The forces from the demand side exactly balance the forces on the supply side, and there is no incentive for change when the equilibrium price is the actual price. If the market price is different from the equilibrium price, forces are set into motion to change the market price, unless hindrances to such change exist. We will take up the possible hindrances after we examine the uninhibited case.

Figure 2–11 shows a single demand curve and a single supply curve, which of course means that all of the determinants other than price are held constant. P_e is the equilibrium price where quantity demanded equals quantity supplied. If the market price were P_a, the quantity demanded would be QD_a and the quantity supplied would be QS_a. In this case, demanders would be at their optimum: When the price is P_a, they wish to buy QD_a, which they are able to do. But at price P_a suppliers wish to sell QS_a, but they can sell only the amount buyers will buy. Thus, there must be sellers who wish to sell more than they are selling. They are not at their optimum. There are suppliers who would prefer to sell at prices below P_a rather than not sell at P_a. There is pressure, then, from sellers who would offer to lower the price. As long as the market price is above equilibrium, some sellers will take steps to lower the price. Notice that, in the process of the price falling, some sellers will prefer not to sell or prefer to sell fewer units at the lower price so that the quantity sellers wish to sell declines from QS_a toward Q_e.

When the market price is below equilibrium, the situation is reversed. At price P_b, sellers are willing to sell the quantity QS_b; and that is the amount they

**FIGURE 2–11   Determination of Equilibrium
Price and Quantity**

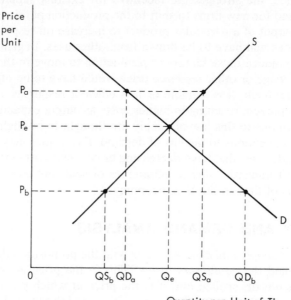

Quantity per Unit of Time

will sell. However, buyers are willing to buy QD_b, but they will be unable to buy any more than sellers will sell. The disappointed buyers would presumably offer to pay a higher price rather than go without the commodity. The market price moves toward the equilibrium price. As it moves higher, suppliers will be willing to sell more; and buyers who were willing to buy a large quantity at the lower price will reduce their purchase rate, bringing the quantities demanded and supplied into equality.

The equilibrium price changes if and only if either the demand or the supply schedules change; and these will change only if the determinants other than price change. If incomes, tastes, or the prices of other commodities change, the demand curve shifts. If technology (productivity), resource prices, or business expectations change, the supply schedule will shift.

An increase in demand causes the equilibrium price to increase, causing producers to expand output as shown in Figure 2–12. The price increases from P_e to P_e'; and the quantity produced, sold, and bought increases from Q_e to Q_e'. Because the public wanted more of this commodity relative to others, more of it was forthcoming. If demand had decreased from D' to D, price would fall from P_e' to P_e and quantity would decrease from Q_e' to Q_e. When the public wants less of this good relative to others, less is forthcoming.

An increase in supply is shown in Figure 2–13, where the supply schedule has shifted from S to S', due, we will presume, to a decrease in the costs of production. At the original equilibrium price of P_e, sellers are willing (after

FIGURE 2–12   Price and Quantity Change because of a Change in Demand

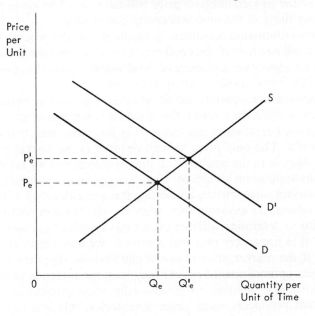

FIGURE 2–13   Price and Quantity Change because of a Change in Supply

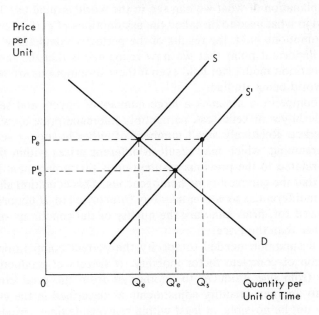

their costs have decreased) to sell at the rate Q_s per time unit; but since buyers are only willing to buy Q_e at that price, some sellers will offer to sell at lower prices and so the new equilibrium price will fall to P'_e. The lower price induces buyers to buy more of the now less costly commodity.

The above discussion describes, in simple terms, the process by which the market price adjusts toward the equilibrium price. To be sure, in such a capsule description we gloss over a number of "real world" issues; but even after these are studied, the basic results seem to stand up.

The question is frequently asked whether a particular observed price is the equilibrium price. In a sense, the question is not meaningful. Equilibrium is a concept—a construct of the mind. It is not something that exists in the empirical world. The only price we can observe is the market price. We can attempt to observe in the marketplace the manifestations we attribute to equilibrium or disequilibrium situations. For example, in our analysis we note that at the equilibrium price, buyers are buying the quantities they wish to buy and sellers are selling the amounts they wish to sell. We can circulate a survey questionnaire to determine whether or not this is indeed the case.

Since this is not a very practical approach, we may approach the question differently. If the market price is above equilibrium, suppliers will be selling less than their optimal quantities. We may look for evidence of this situation. If commodities are building up in unusually large inventories without any indication that producers want larger inventories, this is a clue. Foodstuffs rotting in warehouses may be accounted for in this way. On the other hand, if we observe queues and merchants out of stock, we may conclude that the market price is below the equilibrium price.

What prevents the equilibrating mechanism we have described from being a perfect explanation of what we can see in the world around us? The answer can be found in what used to be called the assumptions of perfect competition. If these assumptions hold, the results of the perfectly competitive model will occur. The important point that we now recognize is that the results of the perfect competition model can hold even if these assumptions are not descriptive of the world being studied.

Perfect competition assumes a large number of buyers and sellers, such that no single buyer or seller can perceptibly influence price by withdrawing from the market. Relatively small numbers of either buyers or sellers allow for some bargaining, which may result in different prices within the market.

Closely related to the previous assumption is the requirement for perfect competition that the commodity be homogeneous. This condition allows transactors to be indifferent as to whom they buy from or sell to. If nonprice competition is allowed for, firms can vary the quality or the conditions surrounding the sales rather than the price.

A third assumption needed to specify the perfect competition model is the assumption of complete factor mobility. If factors of production cannot freely move from one producer to another or from the production of one commodity to another, quantity adjustments as described in the competitive solution may not be possible, at least within reasonable time periods.

The perfect competition case does not allow for interference in the adjustment process by governmental or powerful private agencies. If laws prevent prices from changing in one direction or the other, adjustments will take place, but they will not be just as we described them above. Many applications of microeconomics deal specifically with the impact of artificial constraints such as wage and price controls, rationing, subsidies, taxes, union rules, and monopoly practices.

The four assumptions mentioned above are included in the definition of "pure competition" as well as "perfect competition." A fifth assumption is required for perfect competition, namely, the assumption of perfect knowledge. If buyers and sellers are ignorant of the qualities of different products or even of the existence of some products, or if they are unaware of what prices are or who the buyers or sellers are, the scenario of perfect competition will not be completely accurate.

There is a danger in overemphasizing the importance of these assumptions. One is tempted to say that since the assumptions are obviously not met in practical situations, the analysis must be sterile. This is incorrect. The analysis has great value, even when not adjusted for the existence of imperfections. However, much advanced work in microeconomics deals with adjusting the model to incorporate the significance of relaxing the strict assumptions.

QUESTIONS

1. Compare the communicative aspects of the following markets: wheat at the Chicago Board of Trade, suburban real estate, shampoo, used cars, and "over-the-counter" stocks.
2. What is the difference between "wanting," "needing," and "demanding" a commodity?
3. "The best things in life are free . . . but why does it always cost so much to enjoy free things?" Give some examples of "free," nonmaterial pleasures you could have if you were wealthy, but not if you were poor.
4. Carefully distinguish between "stock demand" and "flow demand" and also between "stock supply" and "flow supply."
5. Conceive of an experiment in an auction-market setting to derive a demand curve from the reservation prices of the participants.
6. What does it mean to say that "a market is cleared"? When is a market not cleared?
7. Suppose that in a particular community the existing stock of (homogeneous) houses and the demand for them are such that the market clearing price is $50,000. Also suppose the cost of producing such a house, including land cost, is constant at $40,000. Construct a diagram which shows the current and the new equilibrium condition.
8. In a competitive industry, why is the demand curve facing any of the firms in that industry a horizontal line, no matter what the shape of the market demand curve for the product?
9. What variables besides price determine the quantity demanded of any commodity?

10. Interpret the following expressions:
    (a) increase in demand
    (b) decrease in supply
    (c) increase in the quantity demanded
    (d) decrease in the quantity supplied
11. Why is the supply curve of a commodity positively sloped?
12. Draw a supply and a demand curve and label the equilibrium price and quantity. If the actual price is above equilibrium, which group is not at its optimum condition and who will take the actions to force the market price downward?
13. List the assumptions necessary for a market to be considered perfectly competitive. Explain why you think each assumption is important in assuring that the scenario of price determination in this chapter will work out as described.

3   Elasticity of Demand and Supply

The concept of elasticity is used in many contexts in economics. Thus, it will be worthwhile to spend some time on the general idea of elasticity before directing attention to the specific notions of the elasticity of demand and supply.

ELASTICITY

Elasticity always deals with the responsiveness or the sensitivity of a dependent variable to a change in an independent variable. Common sense suggests that we can measure such responsiveness by comparing the relative change in the dependent variable with the relative change in the independent variable. If y is the dependent and x the independent variable, $\Delta y/y$ and $\Delta x/x$ are the corresponding relative changes. The elasticity measure then is simply:

$$\text{Elasticity of } y \text{ with respect to } x = \frac{\Delta y/y}{\Delta x/x} \tag{3.1}$$

or

$$\eta_{yx} = \frac{\Delta y}{y} \cdot \frac{x}{\Delta x} = \frac{\Delta y}{\Delta x} \cdot \frac{x}{y} \tag{3.2}$$

where η (eta) is the usual symbol for elasticity.

Equations (3.1) and (3.2) permit measurement of elasticity of any y with respect to any x. If you want to know the sensitivity of gas consumption to automobile horsepower, use the formula:

$$\eta_{MPG,HP} = \frac{\Delta MPG}{MPG} \Big/ \frac{\Delta HP}{HP} = \frac{\Delta MPG}{\Delta HP} \cdot \frac{HP}{MPG}$$

If you want to know the responsiveness of your corn crop to changes in the amount of fertilizer you use, employ the formula:

$$\eta_{bu./acre,f} = \frac{\Delta bu./acre}{bu./acre} \Big/ \frac{\Delta f}{f} = \frac{\Delta bu./acre}{\Delta f} \cdot \frac{f}{bu./acre}$$

and so on for any two variables believed to be related to each other. The dimensions always cancel out, so elasticity is a dimensionless or pure number.

The most important use of the concept of elasticity is in the analysis of elasticity of demand and supply. The unqualified expressions "elasticity of demand" or "elasticity of supply" will be understood to include the phrase, "with respect to its own price." In all other cases the independent variable will be specified. For example, "income elasticity of demand for commodity

x" means the elasticity of the quantity of x demanded with respect to a change in income, or η_{xI}.

The law of demand tells us that ordinarily consumers will respond to a price decline by buying more. But the degree of change in quantity demanded in response to a price change varies considerably, as will be described shortly. *Price elasticity of demand* is a measure of how much the quantity demanded of a commodity responds to a change in its price, given the demand curve. If consumer purchases of a commodity are quite sensitive or responsive to a change in the commodity's price, demand is *elastic;* if the consumption rate is rather unresponsive, demand is described as *inelastic.* More precisely, the demand for a good is elastic over a given price range if a price change (within this range) causes a relative change in quantity demanded that is greater than the relative change in price. If the percentage change in price exceeds the percentage change in quantity demanded, demand is inelastic.[1] If the two percentages are exactly equal, demand is *unit* or *unitary elastic.*

Price Elasticity of Demand Formulas

Letting η stand for the coefficient of "direct" or "own" price elasticity of demand, P_x for the unit price of x, QD_x for the quantity demanded of x, and the sign Δ for a very small change, we may measure η by the following formula:

$$\eta = \frac{\text{percentage change in } QD_x}{\text{percentage change in } P_x} = \frac{\%\Delta QD_x}{\%\Delta P_x} = \tag{3.3}$$

$$\frac{\Delta QD_x}{QD_x} \div \frac{\Delta P_x}{P_x} = \frac{\Delta QD_x}{\Delta P_x} \cdot \frac{P_x}{QD_x}$$

Since η is a "pure number," it is possible to make meaningful comparisons between products. This standardization is needed since a \$1 change in the price of, say, a bushel of wheat is an enormous change, but a \$1 change in the price of an automobile is trivial.

The values for η will generally range from zero to minus infinity. Inasmuch as P_x and QD_x normally move in opposite directions, η is usually negative. However, when economists speak of the magnitudes of demand elasticity, they, as a matter of convention, ignore the minus sign or look at the absolute value of η, i.e., (1) $\eta \equiv |\eta|$ if $\eta \geqq 0$; (2) $|\eta| \equiv -\eta$, if $\eta < 0$. A numerical (absolute) value of η greater than one indicates that demand is elastic; less than one, inelastic; and one, unitary elastic. This fits in with what we said above, for if the percentage change in quantity demanded exceeds the percentage change in P, the numerator in the first formula in (3.3) is greater than the denominator so that η must exceed one in the elastic case.

Because all observed price changes are not extremely small as the formula technically requires, it is often necessary to use a formula that gives a good

---

[1] Some students find it easier to remember elasticity in terms of percentage changes in the two variables. This is permissible since a relative change in a variable is $\Delta x/x$, which can be converted into a percentage change by multiplying $\Delta x/x$ by 100; and in the formula the 100's cancel.

approximation of the "true" value. Geometrically, the problem is that the above point-elasticity formula refers to elasticity at a precise point on a demand curve, whereas elasticity generally must be estimated over an arc or segment of the demand curve. The following formula, which represents an "average" coefficient, should be used for all actual numerical problems, reserving the point concept for more general analysis.

$$
H = \frac{\overbrace{QD_{x2} - QD_{x1}}^{\Delta QD_x}}{QD_{x1} + QD_{x2}} \div \frac{\overbrace{P_{x2} - P_{x1}}^{\Delta P_x}}{P_{x1} + P_{x2}} = \frac{\Delta QD_x}{QD_{x1} + QD_{x2}} \cdot \frac{P_{x1} + P_{x2}}{\Delta P} \tag{3.4}
$$

$$
= \frac{\Delta QD_x}{\Delta P_x} \cdot \frac{P_{x1} + P_{x2}}{QD_{x1} + QD_{x2}}
$$

where QD_{x1}, P_{x1} is one quantity and price of x; and QD_{x2}, P_{x2} is a second quantity and price of x. ΔQD_x and ΔP_x refer to small changes in the quantity and price of x respectively, and H is the arc price elasticity of demand formula. H is an "average" concept since, if we computed the average quantity, $(QD_{x1} + QD_{x2})/2$, and the average price, $(P_{x1} + P_{x2})/2$, the 2's would cancel out, giving the above formula. The reader might wish to verify the elasticity estimates shown in Table 3–1.

The Total Spending Test of Elasticity

While the typical business is vitally concerned with the elasticity of demand for its product, the decision makers do not think of it in terms of an elasticity coefficient. Rather, they look at it in the following way: What will happen to sales or total revenue (TR) as a result of changing the price of the product? A very useful and computationally easy method of testing price elasticity is through observing the effect of price changes on the total amount spent for a good. The total amount spent can be viewed as consumers' total expenditures from the purchasers' viewpoint or total business receipts or total revenue from the seller's viewpoint. (Total revenue equals the price of the commodity times the number of units sold, i.e., $TR = P \cdot Q$.)

For a negatively sloped demand curve, the two factors determining TR, P and Q, have opposite effects. A decline in P reduces TR; the associated increase in Q increases TR, and conversely for a rise in P. Which of the two effects "wins" will determine what will happen to total spending. If the percentage change in P is equal (in absolute value) to the associated percentage change in Q, the two effects offset one another and TR does not change. Since equal proportionate changes mean unitary elasticity, the demand curve must be unitary elastic when TR remains the same after a price change. If the demand is elastic, quantity "wins" — since the percentage change in Q is greater than the percentage change in P — so that TR must rise as price falls. If demand is inelastic, price "wins," so that TR falls as the P falls. The results of this test are summarized in Table 3–2.

TABLE 3–1 Estimates of Coefficients of Arc Elasticity (H)

(1) Price (P) ($ per unit)	(2) Quantity Demanded (QD) (units per day)	(3) $QD_2 - QD_1 = \Delta QD$	(4) $\dfrac{\Delta QD}{QD_1 + QD_2}$	(5) $P_2 - P_1 = \Delta P$	(6) $\dfrac{P_1 + P_2}{\Delta P}$	(7) H [Column (4) x Column (6)]	(8) Elastic, Inelastic, or Unitary Elastic	(9) Total Revenue
$9	0							
8	20	20	20/20	$1	17/1	17	Elastic (H>1)	
7	40	20	20/60	1	15/1	5	Elastic (H>1)	
6	60	20	20/100	1	13/1	13/5	Elastic (H>1)	
5	80	20	20/140	1	11/1	11/7	Elastic (H>1)	
4	100	20	20/180	1	9/1	1	Unitary (H=1)	
3	120	20	20/220	1	7/1	7/11	Inelastic (H<1)	
2	140	20	20/260	1	5/1	5/13	Inelastic (H<1)	
1	160	20	20/300	1	3/1	1/5	Inelastic (H<1)	

TABLE 3–2   Total Revenue Test of Elasticity

Direction of Price Change	Inelastic Demand	Elastic Demand	Unitary Elastic Demand
Price ($P\uparrow$) Increase	$TR\uparrow$	$TR\downarrow$	$TR\leftrightarrow$
Price ($P\downarrow$) Decrease	$TR\downarrow$	$TR\uparrow$	$TR\leftrightarrow$

Fortunately, instead of memorizing Table 3–2, you can learn the following general rule. If as P changes: (1) P and TR move in opposite directions, demand is *elastic;* (2) P and TR move in the same direction, demand is *inelastic;* and (3) TR remains constant, demand is *unitary.* We urge the reader to verify these rules by pencilling in the correct total revenue (expenditure) values in Column (9) of Table 3–1.

This total revenue approach is extremely useful since one needn't know the precise values of elasticity; one must know only if demand is elastic, inelastic, or unitary elastic. The great practical significance of the revenue or expenditure effects of the price elasticity of demand will be demonstrated below.

Graphical Representation of Elasticity

Price elasticity is defined as $(\Delta Q/\Delta P) \cdot (P/Q)$. The first ratio, $\Delta Q/\Delta P$, is the inverse or reciprocal of the slope of the demand curve. The second ratio, P/Q, locates a particular point on a demand curve in the price-quantity plane. Keep in mind that elasticity depends upon both ratios, since there seems to be a temptation to confuse elasticity with slope alone.

Figure 3–1(a) shows a *linear* demand curve, which means that the slope, $\Delta P/\Delta Q$ (and therefore its reciprocal, $\Delta Q/\Delta P$) is the same at every point on the curve. In this case elasticity varies only with P/Q. At point A, P is large and Q is small; and at point B, P is small and Q is large. Elasticity gets smaller in value (less elastic) as we move from A to B.

Now consider Figure 3–1(b), where D_1 and D_2 have different slopes, but at one point they intersect so P/Q is the same. The ratio $\Delta Q/\Delta P$ on D_2 is clearly larger than on D_1 since ΔP is the same, but ΔQ on D_2 is visibly greater than on D_1. This indicates that the elasticity of D_2 is greater than the elasticity of D_1 at point A, but can we make the general statement that D_2 is a more elastic demand curve than is D_1? On both curves elasticity ranges from infinity, where the D curve intersects the price axis, to zero, where the curve intersects the quantity axis; so there must be points on D_1 where the elasticity is greater than points on D_2, and of course vice versa. In other words, we can always compare elasticities at particular points or within particular segments of curves, but to describe a curve as being more or less elastic than another curve is often meaningless.

FIGURE 3-1   Fundamentals of Elasticity

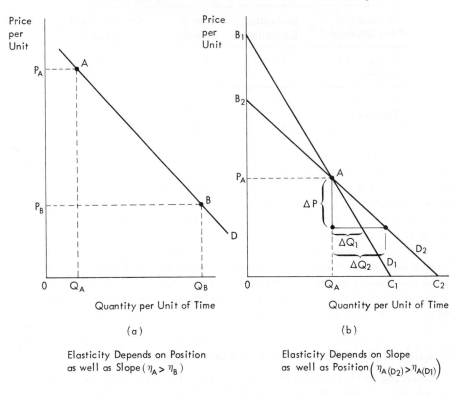

Elasticity Depends on Position
as well as Slope ($\eta_A > \eta_B$)

Elasticity Depends on Slope
as well as Position $\left(\eta_{A(D_2)} > \eta_{A(D_1)} \right)$

There are, at least conceptually, exceptional curves where elasticity is constant throughout their lengths. All of those depicted in Figure 3-2 are constant-elasticity curves. The curve labeled D_1, while not thought to be representative of a demand curve because of its positive slope, is of constant elasticity because it is in the class of linear functions running through the origin. It is easy to see that elasticity is constant because the two components of elasticity are constant. Since it is a straight line, the slope $\Delta P/\Delta Q$ (and therefore $\Delta Q/\Delta P$) is constant; and since the line goes through the origin, the ratio P/Q is constant.

The curve D_2 is, by construction, a rectangular hyperbola, which has the property that, on any point on the curve, any rectangle formed by perpendiculars to the axes has the same area as any other such rectangle drawn from any other point. In economics such a rectangle is price times quantity, and $PQ = TR$. As shown above, if total revenue remains constant as price changes, elasticity equals one. Elasticity on this curve is constant and equal to one throughout its length.

Curve D_3, if it is a demand curve, is a case which is conceivable in some price ranges, although it would be quite unusual. The curve is described as having constant zero elasticity. Again, referring to the elasticity formula $\eta = P\Delta Q/Q\Delta P$, since Q is constant, ΔQ is zero and the numerator is zero; and by

FIGURE 3-2   Constant Elasticity Curves

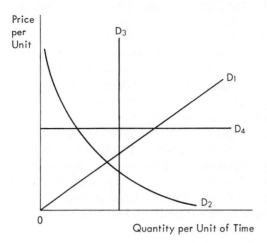

convention zero divided by anything is zero. Economically speaking, there is no quantity response to a change in price.

A case frequently encountered in microeconomics is curve D_4, which could be the demand curve facing a single firm in perfect competition. The idea is that the firm can sell any output at the market-determined price. If the firm set its price even slightly above D_4, it would sell none of the commodity; and there would be no reason to sell at a price below this. D_4 is described as a curve of constant, infinite elasticity, since in this case ΔP is zero, making the denominator of the elasticity formula zero; and anything divided by zero is called infinity.

A method of measuring point elasticity geometrically is presented with the aid of Figure 3-3. The linear function AC represents the demand curve for some commodity, $0E$ the original price, and $0D$ the original quantity. If we

FIGURE 3-3   Geometric Determination of Point Elasticity

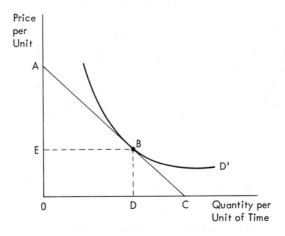

wish to measure the elasticity of demand at point B, we can use the formula $\eta = (\Delta Q / \Delta P) \cdot (P/Q)$. The inverse of the slope of the demand curve, $\Delta Q / \Delta P$, can be measured by DC/BD. The quantity and price at point B are $0D$ and BD respectively. Therefore, $\eta = (DC/BD) \cdot (BD/0D) = DC/0D$. By similar triangles one can also prove that $\eta = BC/AB$ or $\eta = OE/AE$. If the demand curve is nonlinear, the same procedure may be used to find the elasticity at a given point by constructing the tangent line to the demand curve at the relevant point. Thus, if D' is the demand curve, η at B is the same on both D' and on the curve AC, which would now be the tangent to D'.

The relevance of the position on the curve as opposed to the slope of the curve can be shown by making a geometric determination of elasticity of two parallel (i.e., equally sloped) demand curves at a given price $\bar{P}$. Suppose demand curve D_2 is outside demand curve D_1, but they have equal slopes, as in Figure 3–4(a). Which, if either, is more elastic at price $\bar{P}$: D_1 or D_2? In other words, is $\eta_a \gtreqless \eta_b$ where point a is on D_1 and point b is on D_2 at the given price

FIGURE 3–4   Geometric Determination of Equal Elasticity

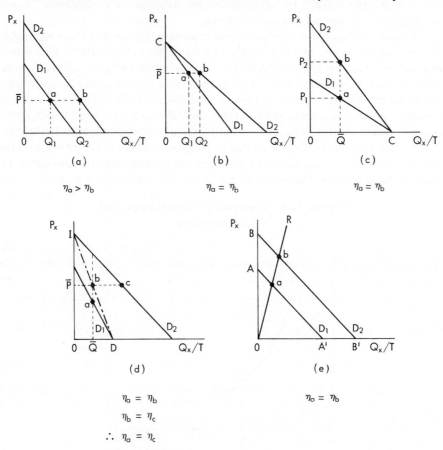

Note: Q_x/T refers to the quantity of commodity x consumed per unit of time.

of $0\bar{P}$? Since $\eta = (\Delta Q/\Delta P) \cdot (P/Q)$ and by definition $\Delta Q/\Delta P$ is the same for two parallel demand curves, and since we are measuring η at a given price $\bar{P}$, we need only compare Q_1 and Q_2 to find η_a and η_b. Clearly, $Q_2 > Q_1$, so $\bar{P}/Q_1 > \bar{P}/Q_2$, and therefore $\eta_a > \eta_b$. In general, parallel shifts to the right for linear demand curves are associated, for a given price, with lower elasticity. To locate points of equal elasticity on two parallel linear demand curves, such as points a and b in Figure 3–4(e), draw a linear ray OR out of the origin. It will always cut points of equal elasticity on the two demand curves; therefore, $\eta_a = \eta_b$ in Figure 3–4(e). The proof depends on the observation that $aA'/aA = bB'/bB$.

As a related exercise, prove that two linear demand curves with a common price intercept have the same elasticity at any given price. Hint: Use one of the geometric measures of elasticity shown above. For instance in Figure 3–4(b) you know that $\eta_a = \eta_b = 0\bar{P}/\bar{P}C$. In this figure D_1 and D_2 are isoelastic ("iso," from the Greek, means "equal") for a given price $\bar{P}$; and therefore along $\bar{P}$, $\eta_a = \eta_b$. Similarly, show that two linear demand curves with a common intercept on the horizontal (quantity) axis are isoelastic for any given quantity of output. Thus, in Figure 3–4(c) $\eta_a = \eta_b = \bar{Q}C/0\bar{Q}$, and so D_1 and D_2 are isoelastic for any given $0Q$. Finally, in Figure 3–4(d) you can extend this analysis to locate points of equal elasticity on demand curves that do not have the same slope or do not have common intercepts by constructing an imaginary demand curve, ID, having a common intercept with each real curve, and then use the above two rules for isoelastic demand curves at a given price or quantity.

For instance, along the given output $0\bar{Q}$ you know that $\eta_a = \eta_b$. Similarly, along a given price $0\bar{P}$, $\eta_b = \eta_c$. Therefore, $\eta_a = \eta_c$. In other words, you can think of Figures 3–4(b), (c), (d), and (e) as showing how, if you were given any point on a linear demand curve D_1, you could find a point on another linear demand curve D_2 that has the identical elasticity.

REVENUE AND ELASTICITY

In the analysis of commodity demand, the relationship of elasticity to the several revenue measures is of great importance. There are three such revenue concepts, all representable by curves, which are to be considered. The first is *total revenue* (or *TR*), which is the sum of the receipts from the sale of the product during a specified time period. Since we normally assume that all units of the commodity sell for the same price, in the given time period *TR* can be described as *PQ*, the unit price times the number of units sold.

$$TR = P \cdot Q \tag{3.5}$$

The second revenue concept is *average revenue* (*AR*). Like any other average, *AR* is the total divided by the number, or, in this case total revenue divided by the number of units of the commodity.

$$AR = \frac{TR}{Q} \tag{3.6}$$

Since, from (3.5), $P = TR/Q$, it is obvious that $AR = P$. If all units sell at the same price, the average revenue, or the per-unit revenue, is of course the price.

Marginal revenue (MR) is the key revenue concept. It is the change in total revenue per unit change in the quantity sold per unit of time.

$$MR = \frac{\Delta TR}{\Delta Q} \tag{3.7}$$

This shows the relationship of MR to TR. It is also sometimes useful to know the relationship of MR to AR. First, we state it; then we prove it.

$$MR = AR + \frac{\Delta AR}{\Delta Q} Q \tag{3.8}$$

or since $AR = P$,

$$MR = P + \frac{\Delta P}{\Delta Q} Q \tag{3.9}$$

First, notice that if a firm can increase sales (Q) without having to lower the product price, ΔP is zero, and $MR = P = AR$. This is a very important observation, because this is what characterizes a firm in pure competition. A firm which is large relative to the market for its output (or an industry made up of many firms) will have to lower its price to increase sales. Thus, for ΔQ to be positive, ΔP will have to be negative. For such a firm or industry, if the quantity sold increases as a result of a decrease in price, its total revenue will change in the following way: $\Delta TR = \Delta Q \cdot P + \Delta P \cdot Q$. That is, total revenue will increase by the increased number of units sold (ΔQ) times the price at which they are sold (P) minus the amount of revenue lost by having to sell the original quantity (Q) at the lower price (ΔP). Starting with the fact that $\Delta TR = \Delta QP + \Delta PQ$, divide both sides by ΔQ: $\Delta TR/\Delta Q = \frac{\Delta Q}{\Delta Q} P + \frac{\Delta P}{\Delta Q} Q$. Since $\Delta TR/\Delta Q$ is MR, and $\Delta Q/\Delta Q = 1$, we have $MR = P + \frac{\Delta P}{\Delta Q} Q$.

Since the total, average, and marginal relationships are so important in so many contexts in microeconomics, it will be beneficial to pursue them further, using graphs as the frame of reference. We can start with the demand curve; and since we have already established the identity of price and average revenue, we can label the curve either D or AR. The demand curve of Figure 3–5 is linear for convenience. Sales are $0Q_1$ when price is P_1, so total revenue is the rectangle $0P_1AQ_1$; and similarly for any other price-quantity combination. Thus, the TR curve is derived from the demand curve. But we could derive the AR curve from the TR curve as well. AR at A is $TR_A/Q_1 = P_1Q_1/Q_1 = $ altitude of triangle $0AQ_1$/base of triangle $0AQ_1 = \frac{AQ_1}{0Q_1}$. This ratio can be measured by angle ϕ_A. It is sufficient for our purpose to observe that $\phi_A > \phi_B$ and that, as we move from the origin to larger sales levels, the ray becomes continuously flatter (i.e., ϕ becomes smaller) and therefore AR is falling, reaching zero only when sales are maximized at zero price.

FIGURE 3-5   Average and Total Revenue Relationships

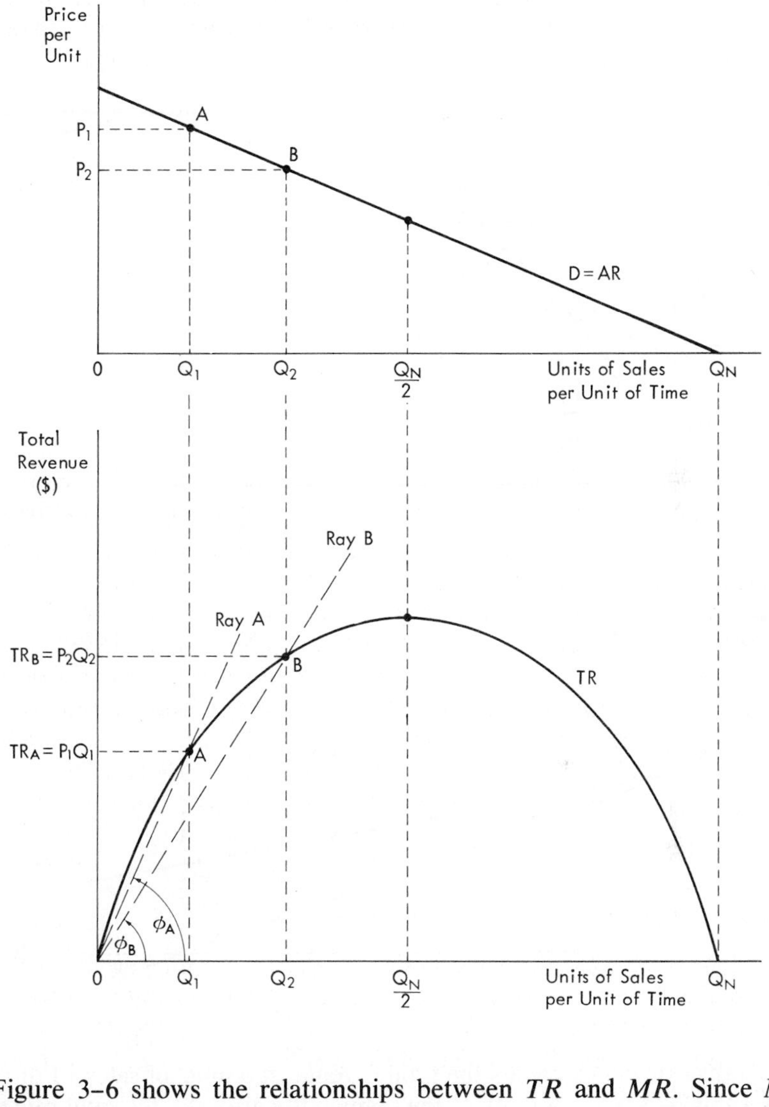

Figure 3–6 shows the relationships between TR and MR. Since $MR = \Delta TR/\Delta Q$, the slope of the TR curve is MR. The slope at any point on a non-linear curve is the slope of a tangent to that point. The slope can be measured from any of the three triangles shown which have tangent A as the hypotenuse, since the ratio of the altitude to the base of each is the same. The slope of TR at A can also be measured by angle θ_A, at B by angle θ_B, and so on. Clearly $\theta_A > \theta_B$; and on a TR curve which is concave from below, MR declines continuously, reaching zero when the slope of TR is zero at the maximum of TR (point C).

In the above paragraph the MR curve was derived from the TR curve. The opposite procedure is also possible. The basic proposition is that the sum

FIGURE 3-6 Marginal, Average, and Total Revenue Relationships

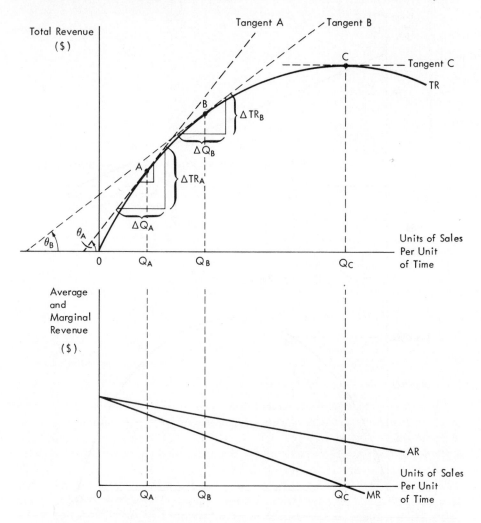

of n marginal revenues equals the total revenue at n units of sales.[2] For example, in Table 3–3 when 5 units of the commodity are sold, the total revenue is 60, which is equal to the sum of the marginal revenues of 20, 16, 12, 8, and 4.

The relationship between marginal revenue and average revenue is shown graphically in Figure 3–7. The first observation to make is that MR always lies below the AR curve. The rule is that whenever the marginal value is below the average value, the average is falling.[3]

---

[2] This proposition is subject to the proviso that the total revenue function goes through the origin.

[3] In other connections it will be important to know that when a marginal value is above the average, the average will be rising.

TABLE 3–3   Relationship between *TR* and *MR*

Price	Quantity	TR	MR
20	1	20	20
18	2	36	16
16	3	48	12
14	4	56	8
12	5	60	4
10	6	60	0
8	7	56	−4

FIGURE 3–7   Average and Marginal Revenue Relationships

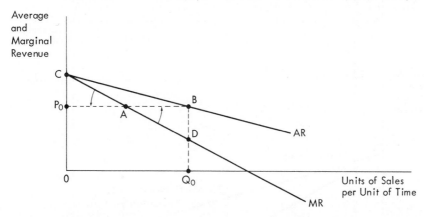

An interesting fact, and one helpful in the geometry of revenue curves, is that the *MR* curve will bisect any perpendicular from the vertical axis to the demand curve. In other words, $P_0A = AB$. To prove this we can show that triangles P_0CA and BDA are similar. We know that the areas of the two triangles are the same from the knowledge that rectangle $0P_0BQ_0$ is equal to total revenue. We also know that the area of $0CDQ_0$ is total revenue,[4] and that $0P_0ADQ_0$ is a common area, so the areas P_0CA and BDA, that are not common, are equal. Since both triangles are right triangles (and thus $\angle CP_0A = \angle DBA$), and since the angles at A are equal ($\angle P_0AC = \angle BAD$), the triangles are similar, which means that $CP_0 = BD$ and $P_0A = AB$. From this result we can always determine the height of *MR* by dropping a perpendicular from a point on the linear demand curve to the horizontal axis, such as BQ_0; and the distance to the *MR* curve is BD, which is equal to CP_0.

With the above discussion of the revenue curves, it is now possible to relate elasticity and the three revenue curves. At the upper range of the demand curve shown in Figure 3–8, elasticity exceeds unity. Since the total revenue tests show that price and total revenue move in opposite directions

[4] From the proposition above that the sum of n marginal revenues equals the *TR* at n, where here n equals $0Q_0$.

FIGURE 3–8   Elasticity and the Three Revenue Curves

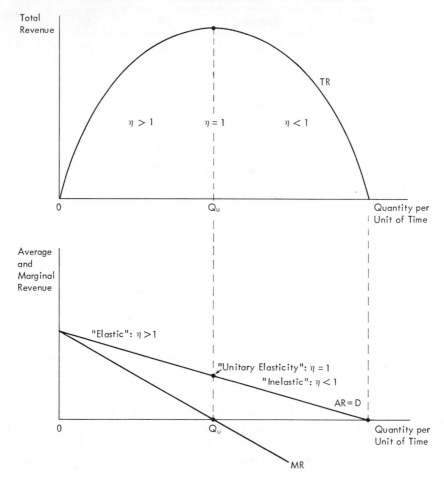

when $\eta > 1$, TR must be rising as Q increases (i.e., P decreases) from zero to Q_u in Figure 3–8. Since TR is increasing as quantity is increasing from zero to Q_u, marginal revenue must be positive. At Q_u, TR reaches a maximum, which means that MR must equal zero. Beyond Q_u units of output, demand is inelastic. When $\eta < 1$, TR must fall as quantity increases (i.e., P falls), and thus MR must be negative.

Obviously no single-product, profit-maximizing firm would ever knowingly produce in the inelastic portion of its demand curve, since TR is smaller than it would be at a smaller output. And, of course, total costs will normally be smaller at the smaller output. Both of these factors make profits larger if output is contracted. Even if there were zero costs, the maximum quantity that would be offered for sale is Q_u where TR is at a maximum. This means with positive costs, where possible, a profit-maximizing, single-product firm will always produce in the elastic sector of its demand curve. It is entirely possible that a competitive industry will operate in the inelastic range of the demand curve for the output of the whole industry. This, of course, is the reason for the complaints by some farmers that while their crop is very large they are getting less money for it than in years when the crop was smaller.

You may recall from equation (3.9) that:

$$MR = P + \frac{\Delta P}{\Delta Q} Q$$

This can be rewritten as: $MR = P \left(1 + \frac{\Delta P}{\Delta Q} \frac{Q}{P} \right)$, and since the expression $\frac{\Delta P}{\Delta Q} \frac{Q}{P}$ is the reciprocal of elasticity, it follows that:

$$MR = P \left(1 - \frac{1}{\eta} \right)$$

If $\eta = 1, MR = 0, TR$ is constant

         $\eta > 1, MR > 0, TR$ is rising

         $\eta < 1, MR < 0, TR$ is falling

DETERMINANTS OF PRICE ELASTICITY OF DEMAND

The degree of price elasticity of demand depends principally upon: (1) the availability of close substitutes; (2) the size or importance of the expenditure on the item in the individual's total budget; (3) the time period involved; and (4) the inherent qualities of the commodity. The first of these is the single most important factor determining elasticity. Since there are no close substitutes for salt, penicillin, eyeglasses (including contact lenses), etc., the elasticity for these commodities is very low (read inelastic) over the usual range of prices for these commodities. In general, the more narrowly defined the commodity in question, the larger the number of available substitutes and the greater the elasticity of demand. Thus, the demand for "Wonder" white bread is more elastic than the demand for white bread, which in turn is more elastic than the demand for bread (white and dark), which in turn is more elastic than the demand for foodstuffs, and so on. With each succeeding case, fewer things can substitute for the commodity. In the first case not only can consumers buy other brands of white bread, but they can also substitute dark bread or even rolls or some other rival commodity for "Wonder" white bread, or they can buy day-old bread or even bake their own.

The availability of substitutes also depends upon the firm's or the industry's product strategies. The more a product can be differentiated in the minds of the consumer, the poorer are other products as substitutes. This differentiation can be accomplished by quality or style variation or through effective advertising. As will be noted in some detail in our discussion of monopolistic competition and oligopoly, price changes and product changes are substitute strategies in that a quality improvement is tantamount to a decrease in price, and a firm might lower the quality of the product rather than raise its price.

For commodities such as condiments, small hardware items, hairpins, chewing gum, matches, pencils, and ink, which take a negligible part of the typical consumer's budget—say, $1/_{100}$ of 1 percent per year—changes in price are likely to have little absolute effect on quantity taken. A closely related argument says that commodities that have expensive complements will tend to be inelastic in demand. Thus, people who pay $500 for a stereo are not going to significantly change their purchases of records if records increase in price from $3.98 to $4.50.

In Chapter 2 we discussed the reasons for expecting demand elasticity to increase with time. Both psychological (e.g., habit and usual perceptual threshold conditions) and institutional (e.g., lack of information and the fact that contracts with suppliers have to expire before a change can be made) rigidities keep consumers from adjusting fully to price changes in the short run. In addition, technological rigidities may operate in the same fashion. For example, for consumers to take advantage of a price reduction for one commodity, they may have to buy some expensive, more durable complementary product. To benefit fully from a fall in the price of electricity relative to gas, consumers will have to buy more electrical appliances. However, this reaction will not likely appear to a large extent in the short run, since consumers will probably wait until their gas appliances wear out before they buy electrical ones.

Ultimately, the elasticity of demand for a commodity depends upon individuals' preferences for the commodity and its characteristics relative to other goods and services. An addictive good would be expected to have a relatively inelastic demand. A life-sustaining good would likewise have an inelastic demand. The elimination of some commodities would have only trivial impact on the consumer's life-style, so these commodities would be expected to have an elastic price demand curve. The demand for a commodity which has many and diverse uses would be elastic since as the price rises, the less urgent uses could easily be eliminated; or if the price falls, the good could be used for trivial purposes. Durable goods are thought to have more elastic demand curves than nondurables since there are alternatives to purchasing durable goods. Consumers can decide to use their old durables longer, or they can employ more careful maintenance and repair to keep their durables operable longer. The inventory stock of durables can also be more readily varied than the stock of perishables, etc.

With the possible exception of the availability of substitutes, none of the above factors are infallible criteria of elasticity of demand; they are only expressions of tendencies. Additionally, in many instances all the elements need not operate in the same direction at the same time. One or more may be working against the others, and the magnitude of elasticity will depend upon the relative strength of the opposing forces. For example, a commodity, such as a refrigerator, may be regarded as a necessity with no close substitutes, which would tend to make the demand inelastic. Yet it may also comprise a large portion of a family's budget, which would tend to make the demand elastic.

Furthermore, the elasticity coefficient can vary for a given product in different price ranges from highly elastic to inelastic. It is implicit in such a statement that it holds only for the price range prevailing in the market when the estimate was made.

Remember the distinction between the individual consumer's price elasticity of demand and the price elasticity of demand for the industry, which is the aggregate of all individual consumers. The elasticity of total demand depends not merely on how a change in price affects the purchases of an individual consumer, but on how it affects the number of consumers. There may be what Kenneth Boulding calls an "industry effect."

> Many commodities may have an almost completely inelastic demand as far as the demand of a single consumer is concerned and yet have an elastic total demand because a change in price causes a large change in the *number* of purchasers.[5]

For example, because of its indivisibility and because the expenditure on it forms a small part of consumers' total expenditures, a single consumer's demand for a newspaper of a given date is probably almost perfectly inelastic within the price range in which the consumer is willing to purchase it. Although the individual will pay 25¢ for one copy, he or she will not be induced to buy a second copy at any price for consumption purposes. Nevertheless, the total demand for the newspaper may be highly elastic because a lower price may induce people not now buying it to do so. Also keep in mind that the elasticity of demand for the output of a firm may be very different from the elasticity of demand for the product.

Some estimates of elasticity of demand for several commodities appear in Table 3-4. Although some of the data are somewhat out of date, they are still of considerable interest in terms of the determinants of elasticity discussed above. For instance, the lower coefficient for automobile parts and accessories compared to the total cost of automobiles can be rationalized by the importance of the item in the budget or the expensive complement argument. We invite the reader to give the reasons for the elasticity of some of the remaining items.

OTHER ELASTICITIES

Before leaving the subject of elasticity of demand, it is worthwhile to mention three further elasticities: cross elasticity of demand, income elasticity, and elasticity of expectations. A change in real income, in the prices of other goods, or in the expectations as to future prices can cause the whole demand curve to shift. While there is, in fact, a separate elasticity for each of the demand "determinants" mentioned earlier, only the three most important — prices of other goods, income, and expectations as to future prices — are discussed here.

---

[5] Kenneth E. Boulding, *Economic Analysis, Volume 1, Microeconomics* (4th ed.; New York: Harper & Row, Publishers, 1966), pp. 540–541.

TABLE 3–4   Estimated Price Elasticity of Demand for Selected Products

Air transportation	1.10
Automobiles	1.5
Automobile parts and accessories	0.5
Bacon and ham	0.88
Business machines	0.50
Butter	0.70
Cooking and heating apparatus	0.26
Cream	0.09
Electric light bulbs	0.33
Flour	0.79
Furniture	3.04
Furs	2.3
Home-produced beef and veal	0.41
Home-produced mutton and lamb	1.47
Jewelry	2.6
Luggage	0.83
Milk	0.31
Motion picture tickets	0.43
Oranges	0.97
Phonographs and radios	1.5
Photographic supplies	1.1
Pork	0.45
Poultry	0.27
Raw apparel wool	1.32
Refrigerators, washing and sewing machines	1.1
Sporting goods and equipment	1.2
Sugar	0.44
Telephone calls (local)	1.0
Transportation of property	0.38

Sources: (1) "Revenue Revision of 1950" (From hearings before the Committee on Ways and Means of the House of Representatives, Eighty-first Congress, Second Session), pp. 980–981.
(2) All foodstuffs are for the U.K., except for those items in (3). Richard Stone *et al., The Measurement of Consumers' Expenditure and Behaviour in the United Kingdom, 1920–1938,* Vol. 1 (Cambridge: Cambridge University Press, 1954).
(3) For the sources of air transportation, furniture, wool, butter, milk, and pork, see C. E. Ferguson, *Microeconomic Theory* (3d ed; Homewood: Richard D. Irwin, 1972), Table 4.3.1, p. 105.

Cross Price Elasticity of Demand

Cross price elasticity of demand measures the responsiveness of sales of commodity x to a change in the price of some other (presumably related) commodity y, *ceteris paribus*. Specifically,

$$\eta_{x,py} \equiv \frac{\text{relative change in quantity demanded of } x}{\text{relative change in price of } y} \qquad \textbf{(3.10)}$$

$$\equiv \frac{\Delta Q_x}{Q_x} \div \frac{\Delta P_y}{P_y} \equiv \frac{\Delta Q_x}{\Delta P_y} \cdot \frac{P_y}{Q_x} \equiv \text{point cross elasticity of demand}$$

The corresponding arc (or average) elasticity formula is $\dfrac{Q_{x2}-Q_{x1}}{P_{y2}-P_{y1}} \cdot \dfrac{P_{y1}+P_{y2}}{Q_{x1}+Q_{x2}}$ for use with numerical calculations. If $\eta_{x,py}$ is positive ($\eta_{x,py} > 0$), the commodities are called *gross substitutes*.[6] This means a decrease in the price of one commodity, say, aluminum, leads to a decrease in the demand for its substitutes, such as steel or plastic, in many manufacturing processes. Most economic commodities are gross substitutes. If $\eta_{x,py}$ is negative ($\eta_{x,py} < 0$), the commodities are called *gross complements*. If $\eta_{x,py} < 0$, then a decrease in the price of any joint product or service, say, dress shirts, leads to an increase in the demand for its complement, ties. Gross complements are commodities that are used together: shoes and shoelaces, right- and left-handed gloves, ham and eggs, ice cream and cake, and costume jewelry and dresses. Of course, what determines a substitute or complement is not invariant for all people at any point in time or even for a particular person at different points in time. For instance, it is entirely possible that ice cream and cake might be substitutes rather than complements under certain circumstances.

The final category is unrelated or independent commodities, in which the cross elasticity is zero ($\eta_{x,py} = 0$). Ham and right-handed gloves, shoelaces and aluminum, and oleo and dress shirts might fit into this category. Figure 3–9

FIGURE 3–9   Alternative Cross Elasticity of Demand Possibilities

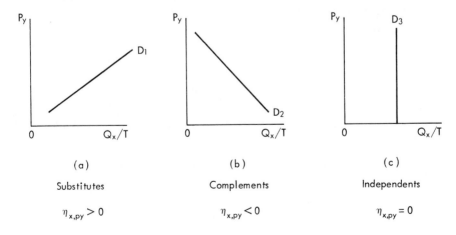

[6] The adjective "gross" is used because no adjustment is being made for the "income effect" of a price change. The income effect arises from the observation that when the price of a commodity changes, a consumer's real income changes, allowing more or less to be purchased of the good in question, as well as other goods. The separation of the price (or substitution) effect and the income effect is explained in Chapters 4 and 5.

graphically illustrates the three general cases of substitutes, complements, and independents.

Some actual estimates of the coefficients of price cross-elasticity of demand have been made. Herman Wold has shown that beef and pork, butter and margarine, and flour and all animal foods are substitutes—e.g., the cross elasticity between the quantity of beef demanded and the price of pork is +0.28, between the quantity demanded of butter and the price of margarine is +0.67, and between the quantity of flour demanded and the price of all animal fats is +0.56.[7]

Cross elasticity of demand has many useful applications. One of the most important is to define the boundaries of an industry. The rule is that a "high" positive cross elasticity between commodities indicates a relationship sufficiently close as to place the commodities in the same industry.[8] The courts have frequently used this concept in defining industries for antitrust cases. A famous example of this is the so-called Cellophane case (involving the Du Pont Company). Rather than confining the cellophane market to those flexible packaging materials having the peculiar physical properties of cellophane, the Court decided to include all waxed paper, glassine, and sulphite paper in the same industry. Although from 1923 to 1947 Du Pont produced almost 75 percent of the cellophane sold in the U.S., this amount constituted less than 20 percent of this broad market or industry. Du Pont was thus cleared of monopoly charges.

Income Elasticity of Demand

The influence of income changes upon demand is also interesting. An increase in an individual's real income generally tends to cause that person's demand for most commodities to rise. Graphically, this would be shown by a shift in the demand curve upward and to the right on the conventional price-quantity diagram.

The effect of changes in income on demand is measured by the income elasticity of demand ($\eta_{x,I}$), defined as the ratio of the relative change in quantity demanded of some commodity at a given price to the relative change in income. Letting I be money income and Q_x the quantity demanded of x at a given price, the income elasticity formulae are (again, the last two formulae are the "average" or "arc" elasticity formulae and are to be employed in numerical calculations):

$$\eta_{x,I} \equiv \frac{\text{relative change in quantity demanded of commodity } x}{\text{relative change in the consumer's money income}} \qquad (3.11)$$

$$\equiv \frac{\Delta Q_x}{Q_x} \div \frac{\Delta I}{I} \equiv \frac{\Delta Q_x}{\Delta I} \cdot \frac{I}{Q_x} \equiv \frac{Q_{x2} - Q_{x1}}{Q_{x1} + Q_{x2}} \cdot \frac{I_1 + I_2}{I_2 - I_1} \equiv \frac{\Delta Q_x}{\Delta I} \cdot \frac{I_1 + I_2}{Q_{x1} + Q_{x2}}$$

---

[7] Herman Wold and Lars Jureen, *Demand Analysis, A Study in Econometrics* (New York: John Wiley & Sons, 1953). It is interesting to note that the cross elasticity for the quantity demanded of pork and the price of beef is +0.14, and the cross elasticity for the quantity demanded of margarine and the price of butter is +0.81.

[8] While, of course, the meaning of "high" is arbitrary, the rule has proven useful.

A "superior" or "normal" good has a positive income elasticity ($\eta_{x,1} > 0$), and an "inferior" good a negative income elasticity ($\eta_{x,I} < 0$). As a general rule, those commodities thought of as necessities tend to have relatively low income elasticities, and those thought of as luxuries tend to have high income elasticities. Since the words "necessity" and "luxury" carry so many connotations, it is probably better to describe the people-goods interface simply in terms of the relevant elasticities. For certain basic commodities, such as some food product, as a consumer's income increases from very low levels, consumption may increase considerably at first. But after a certain income level, the increase in consumption becomes less than proportional to the income increases. (E.g., the following income elasticities were estimated by Richard Stone for the United Kingdom: sugar = .09, home-produced beef and veal = .34, bacon and ham = .55, home-produced mutton and lamb = .70, and oranges = .92.) [9] For certain other items such as housing or meals away from home, as the consumer's income increases, expenditures on these items increase in greater proportion than income. (E.g., the income elasticity for "meals away from home" was estimated at 2.39 in the United Kingdom.) Most budget studies show domestic servants, education, medical care, and restaurant meals are income sensitive (i.e., $\eta_{x,I} > 1$); and food (e.g., grain products), fuel, liquor, and newspapers are relatively income inelastic (i.e., $\eta_{x,I} < 1$).[10]

Actually, there are probably better empirical data — especially that of the U.S. Department of Commerce — available on income sensitivity of consumption purchases. The Department of Commerce has estimated that the following goods have high income sensitivities ($\eta_{x,I} > 1$): air transportation, autos, foreign travel, telephone service, and television repair; whereas those goods with low income sensitivities ($\eta_{x,I} < 1$) include clothing, dental service, local bus transportation, and shoes.

Herman Wold and C. E. V. Leser have estimated a number of income elasticities.[11] For instance, flour (-0.36) and margarine (-0.20) turn out to be inferior goods. Milk and cream (0.07), cream only (0.56), butter (0.42), cheese (0.34), eggs (0.37), meat (0.35), fruits and berries (0.70), and housing (0.38) turn out to be normal goods. All the various income-elasticity cases are illustrated in Figure 3–10. This figure shows functions relating the equilibrium quantity consumed of a commodity to the level of money income. These are called Engel curves after the 19th-century Prussian statistician Christian Engel (although there is some doubt he ever drew one). These Engel curves relate to the concept of income elasticity and derive from income-consumption curves, which are taken up later in the text. Income elasticity can be shown to relate to the slope or curvature of an Engel curve and, in part, to the classification of commodities as superior and inferior. Engel's laws were empirical

---

[9] Richard Stone *et al., The Measurement of Consumers' Expenditure and Behaviour in the United Kingdom, 1920–1938,* Vol. 1 (Cambridge: Cambridge University Press, 1954).

[10] A collection of the empirical results is contained in S. J. Prais and H. S. Houthakker, *The Analysis of Family Budgets* (Cambridge: Cambridge University Press, 1955), and cited in George J. Stigler, *The Theory of Price* (3d ed.; New York: Macmillan Co., 1966), p. 38.

[11] Herman Wold and C. E. V. Leser, "Commodity Group Expenditures Functions for the United Kingdom, 1948–1957," *Econometrica,* Vol. XXIX (January, 1961), pp. 24–32.

FIGURE 3–10 Alternative Engel Curve Possibilities

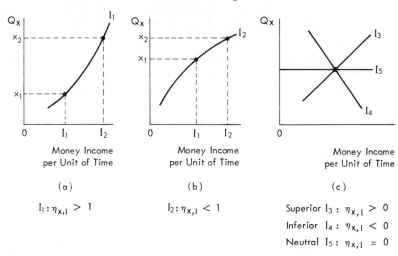

$I_1 : \eta_{x,I} > 1$

$I_2 : \eta_{x,I} < 1$

Superior $I_3 : \eta_{x,I} > 0$

Inferior $I_4 : \eta_{x,I} < 0$

Neutral $I_5 : \eta_{x,I} = 0$

generalizations about the effect of income on consumption. He proposed, for example, that the larger a spending unit's income, the smaller the fraction spent on food. The law has held up remarkably well.

From the definition of income elasticity, it is necessary for all goods consumed by a consuming unit that:

$$\frac{P_x Q_x}{I} \cdot \eta_{x,I} + \frac{P_y Q_y}{I} \cdot \eta_{y,I} + \ldots + \frac{P_z Q_z}{I} \cdot \eta_{z,I} = 1 \qquad (3.12)$$

Elasticity of Expectations

J. R. Hicks introduced another concept of elasticity, the *elasticity of expectations* $(\eta_{Pf,Pt})$.[12] This concept measures the relative change in expected future prices (P_f) to the relative change in current prices (P_t), the other determinants remaining constant. The elasticity of expectations may be written:

$$\eta_{Pf,Pt} \equiv \frac{\Delta P_f}{P_f} \div \frac{\Delta P_t}{P_t} \equiv \frac{\Delta P_f}{\Delta P_t} \cdot \frac{P_t}{P_f} \qquad (3.13)$$

As such, elasticity of expectations is influenced by all sorts of factors, economic, political, social, etc. If $\eta_{Pf,Pt} > 1$, the demand curve will shift to the right as buyers find current goods cheaper than before, relative to future goods, and vice versa for $\eta_{Pf,Pt} < 1$. If $\eta_{Pf,Pt} = 1$, demand remains constant as the current rise in prices is expected to change future prices proportionally. If the current rise in prices leads to the prospect of a smaller rise in future prices, $0 < \eta_{Pf,Pt} < 1$. If the buyers expect the current rise to cause a fall in future prices, then $\eta_{Pf,Pt} < 0$.

---

[12] J. R. Hicks, *Value and Capital, An Inquiry into Some Fundamental Principles of Economic Theory* (2d ed.; London: Oxford University Press, 1939), pp. 203–206.

PRICE ELASTICITY OF SUPPLY

The positive slope of a supply function is its most important property, but the elasticity measure gives additional significant information. However, having devoted a great deal of effort to the analysis of demand elasticity, we need say very little about elasticity of supply.

Supply elasticity refers to the degree of responsiveness of quantity supplied to a change in the price of the good itself, given the supply curve. The formula for "own" (or direct) supply elasticity is identical for "own" (or direct) demand elasticity, except that the phrase "quantity supplied" is everywhere substituted for the phrase "quantity demanded." If we let ϵ represent point price elasticity of supply, Q_x the quantity supplied of good x, P_x the price per unit of good x, and the symbol Δ a very small change, the formula is:

$$\epsilon \equiv \frac{\text{percentage change in } Q_x}{\text{percentage change in } P_x} \equiv \frac{\Delta Q_x}{Q_x} \div \frac{\Delta P_x}{P_x} \equiv \frac{\Delta Q_x}{\Delta P_x} \cdot \frac{P_x}{Q_x} \qquad \textbf{(3.14)}$$

If the percentage change in the quantity supplied of good x exceeds the percentage change in the price of x, supply is elastic; if the percentage change in Q_x is equal to the percentage change in P_x, supply is defined as unitary elastic; and if the percentage change in Q_x is less than the percentage change in P_x, the supply is inelastic. That is, if $\epsilon > 1$, supply is elastic; if $\epsilon < 1$, supply is inelastic; and if $\epsilon = 1$, elasticity is unitary. Inasmuch as P_x and Q_x normally move in the same direction, the elasticity coefficient is normally positive.

We cannot use the same type of movements in total revenue to estimate the elasticity coefficient for an upward-sloping supply function as we used to estimate the elasticity coefficient for a downward-sloping demand function.[13] Since price and quantity have a direct relationship, regardless of the degree of supply elasticity, price and total revenue will always move together for a "typical" supply curve. As price increases (decreases), total revenue must increase (decrease).

Arc Elasticity

An *arc elasticity* formula is an average of the various point elasticities that occur at different prices within the section of the schedule for which the arc elasticity is calculated. This formula is used to work numerical problems. Letting Q_1, P_1 be one quantity and price and Q_2, P_2 a second quantity and price, all for the same good, then ϵ_S, the price elasticity of supply, is:

---

[13] For a discussion of the behavior of supply elasticity and total revenue along linear supply functions, see James P. Houck, "Price Elasticity and Linear Supply Curves," *American Economic Review* (September, 1967), pp. 905–908; or see Note 2 in this chapter's Appendix B, "Mathematical Notes on Supply Elasticities." Houck shows that the elasticity of total revenue, $\epsilon_{TR} = (\Delta TR/TR) \div (\Delta P/P)$, is related to supply (demand) as follows: $\epsilon_{TR} = 1 + (\epsilon_{TR} = 1 + \eta)$. Thus, if price changes by 1 percent, total revenue will change by exactly 2 percent, less than 2 percent, or more than 2 percent, depending on whether $\epsilon = 1$, $\epsilon < 1$, or $\epsilon > 1$ respectively. In the case of unitary demand elasticity, η, the sign is negative; so that, e.g., if price changes by 1 percent, $\epsilon_{TR} = 1 + \eta = 1 - 1 = 0$, and total revenue remains constant. If $\eta > 1$ ($\eta < 1$), the change in TR is negatively (positively) related to the change in price.

$$\epsilon_S \equiv \frac{Q_2 - Q_1}{Q_1 + Q_2} \div \frac{P_2 - P_1}{P_1 + P_2} \equiv \frac{\Delta Q}{\Delta P} \cdot \frac{P_1 + P_2}{Q_1 + Q_2} \tag{3.15}$$

Basically, the elasticity of supply depends upon the ability of resources to shift between alternative employments. This shiftability in turn varies with the amount of time producers have in making adjustments to a given price change. Generally speaking, the greater the amount of time a producer has to adjust to a given price change, the greater the output response and therefore the greater the elasticity of supply. Since the shifting of resources takes time, the longer the time period, the greater the resource shiftability.

Graphic Demonstration of Supply Elasticity

In Figure 3–11 we have illustrated some of the major linear and nonlinear elasticity possibilities. The linear cases depicted in Figure 3–11 (a) are interesting in that the supply curves remain in the same classification over the entire

FIGURE 3-11   Price Elasticity of Supply (ϵ) with Linear and Nonlinear Supply Curves

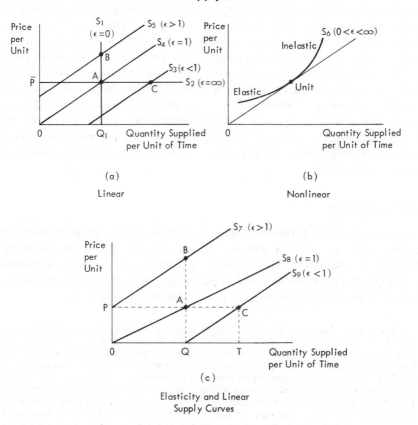

price range—e.g., if initially elastic, the supply curve always remains elastic. S_1 displays zero elasticity or perfect inelasticity over its entire range, as $0Q_1$ will be offered for sale regardless of the price. S_2 is everywhere infinitely elastic, since at a price of $0\bar{P}$, any quantity of the good demanded will be offered for sale. The infinite elasticity of S_2 also means none will be offered below $0\bar{P}$, and a price above $0\bar{P}$ is unnecessary. S_4 illustrates the case of unit elasticity of supply. Any straight-line supply curve passing through the origin, regardless of slope, has an elasticity of unity. S_5 and S_3 are elastic and inelastic respectively throughout their entire lengths. S_6 in panel (b) probably represents the most common form for a short-run supply curve. It exhibits varying elasticity over different price ranges. Initially (at the left), it is very elastic; then it has a range of unit elasticity; but it eventually becomes inelastic. While not true for S_6, a supply curve may eventually turn vertical (i.e., ϵ may become 0) at the "full-capacity" point. A supply curve such as S_6 shows that some minimum supply price is required before any output will be offered.

Proof of Linear Supply Elasticities

It is fairly straightforward to prove that the linear supply functions S_7, S_8 and S_9 are everywhere elastic, unitary, and inelastic respectively, using equation (3.14). This is illustrated in Figure 3–11, panel (c). For instance, for S_8 the ϵ at point A is:

$$\epsilon_A \equiv \frac{\Delta Q}{\Delta P} \cdot \frac{P}{Q} \equiv \frac{0Q}{AQ} \cdot \frac{0P}{0Q} \equiv 1$$

The same procedure may be used for the other two cases. On S_7, ϵ at point B,

$$\epsilon_B \equiv \frac{\Delta Q}{\Delta P} \cdot \frac{P}{Q} \equiv \frac{AP}{AB} \cdot \frac{BQ}{0Q} \equiv \frac{BQ}{AB} > 1. \text{ On } S_9, \epsilon_C \equiv \frac{\Delta Q}{\Delta P} \cdot \frac{P}{Q} \equiv \frac{QT}{CT} \cdot \frac{0P}{0T} \equiv \frac{QT}{0T} < 1.$$

QUESTIONS

1. The generalized concept of "elasticity" was defined in the text. Test your understanding of the idea by developing the elasticity formulae for the following four relationships:
   (a) Grade elasticity with respect to study time
   (b) Elasticity of profit with respect to advertising
   (c) Elasticity of consumption expenditures in the national economy with respect to national income
   (d) Price elasticity of demand
2. Explain the total spending test of elasticity (a) without using numbers, formulas, or graphs; (b) using formulas; (c) using graphs; and (d) by filling in column (9) of Table 3–1.

3. Compare the elasticities of the points marked on the following figure:

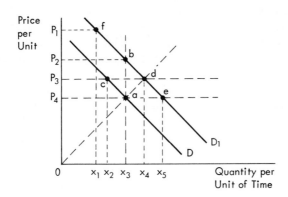

4. Use the ray technique to show what the total revenue curve must look like in order for the demand curve (AR) to be negatively sloped throughout its length.

5. Consider a point on a nonlinear demand curve and show how to determine the corresponding marginal revenue.

6. The demand for cigarettes is quite inelastic, but the demand for any given brand of cigarettes is quite elastic. Explain why this is so.

7. Why are complements and substitutes defined with reference to their respective cross elasticities?

8. What would you conclude if you were told that commodity x and commodity y had a cross elasticity of (plus) infinity?

9. As an individual's income increases from very low to very high, what would you expect to happen to that individual's income elasticity of demand for potatoes? for caviar?

10. Compare the price elasticity of supply of the points marked on the following figure:

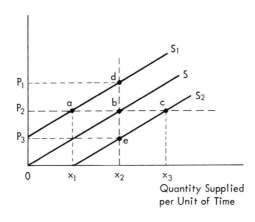

APPENDIX A: MATHEMATICAL NOTES ON DEMAND ELASTICITIES

Note 1. "Own" Price Elasticity of Demand

Letting η = the coefficient of the "own" price elasticity of demand and $q = f(p)$ be the demand function, then η has to do with logarithmic derivatives, since $\eta = \dfrac{\delta(\log q)}{\delta(\log p)}$.

$$\eta = \frac{\delta q}{\delta p} \cdot \frac{p}{q} \tag{3.16}$$

For a linear demand curve $q = a - bp$, the derivative $\delta q/\delta p = -b$, and so (3.16) becomes:

$$\eta = -b\frac{p}{q} = \frac{q-a}{q} \tag{3.17}$$

which varies with q. On the other hand, the basic function $q = ap^{-b}$ gives a family of constant-elasticity curves. The derivative $\delta q/\delta p = -abp^{-b-1}$ and hence:

$$\eta = (-abp^{-b-1})\frac{p}{q} = \frac{-abp^{-b}}{q} \tag{3.18}$$

since $q = ap^{-b}$. In short, the exponent of the price variable in this nonlinear equation is the constant-elasticity value.

η is a pure number independent of the units in which prices and quantities are measured. It is negative if the corresponding demand function is downward sloping. We can derive the total revenue or total expenditure ($=pq$) test for elasticity in the following way:

$$\frac{\delta(pq)}{\delta p} = q + p\frac{\delta q}{\delta p} = q\left(1 + \frac{p}{q}\frac{\delta q}{\delta p}\right) = q(1 + \eta) \tag{3.19}$$

Thus, a consumer's total expenditures on a commodity will increase with price if $\eta > -1$, decrease if $\eta < -1$, and remain constant if $\eta = -1$. (Note that since we have not taken the absolute value of η, for a downsloping demand curve, $\eta < 0$; and therefore the more negative η becomes, the more elastic it becomes.)

Note 2. Income Elasticity of Demand

Like all elasticities, income elasticity assumes all other things are equal. In particular, it assumes that the commodity price is constant. That is,

$$\eta_{x,I} = \frac{\delta q}{\delta I} \cdot \frac{I}{q} \tag{3.20}$$

A linear income demand function can be written as $q = a + bI$, $b > 0$. Since the derivative $\delta q/\delta I = b$, (3.20) becomes:

$$\eta_{x,I} = b\frac{I}{q} \tag{3.21}$$

A hyperbola income-demand function with a constant elasticity, $q = aI^b$, gives the constant elasticity of b, following the same procedure as in (3.18).

If $\eta_{x,I} > 0$, the goods are called superior; and if $\eta_{x,I} < 0$, they are called inferior.

Note 3. Cross Elasticity of Demand

The cross elasticity of demand is defined as:

$$\eta_{y,px} = \frac{\delta q_y}{\delta p_x} \cdot \frac{p_x}{q_y}, \; \eta_{x,py} = \frac{\delta q_x}{\delta p_y} \cdot \frac{p_y}{q_x} \tag{3.22}$$

Suppose the two commodities x and y have linear demand curves.

$$q_x = a_1 + b_1 p_x + c_1 p_y$$

$$q_y = a_2 + b_2 p_x + c_2 p_y$$

The partial derivatives are:

$$\frac{\delta q_x}{\delta p_y} = c_1 \qquad \frac{\delta q_y}{\delta p_x} = b_2$$

Substituting into (3.22) yields:

$$\eta_{y,px} = b_2 \frac{p_x}{q_y} \qquad \eta_{x,py} = c_1 \frac{p_y}{q_x} \tag{3.23}$$

Although these two coefficients are not generally expected to be equal, they could be if the ratio of slopes c_1/b_2 equals the ratio of the original total expenditures on x ($p_x q_x$) and on $y (p_y q_y)$. That is, $\eta_{x,py} = \eta_{y,px}$ if:

$$c_1 \frac{p_y}{q_x} = b_2 \frac{p_x}{q_y} \quad \text{or} \quad \frac{c_1}{b_2} = \frac{p_x q_x}{p_y q_y} \tag{3.24}$$

If $\eta_{y,px} > 0$ (<0), the goods are substitutes (complements). The same holds for $\eta_{x,py}$.

Note 4. General Formulation

If we let the general demand function $q_x = f(p_x, p_y, p_z, I)$ take the following specific functional form:

$$q_x = ap_x^{-b} p_y^{-c} p_z^d I^e \tag{3.25}$$

where a, b, c, d, and e are positive constants, then:

$$\eta = -b \tag{3.26}$$

shows a constant "own" price elasticity. In addition $\eta_{x,py} = -c$ and $\eta_{x,pz} = d$, demonstrating that y and z are substitutes and complements to x respectively; and $\eta_{x,I} = e$ shows that x is a superior good.

APPENDIX B: MATHEMATICAL NOTES ON SUPPLY ELASTICITIES

Note 1. Linear Supply Elasticities

If the supply curve is assumed linear, we can write the functional form as:

$$q = a + bp \text{ (or } p = q - a/b) \tag{3.27}$$

where p is price, q is quantity supplied, and a and b are constants. Concentrating on the first of these formulations, the x (quantity) intercept is a, and the slope of the supply function is b. For normal upsloping supply curves, b is positive. But a can be any value—i.e., $a \gtreqless 0$. It can start at the origin ($a = 0$), in which case q is zero at a zero price. It can cut the x (quantity) axis ($a > 0$), which means some positive amount will be offered for sale even at a zero price. Finally, if it cuts the y (price) axis ($a < 0$), no output will be forthcoming at prices below (or equal to) a.

The elasticity of supply in the linear case is:

$$\epsilon = \frac{\delta q}{\delta p} \cdot \frac{p}{q} = b \frac{p}{q} = \frac{bp}{bp + a} \tag{3.28}$$

Thus, the text's summary of elasticity possibilities with a linear supply curve can easily be shown to hold. If the linear supply curve comes out of the origin, regardless of the value for the slope b, it has unit elasticity. Thus, when $a = 0$, $\epsilon = 1$ in (3.28). Similarly, when $a < 0$, $\epsilon > 1$; and when $a > 0$, $\epsilon < 1$.

Note 2. Linear Supply Curves, Elasticity, and Total Revenue [14]

Using (3.27) to eliminate p in (3.28), we get:

$$\epsilon = 1 - a/q \tag{3.29}$$

Thus, all linear supply curves converge to an elasticity of $+1.0$ as q and p become larger. The precise speed at which they approach it depends on a. With a linear supply curve, total revenue (TR) is given by the parabolic equation:

$$TR = p \cdot q = \frac{q^2 - aq}{b} \tag{3.30}$$

Inasmuch as TR does not reach a maximum as q and p increase, it may be useful to know what proportionate change in TR follows a 1 percent change in price along a given supply curve. This is given by:

$$E_{TR} = \frac{\delta TR}{\delta p} \cdot \frac{p}{TR} = 1 + \epsilon \tag{3.31}$$

---

[14] See James P. Houck, "Price Elasticity and Linear Supply Curves," *American Economic Review* (September, 1967), pp. 905–908.

E_{TR}, the price elasticity of total revenue, is a general expression applying to linear and nonlinear supply curves. As $\epsilon \rightarrow +1.0$, $E_{TR} \rightarrow +2.0$. We can summarize the application of (3.31) as follows: If price increases by 1 percent (i.e., $\Delta p = 1$ percent), TR will increase (ΔTR) by:

	$\Delta TR = 2\%$	$\Delta TR > 2\%$	$\Delta TR < 2\%$	$\Delta TR = 1\%$
If the supply curve is:	unit elastic	price elastic	inelastic	completely inelastic

2 DEMAND—THE ANALYSIS OF CONSUMER BEHAVIOR

Chapter 4 Cardinal Utility Approach to Consumer Behavior

In this chapter and the next, we will employ two separate approaches to explain individual consumer behavior. We will develop the classical cardinal utility approach in this chapter and the more recent ordinal utility or indifference curve approach in the next chapter. Both the cardinal and ordinal utility approaches are useful in that they provide an "explanation" for the "normal" demand curve.

THE CONCEPT OF UTILITY

Before deliberate choices can be made, all goods in the consumer's budget must have some common characteristic which makes comparisons among them possible. And since goods are, in fact, substituted for one another, they must have something in common. This common property is usually called *utility*. Note carefully, however, that while the subjective concept of utility may for some purposes be regarded as equivalent to satisfaction, it carries no connotation whatsoever as to usefulness or social desirability. Bourbon, LSD, bibles, and opera all possess utility in varying degrees. *Utility is simply whatever makes the commodity desired.*

It is very important to distinguish between *ex post* and *ex ante utility. Ex post utility* is the actual satisfaction or an evaluation of the benefits from the act of consumption. This interests the economist only to the extent that it provides some information to the consumer in making future decisions. Almost invariably we are interested in *ex ante* or *expected utility.* Commodity choices have to be made with less than complete knowledge. Sometimes that knowledge is minimal, as in the case of considering the purchase of a movie ticket or a durable commodity one has never bought before. Sometimes consumers can buy with a great deal of confidence in the product, such as when they buy a loaf of bread from their regular baker or when they purchase a frequently used brand-name product.

Objectives, Limitations, Problems

We will assume the typical consumer has a certain *objective,* is confronted with certain *limitations* (called constraints), and has a certain *problem* to solve. The problem that confronts the consumer *qua* consumer is to decide what commodities and how many units of each to buy to maximize total welfare. (In this analysis "savings" is treated as a satisfaction-yielding commodity on a par with bananas, bicycles, and books. The "price" or "cost" of savings is always 1 in that it costs one dollar's worth of goods to save one dollar.)

The objective postulated for the typical consumer is maximization of total welfare, subject to the constraint of a limited budget. We presume the consumer chooses the alternative highest on his or her scale of preferences, and we assume the consumer: (1) knows the relevant alternatives, (2) is able to evaluate these alternatives, and (3) always makes consistent choices. Therefore, we will treat the individual consumer's purchase decisions as deliberate acts of choice in light of the alternative ends available. Alternatively, it would be possible to assume that these consumption decisions are either purely random or that they conform strictly with some customary, purely habitual mode of behavior. Economists, on the whole, reject these last two explanations and accept the first, because even casual observation suggests more consistency and order in choices than an entirely random (stochastic) model would suggest and more variation than a completely habitual model would suggest. Accordingly, we shall assume the typical consumer makes decisions as if pursuing and attempting to maximize a single end.

Actually, we need only ascribe this kind of behavior to a limited proportion of the population. Those individuals who do not behave in accordance with our theory simply become unimportant in determination of price; so even if only a small segment of consumers act as we postulate, they are the ones who significantly impact price.

Budget limitations, positive prices, and time restrain consumers from consuming all they might wish of all commodities. If one had an infinite amount of purchasing power, prices would be irrelevant; or if prices were all zero, there would be no constraint from a budget. But even if purchasing power and prices were not limiting, consumption still takes time; and lifetimes are not perpetuities. One can't play tennis and see a movie at the same time. The time limitation has received relatively little attention from economists because the other two constraints are so effective. In a world of millionaires or a world without physical scarcity, presumably consumption as a function of time would be economists' major preoccupation.

Describing the purchasing power restraint presents a serious problem. Traditionally it has been called the "income constraint" or the "budget constraint," but both of these terms have a time dimension. Is consumption or purchasing during any particular time period restricted to the income during that same time period? The answer is obviously no. After all, it is possible to spend today all of the income one has earned in the past (and not spent) and all of the income one expects to earn in the future (discounted to the present). The effective constraint (and even this is not entirely accurate) is that lifetime consumption is limited to lifetime income, and in a world of uncertainty we might say that expected lifetime consumption is limited to expected lifetime income.[1] So, while an individual's current net worth is the effective restraint, we assume that in a particular (short) time period a prior decision has been made on a budget for that time period.

In analyzing consumer behavior, we take the budget as given. Prices of commodities are given to the individual; that is, they may change but they are not controlled by the buyer. Indeed, all factors presumed to influence quantity demanded except price are held constant in order to study the significance of relative prices.

Cardinal and Ordinal Utility

If the above description of a typical consumer is reasonable, it will be possible with utility theory to explain everyday experiences. For example, we can say that people generally substitute in favor of a commodity which has fallen relatively in price and that people generally do not specialize in the consumption of one commodity or a group of a few goods. (The practice of limiting consumption to one commodity is referred to as "monomania.")

For the laws of utility to be operative, people must be able to choose among and rank all the alternative commodities available. Alternative commodities can be ranked in cardinal or ordinal terms. A *cardinal* ranking puts a precise evaluation on the alternatives. The numerical ratio of two cardinal quantities can be calculated exactly. Height, length, volume, and weight are examples of variables measured with cardinal numbers. It is possible to say that Mr. Hemingway is 1.25 times as tall as Mr. Fitzgerald or that Ms. Stein is 24.5 pounds heavier than Ms. Toklas. The classical economists attempted to do the same thing by measuring utility in arbitrary units called *utils*. Thus, if $A = 5$ utils, $B = 10$ utils, and $C = 40$ utils (where the letters stand for three different bundles or combinations of goods), they can be ranked cardinally: B yields twice the utility of A, and C yields four times the utility of B.

Using *ordinal* utility, commodities can be ranked in order from low to high, but no precise values can be placed on the magnitude of the intervals between them. Brightness, redness, roughness, and wetness are all examples of ordinally representable variables. It makes sense to say that one car is redder than another, but not to say that one car is 2.345 times as red as the other. In the above example an ordinal ranking would merely say that bundle B is preferred to bundle A, and bundle C is preferred to bundle B. In addition, by adding an axiom of consistency, it is possible to say that bundle C is preferred to bundle A. Following the general logical principle known as "Occam's Razor" (or the rule of parsimony) — which states if two theories are equally satisfactory, the one with the fewer and less stringent assumptions is preferred — most economists favor the ordinal utility approach. However, both approaches have

---

[1] Here income is defined to include inheritances, gifts, robberies, etc., which in other contexts might not be included as "income."

their advantages and limitations, both contribute toward a better understanding of consumer behavior, and both have the same implications for demand theory.

TOTAL AND MARGINAL UTILITY

Utility theory starts from the idea that a consumer is able to compare commodities through the common denominator of utility. The *total utility* is the entire amount of satisfaction expected from consuming various amounts of a commodity per unit of time. For example, the total utility (TU) expected from consuming two cups of coffee and a certain set of all other commodities per day might be 30 utils, and that from consuming three cups 35 utils. Up to a point, this positive relation between greater consumption and greater TU is expected to hold.

Marginal utility is defined as the change in total utility per unit change in the quantity of a given commodity consumed per unit of time, when taste and consumption of all other goods remain unchanged. Like any marginal value, marginal utility (MU) refers to the slope or the rate of change of the total utility function, i.e., $MU_x = \Delta TU_x / \Delta Q_x$. In the previous example, the MU of a cup of coffee between two and three cups per day was 5 utils. $\dfrac{\Delta TU}{\Delta Q} = \dfrac{TU_1 - TU_0}{Q_1 - Q_0} = \dfrac{35-30}{3-2} = 5$ utils.

LAW OF DIMINISHING MARGINAL UTILITY

On the basis of economic considerations it is possible to make certain generalizations about the MU (and hence the TU) function. The most important of these concerns the fact that the MU curve or function is negatively sloped. The basis for this belief is the celebrated *law* or *principle of diminishing marginal utility*. The law states that, *ceteris paribus,* the greater the rate of consumption per unit of time of any particular good, the less its marginal utility.

This principle seems to agree with our usual experience that the more we consume of some particular commodity per unit of time, the less valuable to us is one additional unit of it. To illustrate this, assume the commodity is a durable good such as an automobile. The principle claims that a family's desire for a second automobile is less intense than the desire for the first (when they had none), and the desire for the third is weaker than that for the second, and so on.

A casual proof of this principle is the observation that individuals do not spend all their consumption dollars on just one commodity. If the principle were not operative, it is claimed, people would practice "monomania" in the commodity that yielded the highest MU per dollar. Why would anyone ever shift to another good unless this most desired commodity became less desirable as more was consumed?

While seemingly plausible, the "proof," upon closer inspection, turns out to be quite limited. If the MU of any commodity (MU_x) depends only on the quantity consumed of that commodity (Q_x) and not on the quantity consumed of other commodities (Q_y), the argument is valid. However, if the MU_x is not independent of Q_y, MU_x could be increasing and a switch to y (nonmonomania) could still occur. If the increased consumption of x raises the MU_y more than it raises the MU_x, the MU_x has fallen relative to the MU_y, and the switch from x to y will occur.

The above definition of the law of diminishing marginal utility (hereafter *LDMU*) was framed to allow for the fact that the diminishing relative *MU* would suffice in most places where diminishing absolute *MU* is commonly used. In fact, it is a commodity's relative worth and not its absolute worth that is crucial in the theory of consumer behavior. Extending the opportunity cost doctrine to consumption theory, the value of commodity x to a consumer is measured by the amount of other commodities a consumer is just willing to give up to obtain x. If the consumer is willing to sacrifice two units of y to acquire one unit of x, x is "worth" $2y$ to that individual. Since money is generalized purchasing power, the worth of any commodity is expressible in money. A commodity purchased for $2 means the satisfaction yielded by the good is judged to be the same as that which could be obtained from purchasing $2 worth of other commodities.

Several points should be emphasized about the *LDMU*. For instance, the *ceteris paribus* proviso is crucial. It means that tastes and the quantity consumed of other goods remain constant. Thus, MU_x is, in mathematical terms, a partial derivative showing how the TU_x changes as more x is consumed, assuming the quantity of y, z, and all other commodities remains constant. Since the MU_x function equals the slope of the TU_x function, it is possible to depict it graphically, as in Figure 4–1.

In attempting to construct a *MU* curve from a *TU* curve, an easy place to begin is point B, where the *TU* curve reaches its maximal value at x_2 units of x. Since the marginal value must equal zero when the total value is at a maximum (or minimum), one point on the *MU* curve, point A, must lie on the quantity axis at x_2. The economic interpretation of this is straightforward. As long as the extra utility from consuming another unit of a commodity is positive, regardless how small that increment may be, it will increase *TU* from consuming that commodity. Up to x_2, *MU* is positive and thus *TU* is increasing; whereas after x_2, *MU* is negative and hence *TU* is declining. The region after x_2, often called the "saturation" or "disutility" stage, is not normally relevant from an economic point of view. (The annoyance caused by storage or disposal problems of undesired commodities could cause the *TU* function to actually decline like this.) Even if the commodity were free, the consumer would only consume x_2 units and no more of the commodity.

The "per unit of time" qualification in the *LDMU* is also important. Utility and *DMU* must have a time dimension. The consumer is asking the question: If I consume at the rate of one pint of milk per day, what will my total utility be? If I consume at the rate of two pints per day rather than one, how much additional utility will I get? . . . And so on through the feasible range.

Finally, the law involves more than the physiological phenomenon that one gets nauseated after so many ice cream cones, lumps of sugar, breakfasts, or what have you. It is not just a "law of diminishing marginal elasticity of the

FIGURE 4-1   Total and Marginal Utility

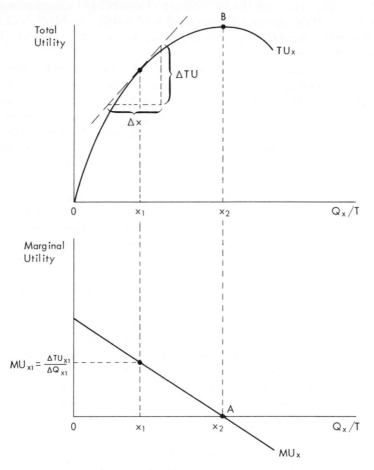

Note: Q_x/T refers to the quantity of commodity *x* consumed per unit of time.

stomach," although it may include that. Psychological as well as physiological considerations are paramount. For this reason, the law is as well exemplified by commodities where physiological considerations are not so obviously crucial.

CONSUMER BEHAVIOR

The concept of utility helps explain consumer behavior, given that the consumer attempts to maximize the utility derived from consumption. The consumer's preferences are assumed to be independent, both of the income level and of commodity prices.

Equimarginal Principle

Following the equimarginal principle of continually balancing marginal gains and losses, the general formula for reaching the most preferred position equates the marginal benefit (MB) to the marginal cost (MC). In this context the marginal benefit is the MU of the commodity and the marginal cost is the price of the commodity. In this last respect, the individual is unlike society as a whole. It was mentioned in Chapter 1 in connection with the production possibility curve that the social marginal opportunity costs normally increase as the total consumption of a commodity expands; yet, for an individual consumer, MC usually remains constant. Most individual consumers purchase an insignificant percentage of the total amount consumed of any commodity. This means most individuals are pure competitors in purchasing commodities. They can purchase all they wish at the prevailing market price, but they can buy none at a lower price. If the market price of eggs is $1 a dozen, a consumer may purchase as many as he or she likes at this price. Measuring MC (i.e., price) on the vertical axis and quantity consumed on the horizontal axis, the curve of an individual consumer's MC would be a horizontal straight line at the going market price of $1 a dozen.

To illustrate, consider the consumer's situation shown in Figure 4–2. This consumer values one unit of the commodity at $5 when consuming at the rate of one unit per unit of time. Thus, this person should consume more than one unit of this commodity since the alternatives sacrificed by purchasing it are only one fifth as great as the benefits received. The consumer should continue purchasing additional units of the commodity up to the point of equality between price (MC) and MU. Because of the $LDMU$ phenomenon, as the individual increases the purchase rate, each unit increase in the consumption

**FIGURE 4–2   Equimarginal Principle
for a Consumer**

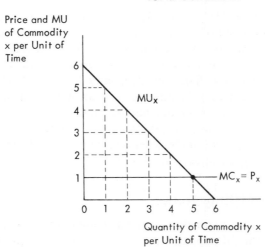

Price and MU
of Commodity
x per Unit of
Time

Quantity of Commodity x
per Unit of Time

rate contributes less extra satisfaction, whereas MC remains constant. If the next unit has an MU of \$4, the individual should increase the buying rate since MC is constant at \$1. This extra unit adds more to total utility than it adds to total costs measured in terms of sacrificed alternatives. The possibility of further net gain is exhausted only at the point where $MC = MU$ or $P = MU$, which in Figure 4–2 is at five units of x.

The equimarginal principle says this rule should be applied to each and every commodity the consumer purchases in order to get an optimum division of expenditures. Consider a simple example where a consumer's entire budget is devoted to the purchase of two commodities, x and y. The unit price of x (P_x) is \$1 and that of y (P_y) is \$2. To reach an optimum, the individual should divide budgetary expenditures such that the $MU_x = MU$ of \$1 and $MU_y = MU$ of \$2. Therefore, the optimum position for the consumer is where:

$$\frac{MU_x}{P_x} = \frac{MU_y}{P_y} \quad \text{or} \quad \frac{MU_x}{MU_y} = \frac{P_x}{P_y}$$

These equations state that a consumer maximizes total utility (i.e., is at the optimum) by buying those quantities of x and y such that the MU per dollar spent on x equals the MU per dollar spent on y. The second expression, stating that the ratio of the MU_x to the MU_y must equal the ratio of their respective prices, can be interpreted as follows: MU_x/MU_y represents the rate at which the consumer is *willing* to substitute y for x, whereas P_x/P_y represents the rate at which the consumer is *able* to substitute y for x on the market. If the rate at which the consumer is willing to substitute equals the rate at which he or she is able to substitute y for x, consumption patterns will not change. If the two rates are not equal, a reallocation will result in a preferred position. For instance, if a consumer is willing to give up four units of y for one unit of x, whereas on the market he or she is able to get one more unit of x by only giving up two units of y, it will pay to do so until the ratios are equal.

When the condition $MU_x/P_x = MU_y/P_y$ is met—the last dollar spent on x yields the same increment of satisfaction (MU) as the last dollar spent on y—the individual is unable to enhance utility by shifting expenditures from one commodity to the other. To illustrate this, assume the equality does not hold. For instance, suppose the following inequality holds: $MU_x/P_x > MU_y/P_y$ (e.g., $4/1 > 2/2$). Under these conditions, the consumer adjusts by spending more on x and less on y. (Because the consumer does this, MU_x falls and MU_y rises.) The extra gain from acquiring more x exceeds the loss from having less y. If the inequality were in the other direction (i.e., $MU_x/P_x < MU_y/P_y$), the consumer would want more y and less x.

Maximization of Utility Rules

Before setting out in precise form the conditions necessary for utility maximization, we should approach the problem with a simple numerical example. Table 4–1 shows the MU_x and MU_y (both measured in utils) for different quantities of x and y (Q_x, Q_y). The table assumes that the MU of each

TABLE 4–1   Two-Good Consumer Optimum, Marginal Utility Approach

Q_x	MU_x (utils)	Q_y	MU_y (utils)
1	28	1	32
2	24	2	29
3	21	3	27
4	20	4	23
5	16	5	20
6	13	6	18
7	9	7	17
8	5	8	16
9	3	9	12
10	1	10	9

Assume: $P_x = \$1$, $P_y = \$1$, $I = \$13$, and $\Delta MU_y/\Delta Q_x = \Delta MU_x/\Delta Q_y = 0$

commodity is unrelated, independent of the quantity consumed of the other commodity—i.e., $\Delta MU_y/\Delta Q_x = \Delta MU_x/\Delta Q_y = 0$. This assumption is made to make the arithmetic manageable. Usually commodities do relate to one another. If the commodities are gross substitutes, a greater consumption of x will tend to lower the MU_y—i.e., $\Delta MU_y/\Delta Q_x < 0$. If the commodities are gross complements, the more of x consumed, the higher the MU_y—i.e., $\Delta MU_y/\Delta Q_x > 0$; but if MU_y does not change as Q_x changes, the commodities are unrelated and $\Delta MU_y/\Delta Q_x = 0$. Thus, the sign of the expression $\Delta MU_y/\Delta Q_x$, whether negative, positive, or zero, provides us with a cardinal utility definition of gross substitutes, gross complements, and unrelated commodities respectively.[2]

The problem is to determine how the consumer in Table 4–1 should allocate the $13 of income between x and y. There are two ways to do this: (1) by the seriatim (order of purchase) method or (2) by the equality (inspection) method. The *seriatim method* says the consumer will purchase one unit at a time, always buying the commodity with the highest MU (per dollar) until income is exhausted. On this basis, what commodity should be purchased first? Since a dollar spent on x is expected to give only 28 units of satisfaction, while a dollar spent on y will yield 32 utils, the consumer will purchase y. The second purchase should also be y since a dollar spent on y increases total utility by 29, whereas a dollar spent on x only increases it by 28. Continuing, one finds that the 3rd, 5th, 7th, 8th, and 13th purchases are of x and the 4th, 6th, 9th, 10th, 11th, and 12th purchases are of y.[3] The consumer will exactly exhaust the $13 income when purchasing five units of x and eight units of y. At this position the MU per dollar of the two commodities is equal. Thus, we have validated the postulate that consumer optimum occurs when, with a given

---

[2] As will be discussed later, this definition as well as the cross elasticity definition of related commodities suffers from the same deficiency; viz., it neglects the income effect. But for now, these definitions will be employed.

[3] When the MU per dollar is equal for both x and y, as is the case after the seventh dollar has been spent, it is irrelevant whether the eighth dollar is spent on x and the ninth on y or vice versa.

income, the consumer purchases those quantities of the different commodities at which the *MU* per dollar of each is equal. This principle holds regardless of the number of commodities confronting the consumer.

The *equality method* looks at all the positions at which the *MU* per dollar is equal and then selects the one for which the consumer's money income is entirely allocated. In Table 4–1, 4*x* plus 5*y* gives a position of equal *MU* per dollar, but only $9 of the consumer's income is spent. The combination 7*x* plus 10*y* yields equal *MU* per dollar, but the consumer's income constraint of $13 has been violated. Only at combination 5*x* plus 8*y* is the consumer able to equate marginal utilities per dollar and exactly exhaust the $13 income. This is the consumer's optimal position, since any reallocation of expenditures would decrease total satisfaction. If $1 per unit of time is transferred from *x* to *y*, the *TU* from consuming one less unit of *x* will decrease by 16, whereas the additional unit of *y* increases total utility by 12—a net loss of four units of satisfaction. Alternatively, a shift from *y* to *x* would result in a net loss of three units of satisfaction.

There is another way to prove this is the optimum point. Compute the total utility associated with any other combination within the consumer's income constraint and compare it with the total utility associated with the combination 5*x* and 8*y*. If this position is truly the best combination, the total utility should be maximized at this point. (And it is, since total utility equals 291 utils for this combination.) The total utility may be computed by adding all the marginal values. For instance, if three units of *x* are consumed, the total utility is 73 (= 28 + 24 + 21).

Of course, in the real world it would be very unlikely that the two commodities (given the natural units) would sell for exactly the same price. When they do sell for the same price, one can speak of equating marginal utilities of the two commodities since that is equivalent to equating marginal utilities per dollar. However, it is the *MU* per dollar rule that is universally applicable. Therefore, we want to look at a slightly more realistic problem involving more than two commodities and involving different prices.

Before attempting such a problem, we should express the necessary and sufficient rules for consumer optimum—i.e., utility maximization—in the form of algebraic equations. There are three separate conditions:

$$\frac{MU_x}{P_x} = \frac{MU_y}{P_y} = \frac{MU_z}{P_z} = \ldots = \lambda \text{ (common } MU \text{ per} \tag{4.1}$$
income dollar)

$$I = Q_x \cdot P_x + Q_y \cdot P_y + Q_z \cdot P_z \tag{4.2}$$

LDMU holds in the case of independent commodities $\qquad$ (4.3)

(4.1) states that at the optimum point, marginal utilities must be in proportion to their prices for all the commodities purchased. (4.2) means the consumer has a budget constraint, so that total expenditure (or the price of *x* times the quantity of *x* purchased plus the price of *y* times the quantity of *y* purchased and so on) cannot exceed income. Since savings are treated here as a commodity, it is assumed that the consumer's income must exactly equal total expenditure. Some of the quantities in (4.2) may be zero. (4.3) states that if the commodities are unrelated, the *LDMU* must hold or condition (4.1) may yield erroneous conclusions. To test this last rule, the reader is invited to reverse the values for the MU_y in Table 4-1, with Q_y of 1 associated with MU_y of 9, Q_y of 2 with MU_y of 12, Q_y of 3 with MU_y of 16, and so on, leaving the values for *x* the same. This yields decreasing MU for *x* but increasing MU for *y*. Further assume that the individual's income is now $10 instead of $13. Under these conditions, what is the new optimal combination?

By the equality method, the $4x + 6y$ combination fits both rules (4.1) and (4.2). The MU per dollar is 20 in each case (remember $6y$ is the old $5y$). But the total utility of consuming this combination is only 185, whereas if the entire $10 income were spent on *y*, purchasing $10y$, total utility would be 203. Since all the numerical consumer-choice problems discussed in the text will assume independence, we must assume that the *LDMU* holds in order to guarantee that when (4.1) and (4.2) are fulfilled, the resulting distribution of expenditures maximizes utility. Put differently, (4.3) along with (4.1) and (4.2) are *sufficient* conditions for a maximum to occur. However, under conditions of interdependence among commodities, (4.3) is not *necessary* for a maximum.

The λ in (4.1) is the marginal utility of a unit of income or money. For the consumer to maximize total utility, the utility of the marginal unit of income must be the same in all uses to which income is put.

All of the above three conditions must be met for a true optimum. Cases have already been demonstrated where (4.1) held but (4.2) did not. These positions would not be optimum. However, if there were no budget constraint — i.e., if prices were zero or incomes were unlimited, which amounts to the same thing — the consumer would consume commodities up to the point at which the MU of each equaled zero. That is, without an income constraint, the individual consumer would continue to increase consumption of *x, y, z, . . . ,* until their marginal utilities became zero.

Several things should be noted about these rules. First, (4.1) does not mean that the respective MUs should be equal. It states that the MUs per dollar of each commodity should be equal. Relative MUs per dollar are always the relevant comparison in allocating consumption expenditures. The MU from possessing a Cadillac may be much higher than that from possessing a Ford, but the considerably higher price of the Cadillac may make the MU per dollar of the Ford higher. A consumer with this evaluation of the marginal utilities would therefore select the Ford.

In addition, (4.1) holds only for commodities that the consumer in fact purchases. Commodities that have very low or negative MUs — such as spoiled eggs, stale beer, and garbage — may not be included in the consumer's final consumption bundle at all because of very low MUs per dollar. A commodity with a negative MU is, of course, excluded since commodity prices are never negative. To avoid the problems involved in those rare cases where there is a "discommodity" or a "bad" — i.e., a nuisance commodity with a negative MU — it is always possible to redefine the product to make it a desirable commodity or a "good." For example, instead of the discommodity garbage, the commodity "garbage removal services" may be used.

The more general formulation of (4.1) is that the MU per dollar of the commodities actually included in the consumer's budget must be greater than or equal to the MU per dollar of the commodities excluded from the budget:

$$\frac{MU_I}{P_I} \geqq \frac{MU_E}{P_E} \tag{4.4}$$

where I refers to included commodities and E refers to excluded commodities.

In any numerical example it may not be possible to attain precisely the optimum position given in (4.1). In such cases the consumer should allocate income so as to get as close as possible to the condition in which the MUs of a dollar's worth of all goods are the same. For instance, if the consumer depicted in Table 4–1 had $14 of income instead of $13, the additional dollar would be spent on x, where MU_x is 13 for the sixth unit, instead of on y, where MU_y for the ninth unit is only 12. This, however, means there would not be an exact solution to (4.1) because of the discontinuity of the units.

With the above three rules, it is relatively easy to find the optimum position in Table 4–2. Table 4–2 assumes three commodities, x, y, and z. The consumer's income is $26 and the commodities are assumed independent of one another. All three commodities are subject to the $LDMU$ so that condition (4.3) is met. To determine the appropriate quantities to consume by satisfying (4.1) and (4.2), we must know the MU per dollar of each commodity. These values are computed in Table 4–2 in columns (3), (6) and (9).

A number of combinations satisfy (4.1) or (4.2), but only one is simultaneously consistent with both (4.1) and (4.2). For instance, the combination $x = 1$, $y = 5$, and $z = 3$ satisfies (4.1) but is associated with less total expenditures than the $26 budget constraint given in (4.2). However, the combination $x = 2$, $y = 6$, and $z = 4$ satisfies both (4.1) and (4.2). And since it has already been established that (4.3) is satisfied, this combination must constitute an

TABLE 4–2   Three-Good Consumer Optimum, Marginal Utility Approach

(1)	(2)	(3)	(4)	(5)	(6)	(7)	(8)	(9)
Q_x	MU_x	$\dfrac{MU_x}{P_x}$	Q_y	MU_y	$\dfrac{MU_y}{P_y}$	Q_z	MU_z	$\dfrac{MU_z}{P_z}$
1	18	9	1	41	13.7	1	15	15
2	16	8	2	40	13.3	2	13	13
3	14	7	3	35	11.7	3	9	9
4	13	6.5	4	30	10	4	8	8
5	12	6	5	27	9	5	7	7
6	11	5.5	6	24	8	6	6	6
7	10	5	7	21	7	7	5	5
8	9	4.5	8	19	6.3	8	4	4
9	8	4	9	17	5.7	9	3	3
10	7	3.5	10	15	5	10	1	1

Assume: $P_x = \$2$, $P_y = \$3$, $P_z = \$1$, $I = \$26$, and $\Delta MU_i / \Delta Q_j = 0$ for all commodities, where i is any commodity and j is any other commodity.

optimal allocation of budget expenditures. The reader may once again test this conclusion by either computing the total utility associated with this optimal combination as compared with other combinations or showing that shifting resources at the optimal combination from x to y, x to z, y to x, y to z, z to x, or z to y causes a net loss.

Algebraic Solution of Optimum Conditions

For those who prefer to work with algebra, it is also possible to determine the optimum distribution of consumption expenditures if the functional forms of the MU schedules and budget are known. Suppose there are two commodities, x and y, and the MU schedules are:

$$MU_x = 20 - 2x, \text{ and } P_x = \$2 \tag{4.5}$$

$$MU_y = 40 - 8y, \text{ and } P_y = \$4 \tag{4.6}$$

We first note that both commodities are subject to the $LDMU$, so (4.3) is satisfied. Next, we should compute the MUs per dollar, as they are needed in satisfying (4.1):

$$\frac{MU_x}{P_x} = \frac{MU_x}{\$2} = \frac{20 - 2x}{2} = 10 - x \tag{4.7}$$

$$\frac{MU_y}{P_y} = \frac{MU_y}{\$4} = \frac{40 - 8y}{4} = 10 - 2y \tag{4.8}$$

Assume the consumer spends the entire income (\$24) on x and y and therefore satisfies the budget constraint (4.2):

$$\$2x + \$4y = \$24 \tag{4.9}$$

$$\$2x = \$24 - \$4y$$

$$x = 12 - 2y$$

This value for x can be substituted into (4.7):

$$\frac{MU_x}{P_x} = 10 - x = 10 - (12 - 2y) = 10 - 12 + 2y = -2 + 2y \tag{4.10}$$

Since at the optimum we know by (4.1) that $MU_x/P_x = MU_y/P_y$, we get:

$$-2 + 2y = 10 - 2y \tag{4.11}$$

$$4y = 12$$

$$y = 3$$

Substituting into equation (4.9) yields:

$$x = 12 - 2y = 12 - 2\,(3) = 12 - 6 = 6 \tag{4.12}$$

Thus, three units of y and six units of x will be consumed at optimality, exactly exhausting the consumer's money income of \$24 (\$4 $\cdot$ 3 + \$2 $\cdot$ 6 = \$12 + \$12).

DERIVATION OF THE DOWNSLOPING DEMAND SCHEDULE FROM THE MARGINAL UTILITY SCHEDULE

On the basis of the utility theory of consumer behavior, we can derive the downward-sloping individual demand curve. An individual demand curve shows, *ceteris paribus,* the different quantities of the commodity the consumer will purchase at various alternative prices. First, we will give an intuitive explanation of how the demand curve may be derived, and then two different rigorous expositions will follow.

Intuitive Approach

The individual consumer is confronted at any moment of time with a given set of consumer-goods prices. Having decided to spend a given amount on consumption (the budget constraint), the individual must choose the composition of expenditures. The more of x purchased, the less of y that can be purchased, the proportions being determined by the prices of x and y. To get the most satisfaction from the total consumer expenditure, the individual will allocate expenditures such that at the margin a dollar's worth of every good or service will yield an equal amount of utility. If the marginal utility of each dollar spent on each good and service were not equal, total utility could be increased by transferring expenditures from the good yielding less to the good yielding more marginal utility. But if the price of one good falls (all other prices remaining the same), a dollar will purchase a greater quantity of that good, and presumably the marginal utility yielded by a dollar's worth of the good will now be greater than before. (If, e.g., $MU_x/P_x = MU_y/P_y$ before, as the P_x falls, with the Q_x, MU_x, MU_y, and P_y remaining constant, the relationship must now be $MU_x/P_x > MU_y/P_y$.) Hence, to restore the equality between the marginal utility of each dollar's expenditure, the individual will buy more of the good at a lower price than at a higher price. (As more x is bought, the MU_x falls because of the law of diminishing marginal utility; so the optimum equality is again established with $MU_x/P_x = MU_y/P_y$.) Thus, the individual demand curve is downward sloping. In addition, the market demand schedule is the sum of the individual demand schedules; and if the individual demand schedules are negatively sloped, so must be the market demand schedule.

Marshallian Approach

Two distinct approaches may be followed in using utility theory to establish individual demand curves for commodities. One was developed by Alfred Marshall (1842–1924) [4] and the other by Léon Walras (1834–1910). [5]

---

[4] Alfred Marshall, *Principles of Economics* (8th ed.; London: Macmillan & Co., 1920), especially Book III, Chapters V and VI. Our presentation draws on George Malanos, *Intermediate Economic Theory* (Philadelphia: J. B. Lippincott Co., 1962), pp. 32–34.

[5] Léon Walras, *Abrégé des eléments d'-économie politique pure* (Paris: R. Pichon et R. Durand-Auzias, 1938), pp. 131–133. Our presentation closely follows Richard H. Leftwich's interpretation of the Walrasian approach in his *The Price System and Resource Allocation* (5th ed.; Hinsdale, Ill: Dryden Press, 1973), pp. 112–116.

The usual Marshallian approach derives demand curves directly from MU schedules. Marshall did this by implicitly assuming that: (1) the prices of all other commodities are constant, and (2) the MU of money is invariant. The second of these assumptions means that he ignored the complication of income effects of price changes. He justified this assumption by arguing that since any single commodity constitutes such a small portion of a consumer's budget, the income effect would be negligible and hence could be ignored. In contrast, the Walrasian approach makes allowance for both income and substitution effects. Many people prefer the Walrasian approach since it makes the cardinal utility analysis more comparable to the ordinal or indifference curve analysis.

In loose terms, the Marshallian approach derives the demand curve for x (D_x) as follows. At the optimum, it is known that $MU_x/P_x = \lambda$ (λ = common MU of money expenditures) and hence that $MU_x = P_x \cdot \lambda$. If λ is assumed constant, the demand curve is the same as the MU curve except for the multiplicative constant. Both the MU_x and D_x curves measure the Q_x on the horizontal axis, whereas the MU curve measures the MU_x on the vertical axis and the demand curve measures the P_x on the vertical axis. The equation $MU_x = P_x \cdot \bar{\lambda}$ (the bar denotes constancy) shows us how to get from MU_x to the D_x.

More precisely, the Marshallian argument can be rendered in terms of Figure 4–3. Given the MU_x schedule, the analysis generates D_x. To derive an individual's D_x, it is necessary to know what quantities the individual will purchase at different market prices — $2.00 a unit, $1.50 a unit, $1.00 a unit, etc. Suppose the MU of money (λ) is constant and equal to four utils, and the $P_x = \$2$. The consumer will, under these conditions, purchase a Q_x such that the MU_x divided by the P_x ($2) equals the MU of money (λ). Figure 4–3(a)

FIGURE 4–3   Derivation of a Demand Curve from a Marginal Utility Curve — Marshallian Approach

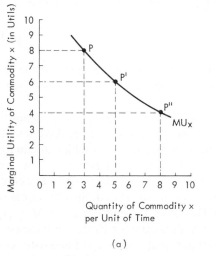

(a)

Marginal Utility Curve for Commodity x

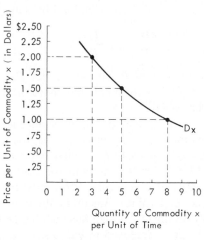

(b)

Demand Curve for Commodity x

indicates that the third unit of x yields eight utils; and since the ratio of MU_x of eight to the P_x of \$2 equals λ, this is the optimum quantity. The consumer would never stop short of consuming three units of x when the $P_x = \$2$. At any Q_x less than three units, a reallocation of, say, \$2 from other commodities, represented by λ, decreases total utility by eight utils; whereas the resulting purchase of an additional unit of x increases total utility by more than eight utils. On the other hand, the individual would never consume more than three units of x when $P_x = \$2$; if he or she consumed more, the additional units would increase total utility by less than the eight utils obtainable from spending the \$2 on other commodities. This information, viz, when $P_x = \$2$ and $Q_x = 3$, can be plotted on Figure 4–3(b).

If we repeat the same experiment for other prices of x, we will obtain the associated optimal Q_x each time. In the end, a continuous figure, such as D_x in Figure 4–3(b), emerges. We recognize this figure as the D_x since it shows various prices and associated quantities as a demand curve is supposed to. Since the MU curve is assumed downsloping (from the $LDMU$) and the MU of money is assumed constant (i.e., the ratio of alternative MUs to prices must remain constant), decreases in P_x must be associated with larger quantities. Under these conditions, when the denominator P_x in (4.1) falls, only the consumption of larger quantities of x can push the numerator MU_x down (with the $LDMU$ and independence assumed) so as to make the ratio again equal to the constant λ (MU of money). Thus, under the Marshallian assumptions, the demand curve is downward sloping.

Walrasian Approach

Walras was able to establish the demand curve for x from the utility analysis as follows. Assume initially that the price of x is P_{x1}, the price of y is P_{y1}, and the respective quantities are x_1 and y_1. Also assume, in order to concentrate on movements in equation (4.1), that at all times the consumer's income is spent. x_1 and y_1 are obtained by satisfying the optimality condition that:

$$\frac{MU_{x1}}{P_{x1}} = \frac{MU_{y1}}{P_{y1}} \tag{4.13}$$

Assuming that P_{x1} is, say, twice P_{y1}, MU_{x1} must be twice MU_{y1} at the optimum. One point on D_x has therefore been established: P_{x1}, x_1. This is shown in Figure 4–4.

To establish a D_x, it is necessary to determine the optimal quantities consumed at other prices, given the consumer's money income. Assuming the price of x rises to P_{x2}, what happens to the other three variables in equation (4.13)? If for the moment we assume that the consumer purchases the same quantity of x as before, $\overline{MU}_x$ must be the same as before (again the bar denotes a constant value). Assuming the commodities are unrelated, the MU_x depends only on the Q_x, which has not changed. However, the entire fraction $\overline{MU}_{x1}/P_{x2}$ will have decreased in value since a larger denominator (from the increase in P_x) is associated with a constant numerator (e.g., $\frac{1}{4} > \frac{1}{7}$). Therefore, even

**FIGURE 4–4   Derivation of a Demand Curve from
Marginal Utility Curves – Walrasian Approach**

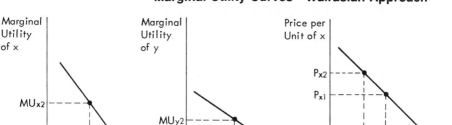

(a)   (b)   (c)

if the right-hand side of the equality in (4.13) remained constant, the entire expression would now be an inequality since the left-hand side has declined. That is,

$$\frac{\overline{MU}_{x1}}{P_{x2}} < \frac{\overline{MU}_{y1}}{\overline{P}_{y1}} \qquad (4.14)$$

Hence, we expect less of x to be consumed.

But there is even an additional reason for expecting this inequality to hold. With an increased price of x and a constant rate of consumption of x, the consumer must be spending more income on x than before, leaving less for y. Since P_{y1} is constant, a decrease in total spending on y necessarily means the consumer must purchase a smaller quantity of y than before, say, Q_{y2}. But decreases in Q_y, given the *LDMU*, means the consumer moves back up the MU_y curve from right to left, arriving at a higher MU_y, such as MU_{y2}. This means that the fraction MU_{y2}/P_{y1} has risen in value. Or,

$$\frac{\overline{MU}_{x1}}{P_{x2}} < \frac{MU_{y2}}{\overline{P}_{y1}} \qquad (4.15)$$

Since the MU_x per dollar is less than the MU_y per dollar, the consumer must reallocate consumption expenditures to reach the optimum. Since the prices of the commodities can now be viewed as given, the only way the individual can change the inequality in (4.15) to an equality is by manipulating the MUs. This is done by changing the quantities consumed. The consumer therefore begins transferring expenditure dollars from x to y. Given the *LDMU* for both, increases in Q_y lead to decreases in MU_y and decreases in Q_x lead to increases in MU_x. This transfer process continues until:

$$\frac{MU_{x2}}{P_{x2}} = \frac{MU_{y3}}{P_{y1}} \qquad (4.16)$$

A second point on this consumer's D_x has been established, P_{x2} with Q_{x2}. The higher price is associated with a lower rate of consumption. In short, the demand function is downward sloping.

If we repeat the same experiment for other prices of *x*, we will obtain the new optimum quantity each time. Eventually, a continuous, downward-sloping function, such as shown in Figure 4–4(c), will emerge. The decrease in the Q_x as the P_x increases is the combined result of the income and substitution effects; that is, the decrease in Q_x is due both to the decrease in the purchasing power of the given money income and to the increase in the price of *x* compared to the price of *y*.

Meanwhile, what has happened to the final quantity consumed of *y?* That is, is $Q_{y3} \leqq Q_{y1}$? Clearly $Q_{y3} > Q_{y2}$, since Q_{y2} assumed the consumer was taking the same Q_x as before even though the P_x had increased. We know, however, that to attain maximum utility as in (4.1), the consumer must increase consumption of *y*. Thus, Q_{y3} must be greater than Q_{y2}. However, is it necessary that $Q_{y3} > Q_{y1}$ as depicted in Figure 4–4(b)? The answer is no. To follow this, an identity may be established: $TE_y \equiv \overline{TE}_{xy} - TE_x$. Given a consumer's money income, total expenditures on the two commodities, $\overline{TE}_{xy}$, must be a constant; whereas expenditures on *y*, (TE_y), directly depend on how much is spent on *x*, TE_x. When the price of *x* rises, what determines the total spending on *x?* Answer: the elasticity of demand for *x*. Only if the demand for *x* is inelastic can an increase in P_x lead to an increase in TE_x. If the demand for *x* is inelastic, the Q_y must be less than its original value, $Q_{y1} > Q_{y3}$, since P_y is constant; if demand for *x* is elastic, $Q_{y1} < Q_{y3}$; and if demand for *x* is unitary, $Q_{y1} = Q_{y3}$.

INCOME AND SUBSTITUTION EFFECTS SEPARATED

It is possible to separate analytically the income and substitution effects, using the classical cardinal utility approach and assuming product demand independence.[6] Suppose the consumer is initially at the optimum point, satisfying equation (4.1) such that (letting MU_{m1}, instead of λ, represent the marginal utility of money):

$$\frac{MU_{x1}}{P_{x1}} = \frac{MU_{y1}}{P_{y1}} = \frac{MU_{m1}}{1} \qquad (4.17)$$

Note that the price of money equals unity, since the price of $1 is $1, the price of $5 is $5, etc. If the price of *x* falls to P_{x2}, the consumer is not at an optimum, since the following inequality holds:

$$\frac{MU_{x1}}{P_{x2}} > \frac{MU_{y1}}{P_{y1}} = \frac{MU_{m1}}{1} \qquad (4.18)$$

---

[6] For a discussion of how the following analysis would be altered if there were interdependence of utilities among consumers, see Richard A. Bilas, *Microeconomic Theory* (2d ed.; New York: McGraw-Hill Book Co., 1971), pp. 51–55. Our discussion assumes that the consumer's income is spent, thereby satisfying equation (4.2).

To restore optimality, the consumer will buy more x and less y, thereby causing the MU_x to fall from MU_{x1} to MU_{x2} and MU_y to rise from MU_{y1} to MU_{y2}, until the following equality is established:

$$\frac{MU_{x2}}{P_{x2}} = \frac{MU_{y2}}{P_{y2}} = \frac{MU_{m1}}{1} \tag{4.19}$$

This equality results from the pure substitution effect alone; and with the *LDMU* and the assumption of independence, this equality assures a downward-sloping demand curve.

Now let's stipulate that a fall in the price of x to P_{x2} results in an increase in the consumer's real income, such that the MU_{m1} falls to, say, MU_{m2}, following the *LDMU*. Once again we have a nonoptimum expression:

$$\frac{MU_{x2}}{P_{x2}} = \frac{MU_{y1}}{P_{y1}} > \frac{MU_{m2}}{1} \tag{4.20}$$

To restore optimality, the consumer must consume more of both x and y so their respective MUs fall in accordance with the *LDMU*.

$$\frac{MU_{x3}}{P_{x2}} = \frac{MU_{y3}}{P_{y1}} = \frac{MU_{m2}}{1} \tag{4.21}$$

This equation reflects the income effect of a price decrease. With a superior good, both the substitution and income effects cause the demand curve to be negatively sloped. The presence of an inferior good would provide a necessary but not a sufficient condition to cause a "Giffen good," i.e., an upsloping demand function.[7]

APPLICATIONS OF CARDINAL UTILITY THEORY

In a market economy, a consumer is able to purchase a commodity for a total sacrifice that is less than the total benefit derived from it. The difference between the total amount of money a consumer *would be willing* to pay for a quantity of a commodity and the amount *required* to be paid for that quantity is called *consumer surplus (CS)*.

Consumer Surplus

Consumer surplus reflects the fact that a consumer's total economic welfare from the consumption of a commodity is greater than the total utility of its monetary value (or total expenditure). Items such as air and water, which currently command zero or extremely low prices, yield considerable amounts of *CS*.

Although the concept of *CS* has been subject to numerous sophisticated measurements (at least 27!), Alfred Marshall's simple and original presentation

---

[7] To ensure a Giffen good, the income effect must be greater (in absolute value) than the substitution effect and the good must be inferior.

is still useful. Marshall assumes that the marginal utility of money is constant $(\bar{\lambda})$, i.e., that there is no income effect. Marshall's approach is particularly useful if one is primarily interested in establishing the existence of CS without being unduly concerned with its precise measurement. For a number of welfare problems, e.g., some tax or public expenditure policies, knowledge of the existence of CS is sufficient. In other cases, range of magnitude measurement is important. For instance, if a public utility everywhere has total costs (TC) greater than total revenue (TR) so that it cannot break even, it is often argued that the government should subsidize the product whenever $TR + CS > TC$.

Table 4–3 and Figure 4–5 present an example of the process of estimating the pecuniary value of CS. The hypothetical data in Table 4–3 show a family's preferences regarding product x, that is, the prices they would be willing to pay for varying rates of consumption. Suppose they buy five units of x. Since they pay $30 for this quantity ($6 \times 5$) while their total welfare is $40, CS is $10. This surplus occurs because all units of this standardized commodity sell for whatever the last unit purchased brings in the market ($6). But we know from the $LDMU$ that the earlier units are worth more to them than the last. Consequently, they receive a surplus on all "previous" units.

TABLE 4–3   Calculation of Consumer Surplus

(1) Price Per Unit	(2) Quantity Bought Per Unit of Time	(3) Total Expenditure $= (1) \times (2)$	(4) Total Welfare (Utility*) $= \sum_{i=1}^{n} (1)$	(5) Consumer Surplus $= (4) - (3)$
$10	1	$10	$10	—
9	2	18	19	$ 1
8	3	24	27	3
7	4	28	34	6
6	5	30	40	10
5	6	30	45	15
4	7	28	49	21
3	8	24	52	28
2	9	18	54	36
1	10	10	55	45

* Total welfare (utility) is measurable in dollars, assuming the *MU* of money $(\bar{\lambda})$ is invariant at 1 util = $1.

Figure 4–5 illustrates this concept. At a price of $10 per unit, the family derives the same utility from one unit of this commodity as they could obtain by spending $10 on other goods – i.e., there is no CS. If the price drops to $9, the family could buy one unit that is worth $10 for $9. CS is $1. At $8, the surplus for the first unit is $2 ($10 - $8) and for the second unit, $1 ($10 - $9). Total $CS = $3. At a price of $6, CS is approximately $4 + $3 + $2 + $1 or $10, as indicated by the shaded area, and so on.

FIGURE 4-5   Consumer and Producer Surplus

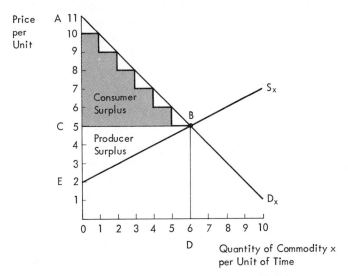

This example deals only with discrete units. If fractional units were not available, the demand curve would be the step function outlined under the D_x curve in Figure 4–5. However, if the commodity is infinitesimally divisible, the smooth demand curve D_x would be relevant and CS would be the area of triangle ABC.

We can see this in another way. From Chapter 3 we know that the area under a marginal curve at any point equals the height of the total curve at that point. Therefore, since the area under the D_x curve is the same as the area under the MU_x curve, under the given assumptions, for six units of x, the total utility equals the area $0ABD$. On the other hand, the total outlay for x equals $P_x \cdot Q_x$ or the area of rectangle $0CBD$. The difference between them, triangle ABC, measures CS. Note that even though a consumer through CS "receives more than he or she pays for," the seller has not been gouged. In fact, the seller may also receive a boon in the form of a *producer surplus*. As demonstrated below, both parties to a voluntary transaction benefit.

Producer surplus is analogous to consumer surplus. Since the supply curve can be interpreted as the quantities sellers are willing to sell per time unit at all possible prices, they would have been willing to sell various amounts at prices below the market price.

Interpersonal Comparisons of Utility

Implicit in the classical utility theory approach was the idea that utility could be compared between individuals. Hence, the sum total of the utilities received by the consumers of a given product could be found by simply adding the utilities of the different individuals together. Most economists today would argue that such interpersonal comparisons are impossible: no one can compare the satisfactions Ms. A and Mr. B derive from consumption. However, as a practical matter some economists are willing, in approaching many of the important economic issues of the day, to provisionally assume that people's utility functions are reasonably alike. Without this assumption there is currently no way to resolve some of these issues. However, this is more a problem for normative or welfare economics than for this book, which deals with economics as a positive discipline.

Exchange

Contrary to frequently expressed opinion, all parties in a voluntary trade or exchange benefit. One person is not made better off as a result of the other being made worse off. This may be demonstrated with the following simple example. Suppose that, on the margin, Ms. White values x twice as much as y, so $MU_x/MU_y = 2$; and Mr. Black values x four times as much as y, so $MU_x/MU_y = 4$. The general principle is that whenever people possess different relative desires for the goods involved, mutually advantageous trade can take place. This means whenever the ratio of MUs differ, trade can be mutually beneficial.[8] Thus, exchange is mutually advantageous when:

$$\frac{MU_{x1}}{MU_{y1}} \neq \frac{MU_{x2}}{MU_{y2}} \tag{4.22}$$

where the subscripts 1 and 2 refer to two different people or groups.

In our example, suppose Ms. White agrees to give Mr. Black one unit of x in exchange for three units of y. Ms. White values x only twice as much as y ($x = 2y$), yet she is getting three units of y in return for sacrificing one unit of x. On the other hand, Mr. Black is delighted to get one unit of x in exchange for only three units of y, since he values x four times as much as y ($x = 4y$). Thus, both parties gain from any exchange with a combination falling between the trading ratios $2y$ for $1x$ and $4y$ for $1x$. At the extremes, one party is as well off as before while the other reaps the entire benefit. For example, if Ms. White instead offered $1x$ in exchange for $4y$, Mr. Black would be indifferent to the trade. If Mr. Black accepts it, Ms. White gets the entire benefit. Or at the ratio $2y$ for $1x$, Ms. White would be indifferent and Mr. Black would get the entire gain. In short, both parties must gain in a voluntary trade or they wouldn't trade.

Economics of Search

Since most of the previous illustrations of utility theory have been rather abstract, let us consider how the theory can more obviously be applied in

---

[8] The word "can" is important. As long as there is a relative disparity in the MUs between any two persons, the allocation of these goods can be revised by trade so that each person is better off, "provided the costs of discovering the people whose values are unequal and negotiating the exchange contracts and transporting goods are not prohibitory." See Armen A. Alchian and William R. Allen, *Exchange and Production; Theory in Use* (Belmont, Calif.: Wadsworth Publishing Co., 1969), p. 53.

everyday life. Consider the question of how much time and effort should be spent in searching for bargains. The rule for conducting search for homogeneous products is, according to George J. Stigler, the following:

> To maximize his utility, the buyer searches for additional prices until the expected saving from the purchase equals the cost of visiting one more dealer. Then he stops searching, and buys from the dealer who quotes the lowest price he has encountered.[9]

Although the cost of search varies, several predictions can be made with this theory. For instance, the theory predicts that the amount of search will depend upon the amount of money the consumer expects to pay for the commodity. A two percent savings in price on an automobile constitutes a much larger saving than a two percent savings on a toaster. Hence, the theory predicts that people will search more for low prices on automobiles than on toasters.

Furthermore, since people search more for items that take up a larger portion of their budgets, high-price sellers will be less likely to survive in these fields. In short, the larger the amount consumers expect to spend on a commodity, the more they will search for low prices. Therefore, the range of prices of heavily-searched items such as automobiles should vary much less (relative to the average price) than do the prices of toasters in retail outlets.

This theory has actually been tested, e.g., with automobiles and automatic washing machines. As predicted, the relative dispersion in automobile prices was significantly narrower than that for washing machines.[10] We urge readers to test this proposition in their own cities. The theory applies to all standardized commodities: e.g., try it with stoves and toasters, refrigerators and radios, color television sets and black-and-white television sets, etc.

The cost of search is different for different people. It depends on the marginal utility of the individual's time and on the onerousness of the process itself as well as on the outlay for search expenses, which in turn depends on the marginal utility per dollar. Thus, we would not expect a person who could be earning $50 an hour working or who values leisure at $50 per hour to engage in search with an expected value which might be less than $50 per hour. Others may find the haggling and the routine of search so distasteful that they would not do so unless the expected value were quite high. Thus, what may seem to be irrational behavior on the part of some individuals who do not "bargain hunt" may in fact be quite reasonable. Some persons seem to find exhilaration (utility) in the pursuit. For them search costs could be negative.

Diamond-Water Paradox

The classical economists (Smith, Ricardo, Mill, Marx, etc.) all rejected the current contention that utility and demand are determinants of price. They

---

[9] George J. Stigler, *The Theory of Price* (3d ed.; New York: Macmillan Co., 1966), pp. 2–3. The entire discussion of search is indebted to his stimulating Chapter 1.

[10] The precise figures are quoted in *ibid.*, p. 4. The data are based on two articles by Allen F. Jung, *The Journal of Business* (October, 1958 and January, 1960).

argued that although water is more "useful" than diamonds, diamonds are more expensive than water; therefore, utility provides no explanation of price. They therefore erected a theory of price that emphasized the cost or supply side, and in particular, labor cost.

Their failure to explain the diamond-water conundrum had many causes besides the dimensional problem.[11] One difficulty involves what it means to be "useful." If this word means only that total utility from consuming water (TU_W) is greater than that of diamonds (TU_D), it is generally true. But if by "useful" the classics meant that water was more functional or more useful from the society's point of view, then their definition was clearly nonsense in terms of price determination. Goods command prices because they satisfy wants, regardless of how meritorious or nonmeritorious these desires may seem from the point of view of anyone other than the consumer.

More crucial to the classics' confusion, however, was their failure to specify units and therefore separate TU from MU—and it is MU, not TU, that determines prices. If diamonds are scarce and hence have a high MU relative to the more abundant water, the price of diamonds will be high to the same degree. Yet at the same time the TU from consuming water can be much higher than that from consuming diamonds because of the much greater quantities of water consumed. Figure 4-6 illustrates just such a case.

In the 1870s the so-called "marginalists," W. S. Jevons, Carl Menger, and Léon Walras, were able to resolve this paradox and usher in an era in which demand and utility came to the forefront. Their solution follows the above line of reasoning and is illustrated in Figure 4-6. Here we see that since only $0D$ units of diamonds are consumed, the MU_D is quite high, equal to $0E$. On the other hand, because $0W$ units of water are consumed, the MU_W is

**FIGURE 4-6   Diamond-Water Paradox
or Paradox of Value**

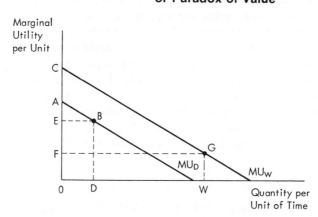

---

[11] The dimensional problem is that the dimensions of water and diamonds are different. Certainly, *some* quantity of water is higher priced than some quantity unit of diamonds, so it is meaningless to compare their prices. As pointed out above, the per-util price of all goods is the same, and utility is the only common denominator.

only $0F$. Hence, diamonds would be dearer than water. Yet note that the TU from consuming water is considerably above that of diamonds. Since any total value equals the area under its marginal curve, the TU_W is $0CGW$, whereas the TU_D is $0ABD$. Clearly $0ABD < 0CGW$ (i.e., $TU_D < TU_W$) even though $0E > 0F$ (i.e., $MU_D > MU_W$), and hence $P_D > P_W$.

QUESTIONS

1. Why is *ex ante* utility important in economic analysis, whereas *ex post* utility is ordinarily of very little interest?
2. Explain the derivation of the marginal utility function from the total utility function.
3. Why does the consumer maximize utility at the rate of consumption at which the marginal utility per dollar of a commodity equals the marginal utility per dollar of all other commodities?
4. If two goods are substitutes, what happens to the MU of x when the quantity consumed of y increases? If two goods are complements, what happens to the MU of x when the quantity consumed of y increases?
5. Using data from Table 4-1 (page 75), determine the optimum quantities this consumer would buy if the price of x $(P_x) = \$2$ per unit, $P_y = \$2$ per unit, and the consumer's income $(I) = \$26$. What quantities would the consumer choose if $P_x = \$1$, $P_y = \$2$, and $I = \$13$?
6. Suppose the government wanted to build a bridge even though the total revenue (tolls) would be less than the costs of building it. Using the concept of consumer surplus, argue in favor of building the bridge.
7. Some people argue that progressive taxes are a fair way to tax because the marginal utility of a dollar for a rich person is much less than that for a poor person. What is wrong with this argument?
8. "Pareto optimality" is a condition where one party can benefit from exchange only at someone else's expense. Show that if two individuals are not at their respective optimal positions, both can benefit from exchange, and after the exchange takes place, Pareto optimum exists.
9. Is it ever possible to say that one commodity is higher priced than another?
10. Can a consumer get more utility from commodity A than from commodity B even though the consumer spent more money on commodity B?

APPENDIX: MATHEMATICAL NOTES

Note 1. Consumer Optimality

There are several alternative ways that the conditions for consumer optimality given in equations (4.1), (4.2), and (4.3) of the text can be derived. First, these three conditions may be rewritten in a slightly more compact form. Assuming that the consumer trys to maximize utility, $U = f(x_1, x_2, \ldots, x_n)$ for a given set of prices (P_1, $P_2, \ldots, P_n$) over which he or she has no influence whatsoever, we may write:

$$\frac{MU_{x1}}{P_{x1}} = \frac{MU_{x2}}{P_{x2}} = \ldots = \frac{MU_{xn}}{P_{xn}} = \lambda \text{ (marginal utility of money)} \qquad (4.23)$$

or more compactly:

$$\frac{MU_{xi}}{P_{xi}} = \frac{MU_{xj}}{P_{xj}}$$

The consumer has a budget constraint such that income per unit of time is I dollars:

$$\sum_{i=1}^{n} P_i x_i = I \tag{4.24}$$

Furthermore, if the commodities are unrelated, the following must hold to ensure that the previous two conditions yield a maximum:

$$\frac{\delta^2 U}{\delta x_i^2} < 0 \text{ for all } i = 1, 2, \ldots, n \tag{4.25}$$

There are two general methods for deriving these conditions: the *substitution approach* and the *LaGrangian multiplier technique*. We will illustrate both these techniques, assuming, for simplicity, a two-commodity world, x and y.

Method 1. Substitution Approach

Given:

Utility function $U = f(x,y)$ $\qquad\qquad$ (4.26)

Income constraint $I = xP_x + yP_y$ $\qquad\qquad$ (4.27)

(4.27) may be written as:

$$\frac{I - xP_x}{P_y} = y \tag{4.28}$$

Substituting this value of y into (4.26), the utility function becomes a function of x alone since income and prices are assumed constant.

$$U = f\left(x, \frac{I - xP_x}{P_y}\right) \tag{4.29}$$

Since x and y bear a fixed relationship to one another via (4.27), the sufficient conditions for a maximum are that $dU/dx = 0$ (first-order condition) and $d^2U/dx^2 < 0$ (second-order condition). Setting (4.26) equal to zero yields:

$$\frac{dU}{dx} = \frac{\delta U}{\delta x} + \frac{\delta U}{\delta y}\left(\frac{P_x}{P_y}\right) = 0$$

This may be rewritten as:

$$\frac{\delta U}{\delta x} = \frac{\delta U}{\delta y}\left(\frac{P_x}{P_y}\right) \tag{4.30}$$

or

$$\left(\frac{\delta U}{\delta x}\right) \div P_x = \left(\frac{\delta U}{\delta y}\right) \div P_y \tag{4.31}$$

This gives us (4.1) in the text: the first-order or necessary condition for a maximum is that the *MU*s must be proportional to their prices. The sufficient or second-order condition for a maximum requires that:

$$\frac{d^2U}{dx^2} = \left[\frac{\delta^2 U}{\delta x^2} + 2\frac{\delta^2 U}{\delta x \delta y}\left(-\frac{P_x}{P_y}\right) + \frac{\delta^2 U}{\delta y^2}\left(-\frac{P_x}{P_y}\right)^2 \right] < 0 \qquad (4.32)$$

Multiplying by a positive number, P_y^2, the inequality still remains:

$$\qquad\qquad\quad A \qquad\qquad\qquad B \qquad\qquad\qquad C \qquad\qquad\qquad (4.33)$$

$$\left[\left(\overbrace{\frac{\delta^2 U}{\delta x^2}\ P_y^2}\right) - \left(\overbrace{2\frac{\delta U}{\delta x \delta y}\ P_x\ P_y}\right) + \left(\overbrace{\frac{\delta^2 U}{\delta y^2}\ P_x^2}\right) \right] < 0$$

$$\qquad\quad + \qquad\qquad\quad +\ + \qquad\qquad\qquad +$$

In the text, the relationship among commodities was defined according to whether $\Delta MU_y / \Delta Q_x \lesseqgtr 0$ (e.g., $= 0$ means independent commodities). Using our present terminology, the definition amounts to whether $\delta^2 U/\delta x \delta y \lesseqgtr 0$.

Since the classical economists assumed an additive utility function, the commodities were unrelated, i.e., $\delta^2 U/\delta x \delta y = 0$. What does this mean in terms of meeting condition (4.33)? The positive signs under the prices indicate that these values are necessarily positive. We therefore need only concern ourselves with the other expressions. The three main components of this equation have been labeled *A, B,* and *C.* With independence, *B* is zero. Since both *A* and *C* are each prefixed by a positive sign and each contains a positive term inside the parentheses, the other term in each case must be negative to ensure that the entire expression is negative (4.33) as required for a maximum. In other words, it is necessary to assume that $\delta^2 U/\delta x^2 < 0$ and $\delta^2 U/\delta y^2 < 0$. The economic interpretation of this is that the *LDMU* is assumed for both commodities. This is another condition for maximization, given as (4.3) in the text. However, the *LDMU* is clearly a necessary and sufficient condition for consumer optimality only when the commodities are unrelated.

Perhaps the most interesting conclusions we can draw from examining (4.33) are that:

(1) the second-order condition can be met even if both commodities exhibit increasing *MU* (provided they are complements), and
(2) the second-order condition may not be met even if both commodities exhibit diminishing *MU* (provided they are substitutes).

If the commodities are substitutes, $\delta^2 U/\delta x \delta y < 0$, *B* is positive. Then even if the *LDMU* holds for both commodities, $\delta^2 U/\delta x^2 < 0$, $\delta^2 U/\delta y^2 < 0$, the entire expression (4.33) may be positive if the positive *B* expression were large enough to overcome the negative *A* and *C* expressions. If the commodities are complements, $\delta^2 U/\delta x \delta y < 0$, *B* is negative. Then even if increasing *MU* holds for both commodities, $\delta^2 U/\delta x^2 > 0$, $\delta^2 U/\delta y^2 > 0$, the entire expression (4.33) may be negative if the negative *B* expression were large enough to overcome the positive *A* and *C* terms.

While it is correct mathematically that the *LDMU* is neither necessary nor sufficient for equilibrium if the goods are unrelated, it is usually assumed that the cross terms, containing the relationship between commodities, are smaller absolute amounts than the direct terms. There are obvious psychological reasons for this assumption and it makes *DMU* compatible with what we deduced.

Method 2. LaGrange Multipliers

We may also find the maximum value of a function of several variables subject to functional constraints by using the technique of LaGrangian multipliers. From the utility function (4.26) and the budget constraint (4.27), we form a third function:

$$V = f(x, y) + \lambda\, f(I - xP_x - yP_y) \tag{4.34}$$

where $\lambda(\neq 0)$ is the yet undetermined LaGrange multiplier. The necessary (first-order) conditions for a maximum are:

$$\frac{\delta V}{\delta x} = \frac{\delta U}{\delta x} - \lambda P_x = 0, \quad \frac{\delta U}{\delta x} = \lambda P_x, \quad \left(\frac{\delta U}{\delta x}\right) \div P_x = \lambda \tag{4.35}$$

$$\frac{\delta V}{\delta y} = \frac{\delta U}{\delta y} - \lambda P_y = 0, \quad \frac{\delta U}{\delta y} = \lambda P_y, \quad \left(\frac{\delta U}{\delta y}\right) \div P_y = \lambda \tag{4.36}$$

$$\frac{\delta V}{\delta U} = I - x \cdot P_x - y \cdot P_y = 0 \tag{4.37}$$

This yields (4.1), i.e., the ratio of the MUs must equal the ratio of the prices for maximum total utility. That is,

$$\left(\frac{\delta V}{\delta x}\right) \div \left(\frac{\delta V}{\delta y}\right) = \frac{P_x}{P_y} \tag{4.38}$$

The sufficient (second-order) condition for a constrained maximum is that the relevant bordered Hessian determinant be positive:

$$\begin{vmatrix} \dfrac{\delta^2 U}{\delta x^2} & \dfrac{\delta^2 U}{\delta x \delta y} & -P_x \\[2mm] \dfrac{\delta^2 U}{\delta x \delta y} & \dfrac{\delta^2 U}{\delta y^2} & -P_y \\[2mm] -P_x & -P_y & 0 \end{vmatrix} > 0 \tag{4.39}$$

which when expanded is the same as (4.33). That is, the second-order condition for a maximum requires that:

$$\frac{d^2 U}{dx^2} = \frac{\delta^2 U}{\delta x^2} + 2\frac{\delta^2 U}{\delta x \delta y}\left(-\frac{P_x}{P_y}\right) + \frac{\delta^2 U}{\delta y^2}\left(-\frac{P_x}{P_y}\right)^2 < 0 \tag{4.40}$$

Multiplying (4.40) by P_y^2, a positive number, we get:

$$\frac{\delta^2 U}{\delta x^2}P_y^2 - 2\frac{d^2 U}{\delta x \delta y}P_x P_y + \frac{\delta^2 U}{\delta y^2}P_x^2 < 0 \tag{4.41}$$

Note 2. Consumer Surplus (CS)

CS has been defined as the excess of total satisfaction a consumer gets from a commodity over the total sum spent to obtain it. Graphically, *CS* is the difference between the total utility—the total area under a demand curve—and the area representing the consumer's total expenditure on the commodity—the area of the rectangle found by multiplying the given market price (p_0) by the quantity consumed (q_0). Since areas are involved, the measurement of CS involves definite integrals.

$$CS = \int_0^{q_0} f(q)dq - p_0 q_0$$

For instance, if the market demand curve is $p = 40 - 2q$, CS at a price of 10 is 225 (hint: at $p = 10$, $q = 15$, and $TE = 150$).

This discussion of CS provides us with a specific place to show, with simple mathematics, the connection between the consumer optimum derived in Note 1 of this Appendix and CS. Given that the prices of other commodities are fixed to a consumer, his or her utility function for commodity x may be written $U_x = f(Q_x)$. Assuming the consumer tries to maximize CS—i.e., the difference between the total utility derived from the consumption of a commodity, $f(Q_x)$, and total expenditures on the commodity, $P_x \cdot Q_x$—the conditions for a maximum require that $V' = 0$, $V'' < 0$ where $V = f(Q_x) - P_x Q_x$. This yields:

$$(1) \quad V' = f'(Q_x) - P_x = 0 \quad \text{or} \quad MU_x = P_x \tag{4.42}$$

$$(2) \quad V'' = f''(Q_x) < 0 \quad \text{or} \quad \text{law of diminishing marginal utility holds}$$

Note 3. Homogeneous Functions

We stated in this chapter that the demand curve is homogeneous of degree zero. In economic terms, if a function is homogeneous it has the same relationship over its entire range. More precisely, a function is said to be homogeneous of degree "i" if, when every independent variable is multiplied by a positive constant, say, λ, the new function is λ^i times the original function. If $f(x, y)$ is the function, it is said to be homogeneous if:

$$\lambda^i f(x,y) = f(\lambda x, \lambda y) \tag{4.43}$$

where $\lambda > 0$ and $i =$ the degree of homogeneity.

The cases where $i = 0$ or 1 (linear) have the most important economic applications. In the case of demand curves, they are said to be homogeneous of degree zero in prices and income. If all prices and incomes are, say, doubled, real demand stays the same and only the nominal values change. Numerical examples of homogeneous functions include: (1) homogeneous of zero degree, $y = (a_1 x + b_1 y)/(a_2 x + b_2 y)$; and (2) homogeneous of degree one, $y = ax^2 + bxy + cy^2$, where a, b, and c are constants.

5 Ordinal Utility or Indifference Curve Approach To Consumer Behavior

The classical cardinal utility approach developed in the last chapter was first challenged late in the nineteenth century by the English economist F. Y. Edgeworth (1845–1926) when he introduced indifference curve analysis.[1] But it was not until the 1930s, largely through the efforts of two other British economists, J. R. Hicks and R. G. D. Allen, that indifference curve analysis became an accepted part of the hard core of economic theory.[2] The ordinal utility approach so won the day that cardinal utility analysis became almost taboo until the very different von Neumann-Morgenstern measurement technique revived interest in it. Later, Nobel Laureate Paul Samuelson championed an alternative approach known as revealed preference. This well-developed theory starts from behavioral axioms and axioms about orderings and shows that consumers act as if they had an indifference map. (The rudiments of the revealed preference theory are considered in Chapter 6.) The most recent attempt to analyze consumer behavior has utilized an apparatus of thought and algebra of reasoning known as axiomatic choice theory.

The ordinal utility approach has several advantages, and these advantages, as described below, have led to its popularity. (1) Edgeworth developed the technique of indifference curves to consider commodities for which utility is a function not only of their own quantities but also of the quantities of other commodities consumed. The Classicists had assumed an additive utility function in which the MU of any commodity was independent of the quantities consumed of other commodities. The indifference curve approach provides a clearer and more rigorous definition of the interrelationships among commodities, i.e., whether they are complements, substitutes, or unrelated commodities. Thus, the graphical indifference curve analysis can be presented using at least two commodities, whereas the classical analysis focused on one commodity. We say "at least two commodities" for often "money income" is used generally to represent all other commodities. (2) Hicks and Allen further developed the indifference curve technique to avoid the notion that utility is measurable in a precise cardinal sense. They also argued that the notion of diminishing MU was not only distasteful but unnecessary. Hence, by Occam's Razor, which cautions against unnecessary assumptions, they found the indifference curve approach more appealing; it requires no assumption of

---

[1] Francis Y. Edgeworth, *Mathematical Psychics* (London: C. K. Paul & Co., 1881).
[2] John R. Hicks and Roy G. D. Allen, "A Reconsideration of Value," *Economica* (February, May, 1934), pp. 52–76, 196–219.

measurable utility or diminishing MU. Put simply, the indifference curve analysis does not require us to know *why* the consumer prefers x to y (the classical analysis had said it was because x has more utility than y per dollar) or to know *by how much* the consumer prefers x to y. (3) The substitution and income effects are easier to see and are more rigorously defined in the indifference curve analysis.

NATURE OF INDIFFERENCE RELATIONSHIPS

The heart of the ordinal utility approach to consumer behavior is contained in five basic assumptions or axioms. These are listed and then discussed seriatim. They are:

1. completeness or complete ordering
2. nonsatiation, or more is preferred to less
3. consistency or transitivity
4. continuity or substitutability
5. optimality

Completeness or Complete Ordering

The completeness assumption states that the consumer has a definite order of preferences or *rank ordering* for every conceivable combination of commodities. With ordinal analysis, we need assume only that the consumer knows his or her preferences but not by how much one combination is preferred to another.

The completeness assumption is sometimes called the trichotomy axiom for the following reason. Suppose there are two different combinations of goods, call them C_1 and C_2. This axiom assumes that the consumer can make one of three statements about these combinations, viz., that (1) C_1PC_2, (2) C_2PC_1, or (3) C_1IC_2, where P stands for a preference relationship and I for an indifference relationship. That is, the consumer can state that he or she: (1) prefers C_1 to C_2, (2) prefers C_2 to C_1, or (3) is indifferent between C_1 and C_2. (Thus, C_1PC_2 is read: C_1 is preferred to C_2).

Indifference is said to be an equivalence relation since it is:

1. *reflexive*, meaning: C_1IC_1, C_2IC_2, and C_3IC_3
2. *symmetrical*, meaning: if C_1IC_2, then C_2IC_1 and so on for all commodity bundle indifference relations
3. *transitive*, meaning: if C_1IC_2 and C_2IC_3, then C_1IC_3

In contrast, the preference relation is:

1. *irreflexive*, meaning: $C_1\not{P}C_1$, $C_2\not{P}C_2$, and $C_3\not{P}C_3$, where $\not{P}$ means "not preferred to"
2. *asymmetric*, meaning: if C_1PC_2, then $C_2\not{P}C_1$ and so on for all preference combinations
3. *transitive*, meaning: if C_1PC_2 and C_2PC_3, then C_1PC_3

Most of these relationships probably meet with your intuition. For instance, if C_1 is preferred to C_2, it is reasonable that C_2 cannot be preferred to

C_1. Similarly, if the consumer is indifferent between C_1 and C_2 and between C_2 and C_3, it seems plausible that C_1 would be regarded as equivalent to C_3.

Nonsatiation, or More is Preferred to Less

The second important assumption underlying utility analysis is that consumers always prefer more goods (as opposed to bads, no-goods, or discommodities) to less. However, no consumer would ever willingly consume a positively priced or zero priced commodity beyond the satiation (i.e., disutility) point. So within the normal range of consumption, we will assume that a consumer always prefers a larger bundle of commodities to a smaller one. In this context, larger and smaller have a very special meaning. One combination is said to be larger than another if and only if it contains as many units of every commodity and more units of at least one commodity.[3] If a combination contains more units of one commodity and less of another, it can be considered neither larger nor smaller.

Consistency or Transitivity

The assumption of consistency or transitivity has already been alluded to in the discussion of completeness. A consistent set of tastes is merely a well-defined order of preference and not necessarily an ethically desirable set of tastes. If a reader prefers to read comic books rather than the *New York Times* and in turn prefers the *Times* to Shakespeare, then this consumer is considered consistent if he or she prefers comic books to Shakespeare. More generally, consistency means that if bundle C_1 (of, say, $10x + 10y$) is preferred to C_2 ($9x + 11y$), and C_2 is preferred to C_3 ($8x + 12y$), then C_1 is preferred to C_3.

Many things in this world are not transitive (the technical name for consistent). Although they do not formally meet all the necessary assumptions to make a valid test,[4] sporting events come close enough that we can use them as obvious examples of nontransitivity. Although, say, Notre Dame beats Michigan State in football, and Michigan State beats Purdue, it does not always follow that Notre Dame will beat Purdue.

Continuity or Substitutability

Substitutability is used in several different senses in ordinal utility analysis. Suppose market basket C_1 is the same as C_2, except that C_2 has less of commodity x in it. From the nonsatiation assumption, C_1 must be preferred to C_2. One meaning of the substitutability assumption is that there is some amount of commodity y which when added to C_2 will make it equivalent or indifferent to C_1. In other words, with one rare exception, some amount of one commodity

---

[3] One combination (A) is said to *dominate* another (B) if the amount of commodity x in A is greater than or equal to the amount of commodity x in B and the amount of commodity y in A is greater than the amount in B. That is, $x_A \geqq x_B, y_A > y_B$ or $x_A > x_B, y_A \geqq y_B$. A is said to *strictly dominate* B if $x_A > x_B$ and $y_A > y_B$.

[4] The major reason for this reservation is that an athletic team on one date is not necessarily isomorphic with that same team on another date, even within, say, a given year.

can substitute for one or a group of other commodities. The exceptional case involves perfect complementarity, when commodities must be used in a fixed proportion to one another, say, one-to-one or two-to-one, etc. (right and left shoes, for example).

Indifference curves are the main analytical tool of the ordinal utility approach. On these graphs the consumption rates per unit of time of two distinct commodities, say x and y, are measured on the axes. Continuity of the curves means that along each axis it is possible to change the quantity consumed of the two commodities by infinitesimal amounts. That is, x and y are assumed continuously divisible. (Gas is an excellent example of a commodity that in fact meets this condition.)

Optimality

Finally, the optimality assumption means that consumers make decisions which they expect will maximize their well-being, always calculating their opportunity costs correctly, given the information they have available. Of course, people do not inexorably act in ways that appear rational. For example, they may amass dollars for Christmas presents by putting their savings in Christmas funds which yield no interest rather than in savings accounts which over the same period yield interest. Also, they may refuse to put extra postage on a letter. If they do not have a stamp of the exact denomination, they would rather pay the cost of a special trip to the post office than pay extra postage.[5] Yet on the whole, most people do behave in a manner tolerably consistent with this assumption of optimality.

It is always dangerous for someone to assert that someone else's behavior is irrational or rational, since the individual making the decision is the only one who knows the relative utilities involved. Rational behavior simply means the systematic and purposive selection of means to achieve given ends or goals, operating within one's capacities and limitations. An outside judgment on rationality can be correct in rare cases, but they rarely occur outside of games or contrived experiments. We can, therefore, assume that whenever a preferred or optimal combination exists, the consumer will choose it. Further, we will assume that any combination is potentially, at least, an optimal one.

Indifference Schedule[6]

Since an indifference curve is based on an indifference schedule, we will discuss the latter first. An indifference schedule is based upon the consumer's

---

[5] And, of course, the cost of this special trip is typically considerably higher than the amount saved by using the minimum postage required. These examples are taken from the always stimulating George J. Stigler, *The Theory of Price* (3d ed.; New York: Macmillan Co., 1966).

[6] The best short exposition we know of on indifference schedules and curves is Milton H. Spencer, "Demand Analysis: Indifference Curves," in *Basic Economics: A Book of Readings*, edited by Arthur D. Gayer, C. Lowell Harriss, and Milton H. Spencer (Englewood Cliffs: Prentice-Hall, 1951), Chapter 22, pp. 91–104; reprinted in *Readings in Microeconomics*, edited by David R. Kamerschen (New York: John Wiley & Sons, 1969), Ch. 5, pp. 59–72. Part of this chapter borrows from his fine analysis.

tastes and preferences and is constructed by confronting the consumer with various bundles and getting his or her reaction to them. From the completeness axiom, the consumer is assumed to be able to tell which market baskets yield equal satisfaction and which ones yield greater or less satisfaction. For simplicity, we again assume that there are only two commodities, x and y. (However, we sometimes use y to represent money income, which can be thought of as a proxy for all other commodities.)

An indifference schedule is based on the relative subjective evaluations of the consumer. More precisely, it is a tabular list showing the various combinations of x and y that the consumer would consider equivalent (i.e., equally satisfactory, of equal total utility, or of indifference). Table 5–1 contains such a schedule. For the moment column C should be ignored. Each of the 11 combinations depicted in column B is equally satisfactory to the consumer. Since they all yield the same total utility or real income, the consumer is indifferent to the choice among them. Combination 1 with $56y$ and $1x$ is just as satisfactory as combination 2 involving $46y$ and $2x$ or combination 3 involving $37y$ and $3x$ and so on.[7]

Note in column B that every time x increases, y decreases. If y did not decrease as x increased, it would be impossible for total utility to remain constant and hence for the consumer to remain indifferent.[8] Clearly, a consumer could not be indifferent between, say, $56y$ and $1x$ and $56y$ and $2x$, for in the latter case he or she would have the same amount of y and more of x.

Actually we could make a stronger statement than we did in the last paragraph. There we argued that as the consumer increased the intake of x, he or she would have to give up some amount of y to remain indifferent. In fact, the consumer is willing to give up only decreasing amounts of y as the consumption of x increases. Between combination 1 and 2, the consumer is willing to give up 10 units of y to secure an additional unit of x. This brings total consumption of x to 2 units. But later, say, between combinations 6 and 7, when the consumer has (or is consuming at the rate of) 6 units of x, he or she is willing to sacrifice only 5 units of y for another unit of x.

Column C in each case shows the exact amount of y that a consumer is willing to give up to acquire an additional unit of x in order to maintain the same level of total satisfaction, total utility, or real income. Economists define this rate at which the consumer is willing to substitute x for y (i.e., give up y to acquire x) as the marginal rate of substitution of x for y (hereafter MRS_{xy}). More formally, MRS_{xy} is defined as the amount of y (Δy) the consumer would be willing to give up to acquire an additional amount of x (Δx), so that a constant level of total satisfaction may be maintained. Since y decreases as x increases, the change in y is negative (i.e., $-\Delta y$), so the equation is:

---

[7] We assume, however, that even if the costs of all combinations were the same, the consumer in fact would choose one of these combinations. In other words, we assume that the consumer will not behave like Buridon's ass. The ass died of hunger because it could not decide between two equally desirable bundles of hay!

[8] Of course, x could be a "discommodity" or "bad" with a negative MU or x could yield zero MU. But the nonsatiation axiom rules out these possibilities.

TABLE 5–1   Indifference Schedule

A	B	C
Combinations	**Indifference Schedule**	**Marginal Rate of Substitution of x for y (MRS_{xy})**
1	56y and 1x	
		10
2	46y and 2x	
		9
3	37y and 3x	
		8
4	29y and 4x	
		7
5	22y and 5x	
		6
6	16y and 6x	
		5
7	11y and 7x	
		4
8	7y and 8x	
		3
9	4y and 9x	
		2
10	2y and 10x	
		1
11	1y and 11x	

$$MRS_{xy} = -\Delta y/\Delta x \qquad\qquad (5.1)$$

and

$$MRS_{yx} = -\Delta x/\Delta y = 1/MRS_{xy}$$

However, as with "own" price elasticity of demand, the convention in economics is to ignore the minus sign and talk about the absolute value of MRS_{xy}—i.e., $MRS_{xy} = |\Delta y/\Delta x|$. Hence, column *C* shows MRS_{xy} as a positive number. It is the (absolute) value of MRS_{xy} that normally declines as more *x* and less *y* is consumed. This is called the *law of diminishing marginal rate of substitution* (*LDMRS*). Whenever we discuss declining MRS_{xy}, we are referring to the absolute value of MRS_{xy}—i.e., $|MRS_{xy}|$.

While the *LDMU* and *LDMRS* concepts are similar in some respects, the *LDMRS* is less restrictive since it deals not with the absolute *MU* of a commodity but with the ratio of *MU*s of two different commodities. This can be shown fairly easily. By definition, total utility is constant in moving from one combination in Table 5–1 to another. The gain in utility from consuming more of *x* must be exactly offset by the loss in utility from consuming less of *y* for the consumer to remain indifferent. Therefore,

$$+\Delta x \cdot MU_x = -\Delta y \cdot MU_y \qquad\qquad (5.2)$$

Suppose one more unit of x is consumed, and the unit carries an MU of 20 utils. Further assume that MRS_{xy} is 5; that is, the consumer is willing to sacrifice 5 units of y to acquire the extra unit of x. For the consumer to remain indifferent, the MU per unit of y must be 4 utils. Only in this way is the gain in utility from consuming more x, 20 utils $\cdot$ 1 = 20 utils, just matched by the loss of utility from consuming less y, 4 utils $\cdot$ 5 = 20 utils.

By simple rearrangement, (5.2) may be rewritten as:

$$-\Delta y/\Delta x = MU_x/MU_y \qquad\qquad (5.3)$$

And from (5.1) we know $MRS_{xy} = -(\Delta y/\Delta x)$, so we can rewrite (5.3) as:

$$MRS_{xy} = -(MU_x/MU_y) \qquad\qquad (5.4)$$

INDIFFERENCE CURVES FROM INDIFFERENCE SCHEDULE

Just as a demand curve may be constructed from a demand schedule, an indifference curve may be constructed from an indifference schedule. To be specific, an indifference curve is defined as a locus of points, each of which shows a combination of commodities, measured on the two axes, among which the consumer is indifferent. Furthermore, there is an entire system of indifference curves called an *indifference map*, which provides a complete description of a consumer's preferences for x and y. There are an infinite number of these indifference curves, and every point in the xy space has an indifference curve through it. One point, R, representing combination 5 in the indifference schedule given in Table 5–1, is shown in the commodity space xy in Figure 5–1. If the entire indifference schedule were plotted, it would provide an indifference curve such as I in Figure 5–1.

For any point such as R the commodity space can be divided into four quadrants. Any point in quadrant 3 is clearly superior to R since it represents either more of x, more of y, or more of both. Just the opposite is true of quadrant 1. To estimate quadrants 2 and 4, the consumer must rank the points relative to R. If the consumer prefers any point to R, label the point "+"; if he or she

FIGURE 5–1   Indifference Curve

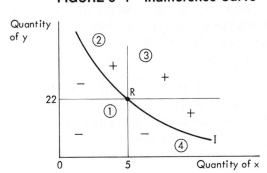

prefers *R* to the point, label the point "−." The boundary line between the +'s and the −'s represents combinations among which the consumer is indifferent. This boundary line of equal real income is called an *indifference curve*. Sometimes it is also called an *iso-utility curve,* where the word "iso" comes from Greek meaning "equal." Hence, an indifference curve shows combinations that yield equal utility.

On an indifference diagram, physical quantities of the commodities consumed per unit of time are represented on the axes. It is also important to notice that while a consumer is indifferent among any combination along a given indifference curve, he or she is most definitely not indifferent among combinations on different indifference curves. To show this, suppose a consumer's tastes and preferences are reflected in the three indifference schedules shown in Table 5–2. Along any given schedule the consumer is completely indifferent as to which combination he or she consumes. However, schedule 3 contains 5 more units of *y* than schedule 2 and 10 more units of *y* than schedule 1 for each quantity of *x*. Using the important axiom that more is preferred to less, every combination in schedule 3 is *ipso facto* superior to any combination in schedules 2 or 1. In short, schedule 3 represents a higher level of real income as compared with schedule 2, and schedule 2 represents a higher level of real income than schedule 1.

TABLE 5–2   Three Indifference Schedules

Schedule 1		Schedule 2		Schedule 3	
y	*x*	*y*	*x*	*y*	*x*
11	0	16	0	21	0
10	1	15	1	20	1
8	2	13	2	18	2
5	3	10	3	15	3
1	4	6	4	11	4

These schedules have been drawn as smooth curves in Figure 5–2 on the assumption that commodities are finely divisible. Under these conditions, the consumer will always be striving to reach the highest attainable indifference curve. These curves represent but three of the infinite number of curves that form the entire indifference map for this consumer.

It is sometimes more revealing, especially to the reader who may have studied contour maps in, say, geology, meteorology, or cartography, to explain the indifference curves in still another way. Since the consumer is assumed to be comparing the combinations of *x* and *y* on the basis of an attribute called utility, common to all commodities, a utility function may be written:

$$U = f(x,y) \qquad\qquad (5.5)$$

For instance, $U = x^2y^2$, $U = xy$, or $U = \sqrt{xy}$ are entirely satisfactory functional forms. In fact, all three of these utility functions yield the same indifference map.

FIGURE 5-2 Three Indifference Curves

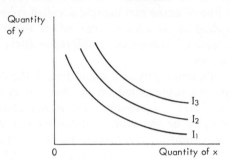

Figure 5-3 shows a representative sketch of such a utility function. This three-dimensional drawing shows that the level of utility depends on the amount of x and y consumed. The more one consumes, the higher one moves up the "hill of pleasure." The purpose of an indifference map is to serve as a contour map, bringing three-dimensional problems down to the more tractable two-dimensional level. The contour map shows the utility "elevation" at various combinations of x and y. Any one contour line (indifference curve) connects points of equal elevation (utility). By cutting a plane through any given level

FIGURE 5-3 Utility Function

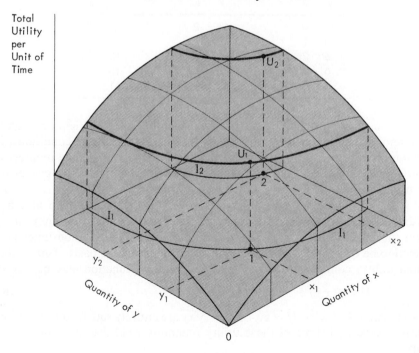

of altitude (utility), a two-dimensional drawing will emerge on the "floor," i.e., in the *xy* plane in Figure 5-3. For instance, in the case of the function $U = xy$, a rectangular hyperbola would emerge on the contour line. Of course, in ordinal utility analysis, the consumer need not know the actual elevation of the utility hill, but only whether one position is higher or lower than another.

Figure 5-4 portrays a closed indifference curve system or map. The indifference curves are labeled from 1 to 6, with the lowest total utility attained on curve 1 and the highest on curve 6. This representation is being used for demonstration purposes only. It is not likely that such a utility function could be relevant for any two goods, but it is a very useful device to visualize a multiplicity of situations.

FIGURE 5-4 A Closed Indifference Curve System or Map

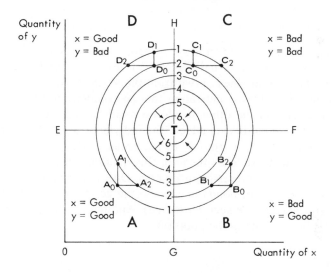

The contours, lines of equal preference (indifference curves), in this diagram are circular around point *T*. This means point *T* is the top of the utility cone or satiation point. If there were no income constraint, the consumer would go immediately to apex point *T*, for it represents the absolutely most preferred point, i.e., the highest real income possible.

The diagram is divided into four quadrants — *A, B, C,* and *D* — by lines *EF* and *GH* which intersect at the top of the cone. These lines are drawn such that they intersect the indifference curves where tangents to the curves are parallel to either the *x* or *y* axis. Along line *EF*, tangents to the curves are vertical lines; so at any point along that line, movements up or down (i.e., infinitesimal increases or decreases of commodity *y*, holding *x* constant) result in no change in total utility, since the consumer would be on the same indifference curve. Thus, $MU_y = 0$ at all points along *EF*. Line *GH* has exactly the same properties as *EF* except that commodity *x* is held constant and amounts of *y* change, and $MU_x = 0$.

Quadrant A

Quadrant A is the only quadrant in which both x and y can be classified as "goods." That is, $MU_x > 0$, $MU_y > 0$. Most price theory is concerned with this case, though some use is also made of the other quadrants.

In this quadrant movements along a straight line from the origin or perpendicular from either axis reflect increases in utility as higher and higher indifference curves are encountered. The marginal rate of substitution is negative for both commodities ($\Delta x/\Delta y < 0$, $\Delta y/\Delta x < 0$) since it is necessary to increase the quantity of one commodity to compensate for any decrease in the other commodity in order to retain the constant amount of utility reflected on a single indifference curve. For instance, decreasing the amount of y from A_1 to A_0 moves the consumer to a lower indifference curve. To get back to the original curve, I_2, the amount A_0A_2 of x must be added.

Quadrant B

In quadrant B, y is a "good" and x is a "bad." Any perpendicular line drawn from the horizontal axis cuts indifference curves of higher values, and conversely for perpendicular lines drawn from the vertical axis. The indifference curves have positive slopes, indicating that to compensate for a loss of one of x or y, a decrease in the other would be required and vice versa. Thus, if B_1B_0 of x (the discommodity) is added, the individual would have to be compensated by an increase in y from B_0 to B_2, because $MU_x < 0$ and $MU_y > 0$.

Indifference curves such as those in this quadrant have been used in the analysis of a number of interesting problems. One of the best known of these is where y is income from bonds or stocks (the good) and x is a measure of risk or price variance of the security (a bad). Another is where work is the no-good (x) and labor income is the good (y).

Quadrant C

In quadrant C both x and y are discommodities. If the amount of either one is increased, the consumer moves to a lower indifference curve, as from C_0 to C_1 or C_0 to C_2. Thus, $MU_x < 0$ and $MU_y < 0$. If the consumer has more of one, he or she can be compensated (stay on the same indifference curve) by getting less of the other. An example in this quadrant might be where x is air pollution and y is water and land pollution. However, we might call x the reduction of air pollution and y the reduction of land and water pollution, and then we would be in quadrant A.

Quadrant D

Quadrant D is the counterpart of quadrant B except that the variables x and y are reversed. Here, $MU_x > 0$ since an increase in the amount of x from D_2 to D_0 moves the consumer to a higher indifference curve, whereas

$MU_y < 0$ since increases in y (from D_0 to D_1 for instance) decrease total utility by moving the consumer to a lower indifference curve.

CHARACTERISTICS OF INDIFFERENCE CURVES

Any system of indifference curves generally contains four basic characteristics. First, indifference curves are continuous and everywhere dense, to use the mathematical terminology. The continuous feature has already been discussed. The "everywhere dense" characteristic, in simple terms, means that through each and every point in the xy plane, called the *commodity space,* an indifference curve passes. Hence, there are an infinite number of different combinations of x and y—e.g., $1x + 1y$, $1.0001x + .9998y$, $.9999x + 1.0001y$, etc. The set of indifference curves taken together form a map describing completely the individual's tastes and preferences.

The second feature of an indifference curve worth noting is that it must be negatively sloping; i.e., $\Delta y/\Delta x$ (or MRS_{xy}) < 0 for all goods.[9] This characteristic of an indifference curve might be easier to understand if we analyze why it would not make economic sense for an indifference curve for goods as opposed to no-goods to assume any other shape. That is, we should analyze why an indifference curve could not be everywhere horizontal, vertical, or upward sloping.

A horizontal indifference curve means the consumer is indifferent between two or more combinations containing the same amount of y and varying amounts of x. In Figure 5–5(a), indifference curve I_1 shows that the consumer is indifferent between $0\bar{y}$ units of good y and any quantity of good x (e.g., $0x_1$, $0x_2$, $0x_3$, $0x_4$, etc.). Since indifference curve I_1 represents the same level of total satisfaction throughout, the consumer must be deriving the total satisfaction from good y, with good x contributing nothing to total satisfaction. The

---

[9] The slope of an indifference curve at any point (M) is measured like any other slope: by constructing a tangent to that point and measuring the intercepts on the x and y axes ($0y_0/0x_0$). In this diagram, the slope, or MRS_{xy}, at M is $\Delta y/\Delta x = \frac{2}{3}$. This means that an exchange of $\frac{2}{3}$ of a unit of y for one additional unit of x will make the consumer no better or worse off.

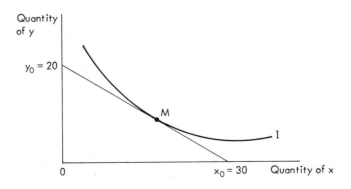

FIGURE 5-5   Three Unusual Indifference Curves

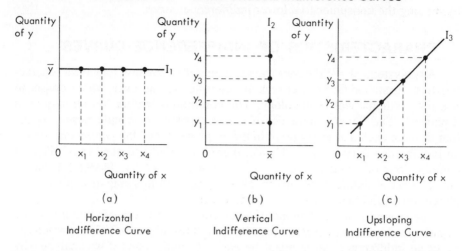

(a)	(b)	(c)
Horizontal Indifference Curve	Vertical Indifference Curve	Upsloping Indifference Curve

fact that the $MU_x = 0$ is shown by the unwillingness of the consumer to re-linquish any of y to obtain more x, the $MRS_{xy} = \Delta y/\Delta x = 0/\Delta x = 0$. But this would mean that the consumer would accept good x only if it were a free good, and therefore any application toward consumer behavior in the general case would be meaningless. At any rate, the nonsatiation assumption of always preferring more to less rules out any product having a zero (or negative) MU.

Figure 5-5(b) shows that the same situation, a saturation point for one of the commodities, would be true if an indifference curve were vertical, such as I_2. This consumer is indifferent between combinations which contain the same amount of x, $0\bar{x}$, and any amount of y (e.g., $0y_1$, $0y_2$, $0y_3$, $0y_4$, etc.). The consumer would not be willing to give up any of x to gain any of y, the $MRS_{xy} = \Delta y/\Delta x = \Delta y/0 = \infty$, and $MRS_{yx} = \Delta x/\Delta y = 0$. Though any indifference curve may be horizontal or vertical at the two extremes, showing saturation of x and y respectively, the relevant area of an indifference curve in nearly all cases would not be either horizontal or vertical.

An indifference curve for two goods could not slope upward to the right, for this would mean that each subsequent point (moving from the origin) represents more of both goods; and the consumer could hardly be indifferent between two combinations if one of them contained more of both goods. Thus, in Figure 5-5(c), along I_3 the consumer would have to be indifferent between the combination $0x_1$, $0y_1$, and the bundle $0x_2$, $0y_2$, which represents more of both x and y. But if a consumer is to be indifferent between two combinations of utility-yielding goods, then substitution must take place; that is, the quantity of one good is increased at the expense of giving up some quantity of the second. Obviously, one of the axes in Figure 5-5(c) must be measuring a dis-commodity or bad which has a negative MU.

Basically horizontal, vertical, and upward-sloping indifference curves are ruled out by the same crucial assumption: as long as one is dealing with two commodities—where a commodity is defined as having an MU greater than zero—a downsloping indifference curve is mandatory.

Given that an indifference curve is negatively sloped at all points, there is still the possibility that it may be linear, concave from the origin, or convex from the origin. The third characteristic of the "normal" indifference curve is that it is, in fact, convex (i.e., the curve is so bent that it is relatively steep at the top and relatively flat at the bottom). The three possibilities are sketched in Figure 5–6.

FIGURE 5–6   Linear, Concave, and Convex Indifference Curves

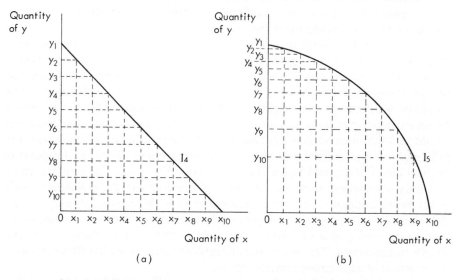

(a)

Linear Indifference Curve --
Constant Marginal Rate of Substitution

(b)

Concave Indifference Curve --
Increasing Marginal Rate of Substitution

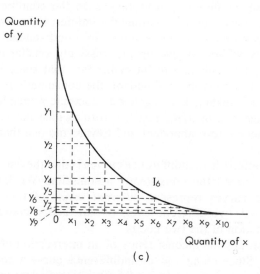

(c)

Convex Indifference Curve --
Diminishing Marginal Rate of Substitution

A useful way to show the logic of convexity is to employ again the process of elimination. Take the linear indifference curve I_4 in Figure 5–6(a). In this diagram, as well as in diagrams (b) and (c), equal units are marked off on the x axis. The resulting changes in y (Δy) associated with the changes in x (Δx) measure the slope of the indifference curve. It is obvious for I_4 that the Δy's are constant, so that the slope ($\Delta y/\Delta x$) must be constant. Since the slope of an indifference curve is the MRS_{xy}, the latter must also be constant. Only for commodities that are perfect substitutes (e.g., two nickels = one dime) would this be true. And as will be discussed presently, perfect substitutability would lead to either monomania or a random vacillation between the two goods by the consumer (depending upon the price relations).

Figure 5–6(b), showing a concave indifference curve I_5, is also very unlikely. In this case Δy is getting larger and larger as more and more x is consumed. This means that the slope or MRS_{xy} is increasing. The economic interpretation of this is that the more x one has relative to y, the more y one would be willing to give up to get even more x. Such distaste for variety would be an extremely unlikely situation. With an increasing MRS_{xy}, the consumer would practice monomania, specializing in the consumption of one good. Put differently, if the indifference curve were everywhere concave, the point of optimal quantities would be on one of the axes. Even if the indifference curve was only somewhere concave (and somewhere convex), the consumer would never be in optimality on any concave part of it. Moreover, although an indifference curve can have a somewhat different shape in different regions of the commodity space, it would be unusual for the curvature to change from convexity to concavity. The economically relevant part of an indifference curve for goods is always in the convex region.

Figure 5–6(c), depicting I_6, is the important diagram. It is apparent that Δy is declining as x changes by equal increments, i.e., the slope is decreasing. The convexity of an indifference curve hinges on the condition of *DMRS*. This means that as a consumer moves along the indifference curve from left to right, he or she is consuming greater amounts of x and smaller amounts of y and is therefore only willing to give up progressively smaller increments of y to gain still more of x. This is a result of the fact that since y is becoming more scarce as x is becoming more abundant, the consumer's personal valuation of y relative to x is higher. It is a general economic principle that, *ceteris paribus*, the exchange rate or *MRS* tends to turn against the commodity (or factor) that is becoming more abundant and toward the one that is becoming more scarce.

The fourth characteristic of indifference curves is that they do not intersect. Intersection would violate the consistency assumption. We know that two distinct indifference curves represent different levels of total satisfaction. But if they intersected, two different levels of satisfaction could be achieved by the same combination of the two goods.

Figure 5–7 illustrates the inconsistency of an intersection of two separate indifference curves. Since along a given indifference curve a consumer is indifferent, on I_1 combination C_1 involving $0x_1$, $0y_1$ is equivalent to C_2 involving

$0x_2$, $0y_2$. Similarly, along I_2 the total satisfaction yielded by combination C_1 involving $0x_1$, $0y_1$ must equal the total expected utility yielded by C_3 involving $0x_3$, $0y_2$. The intersection implies that combination C_2 is equivalent to C_3 or that $0y_2$, $0x_2 = 0y_2$, $0x_3$. Cancelling out the common $0y_2$'s leads to the conclusion that the satisfaction from consuming $0x_2$ is the same as from consuming the greater amount $0x_3$. Given the nonsatiation assumption, it is impossible for the consumer to obtain equal utility from different quantities of the same commodity.

To summarize, we have found "normal" indifference curves to be: (1) continuous and everywhere dense, (2) downward sloping, (3) convex from the origin, and (4) nonintersecting.

FIGURE 5–7   Intersecting Indifference Curves

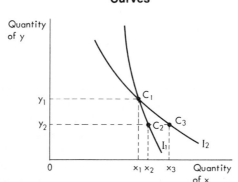

COMPLEMENTS AND SUBSTITUTES

The curvature of an indifference curve may be used to determine whether the commodities are complements or substitutes in the given range. In general, the less convex the indifference curve, the greater the substitutability between the two commodities. In the extreme case of perfect substitutes, shown in Figure 5–8(a), the indifference curve is a downward-sloping straight line. Neglecting the exceptions brought about by vending machines, slot machines, parking meters, etc., nickels are a perfect substitute for dimes at the constant ratio of two to one. Under these conditions, the consumer is completely indifferent between two nickels or one dime.

At the other extreme are commodities known as perfect complements, which have a rigid relationship to one another. In Figure 5–8(b), left and right shoes have a relationship at a ratio of one-to-one. Moving either upward or rightward along I_1 from point T yields no additional utility to the consumer even though greater amounts of y or x are consumed with fixed amounts of the other commodity. For most purposes, the MU of a second right shoe to a consumer who has only one left shoe is zero. Of course, the consumer does move on to a higher level of real income, illustrated by I_2, if he or she has two left and two right shoes.

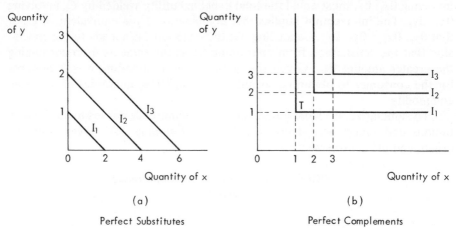

FIGURE 5–8   Perfect Substitutes and Complements

(a)

Perfect Substitutes

(b)

Perfect Complements

BUDGET LINE

Any consumer analysis must incorporate both the available objective information, such as the money income constraint and commodity prices, and the subjective information given by the indifference map. A *budget line* (also called a consumption-possibility line, a line of attainable combinations, or a price-income line) contains the objective information. A budget line is defined as a locus of points, each of which shows a combination of goods that can be purchased if the entire money income is spent.[10] The *budget space* is the area bounded by the budget line and the two axes.

The consumer's possibilities are therefore limited by (1) the price of x (P_x), (2) the price of y (P_y), and (3) income (I). For example, assume that $P_x = \$2$, $P_y = \$1$ (so $P_x = 2P_y$), and $I = \$80$, as in Figure 5–9(a). The shaded area in the diagram represents the consumer's entire budget space, represented by the equation $\$80 \geq \$2x + \$1y$. If the consumer were to spend all of the income on y, he or she could buy $Q_y = I/P_y$ or in this case 80 units of y since $80 = \$80/\$1$. If the consumer spends all of the income on x, he or she could purchase $Q_x = I/P_x$ or in this case 40 units of x since $40 = \$80/\$2$. The straight line (budget line *BL*) connecting these two points represents all the possible combinations of x and y which the consumer is able to purchase given the above prices and an income of $80. For example, one possible combination is $20x + 40y = 20 \cdot \$2 + 40 \cdot \$1 = \$40 + \$40 = \$80$. Of course, the consumer could buy any combination inside the shaded budget space (e.g., $20x + 10y$), but then not all of the income would be spent. In other words, the budget line is a boundary

---

[10] The definition is sometimes worded to include the fact that the typical consumer is a pure competitor by specifying that prices, in addition to income, are also constant. This means the budget line would have to be linear—by definition, the slope P_x/P_y is constant for a pure competitor. While the formulation in the text is more general, allowing for imperfect competition and, say, a concave budget line, the budget line, for simplicity, will generally be drawn as linear.

**FIGURE 5-9   The Budget Line, the Budget Space,
and Shifts in the Budget Line**

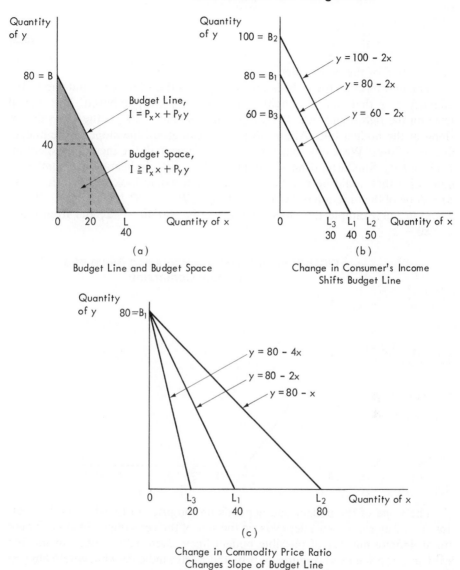

(a)
Budget Line and Budget Space

(b)
Change in Consumer's Income
Shifts Budget Line

(c)
Change in Commodity Price Ratio
Changes Slope of Budget Line

line separating two regions. The shaded region to the left represents the area of possible or attainable combinations; the region to the right represents the area of impossible or unattainable combinations.

Since budget line *BL* is a straight line, there must be a linear equation of the form $y = a - bx$ (where a is the y intercept and b the slope) that fits it. This equation can be derived from the budget constraint $\bar{I} = P_x \cdot x + P_y \cdot y$ (where $\bar{I}$

is a parameter fixed in value) by solving for y: $\bar{I} - P_x \cdot x = P_y \cdot y$, $\dfrac{\bar{I} - P_x x}{P_y} = y$,

or:

$$y = \frac{\bar{I}}{P_y} - \frac{P_x}{P_y} x \qquad\qquad (5.6)$$

the equation of the budget line.

The first term on the right-hand side, $\bar{I}/P_y$, is the y intercept and shows the quantity of y that can be bought if no units of x are purchased. The second term on the right-hand side, $(-P_x/P_y)x$, means that $-P_x/P_y$ is the "b" value or slope of the budget line. Alternatively, we can attain the slope of the budget line as follows: We know that if no x is consumed, all the income is spent on y, $Q_y = \bar{I}/P_y$. Similarly, if no y is bought, $Q_x = \bar{I}/P_x$, indicating the number of units of x that could be purchased. The graph would look like Figure 5–10. The slope of the function is $\Delta y/\Delta x = -(I/P_y)/(I/P_x) = -(P_x/I) \cdot (I/P_y) = -P_x/P_y$. Thus, in our example the slope of the line is $-80/40 = -2$; and from (5.6), $y = 80 - 2x$.

FIGURE 5–10   The Intercepts and Slope of a
Budget Constraint

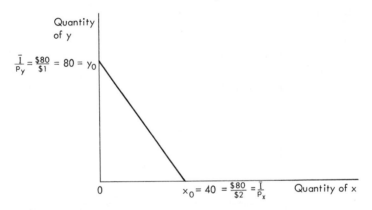

The slope of the budget line depends on the price ratio, whereas the position (i.e., y or x intercept) depends on the size of the consumer's income. There are an infinite number of possible budget lines, each with a different income level and/or price ratio. Figures 5–9(b) and 5–9(c) indicate what would happen if either the consumer's income or the price ratio were changed.

Figure 5–9(b) shows shifts in money income, I, with prices unchanged. In these cases, a parallel shift of the budget line takes place. An increase in income shifts the budget line rightward and outward; a decrease in income shifts it leftward and inward (toward the origin). Starting with B_1L_1 (where $80y$ and $40x$ were the extreme possibilities), Figure 5–9(b) assumes that: (1) income increases by 25 percent for B_2L_2 so that $100y$ and $50x$ are the extreme possibilities, and (2) income decreases by 25 percent for B_3L_3 so that $60y$ and $30x$ are the extreme possibilities. In other words, the equation for

B_2L_2 is $y = 100 - 2x$ and for B_3L_3 it is $y = 60 - 2x$. Notice that the change in income can be expressed in units of x or units of y, viz., $20y = 10x$.

Figure 5–9(c) demonstrates what happens to the budget line when P_x changes, assuming that P_y and income remain constant. Obviously, while the y intercept ($\bar{I}/P_y$) does not change, the slope of the budget line ($-P_x/P_y$) does change. When P_x increases, the slope of the budget line becomes steeper. In Figure 5–9(c), starting from B_1L_1 ($P_x = \$2$), the price of x is assumed to be cut in half along B_1L_2 ($P_x = \$1$), and P_x is assumed to have doubled ($P_x = \$4$) along B_1L_3. This is shown by rotating the budget line around the y intercept, to the right for a price decrease and to the left for a price increase. If $80y$ and $40x$ were the possible extreme quantities initially, the counterclockwise movement resulting from the decrease in P_x means that now $80y$ and $80x$ are possible; the clockwise movement resulting from the increase in P_x means that now $80y$ and $20x$ are possible. In other words, equation (5.6) for B_1L_2 is $y = 80 - x$ and for B_1L_3 is $y = 80 - 4x$.

UTILITY MAXIMIZATION WITH INDIFFERENCE CURVES

We can now put together the *subjective* factors, showing what the consumer *would like to do,* represented by the indifference curve, and the *objective* income and price factors, showing what that consumer *is able to do,* given the income and market prices as represented by the budget line. This will enable us to determine what quantities of x and y the consumer will decide to buy. The consumer maximizes utility by attaining the highest indifference curve possible given the budget constraint. This is shown in Figure 5–11, where three of the consumer's infinite number of possible indifference curves, I_1, I_2,

FIGURE 5–11   **Consumer Optimum, Indifference Curve Approach**

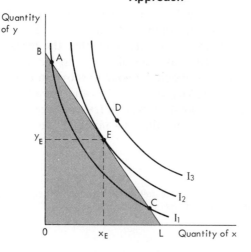

and I_3, are drawn, together with a budget line. There is only one budget line since the relevant prices and income have already been determined.

The budget constraint line, *BL*, bounds the shaded budget space of attainable combinations. The consumer can be anywhere in this shaded area. But if the budget line *intersects* an indifference curve, it is possible for the consumer to reach a higher indifference curve with that same budget line. That is, the consumer will never stop anywhere within the shaded area of attainable combinations but will endeavor to be on the boundary line, *BL*. For instance, although the consumer has the opportunity to be at combination *A* or *C*, both being on I_1 in Figure 5–11, he or she will not choose them because the purchasing power permits the attainment of higher indifference curves, namely all those between I_1 and I_2. The highest indifference curve which the consumer can reach is where the budget line is tangent to the indifference curve. In Figure 5–11 this occurs at combination *E*, representing y_E units of *y* and x_E units of *x*. This combination, therefore, represents the maximum satisfaction which the consumer can achieve, given this consumer's tastes and preferences, income, and the prices of the two goods. Of course, the consumer would like to be on a still higher indifference curve, such as at combination *D* on I_3, representing more of both *x* and *y*. However, combination *D* (or I_3 in general) is impossible because income is too low and/or the prices of the commodities are too high.

At the tangency condition for optimality, the slope of the indifference curve, the MRS_{xy}, equals the slope of the budget line, P_x/P_y. That is, the first-order condition for consumer optimality by the indifference curve approach is:[11]

$$MRS_{xy} = P_x/P_y \tag{5.7}$$

In verbal terms, this condition states that the rate at which the individual is *willing* to substitute *x* for *y* (the MRS_{xy}) must equal the rate at which he or she *can* substitute *x* for *y* (P_x/P_y).

We can see this in another way with the aid of Figure 5–12. Suppose the consumer happened to be at point *A*, where the commodity bundle is composed of y_a amount of *y* and x_a amount of *x*. This person (according to the indifference curve) would be willing to trade $y_a - y_b$ (Δy_1) amount of *y* for only $x_a - x_c$ (Δx_1) of *x*; but the prices are such that the market would allow the exchange of the much larger amount of *x*, $x_a - x_b$ (Δx_2), for the same amount of *y*. Surely this individual would be wise to move to point *B*. At point *A* we can see that MRS_{xy} ($\Delta y_1/\Delta x_1$) > the price ratio ($\Delta y_1/\Delta x_2$). Also, since *B* exhibits the same symptoms as *A*, except in lesser degree, we would expect the consumer to move again, this time to point *E*, the tangency point where $MRS_{xy} = P_x/P_y$.

---

[11] Throughout this section we will follow the economists' common practice of neglecting signs. For example, the formal condition of (5.7) is $|MRS_{xy}| = |P_x/P_y|$.

FIGURE 5-12   Marginal Rates of Substitution and Price Ratios

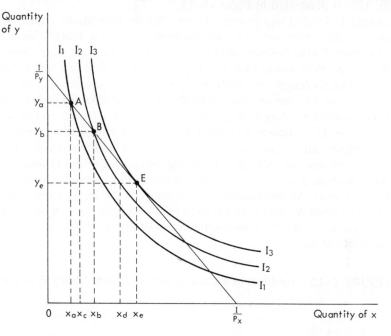

RELATION BETWEEN CARDINAL AND ORDINAL UTILITY APPROACHES

It is possible to relate the ordinal utility optimum condition (5.7) to the cardinal utility optimum condition (4.1) that $MU_x/P_x = MU_y/P_y$. First, we know from (5.4) that $MRS_{xy} = MU_x/MU_y$. Therefore, equation (5.7) can be rewritten:

$$MU_x/MU_y = P_x/P_y \tag{5.8}$$

or

$$MU_x/P_x = MU_y/P_y \tag{5.9}$$

Thus, both approaches reach the same conclusion: consumer optimality requires that the MU derived from the last dollar spent on each commodity be equal (or the last penny spent or whatever is the smallest currency unit defined for the society in question).

We can also relate graphically the cardinal utility approach to the indifference curve analysis.[12] Using a four-quadrant model, we can derive an

---

[12] See David R. Kamerschen, "Cardinal and Ordinal Utility: A Pedagogical Note," *Artha Vijnana*, Vol. 12, No. 3 (September, 1970), pp. 436–438, for a discussion of the limitations of this approach. In particular, it should be noted this pedagogical technique assumes that *x* and *y* are independent goods.

indifference curve from the utility curves for *x* and *y* (if independence is assumed). This is illustrated in Figure 5–13.

The model is divided into four quadrants. The analysis starts in quadrant 1 and moves counterclockwise. TU_y in quadrant 1 exhibits *DMU*. Similarly, TU_x in quadrant 3 also follows *DMU*. If these two functions were drawn in the usual manner, they would look like Figure 5–14. Such a function exhibits *DMU* throughout its length. In quadrant 2 a sum-of-utilities line, U_1, specifies a particular level of *TU*, real income, or total satisfaction from the consumption of the two commodities. Any sum-of-utilities line that is leftward and outward from U_1, such as U_2, specifies a higher level of utility and would generate an indifference curve, call it I_2, in quadrant 4, that would be rightward and outward from the I_1 curve derived from U_1. To fix the intercepts of the *U* lines, start with a point such as *T* on TU_y and zero consumption of good *x* so that the utility from *x* is zero. At that condition total utility is the utility from *y* alone. This establishes point *R*, and point *S* is fixed by consumption of *x* in the amount indicated by point *e* and zero consumption (and utility) of *y*. The utility of $0R$ equals the utility of $0S$.

FIGURE 5–13   Indifference Curves Derived from Utility Functions

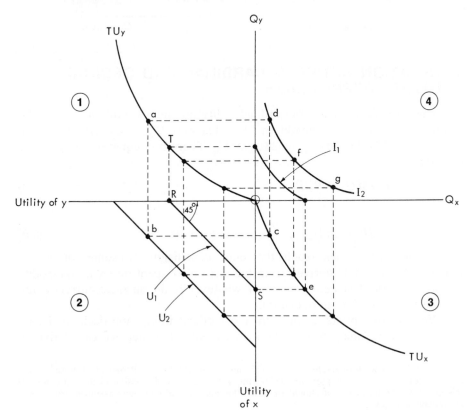

FIGURE 5–14   Total Utility Schedule

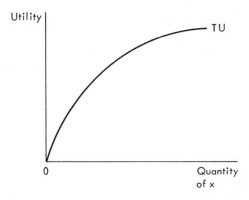

One point, *d*, is located on the indifference curve I_2 by starting from point *a* and moving counterclockwise to point *b*, then *c*, and finally *d*. Every other point on I_2 can be derived in a similar fashion, as shown for points *f* and *g*. In this manner the intimate connection between the indifference curve and cardinal utility approaches can be demonstrated.

OTHER SIMILARITIES

Recall that in Chapter 4 the three conditions required for consumer optimality with the cardinal utility approach were:

$$\frac{MU_x}{P_x} = \frac{MU_y}{P_y} = \frac{MU_z}{P_z} = \cdots = \lambda \ (MU \text{ per dollar}) \qquad \textbf{(4.1)}$$

$$I = Q_x \cdot P_x + Q_y \cdot P_y + Q_z \cdot P_z \qquad \textbf{(4.2)}$$

LDMU holds in the case of independent commodities   **(4.3)**

We showed above that (5.7), $MRS_{xy} = P_x/P_y$, is exactly equivalent to (4.1). The budget constraints of the two approaches are identical, and (4.3) is replaced for the ordinal utility approach by (5.11); i.e., *LDMRS* holds in the case of independent commodities. Thus, the sufficient conditions for consumer optimality under ordinal utility are:

$$MRS_{xy} = P_x/P_y \qquad \textbf{(5.7)}$$

$$I = Q_x \cdot P_x + Q_y \cdot P_y + Q_z \cdot P_z \qquad \textbf{(5.10)}$$

LDMRS holds in the case of independent commodities   **(5.11)**

QUESTIONS

1. Compare the likelihood of satiation occurring for an individual with respect to a single good and with respect to all goods.

2. (a) For an individual, conceive of a particular economic behavior which you would call irrational.

   (b) Argue that it is not possible for anyone to prove that the behavior you described in (a) is, in fact, not rational.

3. Interpret the MRS_{xy} in the two following figures. The difference between the figures is that in (a) the total utility of I_1 is greater than that of I_2, and in (b) the utility of I_2 is greater than that of I_1.

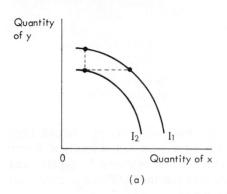
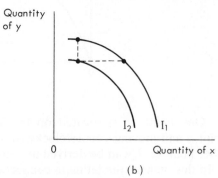

4. On the normally shaped indifference curve, where is the marginal utility of x, and of y, equal to zero? What can be said of the marginal rates of substitution at those points?

5. (a) Prove that indifference curves cannot intersect. (b) Prove that indifference curves involving two goods cannot be positively sloped. (c) Show that it is highly unlikely that indifference curves involving two goods would be concave (to the origin).

6. An individual has an income of $200 per week. The price of y is $2 and the price of x is $8.

   (a) What is the vertical intercept of the budget line?

   (b) What is the horizontal intercept of the budget line?

   (c) What is the equation (using numbers) of the budget line?

   (d) Plot the budget line for (c).

   (e) Plot a new budget line, assuming the individual's income increases to $300.

   (f) Plot a new budget line, assuming the individual's income = $200, P_y = $2, and P_x = $4.

7. If a person were consuming two commodities at rates such that the MRS_{xy} was different from the price ratios of the two goods, explain why the person would benefit from choosing a different combination of x and y.

6 Further Development and Application of Indifference Curve Analysis

This chapter concludes the theory of consumer behavior using the indifference curve analysis begun in Chapter 5. It also examines how the indifference curve technique may be applied to various economic problems and introduces the revealed preference approach to consumer behavior.

SUMMARY OF OPTIMALITY WITH NORMAL INDIFFERENCE CURVES [1]

In the last chapter we found that a consumer's preferences can be represented by a set of indifference curves or an indifference map. These indifference curves are convex to the origin, negatively sloped, and nonintersecting. The consumer's utility is maximized by consuming the combination of goods such that the budget line or iso-expenditure line is tangent to one of the indifference curves. Two implications of this are that: (1) the choice of a particular utility index does not affect the optimum position, provided the utility indices are monotonically increasing transformations of each other; and (2) a proportionate change in money prices and money income does not alter the choice of consumption goods.

CONSUMPTION DETERMINATION WITH NONNORMAL INDIFFERENCE CURVES

There are a number of possible unusual cases where optimality condition (5.7), $MRS_{xy} = P_x/P_y$, developed in the last chapter, would have to be modified. Condition (5.7) provides a maximal result if a tangency solution is possible. If a so-called "corner solution" is called for because the budget line touches the highest indifference curve at one of the axes, the equality in (5.7) becomes an inequality. If, e.g., monomania in either y or x is practiced, the optimal condition becomes:

---

[1] An excellent review of all types of demand theory is contained in Shih-yen Wu and Jack A. Pontney, *An Introduction to Modern Demand Theory* (New York: Random House, 1967); and in John R. Hicks, *A Revision of Demand Theory* (Oxford: Clarendon Press, 1959). For an excellent discussion of all of microeconomics including demand theory, but which requires advanced mathematics, see Trout Rader, *Theory of Microeconomics* (New York: Academic Press, 1972).

(a) $MRS_{xy} < P_x/P_y$ or $MU_x/MU_y < P_x/P_y$ for $x = 0$ (6.1)

(b) $MRS_{xy} > P_x/P_y$ or $MU_x/MU_y > P_x/P_y$ for $y = 0$

Condition (6.1) merely restates general condition (4.4) that $MU_I/P_I \geqq MU_E/P_E$, where the I subscript stands for included and E for excluded commodities. Figure 6-1 provides a sample of the various nonnormal cases in which condition (6.1) is helpful.

Corner solutions hold for the special cases depicted in Figure 6-1. The linear indifference curve in Figure 6-1(a) represents the case of perfect substitutes, such as red shirts and green shirts for a color-blind consumer. There are two possibilities with a linear budget line:

1. If the slope of the budget line (P_x/P_y) equals the slope of the linear indifference curve (constant MRS_{xy}), the two functions will be coincidental and the optimal quantities will be indeterminate in that any combination

FIGURE 6-1 Unusual Indifference Curves

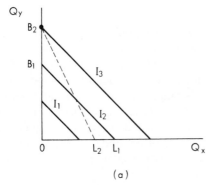

(a)

Perfect Substitutes --
Monomania or Indeterminancy

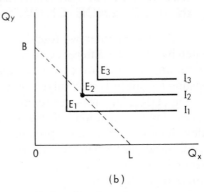

(b)

Perfect Complements --
Consume both Goods in Fixed Ratio

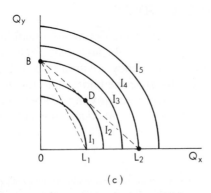

(c)

Concavity -- Increasing MRS --
Monomania

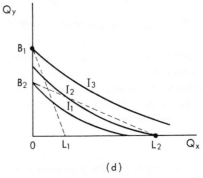

(d)

Steepness Paradox --
Monomania

of x and y will meet optimality condition (5.7) that $MRS_{xy} = P_x/P_y$. Thus, if B_1L_1 is the budget line, it is everywhere coincidental with I_2.

2. If the slope of the budget line, say, B_2L_2, nowhere equals the slope of the indifference curve, monomania will result. The consumer will specialize in the consumption of either x or y, and the slopes will determine which the consumer will choose since the highest indifference curve attainable will always be on one of the axes. In the case depicted in Figure 6–1(a), the consumer will purchase only y, reaching I_3 at point B_2. In short, the difficulty with Figure 6–1(a) in terms of the optimality conditions is that convexity condition (5.11) is not met, and therefore with a linear budget line tangency condition (5.7) also cannot be met.

Figure 6–1(b) depicts the case of perfect complements, in which the commodities are always used in the ratio of $0y/0x$ no matter what the relative prices are. The optimum will occur at the corner of the indifference curve, such as $E_1, E_2,$ or E_3. Given budget line BL, equilibrium will be at E_2.

Figures 6–1(c) and 6–1(d) represent situations where the first-order condition given in (5.7) is not necessary for a maximum. In Figure 6–1(c) the indifference curves are concave, so that (5.11) is also not met. In Figure 6–1(d) the indifference curves are convex, but are everywhere steeper than the budget line. In this case, (5.11) is met. Since in Figure 6–1(c) condition (5.7) is met and (5.11) is not met, the tangency at point D involves minimizing rather than maximizing utility. The consumer can increase utility by moving toward one of the axes, in this case to point L_2 representing monomania in x if the price ratio is BL_2, or to point B if prices are as reflected in BL_1.

In Figure 6–1(d), the highest attainable indifference curve, given budget line B_1L_1, is I_3, at which point only y is consumed. At point B_1, condition (6.1b) is met, but not (6.1a). If the budget line is B_2L_2, just the opposite situation holds, and only x will be consumed at point L_2.

Only in a two-good model, such as those emphasized in most textbooks, are corner solutions considered nonnormal and interior solutions considered normal. In truth, in a many-good world such as we live in, corner solutions are highly realistic inasmuch as an individual never buys all of the goods available.

PRICE-CONSUMPTION CURVE AND DERIVATION OF DEMAND CURVE FROM AN INDIFFERENCE CURVE

Indifference curve analysis concentrates on two objective factors, the price ratio and nominal or money income, and one subjective factor, tastes and preferences. Consumer choices will change if any of these three factors change. The consumer's subjective preferences are assumed independent of both the income level and commodity prices. The taste and preference factor involves shifting the entire indifference curve map and will not be examined in detail here. However, we will take up changes in the price variable and then changes in the nominal income variable in order, assuming all other things remain constant. We will show that changes in prices, given money income, generate points along a given demand curve. Also, shifts in money income, given prices, lead to shifts in the entire demand curve.

Figure 6–2(a) shows the effects of price changes on the quantities consumed of x and y, assuming the consumer's money income is held constant at some level, say, $\bar{I}_1$. The budget line equation facing the consumer is:

FIGURE 6–2   Derivation of Consumer Demand Curve from Price- Consumption Curve

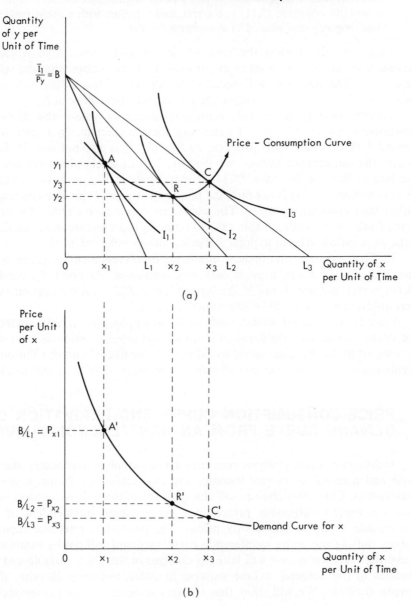

$$y = \frac{\bar{I}_1}{P_y} - \frac{P_x}{P_y} x = \frac{\bar{I}_1}{P_y} - \frac{\Delta y}{\Delta x} x \tag{6.2}$$

The price of x is allowed to fall from the level indicated by the slope of original budget line BL_1 to the price indicated by the slope of budget line BL_2 and finally to the price indicated by the slope of budget line BL_3. In general, with money income held constant, a change in the price of x must change the slope of the budget line, making it flatter for price decreases and steeper for price increases.

Faced with the original budgetary constraint imposed by a fixed money income $\bar{I}_1$ and the set of relative prices given by the slope of budget line BL_1, the consumer reaches the optimum at point A on indifference curve I_1, consuming $0x_1$ units of commodity x. When the price of x falls to that represented by budget line BL_2, the new optimum is at point R on indifference curve I_2, representing $0x^2$ units of x. Finally, when the price of x falls to the level indicated by budget line BL_3, the new optimum point is C on indifference curve I_3 with $0x_3$ units of x being taken.

While Figure 6–2(a) assumes only three separate prices of x, there are an infinite number of price possibilities. Line ARC, joining the tangency points at various prices of x, is called a *price-consumption curve* (PCC). A PCC, such as depicted in Figure 6–2(a), shows how consumption of x varies as its price varies, given the consumer's money income, tastes and preferences, and the price of the other commodities.

Since the PCC shows how the rate of consumption of x will vary as P_x changes, it obviously must bear a close relationship to the demand curve for x. The PCC contains the information necessary to construct the demand for x as a function of price—namely, what happens to Q_x as P_x changes. Figure 6–2(b) demonstrates such a derivation. In both diagrams Q_x is measured on the horizontal axis, whereas in the PCC diagram the quantity of y is on the vertical axis and in the demand diagram P_x is on the vertical axis. Tangency points A, R, and C, forming the price-consumption curve in Figure 6–2(a), give the quantities needed in Figure 6–2(b) to calibrate the demand curve for x. Thus, from points A, R, and C in Figure 6–2(a) one can derive points A', R', and C' respectively in Figure 6–2(b). The price per unit of x is any given amount of wealth or income ($\bar{I}$) divided by the quantity of x for which that amount of money can exchange, namely, $\bar{I}_1/L_i = P_{xi}$. Thus, each of the price-consumption points can be plotted and then connected to form a consumer demand curve, and as expected the law of demand holds in Figure 6–2(b). That is, given money income, money prices of other goods, tastes and preferences, and all the other determinants, quantity demanded tends to vary inversely with price.

A different price-consumption curve could be used to derive other consumer demand curves if any of these determinants were held constant at other levels. For instance, if income were held constant at a level higher than $\bar{I}_1$, a different, higher demand curve would result. Or if consumers' preferences were to change such that the indifference curves all became everywhere steeper, again the demand curve would shift to the right.

DERIVING PRICE ELASTICITY OF DEMAND (η) FROM THE PRICE-CONSUMPTION CURVE (*PCC*)

If we let y represent the numbers of dollars spent on all other goods in the *PCC* diagram, so B is the total income in dollars, we can use the slope of the *PCC* to determine whether $\eta \gtreqless 1$, according to the total-expenditures test covered in Chapter 3. For example, in Figure 6–3(a) at point A, $0x_1$ is the quantity of x chosen and $0y_1$ is the amount of income *not* spent on x. The number of dollars spent on x is $0B - 0y_1$. You will recall that the total-expenditures test for elasticity is:

$$\begin{aligned} \text{if } (\Delta TE_x/\Delta P_x) &> 0, \eta < 1 \\ &< 0, \eta > 1 \\ &= 0, \eta = 1 \end{aligned}$$

Therefore, if the slope of *PPC* > 0, $\eta < 1$; if the slope of *PCC* < 0, $\eta > 1$; and if the slope of *PPC* $= 0$, $\eta = 1$. (η is in terms of absolute value.)

The price-consumption curves in Figures 6–3(b), (c), and (d) reflect demand curves with elasticities equal to, less than, and greater than one respectively over their entire ranges; whereas the demand curve in Figure 6–3(e) changes from elastic to inelastic over different price ranges. Figures 6–3(b), (c), and (d) assume the starting point is BL_1, $0x_1$, and $0y_1$; and P_x falls to P_{x2} (associated with BL_2, $0x_2$, $0y_2$). Thus, the budget lines rotate rightward from point B. In these diagrams, $0B$ represents the consumer's total money income and $0y_1$ represents the quantity of y purchased initially. But since y is money income, total spending on y is also $0y_1$ since $P_y \cdot Q_y = 1 \cdot 0y_1 = 0y_1$. Alternatively, we can think of $0y_1$ as the amount of total money income $0B$ which is not spent on x. Since the consumer's total money income is fixed, total expenditures on x and y combined are a constant, $\overline{TE}_{xy}$, where the bar denotes a constant value. Therefore, by definition Y_1B is the amount spent on x since $TE_x = \overline{TE}_{xy} - TE_y$. This is illustrated in Figure 6–3(a).

In Figure 6–3(b), $0y_1 = 0y_2$, so the total expenditure on y and therefore also on x remains constant as P_x falls. The total-spending test, which states that whenever $\Delta TE_x/\Delta P_x = 0$, then $\eta = 1$, proves that a horizontal *PCC* must be associated with unitary elasticity.

In Figure 6–3(c), as P_x falls to P_{x2}, $0y_1$ rises to $0y_2$ and the amount spent on x, By_1, falls to By_2. Since the amount spent on x falls (by y_1y_2) as P_x falls, $\eta < 1$. An upward-sloping *PCC* means an inelastic demand curve. Figure 6–3(d) shows the opposite situation: as P_x falls to P_{x2}, $0y_1$ falls to $0y_2$ and the total expenditures on x rise from By_1 to By_2 (by y_1y_2). A downward-sloping *PCC* signifies an elastic demand curve.

In Figure 6–3(e), as P_x falls to P_{x2}, $0y_1$ falls to $0y_2$ and the amount spent on x rises from By_1 to By_2, signifying an elastic demand. But as the price falls further to P_{x3}, $0y_2$ rises to $0y_3$ and total expenditure on x, By_2, falls to By_3, denoting an inelastic demand. At point T, elasticity of demand is precisely unitary. Thus, the demand curve is elastic in the range S-T and inelastic from T onward. Actually, a curve with changing elasticity in different price ranges is much more typical than a curve of constant elasticity throughout the entire range.

FIGURE 6-3   Price-Consumption Curves and Elasticity of Demand

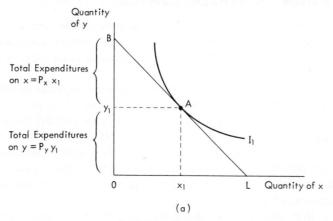

(a)

Total Expenditures on x and y

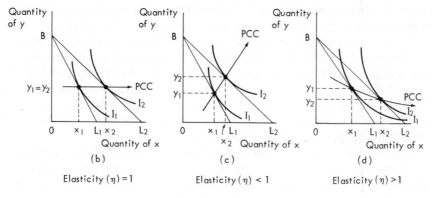

(b)

Elasticity (η) = 1

(c)

Elasticity (η) < 1

(d)

Elasticity (η) > 1

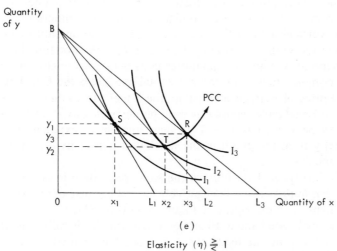

(e)

Elasticity (η) $\gtreqless$ 1

INCOME-CONSUMPTION CURVE AND
THE DERIVATION OF ENGEL CURVES

In the last section, one of the three variables in the usual indifference curve analysis, price, was changed, with the other two variables, nominal income and tastes, assumed to be constant. From the resulting *PCC*, a demand curve was generated.

In this section, all prices and tastes are assumed constant in order to analyze the impact of changes in income on consumption. The resulting points of tangency between the fixed indifference curves and the new parallel budget lines form what is called an *income-consumption curve* (*ICC*). From an *ICC* we can derive an *Engel curve*, which shows, *ceteris paribus*, how a commodity's consumption rate differs at various income levels. On the graphs shown here, y stands for all goods other than x, so total income equals the consumption of x plus the consumption of all other goods.

Since the changes in income are assumed to take place with constant prices, the budget lines shift in a parallel fashion by the proportionate amount that income changes. If income doubles, then the new budget line intersects the two axes at twice the previous quantities. For example, if $I_1 = \$100$, $P_{x1} = \$1$, and $P_{y1} = \$2$, the budget line intersects at $Q_{x1} = 100$ units of x, $Q_{y1} = 50$ units of y; whereas if $I_2 = \$200$, $P_{x2} = \$1$, and $P_{y2} = \$2$, the new budget line intersects the axes at $Q_{x2} = 200$ units of x, $Q_{y2} = 100$ units of y. An *ICC* is found by connecting all the optimum quantities at alternative income levels. As opposed to a *PCC*, however, the points on an *ICC* correspond to points on different demand curves. One of the "givens" in deriving a demand curve is a consumer's income level; if this changes, the whole demand curve shifts.

Figure 6–4(a) (page 130) shows the derivation of an Engel curve from an *ICC*. Forty-five degree lines in the northeast and southwest graphs simply allow the same variable to be measured on both axes. On the northwest graph, the amount of consumption of x is determined in the usual manner, where the indifference curve is tangent to the budget line, and the amount of x is transferred to the vertical axis in the southeast graph. The amount of income is projected from the vertical axis at I_1, I_2, I_3, and I_4 to the horizontal axis in the southeast quadrant. Combining quantities consumed (or bought) on the vertical axis and nominal income on the horizontal axis gives the Engel curve.

Since the price of x (P_x) is a constant, the Engel curve can be converted to an expenditure Engel curve simply by multiplying each x by P_x to give the consumer's outlay on x, namely $P_x x$. This same amount of expenditure can also be read directly from the graph in the northwest corner by measuring I_1–y_1, I_2–y_2, I_3–y_3, and I_4–y_4.

Figure 6–4(b) (page 131) follows the same procedure in constructing the Engel curve, but in this case it is negatively sloped because of the nature of the indifference map. The examples in Figure 6–4(a) in which x is called a "superior" or "normal" good and in Figure 6–4(b) in which x is called an "inferior" good would seem to be the usual cases, but one can conceive of an extreme case where the *ICC* curve is vertical. In this case the Engel curve would be horizontal, indicating complete insensitivity of the consumption of x to changes in income. This is referred to as a "neutral" good. Another extreme is one where the ICC is horizontal and the Engel curve is a straight line at a 45° angle. In this unusual case, a fixed amount would be spent on y (all other goods) and all additional income would be spent on x. If this Engel curve goes through the origin, then income was spent only on x.

ENGEL CURVES AND INCOME ELASTICITY

The shape of Engel curves for particular products and particular individuals may be quite different. The most plausible assumption is that the slope changes as income changes. For example, at very low incomes potatoes might exhibit an Engel curve through the origin at very nearly a slope of one, and the curve might get flatter as income increases and at some point turn negative. Yacht services, on the other hand, might be zero until income becomes quite large; but from that point on, the slope of the Engel curve might very well rise as income increases and perhaps fall at some extremely high incomes.

As with the usual demand curves, our interest is often with the entire market's demand for the commodity rather than the single individual's. The market Engel curve is the summation of the individual curves where both income and quantities are summed. The curvature of the total Engel curve would depend on the distribution of income and on the change in distribution as income changed. Thus, a commodity which has the same-shaped Engel curve for all individuals may have a quite differently shaped Engel curve for the market as a whole. Empirical estimation is the only recourse.

Recall the definition of income elasticity as the ratio of the relative change in the quantity of the commodity purchased (or consumed) to the relative change in income, or $\eta_{xI} \equiv \Delta Q_x/Q_x \div \Delta I/I = \dfrac{\Delta Q_x}{\Delta I} \cdot \dfrac{I}{Q_x}$. Since $\Delta Q_x/\Delta I$ is the slope of the Engel curve and I/Q_x is always positive, as long as the curve is upward-sloping, the income elasticity is positive. Thus, a positive slope to the Engel curve (or the ICC) suggests a superior good; and if the Engel curve (or ICC) is negatively sloped, elasticity is negative and the good is an inferior one. For any point on an Engel curve, the steeper the slope, the higher the elasticity.

In summary, we have found that the ICC can have almost any shape. We do know, however, that it must pass through the origin since with no income the individual can buy no commodities. This means that even with negatively sloped income-consumption curves, such as in Figure 6–4(b), the ICC must be positively sloped or on the x axis at very low incomes. In addition, the ICC must be continuous since the indifference curves are everywhere dense, covering the entire commodity space. Finally, we know that as a consumer's income goes up, with prices remaining constant, consumption of some commodity must increase. However, traditional consumer theory does not tell us what particular commodity the individual will choose to consume.

FIGURE 6-4   Derivation of an Engel Curve from an *ICC*

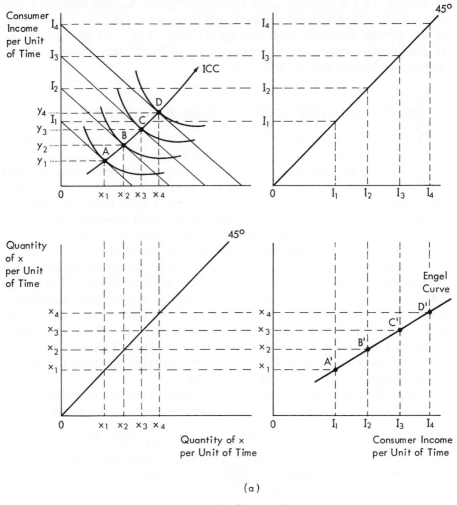

(a)

x and y Superior Goods

THE INCOME EFFECT AND THE SUBSTITUTION EFFECT

One of the advantages of the indifference curve analysis over the cardinal utility analysis is that the substitution and income effects of a price change can be readily isolated. The substitution effect and the income effect are each important in both the cardinal and ordinal analysis of consumer behavior. The substitution effect emphasizes that as P_x falls, a consumer is more *willing* to buy additional units of x because, independent of any increase in real income, x has become *relatively* cheaper (to y, z, etc., prices of which have remained constant). The income effect emphasizes that as P_x falls, the consumer is more

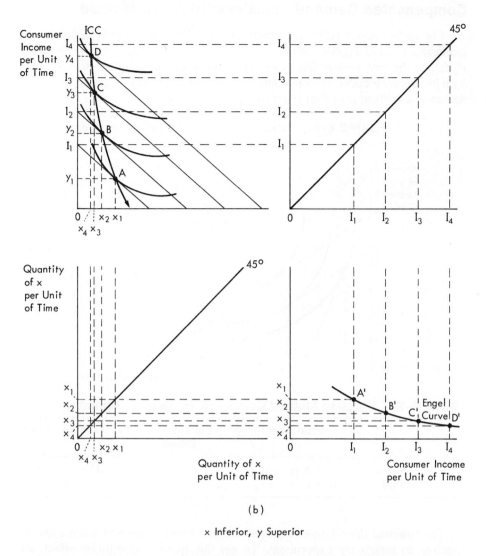

(b)

x Inferior, y Superior

able to buy additional units of *x* since a given money income has *absolutely* more purchasing power than before, independent of any change in relative prices. In short, as P_x falls, the consumer buys more *x* because: (1) it is now less expensive relative to other goods and services; and (2) the consumer's real income has increased. There are two alternative approaches to measuring the substitution and income effects with indifference curves, the Hicksian method and the Slutsky method.[2]

---

[2] John R. Hicks, *Value and Capital* (2d ed.; London: Oxford University Press, 1946), pp. 29–33. Eugene Slutsky, "On the Theory of the Budget of the Consumer," reprinted in *Readings in Price Theory,* edited by Kenneth E. Boulding and George J. Stigler (Homewood: Richard D. Irwin, 1952), pp. 27–56.

Compensated Demand Functions: Hicksian Method

Figure 6–5 is our reference graph. Suppose the consumer is at point *a* on indifference curve I_1, consuming $0x_1$ units of *x*, given budget line *ef*. Now let P_x fall so the new budget line is *eg*. The consumer's new optimum is at point *b* on indifference curve I_3, consuming $0x_4$ units of *x*. The total effect of the price decrease was from *a* to *b* or from $0x_1$ to $0x_4$ units of *x*.

FIGURE 6–5   Hicks and Slutsky Substitution Effect and Income Effect

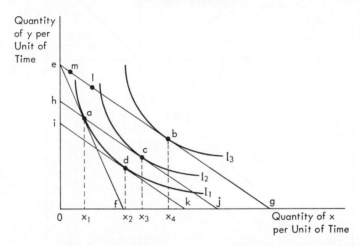

TABLE 6–1   Hicksian Method Compared To Slutsky Method

	Total Effect	=	Substitution Effect	+	Income Effect
Hicksian Method	$a \to b\ (x_1 \to x_4)$		$a \to d\ (x_1 \to x_2)$		$d \to b\ (x_2 \to x_4)$
Slutsky Method	$a \to b\ (x_1 \to x_4)$		$a \to c\ (x_1 \to x_3)$		$c \to b\ (x_3 \to x_4)$

Determining the relative magnitudes of the substitution and income effects requires an imaginary experiment. To get the "pure" substitution effect, we must eliminate any increase in real income that accrued to the consumer as a result of the fall in P_x. By doing this, we isolate the effects of the change in relative prices. To isolate the substitution effect, we confront the consumer with the new relative price ratio but remove the gain in real income, where real income is total utility. The way to do this geometrically is to force the consumer to stay on the same indifference curve (I_1), even though relative prices have changed. Since along a given indifference curve real income is constant, such a procedure will allow us to view the pure substitution effect in operation. Thus, we want the consumer to stay on the original indifference curve, I_1, but with the new relative prices. Therefore, we draw budget line *ik* parallel to the new budget line *eg* so that the former is tangential to the old indifference curve I_1. In short, the consumer now faces the new prices but with the old real income. Thus, the movement from a to d or from $0x_1$ to $0x_2$ units of x must be the substitution effect of the price change. The residual movement from d to b, $0x_2$ to $0x_4$, must be the income effect of the price change. The income effect occurs not because relative prices have changed—as budget line ik parallels eg and therefore has the same slope or price ratio (P_x/P_y)—but because of the gain in real income, depicted by the outward but parallel shift of the entire budget line. If the y axis measures money income, the consumer's income increases in this case from $0i$ to $0e$, which is equal in market value to kg amount of commodity x. While this Hicksian measure is the superior one from a conceptual point of view, it has the shortcoming for empirical work of requiring knowledge about an individual's indifference curve or utility function.

Compensated Demand Functions: Slutsky Method

A good proxy measure for the Hicksian approach is the Slutsky technique. Instead of removing the consumer's entire real income gain from a price decline by forcing the consumer to remain on the same indifference curve, the Slutsky approach confiscates only the consumer's *apparent* real income by leaving enough money income to buy the *original* combination of commodities. In Figure 6–5, the original position is again at point a, where the consumer purchases $0x_1$ units of x, given budget line ef. Now suppose P_x falls so that the budget line is now eg. The total effect is, again, the movement from a to b or from $0x_1$ to $0x_4$. With the Slutsky method, nominal income or apparent real income is reduced such that the consumer could buy the original set of goods, assuming the new price ratio prevailed. Budget line hj would accomplish this. It parallels eg so that the new price ratio holds, yet the income is so reduced that it intersects the old combination of commodities at point a. But note that this new budget line hj is tangential to a new indifference curve I_2, which contains a higher level of total utility than I_1. The consumer therefore will choose combination c, consuming $0x_3$ units of x. Since the consumer deliberately chose the latter combination, c, instead of the former, a, we must suppose that the consumer prefers c to a; consequently, real income must be higher at c than at a. Thus, the consumer ends up on a higher indifference curve, although we apparently stripped the "windfall" income away.

The movement from a to c or from $0x_1$ to $0x_3$ is the substitution effect; the residue $0x_4 - 0x_3$ or the movement from c to b is the income effect. The difference between the Hicks and Slutsky substitution effects is c-d. This difference, $0x_3 - 0x_2$, goes to zero faster than any other difference, making the Slutsky approach a good approximation of the Hicks measure. Slutsky's method overestimates the substitution effect by very little for small price changes. In addition, the Slutsky measure can be computed directly from observable market data on price and quantities consumed. The empirical advantages of the Slutsky analysis partially offset its theoretical shortcomings. Table 6–1 (page 132) summarizes the Hicksian method compared to the Slutsky method as depicted in Figure 6–5.

Ordinary vs. Compensated Demand Functions

A consumer's *ordinary demand function* includes both the substitution and income effects, because it gives the quantity demanded of a commodity as a function of commodity prices and the buyer's income. However, the type of demand function that would be generated if only the substitution effect was allowed to operate is called a *compensated demand function*. We can construct such a demand function by imagining that someone, say, a public authority, taxes (in the case of a price decrease) or subsidizes (in the case of a price increase) a consumer so as to eliminate any income effect after a price change. This "as if" lump-sum tax or payment allows the consumer the minimum income necessary to achieve the initial utility level in the case of a Hicks compensated demand function or the initial consumption combination in the case of a Slutsky compensated demand function.

There is a striking difference between the ordinary and the compensated demand curves. Since the substitution effect is always negative—i.e., price decreases always cause increases in quantity demanded—the Hicks compensated demand curve must be negatively sloped, whereas the ordinary demand curve could conceivably have a positive slope as in the case of a Giffen good. Another difference is that, whereas the ordinary demand curve is homogeneous of degree zero in prices and income—i.e., if all prices and incomes change proportionally, the quantity demanded remains unchanged—the Hicks compensated demand curve is homogeneous of degree zero in prices. This would seem intuitively obvious, since if all prices changed proportionally and the income effect were eliminated, all relative prices would remain the same.

Figure 6–6 shows the most likely shapes for the ordinary and the compensated demand curves, assuming x is a superior good. The ordinary demand curve is labeled OD, the compensated demand curve is labeled CD, and their point of intersection—assumed to be current price $0P_1$ and quantity $0x_1$—is

FIGURE 6–6   **Ordinary Demand Curve**
(OD) and Compensated
Demand Curve (CD)

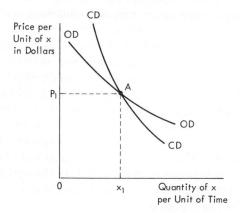

labeled A. With prices falling from P_1, CD will be associated with lower quantities for each price than OD, and therefore lies below OD. A lower price means that real income has increased, which necessitates a negative income compensation along CD; but OD includes both the income and substitution effects, each of which tends to cause an increase in quantity demanded for a superior good when its price has fallen. However, CD includes only the increase in consumption of x that results from the substitution effect since the income effect, by definition, has been removed. By the same line of reasoning, for price increases above P_1, the income effect on consumption will be negative, and OD will be below CD and will therefore be associated with smaller quantities for each price as compared to CD.[3]

Giffen Good vs. Inferior Good

A negative income effect is a necessary but not a sufficient condition for a Giffen good. An inferior good is a commodity whose consumption rate falls as income rises; i.e., the income effect is negative. A Giffen good requires even a stronger condition than a negative income effect, however. It requires that the demand curve be upward sloping, which requires not only a negative income effect, but an income effect greater, in absolute value, than the substitution effect. The convexity of indifference curves ensures that the substitution effect will always be negative. That is, the quantity consumed of x will always move in the opposite direction of the price change if income is held constant. The substitution effect alone always tends to make the demand curve downward sloping. Hence, only the income effect can make the demand function upward sloping.

If x is a normal (or superior) good, both the income and substitution effects will move in the same direction, ensuring a downsloping demand curve. If x is an inferior good, the income effect will work in an opposite direction from the substitution effect. Since the substitution effect is normally much larger than

---

[3] A Slutsky apparent-real-income compensated demand curve would fall between OD and CD for prices lower than P_1 and would be above CD for prices above P_1 for a superior good such as in Figure 6–6. The Slutsky curve includes both the substitution effect and a partial income effect. But what is tricky about this demand curve is that, after compensation to allow purchase of the original combination of goods, a consumer's real income is always higher whether the price has increased or decreased. This results because, after relative prices have changed, the consumer will not, in fact, buy the original combination of goods, but will purchase some preferred combination involving more of the commodity for which the relative price has fallen. Thus, for prices above P_1 in Figure 6–6, the consumer cuts back purchases with OD the most, inasmuch as both the substitution and income effects are operating in this direction—good x's relative price has gone up and real income has fallen. Hick's CD will involve a smaller reduction in quantity consumed since only the substitution effect is involved. But the Slutsky compensated demand curve will involve the smallest reduction in quantity demanded because it involves a slightly higher real income coupled with a substitution effect. In the case of inferior goods, the relative positions of all three curves will be exactly reversed. An extended discussion of these various demand curves can be found in Milton Friedman, *Price Theory: A Provisional Text* (Chicago: Aldine Publishing Co., 1962), Ch. 2, especially pp. 48–55. Martin J. Bailey, "The Marshallian Demand Curve," *Readings in Microeconomics*, edited by David R. Kamerschen (New York: John Wiley & Sons, 1969), pp. 169–179, takes Friedman's analysis one step further by introducing a "constant-apparent-production" demand curve and a "constant-production" demand curve.

the income effect, the demand curve will usually be negatively inclined, even for an inferior good. Do not be misled by the highly exaggerated price changes and income effects shown in Figure 6–5. We exaggerated this example only to make the exposition clearer. Normally, the price changes are much smaller, and any single commodity accounts for such a small fraction of a consumer's total budget that the income effect is quite small. For instance, if an item comprises, say, $\frac{1}{10}$ of a consumer's $100 weekly budget ($10), an unusually large percentage, and if its price falls by, say, $\frac{1}{10}$, a relatively large change, the income effect will be only $\frac{1}{100}$ of the budget. This amount of increased income will then be allocated among all goods. In brief, for x to be a Giffen good: (1) it must be an inferior good, and (2) it must comprise such a large portion of a consumer's budget and/or the price change must be so large that the income effect is, neglecting signs, larger than the substitution effect.

APPLICATIONS OF ORDINAL UTILITY THEORY

In Chapter 4 we learned that the cliché, "you get what you pay for," was at best misleading; consumers sometimes get more than they pay for. They get a surplus.

Consumer Surplus

Consumer surplus, according to Marshall, was the difference between the (total) amount a person would be *willing* to pay for a good rather than go without it and the amount which the person actually pays.[4] In Chapter 4, consumer surplus was estimated by the cardinal utility approach. It may also be measured with the indifference curve analysis. This is demonstrated in Figure 6–7.

FIGURE 6–7   Two Indifference Curve Measures of Consumer Surplus

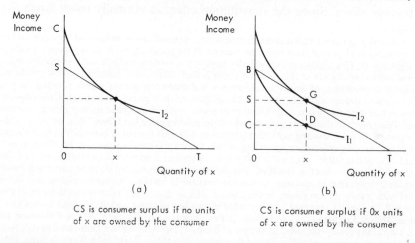

(a)

CS is consumer surplus if no units
of x are owned by the consumer

(b)

CS is consumer surplus if 0x units
of x are owned by the consumer

---

[4] See John R. Hicks, *Value and Capital* (2d ed.; London: Oxford University Press, 1946), pp. 38–41, or George J. Stigler, *The Theory of Price* (3d ed.; New York: Macmillan Co., 1966), pp. 78–81.

In this diagram, money income, our proxy for all other goods, is measured on the *y* axis and the commodity in question on the *x* axis. Two approaches may be taken here. Figure 6–7(a) assumes that the consumer has no units of *x* initially. We then determine what income, without the right to buy 0*x* units of *x*, would equal the consumer's income with the privilege of buying 0*x* at the price ratio given by the slope of budget line *ST*. If the consumer could purchase no units of *x*, he or she could reach indifference curve I_2 only with an income of 0*C*. Alternatively, if the consumer were allowed to purchase 0*x* units of *x*, he or she could reach I_2 with an income of only 0*S*. *CS* is therefore a measure of the consumer surplus.

Figure 6–7(b) assumes that the consumer has purchased 0*x* units of *x* for which he or she pays a sum equal to *SB*. This places the consumer on indifference curve I_2. However, this individual would have been willing to pay *BC* for 0*x* units of *x* rather than go without it. Without any *x*, the consumer would be at point *B* on indifference curve I_1. He or she would still be on I_1, even if as much as *BC* was paid for 0*x* units of *x*. This would put the consumer at point *D* on I_1. Therefore, *CS* in Figure 6–7(b) is the consumer surplus. The Marshallian cardinal utility analysis needed to assume no income effect existed, i.e., to assume the *MU* of money income was constant, for the area under the demand curve and above the price line to represent consumer surplus. The indifference analysis must make this same assumption in order for the two estimates given in Figure 6–7 to be the same.

Exchange

Chapter 4 demonstrated, with cardinal utility analysis, why exchange takes place. In particular, (4.22) noted that whenever the ratios of the *MU*s are not equal for two people (or groups), mutually beneficial trade will take place. Since the MRS_{xy} is equivalent to the ratio of *MU*s ($MRS_{xy} = MU_x/MU_y$), this same condition can be stated as:

$$MRS_{xy1} \neq MRS_{xy2} = \text{condition for mutually beneficial exchange} \qquad (6.3)$$

where the subscripts 1 and 2 refer to different people or groups. Both parties can therefore gain by exchange until such time as expression (6.3) becomes an equality. This is illustrated in Figure 6–8 for *A* and *B* (which can represent different people, groups, regions, nations, etc.).

A diagram such as Figure 6–8 is referred to as an *Edgeworth-Bowley box diagram*. Assume there are two individuals, *A* and *B*, who each hold endowments of the two goods *x* and *y* for future consumption or trade. The tastes and preferences of each are indicated by their indifference curves, labeled A_1, A_2, and A_3 for consumer *A*, and B_1, B_2, and B_3 for consumer *B*. Only three of an infinite number of such curves have been shown for each consumer to make the diagram clearer. The curves have the usual convex, downward-sloping shape, with the higher numbers indicating higher levels of satisfaction, A_2PA_1, A_3PA_2, etc. We can easily see this for *A*, whose origin is at the lower left, 0_A. *B*'s origin is at the upper right, which means this person's indifference

FIGURE 6-8 The Basis of Exchange

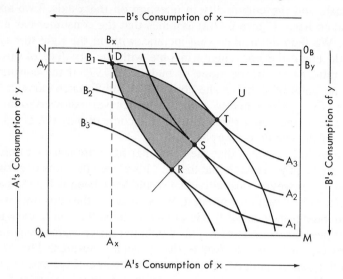

map has been rotated 180° and superimposed on that of A so that the axes form a box. (Although B's curves may look peculiar, if you turn the page upside down, you will see they form a typical indifference map.) Point D represents their assumed initial stocks. The width of box $0_A x$ represents the sum of the stocks of x held by both A and B. The vertical height of the box equals the sum of y's held by both parties. Therefore, at point D, A holds $0_A A_x$ units of x and $0_A A_y$ units of y. B holds the residue on each axis or $A_x M \ (= 0_A M - 0_A A_x)$ units of x and $A_y N \ (= 0_A N - 0_A A_y)$ units of y. This places A on the indifference curve labelled A_1 and B on indifference curve B_1.

Whenever the indifference curves of A and B are intersecting rather than tangential, either or both parties may gain from trade. Starting from point D, either or both may gain from exchange anywhere in shaded area DRT. Starting from point D, if curve A_1 is followed downward to the right, B can reach higher levels of satisfaction; whereas A, by the definition of an indifference curve, is no worse off. Only at points such as R, S, and T, at which A's and B's indifference curves are tangential, will this no longer be true.

Just the reverse holds if indifference curve B_1 is followed. Then B's utility would be constant, but A would get progressively better off by reaching higher valued indifference curves. Anywhere in shaded area DRT both may benefit from exchange as compared to their situation at point D. The locus of tangency points is called a *contract* or *conflict curve*. In Figure 6–8 the contract curve is labeled RST. It shows all the allocations of goods between the two parties such that the MRS_{xy} is the same for both parties at each point. The term "conflict" curve rightly suggests that along this curve, what one party gains the other must lose. The farther northeast A can put the bargain, i.e., the closer to point T, the better off A is. B achieves more welfare the closer the bargain can be pushed toward R. The term "contract" curve is sometimes used since, if free exchange is allowed, the parties will end up somewhere on the curve because the curve represents an optimal — any point not on the "contract" curve is necessarily worse than some points on the curve. Although points R, S, and T are all better than point D, we cannot judge between points D and U, for example, for B is worse off at U than at D.

Supply of Labor Services

It is easy to derive a supply curve of labor services with indifference curve analysis, as can be seen in Figure 6–9. In Figure 6–9(a), money income per day is measured on the vertical axis, and hours of work offered (and withheld) in the labor market is measured on the horizontal axis; whereas in Figure 6–9(b) the wage rate per hour is measured.

Income earned from hours of work and leisure are substitute goods, and the sum of labor time and leisure time must total 24 hours per day. This analysis assumes that the worker is free to choose to work any number of hours, based upon the worker's tastes and preferences and the wage rate (i.e., the price of labor service per hour). The indifference curves are positively sloped because work is a discommodity which requires more income if additional leisure is to be given up. In addition, these indifference curves are concave from above (i.e., they get steeper as the number of hours of work increases) for two reasons: (1) There is something approaching a physical maximum to the number of hours of work that can be performed in a day — e.g., perhaps 16–18 hours. The curves become nearly vertical at this limit. (2) Marginal disutility from work and MU of leisure both increase as hours of leisure decline. That is, the indifference curves are concave from above because of $DMRS$ between income and leisure.

The hourly wage rate is measured by the slope of a ray from the origin. For example, in Figure 6–9(a), 24 hours of work would yield y_1 dollars of income, so the income per hour is $y_1/24$ hrs (= slope of ray $0y_1$). Since the individual worker will want to be on the highest attainable indifference curve, the optimum, as in any other indifference curve analysis, is at the point of tangency of the price line (here the wage, or price per hour of leisure) and the indifference curve. At this point the MRS between income and work equals the trade off determined by the market between them — that is, the wage. The *wage-work (W-W) curve* connecting points of tangency ABC is an exact analog to the price-consumption curve (PCC) described earlier. Up to point B, increases in the wage rate lead to increasing hours of work; but after point B, the reverse is true. Notice that the individual's income from labor per day (I) is the wage (P) times the number of hours worked per day (H), so $I_1 = P_1H_1$, etc. Notice also that all the information for deriving a demand for leisure as a function of the wage rate is contained in the diagram.

The supply curve of labor is projected from Figure 6–9(a) to Figure 6–9(b). Points A, B, and C in panel (a) correspond to points A', B', and C' in panel (b). At a wage or price of P_1, H_1 hours of labor effort will be forthcoming, and so on.

FIGURE 6-9   Supply of Labor Services
of an Individual Worker

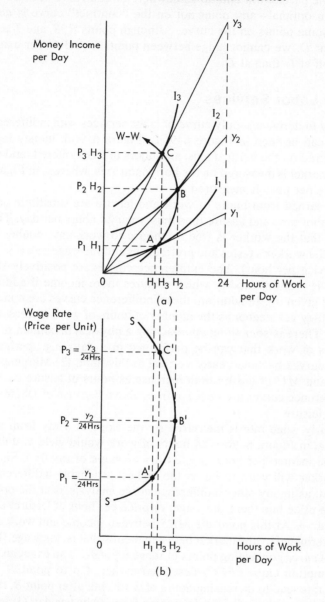

Up to point B' in panel (b), the substitution effect is said to dominate the income effect. That is, as the wage rate goes up, two things happen: (1) Leisure becomes more expensive since the income lost from each hour of work given up has risen. A worker will want to work more hours. He or she will substitute more work for less leisure. This is the substitution effect. (2) On the other hand, as the price of labor goes up and if the individual works the same number of hours as before, total money income will rise. This will lead to a desire to consume more of all (superior) goods, including leisure. Hence, there will be an income effect tending to cause the individual to work fewer hours as the wage rate goes up.

At wages above B', the supply curve is backward-bending. The income effect dominates the substitution effect beyond this point, causing an overall reduction in the number of hours worked per unit of time as the wage rate goes up. Some labor economists think these backward-rising supply curves for labor are fairly common for certain people in all nations. They are not restricted to the natives of low-income countries as some studies have suggested. The shape of the supply curve depends upon the person's or group's tastes and preferences regarding leisure and income.

Additional Applications

The indifference curve analysis can be applied in numerous other situations in our everyday life. For instance, we can readily demonstrate that the cost of subsidies in kind, such as providing public housing to low-income groups, is always greater than the money equivalent of the subjective gain to subsidized groups.[5] The general principle is that, apart from etiquette and sentimental considerations, a cash gift will always put the donee on a higher indifference curve (make the donee happier) than a gift in kind, even if the gift is a commodity that the person wants, such as housing!

The same is true of fringe benefits as opposed to money income in an employee's total compensation. Consider the following case. A firm subsidizes lunch for its employees at 50 percent of the price to the firm of providing the meals. Figure 6–10 shows one employee's preferences and budget constraints, LM being the full price situation and LN the subsidized price relation. At the subsidy price this employee consumes amount $0x_A$ per month, spending RL of income for it. The firm spends an equal amount, which happens to be RS since LS is the full price of $0x_A$. RS is thus the amount of the monthly subsidy per employee.

Suppose the firm were to abandon the subsidy program and increase each employee's income by the amount of the subsidy. The employees would then have to pay the full price for lunches, so that with the higher income the new budget constraint would be TU, $(TL = RS)$. The worker's new optimum point is B, which is on a higher indifference curve. In this case the employees are better off.

Now notice that the firm could, instead of increasing employee compensation by the full amount of the subsidy, raise incomes by just $T'L$, which would allow the workers to remain on the original indifference curve and thus be just

[5] See, e.g., Donald S. Watson, *Price Theory and Its Uses* (3d ed.; Boston: Houghton Mifflin Co., 1972), pp. 111–113. He also demonstrates, pp. 109–111, the superiority of an income tax over an excise tax. That is, he demonstrates that an excise tax puts a taxpayer on a lower indifference curve than does an income tax of an equal amount. However, the validity of this proposition is open to some question.

FIGURE 6-10 Economic Effects of Subsidies

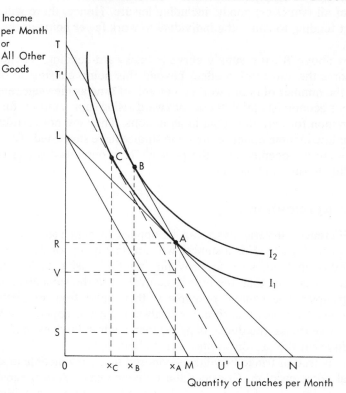

as well off. But the firm outlay of $T'L$ is less than the subsidy amount RS ($T'L = VS$). In this case the firm is better off. Both parties would be better off (than with the subsidy plan) if income is raised by anywhere between LT' and LT.

Similarly, one can analyze, with the indifference curve apparatus, the effects of overtime rates, work restrictions, and general assistance payments on the labor supply.[6] The general principle again emerges that restrictions of any kind placed on a person's freedom of choice in the market can never increase his or her utility. In other words, an individual with freedom of choice is always at least as well off, and generally better off, than an individual whose choice is restricted. In addition, an individual's optimal allocation between present and future consumption, including borrowing and lending decisions, can be determined by the indifference curve technique. In general, the optimal point is where the rate of time preference exactly equals the rate of interest.

---

[6] See, e.g., Charles E. Ferguson, *Microeconomic Theory* (3d ed.; Homewood: Richard D. Irwin, 1972), Ch. 3, especially pp. 83–92.

REVEALED PREFERENCE THEORY

Although two approaches have been used in addition to the cardinal utility and indifference curve approaches to explain consumer behavior, the mathematical prerequisites for examining in detail these alternative approaches are beyond the bounds of this book. These two more mathematical approaches are the *revealed preference theory*, which was originally developed in the 1930s by Nobel Laureate Paul A. Samuelson,[7] and the *modern axiomatic choice theory*.[8] Happily, we can develop the rudiments of the revealed preference approach with some modest geometric techniques. In this section, we will analyze the revealed preference theory in this pictorial way.

The revealed preference approach requires even less stringent assumptions than the indifference curve technique. The revealed preference approach requires only observable price-quantity information.[9] If a consumer buys some basket of goods, call it *A*, rather than any other basket, call it *B*, the individual must have done so either because he or she likes *A* better than *B* or because *A* is cheaper. It is important to note that without additional information on relative prices we cannot infer that because the consumer purchases basket *A* over basket *B* that he or she prefers *A* to *B*. If *A* is at least as expensive as *B* and the consumer buys *A*, then one can conclude that *A* is preferred over *B*. In such a case, we have, by assumption, removed the possibility that *B* was preferred, but the consumer's income was not large enough to buy it. If a consumer selects *A* when it is more expensive than (or equally expensive as) *B*, we say that *A* has been revealed preferred to *B*, or *B* has been revealed inferior to *A*.

The theory of revealed preference is based on three axioms. Letting the symbol P ($\not{P}$) represent revealed preferred (not revealed preferred), APB ($A\not{P}B$) means *A* is revealed preferred (is not revealed preferred) to *B*.

1. *Two term consistency.* If APB, then $B\not{P}A$.
2. *Three term consistency.* If APB and BPC, then APC. (This was called transitivity in Chapter 5.)
3. *Budget line existence.* There exists some set of relative prices that will induce the consumer to buy any given basket of goods.

Observing a consumer's actual choices when faced with particular price ratios and given incomes can reveal a surprising amount of information about

---

[7] See, e.g., his *Foundations of Economic Analysis* (Cambridge: Harvard University Press, 1965), especially pp. 107–111 and 146–163.

[8] The originator of this approach is not so easily determined. However, for a thoroughly delightful, albeit watered-down version of modern axiomatic choice theory, see Vivian Charles Walsh, *Introduction to Contemporary Microeconomics* (New York: McGraw-Hill Book Co., 1970).

[9] For this reason many economists felt that the revealed preference approach would be subject to intensive empirical investigation. It has not been. One of the best of the modest number of statistical studies on revealed preference is A. C. Y. Koo, "An Empirical Test of Revealed Preference," *Econometrica* (October, 1968), pp. 646–664.

the person's indifference curves. If we could practically conduct enough experiments, we could construct the (almost) complete indifference curve. However, with just one observation we can deduce quite a bit. First, by the rule that more is preferred to less, in Figure 6–11 any market basket within *BAC* is preferred to *A*, and any combination within *DAE* is inferior to *A*. If, in addition, we know the consumer's budget constraint is, say, *LM* in Figure 6–11, all combinations in *LAD* and *MAE* are revealed inferior to *A* since these choices were available but rejected. This is all we can know from one observation. The indifference curve through point *A* must be in the unshaded areas *LAB* and *MAC*.[10] *BAC* can be considered the *superior boundary* and *LM* the *inferior boundary*.

FIGURE 6–11   **Revealed Preference:**
inferior Area *0LM,*
Superior Area *BAC*

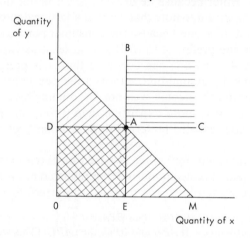

We wish to construct an experiment which, at least conceptually, will allow us to deduce the shape of a single indifference curve. We do this by constructing the superior and inferior boundaries such that they come closer together. We will assume the relative prices and consumer's income can be controlled in the experiment. We will also assume the consumer's preferences will not vary during the experiment.

Constructing the Superior Boundary

We can find combinations of commodities the consumer prefers to bundle *A* by varying relative prices of the commodities such that the consumer could still buy *A*. For example, raise the price of *x* in Figure 6–12(a) to the ratio

---

[10] The point was made earlier, but it is worth repeating in this context: the indifference curve through *A* cannot be concave since if it were, it would have to pass through the inferior zone *L0M*.

FIGURE 6–12   Revealed Preference: Determination of Superior Areas

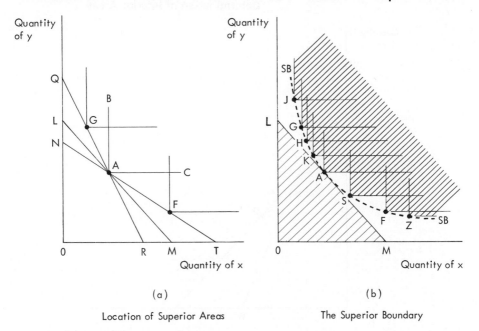

(a)

Location of Superior Areas

(b)

The Superior Boundary

reflected on line QR, which runs through point A. We would expect the subject to buy less of x than when the price ratio was reflected by line LM. If the consumer selects point G, then that combination is preferred to combination A, since A is no more expensive. Now try a price ratio less than LM while still requiring the budget line to run through point A, e.g., line NT. We expect more of x to be bought; so suppose the buyer chooses bundle F, revealing that F is preferred to A. Thus, G and F are on higher indifference curves than A. Our experiment would proceed in this fashion until we tire of it, or we have as much information as we need, or our budget for the experiment is getting low.

A set of points such as J, G, H, K, S, F, and Z would then trace out something like a superior boundary line SB-SB in Figure 6–12(b). The indifference curve through point A must be below (or to the left of) these points. The inferior boundary is still LM, so the indifference curve we are looking for lies to the right of (or above) LM. The project now is to reduce some of the space between SB and LM.

Constructing the Inferior Boundary

Figure 6–13(a) is our reference for the construction of the inferior boundary. The experiment now must be designed to find commodity bundles in the space between SB and LM which are revealed inferior to point A. Starting

**FIGURE 6–13   Revealed Preference:
Determination of Inferior Areas**

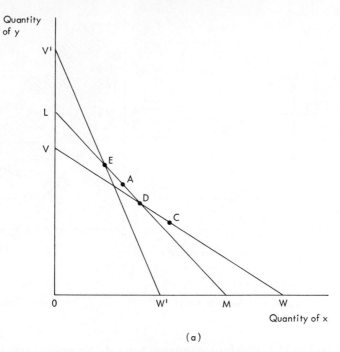

(a)

Location of Inferior Areas

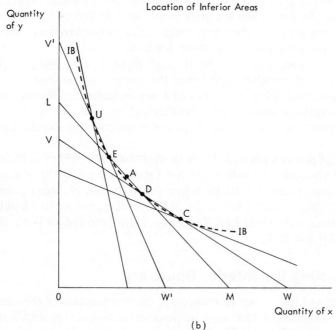

(b)

The Inferior Boundary

from the knowledge that any other point on budget line *LM* has been revealed inferior to *A*, if we can choose income-price relationships which will induce the subject to prefer a point on *LM* to points in the space between *LM* and *SB*, we will be able to eliminate some additional area of ignorance.

The third axiom of revealed preference theory is that some set of relative prices will induce the consumer to buy any given basket. In other words, we can find a budget line such that the individual will select bundle *D*. This will require some experimentation. For instance, if the budget line chosen induced the consumer to buy a bundle to the right of *D*, such as point *C*, we would have to raise the price of *x* (that is, make the budget line steeper) to reduce the consumption of *x*, and we would have to continue to do this until *D* is in fact chosen. At that point we know that all bundles in area *MDW* are revealed inferior to *D*; and since *D* was earlier revealed inferior to *A*, *MDW* points are inferior to *A* (assuming transitivity, of course).

To reduce the area of ignorance above point *A* between *SB* and *LM* [of Figure 6–12(b)], we will follow the above procedure analogously, only now the prices chosen will be higher for *x* than the *LM* price ratios. This would be the case for budget line *V'W'*. Here the subject would be persuaded to buy bundle *E* by proper price manipulation, which would then reveal a preference for *E* over all bundles in *LEV'*. At this stage the inferior boundary is *V'EDW*. We can further delineate the boundary by forcing points *C* and *U* and so on, as shown in Figure 6–13(b), with a curve something like *IB-IB* tracing out the inferior boundary. The more experiments we conduct, the closer *IB* and *SB* will come together, forming the indifference curve.

QUESTIONS

1. Give as many reasons as you can why people don't consume some products at all.
2. Using indifference curve analysis, interpret the assertion, "I love steak, but I can't afford it, so I eat hamburger."
3. If the variable on the *y* axis of an indifference curve graph represents all other goods, explain how to determine the total expenditure on commodity *x*.
4. Explain how we know that if *PCC* is positively sloping, the individual's demand for the commodity is inelastic. What can be said about a horizontal *PCC?* A negatively sloped *PCC?*
5. Draw the indifference curve graph necessary to construct a horizontal Engle curve. Explain the meaning of such a curve and evaluate its practicality.
6. Draw an indifference curve graph in which the income effect of a price decrease is negative and greater in absolute terms than the substitution effect. (This is called a "Giffen good.")
7. The Hicks and the Slutsky approaches differ in their definition of constant real income. Which definition seems most satisfying intellectually, and which one seems most practical for measurement purposes? Why?
8. The text does not show the graphics of the construction of a compensated demand curve. Using the Hicks approach, derive three points on an ordinary demand curve and three points on a compensated demand curve. The three points should be the current price, a price above the current one, and a price below the current one.

9. Using the Edgeworth-Bowley box technique, show that an equal distribution of all goods to consumers is not necessarily the "best" distribution, even if the goods are free to the society.
10. Under the heading "Supply of Labor Services" (pages 139–141), a supply curve of an individual's labor effort is constructed. Using the same individual as the one in Figure 6–9, construct a demand curve for leisure as a function of the price (wage).
11. Without actually drawing the graph, explain how an indifference curve could be derived through the use of the revealed preference method.

7 Market Structure and the Firm's Demand Curve

In the last few chapters our primary concern has been with the demand curve of an individual consumer. This chapter will emphasize the demand curve as it appears to individual business firms and the demand curve for a given commodity.

FOUR BASIC MARKET MODELS

A *market* in economics exists when buyers and sellers are able to get together to carry out economic transactions. The essence of a market is *communication* or the spread of information among buyers and sellers. There may or may not be a well-defined physical area within which the communication takes place. Certainly the buying and selling of most homogeneous agricultural and primary products has no geographical barriers, with trade taking place in world markets via transoceanic telephone and cable.

The nature of a firm's demand curve is closely associated with the type of market organization in the industry to which that firm belongs. After giving a verbal description of the major market models in the U.S. economy, we will give a graphical and verbal demonstration of the connection between market structure and the elasticity of the firm's demand curve.

The four basic market types on the selling side are: pure or perfect competition,[1] monopoly, monopolistic competition, and oligopoly. The last three are sometimes lumped together into the classification "imperfect competition" or just "monopoly" as distinct from perfect competition. All of these various categories are arbitrary, with many "real world" firms or industries not falling unambiguously into any one of them. It is even possible for a single firm to have a monopoly in one product, be oligopolistic for others, and be a pure competitor in still other markets. It is best to look at these four models as points in a

---

[1] Economists sometimes distinguish between "pure" and "perfect" competition by defining the latter to include all the conditions necessary for the former plus one additional condition, namely, that all economic entities possess perfect information regarding all the alternatives open to them. Such a distinction will not be maintained in this book. Instead, pure and perfect competition will be used interchangeably. The primary reason for this attitude is the belief that with such a distinction the idea of perfect competition begins to sound like something much more desirable than merely pure competition. This is simply not true. "Perfect" knowledge is in general as foolish a goal as "perfect" ignorance. Since costs are always involved in seeking information, no consumer would ever seek out perfect knowledge (even if it could be defined unambiguously, which is also dubious). Instead, the search for information should extend only to the point at which the marginal benefit from any additional information just equals the marginal cost of obtaining it.

spectrum ranging between the two polar cases of pure competition and pure monopoly, with monopolistic competition being closer to pure competition and oligopoly closer to pure monopoly.

PURE COMPETITION

Two approaches can be taken in describing the conditions in these various markets. It is possible to indicate either the *necessary* or the *sufficient* conditions for a given model to hold. Economists are wont to use the latter approach. For instance, pure competition is often defined as requiring a large number (relative to the size of the market) of independently acting small firms producing a homogeneous product in an industry free of legal or other artificial restraints such that entry (and exodus) is relatively easy. There are so many firms that one firm's withdrawal from the market would affect output and price infinitesimally. Implicit in this concept is also the belief that each competitor is reasonably aware of prevailing or impending opportunities and is willing to take advantage of them (i.e., resources are mobile).

While the above structural conditions—large numbers, homogeneous products, informed people, etc.—are sufficient to ensure competitive results, they are not necessary. The necessary conditions are: (1) each firm *believes* it cannot significantly influence the market price—it is a *price-taker;* and (2) freedom of entry and exit exists. The really important ingredient in making competitive conditions is the subjective factor of the entrepreneurs feeling they are price-takers. However, certain objective structural conditions, such as those described above, make the assumption more plausible.

In light of the necessary conditions, competitive conditions could possibly be approximated with a very small number of firms (ten, two, even one!) as long as the entrepreneurs feel they cannot influence the market price. However, since economic literature continues to utilize the sufficient conditions, this text will, for the most part, follow this tradition.

Following the structural approach, it is difficult to find exact "real-world" examples of pure competition. The New York Stock Exchange provides a very close approximation. Agriculture, fishing, and trucking (except for government intervention) are reasonably close examples. Thus, for example, individual wheat farmers produce such a trifling part of the total wheat output that they feel they cannot significantly influence the price. They must accept the given market price, which is determined by the demands of all users and the supply of all wheat farmers. Individuals merely adjust their output to achieve the best profit possible. They are *price-takers* (or *quantity-adjusters*). In contrast, a monopolist can influence price and hence has a price policy and can be considered a *price-maker.*

Other Competitive Dimensions

In addition to the number of firms and type of product (i.e., homogeneous or not), other dimensions of market structure can be examined. Probably the most important are: (1) the condition of entry into the industry (Do any significant financial, legal, or technical barriers hinder entry?); and (2) the type of competition (Do firms attempt to gain customers by changing prices or by adjusting nonprice variables such as advertising expenditures or product quality?).

In general, it turns out to be more difficult to enter imperfectly competitive than perfectly competitive industries in roughly the degree suggested by our continuum. That is, it is generally more difficult to enter purely monopolistic than oligopolistic industries; in turn, it is generally more difficult to enter oligopolistic than monopolistically competitive industries. Also, competition through nonprice channels—heavy advertising outlays and frequent quality changes—is generally more prevalent in imperfect competition, especially oligopoly and monopolistic competition. Nonprice strategies are nonexistent in pure competition and infrequent in pure monopoly.

Characteristics of Competitive Markets

As we will discuss in a later chapter, a major result of pure competition is to force prices down to the minimum level of average cost. For the present, the two most important characteristics of competitive markets are that: (1) each economic unit tries to buy cheap and sell dear; and (2) a single price prevails for any one good or service.

This second characteristic is so important that some economists define a competitive market as an area within which the price tends toward uniformity, with allowance for transportation costs. The reasoning behind this definition is fairly obvious. If a price differential did occur for some homogeneous product, buyers and sellers would quickly close the gap by shifting buying from the more expensive to the less expensive markets and selling in the market with the higher prices. Similarly, speculators stabilize price over time, such as for agricultural commodities, by buying them at harvest time when supplies are high and prices are low and storing them to sell in time of limited supply and high prices. Both at a given point in time and over time, speculators fulfill a valuable economic function by equalizing prices between different geographic areas and different time periods. Typical speculators do not deserve the abuse the public generally heaps upon them. In competitive situations, speculators provide a valuable economic function and are only repaid with a "reasonable" rate of remuneration over the long run. Should this return become excessive compared with storage and other costs, a host of new speculators would enter the market until profits disappeared.

PURE MONOPOLY

Pure monopoly violates the numbers requirement for pure competition since there is only one seller of a given commodity in a given market. A pure monopolist is a single seller of a product which has no close substitutes.

Although clear-cut examples of pure monopoly are rare, local public utilities are often in approximately this position. Usually only one company, which is typically regulated by a public body, furnishes telephone or electric service to a community. At times, Alcoa and IBM were examples of near pure monopoly in the private sector of the economy. Other industries that at times have come close to meeting the standards of pure monopoly include the manufacture of locomotives, shoe machinery, and telephone equipment and the production of magnesium and nickel. In terms of the type of product, the pure monopolist can be said to have a unique product.

MONOPOLISTIC COMPETITION

Monopolistic competition lacks one of the major structural requirements for pure competition—namely, homogeneity of the product. It fulfills the basic structural condition of a large number of firms. The basic characteristic of the monopolistically competitive type of market structure is the close substitutability among the only slightly differentiated goods produced by the relatively large number of firms in the industry. Some economists refer to monopolistic competition as the case of "product differentiation and large numbers." The competition found in much of the retail trade in large cities, the cotton textile industry, the food processing industry, and the shoe industry approximates this model.

OLIGOPOLY

Under oligopoly, both the homogeneity and large numbers criteria can be met, but seldom are. Usually one, if not both, are absent. Oligopoly is difficult to pinpoint because it is a residual model which must include all industries that do not fit neatly into one of the other three models. Although oligopoly is usually thought of as consisting of a few large firms, say, two to six, there can be many firms in the industry. However, in this case a few firms produce the bulk of the output and the rest form a competitive fringe, dividing the remaining industry among themselves. "Duopoly" is the special term used to describe the case of exactly two sellers.

The real test for oligopoly is to determine if interdependence exists. The relevant question to ask in this context is: Do the firms in the industry regard themselves as rivals and take account of their competitor's adjustments to output, price, etc.? If the answer is yes, the essence of oligopoly is present in the industry. The interdependent behavior present in oligopoly is in sharp contrast to the other market models. Under pure and monopolistic competition there are so many other firms that no one entrepreneur looks at others as rivals in the sense that he or she feels the firm's economic position will be affected by what others do. Any single wheat farmer is unconcerned with the economic actions of any other wheat farmer since each individual's annual production is too small a fraction of total wheat production to influence the market price. Interdependence is also not a feature of pure monopoly since, by definition, the pure monopolist has no close rivals.

The four largest firms in the American automobile industry illustrate the classical oligopoly model that features fewness. In contrast, the steel industry, which is also considered an oligopoly market, has several dozen firms, but the four largest produce the bulk of the output. A small number of firms is sometimes a sufficient, but not a necessary, condition for oligopoly. What is necessary for oligopoly is the subjective feeling that has been described as mutual interdependence.

It is also possible to distinguish between homogeneous and heterogeneous (differentiated products) oligopoly. The first group includes many raw materials or semifinished goods industries, such as most metal products (aluminum, copper, lead, steel, and zinc), cement, rayon, explosives, alcohol, and some building materials. The second category contains finished consumer goods, such as automobiles, tires, petroleum products, soap, toothpaste, cigarettes, fountain pens, breakfast foods, electrical appliances, electric razors, radios, refrigerators, and some producers' goods such as aircraft and farm implements.

FURTHER STRUCTURAL CHARACTERISTICS

In addition to the above factors influencing market structure – number of firms, degree of product differentiation, extent of entry barriers, etc. – other important factors bear on the "competitiveness" of an industry. They include (1) proximity, (2) interindustry competition, and (3) technological change.

Proximity

The geographical factor is important in any meaningful discussion of market structure. The size of the market is crucial in determining competitiveness. Looking only at the number of firms may sometimes be deceptive. For example, although there are about 14,000 commercial banks in the U.S., many people in rural areas would never think of using, say, the Chase Manhattan Bank in New York City. The importance of the geographical factor is also evidenced in the cement industry, which has about 50 producers. Yet because the cost of transportation is so high, the market for any one producer ordinarily does not extend beyond approximately 300 miles. The geographic radius of sales of the ready-mix concrete industry, which has about 5,000 producers nationally, is even more restrictive. Approximately 90 percent of all ready-mix concrete sales take place within 16 miles of the plant.

Interproduct and Interindustry Competition

The number of firms in an industry may provide a misleading indication of the competitive pressures when the industry's product has close substitutes in other markets. Industries with only a few firms may face stiff competition from products or firms in closely related industries. For example, Alcoa, Kaiser, and Reynolds dominate the aluminum market; yet they face serious competition from substitute materials – copper, steel, or even plastics and wood. Similarly, the giants of the metal container industry – American and Continental Can – face competition from glass, paper, and plastic containers.

Technological Change

Finally, technological advance over time can undermine entrenched monopoly positions that may exist at a given point in time. Some economists, particularly the late Joseph A. Schumpeter, argued that often the industries that look socially undesirable from a static point of view lead to more progressive results from a dynamic point of view. He argued that the monopolistic firms have both greater means and greater incentive to foster technological advance. These firms have previous earnings they can plow back into research and development (R&D), and they have the desire to do so since this may permit them to persistently earn large profits in the future. Under purely competitive conditions, there are no past long-run profits to finance R&D; and the incentives are only very short-run since rivals will emulate any successful innovation, thereby dissipating any short-run abnormal returns. In short, the Schumpeterian hypothesis asserts that the prerequisites for undertaking risky and uncertain innovations—possession of accumulated profits, prospects of further such returns in the future, and the security attending market power— are clearly most likely found under monopoly conditions. The Schumpeterian School says look at our most competitive industry: agriculture. Have significant technological innovations developed in agriculture? While the answer is yes, they add that the technical progress has not come from the farmers themselves, but from government and university research and from the efforts of oligopolistic farm equipment, chemical, and seed concerns.

The proponents of the anti-Schumpeterian School say pure competition is best for fostering innovations. They cite the relative unprogressiveness of the monopolistic, regulated public utilities. For example, they point out the relative slowness in cutting rates and improving service shown by electric and gas companies and railroads. However, government regulation may be the culprit rather than the structure of industry for these results. The anti-Schumpeterians believe that the discovery and introduction of new products, new sources of raw materials, new methods of production, and new markets (Schumpeter's categories of innovation) are more likely when large numbers of firms are involved. In addition, bureaucratic rigidities, which are frequently attributed to large scale enterprise, are not found in the smaller, more flexible competitive firms.

The empirical evidence that has been marshalled to date on this question is indecisive.[2] Some of the data are consistent with both approaches. But the fact remains that under monopoly there is both a short-run and a long-run incentive to innovate and reduce costs, whereas under pure competition there is only a short-run incentive. Oligopoly may well be the market structure most conducive to technological development.

---

[2] An excellent short review of the literature is contained in Jesse W. Markham, "Market Structure, Business Conduct, and Innovation," *American Economic Review*, Vol. LV (May, 1965), pp. 323–332, reprinted in *Readings in Microeconomics*, edited by David R. Kamerschen (New York: John Wiley & Sons, 1969), Chapter 25, pp. 344–354.

FIRM DEMAND CURVES AND MARKET ORGANIZATION

The elasticity of a firm's demand curve greatly depends upon the type of market in which a firm sells its output. We have already discussed four pure classifications of markets. We will now analyze the firm's demand curve under the somewhat heroic assumption that any firm falls neatly into one of these four rubrics. As one might expect, the concept of a firm's demand curve shows, *ceteris paribus*, the different quantities which the firm believes it can sell at various alternative prices.

The rule we can employ as a first approximation is the following: *Ceteris paribus*, the elasticity of a firm's demand tends to vary directly with the degree of competition it faces in its relevant market area. The greater the degree of competition, the more elastic the demand function. In the case of perfect competition, the firm's demand curve would be perfectly or infinitely elastic or, in geometric terms, horizontal. This means the firm is a price-taker, too small to individually influence the market price. It can sell all that it cares to at the market price, but none at a higher price. Buyers will shift to its competitors if it tries to get even a penny more for the completely homogeneous product it sells. Figure 7–1 illustrates the competitive case.

FIGURE 7–1 The Firm and the Industry under Perfect Competition

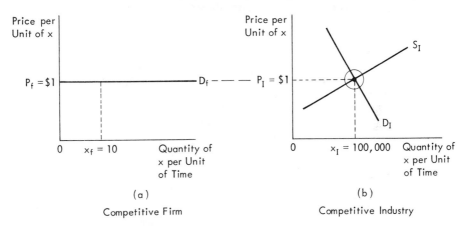

(a)
Competitive Firm

(b)
Competitive Industry

Perfect Competition

Panel (a) of Figure 7–1 shows the firm's demand schedule, D_f, and panel (b) shows the industry demand, D_I, and industry supply, S_I, schedules. At the price of \$1, the representative firm, depicted in panel (a), supplies 1/10,000 of the aggregate output of 100,000. There are 10,000 of these "typical" firms in this industry, with each supplying $x_f = 10$. Thus, while the y axis on both diagrams measures price per unit and the x axis quantities per unit of time, the scale on the x axis differs considerably between diagrams.

The firm's demand curve is actually an infinitesimal segment of D_I near output x_I stretched out over the firm's diagram. This area is circled in panel (b).

The typical firm, depicted in panel (a), is viewed as supplying this last small amount of the large quantity x_l, so that its demand curve appears horizontal to it. While this explanation is a plausible one for the infinite elasticity of demand for a competitive firm, the only explanation necessary is that the firm believes it can sell the total amount shown on the diagram at the prevailing price, and it can.

Figure 7–2 shows the firm and industry demand curves for all four market types. However, before examining this figure, a very brief review of the revenue concepts should prove helpful: (1) total revenue (TR) equals price (average revenue) times quantity, $TR = P \cdot Q$; (2) average revenue equals total revenue divided by quantity, $AR = TR/Q = PQ/Q = P$; and (3) marginal revenue is the change in total revenue resulting from a change in the quantity sold, $MR = \Delta TR/\Delta Q$. Furthermore, we know from Chapter 3 that $TR = AR \cdot Q$, $TR_n = \sum_{i=1}^{n} MR$, and $MR = AR + \dfrac{\Delta AR}{\Delta Q} Q$.

We can establish several important points from Figure 7–2. First, under perfect competition, price (AR) equals marginal revenue (MR). If a bushel of wheat sells at \$4, every additional bushel of wheat a farmer sells brings in

FIGURE 7–2 Firm and Industry Price Elasticity of Demand under Various Market Conditions

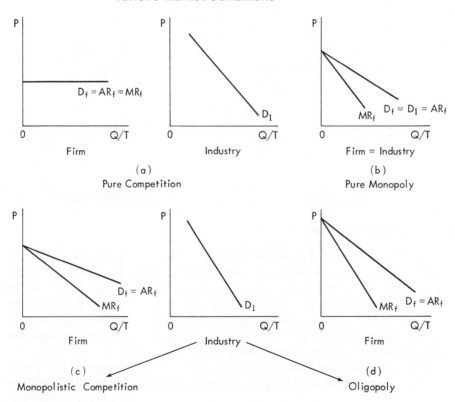

an additional $4 of revenue. This equality between *P* and *MR* will have important welfare implications later when we compare performance under competitive versus monopolistic markets.

Imperfect Competition

Secondly, Figure 7-2 illustrates that the demand schedule facing an imperfectly competitive firm is always downsloping and therefore less than perfectly elastic. This proposition may best be seen in the case of pure monopoly, which features but one seller. We know that all industry or market demand curves are downsloping, and since under pure monopoly the firm is the same as the industry, the firm's demand curve must therefore be downsloping and less than perfectly elastic. Furthermore, the fact that the *AR* schedule is downsloping necessarily means that the *MR* schedule falls faster. Thus, if an imperfectly competitive firm lowers its price to sell more units, the lower price will apply not only to the extra units sold but also to all prior units which otherwise could have been sold at a higher price.[3] In short, under (nondiscriminating) imperfect competition, price is always greater than marginal revenue.

Panels (c) and (d) in Figure 7-2 illustrate that while a monopolistically competitive firm and an oligopolistic firm are like a purely monopolistic firm in that their demand schedules are downsloping, they are different in that the firm is not identical with the industry. In the oligopoly case, each firm's output comprises a significant portion of total output, but it does not constitute the entire supply as in pure monopoly. In the case of monopolistic competition, the concept of an industry loses some meaning and most economists concentrate their analysis on the firm level. This is easy to understand. There is no unique equilibrium price or quantity to measure on the axes of an industry diagram. Each firm is in a sense a monopolist for the differentiated product it sells. Since these products are close, but not perfect, substitutes for one another, there is no rigorously precise way to draw industry curves, which require standardized units. Instead of a single price prevailing in the market at any given point in time, there may be a cluster of prices.

The demand curve facing a monopolistically competitive firm is expected to be highly elastic because of the relative freedom of entry and large number of close substitute products available. The precise degree of elasticity depends upon the numbers and proximity of rival sellers and on the degree of product differentiation, real or imagined, for the product. In contrast to a pure competitor, a monopolistic competitor changes the quality of the product and engages in persuasive advertising to create a difference in the customers' minds between the firm's product and that of competitors. This product differentiation, no matter how slight, means the demand schedule can never become horizontal. If a monopolistic competitor raises its price, it will not lose all its sales as would a pure competitor selling a standardized product.

---

[3] This assumes the inability to charge different prices to different buyers. Where such discrimination is possible, another analysis is required. This analysis is discussed in Chapter 14.

Oligopoly

As a first approximation, the oligopolistic firm's demand schedule would seem likely to stand somewhere between the rather inelastic demand schedule of the pure monopolist and the highly elastic demand schedule of the monopolistic competitor. It would have greater elasticity than the former and less than the latter. If so, this would form the continuum we suggested earlier, with the high to low range of elasticity for the firm's demand curve following the continuum of market structures from pure competition to pure monopoly.

Unfortunately, the symmetry of Figure 7–2 is not assured because of the complexity of an oligopoly market in practice. This complexity stems from two factors: (1) The oligopoly classification is a residual category embracing all industries not falling neatly into any of the other three. It includes industries with: (a) large and small numbers of firms, (b) differentiated and homogeneous products, (c) collusion and no collusion among firms, and (d) strong and weak barriers to entry. (2) Mutual interdependence usually causes uncertainty, which makes the economic actions of oligopolists difficult to predict.

Mutual interdependence is the distinguishing feature of oligopoly. This means that the precise position and shape of any oligopolist's demand curve will depend on the exact nature of the reactions of its rivals. If there is no known way to predict the behavior of rivals, the oligopolist's demand curve will be indeterminate. If a given oligopolist lowers its price, a rival can follow this cut to the last cent, follow it only partially, neglect it entirely, or counteract it by changing the product quality, product characteristics, advertising outlays, etc.[4]

At the other extreme, oligopolistic firms may get together and form a collusive cartel to maximize the joint profits of the industry. In essence, such an arrangement would bring us back to the pure monopoly model discussed earlier. Under a cartel arrangement, the industry demand curve becomes most important and any single firm's demand curve is no longer relevant.

One case of interdependence that produces a determinate solution occurs when the oligopolist feels that rivals will match any price cut but will not follow a price rise. This behavior produces a curve that is "kinked" at the current market price, being relatively inelastic at prices below this and elastic at prices above the going price.

---

[4] For this reason, some economists would argue that, in general, an oligopolistic demand curve does not exist. They argue as follows: The usual demand curve is drawn on the assumption that all other prices are constant. This assumption is not reasonable for an oligopolist. Therefore, the usual demand curve is not defined. The indeterminate case is more serious than this. The pure case of oligopoly is that firm A's demand curve depends on firm B's reaction to firm A's action. But that in turn depends on firm B's price demand curve which in turn depends on firm A's reactions to firm B's prices which in turn depend upon firm A's demand curve and so on, unless oligopolists behave and are thought to behave in very particular ways. It's not just a matter, they argue, of not knowing where the demand curve is. The problem is that the curve is not defined at all. This, they claim, is the central feature of homogeneous oligopoly.

Figure 7–3 illustrates a "kinked" demand curve. This curve is particularly convincing in explaining price rigidity in mature industries. Suppose the current market price is $0P$ and quantity for an oligopolistic firm is $0Q$. Above $0P$ the demand curve is highly elastic, reflecting the fact that the rivals are not expected to follow this firm's price increases. Thus, the oligopolist who initiates the price increase will be "priced out of the market" as customers turn to available close or even perfect substitutes. Below $0P$ the demand curve is relatively inelastic, reflecting the fact that rivals are expected to follow a price cut. Thus, no one firm within the industry can gain any advantage on intra-industry rivals. However, a lower price allows some increase in total industry sales. In that case, each firm would be likely to merely gain its proportionate share of the enlarged quantity demanded along the given industry demand curve.

FIGURE 7–3   The "Kinked" Oligopoly Demand Curve

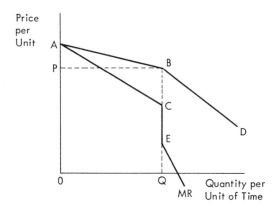

In other words, any single oligopolistic firm will not raise its price, because it expects its rivals will not follow suit (since the rivals will thereby gain increased demand). On the other hand, the firm will not lower its price, because it expects its rivals will follow its lead (since the rivals otherwise would suffer a loss in demand). Thus, unless some fundamental force changes either on the cost or demand side, such that all firms could be expected to act in concert, prices are not likely to change. While this kinked demand curve is a plausible explanation of the observed relative inflexibility of prices in oligopolistic markets, it doesn't explain why prices are what they are.

QUESTIONS

1. Explain the demand-side differences between a firm, an industry, and a market.
2. If a firm views itself as a price-taker, why are the conditions of perfect competition unnecessary for the competitive result?

3. What are the most important characteristics of a competitive market?
4. Explain why a single price would exist in a market for a homogeneous good. What would you do if you observed the price of wheat was $5 a bushel in St. Louis and $4 a bushel in Kansas City?
5. How does the demand situation for a monopolist differ from that of a firm in monopolistic competition?
6. Write an essay on the likelihood of inventions and innovations occurring under the different market structures.
7. "The kinked demand curve explains why oligopoly prices are rigid, but is of no help in explaining why the existing price is what it is." Explain.

SUPPLY—THE ANALYSIS OF PRODUCTION AND COST

Theory of Production

Chapters 4–7 investigated the determinants of demand. The next several chapters will do the same thing for the supply side. To this point it has only been suggested that costs of production help determine the shape and position of the supply curve. But underlying the costs of production are the technological production conditions facing the firm. In fact, the principles of production play a dual role in the determination of relative prices, helping to explain both product and factor prices. In the first case, the theory of production underlies the costs of production and supplies of particular goods. That is, production influences cost and cost influences supply, which together with demand determines product prices. The principles of production also provide a foundation for the analysis of a firm's demand for productive services. In general, the greater a resource's productivity, the greater the demand for it. The firm's demand for resources and the supplies of these resources determine resource prices.

Our explanation of the theory of the firm will parallel in many respects the theory of demand, since these two analyses have a great deal in common. Instead of an individual consumer, however, the individual firm becomes the center of attention. The behavioral assumptions of the two economic entities are similar. Consumers are presumed to act as if they are trying to maximize their satisfaction, and firms act [1] as if they are trying to maximize their profits.[2] In other words, the consumer tries to maximize utility for a given rate of consumption outlays, and the firm tries to maximize production for a given rate of cost outlays.

Of course, there are also differences in the two analyses. The subjective utility function in consumption analysis is replaced by the objective production

---

[1] Of course, since the firm is a technical unit in which goods and services are produced, it formally cannot "act"; but rather, the decision-maker or entrepreneur does. However, we shall retain the grammatical fiction that a firm "acts" for purposes of exposition.

[2] A later chapter will examine criticisms and alternatives to the assumption that firms make decisions such that profit will be as large as possible. For now, we make this assumption because: (1) some assumption about the motives of decision-makers must be made if the theory is to predict their actions; (2) numerous predictions based on this assumption have been confirmed by both casual and systematic observation; and (3) no alternative assumption has emerged that yields significantly better results.

function in production analysis. The latter, unlike the former, can be measured unambiguously with a cardinal measure (although it is sometimes very difficult to define the output, as in education for example). Furthermore, while a consumer's income is assumed fixed for any given period of time, the firm's possible outlays are variable, depending upon the planned level of output aimed at maximizing profits.

The two approaches used to explain the theory of production have their counterparts in those used to explain the theory of demand. The classical production function approach discussed in this chapter is analogous to the classical cardinal utility approach. The more recently developed isoquant analysis, the topic of the next chapter, is analogous to indifference curve analysis.

THE PRODUCTION FUNCTION

The concept of a *production function* summarizes the technical conditions facing the firm. It shows the functional relationship given by technology between a firm's physical rates of input and its physical rates of output per unit of time. For obvious economic reasons, it is defined only for nonnegative values of the factors and the output level. In general mathematical terms, a production function may be represented as follows:

$$q_i = f(a,b,c, \ldots , n) \tag{8.1}$$

where a, b, c, . . . , n represent quantities of the productive services per time period and q_i represents the quantity of output of the ith good per unit of time. (For simplicity, we will assume our firms produce a single homogeneous good.)

A number of important points must be stressed about this concept. First of all, "production" refers to the transformation of inputs into output. This output can take the form of services rendered—e.g., financial, retail, transportation, entertainment, etc.—as well as physical changes in matter—e.g., farming, or transforming steel, glass, etc., into an automobile.

Secondly, a production function is a flow concept. It relates flows of inputs with their resulting flows of output during some specified period of time. And the flow of the services of inputs, not merely the quantities of the inputs, is always relevant. It is the hours of human labor and machine-hours of capital, i.e., the flows of services, that are crucial. The outputs of other firms may be inputs to the firm being studied.

Thirdly, in some senses the production function concept is merely a physical, technological, or engineering concept; and yet it has an economic dimension to it. It is a technical relationship in that it relates only to physical units, not dollar units; and consulting engineers and other technical personnel gather the information, not economists, business consultants, etc. It has nothing to do with economics in that it concerns physical relations and leaves prices or economic valuations aside.

In another sense, the concept of a production function is more than just technological. It does not merely relate any combination of resources to levels of output. Rather, it is the technical relationship showing the maximum quantities of output that can be produced by each set of specified factors of production. Numerous possible or attainable levels of output correspond to each combination of inputs, but only this maximal level, rather than all possible levels of output, is of interest to the firm. For example, a production function for an automobile factory would show the maximum number of autos that can be produced per unit of time, say, 100 per day, given particular quantities of labor, steel, glass, rubber, etc. Many combinations of resources correspond to each level of output. For instance, it may take 5 minutes of labor and 5 minutes of milking machine time to produce one-half gallon of milk or, alternatively, it may take 20 minutes of labor without the use of the milking machine for the same output of milk. A production function can also be thought of as a minimum as well as a maximum concept. For example, the production function for the automobile manufacturer producing 100 autos per day shows the minimum quantities of labor, steel, glass, rubber, etc. that are required to produce the 100 autos.

Finally, for convenience, the assumption is often made in production analysis that factors can be separated into two categories: fixed and variable. A fixed factor, as contrasted to a variable factor, is often defined as one whose quantity cannot be quickly changed when market conditions indicate a need for a change in output. In fact, no factor is absolutely fixed in quantity no matter how short the time period. However, immediate variation of so-called "fixed" factors would cost so much that such a change would not be economically relevant. In other words, "fixity" is not a real world fact. It is a convenience for certain theoretical purposes.

Technical and Economic Efficiency

Suppose, to use a simplified illustration, that a firm produces a homogeneous product that uses only two productive services, capital and labor. Further assume that the state of technology is such that there are only four known ways to produce the desired output of 100 units per day. These alternatives are shown in Table 8–1.

TABLE 8–1 Technical and Economic Efficiency (Output of 100 Units Per Day)

	Quantity of Inputs Required	
	Capital	Labor
Method *A*	5	100
Method *B*	10	150
Method *C*	10	50
Method *D*	25	25

Which method should be used? To answer this question, we must distinguish between *technological* or *engineering efficiency,* which measures inputs in terms of physical units, and *economic efficiency,* which measures inputs in dollar terms. For any given output, the best process is the one that is technologically most efficient or, in other words, uses the least inputs (assuming positive values of inputs).

Method *B* in Table 8–1 is *technologically inefficient* because it is wasteful, using more of both inputs than method *A,* and can therefore be disregarded. The other three methods are all *technologically efficient,* since none uses less of both inputs than the others. Method *A* is capital saving and labor using relative to methods *C* and *D,* whereas method *C* is labor saving and capital using relative to method *A.* Method *D* is labor saving and capital using relative to methods *A* and *C.*

Principle of Substitution

Which of the technologically efficient methods is economically most efficient, involving the least sacrifice or cost to the firm, depends on factor prices. Try different factor prices, e.g., $3 or $4 for capital and $1 for labor, or the reverse, to demonstrate this. You will discover that economic efficiency dictates that the choice of production methods depends upon the relative factor prices.[3] Economists, following Alfred Marshall, the great English economist, refer to this idea as the *principle of substitution.* This principle merely states that, given the technological horizon (possibilities), economically efficient production will involve substituting cheaper factors for dearer ones when relative factor prices change. One of the economic realities that most intrigues students of price theory is the wide latitude over which this substitution can take place. It is particularly easy to underestimate the possible degree of substitution in manufactured goods. In agriculture, it is fairly easy to see how a farmer can substitute fertilizer, tractor time, additional land, etc., for labor to produce a bushel of wheat. But in manufacturing, many people seem to believe that inputs must be used in fixed proportions. Yet to take an extreme example, two apparently nonsubstitutable products like glass and sheet steel can be good substitutes over a wide range in automobile production if the designers merely vary the dimensions of the windows. As the relative price of sheet steel (glass) rises, they can design cars with bigger (smaller) windows. If house-building carpenters are told not to pick up nails that are dropped, nail input is being substituted for labor.

---

[3] More accurately, the relevant factor prices are expected future factor prices, or those that will prevail when the factors are actually used. If the firm is a monopsonist, which by definition influences input prices, or if it knows its prices are going to change because of influences beyond its control, it must consider future factor prices in making a decision. For example, the movement of the U.S. cotton textile industry from New England to the South, presumably to take advantage of the less expensive Southern labor, has resulted in scarcer and more expensive labor because of both the increased demand by new firms and the increased efforts to unionize the previously unorganized Southern labor market.

In other words, the behavioral assumption of profit maximization coupled with the principle of substitution allows us to predict that the production methods used tend to change as relative factor prices change. Since scarcer factors are usually high priced, relatively more of the abundant and cheaper factors will tend to be used and less of the relatively scarcer and more expensive ones. If this theory is correct, we can predict, e.g., that in countries (or regions of the U.S.) where lumber is relatively abundant and cheap, relatively more frame than brick houses will be constructed. Similarly, one would expect most products to be made with more labor (relative to land and capital) in Hong Kong than in the U.S.

Importance of Technology

A production function's form is determined by the state of technology. As the level of technology improves, the production function shifts, either showing a smaller flow of inputs for a given level of output or a larger flow of output for a given level of inputs. However, only in the very long run are the firm's technological possibilities subject to change.

The Time Element

This brings us to our final point about production functions, namely, that their shape and position depend upon the time period considered. The production function always involves a time element since some time is necessary for transferring from one production process to another. Thus, our earlier comment that the degree of substitutability between factors is usually quite high assumes that some transitional period of adjustment is allowed. In this connection we have already distinguished between the short run, where at least one input is fixed in supply to the firm, and the long run, where all inputs, including plant and equipment, are variables, but the state of technology is fixed. With an improved technology, equation (8.1) would become:

$$q = f^* (a,b,c, \ldots , n) \tag{8.2}$$

where f^* represents a different relation between inputs and outputs than f. A family of an infinite number of short-run production functions can be distinguished on the basis of: (1) which particular inputs are held constant; and (2) the level at which they are held constant. Suppose a and b are the only two factors participating in the production of the commodity, q, so that the production function can be written as:

$$q = f(a,b) \tag{8.3}$$

Then either a or b may be held constant and the other can be the variable input. For instance, one family of short-run production functions can be defined by making a a fixed factor and b a variable factor. Suppose a is held constant at level $\bar{a}_i$ (where $\bar{a}_i$ can be, say, 10 acres of land):

$$q = f(b) \mid a = \bar{a}_i \tag{8.4}$$

The functions of the family differ from each other according to the level at which a is held constant. For example, $a = \bar{a}_2$ would provide another production function with a held constant at, say, 25 acres of land. Similarly b can be held constant and a can vary.

$$q = f(a) \mid b = \bar{b}_i \tag{8.5}$$

where $\bar{b}_i$ can be set at various levels. Suppose the long-run production function were:

$$q = 100 \sqrt{ab} \quad \text{(or the same thing, } q = 100[ab]^{1/2}) \tag{8.6}$$

Fixing b, the short-run production function becomes:

$$q = k \sqrt{a} \tag{8.7}$$

where $k = 100 \sqrt{b}$. However, the precise relation between q and a depends on the level at which b is held constant. Since we have used a functional form involving square roots, four obvious numerical values that would satisfy equation (8.7) are:

$$
\begin{aligned}
q &= 100 \sqrt{a}, \text{ for } b = 1 \\
q &= 200 \sqrt{a}, \text{ for } b = 4 \\
q &= 300 \sqrt{a}, \text{ for } b = 9 \\
q &= 400 \sqrt{a}, \text{ for } b = 16
\end{aligned}
\tag{8.8}
$$

Cobb-Douglas Production Function

A famous statistical production relation, of which our illustration $q = 100 \sqrt{ab}$ is an example, is the *Cobb-Douglas production function*.[4] It is written:

$$q_i = A K^{\alpha} L^{\beta} \tag{8.9}$$

where q_i is the output of the ith good; L is the quantity of labor services; K is the quantity of capital services employed; and A, α $(0 < \alpha < 1)$ and β $(= 1 - \alpha)$ are positive, constant coefficients.[5] This function can be applied to a given sector of the economy, as Cobb and Douglas did to manufacturing, or to an entire economy. In U. S. manufacturing, it turned out that $\alpha = \frac{3}{4}$, $\beta = \frac{1}{4}$, which means that labor contributed about three quarters of increases in production and capital the remaining one quarter. Not only has the Cobb-Douglas function

---

[4] Named after its main proponents, the former Senator from Illinois, Paul H. Douglas, who was a distinguished economist before his tenure in the Senate, and Charles W. Cobb, a mathematician. See their "A Theory of Production," *American Economic Review* (March, 1928), pp. 139–165, and Paul H. Douglas, "Are There Laws of Production?" *American Economic Review* (March, 1948), pp. 1–41. Also, see Martin Bronfenbrenner and Paul H. Douglas, "Cross-section Studies in the Cobb-Douglas Function," *Journal of Political Economy* (December, 1939), pp. 761–785.

[5] Thus, in our illustration $q = 100 \sqrt{ab}$, $A = 100$, $\alpha = \frac{1}{2}$, and $\beta (= 1 - \alpha) = \frac{1}{2}$ (since $\sqrt{a}$ may be written as $\alpha^{1/2}$). A Cobb-Douglas production function is mathematically linear and homogeneous, or in economic terms it exhibits constant returns to scale.

provided good empirical results, but it has the desirable analytical properties of diminishing marginal productivity to all factors, constant returns to scale, and positive dependence. These properties are all discussed later in this chapter. (Another important property of the Cobb-Douglas production function is that it is consistent with Euler's theorem, which is discussed in a later chapter.)

SHORT-RUN PRODUCTION FUNCTIONS

To better understand the classical theory of production, it is convenient to divide the analysis into an investigation of short-run and long-run production functions. In the first instance, the law of proportionality (also called the law of variable proportions or the law of diminishing returns) is crucial in explaining the shape and position of the production function; whereas in the long run, the so-called law of returns to scale will be prominent. In other words, short-run analysis deals with the behavior of output as the *proportions* of productive services are varied. It says nothing about the effect on output of proportionate changes in the amount of resources employed by the firm. In contrast, the long-run analysis deals with changes in the *size* or *scale* of production rather than with changes in proportions.

Variable Proportions and the Law of Proportionality

In the short run, the *law of proportionality,* one of the oldest and most firmly established principles of economics, describes the rate of change of a firm's output in response to a change in one of the inputs, with one or more of the remaining inputs held constant. This law states that, *ceteris paribus,* as equal increments of one variable resource are applied to fixed amounts of other resources per unit of time, after a certain point the resulting increases in total output become smaller and smaller; i.e., the increase in output per unit change of the variable input will fall.

In what will later be described as the economically relevant region, total output will always increase in response to an increase in one of the inputs. Thus, it is not total output itself that diminishes, but rather the size or the rate of the increases in total output. Only under extreme conditions would total product actually diminish from the application of additional inputs.

The reason the term "law of proportionality" or "law of variable proportions" is preferred to the term "law of diminishing returns" (*LDR*) is twofold. First, as will be discussed shortly, the term *LDR* is ambiguous since it is not clear whether the total, average, or marginal value is declining. And unfortunately, it is the least important of these laws, the total version, that often gets into the newspaper. Secondly, the names involving some derivative of the word "proportions" are preferred since they are more descriptive of the essence of the phenomenon. The fundamental explanation for the operation of this law is that the proportions among the inputs are being varied. The returns diminish because the factor that is being increased—the variable factor—has progressively less and less of the other factor—the fixed factor—to work with. For instance, as more and more laborers are added to a fixed amount of land (and capital), less and less land (and capital) are available per worker. If one input is fixed and the other is increased, the proportions between the inputs are obviously changed. If the ratio between labor and land is originally one-to-one (i.e., each laborer hired has one unit of land on which to work), as the number of laborers increases and the quantity of land remains constant, the ratio declines. If one input increases by 100 percent and the other by 50 percent, the proportions are also varied. However, for convenience the text's discussion for the most part will be limited to the more easily understood cases of varying proportions in which one input is held fixed.

Qualifications of the Law of Proportionality

The qualification *"ceteris paribus"* in the definition of the law of proportionality is important. It emphasizes that the phenomenon assumes that the only change is in the proportions between the inputs. Such things as the state of technology, the quality of the inputs, the quantities of the fixed inputs, and the social and economic organization are all assumed unchanged.

The phrase "per unit of time" reminds us that the hypothesis really is not concerned with what would result from the chronological application of additional quantities of input. For purposes of exposition, we will assume that first one worker is hired, then the second, and so on. In reality the law of proportionality describes a set of alternatives. It shows the results of using alternative amounts of a variable input with constant amounts of other inputs. It says if a firm hires, say, three workers, total output will be 100 units; whereas if it instead hires four workers, total production will be 125 units, and so on. The statement "after a certain point" in the law of proportionality reminds us that the firm may experience an increasing range of productivity before the diminishing phase sets in.

Wherever the law of proportionality refers to increasing the units of the variable input, say, labor, it assumes these workers are equally skilled and vigorous—i.e., they are homogeneous from an economic standpoint. Diminishing returns are not due to the employment of successively less and less efficient workers (though that could also happen), but rather they are due to people of equal ability being employed in a less efficient combination. Nor is the diminishing rate of increase of total product caused by ignorance or mistakes of the entrepreneurs; the rate would diminish even if they were omniscient, as long as factor proportions vary.

Three Ways of Looking at Variable Proportions

As has already been suggested, we can state the law of proportionality in terms of the behavior of any one of three product curves—total, average, or marginal. Popular discussions of economic questions often allude to the "point of diminishing returns." However, any such allusion will be ambiguous unless it refers specifically to total, average, or marginal returns. As we will demonstrate, each of these three points almost invariably involves a different quantity of the variable input. Therefore, in referring to this law, one should specify the relevant version whenever confusion could possibly result without such specification.

Average product is found, as is any average value, by dividing the total value (a sum) by the number of units of the variable in question. The average product of a resource is the total product divided by the number of units of that resource. Outputs and resources are measured per unit of time, and the term "resource" (factor, productive service, input) is a shorthand notation for flows of services, worker-hours, land-hours, or machine-hours. For example, if 100 person-years of labor cultivating 100 acres of land produce 1,000 bushels of wheat, the average product of a worker-year of labor is 10 bushels of wheat, and the average product of an acre of land is 10 bushels of wheat per year. We will hereafter refer to the average product of input a as APP_a, for average *physical* product of a. Symbolically, it can be represented by:

$$APP_a = TPP/Q_a \tag{8.10}$$

where TPP is the total physical product and Q_a the quantity of input a. The expression emphasizes that the output described is in physical terms—bushels, pounds, etc.—and not in dollar values.

The *marginal physical product* of a factor is the change in the total physical product resulting from a very small change in the quantity of the factor when all other inputs are held constant. Formally, the marginal physical product of factor a is:

$$MPP_a = \Delta TPP/\Delta Q_a \tag{8.11}$$

where ΔTPP is the change in total output and ΔQ_a is the change in the (flow) amount of the service of factor a, assuming factors b, c, and so on are held constant.

To illustrate the computation of the MPP_a, suppose the addition of an extra worker-year of labor results in an increase in the total production of wheat from 1,000 to 1,050 bushels. The extra 50 bushels of wheat are the marginal product of a worker-year of labor.

A Tabular Illustration. We can illustrate the law of proportionality both numerically and graphically. Suppose a certain farm has 100 acres of land, together with a fixed amount of capital in the form of buildings, farm machinery and equipment, services, fertilizers, and seed. The farmer must decide how many workers to hire on the basis of the technologically given productivity figures shown in Table 8–2. This table depicts the physical output of wheat, measured in bushels, resulting from the application of various alternative quantities of labor, assuming the other factors are held fixed at what can be called one unit. Diminishing marginal returns begin with the fourth unit of labor, diminishing average returns begin with the fifth unit of labor, and diminishing total returns begin with the ninth unit of labor. The constant value (in this case

TABLE 8-2   **Law of Proportionality (or Law of Diminishing Returns)**

(1) Worker-Years of Labor	(2) Total Output of Wheat Per Year TPP (in Bushels) [(1) × (3) or Σ(4)]	(3) Average Physical Product of Labor APP_L (in Bushels) [(2)/(1)]	(4) Marginal Physical Product of Labor MPP_L (in Bushels) [Δ(2)/Δ(1)]	
0	0	0	0 ⎫	
1	500	500	500 ⎪	
2	1,500	750	1,000 ⎬ Stage 1	
3	3,000	1,000	1,500 ⎪	
4	4,000	1,000	1,000 ⎭	
5	4,800	960	800 ⎫	
6	5,400	900	600 ⎪ Stage 2	
7	5,600	800	200 ⎬	
8	5,600	700	0 ⎭	
9	5,500	611	−100 ⎫ Stage 3	
10	5,300	530	−200 ⎭	

the maximum value) of the average occurs at the fourth unit of labor, at which point the marginal product equals the average product. We will demonstrate the reason for this equality later.

The initial stage of increasing average and marginal returns results from using a very inefficient ratio of the variable to the fixed input. Too little of the variable resource, labor, is being employed with a given quantity of land. The variable factor is spread so thin that additional units of it cause total output to increase at an increasing rate. Eventually, however, diminishing returns to both the average and the marginal products set in. Finally, the quantity of the variable input increases to such an extent that it reduces the efficiency of the previous units, resulting in an actual decline in output. In Table 8-2, the total physical product continues to rise up to seven worker-years of labor; but beginning with the ninth unit, the fixed factor, land, becomes so inadequate relative to the variable factor, labor, that negative returns—a negative MPP_L —set in. To take an extreme case, if so little of the fixed resource, say, land, is available that an additional worker merely bumps into the other workers and thereby reduces their output by more than the added worker's contribution, total output declines after the employment increase.

Two Economically Irrelevant Regions. There are two regions that we know the entrepreneur will avoid. Insofar as possible, a firm will never operate in a region where any factor has a negative marginal physical product. Beyond eight units of labor, the total output declines because of the superabundance of labor. Even if labor costs nothing, no one would hire workers with a negative *MPP*.

A firm could get into the uneconomical range because the quantities of some factors are outside its control or because the factors are sometimes indivisible. Let us postpone the second reason for now and consider only the first. If the firm cannot control the quantities of some factors of production, it could end up in the negative-returns stage. For instance, in the illustration given in Table 8–2, suppose the firm had its choice of using zero labor units or ten labor inputs. While the total physical product is only 5,300 with ten units of labor ($MPP_L = -200$), whereas if the firm used only, say, eight worker-hours of labor it could produce more (5,600 bushels of wheat), the firm may still prefer to use ten units of labor if faced with a "ten-units-or-nothing" alternative. Depending upon the price of labor and wheat, the firm is very likely to be better off with ten units of labor than with zero (or even more, say, 2, 3, 4, etc.) units of labor. While a firm might be required to hire, own, or purchase a particular quantity of some factor because of government regulations, union agreements, or certain other circumstances, the firm would often not have to use all of that factor. For example, while railroads were required to employ firemen on diesel engines, such workers were not involved in the production of railroad service.

The other region a firm will avoid, in addition to the range where the *MPP* of the variable input is negative, is the range where the marginal physical product of the fixed input is negative. In other words, a firm will avoid a region where the *APP* of the variable factor (labor) is increasing. For reasons demonstrated below, the range of increasing average physical product for one factor necessarily coincides with negative marginal physical product for the other factor.[6] It is this fact that gives the paradoxical result that something seemingly desirable, like increasing average physical product, turns out to be something to avoid.

To see why a firm will have an incentive to expand beyond the stage where the *APP* of labor is rising, note that a stage of increasing *APP* can be translated into a stage of falling average cost. Suppose we have a profit-maximizing firm, say, a wheat farmer. Profits per unit equal the selling price minus the average cost of production. If a bushel of wheat sells for $1 and the average cost is $.75, a profit of $.25 is made on each unit sold. If 100 units are sold, the total profits are $25. Since our wheat farmer is assumed to be a pure competitor in

---

[6] The equivalence between increasing *APP* for one factor and negative *MPP* for the other is necessarily valid only for a production function that exhibits constant returns to scale, i.e., is homogeneous of the first degree.

the output market, any output can be sold at the given market price of $1. Therefore, whenever average costs are falling, output per unit and more importantly total profits can be increased by expanding output. For example, if average cost falls to $.50 per unit when sales are at the rate of 200 units, total profits are $100 = ($1.00 − $.50)200. Total profits are larger since both the profit "margin" has increased (from $.25 to $.50 per unit) and output has expanded (from 100 to 200 units). Since we assume firms always attempt to maximize total profits, they will never cease production when average returns (costs) are increasing (decreasing), since profits must be rising in that range. In other words, an entrepreneur will never employ the variable factor in the range where *APP* is increasing because a rising *APP* for the variable factor necessarily means a negative marginal physical product for the fixed factor. The fixed factor, land, is so superabundant relative to the variable factor, labor, that total output will actually increase if some land is allowed to lie fallow. For example, three cowhands will produce a greater total output if they try to work a 50-acre spread than if they try to work an enormous area such as the King Ranch.

One factor's average returns often increase because the other factor is indivisible. Suppose our wheat farmer can buy tractors of only two sizes, large and small, where the large tractor is twice the size of the small one. For some given amount of land and labor, the total product with the large tractor may be less than with the small tractor because the large one tramples down more wheat in turning corners than the small one. In this case the large tractor has a negative *MPP,* whereas land exhibits an increasing *APP.* Yet if the large tractor is the minimum size available, the farmer will still want to purchase it rather than do things by hand. Although the farmer in these circumstances would like to throw "half" the tractor away, it is, of course, not physically possible to do so.

In addition to the above case, where it is physically not possible to dispense with some of the indivisible input and hence the firm may operate in the range of increasing *APP,* is the circumstance where it costs something to reduce the use of a factor. If there are such disposal costs, it is also possible that the firm would produce in the so-called "uneconomic" range rather than incur such costs.

A Graphic Illustration. The law of variable proportions may be seen in Figure 8–1, which is a smoothed-out version of data similar to that of Table 8–2. Figure 8–1 shows what would happen to the *TPP* and to the *MPP* and *APP* of labor if the factors were not increased proportionately. However, this figure assumes that if the factors were increased proportionately, the output would increase proportionately. If, for instance, all inputs were doubled, output would double. Such a production function is said to be linear and homogeneous (homogeneous of the first degree) or, in economists' terms, a "constant-returns-to-scale" production function. These production function concepts are developed in detail below. Suffice it to say now that stage 2 of production, emphasized in the following pages, is uniquely defined only for a linear and

FIGURE 8-1 Three Stages of Production

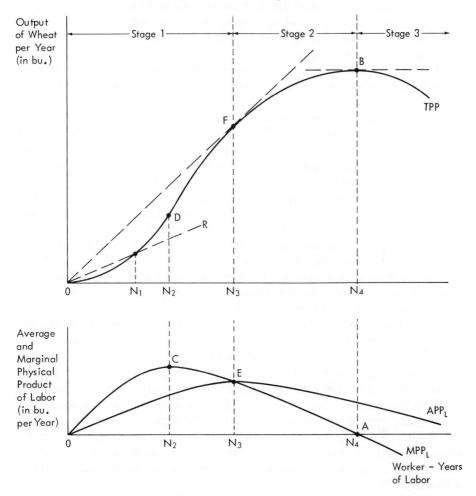

homogeneous production function. To repeat, Figure 8-1 shows what would happen to the total, average, and marginal products of the inputs if they were not changed in equal proportions, assuming that if they were changed proportionately, output would change proportionately.

The vertical axes measure output, which in this case is bushels of wheat. This is output per unit of labor for the average and marginal curves and total output for the total curve. The horizontal axes measure the flow of labor services divided by the (constant) flow of land services. Reading these axes from left to right, the ratio of labor to land is increasing.

The total product rises at an increasing rate up to point D (N_2 units of labor) and at a decreasing rate to its maximum value at point B (N_4 units of labor) and declines beyond that point. The APP_L and MPP_L curves are derived from the TPP curve. Since the $APP_L = TPP/Q_L$, the slope of any ray out of the origin to any point on the *TPP* curve measures the APP_L. For instance, in Figure 8–1, ray OR measures the *APP* of N_1 units of labor. Up to N_3 units of labor the slope of the ray out of the origin, $TPP/Q_L = APP_L$, is increasing. The APP_L reaches its maximum at point *F* on the *TPP* curve or at point *E* on the APP_L curve and declines after that.

The MPP_L curve is derived by computing the value of the slope of the *TPP* curve at each point. Point *A* on the MPP_L curve or point *B* on the *TPP* curve represents the point where the slope of the *TPP* curve or the MPP_L is zero and *TPP* is at its maximum. In the range to the left of point *A*, an additional worker has a positive MPP_L and hence must increase total output if hired. This is not to say that it is economically prudent to hire the worker. But it is true that the total physical volume of output will increase whenever a factor with a positive MPP_L is added. To the right of point *A*, an additional worker's output is negative and thus must decrease *TPP* if employed. The MPP_L curve reaches its maximum value at point *C*, which corresponds on the *TPP* curve to inflection point *D*, where the change from concave upward to concave downward occurs. The law of diminishing marginal returns therefore is operative after point *C* (or *D*), associated with N_2 units of labor.

The *TPP* curve in Figure 8–1 has been drawn out of the origin. While this is considered the most likely possibility, the *TPP* curve could begin either above or to the right of the origin. The *TPP* curve would begin above the origin if the input measured on the *x* axis was not indispensable to the production measured on the *y* axis. For instance, a positive *TPP* of wheat could be produced with a zero quantity of an input such as fertilizer. On the other hand, *TPP* might be zero even after the application of several units of the input if a certain threshold level of inputs is required to obtain any output. For instance, for a professional baseball team to perform, a certain minimum number of labor inputs, nine, are necessary before the *TPP* becomes positive.

The law of diminishing total returns becomes operative after point *B* (or *A*), associated with N_4 units of labor. Stage 3 encompasses from N_4 units of labor on, in a rightward direction, where *TPP* is declining and the MPP_L is negative.

The law of diminishing average returns begins after point *E* (or *F*), associated with N_3 units of labor. From the total-average-marginal relationships, we know the MPP_L and the APP_L are closely associated. It can be proved that: (1) whenever the APP_L is increasing (decreasing), the $MPP_L > APP_L$ ($MPP_L < APP_L$); and (2) whenever the APP_L is at a maximum, $MPP_L = APP_L$. Thus, the average-marginal relations state that if we are given information on the direction (rising, falling, constant) of the average value, we can state something definite about the position (above, below, or equal to) of the marginal value relative to the average value. For instance, in Figure 8–1, the APP_L is rising from 0 to *E*, so we know the MPP_L is above the APP_L in this range. Note, however, we cannot say that the MPP_L is rising (or falling, or anything about its direction); in fact, from *C* to *E*, the MPP_L is falling, yet the APP_L is rising since $MPP_L > APP_L$.

Stage 1 is the area from the origin to point E (or F). In this stage the APP_L of labor is increasing, whereas land has a negative marginal physical product. Stage 2 begins after point E (or F) and continues to point A (or B). In this stage both inputs have positive but declining marginal and average products. In stage 3, beginning after point A (or B), the marginal physical product of labor is negative and the average physical product of land is increasing.

In summary, then, when the production function is linearly homogeneous, except for a few trivial exceptions, an economical combination of factor inputs will always occur in stage 2. The exact volume and quantity of inputs that will be hired within stage 2 depend on relative prices, as we will demonstrate shortly.

Profit-Maximizing Conduct

The law of proportionality that is relevant for economics concerns not average or total returns but marginal returns. If we assume that the prices of all factors of production are positive, the relevant economic range of production for the firm is the region in which all marginal products are positive and declining. If any factor is employed where its MPP is negative, using less of that factor will increase TPP. If MPP is not declining, the firm's incremental costs are not rising as output expands, and it will benefit the firm to expand output to enhance profits. Thus, profit maximization requires that the MPP of each factor be positive and declining.

We can therefore demonstrate in Figure 8–1 that the precise number of laborers hired will be between points F (E) and B (A), involving from N_3 to N_4 units of labor. Business decision-makers will not hire more than N_4 workers since the MPP_L would be negative. Nor will they employ fewer than N_3 workers since the average physical output of labor is rising, which means that the marginal physical product of land is negative and hence greater total profits can be made by expanding output and the employment of inputs. Just where the final position will be depends upon the prices of inputs and the market price of the output. The cheaper the labor (land), the closer the firm will be to point $A(E)$, where the MPP of labor (land) is zero. Only in the extreme case of zero input prices would any employer be at either boundary line of stage 2 rather than within it. We can generalize from this conclusion that the greater the relative scarcity of any factor, the higher its marginal productivity and, therefore, the higher its earnings. This is simply an application of the general economic law that, other things being equal, the smaller the supply of any good or service, the higher its price.

The commonsense version of the principle of proportionality, which so far has only been discussed in terms of a single firm, can be applied to a national economy as a whole. For instance, one reason why the real wages in the United States are so high compared to underdeveloped countries like China and India is that in the United States the working population is very small compared to the quantity of capital and land available, whereas in China and India the labor force is very large compared to the supply of capital and land. The result is that in the United States capital-intensive methods of production tend to be used and wages are relatively high, whereas in China and India labor-intensive techniques are predominant and wages are relatively low.

Factor Symmetry of Stages 1 and 3

We can demonstrate the interfactoral symmetry in stages 1 and 3 for a constant-returns-to-scale production function. That is, stage 1 for labor is stage 3 for land and stage 1 for land is stage 3 for labor. Or in general, stage 1 for one input is stage 3 for some other input and vice versa. As will be developed more fully in a moment, factor symmetry means in stage 1 the low variable-fixed-factor ratio produces a positive *MPP* for the variable factor and a negative one for the other factor, whereas in stage 3 the high variable-fixed-factor ratio yields a negative *MPP* for the variable factor and a positive *MPP* for the other factor.

To demonstrate factor symmetry, we will assume that the production function is mathematically linear and homogeneous. Since we will discuss the long-run production function and returns to scale in some detail later, suffice it to say now that such a production function means that proportionate changes in the two inputs will produce proportionate changes in *TPP*. For example, if 100 units of output can be produced with 2 units of labor and 1 unit of land, then 200 units of output can be produced with 4 units of labor and 2 units of land, and 50 units of output can be produced with 1 unit of labor and $\frac{1}{2}$ unit of land. With such a production function, only factor proportions, not the absolute factor amounts, determine the output per "dose" of the factors. It is useful to be able to separate the short-run proportionality effects from the long-run scale effects.

In Table 8–3 the ratio of labor to land is increasing from top to bottom (see column 3), and the ratio of land to labor is increasing from bottom to top (see column 9). The maximum quantity of labor is assumed to be ten units and of land one unit. The last entry in column 3 shows the full ten units of labor being used with one unit of land. This ratio of 10 to 1 is the same as if $\frac{1}{10}$ unit of land were used with one unit of labor; hence the entry $\frac{1}{10} = (\frac{1}{10})/1$ in column 9. Moving up from bottom to top, the ratio five units of labor per unit of land is the same as $\frac{1}{5}$ of a unit of land per unit of labor, and so on until the ratio one-to-one is reached at the top.

Since columns 1–6 in Table 8–3 are the same as in Table 8–2, we will skip the explanation of them. Columns 7–9 have already been explained. We will therefore concentrate on determining *TPP, MPP,* and *APP* for land. First, the last entry in column 10, 530, was computed as follows: Since we know from column 4 that 10 units of labor combined with 1 unit of land produces 5,300 units of output, $\frac{1}{10}$ of a unit of labor coupled with 1 unit of land should produce a *TPP* of $\frac{5,300}{10}$ or 530 units. Similarly, since the labor/land ratio 5 to 1 yields a *TPP* of 4,800, the land/labor ratio of $\frac{1}{5}$ to 1 should produce $\frac{4,800}{5} = 960$ units of output.

TABLE 8-3   Factor Symmetry

(1) Labor	(2) Land	(3) Labor/Land	(4) Total Physical Product (Land = 1 unit)	(5) Marginal Physical Product of Labor	(6) Average Physical Product of Labor	(7) Land	(8) Labor	(9) Land/Labor	(10) Total Physical Product (Labor = 1 unit)	(11) Marginal Physical Product of Land	(12) Average Physical Product of Land
1	1	1	500	500	500	1	1	1	500	−500	500
2	1	2	1,500	1,000	750	$1/2$	1	$1/2$	750	−1,500	1,500
3	1	3	3,000	1,500	1,000	$1/3$	1	$1/3$	1,000	0	3,000
4	1	4	4,000	1,000	1,000	$1/4$	1	$1/4$	1,000	800	4,000
5	1	5	4,800	800	960	$1/5$	1	$1/5$	960	1,800	4,800
6	1	6	5,400	600	900	$1/6$	1	$1/6$	900	4,200	5,400
7	1	7	5,600	200	800	$1/7$	1	$1/7$	800	5,600	5,600
8	1	8	5,600	0	700	$1/8$	1	$1/8$	700	6,403	5,600
9	1	9	5,500	−100	611	$1/9$	1	$1/9$	611	7,290	5,500
10	1	10	5,300	−200	530	$1/10$	1	$1/10$	530	5,300	5,300

Column (6) Average Physical Product of Labor: Stage 1 (500, 750, 1,000); Stage 2 (1,000, 960, 900, 800); Stage 3 (700, 611, 530).

Column (12) Average Physical Product of Land: Stage 3 (500, 1,500, 3,000); Stage 2 (4,000, 4,800, 5,400, 5,600); Stage 1 (5,600, 5,500, 5,300).

1 unit of land = 100 acres.

The *MPP* schedule for land shown in column 11 is computed as follows: We know that the *MPP* of land equals, by definition, the change in *TPP* per full unit change in land—i.e., the *MPP* of land $= \Delta TPP/\Delta Q_{Land}$. For example, since the first $\frac{1}{10}$ of a unit of land increases *TPP* from zero to 530 units, the *MPP* of land is $530 \div \frac{1}{10} = 5,300$. (Substituting, $\Delta TPP = 530$, $\Delta Q_{Land} = \frac{1}{10}$.) Similarly, an increase in land from $\frac{1}{5}$ to $\frac{1}{4}$ of a unit increases *TPP* from 960 to 1,000. Thus, $\Delta TPP = 40$, $\Delta Q_{Land} = \frac{1}{20}$, so that the *MPP* of land $= (40)/(\frac{1}{20}) = 800$.

Finally, column 12 shows the *APP* of land, defined as $\dfrac{TPP}{Q_{land}}$. At the bottom of this column, we get $\dfrac{530}{\frac{1}{10}} = 5,300$. Or at the $\frac{1}{5}$ ratio, we find the *TPP* of land is 960, so that the *APP* of land is $960 \div \frac{1}{5} = 4,800$.

It is left to the reader to prove that the *TPP* using one unit of land is the same as the *APP* of land using one unit of labor—i.e., column 4 = column 12. Similarly, the *APP* of labor using one unit of land gives the same values as the *TPP* using one unit of labor—i.e., column 6 = column 10.

Least-Cost or Maximum Output

Previously we indicated that the precise proportions in which the inputs should be hired depends on their relative prices. In this section we will demonstrate this, assuming competition prevails in both the input and output markets and that there are only two inputs, *A* and *B*.[7] We shall further assume that the firm would like to obtain a given amount of output for the least possible cost or, in other words, it strives to obtain the largest possible output from a given cost outlay. Finally, we assume that Table 8–4 gives the firm's technical production possibilities for producing commodity *x*.

The maximum total product that can be produced from given expenditures or given cost outlays on factors is at the point at which the ratios of the marginal productivities of the different factors to their prices are equal. That is, when at an optimum the *MPP* obtained from spending the last dollar on all factors must be the same. Symbolically, this condition can be stated as follows:

$$\frac{MPP_A}{P_A} = \frac{MPP_B}{P_B} = \ldots = \frac{MPP_N}{P_N} = \lambda \tag{8.12}$$

where $P_A, P_B, \ldots, P_N$ are all the prices of inputs and λ represents the *MPP* of money on a dollar's worth of output. If condition (8.12) is met, the quantity of output obtained from an additional dollar's worth of cost outlays on one

---

[7] Note that we are only concerned at this stage of the analysis with determining the correct ratio or proportion of inputs to hire, not with the scale or absolute amounts. It may be that a firm would employ labor and land in the ratio of 2 to 1. However, another question that we ultimately must answer is one of scale. Later we shall discover that the absolute amounts of inputs to hire will be determined by the location of the profit-maximizing output position. Using inputs in the correct proportion will give the firm the least cost for producing any output. But the firm is not interested in producing just any output, but only in producing the profit-maximizing output. In other words, condition (8.12) below must always be met for all variable inputs; but it is attained for all inputs, fixed and variable, only at one point.

TABLE 8-4   Production Function for Commodity x

Factor A (Physical Units)	MPP_A (Units of x)	Factor B (Physical Units)	MPP_B (Units of x)
1	60	1	38
2	52	2	34
3	44	3	30
4	32	4	28
5	22	5	26
6	16	6	22
7	8	7	16
8	2	8	8

Assume $P_A = \$2$, $P_B = \$1$, cost outlay = $15, and $\Delta MPP_B / \Delta Q_A = 0$.

variable factor (or λ) will exactly equal that obtained from an additional dollar spent on any other factor. Marshall referred to condition (8.12) as the "principle of substitution," since if it is not met, total output can be increased with a given amount of cost outlays by purchasing more of the relatively cheap factor(s) and less of the relatively dear factor(s).

In Table 8-4, the least-cost combination of factors as formulated in condition (8.12) involves four units of A and seven units of B when $P_A = \$2$, $P_B = \$1$, and the firm's given expenditures are $15. This analysis provides an exact analogue to the MU analysis of Chapter 4. Thus, we will say very little as to why the ratio A/B of $4/7$, involving an MPP per dollar of 16, is optimal.

Three Possible Interrelationships Among Factors

The numerical example in Table 8-4 assumes the factors are independent, i.e., that $\Delta MPP_B / \Delta Q_A = 0$. The same kind of definition of complements, substitutes, and independent commodities that was used in consumption analysis can be used in production analysis. Thus, the following definitions can be made:

$$\frac{\Delta MPP_B}{\Delta Q_A} \begin{array}{l} > 0 \text{ gross complementary inputs} \\ = 0 \text{ gross unrelated or independent inputs} \\ < 0 \text{ gross substitute inputs} \end{array} \qquad \text{(8.13)}$$

The word "gross" is included because this definition includes both substitution and output effects, whereas "net" relations involve only the substitution effect. The *substitution effect* refers to the fact that even if output were kept constant, when the relative prices of inputs change, lower priced inputs would be substituted for higher priced ones. The *output* (or *expansion*) *effect* refers to the fact that as an input's price is lowered, (marginal) costs for any given output are also lowered, and a firm will want to expand its output and hence its input usage.

Typically, factors are gross substitutes the longer the time period involved, since an increase in the quantity of A usually leads to a decrease in the MPP_B

(and hence in the demand for B). For instance, the rise in labor costs in the U. S. has historically led to the development of labor-saving machinery and the substitution of capital for labor. In turn, generally a drop in the price of labor will lead to an increase in its usage and a decline in the demand for capital in order for the firm to reach the least-cost point. However, this substitution effect can be offset wholly or in part by an accompanying output effect. A lower price of labor means lower (marginal) costs and a higher equilibrium level of output. A larger output necessitates more inputs and a greater demand for all ("normal") factors, including machinery. The net effect of the decline in the price of labor on the demand for machinery depends upon the relative magnitudes of these two effects. As in the commodity market, the substitution effect normally is considerably larger than the output effect.

If the inputs are gross complements in that they are used in relatively fixed proportions, the lower price of, say, computers is associated with an increased productivity and demand for computer programmers, operators, key punchers, etc. The results are unambiguous in this case. Both the substitution and the output effects are in the same direction. In general, the longer the time period, the more likely any complementary input is to change to a substitute input.

We made the assumption of independence in Table 8–4, strictly for convenience, and it in no way invalidates the end result.[8] To illustrate this, suppose that the $MPP_A/P_A > MPP_B/P_B$ so that the firm would be tempted to use more A and less B. Furthermore, assume that there is a positive dependence between the MPP_A and Q_B and between the MPP_B and Q_A—i.e., that the factors are gross complements. That is, the MPP_A, for example, is greater—i.e., the MPP_A curve shifts rightward—as more of the other factors (represented by Q_B) are used. Therefore, as expenditures are transferred from factor B to factor A, the MPP_A declines: (1) because of the law of diminishing marginal productivity along the given MPP_A curve; and (2) because of complementarity, the smaller Q_B shifts the entire MPP_A curve downward. Alternatively, the MPP_B is larger: (1) because, following the law of diminishing marginal productivity, less B means a greater MPP_B; and (2) because of the positive dependence, the larger Q_A shifts the MPP_B curve upward. This process is illustrated in Figure 8–2(a), where, when Q_A increases from A_1 to A_2, the MPP_A falls from $MPP_{A(B=B_1)}$ to $MPP_{A(B=B_2)}$ as a result of the combined effects of a movement along a downward-sloping MPP_A curve and a shift downward of the entire MPP_A curve. Both the law of diminishing marginal productivity and positive dependence explain the new level of marginal physical product. Exactly the reverse process is simultaneously occurring for factor B, as shown in Figure 8–2(b).

If there were no such positive dependence between factors and if there were constant or increasing MPPs, entrepreneurs would use only one factor (monomania in the factor market). For example, if the $MPP_A/P_A > MPP_B/P_B$

---

[8] As in demand analysis, the possibility of output effects does make the definitions given here less precise. Strictly speaking, net complementarity and substitutability deal only with the substitution effect. That is, they are strictly defined only for a fixed output. If only two factors are employed in producing a certain product, they cannot be net complements, since more of both labor and machinery would entail a larger output, which violates the assumption of a fixed output.

FIGURE 8-2 **Diminishing Marginal Productivity and Positive Dependence**

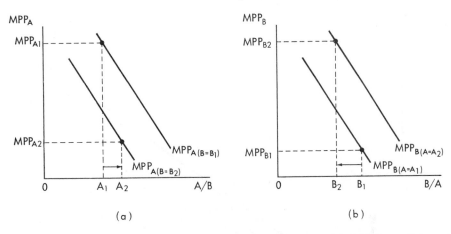

(a)   (b)

and if the MPP_A and MPP_B were constant, the firm would shift its entire cost outlays to input A.

VARYING THE "FIXED" FACTOR

Much of this chapter has dealt with the short-run situation, where we arbitrarily hold constant a certain category of factors of production and observe how output changes as we vary another factor. We extend the analysis in this section to observe the impact on output of changes in the "fixed" factor. Figure 8-3 graphs output as a function of resource input x when the other factor is y_1 and when y_1 is doubled to $2y_1$. These are drawn for the linear homogeneous case.

When the "fixed" factor is y_1, output is Q_1 if the "variable" factor is x_1. When the "variable" factor is doubled to $2x_1$ and the "fixed" factor is doubled to $2y_1$, total output doubles to $2Q_1$. The same is true for any other point x. The particular points x_1, Q_1 and $2x_1$, $2Q_1$ happen to be the points where the APP of the variable factor x is a maximum for both production functions; and note very carefully that the maximum values of the APPs equal each other, as seen in the lower graph. This is clearly the case since ray $0R$ is the ray with the greatest angle that can touch either production function.

Another point of some interest is at x_0 use of the "variable" factor. Since the total physical product is the same, APP_x is the same; but only half as much of the "fixed" factor is being used on the $TPP_{y=y1}$ production function.

Figure 8-4(a) shows a more complete linear homogeneous production relation. Constant returns to scale are exhibited in such a function. The number of short-run production functions possible depends only on the divisibility of factor y. Figures 8-4(b) and 8-4(c) portray increasing and decreasing returns to scale, respectively. The maximum APPs of the "variable" factor increase as the two factors increase in Figure 8-4(b) and decrease in Figure

FIGURE 8–3 **Production Functions with Different Amounts of the "Fixed" Factor**

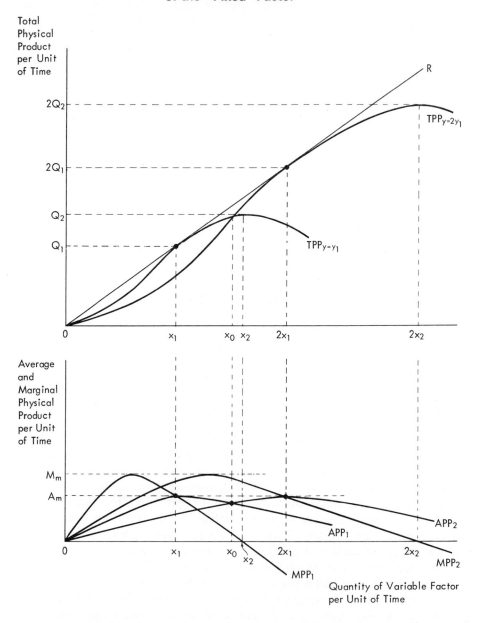

8–4(c). Increasing returns to scale means that if all factors are increased by a given percentage, output will increase by more than that percentage. Decreasing returns implies that if all factors are increased by a given percentage, output will increase by less than that percentage. This means that the average physical product of the factors increases with increasing returns and decreases with decreasing returns.

FIGURE 8-4 Long-Run Production Functions

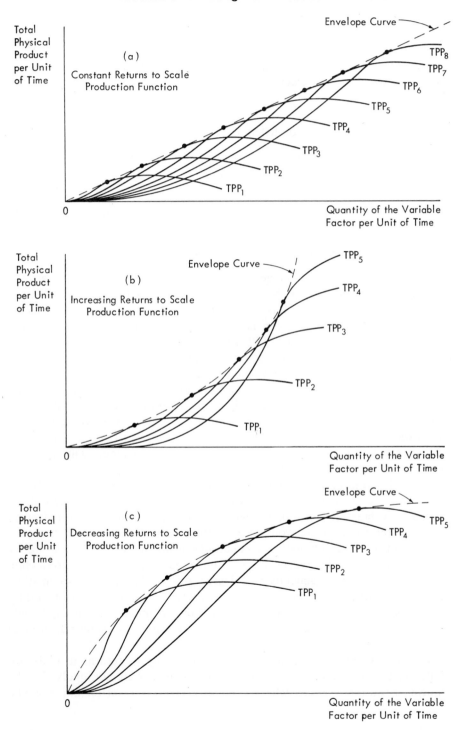

Algebraic Formulation of Returns to Scale

Starting from the production function:

$$q = f(a,b,c, \ldots, n) \tag{8.14}$$

suppose all inputs are multiplied by a fixed amount λ, and the resulting proportion by which output changes is α. Then we may write:

$$\alpha q = f(\lambda a, \lambda b, \lambda c, \ldots, \lambda n) \tag{8.15}$$

The three possibilities can be listed as follows:

$\alpha = \lambda$ constant returns to scale
$\alpha > \lambda$ increasing returns to scale
$\alpha < \lambda$ decreasing returns to scale

In mathematical terms, any homogeneous (production) function can be written as:

$$\lambda^i q = f(\lambda a, \lambda b, \lambda c, \ldots, \lambda n) \tag{8.16}$$

where i = the degree of homogeneity. Thus, if all inputs are increased by λ (e.g., they are all doubled or halved for $\lambda = 2$ and $\lambda = 0.5$ respectively), any homogeneous function will have its output increased by λ^i. With constant returns, the production function is homogeneous of degree one or linearly homogeneous, since when $i = 1$, *TPP* increases in the same proportion as do the inputs. In economic terms, the word "homogeneous" means that the same returns apply for the entire production function. (For example, a 10 percent increase in all inputs always results in a 5 percent increase in output.) "Linear" means a given proportionate change in all the factors yields an equal proportionate change in total output. (For example, a 10 percent increase in all inputs always results in a 10 percent increase in output.) If $i > 1$, increasing returns prevail; e.g., if $i = 2$, $\lambda = 2$, then a doubling of inputs will quadruple *TPP* since $\lambda^i = 2^2 = 4$. With decreasing returns to scale, $i < 1$; e.g., if $i = \frac{1}{2}$ and $\lambda = 4$, then a quadrupling of factors will double *TPP* since $\lambda^i = 4^{1/2} \, (=\sqrt{4}) = 2$.

From an economic viewpoint, a production function is not likely to be continuously homogeneous of a degree greater than one. This would mean increasing returns to scale would prevail throughout the entire range of production. Since under competitive conditions firms subject to increasing returns to scale would never want to stop expanding output, a production function which is homogeneous of a degree greater than one is incompatible with competition. A firm most likely operates with a nonhomogeneous rather than a homogeneous production function. For example, it could experience increasing returns to scale at first, followed by a stage of constant returns, and finally by a stage of decreasing returns.

Before enumerating the likely causes of the various returns to scale, we would like to state explicitly that changes in technology are not involved in the concept of returns to scale, which assumes a given state of technology. The concept of returns to scale involves only the relation between size and efficiency, where the efficiency is measured by the ratio of the value of the output to the value of the input. (Efficiency in the economic sense must involve the ratio of useful output to useful input, both measured in dollar terms, because the first law of thermodynamics tells us that the ratio of physical output to physical input is always unity.)

Causes of Returns to Scale

The most important causes of increasing returns to scale are specialization and indivisibilities. Since Adam Smith's celebrated pinmaking example, economists have been aware of the possible economies resulting from a higher degree of specialization of all factors (not just labor as might be suggested by the frequent use of the phrase "division of labor" with the term "specialization"). Workers and machines can often be more efficient if utilized on a smaller range of tasks, with the ultimate limit to further specialization being what Smith called the "extent of the market" or the volume that can be sold.

Indivisibility or "unavoidable excess capacity" means that workers or machines are available only in certain (minimal) sizes. The larger the firm's output, the greater the possibility that it can use the minimum size equipment. For many operations the minimal level of operation necessary for efficiency is substantial, e.g., a blast furnace. That is, the point of minimum efficient scale of a production process can be quite high; but once reached, substantial economies can be obtained.

The classic example of technological relationships resulting in increasing returns is containers (such as boxes or warehouses) which have the property that their contents increase by the cube of their dimensions, but their surface and required materials only increase by the square. This is one reason the price per unit is less at larger quantities than at lower quantities.

Finally, the celebrated "law of large numbers" may give rise to economies of scale. For example, because there is greater stability—less random, stochastic, or chance variation—in the aggregate behavior of a larger number of customers, a firm need not increase its inventory in proportion to its sales. A firm with $100,000 in sales of a given product may need to keep 3 percent in inventories, whereas another seller of the same product with $1,000,000 in sales may require only 1 percent.

Eventually in most industrial processes, decreasing returns to scale do set in. They arise primarily because of the difficulties and inefficiencies of coordination and control as a firm's management shifts from an entrepreneur—e.g., a Henry Ford I—to a management team—e.g., the present day Ford Motors leadership. Beyond a certain point, proportionate increases in the number of administrators do not produce proportionate increases in entrepreneureal capacity. Communication, coordination, and control problems exist with three in the management team that simply do not exist with one (or even two) executives.

QUESTIONS

1. An innovation or improvement in technology is defined as a shift in the production function, meaning that a greater output is possible from a given quantity of inputs or the same output is possible with fewer inputs. Graph the production functions that describe an innovation in these two ways.
2. What is the essential analytical difference between what is called the "long run" and the "short run" in production theory? Do you think there is a real-world counterpart to this distinction?
3. "Since diminishing returns always set in eventually, there is a natural limit to any firm's production." Discuss the errors and ambiguities in this statement.
4. Try to describe in a way that is understandable to noneconomists how the law of diminishing returns works in the production of pork products, using the rate of corn input per day as the variable factor. (This is an important feature of a phenomenon you may have heard of called "the corn-hog cycle.")
5. Explain why a firm would find it unwise to produce in a range of variable input utilization where the average physical product of that factor is increasing.
6. Prove the following statements:
   (a) *MPP* of the variable factor is zero when *TPP* is at its maximum.
   (b) *MPP* = *APP* at the maximum of *APP*.
   (c) *APP* is rising when *MPP* > *APP*.
   (d) *APP* is rising when *TPP* is convex (from below).
   (e) *APP* is falling when *TPP* is concave (from below).
   (f) *MPP* is at its maximum when *TPP* changes from convex to concave.
   (g) *MPP* is negative when *TPP* is falling.
7. When the average physical product of the variable factor is rising, the marginal physical product of the other factor (called the "fixed factor") is negative. Show this using graphs like those of Figure 8–3. (This question assumes a linear homogeneous production function.)
8. Draw a series of production functions which, when envelope curves are drawn to them, exhibit a production process with a stage of increasing, constant, and decreasing returns to scale.

APPENDIX: MATHEMATICAL NOTES

Note 1. Production Functions

Suppose there are two factors, *a* representing units of labor and *b* denoting units of land, and therefore the generalized production function is:

$$q = f(a,b) \tag{8.17}$$

This production function is typically assumed in economics to be a single-valued continuous function with continuous first- and second-order partial derivatives.

If we assume the quantity of land (labor) is held constant and labor (land) is varied in amount, the *MPP* of labor (land) is given by the partial derivative:

$$MPP_a = \frac{\delta q}{\delta a} = f_a(a,b) \qquad\qquad MPP_b = \frac{\delta q}{\delta b} = f_b(a,b) \tag{8.18}$$

Further, it is assumed in the economically relevant range that these marginal products are: (1) positive:

$$MPP_a = \frac{\delta q}{\delta a} > 0 \qquad MPP_b = \frac{\delta q}{\delta b} > 0 \qquad \text{(8.19)}$$

and (2) subject to diminishing returns:

$$\frac{\Delta MPP_a}{\Delta Q_a} = \frac{\delta^2 q}{\delta a^2} < 0 \qquad \frac{\Delta MPP_b}{\Delta Q_b} = \frac{\delta^2 q}{\delta b^2} < 0 \qquad \text{(8.20)}$$

To take a specific example, suppose the production function is:

$$q = 10a - 5a^2 + 5ab \qquad \text{(8.21)}$$

Then the marginal products are:

$$MPP_a = \frac{\delta q}{\delta a} = 10 - 10a + 5b \qquad MPP_b = \frac{\delta q}{\delta b} = 5a \qquad \text{(8.22)}$$

If, for example, $a = 1$ and $b = 3$, the $MPP_a = 15$ and the $MPP_b = 5$.

Note 2. Optimality Conditions

The validity of the principle of substitution in guiding decision-makers to the proper combination of inputs can be shown in two separate ways: (1) as a constrained output maximization problem, or (2) as a constrained cost minimization problem. Either problem is analogous to consumers' maximizing their utilities subject to budget constraints, a concept developed in Chapter 4 employing the technique of LaGrangian multipliers.

First, we assume the firm wishes to maximize its output subject to a cost constraint. To demonstrate how the entrepreneur can obtain the greatest possible output from a given cost outlay, let $q = f(a,b)$ be the production function and $C = P_a \cdot a + P_b \cdot b + F$ be the total cost (C) function, where P_a and P_b are the prices of inputs a and b respectively, a and b are the quantities of the two factors, and F represents the firm's fixed costs. Next, we must form a third function combining these two functions:

$$V = f(a,b) + \lambda(C - P_a \cdot a - P_b \cdot b - F) \qquad \text{(8.23)}$$

where $\lambda(\neq 0)$ is an undefined LaGrangian multiplier.

The necessary (first-order) conditions for a maximum require that we set the partial derivatives of V with respect to a, b, and λ equal to zero:

$$\frac{\delta V}{\delta a} = \frac{\delta q}{\delta a} - \lambda P_a = 0, \qquad \frac{\delta q}{\delta a} = \lambda P_a, \qquad \frac{\delta q}{\delta a} \div P_a = \lambda \qquad \text{(8.24)}$$

$$\frac{\delta V}{\delta b} = \frac{\delta q}{\delta b} - \lambda P_b = 0, \qquad \frac{\delta q}{\delta b} = \lambda P_b, \qquad \frac{\delta q}{\delta b} \div P_b = \lambda \qquad \text{(8.25)}$$

$$\frac{\delta V}{\delta \lambda} = C - P_a \cdot a - P_b \cdot b - F = 0 \qquad \text{(8.26)}$$

By moving the price terms to the right of the first two equations and dividing the first by the second, we obtain the text's equation, stating that the necessary conditions are that the ratio of the MPPs must equal the ratio of their prices:

$$\frac{\delta q}{\delta a} \div \frac{\delta q}{\delta b} = \frac{P_a}{P_b} \text{ or } \frac{\delta q}{\delta a} \div P_a = \frac{\delta q}{\delta b} \div P_b = \lambda \tag{8.27}$$

λ may be interpreted as the contribution to output of the last dollar spent on each factor.

The sufficient (second-order) conditions require that the relevant bordered Hessian determinant be positive:

$$\begin{vmatrix} \dfrac{\delta^2 q}{\delta a^2} & \dfrac{\delta^2 q}{\delta a \delta b} & -P_a \\[2ex] \dfrac{\delta^2 q}{\delta b \delta a} & \dfrac{\delta^2 q}{\delta b^2} & -P_b \\[2ex] -P_a & -P_b & 0 \end{vmatrix} > 0 \tag{8.28}$$

Alternatively, a firm may desire to minimize the cost of production, $C = P_a \cdot a + P_b \cdot b + F$, at some given level of production, $q = f(a,b)$, for the function:

$$Z = P_a \cdot a + P_b \cdot b + F + \mu \, [q - f(a,b)] \tag{8.29}$$

Again we set the partial derivatives of Z with respect to a,b, and μ equal to zero:

$$\frac{\delta Z}{\delta a} = P_a - \mu \frac{\delta q}{\delta a} = 0 \qquad P_a \mu = \frac{\delta q}{\delta a} \qquad \frac{\delta q}{\delta a} \div P_a = \mu \tag{8.30}$$

$$\frac{\delta Z}{\delta b} = P_b - \mu \frac{\delta q}{\delta b} = 0 \qquad P_b \mu = \frac{\delta q}{\delta b} \qquad \frac{\delta q}{\delta b} \div P_b = \mu \tag{8.31}$$

$$\frac{\delta Z}{\delta \mu} = q - f(a,b) = 0 \tag{8.32}$$

Since P_a, MPP_a, and μ are all positive, moving the price terms of the first two equations to the right and dividing the first by the second yields:

$$\frac{\delta q}{\delta a} \div \frac{\delta q}{\delta b} = \frac{P_a}{P_b} \text{ or } \frac{\delta q}{\delta a} \div P_a = \frac{\delta q}{\delta b} \div P_b = 1/\mu \tag{8.33}$$

The multiplier μ is the reciprocal of the multiplier λ, or the total derivative of cost with respect to output (formally defined in Chapter 10 as marginal cost). Thus, the necessary (first-order) conditions for cost minimization subject to an output constraint are identical to those for output maximization subject to a cost constraint.

The sufficient (second-order) conditions require that the relevant bordered Hessian determinant be negative:

$$\begin{vmatrix} -\mu \dfrac{\delta^2 q}{\delta a^2} & -\mu \dfrac{\delta^2 q}{\delta a \delta b} & -P_a \\[2ex] -\mu \dfrac{\delta^2 q}{\delta b \delta a} & -\mu \dfrac{\delta^2 q}{\delta b^2} & -P_b \\[2ex] -P_a & -P_b & 0 \end{vmatrix} < 0 \tag{8.34}$$

Since $\mu > 0$, by substituting and multiplying it is possible to arrive at exactly the same second-order condition as given in (8.28).

9 Isoquant Approach to Production Theory

Paralleling the indifference curve analysis of consumption theory is the isoquant approach to production theory. In fact, the indifference curve analysis may be thought of as consumption indifference curve analysis and the isoquant approach as production indifference curve analysis. Rather than dealing with iso-utility (equal-utility) curves as in the indifference curve analysis, the isoquant approach utilizes iso-product (equal-product or equal-output) curves.

As we have previously argued, the big advantage the indifference curve analysis has over the older classic cardinal utility approach is that it does not require cardinal measurement of a consumer's subjective feelings. However, this is not an issue in production theory. Each contour line can represent a specific known volume of physical output rather than represent merely a ranking of output combinations. An isoquant is obtained directly from the production function and is just a different way of looking at the same thing. Isoquant analysis is operational and therefore easily subjected to empirical testing.

This chapter will first develop the concept of an isoquant. Next, we will introduce factor cost or isocost curves, exact analogs to budget constraint lines. Together isoquants and isocost curves permit us to develop the optimality conditions. Furthermore, throughout this chapter we will indicate the interrelationship between the modern isoquant approach and the traditional production function approach. Because of the close connection between the mechanics in the production and consumption indifference curves, this chapter will cover some points only briefly, assuming some familiarity with the techniques introduced in Chapter 5.

ISOQUANTS

An *isoquant* shows all the various combinations of factors, here labeled a and b, that a firm may use to produce a given quantity of output. Neglecting the extreme (and possibly nonexistent) case of fixed proportions, in which factors must be combined in a rigidly predetermined pattern, a given amount of output can be produced using a number of different combinations of factors, provided sufficient time is allowed for adjustment. In fact, it is assumed that the factors of production can be continuously substituted for one another in most ranges of the production space. However, for any given output level some minimum amount of each input is generally required.

Consider the Cobb-Douglas production function equation, number (8.6) in the last chapter, $q = 100 \sqrt{a \cdot b}$, where q = total output and, say, factor a is hours of labor and factor b is hours of some piece of capital equipment. As Table 9–1 indicates, 1,000 units of output can be produced using several different sets of inputs. For example, the entrepreneur can use 4 hours of labor and 25 machine-hours and get 1,000 units of output; for $100 \sqrt{4 \cdot 25} = 100 \cdot 10 = 1,000$. If the relative price of capital services rises, an entrepreneur, following the principle of substitution (8.12), would want to cut down on the relatively expensive factor, capital, and use more of the relatively inexpensive factor, labor. The specified production function indicates that if a reduction of 5 machine-hours of capital takes place, 1 additional hour of labor must be used to maintain the same level of production; for $100 \sqrt{(4+1) \cdot (25-5)} = 100 \sqrt{5 \cdot 20} = 1,000$. If 15 machine-hours are to be used, then $6\frac{2}{3}$ hours of labor must be employed to maintain production at 1,000 units. At 25 machine-hours, it takes 1 additional hour of labor to compensate for the loss of 5 machine-hours; whereas at 20 machine-hours, it takes an additional $1\frac{2}{3}$ hours of labor to compensate for the loss of 5 machine-hours. This illustrates a general principle in production, viz., the scarcer any factor is, the more difficult and costly it becomes to replace it with another factor. This principle follows from the law of diminishing marginal returns.

TABLE 9–1   Variable Inputs to Produce a Given Output

Quantity of Factor a Per Unit of Time (Labor)	Quantity of Factor b Per Unit of Time (Capital)	Total Output from Cobb-Douglas Production Function $q = 100 \sqrt{a \cdot b}$
1	100	1,000
2	50	1,000
3	$33\frac{1}{3}$	1,000
4	25	1,000
5	20	1,000
6	$16\frac{2}{3}$	1,000
$6\frac{2}{3}$	15	1,000
7	$14\frac{2}{7}$	1,000
8	$12\frac{1}{2}$	1,000
9	$11\frac{1}{9}$	1,000
10	10	1,000

We know that along a given isoquant, output is constant so that any change in factor combinations must leave total output unchanged. The increase in total output from using more of, say, factor a must be exactly offset by the decline in total output from using less of factor b, so that the change in total output is zero. The general equation for maintaining a given level of output along a given isoquant as factors are substituted is:

$$\text{(a)} \quad \Delta Q_a \cdot MPP_a + \Delta Q_b \cdot MPP_b = 0 \tag{9.1}$$

or

$$\text{(b)} \quad \Delta Q_a \cdot MPP_a = - \Delta Q_b \cdot MPP_b$$

along a given isoquant

(9.1b) states that the change in the quantity of a times the marginal physical product of a must equal the change in the quantity of input b times its marginal physical product. Thus, if 3 machine-hours of capital with marginal physical productivity of 4 each are withdrawn from production (reducing output by $-3 \cdot 4 = -12$ units), 6 additional hours of labor, each with marginal physical productivity of 2, are necessary to keep the same level of output ($+2 \cdot 6 = 12$).

Graphic Illustration

The geometric representation of a table such as Table 9–1 would trace an isoquant. That is, an isoquant (IQ) is a locus of points, each of which shows a different combination of the two factors that may be used to produce a given quantity of output. Figure 9–1 illustrates a family of such isoquants. These curves show the different combinations of factors a and b (or labor and capital) that can be used to produce 1,000, 2,000, 3,000, and 4,000 units of output respectively. As the firm moves up successive isoquants, from IQ_1 to IQ_4, it moves up the "hill of production." In contrast to the indifference curve analysis, we know by exactly how much one curve is above the other. Since these isoquants are based on known technological information, there is no objection to saying IQ_2 is greater than IQ_1 by 1,000 units.

Along a given isoquant, output is constant. Points along IQ_1, for example, show that 1,000 units of output can be produced using a_1 units of factor a and b_1 units of input b or a_2 units of a and b_2 units of b or a_3 units of a and b_3 units of b and so on. Note, however, that b_3 (a_1) is the minimum amount of b (a) that can produce the given level of output, 1,000 units. Since any given level of output most often requires certain minimum amounts of the factors, only when both factors are above these minimal requirements, such as between points b_3 and a_1 along isoquant IQ_1, can substitution take place.

FIGURE 9–1   A Family of Isoquants

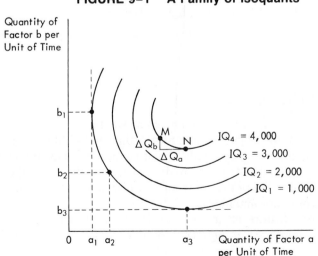

Slope of an Isoquant

The exact rate of trade off between one factor and another along a given isoquant is represented by the slope of the isoquant, shown as $\Delta Q_b/\Delta Q_a$ in Figure 9–1. In economic terms, the slope of an isoquant is called the *marginal rate of technical (or factor) substitution of factor a for b* ($MRTS_{ab}$). That is, the slope of an isoquant $= \Delta Q_b/\Delta Q_a = -MRTS_{ab}$. Again the convention in economics is to ignore the minus sign and talk about the absolute value of $MRTS_{ab}$—i.e., $MRTS_{ab} = |\Delta Q_b/\Delta Q_a|$ so that the trade-off rate is always expressed in positive terms. Thus, in the numerical examples given in Table 9–1, the $MRTS_{ab}$ between 25 and 20 units of factor b and 4 and 5 units of a is $(25 - 20)/(4 - 5) = 5/-1 = |5|$. Similarly, between 20 and 15 units of b, it is $3 = (20 - 15)/(5 - 6\frac{2}{3})$.

In other words, the $MRTS_{ab}$ shows the amount of factor b that must be sacrificed per unit increase in factor a so as to maintain a constant level of output. From the figures given in the last paragraph you may have already surmised that the $MRTS_{ab}$ typically diminishes (in absolute value) as more of factor a is added while the firm moves from left to right along an isoquant. That is, it takes a smaller and smaller amount of b to compensate for a given increase in a; or the other way around, it takes continuously more a to compensate for any given reduction in b. This phenomenon of the *diminishing marginal rate of technical substitution between factors a and b* ($DMRTS_{ab}$) is consistent with the principle of diminishing marginal product. As more of factor a is used in place of factor b, factor a becomes a poorer and poorer substitute for factor b.

Since along a given isoquant output is constant, the gain in output from using a little more of factor a must exactly equal the loss from using a little less of factor b. Equation (9.1) shows that the gain in output equals the loss in output since (neglecting signs) $\Delta Q_a \cdot MPP_a = \Delta Q_b \cdot MPP_b$. Dividing both sides by ΔQ_a, we can see that $MPP_a = (\Delta Q_b/\Delta Q_a) \cdot MPP_b$ and then further dividing both sides by MPP_b yields:

$$-(MPP_a/MPP_b) = \Delta Q_b/\Delta Q_a = MRTS_{ab} \tag{9.2}$$

That is, neglecting signs, the $MRTS_{ab}$ equals the ratio of the MPP_a to the MPP_b. This is seen in Figure 9–2.

Characteristics of Isoquants

Isoquants are: (1) continuous and everywhere dense, (2) negatively sloping, (3) convex to the origin, (4) nonintersecting, and (5) do not cut the axis for an indispensable input. The continuity of isoquants means the factors can be continuously substituted for one another, at least within the rather wide range between the points where the constraint requirement of some minimal quantity of either factor is not binding.

The second feature of an isoquant is that it must be negatively sloping, under our assumption; i.e., $\Delta Q_b/\Delta Q_a$ (or $MRTS_{ab}$) < 0. The qualifying phrase

FIGURE 9-2 Isoquants, the Marginal Rate of Technical Substitution, and Marginal Physical Products

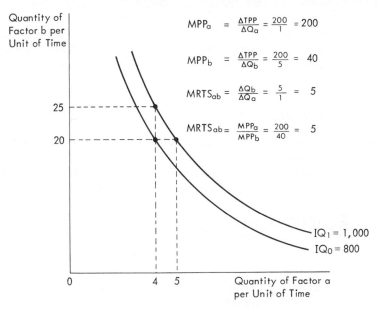

Quantity of Factor b per Unit of Time

$$MPP_a = \frac{\Delta TPP}{\Delta Q_a} = \frac{200}{1} = 200$$

$$MPP_b = \frac{\Delta TPP}{\Delta Q_b} = \frac{200}{5} = 40$$

$$MRTS_{ab} = \frac{\Delta Q_b}{\Delta Q_a} = \frac{5}{1} = 5$$

$$MRTS_{ab} = \frac{MPP_a}{MPP_b} = \frac{200}{40} = 5$$

25

20

$IQ_1 = 1,000$
$IQ_0 = 800$

0   4 5   Quantity of Factor a per Unit of Time

will be explained in a moment. Since inputs are generally technical substitutes for one another, if one factor is increased, the quantity of the other must be decreased to maintain output at a given level. The economically relevant section of the isoquants is limited to the downsloping range by the assumptions that firms are profit-maximizers and that we are dealing only with factors with a $MPP \geqq 0$, not with disfactors with a $MPP < 0$. Beyond b_1 and a_3 in Figure 9-1, the isoquant is upward sloping, curling up and away from the two axes. This shape means in these ranges the inputs are worse than redundant; they have become a positive nuisance and interfere with production. Beyond b_1 and a_3 they become disfactors with negative marginal products. For example, beyond a_3, to keep output constant, more of factor b must be used as more of factor a is added. Obviously, no profit-maximizing entrepreneur will ever willingly produce a given output in a range that requires more of both factors. At a_3 the isoquant is horizontal, indicating the MPP_a is zero; and at b_1 the isoquant is vertical, indicating the MPP_b is zero. In those cases where the inputs do not actually become economic nuisances or disfactors but merely do not add to total output (i.e., their $MPP = 0$), the isoquant will continue being horizontal (vertical) instead of curling away from the axis.

Thirdly, and perhaps most importantly, an isoquant is assumed to be convex. This is a reflection of the *law of diminishing marginal rate of technical substitution of factor a for factor b (LDMRTS_{ab})*. While akin to the law of diminishing marginal productivity, the *LDMRTS* is not quite the same thing, since the *MRTS* is the *ratio* of the marginal products of the two factors.

The curvature of an isoquant is used to determine the substitutability between factors. A straight-line isoquant means the factors are perfect substitutes; a right-angled isoquant reflects complements or factors that must be used in fixed proportions; and finally a "conglomerate" is where two factors are both complements and substitutes in different ranges. In general, the poorer the substitutes, the more convex the isoquants; the better the substitutes, the less convex the isoquants.

Elasticity of Substitution

A more precise way to express substitutability in economics is in relative terms, using the concept of the elasticity of technical substitution (σ). This concept measures the relative rate of change of the proportions between factors a and b divided by the relative change in the $MRTS_{ab}$.[1] That is,

$$\sigma = -\frac{\text{relative change in the proportions of the factors } (b/a)}{\text{relative change in the } MRTS_{ab}} \quad \text{(9.3)}$$

or

$$\sigma = -\frac{\Delta(b/a)}{b/a} \div \frac{\Delta MRTS_{ab}}{MRTS_{ab}} = \frac{\Delta(b/a)}{\Delta MRTS_{ab}} \cdot \frac{MRTS_{ab}}{b/a} \quad \text{(9.4)}$$

Since the expected sign of σ is negative, economists conventionally multiply by -1 as in (9.3) to make σ positive. Therefore, perfect complements are said to exist when $\sigma = 0$, and perfect substitutes exist when $\sigma = \infty$.

Strictly speaking, σ describes a property along a given isoquant and thus assumes that output remains constant as factor prices (or the $MRTS_{ab}$) change. Suppose the price of factor a (P_a) falls relative to the price of factor b (P_b). This leads to a decrease in the $MRTS_{ab}$ since more of factor a and less of factor b is used, causing the firm to move downward and rightward along its isoquant. If $\sigma > 1$ ($\sigma < 1$, $\sigma = 1$), total factor earnings of input a would have fallen (increased, remained the same) relative to those of factor b.

Thus, σ is an important concept in both production and distribution theory. For instance, we can predict that if σ is inelastic, i.e., $\sigma < 1$, an increase in wage rates will lead to an increase in labor's relative share of national income. This is apparently what happened in U. S. manufacturing over the postwar years. When $\sigma < 1$, this means that, say, a 10 percent increase in labor's wage rate will lead to a less than 10 percent, say, 8 percent, decline in the numerator of σ or the relative quantity of labor employed. Obviously if only 8 percent less labor is used in response to a 10 percent rise in wage rates, labor's earnings

---

[1] Instead of using the relative change in the $MRTS_{ab}$ in the denominator, economists sometimes use the proportionate change in the ratio of their marginal productivities (or the proportionate change in the ratio of their prices). And sometimes they compare changes in a/b with changes in MPP_b/MPP_a (or P_b/P_a) to keep the elasticity positive.

have increased relative to those of input *b*, say, capital.[2] While there is considerable evidence that, for the U. S. economy as a whole and for the manufacturing sector as a whole, σ is substantially less than one,[3] there are subsectors or specific industries and groups with production functions in which σ is greater than one.[4] If $\sigma > 1$, the relative per-unit return to capital diminishes as wage rates increase, whereas capital's total share increases.

The reason σ is called a relative measure can be seen by examining points *M* and *N* in Figure 9–3. If the firm moves from *M* to *N*, $\Delta Q_b/\Delta Q_a$ (or $\Delta b/\Delta a$) changes by decreasing in (absolute) value. But the ratio *b/a* also declines. σ attempts to determine which change is relatively greater. That is, if *b/a* is denoted by *E* and $\Delta Q_b/\Delta Q_a$ by *e*, then $\sigma = \dfrac{\Delta E/E}{\Delta e/e}$.

FIGURE 9–3   Elements of the Elasticity of Substitution

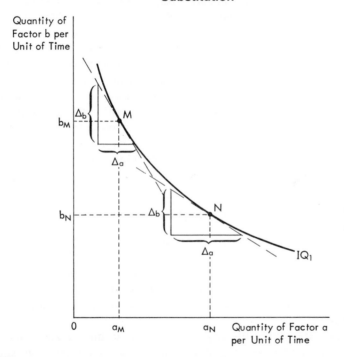

[2] Note that we have talked only about relative, not absolute, shares. Thus, it is possible, for example, for factor *b* to be earning relatively more than before, although it and factor *a* are earning absolutely less than before as a result of a decline in the P_a.

[3] See, for example, J. W. Kendrick and Ryuzo Sato, "Factor Prices, Productivity, and Growth," *American Economic Review,* Vol. LII (December, 1963), pp. 974–1003.

[4] See Charles E. Ferguson, "Time-Series Production Functions and Technological Progress in American Manufacturing Industry," *Journal of Political Economy,* Vol. LXXIII (April, 1965), pp. 135–147. To be sure, changes in relative shares also depend on the nature of technological progress over time. If it has been labor-using in the U. S. economy, as some evidence suggests, this would also tend to explain some of the increase in labor's share. See Charles E. Ferguson, "Substitution, Technical Progress, and Returns to Scale," *American Economic Review,* Vol. LV (May, 1965), pp. 296–305.

Additional Characteristics

Returning to the characteristics of isoquants, we can also add that they are nonintersecting. If they did intersect, a given combination of factors a and b could produce two different levels of output with an invariant technology. More simply, if two isoquants did intersect, such as the 1,000 units of output curve and the 2,000 units curve, the implication would be that $1,000 = 2,000$.

The final characteristic of an isoquant is that when a factor is indispensable (i.e., a certain minimum amount of the factor is essential to obtain a particular level of output), the isoquant cannot cut the axis representing zero units of this factor. For instance, the production of gold watches requires a certain minimum amount of gold. However, even in this case much more substitution can take place than is ordinarily thought possible. For instance, it has been documented that the coefficient of gold production into gold leaf is not fixed, as, e.g., the noted Italian economist, Vilfredo Pareto (1848–1923), had once argued.[5] It is not true that only so much gold leaf can be hammered out of an ounce of gold. In the U. S., where labor was expensive, only 262,000 leaves to the inch were obtained, whereas in Germany, where labor was relatively cheap compared to gold, the leaf was pounded thinner, with 350,000 leaves to the inch. It is sometimes thought that chemical combinations represent examples of fixed coefficients of production. It takes exactly two molecules of hydrogen to one of oxygen to form water, but notice that this is almost irrelevant economically. In the process of water production the firm might very well use 10 or 100 times as much oxygen as hydrogen if the price of hydrogen is very high and the price of oxygen very low. One could say that economics is the science of being wasteful wisely.

Short-Run and Long-Run Relations

The previous chapter used the production function approach to make the distinction between short-run and long-run relations. Short-run changes in output due to changing proportions between factors must be distinguished from long-run changes in production due to changing scale or absolute amounts of the factors employed, proportions remaining the same. Figure 9–4 illustrates this distinction.

A straight line out of the origin is used to determine scale; whereas a horizontal line (or a vertical one), starting at any arbitrary position, such as $0\bar{b}_1$ units of factor b and varying amounts of a, shows changing proportions. With a and b the only two factors, the fact that the isoquants are equidistant along rays $0R_i$ means that constant returns to scale must prevail, with proportionate changes in both factors a and b giving rise to equal proportionate changes in output. On the other hand, if the quantity of factor b is held constant, say, at $0\bar{b}_1$ units, the resulting increases in output from expanding only factor a are

---

[5] Cited in G. J. Stigler, *The Theory of Price* (3d ed.; New York: Macmillan Co., 1966), p. 117. The source is the U. S. Tariff Commission. *Gold Leaf* (1926), p. 6.

FIGURE 9-4 Scale vs. Proportions in Input Use

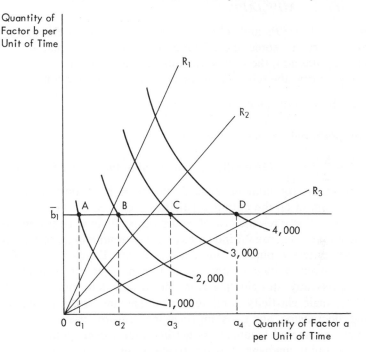

indicated along line $\bar{b}_1 D$. The initial 1,000 units of production can be obtained using $0a_1 (= \bar{b}_1 A)$ units of factor a; whereas the next 1,000 units of production require $a_1 a_2 (= AB)$ units of factor a, and the next 1,000 units of output require $a_2 a_3 (= BC)$ units of factor a, and so on. Since $0a_1 < a_1 a_2 < a_2 a_3 < a_3 a_4$, factor a must be subject to the law of diminishing marginal productivity; equal increments in production require progressively greater quantities of factor a.

Economists use two different elasticity concepts to distinguish between short-run changes in proportion and long-run changes in scale. Given the short-run production function, $q_x = f(a,b)$, the *output elasticity* of a, called ϵ_a, is the relative change in the total output of x resulting from a given relative change in the quantity of factor a, the quantity of factor b held constant. Thus,

$$\text{(a)}\quad \epsilon_a = \frac{\Delta q_x}{q_x} \div \frac{\Delta q_a}{q_a} = \frac{\Delta q_x}{\Delta q_a} \cdot \frac{q_a}{q_x} = \frac{\Delta q_x}{\Delta q_a} \div \frac{q_x}{q_a} \tag{9.5}$$

$$\text{(b)}\quad \epsilon_b = \frac{\Delta q_x}{q_x} \div \frac{\Delta q_b}{q_b} = \frac{\Delta q_x}{\Delta q_b} \cdot \frac{q_b}{q_x} = \frac{\Delta q_x}{\Delta q_b} \div \frac{q_x}{q_b}$$

Since $\Delta q_x/\Delta q_a$ and $\Delta q_x/\Delta q_b$ are the marginal physical products of factors a and b respectively, and q_x/q_a and q_x/q_b are the average physical products of factors a and b respectively, the right-most terms in the two equations in (9.5) mean that the output elasticity of a factor equals its marginal physical product divided by its average physical product.

(a) $\epsilon_a = MPP_a/APP_a$ **(9.6)**
(b) $\epsilon_b = MPP_b/APP_b$

While in general, *MPP*s and *APP*s vary and hence output elasticities vary as input ratios vary, in some special types of production functions, such as a homogeneous function, the output elasticities are constant.

In the long run, the relevant elasticity is called the function coefficient (E) and shows the proportional change in the total output of $x \left(= \dfrac{\Delta q_x}{q_x}\right)$ resulting from a proportional change in the quantity of all inputs $\left(= \dfrac{\Delta \lambda}{\lambda}\right)$. Thus, $E = \dfrac{\Delta q_x}{q_x} \div \dfrac{\Delta \lambda}{\lambda} = \dfrac{\Delta q_x}{\Delta \lambda} \cdot \dfrac{\lambda}{q_x}$. Generally, E is a variable that depends on the level of output. However, for homogeneous functions E is a constant. E is always equal to the sum of all the output elasticities; i.e., $E = \epsilon_a + \epsilon_b + \cdots + \epsilon_n$.

Figure 9–5 illustrates the law of returns to scale in what is considered the most typical case: viz., ray OR indicates that the (nonhomogeneous) production function first enters a phase of increasing returns, then a period of constant returns, and finally a stage of decreasing returns. The intervals at which the isoquants cross any straight line from the origin determine the type of returns. Thus, scale elasticity is related to the spacing of the isoquants. When increasing, decreasing, and constant (marginal) returns prevail, the spacing of successively numbered isoquants is getting ever closer, getting ever farther apart, or remaining unchanged, respectively. Going from 0 to 1,000 to 2,000, and from 2,000 to 3,000 units of output, ray OR intersects the isoquants at

FIGURE 9–5   **Changing Returns to Scale**

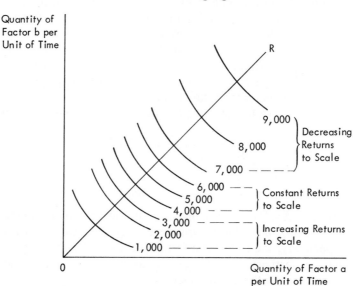

smaller and smaller intervals, indicating increasing returns with given proportionate increases in the inputs, giving rise to ever greater proportionate increases in production. From 3,000 to 6,000 units of output, ray OR crosses the isoquants at equal intervals, indicating constant returns. Finally, from 7,000 to 9,000 units of output, the intersection is at increasing intervals, which means decreasing returns to scale. While Figure 9–5 illustrates a nonhomogeneous function or one where the same returns do not prevail over the entire production range, we can use the identical procedure to demonstrate homogeneous functions. For instance, if constant returns prevailed everywhere (homogeneity of the first degree), all the isoquants would cross ray OR at equal intervals; i.e., they would be equally spaced.

Isoclines and Ridge Lines

To show which part of an isoquant is relevant from an economic point of view and to show the intimate connection between isoquant and product curves, we must define some terms. The two ideas that are important in this connection are the general concept of isoclines and the specialized concept of ridge lines, which are special kinds of isoclines. An *isocline* is a locus of points cutting the isoquants at points of equal slope. In Figure 9–6, $0A$ and $0B$ are isoclines drawn through the isoquants at the point where each isoquant is tangent to a vertical line for $0A$ and a horizontal line for $0B$. The shapes of the isoclines depend upon the production function.[6] When isoclines such as

FIGURE 9–6   Ridge Lines and the Relevant Range of Input Utilization

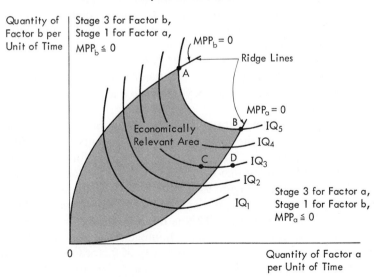

---

[6] The isoclines of homogeneous production functions are rays, or straight lines, passing through the origin.

$0A$ and $0B$ connect the points where the isoquants become respectively vertical (i.e., $MPP_b = 0$) and horizontal (i.e., $MPP_a = 0$), they are called *ridge lines*.

The shaded area in Figure 9–6 lying between the ridge lines is the only economically relevant part of the isoquant map. In this region, the isoquants are negatively sloped and convex. The firm would never operate above $0A$ or below $0B$, since such operation would use more of both factors to produce the same level of total output that fewer units of both factors could produce. Thus, in Figure 9–6 a movement along IQ_3 from C to D would involve a redundancy of both factors a and b; with positive factor prices, point C is obviously preferable to D. In short, ridge lines $0A$ and $0B$ enclose the economically relevant area because an entrepreneur will never use a factor combination which will produce a negative marginal product for any of the factors. Inside the cigar-shaped area enclosed by ridge lines $0A$ and $0B$, the marginal products of both factors are positive. Whenever the isoquant becomes upward sloping, the marginal product of one of the factors is negative.

Ridge line $0A$ connects points for which the $MPP_b = 0$ or, saying the same thing, the $MRTS_{ab} = \infty$; and ridge line $0B$ connects points for which the $MPP_a = 0$, or the $MRTS_{ab} = 0$ (see equation [9.2]). Beyond ridge line $0A$ ($0B$), the MPP_b (MPP_a) becomes negative.

Now turn to Figure 9–7(a), ignoring panels (b) and (c) for the moment. Ridge line $0A$ ($0B$) shows the minimum amounts of factor a (b) necessary to produce the different quantities of output associated with the isoquants cut by it. For example, at point C in panel (a), no more of factor a can be substituted for factor b if the level of output indicated by IQ_5 is to be produced. At this point, the slope of IQ_5 is zero, which means the MPP_a is zero and hence the $MRTS_{ab}$ is zero. Beyond this point, the MPP_a is negative and would involve higher production costs to produce IQ_5 than would some other combination of factors. If the firm is operating at point D, it could continue to produce IQ_5 by successively reducing the use of factor b as long as it increases factor a at the same time. But at point C, any decreases in b would reduce output (say, to point E) and increases in a would only reduce output further (to point G on IQ_3). In other words, beyond ridge line $0B$, factor a is no longer a substitute for factor b.

We have implicitly demonstrated the connection between the production function approach used in the last chapter and isoquants. The region above ridge line $0A$ represents stage 3 for factor b and stage 1 for factor a, whereas the region rightward of ridge line $0B$ depicts stage 3 for factor a and stage 1 for factor b, as illustrated in Figure 9–6. With the isoquant map, we can derive the total, average, and marginal physical product curves similar to those given in Figure 8–1 of the last chapter. This is done in Figure 9–7(b) and 9–7(c), assuming panel (a) represents a linear homogeneous production function.

Along line $\bar{b}_1 F$ in Figure 9–7(a), the quantity of factor b is held constant at level $\bar{b}_1$, while the quantity of factor a is increased. The total output is represented by the isoquant intersected by $\bar{b}_1 F$ at the different quantities of factor a. For example, the output with a_4 units of factor a (and $\bar{b}_1$ units of factor b) is that

FIGURE 9–7 **Product Curves and Isoquant Relationships**

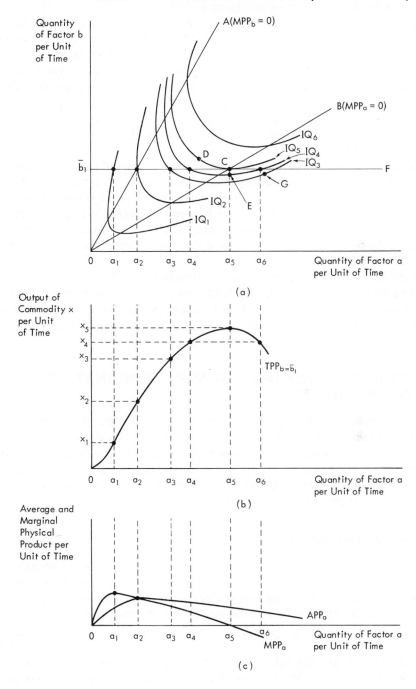

(a)

(b)

(c)

associated with IQ_4. Assume the commodity produced is x and the production level associated with IQ_4 is x_4 in Figure 9–7(b).

The easiest point to locate on the TPP curve is at a_5 units of factor a, where ridge line $0B$ indicates that the MPP_a is zero. Since the TPP curve increases up to this point and decreases thereafter, this must be a maximum. From the definition of MPP, we know that a maximal value for the total occurs where the marginal value equals zero, as seen in Figure 9–7(c). On the other hand, anywhere in the region above ridge line $0A$, the MPP_b is negative. And we know from the last chapter that when the MPP of one factor is negative, the APP of the other is increasing. Therefore, from zero to a_2 units of factor a, the APP_a is increasing.

When a_1 units of factor a are combined with $\bar{b}_1$ units of factor b, output x_1 on isoquant IQ_1 is outside the ridge line. Thus, the MPP_b is negative. When the combination $a_2\bar{b}_1$ is used, production takes place on ridge line $0A$, where the MPP_b is zero and the APP_a is at a maximum. The MPP_a is increasing up to a_1 units of factor a and decreasing after that. TPP is increasing at an increasing rate up to the inflection point at a_1. This is the point at which the MPP_a reaches its maximum.

Actually, we could use the isoquants given in Figure 9–7 to derive a whole family of TPP (and related APP and MPP) curves, one for each level of factor b assumed. Alternatively, we could turn the analysis around by assuming that factor a is constant to see how the law of proportionality affects the TPP by varying the quantities of factor b employed.

ISOCOSTS AND THE OPTIMUM COMBINATION OF INPUTS

All combinations along a given isoquant yield the same total output. But the total cost of producing this given level of output varies along the isoquant, given factor prices. The combination of factors that produces the given output for the lowest total cost is known as the economically most efficient factor combination. It is this economically most efficient factor combination that is of interest to our profit-maximizing producers.

Factor-Cost or Isocost Equation

To determine total cost and the economically most efficient combination, we must work with the concept of *factor-cost* or *isocost curves*, the exact analogue to budget lines in indifference curve analysis. Assume a firm's total cost of production (C) can be represented by the linear equation:

$$C = P_a \cdot Q_a + P_b \cdot Q_b + F \tag{9.7}$$

where P_a and P_b are the respective prices of the variable factors a and b, and F is the cost of the fixed factor. An *isocost function* is then defined as a locus of points, each of which shows a combination of factor inputs that the firm may purchase for a specified constant total cost outlay. If the firm is a competitor in the input market with no control over prices, this isocost function can be represented by a linear equation of the form $y = a - bx$, where a is the y intercept and b the slope. If in contrast to (9.7), total cost is fixed, $\overline{C}$, the isocost function can be written $C = P_a \cdot Q_a + P_b \cdot Q_b + F$. Solving for Q_b gives $P_b \cdot Q_b = \overline{C} - (P_a \cdot Q_a) - F$, and:

$$Q_b = \frac{\overline{C} - F}{P_b} - \frac{P_a}{P_b} \cdot Q_a \qquad (9.8)$$

The y intercept $(\overline{C} - F)/P_b$ gives the amount of factor b that can be purchased if the entire cost outlay, excluding the expenditure on fixed factors, is spent on b. The x intercept, if we solve for Q_a, shows the total amount of factor a that can be obtained if the total cost allotment is expended upon a. The total quantity of any input, the ith input, that can be bought if the entire cost outlay $\overline{C}$ is spent on this factor is $Q_i = (\overline{C} - F)/P_i$. The greater the total outlay $\overline{C}$, the greater the intercepts of the isocost line axes and the further from the origin the isocost line lies; e.g., $\overline{C}_4 > \overline{C}_3 > \overline{C}_2 > \overline{C}_1$, in Figure 9–8. Equation (9.8) also shows that the slope of an isocost function equals the negative of the factor price ratios (slope $= -P_a/P_b$). We can also demonstrate this by solving geo-

metrically for the slope in Figure 9-8. That is, slope $= \Delta y/\Delta x = -\left(\dfrac{\overline{C} - F}{P_b}\right) \div$

$\left(\dfrac{\overline{C} - F}{P_a}\right) = -\left(\dfrac{\overline{C} - F}{P_b}\right) \cdot \left(\dfrac{P_a}{\overline{C} - F}\right) = -\left(\dfrac{P_a}{P_b}\right).$ In Figure 9-8 the slopes of the iso-

cost functions—i.e., the price ratios—are assumed constant. When only the

FIGURE 9–8 Isocost Lines

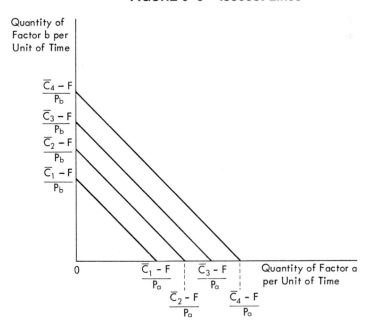

cost outlay and not the price ratios are changed, the isocost lines shift in a parallel fashion.

The Optimum Combination of Factors

In the short run, the outlays for fixed inputs F are constant. While it is possible to measure the additions to cost in excess of F, to simplify the analysis of the optimum combination of factors without changing anything essential, let us neglect entirely the payments to fixed inputs, that is, assume $F = 0$. Or if the reader prefers, we can assume we are examining the long-run least-cost conditions in which all factors are variable and hence F in fact equals zero. Further, we will assume the firm either (1) seeks the greatest total output that can be produced with the given total cost outlay—i.e., wants to get on the highest possible isoquant that the given isocost constraint will allow—or (2) seeks to produce a given output at the lowest possible total cost—i.e., wants to get on the lowest possible isocost function that its given isoquant will allow.

To show the optimum conditions, the isocost function can be thought of in exactly the same way as the budget line: viz., as separating the attainable from the unattainable combinations. All combinations that are equal to or inside the isocost line are considered to be in the factor-cost or isocost space. This area has the equation $\overline{C} \geq P_a \cdot Q_a + P_b \cdot Q_b$. However, to get the largest output possible with a given $\overline{C}$, the firm must actually get on the isocost line and not be within the isocost space.

To keep the diagram simple, we have superimposed only four isoquants, IQ_1, IQ_2, IQ_3, and IQ_4, on the four isocost functions to form Figure 9–9. Suppose the firm's total cost outlay is C_2. What is the greatest total output

FIGURE 9–9   Optimum Input Determination

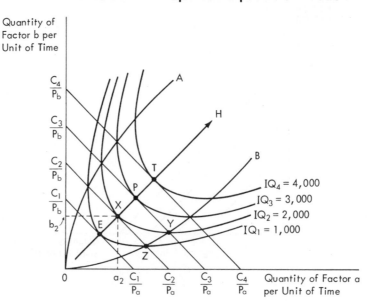

that can be produced with this outlay? Clearly, it can produce the output at point Z, where C_2 intersects $IQ_1 = 1,000$ units. But this output would not be optimal since, with that outlay, it can move from point Z to point X; and X lies on IQ_2 with a total output of 2,000 units. The firm wants to reach the highest isoquant it can, given its cost constraint. The optimum output is therefore where the given isocost function is tangent to an isoquant. If the isocost function is C_2, Figure 9–9 shows that a_2 units of factor a and b_2 units of factor b should be used.

Turning the problem around, what is the lowest cost at which 2,000 units of output can be produced? Once again, the optimum point occurs where the isoquant (representing 2,000 units of output or IQ_2) is tangent to an isocost function. Any other point on this isoquant gives the same output, but at a higher cost than the minimum cost tangency point. Point Y in Figure 9–9, for instance, still produces the desired output of 2,000 units; but by being farther to the right than C_2, namely on C_3, it involves a higher cost. Thus, 2,000 units of output can be produced at the lowest total cost when b_2 units of factor b and a_2 units of factor a are used.

If the firm should decide to produce a different amount of output, say, 3,000 units, then, with given relative factor prices, its entire isocost function would have to shift outward in a parallel fashion. The new optimum point for 3,000 units of output would be at point P. If factor prices are constant, isocline EH traces the optimal combination of inputs involving all the tangency points. This curve is called the *expansion path* or *scale line* of the firm. In the case of a linearly homogeneous production function which has constant returns to scale operating at all output levels, the expansion path is a straight line out of the origin, as in Figure 9–10(a).

Figure 9–10(b) shows the expansion path of a firm whose production function exhibits decreasing returns to scale. Such a firm can maximize output for any given expenditure ($\bar{C}_i$) by varying the proportions of the two factors used while increasing the use of both. The result is a nonlinear expansion path, which could be convex as well as concave, or could be convex in some ranges and concave in others.

The general equation for obtaining the optimum combination of inputs is then:

$$MRTS_{ab} = -P_a/P_b \tag{9.9}$$

At the point of tangency of the isocost line and the isoquant, the slopes of the two functions are equal. The slope of the isocost function is $-P_a/P_b$. The slope of the isoquant is the $MRTS_{ab}$. But from (9.2) we know that the $MRTS_{ab} = -MPP_a/MPP_b$. Therefore, neglecting signs as usual, expression (9.9) can be written as:

$$\frac{MPP_a}{MPP_b} = \frac{P_a}{P_b} \text{ or } \frac{MPP_a}{P_a} = \frac{MPP_b}{P_b} \tag{9.10}$$

Thus, we can see the formal equivalence of the traditional production function and the modern isoquant analysis, and the conclusions are the same: For a

FIGURE 9–10   Construction of Expansion Paths

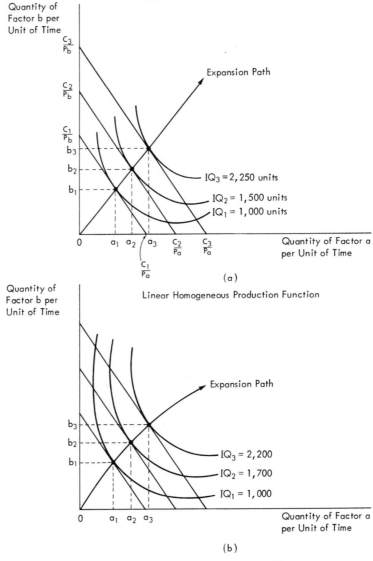

(a)

Linear Homogeneous Production Function

(b)

Nonhomogeneous Production Function

factor combination to be the optimum or least-cost combination, the ratio of the factor marginal physical productivities must equal the ratio of their respective prices; or alternatively, the *MPP* of a dollar's worth of any factor must equal the *MPP* of a dollar's worth of every other factor employed.

Substitution and Output Effect

In discussing consumer goods, we indicated that a change in a commodity's price has two theoretically discernible effects, a substitution effect and an income effect. The substitution effect is always negative — that is, price changes always lead to quantity changes in the opposite direction; e.g., a decline in the P_x leads to an increase in the QD_x. Also, the income effect normally is negative, reinforcing the substitution effect — a decline in the P_x leads to an increase in real income and hence usually (i.e., for a "normal" good) to an increase in the QD_x. The firm experiences similar types of reactions, only these reactions are referred to as the substitution effect and the output effect. The *substitution effect* shows how a fall in a factor's relative price leads to more of it being employed, even if the firm's total production remains constant. The *output effect* also leads to more of any (superior) factor being employed, since lower factor prices mean lower costs. These lower costs lead the firm to expand total output and hence use more of the cheaper factor. In this context, a factor is superior (inferior) when a firm employs more (less) of the input as its real cost outlays increase. Figure 9–11 depicts this distinction between the substitution effect and the output effect.

Figure 9–11 assumes that: (1) there are two inputs, labor (L) and capital (K); (2) the wage rate has fallen so that the isocost line is now IC_2 instead of IC_1; (3) IQ_1 and IQ_2 are the pertinent production isoquants; and (4) the firm is initially at its optimum at point X, using $0K_1$ units of capital and $0L_1$ units of labor. After the relative price change, the new optimum is at point $Z;$ but this

FIGURE 9–11   **Substitution and Output Effects of a Change in the Price of a Factor of Production**

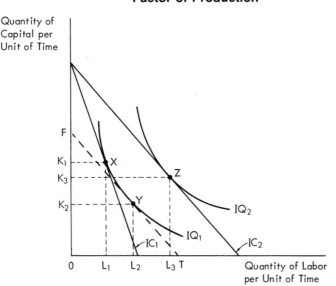

movement represents the total effect, composed of both the substitution and output effects.

A movement along original isoquant IQ_1 from point X to point Y represents the pure substitution effect. At Y, $0K_2$ and $0L_2$ units of the inputs are used. Point Y is obtained by constructing the fictional isocost line FT parallel to IC_2, so that the new factor price ratio prevails and is tangent to IQ_1, which keeps the output level constant.

The movement from Y to Z is the output effect. The output expands because of the lower factor price for labor, causing the original budget to command more total resources or a lower total cost for any given output, thereby inducing the firm to use $L_2 - L_3$ units more of labor, and $K_2 - K_3$ units more of capital than it would use if only the substitution effect were present.

For the most part, the substitution effect and the output effect in production theory are analogous to the substitution effect and the income effect in consumption theory. But there is one notable difference. While both analyses allow for inferior goods or inferior inputs, the Giffen good has no equivalent on the production side. Put differently, a factor's demand curve is always negatively sloped, whereas a Giffen good or positively sloped output demand curve is possible. While the output effect can be in the opposite direction from the substitution effect, as in the case of an inferior input, the output effect can never be large enough to offset the substitution effect. This fact represents one of the few nonsymmetries between the input and output demand analyses.

Basically, the reason for this nonsymmetry is this: The output effect for production theory is capable of definition and parallels the income effect for consumer theory. But the output effect is an economic construct in a way that the income effect is not. The firm, in deciding what to do when the price of a factor changes, does not in fact operate with an output constraint. It operates to maximize its profits. This means that, in the firm's demand for factors, there is not in fact an output effect in the same way that there is an income effect for the consumer. The firm's demand for factors depends upon all the prices but not upon its own output, which is also a decision variable. It is this consideration that results in the absence of Giffen goods in the demand for factors.

TECHNICAL PROGRESS

To this point, the analysis has implicitly assumed that the production function is static. But technological progress does occur. Nobel Laureate John R. Hicks defines technical progress as capital-using, neutral, or labor-using, depending upon whether the $MRTS_{LK}$ diminishes, remains unchanged, or increases at the originally given capital-labor ratio. Put differently, technical change is labor-using if the MPP_L increases by more than the MPP_K (at a given capital-labor ratio), thereby encouraging the firm to use relatively more labor. In graphic terms, a labor-saving technological development would shift the isoquant map downward toward the origin; and with labor measured on the x axis, the slope of the isoquant would get steeper, indicating the MPP_L has increased relative to the MPP_K. Of course, the slope of an isoquant is called the $MRTS_{LK}$ and equals the ratio of the MPP_L/MPP_K. For capital-using and neutral technological progress, the isoquants shift downward but the slopes become flatter or remain unchanged respectively.

QUESTIONS

1. Prove algebraically that the slope of an isoquant is equal to the ratio of the marginal physical products of the two inputs.
2. Draw an isoquant and mark on it point A where the marginal physical product of factor a is zero, and point B where the marginal physical product of b is zero. Are there ranges on the isoquant you have drawn where the MPPs of the two factors are negative?
3. The text states that, "A straight-line isoquant means the factors are perfect substitutes." Explain in commonsense terms why this is so.
4. Refer to Figure 9–4. How is the MPP_a calculated along horizontal line $\bar{b}_1$? Can you tell by looking at the graph that the MPP_a is falling between A and D? If factor a were held constant at a_3, what can be said from the graph about the MPP_b?
5. Show that with a given cost outlay any combination of the two factors on an isocost function is possible.
6. Show the equivalence of these two statements concerning the objectives of the firm:
   (a) A firm wishes to produce a given output for the least cost.
   (b) A firm wishes to produce the largest output for a given cost.
7. Explain why a firm would find it unwise to utilize factor proportions where $MRTS_{ab} > P_a/P_b$ or where $MRTS_{ab} < P_a/P_b$.
8. Graph and explain the substitution effect and the output effect of a change in the price of a factor of production.

APPENDIX: MATHEMATICAL NOTES

Note 1. Factor Optimum

We can use the discussion of consumer optimum in note 1 of Chapter 4's Appendix to prove the factor optimum condition given in (9.10). We need only change MUs to MPPs, commodity prices to input prices, and income to cost outlay, and let U represent output instead of utility. Even the second-order conditions are the same.

Note 2. Proof that Factor Demand Curves Are Downsloping

If $q_x = f(a,b)$ is the production function, a firm's total profits (π) – equal to its total revenue (or $P_x \cdot q_x$) minus its total costs (or $P_a \cdot a + P_b \cdot b + F$, where F is fixed costs) – from producing commodity x are:

$$\pi = TR_x - TC_x = P_x \cdot f(a,b) - a \cdot P_a - b \cdot P_b - F \qquad (9.11)$$

The first-order or necessary conditions for maximizing profits are:

$$P_x \frac{\delta q}{\delta a} - P_a = 0, \quad P_x \frac{\delta q}{\delta a} = P_a \tag{9.12}$$

$$P_x \frac{\delta q}{\delta b} - P_b = 0, \quad P_x \frac{\delta q}{\delta b} = P_b$$

Since $\delta q / \delta a = MPP_a$, $\delta q / \delta b = MPP_b$, these conditions say that, for factor optimum to exist, the VMP_a (the value of the marginal product of factor $a = P_x \cdot MPP_a$) must equal the P_a and the VMP_b ($= P_x \cdot MPP_b$) must equal the P_b. The second-order or sufficient condition for a maximum requires that:

$$\frac{\delta^2 q}{\delta a^2} < 0, \quad \frac{\delta^2 q}{\delta b^2} < 0 \quad \text{and} \quad \frac{\delta^2 q}{\delta_a^2} \cdot \frac{\delta^2 q}{\delta b^2} > \left(\frac{\delta^2 q}{\delta a \delta b}\right)^2 \tag{9.13}$$

In economic terms, these first two conditions state that the marginal productivities of the inputs must be declining.[7] If the necessary conditions given in (9.12) are differentiated with respect to the P_a, holding the P_b and P_x constant, the results are:

$$P_x \left(\frac{\delta^2 q}{\delta a^2} \cdot \frac{\delta a}{\delta P_a} + \frac{\delta^2 q}{\delta a \delta b} \cdot \frac{\delta b}{\delta P_a}\right) = 1 \tag{9.14}$$

$$P_x \left(\frac{\delta^2 q}{\delta b \delta a} \cdot \frac{\delta a}{\delta P_a} + \frac{\delta^2 q}{\delta b^2} \cdot \frac{\delta b}{\delta P_a}\right) = 0$$

from which we get:

$$\frac{\delta a}{\delta P_a} = \frac{\dfrac{\delta^2 q}{\delta b^2}}{P_x \left[\left(\dfrac{\delta^2 q}{\delta a^2} \cdot \dfrac{\delta^2 q}{\delta b^2}\right) - \left(\dfrac{\delta^2 q}{\delta a \delta b}\right)^2\right]} \tag{9.15}$$

The second-order conditions show therefore that the slope of a factor demand curve is negative, given the required signs in (9.13). Since the $P_a = P_x(\delta q / \delta a)$, i.e., $P_a = VMP_a$ from (9.12), differentiating this with respect to P_a, assuming factor b and P_x are constant, yields:

$$\frac{\delta a}{\delta P_a} = \frac{1}{P_x \dfrac{\delta^2 q}{\delta a^2}} \tag{9.16}$$

Thus, the slope with respect to the price axis of the long-run factor demand curve, which assumes the price of other inputs is constant $(\overline{P}_b)$, is numerically larger than the short-run factor demand, which assumes the quantity of other factors is constant $(\overline{b})$.

Note 3. Homogeneous Functions

The partial derivatives of a production function homogeneous of degree n are homogeneous of degree $n - 1$. Note, a production function, $q = f(a,b)$, is homogeneous of degree n if:

---

[7] The second-order conditions given in equation (9.13) are violated under constant returns. In economic terms, all conditions together state that the marginal product of any linear combination of factors must be declining.

$$\text{(a)} \quad \lambda^n q = f(\lambda a, \lambda b) \tag{9.17}$$

or

$$\text{(b)} \quad \lambda^n f(a,b) = f(\lambda a, \lambda b)$$

where n is a constant and λ is any positive real number. Differentiating (9.17b) partially with respect to factor a (letting f_a denote partial differentiation) using the function of a function rule on the right, yields:

$$\lambda^n f_a(a,b) = \lambda f_a(\lambda a, \lambda b) \tag{9.18}$$

Dividing through (9.18) by λ yields:

$$\lambda^{n-1} f_a(a,b) = f_a(\lambda a, \lambda b) \tag{9.19}$$

which is the definition of a function which is homogeneous of degree $n-1$.

Note 4. Expansion Path

Given a general production function, $g = f(K,L)$, the expansion path is an implicit function of factors capital (K) and labor (L):

$$g(K,L) = 0 \tag{9.20}$$

for which the first- and second-order conditions for constrained maxima (for output given cost outlay) or minima (for cost outlay given output) are fulfilled. If the isoquants are convex, the second-order conditions are always satisfied, and the expansion path can be derived from the first-order conditions. Thus, for instance, for the Cobb-Douglas function, $q = AK^\alpha L^{1-\alpha}$, the expansion path is given by the implicit function:

$$(1-\alpha) P_K \cdot K - \alpha P_L \cdot L = 0 \tag{9.21}$$

which is a linear function emanating from the origin in the isoquant plane.

Note 5.[8] A Summary of the Mathematical Properties of a Homogeneous Production Function of Degree One (i.e., Linear Homogeneous), $q = f(a,b)$

1. $q = f(a,b)$ can be written in the following form: $q = a\phi(b/a)$, or $q = b\psi(a/b)$.
2. The first partial derivatives f_a, f_b are homogeneous of degree zero, i.e., f_a and f_b are functions of the ratio a/b only.
3. $q = af_a + bf_b$ (Euler's Theorem).
4. $af_{aa} = -bf_{ab}$ and $bf_{bb} = -af_{ab}$, i.e., $f_{aa} < 0$ or $f_{bb} < 0$ implies $f_{ab} > 0$.
5. $f_{bb} = \dfrac{a^2}{b^2} f_{aa}$.

From 4 and 5 it follows that:

6. $f_{aa} = f_{bb} = f_{ab} = 0$ when any one of the three is zero and $a,b > 0$.
7. $q^2 = a^2 f_a^2 + 2abf_af_b + b^2 f_b^2$.
8. $f_{aaa} = -\dfrac{1}{a} f_{aaa} - \dfrac{b^3}{a^3} f_{bbb}$.

---

[8] See, e.g., Charles E. Ferguson, *The Neoclassical Theory of Production and Distribution* (Cambridge: Cambridge University Press, 1969). The subscripts indicate partial differentiation, e.g., $f_a = \delta q / \delta a$.

9. $\sigma = \dfrac{f_a f_b}{a f_{ab}} \left(\text{in general, } \sigma = \dfrac{f_a f_b (a f_a + b f_b)}{ab(f_{aa} f_b^2 - 2 f_{ab} f_a f_b + f_{bb} f_a^2)} \right).$

10. The isoclines are linear.

Note 6. A Summary of the Mathematical Properties of Homogeneous Production Functions of Degree n, $q = f(a,b)$

1. $q = f(a,b)$ can be written as $q = a^n \phi(b/a)$ or $q = b^n \psi(a/b)$.
2. The first partial derivatives f_a and f_b are homogeneous of degree $n - 1$.
3. $nq = af_a + bf_b$ (Euler's Theorem).
4. $n(n - 1)q = f_a^2 f_{aa} + 2ab f_{ab} + f_b^2 f_{bb}$.
5. $\sigma = \dfrac{f_a f_b}{(1 - n) f_a f_b + nq f_{ab}}.$
6. The isoclines are linear.

10   Costs of Production

The interaction of the forces of supply and demand determines commodity prices. Chapters 4–7 explored the basic factors underlying demand. Chapters 8 and 9 laid the bases for understanding supply. The basic factor underlying the ability and willingness of a firm to supply a product is its cost of production. The principles of production, described in Chapters 8 and 9, along with factor prices explain the theory of cost. Costs are obviously important in supply decisions since the production of any economic good requires the use of economic resources which, because of their relative scarcity, bear price tags. But cost information is not sufficient to predict supplies. The amount of any commodity which a firm is willing to supply in the market depends upon the price or cost of resources essential to its production and the price or revenue the commodity will bring in the market. In this chapter, we will describe in some detail the firm's short-run and long-run costs. But first we will briefly discuss the firm's decision-making process.

DECISION-MAKING BY THE FIRM IN DIFFERENT TIME HORIZONS

Before a firm can decide what quantity to produce and what price to sell for, it needs to know what production costs and sales revenue to expect. It can obtain the relevant data on cost curves from production function figures and factor prices. For instance, if the firm knows that the services of an extra laborer cost $10 a day (assuming labor services are the only variable input) and the marginal physical product of labor is five units, the extra or marginal cost of producing an additional unit of output is $2 ($10/5 units = $2 per unit). Physical production conditions together with factor prices determine production costs.

Revenue or demand conditions, on the other hand, depend upon the market structure. In other words, the revenue conditions facing the firm are determined by whether the market is one of pure competition, pure monopoly, monopolistic competition, or oligopoly. After the cost conditions have been fully described in this chapter, succeeding chapters will take up the revenue conditions in each of these markets separately.

The firm needs information on both cost and revenue to determine its profits. The firm acts as if it is trying to maximize its total profits. The total profits from producing commodity x (π_x) may be expressed in either total or average terms. In total terms, $\pi_x = TR_x - TC_x$, where TR_x is total revenue and TC_x is total cost. In average terms, $\pi_x = (P_x - ATC_x)\, Q_x$, where ATC_x is the average total cost of producing and selling. If a firm has total sales of $100 and total costs of $80, $\pi_x = \$100 - \$80 = \$20$. Alternatively, profit per unit (or the profit margin) can be computed by subtracting the ATC_x of $.80 from the P_x of $1. The resulting profit per unit, $.20, may be multiplied by the number of units sold, 100, to arrive at the same total profits, $20.

Equimarginal Principle

The *equimarginal principle* can be used to describe a firm's behavior just as it was used to rationalize the actions of a consumer. In addition to the marginal approach, we can also identify the firm's maximum-profit (minimum-loss) output as the particular output yielding the greatest excess of total revenue (TR) over total costs (TC) (or least excess of costs over revenue).

The firm's decision-maker tries to reconcile the conflict between the desire to maximize TR, which ordinarily increases with output, and the desire to minimize TC, which also increases with output. Therefore, the entrepreneur must always determine what effect changes in output will have on both TR and TC. If TR increases more than TC increases, it pays to expand output. If TR increases by $5 and TC by only $4 from selling one more unit of output, the change results in $1 more profits (or $1 less losses). If TR decreases less than TC decreases when output is reduced, it pays to contract output.

The change in total revenue resulting from a unit change in quantity sold is marginal revenue. The change in total cost resulting from a unit change in quantity produced is marginal cost. The equimarginal principle on the production side states that a firm maximizes its profits (or minimizes its losses) by producing where marginal revenue (MR) equals marginal cost (MC). When MR is not equal to MC, it always pays a firm to change output. When $MR > MC$, it is preferable to expand output. When $MR < MC$, it is best to contract output.

Meaning of Costs and Profits

Before we can understand why firms seek to maximize profits, we must have a clear definition of the concept of profits. The accountant defines profit as the residual from subtracting the explicit expenses of production from sales receipts. But to the economist, *profit* is total revenue minus all costs—explicit and implicit. Implicit costs involve no direct money outlay or out-of-pocket costs as do explicit costs.

The distinction between implicit and explicit costs stems from the economist's use of costs in the sense of alternatives or opportunities given up. The *alternative cost doctrine* states that the cost of any action is measured in terms of the alternatives sacrificed or opportunities foregone in pursuing that course. The cost of producing some particular commodity x is the value of the alternative products foregone to which the resources used in the production of x could have been devoted. The classic illustration of this is "guns vs. butter": the cost to society of producing war goods is measured in terms of the reduced production and hence consumption of civilian goods. The real cost of resources to the firm is the payments which must be made to obtain or retain the resource services in their present employment, and these payments are their values in the next best alternative use.

It is in translating the real economic costs into money terms that the explicit-implicit distinction occurs. Everyone would consider the money payments or cash outlays to resource suppliers outside the firm as costs. These explicit business costs would include all the following types of expenses: $100,000 in wages for labor, $50,000 for materials, $60,000 for land rent, etc. In addition, the economist — but not the accountant — would include in total costs implicit costs, i.e., the remuneration of self-owned, self-employed resources. In money terms, implicit costs are the money payments which the self-employed resources could have earned in alternative employments if the owners had not put them to work in their own firm. Thus, business profits equal a firm's total revenue minus its business costs, whereas economic profits are the difference between a company's total revenue and its total or full costs.

Suppose two similar firms in the same industry were both considering expanding productive facilities by $100,000, one by retained earnings or past profits not paid out in dividends and the other by borrowing at the going market rate of interest. The first firm, call it firm A, would have no explicit interest cost, while the second, call it firm B, would. Yet firm A has implicit costs which firm B does not have, the exact amount of which is determined by the going market price of the resources owned by the firm. The implicit cost to firm A is the interest rate obtainable in the market if the money were loaned out instead of invested in the firm. If the current market rate of interest is 8 percent, there is an implicit cost of $8,000 because the $100,000 is being used for expansion within the firm rather than being lent out. This "lost" interest represents the alternative or opportunity sacrificed. The same conclusion holds for owned building and land that likewise would bear an explicit rental charge; the services of a business owner who also manages his or her own firm, thereby avoiding the explicit costs of a hired manager; etc. Note that accountants already recognize some implicit costs and the tendency seems to be towards recognizing more. Depreciation is a good example of an implicit cost that accountants actually record.

Time Considerations

In the long run, the quantity of all factors is variable. Put differently, the long run is a period of time sufficiently long to allow existing firms to expand or liquidate their plant and equipment and to permit new firms to enter the industry. In contrast, in the short run, some factors are relatively fixed in quantity in that altering their quantity would not be economically feasible. That is, in the short run, existing firms are unable to alter their plant and equipment, except to scrap them, and new firms do not have time to enter the industry.

To repeat a point made earlier, the distinction between the short run and the long run has little to do with a calendar time period, such as a year. Rather these runs refer to operational time periods or to sets of conditions relating to the possible adjustments that may be made. For example, the short run could possibly be longer than the long run because it takes a longer time for existing firms to build new plant and equipment than for new firms to come into the industry. There are two more periods of adjustment or time periods that are considerably less well developed theoretically in economics: the very long-run (or secular) period in which technology as well as all factors are variable, and the very short-run (or market or immediate) period in which only a fixed quantity of output is available.

The long-run liquidation of plant and equipment may be accomplished by the failure to replace items wearing out or becoming obsolete. However, in the short run, a firm may be "stuck" with its plant and equipment. Under these circumstances, a firm may be better off continuing to produce even though it is suffering losses. In the short run, the immediate alternatives facing a firm which has total costs exceeding total revenue are: (1) to close down, thereby losing its investment in plant and equipment (minus its scrap value); or (2) to continue producing into the long run, during which time the plant and equipment depreciate out of existence. The second possibility results in smaller losses than the first whenever the firm's total sales revenue is greater than its total variable costs, even though total costs are not covered.

A firm's variable costs vary with its output, whereas total fixed costs remain the same regardless of the firm's rate of production (i.e., they are independent of the rate of output). Fixed costs include all payments on a long-term contractual basis: interest expenses on borrowed funds, rent on buildings and land, insurance premiums, property taxes, some depreciation charges (to the extent that depreciation is a function of time alone), wages and salaries of certain key personnel, etc. In contrast, variable costs include only those payments which depend upon the rate of output: costs of raw materials, fuel, power (above basic charges), noncontractual wage and salary payments, depreciation (to the extent that depreciation depends on output), etc. Total costs are the sum of variable and fixed costs. As an empirical fact, in most industries fixed costs are usually smaller than variable costs. A more detailed discussion of all the conventional cost functions and curves is provided below.

It is important to understand why a firm would produce in the short run if its variable costs are met by its sales revenue, regardless of whether fixed costs are covered. Even if a firm stops producing, it is still obligated for its fixed costs. Therefore, any excess of total revenue over total variable costs helps to meet total fixed costs. In other words, whenever a firm's net revenue, defined as total revenue minus total variable costs, is positive, the firm will benefit from producing in the short run. It is better to take a smaller loss while producing than a larger loss (equal to total fixed cost) when not producing. Of course, if this situation is expected to persist in the long run, the firm will start making adjustments; namely, depreciating its plant and equipment and eventually quitting the industry. If variable costs are not met by sales revenue, the firm should shut down immediately to avoid incurring unnecessary losses.

Costs, Profits, and Supply

The supply of a commodity is generally closely related to its production costs. The exceptions to this general rule include physically nonreproducible goods—such as Velázquez' painting *Portrait of Juan de Parejo,* which was purchased by the Metropolitan Museum of Art in New York City in 1971 for $5,544,000—and goods physically reproducible in the short run and long run but not in the immediate period. In such cases the "bygones are bygones" rule is applicable. However, once beyond the very short-run period, costs of production become the main determinant of supply for the physically reproducible good that is the main concern of this text.

The role of costs in the short run is quite different from their role in the long run. In the long run, a firm must receive no less than zero economic profits to stay in business. In the short run, production will continue if sales revenue covers variable costs even though business profits are less than zero. By at least partially meeting its fixed charges, a firm loses less by producing than by closing down, in which case the entire total fixed costs must still be met. In other words, the analysis of competitive pricing rests upon the fundamental thesis: In both the short run and long run, every competitive firm's supply curve of a physically reproducible commodity is a cost curve, although not vice versa. Goods whose production cannot be altered and therefore whose costs of production have already been incurred account for our time-period qualification. In the immediate run, costs (and profits) may have little or no connection with supply. The "not vice versa" qualification refers to the fact that some cost curves are never supply curves.

SHORT-RUN COST FUNCTIONS

Fixed and variable costs can be divided into several important subcategories. To be sure, some cost items may be hard to classify as fixed or variable. One such example might be the depreciation costs of a piece of capital equipment, such as a machine. The more the machine is used, the more it wears out; this can be regarded as a variable cost. In addition, the machine depreciates each year just because it grows older or becomes obsolete; this is a fixed cost.

The lowest costs which a firm or industry can achieve will depend upon the type of adjustments it is able to make in the amounts of resources it employs. That is, the classification of costs depends on the length of the "run." In fact, only in the short run does the distinction between fixed and variable costs hold. Since the long run is a period of time sufficiently long for a firm to vary the amounts of all resources used (including the size or scale of the firm's plant), all costs are variable in the long run.

Importance of the Law of Proportionality

Since at least some factors are, by definition, fixed in the short run, the law of proportionality is operative and provides the fundamental explanation for the shapes of the various cost curves in that period. A firm's cost of producing any level of output depends on both the prices and the quantities of needed resources. Under competitive conditions in the factor market, the prices of factors to any firm are constant at the market price. Since factor prices are constant, variations in the quantity of factors determine the shape of the cost curves. The law of diminishing returns explains how the required amount of factors varies as output changes.

Total Cost Curves

In depicting short-run cost curves, both the average and marginal versions of the law of diminishing returns are important. The law's marginal physical product formulation explains the shape of marginal costs and the average physical product version explains average variable costs. In addition to explaining these per-unit curves, the law provides underpinnings for the total curves, which we shall take up first. Table 10–1 illustrates the various cost concepts, total and per unit, and shows the way the costs of producing commodity x might change as plant output in a given time period (say, per day) increases from 0 to 11 units. Only the total figures given in columns (1) through (4) are relevant for the moment.

Total Fixed Costs. *Total fixed costs* (*TFC*) represent the obligation that the firm has to pay for its fixed resources. *TFC* is the number of units of the fixed factors times their respective prices. $TFC = FF_a \cdot P_a + FF_b \cdot P_b + \cdots + FF_n \cdot P_n$, where FF_i are the time rates of services of the different fixed factors. Since the quantities of the fixed factors are by definition fixed in the short run, the aggregate outlay on them must remain constant irrespective of what happens to the firm's level of output. There is a rough correspondence between what economists term "fixed" costs and the business term "overhead" costs.

Actually, from an opportunity-cost doctrine, the term "costs" in "fixed costs" is a misnomer. That is, costs are measured in economics in terms of

TABLE 10–1   Cost Concepts Illustrated

Total Costs				Per-Unit Costs			
(1)	(2)	(3)	(4)	(5)	(6)	(7)	(8)
$TPP = Q_x$	TFC	TVC	TC	AFC	AVC	ATC	MC
			(2) + (3)	(2) ÷ (1)	(3) ÷ (1)	(4) ÷ (1)	Δ(3)/Δ(1) or Δ(4)/Δ(1)
0	$100	$ 0	$ 100	$ ∞	$ 0	$ ∞	$ 0
1	100	100	200	100.00	100.00	200.00	100
2	100	190	290	50.00	95.00	145.00	90
3	100	270	370	33.33	90.00	123.33	80
4	100	340	440	25.00	85.00	110.00	70
5	100	420	520	20.00	84.00	104.00	80
6	100	510	610	16.67	85.00	101.67	90
7	100	610	710	14.29	87.14	101.43	100
8	100	720	820	12.50	90.00	102.50	110
9	100	840	940	11.11	93.33	104.44	120
10	100	990	1,090	10.00	99.00	109.00	150
11	100	1,190	1,290	9.09	108.18	117.27	200

the alternatives or opportunities foregone; but in the case of fixed costs, once the contractual arrangements have been made, alternatives are no longer available to the firm. Hence, some economists prefer the terms "noncost outlay" or "fixed outlay" in place of "fixed costs." However, since the "fixed costs" terminology is so widely employed, we will continue to use it here.

Total Variable Costs. In contrast to fixed costs, *total variable costs* (*TVC*) vary with a firm's rate of production since a larger output requires a larger quantity of variable inputs. However, the rate of increase in variable costs is not constant because of the law of diminishing returns. At first, if there is a stage 1 of productivity, *TVC* will increase, but at a decreasing rate. Eventually, however, *TVC* will increase at an increasing rate as diminishing returns set in. This occurs after the fourth unit of output in Table 10–1.

To show the relationship between the input expense and the output cost, consider Figure 10–1. The southeast quadrant is the familiar *TPP* curve showing output as a function of the variable inputs, though to make it look familiar you will have to turn your book on its side. The southwest quadrant just has a 45° line from the origin so that quantities measured vertically equal quantities measured horizontally, which allows us to determine the variable factor quantities on the northwest quadrant. In that quadrant is a straight line from the origin, which with a constant price of the variable factor gives *TVC* as a function of Q_v, the quantity of the variable *input*. The slope of the line is the price

FIGURE 10–1   Construction of *TVC* Curve

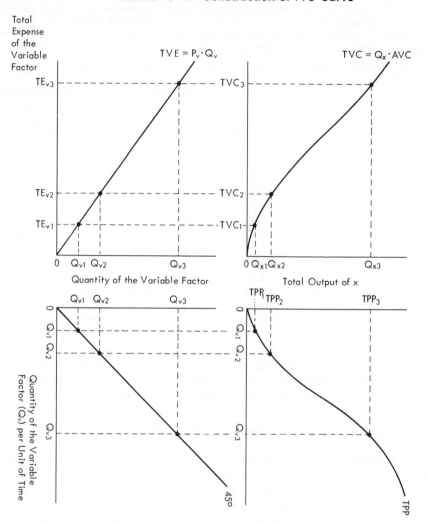

of the variable input. The amounts of *TVC* are then plotted in the northeast quadrant, where *TVC* is a function of *output*.

Total Costs. *Total costs* (*TC*) are the sum of fixed and variable costs at each level of output. That is,

$$TC = TFC + TVC \qquad\qquad (10.1)$$

Thus, at five units of output in Table 10–1, $TC = \$100 + \$420 = \$520$. Alternatively, we can define total costs as:

$$TC = Q_a \cdot P_a + Q_b \cdot P_b + \cdots + Q_n \cdot P_n \qquad\qquad \text{(10.2)}$$

where Q_a, Q_b, Q_c, ..., Q_n are the flow of factor services rendered per unit of time, and P_a, P_b, P_c, ..., P_n are the prices of the factor services. In the short run, no more than n-1 of these factors are variable; or to turn it around, at least one of the n inputs must be fixed in total quantity. Graphically, the TC curve starts at the level of the TFC curve and then assumes the general contours of the TVC curve. In other words, the *level* of the TFC curve determines the y intercept and the *shape* of the TVC curve determines the slope of the TC curve. Since changes in output do not affect TFC, the TVC and TC curves must have the same slope at any given level of output. The vertical distance between TC and TVC measures TFC and represents a smaller and smaller percentage of total cost as the rate of production becomes larger and larger. The three total cost curves are shown in Figure 10–2.

Per-Unit Cost Curves

For many purposes, per-unit cost curves are more helpful than total curves. For instance, since product price is a per-unit (revenue) concept, per-unit costs are more useful for comparison than total costs.   The four per-unit cost

FIGURE 10–2   Total Cost Curves

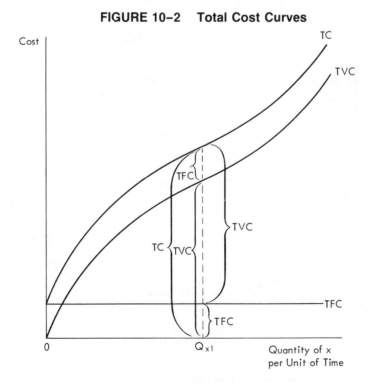

curves include the average fixed cost curve, the average variable cost curve, the average total cost curve, and the marginal cost curve. Table 10–1 illustrates all of these per-unit costs numerically with their corresponding total costs.

Average Fixed Costs. *Average fixed costs* (*AFC*) at different levels of production are found by dividing *TFC* by the corresponding output. That is,

$$AFC = TFC/Q_x \qquad\qquad (10.3)$$

where *TFC* is the constant total fixed costs and Q_x is the total output. Since the numerator is a constant, as the denominator, total output, becomes larger and larger, the entire fraction (*AFC*) must get smaller and smaller. This continuously falling *AFC* as output expands is what business people commonly call "spreading the overhead."

Figure 10–3 illustrates all four per-unit cost curves. The average fixed cost curve is shown explicitly only in panel (a), since indirectly it is already shown in panel (b) as the vertical distance between *ATC* and *AVC*.

Geometrically, the *AFC* curve is a rectangular hyperbola. Such a geometric figure is constructed of rectangles of equal area. These rectangles are formed by dropping lines to the *y* and *x* axes at all points on the *AFC* curve. Five such

FIGURE 10–3   Per-Unit Cost Curves

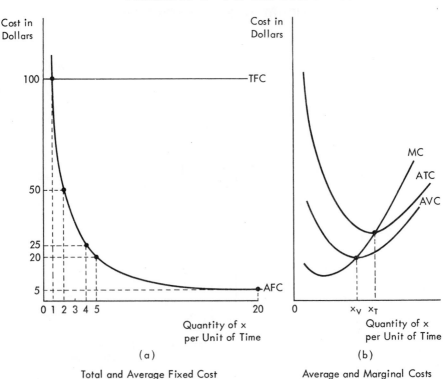

(a)
Total and Average Fixed Cost

(b)
Average and Marginal Costs

rectangles have been constructed in Figure 10–3(a). By the definition of a rectangular hyperbola, these areas must all be equal. Since the vertical axis measures AFC, the area of the rectangles is equal to TFC. Since we know TFC is constant at \$100, the AFC curve must be a rectangular hyperbola.

Average Variable Costs. *Average variable costs* (AVC) are found by dividing TVC by total output. Symbolically,

$$AVC = TVC/Q_x \qquad \qquad (10.4)$$

The law of diminishing average product provides the fundamental explanation for the shape of this curve. The AVC curve is a reflection of the APP curve. This is illustrated in Figure 10–4.

FIGURE 10–4   Construction of the AVC Curve

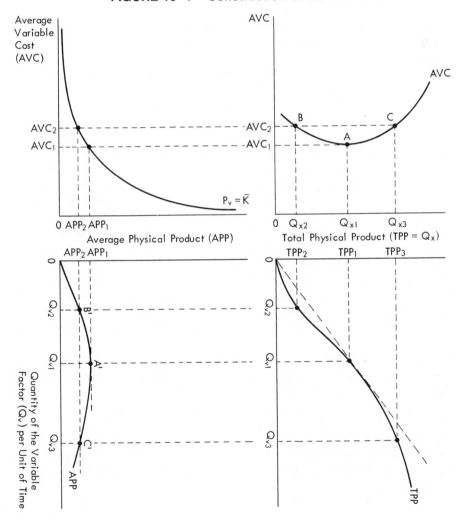

To read this graph, first turn your book on its side so the TPP and APP curves look normal. The TPP curve is the fundamental one, showing how the output of the commodity being produced varies as inputs of the variable factor change. The APP curve is derived from the TPP curve, as demonstrated in earlier chapters. A point of orientation is at Q_{v1} amount of variable factor use where the APP is at its maximum.

The curve labeled $P_v = \bar{K}$ in the northwest quadrant requires explanation. First we need to show the relationship between AVC and APP by the following substitutions:

$$AVC = \frac{TVC}{Q_x} = \frac{Q_v \cdot P_v}{Q_v \cdot APP} = \frac{P_v}{APP} \tag{10.5}$$

and therefore:

$$P_v = AVC \cdot APP = \bar{K} \text{ (a constant)} \tag{10.6}$$

where Q_v, P_v, and APP are the quantity, price, and average physical product, respectively, of the variable input, and Q_x is the total output or TPP of commodity x.

By definition, TVC equals the quantity of variable inputs hired times their respective prices. For example, if 10 units of labor (labor being the only variable input) are hired at \$2 each, TVC equals \$20. Total physical product, Q_x, equals the average physical product times the number of units of the variable factor. In this case $Q_x = APP_L \cdot Q_L$, where APP_L is the average physical product and Q_L the quantity of labor. If each laborer, on the average, produces 6 bushels of wheat, and there are 10 workers, the total output of wheat is 60 bushels. In (10.5), the Q_v term is common to both the numerator and the denominator and may be eliminated. This gives us $AVC = P_v/APP$. Since under competitive conditions in the input market the firm may hire all the inputs it wants at the going market price, P_v is a constant, so we may write $AVC = \bar{K}/APP$. Therefore, AVC is inversely and proportionately related to APP. When AVC is at a minimum, APP is at a maximum, such as points A and A' in Figure 10–4. This also makes good economic sense. If workers are paid a constant wage of, say, \$10 per hour per worker, the point at which AVC is minimized occurs where APP is maximized. Thus, with $P_L = \$10$, if $APP = 2$ bushels, AVC is \$5; at $APP = 5$ bushels, $AVC = \$2$; at $APP = 10, AVC = \$1$; and so on.

Returning to the $P_v = \bar{K}$ curve in Figure 10–4, since $P_v = AVC \cdot APP = \bar{K}$, the curve is a rectangular hyperbola. For a given amount of variable factor used (say, $Q_{v1} = 10$ workers), we know the APP is APP_1 (say, 6 bushels). Now, if $P_v = \bar{K}$ is \$2 per worker, we know the AVC (that is, the average labor cost per unit of output of x) is $AVC_1 = P_r/APP_1 = \$2/6 \ bu. = \$.33$. The AVC_1 amount can now be transferred to the northeast quadrant to determine a point (A) on the average variable cost curve at total output $Q_{x1} = TPP_1$. Every point on the AVC curve is derived in the same way, though only the construction of points A, B, and C is shown.

If the price of the variable input were to increase, the rectangular hyperbola would shift to the right; and if you then traced the new AVC curve, you would find that the AVC curve shifts upward. Try it.

If there is first a stage of increasing APP and then a phase of decreasing APP, the AVC curve will be U-shaped, as depicted in Figure 10–3(b) and 10–4. The range of decreasing AVC corresponds to stage 1 in our earlier discussion of a linear homogeneous production function. At low levels of output, capital equipment in the plant is underutilized and production is inefficient and costly, reflecting the fact that not enough variable resources are being combined with the fixed plant. As output expands, greater specialization and a more complete utilization of a firm's capital equipment will result in more efficient production and a declining AVC. For instance, a dozen or so workers can hardly operate a modern steel mill as efficiently as, say, 100 or so. Additional workers lead to greater efficiency up to a certain point, point A in Figure 10–4. After diminishing average returns set in, the AVC curve will turn up.

Average Total Costs. The *average total cost* (ATC) curve can be found by dividing total costs (TC) by total output or by adding AFC and AVC. That is,

$$ATC = TC/Q_x = AFC + AVC \tag{10.7}$$

As depicted in Figure 10–3(b), the ATC curve is typically thought to be U-shaped. This reflects the fact that, given the scale of plant, the larger the firm's output, the greater the efficiency of the fixed resources. This is true because the larger the output, the smaller the AFC. At low levels of output, both components of $ATC-AFC$ and $AVC-$ are falling, so of course ATC is falling. Eventually the law of diminishing average product applies, causing AVC to rise. But over a certain range, AFC falls more rapidly than AVC rises. This means ATC continues to fall. The minimum point on the AVC lies at a lower output level, X_V in Figure 10–3(b), than does the minimum point on the ATC curve, X_T, because the ATC curve is a combination of both the rising AVC curve and the monotonically falling AFC curve. That is, the shape and position of the ATC curve depends upon the efficiency level of both the variable and the fixed factor.

Marginal Costs. *Marginal cost* (MC) is the extra cost of producing one additional unit of output; or more generally, MC is the change in total cost resulting from the change in total output. Algebraically, the MC of producing commodity x is:

$$MC_x = \frac{\Delta TC}{\Delta Q_x} = \frac{\Delta TVC}{\Delta Q_x} \tag{10.8}$$

or

$$MC_n = TC_n - TC_{n-1} \text{ (if } \Delta Q_x = 1) \tag{10.9}$$

where n stands for any volume of production.

We can use either ΔTC or ΔTVC in the numerator of (10.8) because TC changes only when TVC changes, since the other component is fixed cost. Put differently, marginal fixed cost is always zero. We can verify in Table 10–1 that TC and TVC always change by the same amount by examining columns (3) and (4). In short, MC depends only on variable costs.

MC is a very strategic concept in that it represents those costs over which the firm has direct influence. MC shows what expenditures are necessary to produce another unit of output or what expenditures can be saved by reducing output by one unit. *Incremental cost,* which is a generalization of MC, is defined as the added cost of any added activity, such as covering an additional sales territory or starting a delivery service. Thus, incremental cost applies to any number of additional units, not to just one, as does MC.

The MC curve is typically drawn U-shaped, reflecting the law of diminishing marginal returns. This follows since:

$$MC = \frac{\Delta TVC}{\Delta Q_x} = \frac{\Delta Q_v \cdot P_v}{\Delta Q_v \cdot MPP} = \frac{P_v}{MPP} = \frac{\bar{K}}{MPP} \qquad \text{(10.10)}$$

The change in TVC (or TC) equals the change in the number of variable factors hired multiplied by their prices. The change in total output equals the change in the number of variable factors multiplied by their marginal physical product (from the definition of $MPP = \Delta TPP/\Delta Q_v$). Taking out the common ΔQ_v term leaves MC equal to the price of the variable factor (which under competition is constant) divided by the MPP. Therefore, MC is inversely and proportionately related to MPP. (Incidentally, relaxing the assumption of constant factor prices would not materially change the shape of the curves in Figure 10–3(b); it would only make $AVC, ATC,$ and MC rise earlier and sharper.)

Figure 10–5 shows the graphical derivation of the marginal cost curve from the marginal physical product curve. The principles of its construction are the same as those for the derivation of the AVC curve, with the only difference being that in Figure 10–5 the hyperbola value (P_v) in the northwest quadrant equals marginal cost (MC) times marginal physical product (MPP). Again, the reader may wish to change the price of the variable factor to observe the effect on MC.

Table 10–2 shows numerically the same interrelationships between the product side and the cost variables. Assuming that labor services are the only variable inputs employed by the firm, the table demonstrates that the MC of output changes inversely with the MPP of labor, and the AVC of output varies inversely with the APP of labor. Assuming the firm is a pure competitor in the factor market, hiring at the prevailing wage rate of $20 per unit of labor service (a day's labor, for example), the entries presented in columns (6) and (7) can be obtained from just the information given. For example, at three units of labor employed, $MC_x = P_L/MPP_L = \$20/15 = \$4/3 = \$1.33$; or alternatively we can solve for $MC_x = \Delta TVC_x/\Delta TPP = (\$60 - \$40)/(37 - 22) = \$20/15 = \$4/3 = \$1.33$. Similarly, at three units of labor, the $AVC_x = P_L/APP_L = \$20/$

FIGURE 10-5 Construction of the *MC* Curve

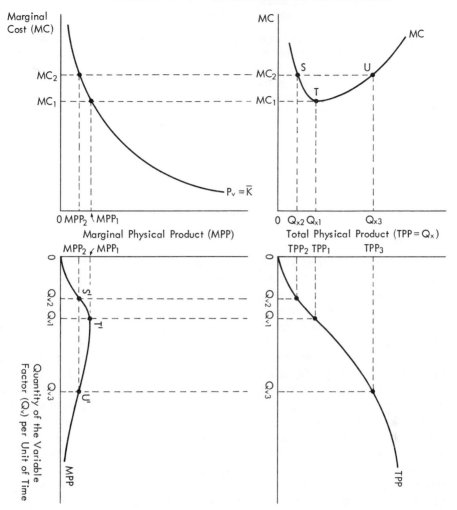

12.33 = \$1.62; or alternatively we can solve for $AVC_x = TVC_x/TPP = \$60/37 = \$1.62$.

Figure 10-6 helps show the relationships among the cost curves. In panel (a) are the total cost curve (TC) and the total variable cost curve (TVC), with the vertical distance between them being the total fixed cost. Since the average cost per unit of output is the total cost divided by the output, the average value can be measured by the slope of a ray drawn from the origin. That slope is given by (for just one example) Q_1T_1 divided by $0Q_1$ for point T_1. The steeper the angle of the ray at the origin, the higher the average. Thus, considering the point on the total cost curve as we move from small outputs to larger outputs,

TABLE 10–2   Production and Cost Relationships

(1) Units of Labor Employed Q_L	(2) Total Physical Product TPP_L	(3) Average Physical Product of Labor APP_L	(4) Marginal Physical Product of Labor MPP_L	(5) Total Variable Cost (Wages) TVC_x	(6) Average Variable Cost of Output AVC_x	(7) Marginal Cost of Output MC_x
1	10	10	10	$ 20	$2.00	$2.00
2	22	11	12	40	1.82	1.67
3	37	12.33	15	60	1.62	1.33
4	49	12.25	12	80	1.63	1.67
5	58	11.60	9	100	1.72	2.22
6	64	10.67	6	120	1.88	3.33

This table assumes the price of labor is constant at $20 and labor is the only variable input.

the average declines from zero output to point T_A on the TC curve and to point T_B on the TVC, where the ray is tangent to the total curves so that all other points on the total curves have steeper rays intersecting them.

Marginal cost is the slope of the total cost at any point on either total curve. At points T_x and T_y the slopes of the curves, as measured by the slopes of the tangents of the curves at those points, are shown as $\Delta TC = \Delta TVC$ divided by ΔQ. The steeper the slope of the tangent, the larger the marginal cost. Since the slope of the TC and the TVC are the same for any given level of output, there is only one marginal cost curve. Notice that $MC = AVC$ at the point where AVC is at its minimum, and $MC = ATC$ where ATC is at its minimum. This is necessarily true geometrically because the ray measuring the average is the same as the tangent which measures the marginal.

There is another way to see the same proposition dealing with the average and marginal curves. Whenever the marginal value is below the average value, the average must be falling; and whenever the marginal value is above the average, the average must be rising (as we move from left to right). The justification for these statements comes directly from the definitions of marginal and average. Marginal cost is the increase in total cost per unit increase in output. If this increase is less than the average, the average must be smaller than it was before the unit of output increase. If the addition to a total is greater than the average, the average must increase; and finally if the total increases by an amount equal to the average, the average won't change. Thus, for our cost curves, the average curves are falling when the marginal is below the average (even if MC is rising); and when MC is above ATC or AVC, these curves are rising. When MC equals AVC, AVC is constant at its minimum. MC, of course, also equals ATC at the ATC minimum.

An additional fact, which is simply another application of a principle demonstrated with reference to product curves, is that the area under the marginal

FIGURE 10–6   Total and Per-Unit Cost Curves

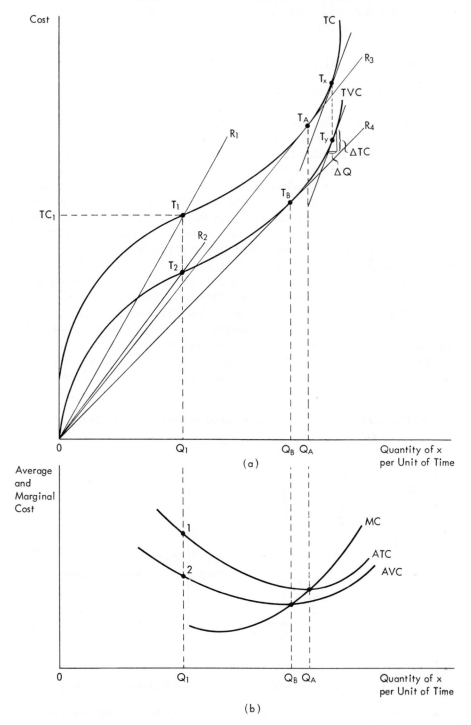

(a)

(b)

cost curve at any level of output equals TVC at that same level of output. Similarly, the area under the marginal cost curve plus total fixed cost at any output equals TC at that output.

THE LONG RUN

Since the typical average cost curves presented here always fall to a certain point and then rise after that, they must have a minimum point. In Figure 10–6 the short-run ATC curve is at its minimum level at output Q_A. The output at which the short-run ATC curve is at its lowest or minimum point, for any scale of plant, is called the *technical optimum rate of output*. This is simply the rate of output, given the particular size of plant (combination of fixed factors), which has the smallest average cost. Fewer inputs are used per unit of output than at any other output level, assuming some inputs are held fixed.

The fixed factors in an analysis such as this are usually considered to be the physical plant, though that is too narrow an interpretation to get the full benefits of the theory. In the planning stage, before any factors are fixed, there may be a multitude of possible plant designs and production technologies. If the firm knew the level of output it would produce, and if that output would not change for many years, the firm could choose the fixed factors and plant design to produce that level of output at the lowest possible average total cost. This is a technical or engineering problem, and the ATC curve might look like the one in Figure 10–7(a), constructed to produce output $0x_0$.

However, if the demand for the product is variable, the firm's output decision may at times be near $0x_1$ and at other times $0x_2$, in which cases average

FIGURE 10–7   Alternative Technologies and the Average Cost Curves

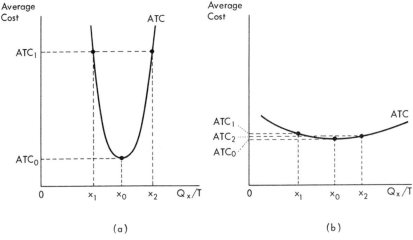

(a)

Best Plant Design for Certain Outputs

(b)

Best Plant Design for Uncertain Outputs

Note: Q_x/T refers to the quantity of commodity x produced per unit of time.

total cost will be very high. The firm may be better off designing a plant with an average cost curve such as that in Figure 10–7(b), where ATC never gets as small as in Figure 10–7(a) but within relevant production ranges may be lower, such as shown for outputs $0x_1$ and $0x_2$. A fairly simple example of the situations portrayed in Figure 10–7(a) and (b) is where (a) involves a large machine which is very efficient at what engineers might call "capacity"; whereas (b) involves a large number of smaller machines, an arrangement which may adjust more efficiently to changing output needs.

LONG-RUN COST FUNCTIONS

The firm's long-run problem is to choose the plant size which is most efficient at producing the anticipated future range of outputs.[1] The set of cost curves we have been discussing in this chapter can describe each possible plant size. Suppose, for simplicity of exposition, that five plant sizes are being considered. Figure 10–8 shows the short-run ATC and MC curves for each plant

FIGURE 10–8   Long-Run Average Costs – Discontinuous Case

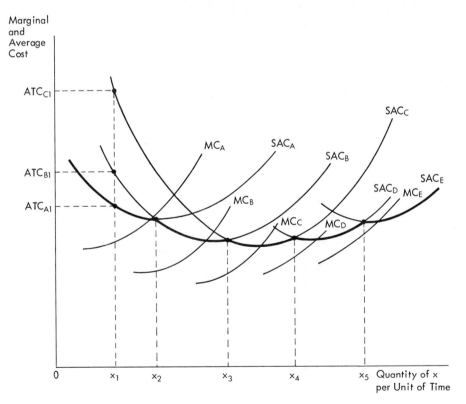

------

[1] We are still keeping secret why a firm would wish to produce any particular output. The solution is revealed in Chapter 11.

size, A, B, C, D, and E. If the firm knew it would be producing less than $0x_2$, it would prefer plant size A, since the average cost is less with that size than with any of the larger plants. Since the average cost is least for that given output, total cost is also least. We can clearly see this at output $0x_1$, where $ATC_{A1} <$ $ATC_{B1} < ATC_{C1}$, and for D and E average cost would be even higher. From output $0x_2$ to output $0x_3$, plant size B is the most economical; from $0x_3$ to $0x_4$, size C is best; from $0x_4$ to $0x_5$, D has the lowest average cost; and beyond $0x_5$, plant size E is preferred. The long-run average cost curve (LAC) is the heavy line for this discontinuous case.

We will now take up the case where the fixed factors are continuously divisible, that is, where an infinite number of plant sizes are possible. To begin, suppose the firm has ascertained that ATC_{A1} in Figure 10–8 is the lowest possible ATC that can produce $0x_1$; but if it plans to produce a slightly larger output (say $0x_1 + 1$), it could increase the scale of plant slightly and arrive at another SAC curve, as shown in Figure 10–9 as SAC_F. The lowest average cost of producing $0x_1 + 1$ is thus attained with plant size F. The lowest average cost of producing $0x_1$ can be attained with plant size A. If we continued the analysis in this way, determining the lowest ATC for every level of output and connecting all points with the characteristics of points 1 and 1' in Figure 10–9, we would arrive at a smooth curve. Points 2, 3, 4, and 5 in Figure 10–9 are such points. The envelope curve LAC is a locus of tangency points of the

FIGURE 10–9   Long-Run Average Costs—Continuous Case

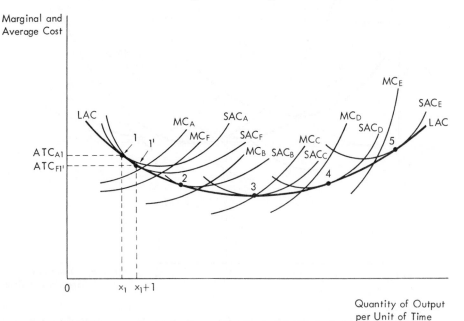

Quantity of Output
per Unit of Time

SAC curves, each point representing the lowest possible cost of producing any given output. This curve is sometimes called the "planning curve."

The negatively sloped portion of the *LAC* curve (from zero output to $0x_c$) is the situation referred to as "increasing returns to scale." From $0x_c$ to larger outputs is described as "decreasing returns to scale"; and right at $0x_c$, where *LAC* is at a minimum and constant, "constant returns to scale" exist.

We can also derive the long-run marginal cost *(LMC)* curve graphically. Since *LMC* is the change in total costs per unit change in output when all factors are variable, the slope of the long-run total cost *(LTC)* curve is the *LMC*. The *LTC* curve is derivable by multiplying *LAC* by output at all levels of output, just as short-run total cost can be found by multiplying *SAC* times output. Figure 10–10 shows the *SAC-LAC* relationship. *STC* is tangent to *LTC* at the level of output where *SAC* is tangent to *LAC*. Since the slope of the short- and long-run total cost curves is the same at their points of tangency, the marginal costs must also be the same. (See points *A*, *B*, and *C* in Figure 10–10, for example.)

Figure 10–11 shows more points and the construction of a more continuous *LMC* from the *SMC*s. If the fixed factors are completely divisible and flexible, the *LMC* curve is a locus of points of *SMC*s at all points at which the *SAC* is a minimum for each level of output. Notice that the relations among *LAC*, *LMC*, and *LTC* that we have stressed with reference to the corresponding short-run curves hold as well. For example, when *LMC* is below *LAC*, *LAC* is falling, and vice versa.

INTERNAL VS. EXTERNAL ECONOMIES OF SCALE

In the above discussion of returns to scale, we implicitly assumed that we were discussing internal, not external, economies and diseconomies of scale. Internal effects can result from a firm's own action; the effects are internal to the firm in that a firm can cause them by enlarging its scale of plant. External effects are so-called because they are outside the control of any one firm. They result from the actions of the entire industry (or group of industries) and cannot be attained by a single firm changing its rate of output. An internal effect involves a movement along a given cost function, whereas an external effect involves a shift in the entire cost function.

An external economy or diseconomy exists when a firm's production function or cost function contains as a variable the output of the entire industry. An external economy (diseconomy) is said to be present if the simultaneous expansion of all firms in the industry changes the production function of the individual firm in such a way as to raise (lower) output or lower (raise) the cost curve. Suppose expansion of output by neighboring firms created an increased outpouring of smoke, imposing extra cleaning costs on all firms. While no change occurred in factor prices, the entire cost function shifted up. Similarly, if several companies pumped oil from the same pool, the more oil one firm

FIGURE 10–10   Long-Run Total and Per-Unit Cost Curves

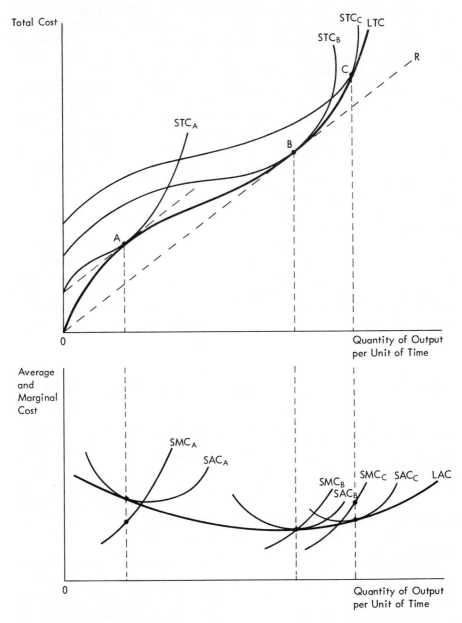

secured from the pool, the less would be available or the greater the cost to the other companies.

The external effects are further subdivided into *technical* and *pecuniary* varieties. An external technical economy of scale can be exemplified by adjacent coal mines, where the more water other firms pump from their shafts,

FIGURE 10-11   Long-Run Average and Marginal Costs

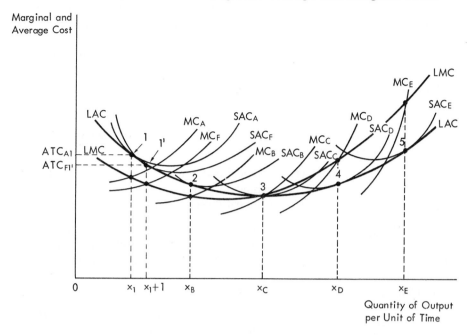

the less the remaining firms need remove. The cost curves of the parasitic firm would shift downward.

The most general type of external influence is pecuniary, in which the prices of factors of production change because of changes in the size of the industry. One firm generally does not buy enough of any one input to be able to do this alone; if it did, the effect would be internal for it, external for others. A real world example of external pecuniary economies is the electronics industry in the U. S. As the industry expanded, trade schools formed in which the trainees paid to learn. This allowed the electronics industry to hire relatively more efficient workers per dollar of cost outlay. This would not have occurred if, say, just the ABC Electronics firm expanded; it was only worthwhile when the entire electronics industry expanded. Similarly, it becomes worthwhile to bring a railroad into a business district if, say, all the firms in that area expand. It might not be feasible if only one of them expands. The savings in transportation costs from having the railroad in such close proximity would be an external economy.

The most likely external effect is pecuniary diseconomies as an industry expands. This results in an increasing-cost industry and the upward-sloping (long-run) industry supply curve that economists maintain is typical. Suppose the demand for gadgets increases. What will likely happen? The attempt by each existing firm to expand its output and the simultaneous attempt by newly entering firms to initiate production is equivalent to an increased demand for resources. Since resource supply curves for an industry are, except in the rarest of cases, upward sloping, all these firms cannot obtain greater amounts of resources at unchanged resource prices. The result is higher factor prices and hence external pecuniary diseconomies.

In terms of a generalized production function, these external effects can be formally admitted into the analysis by including the output of the industry, designated by TPP_I, as an independent variable:

$$TPP_i = f(a, b, c, \ldots, n, TPP_I) \qquad \text{(10.11)}$$

Looking first at external technical effects for a particular set of values of $a, b, c, \ldots, n$, we may define the following:

$$\frac{\Delta TPP_i}{\Delta TPP_I} \begin{array}{l} > 0 \text{ external technical economies} \\ = 0 \text{ external technical neutrality} \\ < 0 \text{ external technical diseconomies} \end{array} \qquad \text{(10.12)}$$

Thus, assuming a constant product price, if the increase in industry output TPP_I leads to a decrease in the firm's output TPP_i, as in our smoke example, the above expression is negative and we have an external technical diseconomy, and so on.

External pecuniary effects may also be defined formally as:

$$\frac{\Delta P_i}{\Delta TPP_I} \begin{array}{l} < 0 \text{ external pecuniary economies} \\ = 0 \text{ external pecuniary neutrality} \\ > 0 \text{ external pecuniary diseconomies} \end{array} \qquad \text{(10.13)}$$

where ΔP_i designates the change in price of the ith factor. If the change is positive as TPP_I expands, as expected in the majority of cases, external pecuniary diseconomies are said to be present, and so on.

QUESTIONS

1. "Opportunity" cost, "alternative" cost, "implicit" cost, and "paper" cost (more often used in the expression "paper profit" or "paper losses") are synonymous terms. Explain the basic concept of each.
2. "The distinction between the long run and the short run is a fiction, with no counterpart in the real world." Evaluate this criticism, explaining why someone might make the statement, and how the use of this artificial distinction might be defended.
3. Why might a firm continue to produce a positive output even though it is not meeting all of its costs with the revenue from sales? Under what circumstances would a firm elect to discontinue production entirely?
4. Using Figure 10–1, show the effect on the total variable cost curve of (a) an upward shift of the production function (the TPP curve), and (b) an increase in the price of the variable factor.
5. Using Figure 10–4, show the effect on the AVC curve of (a) an upward shift of the production function, and (b) an increase in the price of the variable factor.

6. The following statements point out important relationships between average and marginal variables: Whenever the marginal is above the average, the average is rising. Whenever the marginal is below the average, the average is falling. Whenever the average is constant, the average is equal to the marginal. Use the following data on a baseball player's hitting to show the truth of the statements. Consider each week's batting average as the marginal value.

week	hits	times at bat	total hits	total at bat	batting average	marginal value
1	10	20				
2	8	24				
3	9	28				
4	7	26				
5	12	27				
6	11	30				
7	8	16				
8	9	22				

7. With the use of a graph, explain why a firm with a falling *LAC* curve would not produce at the level of output at which the *SAC* curve is at its minimum.
8. What is the distinction between external and internal economies (or diseconomies) of scale? What is the distinction between technical and pecuniary economies (or diseconomies) of scale?

APPENDIX: MATHEMATICAL NOTES

Note 1. Short-Run Cost Functions

The short-run total cost function can be written as:

$$TC = f(q_x) + F \tag{10.14}$$

which states that total cost (TC) is a function both of the output of x, $f(q_x)$, and fixed costs, F. The form of the function depends on the technical conditions of production reflected in the technologically given production function and the conditions of supply of the variable factors of production.

The per-unit cost curves are defined as follows:

$$ATC = \frac{f(q_x) + F}{q_x} \tag{10.15}$$

$$AVC = \frac{f(q_x)}{q_x} \tag{10.16}$$

$$AFC = \frac{F}{q_x} \tag{10.17}$$

$$MC = \frac{d(TC)}{dq_x} = \frac{d(TVC)}{dq_x} = f'(q_x) \tag{10.18}$$

Since the derivatives of TC and TVC are identical inasmuch as the fixed-cost term F vanishes upon differentiation, there is only one MC curve. $MC = AVC$ (ATC) when AVC (ATC) is at a minimum. This is easily proved. The first-order condition for a minimum is that the first derivative of AVC be set equal to zero.

$$\frac{d(AVC)}{dq_x} = \frac{d[f(q_x)]}{dq_x} = \frac{q_x f'(q_x) - f(q_x)}{q_x^2} = 0 \tag{10.19}$$

by the quotient rule for differentiating. Therefore,

$$\frac{d(AVC)}{dq_x} = \frac{f'(q_x)}{q_x} - \frac{f(q_x)}{q_x^2} = 0 \text{ and } f'(q_x) = \frac{f(q_x)}{q_x} \tag{10.20}$$

Substituting with (10.18) and (10.16) respectively, we get $MC = AVC$. Similarly, we can prove that if AVC is rising (falling) $MC > (<) AVC$ by merely changing the equality in (10.19) and (10.20) to the proper inequality.

Note 2. Long-Run Cost Functions

The long-run total cost (LTC) curve is a function both of the output level and the plant size or scale:

$$LTC = f(q_x, x) + g(s) \tag{10.21}$$

where the parameter s represents the levels of the firm's fixed input or size (scale) of plant. The larger is s, the larger the firm's scale of plant. Thus, fixed cost is an increasing function of plant size: $g'(s) > 0$. Since (10.21) describes a whole family of LTC curves as soon as a particular plant size is selected, say, $s = \bar{s}_1$, this equation becomes equivalent to the short-run function given in (10.14).

A linear homogeneous production function generates a linear LTC function:

$$LTC = aq_x \tag{10.22}$$

where $a = P_a \cdot q_a + P_b \cdot q_b$, and $LMC = LAC = a$.

Note 3. Normal Cost Conditions

In the text several normal cost conditions were discussed. The simplest short-run total cost (STC) function satisfying these conditions is the quadratic form:

$$STC = aq_x^2 + bq_x + c \tag{10.23}$$

where a, b, and c are positive constants, and fixed costs are c. This functional form yields the following elasticity of total cost, κ, where κ is defined as $\Delta TC/TC \div \Delta q_x/q_x$:

$$\kappa = \frac{q_x(2aq_x + b)}{aq_x^2 + bq_x + c} \text{ with } \frac{\delta \kappa}{\delta q_x} > 0 \tag{10.24}$$

as required in the normal case. However, as Figure 10–12 indicates, the quadratic function does not generate exactly the curves drawn in the text. In particular, the MC curve does not have a minimum point at some level of output smaller than that at which ATC is at a minimum. Therefore, the simplest equation that meets the normal condition and this additional property is the cubic functional form:

$$TC = aq_x^3 - bq_x^2 + cq_x + d \tag{10.25}$$

where a, b, c, and d are positive constants or parameters and fixed cost is d. Shifts in a, b, or c affect both the shape and position of the equation, whereas shifts in d affect only position. The other equations corresponding to (10.25) in the usual textbook graphs are:

$$ATC = aq_x^2 - bq_x + c + d/q_x \tag{10.26}$$

$$AVC = aq_x^2 - bq_x + c \tag{10.27}$$

$$MC = 3aq_x^2 - 2bq_x + c \tag{10.28}$$

FIGURE 10–12   Quadratic Cost Function

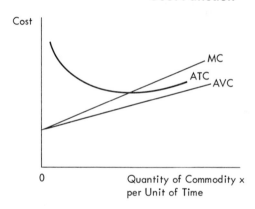

Note 4. Derivation of Cost Functions

The short-run cost function given in (10.14), $STC = f(q_x) + F$, can be derived from the information given in a system of equations consisting of the production function (10.29), the cost equation (10.30), and the expansion path (10.31).

$$q_x = f(q_a, q_b) \tag{10.29}$$

$$STC = P_a \cdot q_a + P_b \cdot q_b + F \tag{10.30}$$

$$0 = h(q_a, q_b) \tag{10.31}$$

This system of three equations in four variables can be reduced to single equation (10.14), which states cost as an explicit function of the level of output, q_x, and the cost of fixed factors, F.

Alternately, the long-run cost function (10.21) can be derived in the same manner, with the production function, cost equation, and expansion path function, letting the parameter s be the scale of plant, which is a continuous variable.

$$q_x = f(q_a, q_b, s) \tag{10.32}$$

$$LTC = P_a \cdot q_a + P_b \cdot q_b + g(s) \tag{10.33}$$

$$0 = h(q_a, q_b, s) \tag{10.34}$$

For example, the long-run total cost function for the Cobb-Douglas production function can be derived using this system of equations:

$$q_x = A q_a^\alpha q_b^{1-\alpha} \tag{10.35}$$

$$LTC = P_a \cdot q_a + P_b \cdot q_b \tag{10.36}$$

$$(1 - \alpha)P_a \cdot q_a - \alpha P_b \cdot q_b = 0 \tag{10.37}$$

This yields a total cost function:

$$LTC = c \cdot q_x \tag{10.38}$$

where:

$$c = \frac{P_a^\alpha P_b^{1-\alpha}}{A \alpha^\alpha (1 - \alpha)^{1-\alpha}}$$

MARKET ORGANIZATION AND THE THEORY OF THE FIRM

Short-Run Pricing and Production under Pure Competition

The last four chapters forged the tools necessary to analyze a firm under any type of market structure. This chapter develops the short-run pricing and production behavior of a purely competitive firm. The following chapter is devoted to the long-run production and pricing decisions in competitive markets.

We have previously argued that, as a *necessary* condition for pure competition, each firm must subjectively regard itself as a price-taker. However, we also indicated that several objective, structural conditions are often *sufficient* to bring about pure competition: (1) a large number of independent sellers; (2) economic homogeneity of the product so that the many buyers are indifferent among the many sellers; (3) buyers and sellers are reasonably informed about economic quantities and are guided by the information; and (4) free entry and exit of firms exists. Thus, a competitive market is often characterized by rapidly changing prices, a changing identity of buyers and sellers, and excellent dissemination of information.

The demand schedule a price-taker faces can be visualized as a horizontal line with an elasticity approaching infinity. This means the total revenue (TR) function will also be linear and will usually emanate from the origin. Since $TR = P \cdot Q$ and $P = MR =$ a constant, TR must be linear with a constant slope (MR).

The statement that a perfectly competitive firm acts as if it can alter its production rate without affecting the product price implicitly means within any normal range, say, up to a doubling or tripling of sales at most. In other words, we assume that any variation in production that raises a firm's output by a very large amount, say, 100-fold, is normally not practicable. The horizontal demand curve does not mean the firm can actually sell an infinite amount at the going market price, but rather that within any reasonable range, changes in production will leave prices virtually unaffected.

RULES FOR SHORT-RUN PROFIT MAXIMIZATION

As before, we will assume that the firm acts as if it is trying to maximize its profits (π), defined as total revenue (TR) minus total cost (TC), or price (P) minus average total cost (ATC) times the quantity produced (Q). Since $\pi = TR - TC$ [or $\pi = (P - ATC)\,Q$], profit-maximizing on behalf of the firm calls for maximizing the excess of TR over TC. As discussed below, there are theories other than profit maximization to explain firm behavior. Yet economists, for the most part, assume the objective of profit maximization. This is not merely out of habit. For one reason, many of the other alleged goals of the firm — such as prestige, power, and security — are highly correlated with profits, making it almost impossible to disentangle their separate influences. And more importantly, profit maximization may automatically bring about the others. In addition, the profit-maximization assumption has provided predictions about firm behavior as well as or better than any of the alternative theories.

Three Possible Outcomes

In the short run, the competitor [1] has a fixed plant and attempts to obtain an optimal position by adjusting output through changes in the amounts of the variable factors used. This behavior will always cause one of three possible outcomes: (1) profit maximization by producing; (2) loss minimization by producing; or (3) loss minimization by closing down. When we say that the firm's goal is profit maximization, interpret this as a generic statement that includes loss minimization if that course is the best alternative available. In the short run, a firm will continue to operate, even if it is incurring losses, as long as its sales revenue exceeds its variable costs so that losses are smaller than they would be if the firm ceased production altogether. In the long run, the firm must make at least zero economic profits to continue production. It is important to emphasize that even if a firm closes down and produces no output in the short run, there may be certain fixed or unavoidable costs that it still must meet. In the long run, however, all costs are variable and avoidable.

In the short run, decision makers in a competitive firm must concern themselves with the following two questions: (1) Should the firm produce or close down? (2) If the firm is to produce, at what level should it produce? We can answer the first question as follows: Produce if total sales revenue exceeds total variable cost ($TR > TVC$). Since total profits (π) = $TR - TC$, the firm should clearly operate its plant when $TR > TC$ or $\pi > 0$. A less obvious case in which a firm may still produce involves a situation in which no profitable rate of output is possible. The firm will still produce if, by so doing, it can incur a smaller loss than it necessarily stands to suffer by closing down. By definition, fixed costs are unavoidable outlays that must be paid even if output were to cease. In contrast, variable costs are avoidable expenditures that change with output and cease altogether when output is zero. Since only variable costs

---

[1] Hereafter the words "competitor" and "competitive" will always refer to a "pure competitor" or a "purely competitive" situation unless otherwise indicated.

can be avoided by closing down, it is the variable costs that are crucial in the short run in determining whether the firm produces or not. In brief, the firm will produce in the short run if it either: (1) earns a profit ($TR > TC$) or (2) incurs a loss ($TC > TR$) that is less than or equal to its TFC ($TR \geq TVC$). Any excess of price over the avoidable average variable cost ($P > AVC$) can be used to reduce the loss below the amount the firm would have incurred had it closed down, namely, its unavoidable fixed costs.

If a firm decides not to produce, the answer to the second question is that the optimal output is zero. If the firm decides to produce, the answer to the second question is to select the profit-maximizing (or loss-minimizing) rate of output. Under the total analysis, this amounts to producing where the excess of TR over TC is at a maximum (or where the excess of TC over TR is at a minimum). Maximizing ($TR - TC$) and minimizing ($TC - TR$) are the profit-maximizing and loss-minimizing outcomes respectively.

The marginal-analysis answer to the second question is in a sense less complex than that of the total approach. The marginal analysis indicates that if it pays to produce at all, it will be most profitable to produce where marginal revenue (MR) equals marginal cost (MC). This conclusion once again follows from the application of the equimarginal principle, which states that the most preferred position is always one where marginal benefit, here marginal revenue, equals marginal cost. Obviously, the firm should produce any unit of output for which $MR > MC$, because the revenue from selling such a unit will exceed the cost of producing it. If $MC > MR$, the firm should avoid producing that unit, for it will add more to cost than to revenue. In short, $MR > MC$ calls for an expansion of output, and $MR < MC$ calls for a contraction of output. The (nonzero) optimum output, therefore, occurs where $MR = MC$. A qualification to this rule is that a competitive firm should always produce within an output range in which its marginal costs are rising. As long as MC is falling, enlarging output increases profits.

Restatement and Proof of the Basic Profit-Maximizing Algorithm

It is possible to restate and prove with elementary algebra the above rules for profit-maximizing behavior. We can put our rules in the form of three necessary conditions to attain maximal profitability. For a given output n to be the optimum, profit-maximizing rate of production, under any type of market structure, the following three conditions must hold:

$$MR_n = MC_n \quad \textit{marginal equality} \qquad \textbf{(11.1)}$$

(a) $MR_{n+1} < MC_{n+1}$ at larger outputs $\left.\vphantom{\begin{matrix}a\\b\end{matrix}}\right\}$ *marginal inequality* **(11.2)**
(b) $MR_{n-1} > MC_{n-1}$ at smaller outputs

(a) Short run: $TR_n \geq TVC_n$ (i.e., $P_n \geq AVC_n$)[2] **(11.3)**
(b) Long run: $TR_n \geq TC_n$ (i.e., $P_n \geq LAC_n$)

---

[2] This is shown as follows: By definition, $TR_n = P_n \cdot Q_n$ and $TVC_n = AVC_n \cdot Q_n$, where Q_n is the number of units sold and P_n is the price when n units are sold. Therefore, $TR_n \geq TVC_n = P_n \cdot Q_n \geq AVC_n \cdot Q_n$; and if we divide by Q_n, we get $P_n Q_n / Q_n \geq (AVC_n \cdot Q_n)/Q_n = P_n \geq AVC_n$.

While *marginal equality,* (11.1), is often considered the most important condition, *marginal inequality,* condition (11.2), is actually the crucial one. In fact, the next chapters will give several examples to show the greater generality and greater power of marginal inequality in finding optimal solutions. However, it is useful to keep all three conditions of the basic profit-maximizing algorithm in mind when searching for possible optimal values.

To show that the above conditions produce the best level of output, let us define π_n as the total profit when n units of output are sold:

$$\pi_n = TR_n - TC_n \tag{11.4}$$

and define $\Delta\pi_n$ as the change in total profit as a result of selling the nth unit of output. $\Delta\pi_n$ is sometimes referred to as *marginal profit.*

$$\Delta\pi_n = \pi_n - \pi_{n-1} = marginal\ profit \tag{11.5}$$

If the firm is in fact maximizing its profits by producing n units of output, its profits must be greater than or equal to the profits at the alternative outputs of: (1) zero (closing down); (2) $n - 1$ (smaller outputs), and (3) $n + 1$ (larger outputs). That is, if n is the profit-maximizing rate of production,

$$\pi_n \geqq \pi_0 \tag{11.6}$$
$$\pi_n \geqq \pi_{n-1} \tag{11.7}$$
$$\pi_n \geqq \pi_{n+1} \tag{11.8}$$

Expression (11.6) emphasizes that the profits from producing must not be smaller than those from closing down. Expressions (11.7) and (11.8) state that a change to a smaller or larger rate of production cannot increase profits if n is the maximal profit or optimal output.

We can easily demonstrate that if it pays to produce rather than close down —that is, if (11.6) holds—then (11.3) is necessarily fulfilled. First, from (11.4) and the fact that $TC_n = TVC_n + TFC_n$, we can rewrite (11.6) as:

$$TR_n - TVC_n - TFC_n \geqq TR_0 - TVC_0 - TFC_0 \tag{11.9}$$

By definition, we know:

$$TR_0 = TVC_0 = 0 \tag{11.10}$$
$$TFC_n = TFC_0 = \bar{C} \tag{11.11}$$

where $\bar{C}$ is a constant. Substituting (11.10) and (11.11) into (11.9) yields:

$$TR_n - TVC_n - \bar{C} \geqq 0 - 0 - \bar{C} = TR_n - TVC_n \geqq 0 \tag{11.12}$$

or

$$TR_n \geqq TVC_n \quad or \quad P_n \geqq AVC_n \tag{11.13}$$

Hence, we have proved that it is always better to produce than to not produce if (11.13) holds.

To prove (11.7) or (11.8), it is necessary to show that only when $MR_n = MC_n$ can the firm not increase its profits by changing output; i.e., we must show $\Delta\pi_n = 0$ when $MR_n = MC_n$. This can be done by substituting (11.4) into (11.5) to get:

$$\Delta\pi_n = \pi_n - \pi_{n-1} = (TR_n - TC_n) - (TR_{n-1} - TC_{n-1}) \qquad \textbf{(11.14)}$$
$$= (TR_n - TR_{n-1}) - (TC_n - TC_{n-1})$$

or

$$\Delta\pi_n = MR_n - MC_n \qquad \textbf{(11.15)}$$

i.e., marginal profit $= MR_n - MC_n$. $\Delta\pi_n = 0$ only when $MR_n = MC_n$. If $MR_n - MC_n > 0$ (i.e., $MR_n > MC_n$), the increase in total revenue is greater than the increase in total cost, so profit increases. Thus, it pays to expand output and (11.8) cannot hold. If $MR_n - MC_n < 0$ (i.e., $MR_n < MC_n$), contracting output increases profits and (11.7) does not hold. Put differently, when a firm's marginal profits, $\Delta\pi_n$, are positive (negative), it can increase its total profits by expanding (contracting) output. With a discontinuous production function, the best the firm can do is satisfy $\Delta\pi_n \leq 0$.

Thus, for profit maximization, $MR_n = MC_n$ and $MR_{n+1} - MC_{n+1} < 0$ (i.e., $MR_{n+1} < MC_{n+1}$), and $MR_{n-1} - MC_{n-1} > 0$ (i.e., $MR_{n-1} > MC_{n-1}$). This means at n units of output, the slope of MC must be greater than the slope of MR. If pure competition exists and the firm faces a horizontal demand curve, this last condition means that MC_n must cut MR_n from below at n. Thus, under pure competition the necessary condition for maximum profits, shown as (11.2) above, requires that the MC curve be rising. (Note 2 in the Appendix demonstrates that these conditions are merely the general conditions for finding a maximum, familiar to any student in calculus.)

ILLUSTRATION OF THE THREE POSSIBLE OUTCOMES

The necessary profit-maximizing conditions in the short run can perhaps best be seen if we first give a numerical example and then a graphic illustration based on these same numbers. Table 11–1 presents the basic data.

Tabular Analysis

Table 11–1 presents the three general possibilities facing a firm in the short run: (1) the profit-maximization case is illustrated with a price P_1 and marginal revenue MR_1 of \$111; (2) the loss-minimization case with a P_2 and MR_2 of \$91; and (3) the shut-down case with a P_3 and MR_3 of \$81. The table shows these cases using both the total and marginal approaches. The left-hand side of the table, columns (1) to (10), presents the total analysis, whereas columns (11) to (18) provide equivalent results using the marginal approach.

Looking first at the total analysis, column (1) shows total product; columns (2), (3), and (4) show the TR figures for the three different prices — TR_1 associated with $P_1(MR_1)$, TR_2 with $P_2(MR_2)$, and TR_3 with $P_3(MR_3)$; and columns (5), (6), and (7) show the total cost figures — TFC, TVC, and TC respectively. The important columns for making pricing and production decisions by the

TABLE 11-1 Output Determination for a Firm in Pure Competition

Total Analysis

(1) Total Physical Product TPP	(2) Total Revenue (TR_1) Price = $111	(3) Total Revenue (TR_2) Price = $91	(4) Total Revenue (TR_3) Price = $81	(5) Total Fixed Cost TFC	(6) Total Variable Cost TVC	(7) Total Cost TC	(8) $TR_1 - TC$ (2)-(7)	(9) $TR_2 - TC$ (3)-(7)	(10) $TR_3 - TC$ (4)-(7)
0	$ 0	$ 0	$ 0	$100	$ 0	$ 100	$ -100	$ -100	$ (-100)
1	111	91	81	100	100	200	-89	-109	-119
2	222	182	162	100	190	290	-68	-108	-128
3	333	273	243	100	270	370	-37	-97	-127
4	444	364	324	100	340	440	+4	-76	-116
5	555	455	405	100	420	520	+35	-65	-115
6	666	546	486	100	510	610	+56	(-64)	-124
7	777	637	567	100	610	710	+67	-73	-143
8	888	728	648	100	720	820	(+68)	-92	-172
9	999	819	729	100	840	940	+59	-121	-211
10	1,110	910	810	100	990	1,090	+20	-180	-280
11	1,221	1,001	891	100	1,190	1,290	-69	-289	-399

Marginal Analysis

(11) Total Physical Product TPP	(12) Average Fixed Cost AFC	(13) Average Variable Cost AVC	(14) Average Total Cost ATC	(15) Marginal Cost MC	(16) Price = P_1 = Marginal Revenue $MR_1 = \$111$	(17) Price = P_2 = Marginal Revenue $MR_2 = \$91$	(18) Price = P_3 = Marginal Revenue $MR_3 = \$81$
0	$ ∞	$	$ ∞	$ 0			
1	100.00	100.00	200.00	100	$111	$91	$81
2	50.00	95.00	145.00	90	111	91	81
3	33.33	90.00	123.33	80	111	91	81
4	25.00	85.00	110.00	70	111	91	81
5	20.00	84.00	104.00	80	111	91	81
6	16.67	85.00	101.67	90	111	91	81
7	14.29	87.14	101.43	100	111	91	81
8	12.50	90.00	102.50	110	111	91	81
9	11.11	93.33	104.44	120	111	91	81
10	10.00	99.00	109.00	150	111	91	81
11	9.09	108.18	117.27	200	111	91	81

total approach are (8), (9), and (10), which show the economic profits (+) or losses (−) at different output levels for each of the three prices. The profit-maximizing firm will try, provided $TR \geq TVC$, to either maximize the difference if $TR > TC$ or minimize the difference if $TR < TC$. Reading vertically down column (8), which shows the profit figures for $P_1 (MR_1) = \$111$, we can see that the maximum profit can be made at eight units of output, at which point total profits are +$68. Checking column (9), in which P_2 is assumed to equal $91, the best the firm can do is produce six units of output. The firm minimizes losses (−$64) by producing at this level of output, since closing down would involve larger losses equal to the amount of unavoidable fixed costs ($100). Finally, column (10) assumes $P_3 = \$81$ and shows the best non-zero outcome is at five units of output where losses equal $115. However, since closing down involves only the loss of the unavoidable TFC of $100, production will cease.

The right-hand side of Table 11–1 assumes the same cost and price data and allows us to demonstrate that the identical results are obtained using the marginal analysis. The short-run rule for the most preferred position via the marginal approach is to produce where $MR = P = MC$, provided MC is rising and $P \geq AVC$. If $P < AVC$, the firm should not produce since its losses would be less if it shut down. The "MC is rising" qualification is necessary because if MC is falling, the competitor has every reason to expand output since each additional sale lowers MC while MR remains constant. Falling MC (or ATC) is incompatible with competition; a competitive firm would always expand with a falling MC (or ATC) until it either produced a significant enough portion of the entire industry's output that it ceased to be a competitor or until the cost curves stopped falling. Put differently, the rising MC qualification is necessary to meet what mathematicians call the second-order (or loosely sufficient) conditions for a maximum. The MR and MC equality means that profits are constant; i.e., the profit (π) function has a horizontal slope. But this constancy can occur at a "top-of-the-hill" point a or at a "bottom-of-the-valley" point b of the function in Figure 11–1. To summarize,

**FIGURE 11–1   Constant Maximum
or Minimum Values**

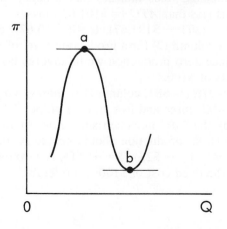

the equation $MR = MC$ tells us the firm is either experiencing a maximum or a minimum profit. If, in addition, we know that MC is rising, we know that profit is at a maximum.

Columns (11) through (15) in Table 11–1 repeat for convenience the cost data presented in Table 10–1. To find the optimal position with the marginal analysis, we must peruse the MC column (15) to find the rate of output which has a MC that has approximately the same value as MR. For most sets of data, there will not be any nonfractional level of output at which MR and MC are precisely equal. In such instances, the firm should produce the last integral unit of output for which MR exceeds MC. In this case, that output would be eight units, where the MR of $111 is associated with a MC of $110.

The second step to ensure that an output of eight is the profit-maximizing optimal is to make sure MC is rising. Since MC is rising at eight units of output, this rate of output is the desired "top-of-the-profit-hill" level of operation.

After first finding where $MR = MC$ and second ensuring that MC is rising, the third step is to see if $P \geqq AVC$; if not, the firm should close down. At eight units of production, AVC equals $90, which is less than the price of $111, so the firm should produce this output. Since the ATC of $102.50 is less than the price of $111 at this output, an economic profit will be realized. We can compute the exact level of profit with the formula $\pi = (P - ATC)Q$. In this case it would be ($111 − $102.50) $\cdot$ 8 = ($8.50) $\cdot$ 8 = $68.00, which is the figure that appears in column (8) for eight units of output.

Table 11–1 also illustrates the point that the firm seeks to maximize total, not per-unit, profit. The highest per-unit profit, or where output level P exceeds ATC by the greatest amount, occurs at seven units of output, where the constant P_1 of $111 is matched with the (minimum) ATC of $101.43. At this output, per-unit profits are $9.57, compared with a per-unit profit margin of $8.50 at eight units of production; but total profits are only $67 at seven units of output, which is less than the total profits of $68 at eight units of output.

Examining the $P_2 = MR_2 = $91 alternative, column (15) indicates that $MC = $90 at both two and six units of output. However, the second-order condition requiring that MC be rising eliminates a production rate of two units from consideration. Since P (= $91) exceeds AVC (= $85) at six units of output, the profit-maximizing rules indicate that production should occur. But because P (= $91) is less than ATC (= $101.67), losses are incurred. That is, $\pi = (P - ATC)Q = ($91 − $101.67) \cdot 6 = (-$10.67) \cdot 6 = -64.02 or the rounded off $-$64 in column (9) for a production level of six. This is the loss-minimizing case, since zero production would involve losses equal to the unavoidable fixed costs of $100.

Finally, for $P_3 = MR_3 = $81, column (15) shows two possible production rates where $MR = MC$: three and five units of output. The rate of three units can be eliminated by the "MC must be rising" rule. At an output of five, AVC (= $84) > P$ (= $81), so production should cease. At this output $\pi = (P - ATC)Q = ($81 − 104) \cdot 5 = (-$23) \cdot 5 = -$115$. A zero rate of output, involving losses equal to the fixed cost of $100, is preferable.

Graphic Analysis

Figure 11–2 presents these same three general cases graphically. Panel (a) presents the profit-maximizing case. The top diagram in each case represents the total approach; the middle diagram, the profit function; and the bottom diagram, the marginal analysis. A good understanding of Figure 11–2 at this point will make the similar diagrams employed in imperfect competition and in the factor markets much easier to handle. The diagram for the imperfectly competitive cases will look exactly the same with two important exceptions: (1) the *TR* curves will be curvilinear rather than linear, and (2) the *MR* curve will be downsloping and less than *P* rather than horizontal.

The reason the *TR* functions are linear and upward sloping in the purely competitive case is clear from the total-average-marginal relationships and our rules concerning slope. A linear function necessarily means that the slope is constant. The slope of *TR* is *MR*. Under competitive conditions, *MR* and *P* are horizontal or constant since the firm is a price-taker. The *TR* function is upsloping since a greater level of output always increases total receipts for a competitor.

In the great majority of cases *TR* would start at the origin, signifying there is no revenue if there is no output. However, it is possible, but unlikely, for *TR* not to start at the origin. For instance, if a firm sells (nonrefundable) season passes, it can have a positive sales revenue without any output, in which case *TR* would start above zero on the *y* axis. Alternatively, if a firm decides to temporarily sell its product only in, say, units of five, permitting no smaller size purchases, *TR* would intersect the *x* axis, depicting zero revenue from zero to five units of output.

The exact value of the slope of the *TR* function depends on the level of the *MR* function. Since the slopes are getting flatter or smaller in algebraic value as we move from panel (a) to panel (b) to panel (c) in Figure 11–2 (that is, as price changes from $111 to $91 to $81), naturally *MR*, which is the slope of *TR*, decreases in magnitude.

The function labeled π, which falls between the total and marginal diagrams, is the profit function. It relates total profits (π), measured on the vertical axis, to the quantity sold, measured on the horizontal axis. When the π function falls below the horizontal axis, negative profits, or losses, are being incurred. It is important to note that we have explicitly marked off distances $0F$ and $0F'$, where $0F = 0F' = TFC$, on the π diagrams. They are drawn in so that the results of producing the best possible level of output can be directly compared with the alternative of closing down. In other words, if the firm ceases production, its unavoidable losses will be $0F'$ or $100. In those cases presented in panel (b) and panel (c) where the firm is not making a positive profit, it is important that the losses from producing can be compared with the alternative of closing down. In general, if the profit function is closer to the horizontal axis than is $0F'$, the firm should produce.

FIGURE 11-2 Output Determination for a Firm in Pure Competition

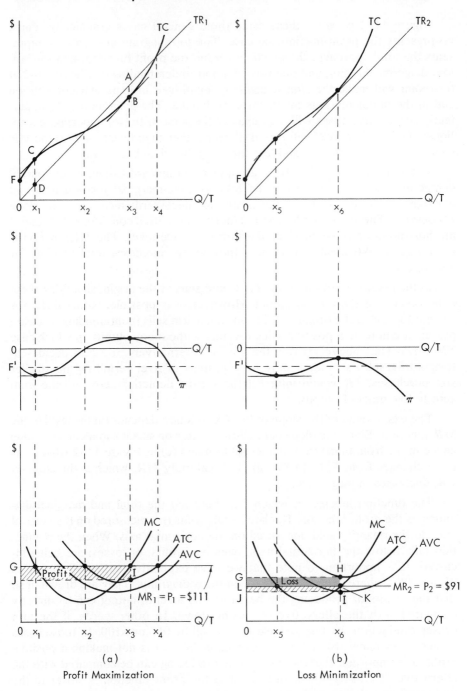

(a)
Profit Maximization

(b)
Loss Minimization

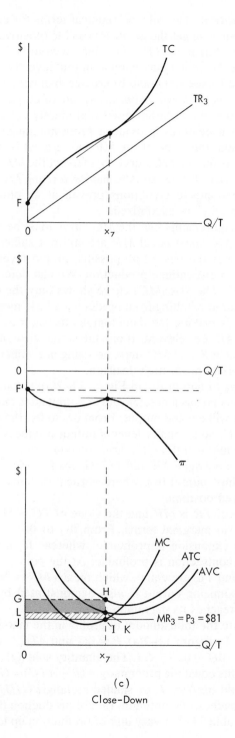

(c)
Close-Down

Profit Maximization. The rule in graphical terms for profit maximization with the total analysis is to get the greatest possible (positive) vertical distance between TR and TC. Since $\pi = TR - TC$, this necessarily follows. In panel (a), the vertical distance AB is at a maximum at output level $0x_3$. At an output such as $0x_1$, the vertical distance CD could be greater than vertical distance AB. But since $TC > TR$, this is the *loss-maximization* rate of output! This also demonstrates the importance of our earlier point that merely equating MR with MC is not sufficient to necessarily provide a profit-maximizing output, even if $P \geqq AVC$. In addition, the slope of the MR curve must be less than the slope of the MC curve, causing the MC curve to intersect the MR curve from below. In the competitive case this amounts to having a rising MC curve (since MR is horizontal). The opposite conditions prevail at an output of $0x_1$, where losses rather than profits are maximized.

Of course the requirements that the MC curve must be rising more rapidly than MR and that MC must equal MR are still not sufficient to ensure that this production rate is the best of all possible output levels. The firm's best alternative may be to discontinue production. We can determine this by comparing AR and AVC. The MR (MC) curve shows only the change in revenue (cost) per unit of output resulting from producing a little more or less. In short, whenever the firm is making the dichotomous decision to produce or not to produce, AVC and AR are relevant. If one takes this view of the firm, the rules that MC must equal MR and MC must be rising are sufficient to always give the firm the appropriate production decision.

From output $0x_2$ to output $0x_3$ in Figure 11–2(a), the slope of TR exceeds the slope of TC. This means a greater rate of output adds more to revenue than to cost, so the firm will expand output. From $0x_3$ to $0x_4$ the slope of TR is less than the slope of TC, so a smaller level of output produces a greater decrease in cost than in revenue; therefore, the firm will contract output. Put differently, the vertical distance between TR and TC widens from $0x_2$ to $0x_3$ and narrows from $0x_3$ to $0x_4$. Thus, output $0x_3$, where vertical distance AB is maximized, must be the preferred position.

Since the slope of TR is MR and the slope of TC is MC, it is possible to couch the analysis in marginal terms. From $0x_2$ to $0x_3$, MR is greater than MC, which means expansion is profitable; whereas from $0x_3$ to $0x_4$, MR is less than MC and contraction is profitable. At the point of maximum profits, the slopes of TR and TC are equal, which means $MR = MC$. That this is, in fact, the profit-maximizing output is also demonstrated by the fact that the profit function (π) reaches its maximum at $0x_3$.

We can compute the total amount of profits in the marginal diagram, since $\pi = (P - ATC)Q$. In Figure 11–2(a), $P = 0G$ and $ATC = 0J$, so the per-unit profit $(P - ATC) = (0G - 0J) = GJ$. The quantity sold ($Q$) at the optimal point $0x_3$ is JI. Total profits equal the profit margin $(P - ATC) = GJ$ multiplied by the number of units sold $(0x_3) = JI$, or shaded rectangle $GHIJ$. In both the total and marginal approaches, the optimum rate of production ($0x_3$) is shown to be eight units, as in Table 11–1. Every unit of production up to and including the eighth unit of output adds more to TR than to TC. For the ninth unit of output, MC ($120) exceeds MR ($111); and the firm will not produce that unit.

Of course, $0x_3$ is not the output level at which the per-unit profit margin is maximized. The firm's goal is to maximize its total profits, not its per-unit profits. As Table 11–1 previously indicated, the profit per unit is maximized at seven units of output. This is easily demonstrable in Figure 11–2(a). Since under pure competition the price line is horizontal, the per-unit profit margin is maximized at the minimum point on the ATC curve. This occurs where the MC curve intersects the ATC curve.

Loss Minimization. Figure 11–2(b), showing a price of $91, represents the loss-minimization case. Since TC (ATC) everywhere exceeds TR (P_2), a positive profit is not possible at any level of output. The best the firm can do is minimize the vertical distance between TR and TC, as is done at $0x_6$ (= six units of output). The loss if production is discontinued is the unavoidable TFC of $100 or $0F'$. As the middle diagram illustrates, the profit function is inside this $0F'$ distance, which indicates that the production of six units of output results in a smaller loss than stopping production.

In the bottom diagram, profits are $(P - ATC)Q$. Substituting $P = \$91 = 0L$, $ATC = 0G$, and $Q = 0x_6 = LK$ yields $(P - ATC)Q = (0L - 0G) \cdot LK = (GL) \cdot (LK)$. Losses, therefore, equal the area of shaded rectangle $GHKL$. These losses can be graphically compared with TFC ($100), the losses that would be incurred by closing down. Since $TFC = (AFC) \cdot Q$, the shut-down losses would be rectangle $GHIJ$. This can be derived as follows: $AFC = ATC - AVC = HI$ at output $0x_6 = 6$ and $Q = 0x_6 = JI$; therefore, $TFC = (AFC)Q = (HI) \cdot (JI)$ or rectangle $GHIJ$. In other words, the reduction in losses by producing rather than closing down equals crossed rectangle $LKIJ = \$36$. Whenever $TR > TVC$, the competitor will be better off producing in the short run. The amount by which TR exceeds TVC is rectangle $LKIJ$.

Close-Down. In Figure 11–2(c), representing a price of $81, TC everywhere exceeds TR; in fact, TVC is everywhere larger than TR. The firm cannot cover AVC, much less ATC. The profit function (π) is outside the TFC loss of $0F'$, representing the profit level at zero output. Since $0F'$ is closer to the horizontal axis depicting zero profits than is the profit function when the firm is producing its "best" nonzero output possible of five units, the firm should stop producing. The firm will lose at least $115 if it produces, and it will lose $100 if it does not produce.

We can again figure the firm's exact losses from producing at the best (positive) output possible, $0x_7 = 5$, by $(P - ATC)(Q) = (0J - 0G)0x_7 = (GJ) \cdot (JI)$. Losses equal the area of rectangle $GHIJ$ or $115. If the firm shuts down, its losses are $TFC = (AFC)Q = (HK) \cdot (0x_7) = (HK) \cdot (LK)$ or the area of rectangle $GHKL$ equal to $-\$100$. Therefore, the reduction in losses by not producing is the area of crossed rectangle $LKIJ$ or $15 in total.

COMPETITIVE FIRM'S SHORT-RUN SUPPLY CURVE

In Table 11–1 and the accompanying diagrams, we selected three different prices and determined what quantity the profit-seeking competitive firm, faced with certain costs, would choose to offer in the market at these prices. The schedule of prices and the corresponding quantities supplied obviously constitute that firm's supply curve. Applying the qualified MR $(P) = MC$ rule to still other prices, we generate an upward-sloping supply curve. At any given selling price, equal to MR, the competitive firm's output is at a point where its MC equals the price. If now P (MR) should rise, MR exceeds MC, and profits can be increased by expanding output until MC increases to the new higher MR. Therefore, the higher the price, the greater each firm's output and quantity supplied on the market. Since the supply curve is derived from the MC curve and the MC curve depends on the law of diminishing returns, it is the $LDMR$ that lies behind or explains the "typical" upsloping supply curve.

Of course, the entire MC curve is not relevant for supply analysis. The qualified profit-maximum rule states that MC must be rising and P must be greater than or equal to (minimum) AVC. The supply function is not defined or shows zero quantity supplied for all prices (quantities) less than the ordinate (abscissa) of the point where MC and AVC intersect. In the numerical example given in Table 11–1, price must be equal to or greater than \$84 (the minimum AVC) before any output will be produced. Some of the numerical values for the firm's supply curve derived from Table 11–1 would be as shown in Table 11–2.

TABLE 11–2 Short-Run Supply Schedule of a Competitive Firm

Price Per Unit	Quantity Supplied Per Unit of Time	Profit (+) or Loss (−)	
\$ 71	0	\$−100	*CD*
81	0	−100	*CD*
91	6	−64	*LM*
101	7	−3	*LM*
111	8	+68	πM
121	9	+149	πM
151	10	+420	πM

Legend: *CD* = close down
　　　　LM = loss minimization
　　　　πM = profit maximization

The link between production costs and short-run firm supply may be summarized as follows: The purely competitive firm's short-run supply curve is that portion of its rising marginal cost curve which lies above the minimum point on the average variable cost curve. The difference between the MC curve and the supply curve is that the dependent and independent variables are reversed. Thus, at any given output on the MC curve, the marginal cost is the vertical distance to the curve; whereas at any given price on the supply curve, the output is the horizontal distance to the curve. This is illustrated in Figure 11–3. Line segment $0ABC$ constitutes the competitive firm's short-run supply curve. At any price above $0P_2$, the firm maximizes profits or minimizes losses by producing that quantity at which $MC = P$ (MR). At prices below $0P_2$, such as $0P_1$, the quantities offered are zero. Below a price of $0P_2$, the firm will lose less money by closing down than by producing. Between the close-down price of $0P_2$ and the break-even price of $0P_4$ lies the loss-minimization zone. In this range, the firm will lose less by producing the "best" output than by stopping production. For prices greater than $0P_4$, the firm realizes positive profits by producing the optimal output.

FIGURE 11–3   Competitive Firm's Short-Run
Supply Curve

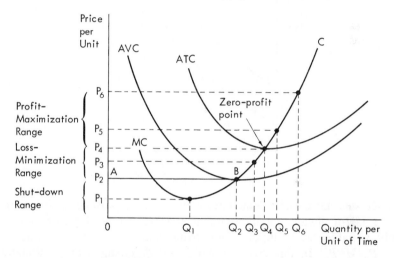

SHIFTS IN SUPPLY CURVES

A firm's marginal cost (and supply) schedule is based on the assumption that everything remains constant except the price and quantity of the commodity. In particular, changes in the costs of production due to changes in the state of technology and changes in the prices of productive factors are presumed not to occur. If technology and factor prices change, the entire MC schedule (and thereby the firm's short-run supply schedule) will shift.

Lower factor prices or improved technology cause the marginal costs for any given output to fall. As a consequence, the firm's supply curve increases. Graphically, an increase in supply (or decrease in marginal cost) is represented by a rightward (downward) movement of the function, such as in Figure 11–4. Suppose initially the firm's marginal cost curve is MC_1 and at a price of $0P_1$ its output is $0q_1$. After, say, better technology is introduced or factor prices are lowered, the marginal cost curve falls to MC_2, and the output at $0P_1$ is $0q_2$. If a firm's costs are lowered, it makes sense that the firm would be willing to put a greater output $(0q_2)$ on the market at the same price $(0P_1)$ or the same quantity $(0q_1)$ on the market at a lower price $(0P_2)$. A rise in costs—due, for example, to an increase in the prices paid for factors—decreases the firm's supply curve. If marginal costs were originally shown by MC_2, they would rise to MC_1.

Note that MC does not change proportionately to changes in factor prices. This follows from our principle of substitution. With variable factors, the entrepreneur will shift from higher to lower priced factors, thereby increasing the proportion used of the relatively inexpensive factors.

FIGURE 11–4   A Shift in the Firm's Supply Curve

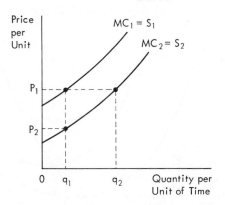

To see this, let us first demonstrate that, *ceteris paribus,* a change in the price of a factor always entails a shift in the MC curve. Suppose factor a is the only variable factor input. Then from equation (10.10) we know that $MC_x = P_a/MPP_a$. In this case the MC_x and P_a changed proportionately—e.g., a 100 percent increase in P_a increases P_a/MPP_a and hence MC_x by 100 percent. If, on the other hand, the P_a increases and all factors are variable, the entrepreneur will substitute other factors for input a to satisfy the least-cost rule $MPP_a/P_a = 1/MC_x$ or, taking reciprocals,

$$MC_x = P_a/MPP_a = P_b/MPP_b \tag{11.16}$$

This rule holds provided the firm is a competitor in the factor market.[3] By following the principle of substitution, the entrepreneur can reduce the cost-increasing effect of a rise in the price of one factor by employing proportionately more of the now relatively inexpensive factor b.

---

[3] Otherwise, as we shall see later, the more general expression $MC_x = MFE_a/P_a = MFE_b/P_b$ holds if monopsony exists, where MFE is the marginal factor expense of hiring one more unit of a factor. Also note that this entire section assumes that the factors discussed are noninferior. An inferior factor's price and MC curve move inversely rather than directly as in the case of superior and normal factors. See Charles E. Ferguson, *The Neoclassical Theory of Production and Distribution* (Cambridge: Cambridge University Press, 1969), especially section 9.6, pp. 193–199.

COMPETITIVE INDUSTRY'S SHORT-RUN SUPPLY CURVE

In the simplest case in which no external effects are present, the short-run aggregate, industry, or market supply curve is the sum of the supply curves (i.e., the *MC* curves) of all the firms in the industry. If there are *n* different firms in the industry, we obtain the aggregate supply function by summing all the individual firms' supply curves. That is,

$$S = \sum_{i=1}^{n} f_i(p) \tag{11.17}$$

Since all the individual firms have rising *MC* curves and hence rising supply curves because of the *LDMR*, the industry supply curve must also be rising.

However, the industry supply curve is the sum of the firms' *MC* curves (above the minimum *AVC*) only if there are no external pecuniary or technical economies or diseconomies of scale. There is some debate in economics as to whether external effects are more or less likely to occur in the long-run period. The argument that external effects are more likely in the long run goes as follows: External effects require expansion of the entire industry's output. The longer the time period, the greater the possibility of expanding output. In the short run, expansion can come only from existing firms using their prevailing scales of plant. In the long run, new firms can start producing and existing firms can build larger scales of plant.

With external effects, a firm's costs depend on other firms' production levels. If expansion of other firms lowers (raises) the given firm's costs, an external economy (diseconomy) is said to have occurred. Events such as newer and cheaper raw material sources and the diffusion of newer and better technological knowledge can lead to external economies. However, most economists feel that external diseconomies are much more common. In particular, they feel that as an industry as a whole expands, the only way it can attract a sufficient quantity of factors is to raise the prices paid to these factors.

Thus, in Figure 11–5 a firm producing $0q_1$ can expand along MC_1 if it is the only firm that decides to expand and if it is a competitor in the factor market.

FIGURE 11–5   External Diseconomies and Marginal Costs

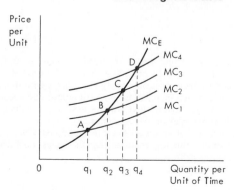

However, if all firms in the industry decide to expand simultaneously, factor prices do not, in fact, remain constant. The higher factor prices needed to attract the additional factors impose on all firms an external diseconomy which shifts the entire marginal cost function from MC_1 to MC_2.

With external diseconomies present, the firm's actual or quasi MC and supply curve becomes $ABCD$ (MC_E). However, one school of thought argues that such effects are more likely in the short run than in the long run, because in the long run the expanding industry may be able to use factors that contracting industries have laid off. The longer the time period, the more mobile the factors. This means the released factors will be attracted to the expanding industries where factor prices are rising. This increases the supply of factors and the MC curve shifts downward and rightward.

In general, the effect of external diseconomies (economies) is to make the industry supply curve more inelastic (more elastic) than it would otherwise be. In fact, external economies can possibly produce a negatively sloping aggregate supply. However, while external economies are necessary to produce a downward-sloping industry supply curve, they are not sufficient. That is, an industry supply function can have a positive slope in spite of external economies.[4] If factor prices rise in response to industry X expanding, firms in industry X experience rising total, average, and marginal costs which cause them to "pull in their horns" a bit with respect to expanding their own output. Instead of a simple summation, when external effects are present the industry supply curve becomes a more complex summation, involving all the optimum outputs for each firm at every possible industry price. In other words, the aggregate supply curve becomes a summation of the firm's actual or quasi supply curves, such as $ABCD$ in Figure 11–5.

The precise elasticity of this industry supply curve depends upon: (1) the magnitude and direction of the external effects, (2) the magnitude of the cost differences among firms, and (3) the shape of the MC curves of the individual firms. The industry supply curve tends to be more inelastic: (a) the greater the external diseconomies, (b) the greater the interfirm cost differences, and (c) the steeper the MC curves (or the greater the severity of the $LDMR$). Points (a) and (c) are fairly obvious. Point (b) simply means that if cost differences are great, the commodity's price would have to rise substantially before a firm with costs substantially higher than the marginal firm could profitably start producing.[5]

---

[4] For a mathematical proof of this, see J. M. Henderson and R. E. Quandt, *Microeconomic Theory; A Mathematical Approach* (2d ed.; New York: McGraw-Hill Book Co., 1971), pp. 111–113. Note that external effects need not apply to all firms with the same force and perhaps not even in the same direction. An increase in industry output can cause some firms' total cost curves to fall and others to rise. In this text we will assume for convenience that the external effects are unambiguously economies or diseconomies.

[5] Of course, at the optimum position all firms in the industry must have the same marginal cost for their optimum outputs. But this requires that the lowest cost firms produce a larger optimal output than the higher cost firms.

To repeat, external effects are absent when factor supplies to the industry are infinitely elastic and the industry's product expansion does not affect the individual firm's physical production functions. Only when external effects are absent can the horizontal aggregation of the short-run supply curves of all firms in the industry in fact give the market supply curve.

SHORT-RUN EQUILIBRIA: FIRM AND INDUSTRY

Figure 11–6 represents the short-run equilibrium conditions for the industry and for a representative firm. While the price (MR) of the product measured on the vertical axis is the same for both the firm and the industry, the output for the industry is measured in units of, say, 1,000 bushels of wheat if the representative firm's output units are single bushels of wheat. Since there are, say, 1,000 firms in the industry, the output has to be measured in substantially larger units for the length of the horizontal axis in the two diagrams to be approximately the same as depicted in Figure 11–6. Assuming no external effects exist, we obtain the industry supply curve S_I by taking the amounts produced by all firms at each possible price where their marginal costs equal their prices. The firm depicted in Figure 11–6(b) is representative of the firms in the industry. The industry supply curve S_I interacts with the industry demand curve discussed in previous chapters to determine the market price P_I. The competitive firm accepts this price as given, so that $P_f = MR_f = P_I$.

FIGURE 11–6   Short-Run Equilibria: Firm and Industry

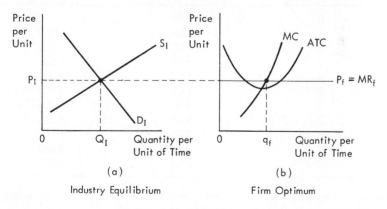

(a)

Industry Equilibrium

(b)

Firm Optimum

Figure 11–6 is said to represent full equilibrium because both the firm and the industry are in equilibrium. For the firm to be at its optimum, it must be maximizing its profits, producing according to the qualified $MR = MC$ rule. The industry is in equilibrium when the total industry demand equals the total industry supply. If these conditions hold, there is no tendency to change the level of output, at least in the short run.

Although Figure 11-6 depicts "full" equilibria in which short-run production and consumption decisions are in balance, firms are earning profits. Short-run equilibrium is compatible with any condition of profitability for the industry. Only in the long run does the competitive mechanism for eliminating profit—free entry—operate.

QUESTIONS

1. At the beginning of this chapter, the sufficient conditions for pure competition to exist are listed. It is also pointed out that the only necessary condition is that the firms in the industry regard themselves as price-takers. Try to relate these sufficient conditions to the necessary condition by asking why the demand curve *might* not be infinitely elastic if one of them did not hold, but showing that it would still be infinitely elastic as long as the necessary condition holds.
2. Precisely under what circumstances would a firm be better off stopping production altogether than continuing to produce at the level of output at which $MC = MR$? Why?
3. A purely competitive firm has the following cost information. If the price of the product it sells is $61, what is the optimal output decision for this firm? Determine the values of marginal cost, average total cost, average variable cost, average fixed cost, average revenue, and marginal revenue. Show what would happen to its profit if the firm produced one more or one less than the optimal amount.

Total Physical Product	Total Fixed Cost	Total Variable Cost
0	$50	0
1	$50	$50
2	$50	$95
3	$50	$135
4	$50	$170
5	$50	$210
6	$50	$255
7	$50	$305
8	$50	$360
9	$50	$420
10	$50	$495

4. From the data in question 3, construct a supply schedule and draw the graph of it. Use these prices: $36, $41, $46, $51, $56, $61, and $76.
5. Suppose labor is the only variable factor used by the firm of questions 3 and 4, and suppose wages are cut 10 percent. Calculate the new supply schedule and graph it on the same diagram used in question 4.
6. Suppose the cost of the fixed factor is cut in half. What happens to the supply curve of the firm of the preceding questions? Explain.
7. Using graphic analysis, show and explain how external economies affect the supply curves of the firm and the industry.

APPENDIX: MATHEMATICAL NOTES

Note 1. Industry Supply and Demand Curves

Suppose price is held constant at some level, say, P, the industry supply is Q_I, and q_A, q_B, q_C, ..., q_N is the quantity supplied by firm A, firm B, firm C, etc., and there are no external effects, then:

$$Q_I = q_A + q_B + q_C + \ldots + q_N \qquad (11.18)$$

If (11.18) is differentiated with respect to price P, we get:

$$\frac{dQ_I}{dP} = \frac{d(q_A + q_B + \ldots + q_N)}{dP} \qquad (11.19)$$

(11.19) can be substituted into the formula for the price elasticity of industry supply, ϵ_I, to yield:

$$\epsilon_I = \frac{P}{Q_I} \cdot \frac{dQ_I}{dP} = \frac{P}{Q_I} \cdot \frac{d(q_A + q_B + q_C + \ldots + q_N)}{dP} \qquad (11.20)$$

$$= \frac{P}{Q_I} \cdot \left(\frac{dq_A}{dP} + \frac{dq_B}{dP} + \frac{dq_C}{dP} + \ldots + \frac{dq_N}{dP} \right)$$

$$= \frac{q_A}{Q_I} \cdot \frac{P}{q_A} \cdot \frac{dq_A}{dP} + \frac{q_B}{Q_I} \cdot \frac{P}{q_B} \cdot \frac{dq_B}{dP} + \ldots + \frac{q_N}{Q_I} \cdot \frac{P}{q_N} \cdot \frac{dq_N}{dP}$$

$$\epsilon_I = K_A \cdot \epsilon_A + K_B \cdot \epsilon_B + K_C \cdot \epsilon_C + \ldots + K_N \cdot \epsilon_N \qquad (11.21)$$

where K_A is the relative share of firm A in the total production of the industry, ϵ_A is the price elasticity of supply for firm A, and so on for all N firms.

By a similar proof, we can demonstrate that:

$$\eta_I = K_A \cdot \eta_A + K_B \cdot \eta_B + K_C \cdot \eta_C + \ldots + K_N \cdot \eta_N \qquad (11.22)$$

where K_A is the relative share of consumer A in the total consumption of the product, η_A is the price elasticity of the demand curve of consumer A, and so on; and η_I is the price elasticity of demand for the entire market demand curve.

Note 2. Optimality Conditions

Rather than prove the special conditions for pure competition, let us first derive the general optimality solution and then indicate how this would differ if pure competition, in fact, existed. Suppose $p = f(q)$ is the inverse demand function, $TR = qf(q)$ is the total revenue function, $TC = g(q) + F$ (where F represents fixed costs) is the total cost function, and $(\pi) = TR - TC = qf(q) - g(q) - F$ is the profit function.

$$\pi = qf(q) - g(q) - F \qquad (11.23)$$

The first- and second-order conditions for a maximum are that $d\pi/dq = 0$ and $d^2\pi/dq^2 < 0$ (the second condition ensures that we have a local maximum). Taking the first derivative of (11.23) and setting it equal to zero yields:

$$d\pi/dq = f(q) + qf'(q) - g'(q) = 0 \tag{11.24}$$

or

$$f(q) + qf'(q) = g'(q) \tag{11.25}$$

Marginal revenue is $\dfrac{d[q \cdot f(q)]}{dq} = f(q) + qf'(q)$ and marginal cost is $dTC/dq = g'(q)$. Thus, the first-order condition for profit maximization is that $MR = MC$.

The second-order condition requires that:

$$d^2\pi/dq^2 = 2f'(q) + qf''(q) - g''(q) < 0 \tag{11.26}$$

or

$$d^2\pi/dq^2 = 2f'(q) + qf''(q) < g''(q) \tag{11.27}$$

The term $2f'(q) + qf''(q)$ is the slope of MR, whereas the last term, $g''(q)$, is the slope of MC. Hence, the second-order condition for profit maximization requires that the slope of MC must be greater than the slope of MR (with respect to the quantity axis). With monopoly, in contrast to pure competition, MC may be downward sloping at the $MC = MR$ point and an optimum will still result if the slope of MC is flatter (smaller in absolute value) than that of MR. Clearly if MC is upsloping and MR is downsloping, as we would normally expect, (11.26) is satisfied.

In addition to these two conditions, there is what we can call a third-order condition that must be fulfilled before a given rate of production is definitely optimal. This condition ensures that it is better to produce than to close down.

$$TR \geq TVC \text{ in the short run} \tag{11.28}$$
$$TR \geq TC \text{ in the long run}$$

Third-order condition (11.28) is identical for competition and monopoly. The difference between perfect and imperfect competition occurs in equations (11.24) and (11.25) which, because $p = f(q)$ is a constant in the case of pure competition,

$$d\pi/dq = f(q) - g'(q) = 0 \tag{11.29}$$
$$f(q) = g'(q) \tag{11.30}$$

This means that since both MR and P are given by $f(q)$, the first-order condition is that $P(=MR) = MC$. The second-order condition, (11.26), now becomes:

$$d^2\pi/dq^2 = 0 - g''(q) < 0 \tag{11.31}$$
$$= -g''(q) < 0$$

or

$$g''(q) > 0 \tag{11.32}$$

The second-order condition is therefore that MC be positively sloping.

Note 3. Derivation of Elasticity of Demand for a Firm

The text stated that a large number of firms was a sufficient, but not necessary, condition for competition. Thus, two firms could conceivably behave as price-takers. This can be demonstrated. Let D_f represent the demand facing any one of the n firms in the industry, S_0 the quantity supplied by other producers, and D_T the total or aggregate quantity demanded. By definition.

$$D_f = D_T - S_0 \tag{11.33}$$

and

$$\Delta D_f = \Delta D_T - \Delta S_0 \tag{11.34}$$

Let us divide all three expressions by a common term, the change in the price of the product, ΔP.

$$\frac{\Delta D_f}{\Delta P} = \frac{\Delta D_T}{\Delta P} - \frac{\Delta S_0}{\Delta P} \tag{11.35}$$

Now we can multiply each term by the common element P/D_f without changing the relationship.

$$\frac{P}{D_f} \cdot \frac{\Delta D_f}{\Delta P} = \frac{P}{D_f} \cdot \frac{\Delta D_T}{\Delta P} - \frac{P}{D_f} \cdot \frac{\Delta S_0}{\Delta P} \tag{11.36}$$

The expression on the left is the price elasticity of the demand curve facing the firm, η_f.

$$\eta_f = \frac{P}{D_f} \cdot \frac{\Delta D_T}{\Delta P} - \frac{P}{D_f} \cdot \frac{\Delta S_0}{\Delta P} \tag{11.37}$$

Since $\dfrac{P}{D_f} = \dfrac{D_T}{D_f} \cdot \dfrac{P}{D_T}$ and $\dfrac{P}{D_f} = \dfrac{S_0}{D_f} \cdot \dfrac{P}{S_0}$, (11.37) may be written as:

$$\eta_f = \underbrace{\frac{D_T}{D_f}}_{A} \underbrace{\left(\frac{P}{D_T} \cdot \frac{\Delta D_T}{\Delta P} \right)}_{B} - \underbrace{\frac{S_0}{D_f}}_{C} \underbrace{\left(\frac{P}{S_0} \cdot \frac{\Delta S_0}{\Delta P} \right)}_{D} \tag{11.38}$$

The term associated with B on the right side is the price elasticity of the total demand curve, η_T, and the term associated with D is the price elasticity of the supply curve of all other firms, ϵ_0. Therefore,

$$\eta_f = \frac{D_T}{D_f} \eta_T - \frac{S_0}{D_f} \epsilon_0 \tag{11.39}$$

For competition to exist, $\eta_f \to -\infty$. But clearly ϵ_0, to name but one element, is important in determining η_f in addition to the number of firms. It is true that η_f gets larger, the smaller the share of the firm; i.e., η_f gets larger as D_T/D_f or S_0/D_f gets larger. If the shares are quite small, and hence η_f is quite large, the results are for all practical purposes the same as if the demand is horizontal ($\eta_f \approx -\infty$). For instance, if the share of the firm is 1/1,000 of the total output, $\eta = -1$, and $\epsilon_0 = 2$, then:

$$\eta_f = \frac{1,000}{1}(-1) - \frac{999}{1}(2)$$
$$= -1,000 - 1,998$$
$$= -2,998$$

In economics this number is sufficiently large that the firm's demand curve can be regarded as virtually horizontal.

12 Long-Run Pricing and Production under Pure Competition

In this chapter we will derive the long-run supply curves for the firm and for the industry. From the firm's point of view, the primary difference in the long run is that, since all factors are variable, expected total revenue must at least cover expected total cost. As far as the industry is concerned, long-run equilibrium is achieved only when no profits or losses are earned. Of course, the requirement that total profits ($\pi = LTR - LTC$, where the prefix L represents long run) equal zero allows entrepreneurs to earn a "normal" return on what their contributed inputs of labor and capital could earn in alternative employments. The implicit costs in LTC must be sufficiently high to retain entrepreneurial ability.

The discussion of "normal" conditions of supply will be limited to purely competitive situations. However, on the supply side, pure competition is more than a simplifying assumption; it is an imperative. As revealed in the next chapter, a monopolist does not even have a "supply curve" as that concept is conventionally defined. That is, in monopoly there is no single unique supply price (quantity) associated with each quantity (price).

The supply function in this chapter is assumed continuous, nonnegative, single-valued, monotonically increasing, and homogeneous of degree zero. In addition, the supply function is assumed to have an elasticity (ϵ) that is: (1) between zero and infinity, (2) continuously decreasing as output increases, and (3) greater in value in the long run than in the short run. The only point that perhaps needs further discussion is why ϵ is assumed to be continuously decreasing. This is assumed because returns to scale are presumed to become increasingly unfavorable along a conventionally shaped (nonhomogeneous) cost curve. Therefore, if factor prices are assumed to remain constant, ϵ will decline continuously.

LONG-RUN SUPPLY CURVE

The long-run analysis is in one respect quite different from the short-run analysis and in another respect quite similar. The long run allows for a much wider range of potential output than does the short run. The long-run firm and industry supply is much more elastic than that of the short run. In the long run, established firms have ample time to expand or curtail their scale of plant and firms may enter or leave the industry. In contrast, in the short run the only avenue for expanding the industry's output is for existing firms to use their prevailing scale of plant more intensively.

On the other hand, the long-run analysis is similar to the short-run in that in both periods, the firm must produce where $MR = MC$. In the long-run case, this means producing where long-run marginal costs (LMC) equal long-run marginal revenue (LMR). However, the long-run analysis differs from the short-run in that the minimum remuneration required to keep a firm producing in the long run is zero economic profits. In the short run, a firm may produce to minimize losses because it is stuck with its plant and equipment and therefore has unavoidable fixed costs. But in the long run, if the firm is not earning profits, it will leave the industry by not replacing worn-out or obsolete plant and equipment. This means that the firm's long-run expected total revenue (LTR) must not be less than its long-run expected total cost (LTC), or its price (or long-run average revenue, LAR) must not be less than its long-run average costs of production (LAC). Economic losses will occur if $LTR < LTC$ (or $LAR < LAC$). Therefore, the competitive firm's long-run supply curve is that portion of its rising long-run marginal cost curve which lies above its long-run average cost curve.

In Figure 12–1, the thicker portion, *AB,* of the *LMC* curve represents the competitive "representative" firm's long-run supply curve. To see how the firm adjusts to changes in demand, assume that entry into the industry is blocked temporarily and that the firm is originally producing output $0q_1$ at price $0P_1$. If demand increases to D_2, in the long run the firm will want to move along *LMC* to output $0q_2$. It would do so by using a larger scale of plant, namely, the one represented by the subscript *a*. Hence, the segment of the *LMC* curve labeled *AB* represents the firm's long-run supply curve. The portion of the *LMC* curve below the (minimum) *LAC* curve is not relevant since the firm must at least earn zero economic profits to remain in the industry.

FIGURE 12–1 A Purely Competitive Firm's Long-Run Supply Curve *(A–B)*

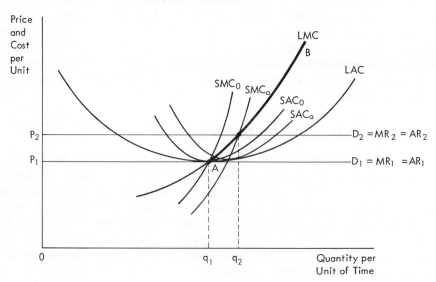

Of course, at output $0q_2$ the firm is earning profits. This is why we assume entry is blocked. With free entry, the competitive firm cannot earn profits if the industry is to be in long-run equilibrium. The firm will be forced—through entry and exit—to operate at point A, producing an output of $0q_1$ with plant scale SAC_0, and the price will remain at $0P_1$ or the level of the lowest average costs possible. It is for this reason that the technical optimum scale of plant associated with SAC_0 takes on particular significance in long-run competitive equilibrium.

CAPITALIZATION OF RETURNS TO FIXED FACTORS

The theory of the firm concludes that in the long run all firms will be at the zero profit level and that all firms in the industry have the same "costs." These conclusions seem highly unrealistic. However, once the concept of costs is fully understood, the conclusions will appear eminently reasonable.

To clarify the issues, consider the case of a large number of truck farms serving a community. The farms are identical in all respects except that one farm (farm A) is twenty miles closer to the market than the others. Suppose the farmer of farm A pays the same rent as all of the other competitors per acre of land. Since transportation costs per unit of output are less for farm A than for the others, the cost curves will appear as in Figure 12–2.

AVC is lower for farm A than for the others. AFC is the same, so ATC is less for A. The owner of the land of farm A would be expected to raise the rent on that land until all "profit" (rectangle $ABCP_0$) is eliminated. The land-owner can do this because any other entrepreneur would be willing to pay up to amount $ABCP_0$ in addition to the current rent for the use of this favored location. Thus, the fixed cost for farm A increases by the full amount of what had been considered "profit" before. The AVC curve remains where it was, but the ATC curve shifts upward to ATC' to become tangent to the price line.

FIGURE 12–2 Shift in Cost by Capitalization of Returns

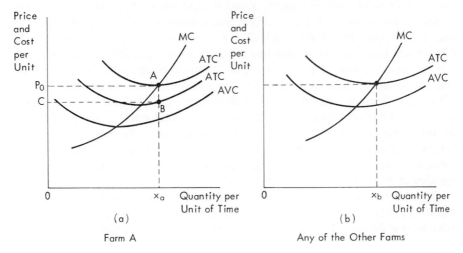

(a)

Farm A

(b)

Any of the Other Farms

Since the land used by farm *A* yields a greater expected future return to its owner than before, its present value has increased. In other words, when it is realized that the earnings of a piece of wealth (in this case, the land) will be greater in the future than had been expected, that piece of wealth is recapitalized to a higher present value than before; and given its new present worth, it will yield the same rate of return as all other wealth.

Notice two things. First, it makes no difference who owns the land, the entrepreneur or someone else. The process should be the same. In the owner-user case the added costs would not be out-of-pocket, but opportunity or implicit costs; but they would be very real in the decision process, nevertheless.

Secondly, the process described here is applicable to any factor responsible for the lower apparent cost for one firm compared to the others. (Incidentally, the process works in reverse where a particular factor is responsible for higher apparent *AVC*s.) The lower *AVC* could be due to a productive process not available to other firms (because of patent rights, for example) or to unusual talents of the entrepreneur or particular employees, or it could be due to a number of other factors of production with superior productivities.

LONG-RUN INDUSTRY SUPPLY CURVES

In the short run the industry supply schedule can be derived by summing horizontally the supply curves for established firms. This is clearly not permissible, however, in the long run where free entry and exit make the number of firms in a given industry a variable.

The Triple Equality $P = MC =$ (minimum) *AC*

Before describing the long-run equilibrium adjustments necessary to obtain a long-run industry supply schedule, it is perhaps best to state in advance the basic result of these adjustments. We conclude that after all long-run adjustments are completed (that is, after long-run equilibrium is attained), the product price will be exactly equal to and production will occur at the minimum point on each competitive firm's long-run average cost curve. In final equilibrium P $(LMR) = LMC = LAC$. Not only is price equal to the *LAC*, but it turns out to be equal to the lowest *LAC* possible at the bottom of the U-shaped curve. This means that all firms have built the technically optimum scale of plant and are operating it at its technically optimum rate of output. Furthermore, as Figure 12–1 illustrates, the minimum point on *LAC* is also the minimum point of the technically optimal scale of plant, SAC_0. At the minimum point on SAC_0, SMC_0 must equal SAC_0. We therefore have the "everything is equal" result of P $(LMR) = LAC = LMC = SAC_0 = SMC_0$. However, the first three of these are crucial and are referred to as the *triple equality* or $P = LMC =$ (minimum) *LAC*.

This triple equality follows from two facts: (1) firms attempt to maximize profits; and (2) free entry and exit of firms exist. Suppose, for example, starting from an equilibrium position, that the demand for the products of a given industry increases such as from D_1 to D_2 in Figure 12-1. With price now greater than *LAC*, profits exist, which will attract new firms into the industry and will cause expansion of output by established firms. Expansion of the industry will increase product supply until price is brought back into equality with *LAC*. In Figure 12-1, this would involve a shift downward of the firm's demand curve from D_2 back to D_1. The reverse phenomenon—contraction in the number of firms and industry output—will occur if $P < LAC$ and losses are incurred. In either case, for the industry to be in long-run equilibrium, profits or losses must not exist. Entry or exit will force a break-even solution where $P = LAC$.

The entire adjustments process involves not only a shifting downward (or upward in the case of losses) in the representative firm's demand curve as entry (exodus) occurs, but typically the cost functions also shift as new firms enter an industry. Thus, the equilibrating process is the result of two forces: demand and cost shifts. The exact nature of the cost adjustments depends upon whether the industry is one of increasing, constant, or decreasing costs. In turn, the type of cost conditions in the industry depends upon whether the industry experiences net external diseconomies, external neutrality, or external economies as expansion takes place. We will examine each of these possibilities.

Increasing Costs. Figure 12-3(a) depicts a representative firm initially in long-run equilibrium, operating where $LMC_1 = LMR$ at price $0P_1$ and producing output $0q_1$. (To keep the diagram less cluttered, the *SAC* curves are omitted.) Figure 12-3(b) illustrates the industry in long-run equilibrium

FIGURE 12-3   Long-Run Supply Curve of a Purely Competitive Industry with Increasing Costs

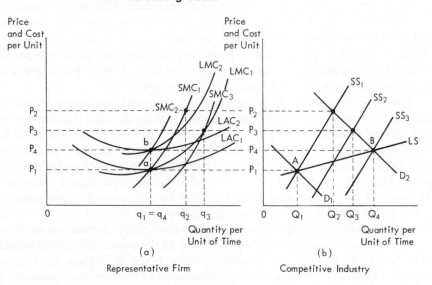

producing $0Q_1$ at $0P_1$, since zero profits are being earned where $QD = QS$. In other words, the firm is assumed initially to be in long-run equilibrium at point a and the industry at point A. The industry's short-run supply curve is SS_1 and the industry's initial demand curve is D_1. Suppose a change in tastes, incomes, or expectations, etc., occurs, shifting demand from D_1 to D_2. This new demand function intersects SS_1 at an output level of $0Q_2$ and a price of $0P_2$. The firm expands its output to $0q_2$, moving along its SMC_1 curve to achieve short-run equilibrium. Although the SAC curves have been omitted, the firm must now be making profits since demand has increased from the zero-profit point and for the moment the cost functions are assumed stationary.

In the long run, two further things will happen to change equilibrium price and quantity: (1) The firms will adjust their plant size so as to produce the desired output in the cheapest manner possible. In terms of Figure 12–3, the representative firm will adjust its capacity by moving along LMC_1 to where output is $0q_3$ and price is $0P_3$. (2) New firms will enter the industry, attempting to capture some of the profits.

Although these two movements occur simultaneously, it is easier to assume that the expansion of output by established firms precedes the entry of new firms. The expansion of output by existing firms pushes the supply curve outward to SS_2, associated with a decrease in price to $0P_3$ and an increase in industry output to $0Q_3$. With profits still being made, new firms begin entering the industry, increasing supply to SS_3, at which point profits equal zero. This occurs at a price of $0P_4$, a level of output by the firm of $0q_4$, and a rate of production for the entire industry of $0Q_4$.

Note $0P_4 > 0P_1$ because the expansion of industry output imposes an external diseconomy on all the firms in the industry. That is, the increase in demand for this commodity causes an increase in demand for the factors involved in its production, which in turn causes factor prices to rise. An industry that experiences external diseconomies as output expands is known as an "increasing-cost" industry. In such cases, any short-run profits are squeezed out in two ways: (1) the demand and MR curves for each firm shift downward, and (2) the cost curves shift upward. In final long-run equilibrium, the representative firm ends up at point b, producing $0q_4$ units of output at a per-unit price of $0P_4$ (decreasing its scale from SMC_3 to SMC_2), and the industry winds up at point B, producing $0Q_4$ units of output at price $0P_4$.

The new firm equilibrium output, $0q_4$, is exactly the same as the old equilibrium output, $0q_1$, because we assumed that the external diseconomy was such that all factors had proportionate increases in their prices. From the law of substitution, it follows that the minimum point on the new LAC_2 curve must be the same as on the LAC_1 curve. Since the least-cost combination requires $MPP_a/P_a = MPP_b/P_b = \cdots = MPP_n/P_n$, a proportionate increase in the price of all factors would yield exactly the same equilibrium values. If factor prices change disproportionately, there is no parallel shift of the cost curves and the firm's long-run equilibrium output might increase or decrease.

The industry long-run supply curve joins all the points of long-run equilibrium. In Figure 12–3(b), LS connects points A and B. Hence, the long-run industry supply curve is a horizontal summation of the minimum points on all the individual firms' *LAC* curves after the external effects have worked themselves out. Geometrically, it is the locus of successive minima on the *LAC* of the firms in the industry, given time for plant scale adjustments and entry and exit.

The crucial factor in determining the shape of the industry's long-run supply function is the effect, if any, which changes in the number of firms in the industry have on the cost curves of the individual firms which comprise the industry. Typically, the effect of entry is to shift cost curves upward. This, the increasing-cost case, is caused by external diseconomies of scale. Although the external diseconomies theoretically can be of a technical or a pecuniary variety, the former is generally minor. Typically the externality is of a pecuniary variety, raising factor prices.

Constant Costs. In some circumstances, an industry might be a constant-cost industry. In fact, several empirical studies suggest that constant costs may be more common than once thought. In the constant-cost case, the entire expansion of output will occur solely because the number of firms producing the same given level of output increases, not because the previously established firms expand their rate of output. Of course, in the short-run period the established firms expand their output; but, after all long-run adjustments have been completed, they return to their original rate of production. In terms of Figure 12–4, a constant-cost industry, the representative firm in panel (a) would experience no change in any of the cost curves from an expansion of industry output, and therefore its output would remain at $0q_1$. In panel (b) the industry would increase output by the amount of the change in demand, all of which will be supplied by new firms. The long-run industry supply curve *LS* is linear and horizontal at price $0P_1$.

FIGURE 12–4   Long-Run Supply Curve of a Purely Competitive Industry with Constant Costs

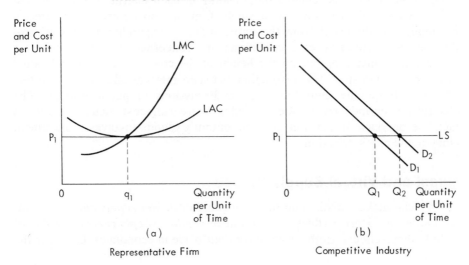

(a)
Representative Firm

(b)
Competitive Industry

For an industry to be one of constant cost, its demand for factors must be small in relation to the total demand; it must not employ any specialized factors whose supply is not easily augmentable; and it must not use factors in unique proportions. In short, it must have no net external economies or diseconomies of scale. In such cases, external neutrality is said to exist. For instance, the hairpin industry could no doubt buy all the steel input it desires without influencing the price of steel, since it uses a small percentage of the annual total consumption of steel. In contrast, the automobile industry, in terms of steel consumption, is likely to be an increasing-cost industry.

Decreasing Costs. The final theoretical possibility is a decreasing-cost industry in which factors become cheaper as the industry expands. Economists think the likelihood of decreasing costs, especially over any extended period of time, is quite small. Since the factor supply curves facing most industries are much more likely to be upward sloping—indicating that higher factor prices are required to attract additional units of a factor—the idea of external economies and perhaps a downsloping industry supply curve is not appealing to most economists. Furthermore, if downward-sloping industry supply curves were fairly prevalent, we would expect to find many more unstable markets than we do. In the case of a decreasing-cost industry, Figure 12–3 would have to be redrawn, showing a shift downward from LAC_1 to LAC_2 in panel (a); and point B would be below point A in panel (b), producing a downsloping LS curve.

To summarize, increasing-cost, constant-cost, and decreasing-cost industries are associated with net external diseconomies, external neutrality, and external economies of scale, respectively. External effects should be sharply distinguished from internal effects. External effects refer to a shift of the whole cost function, whereas internal effects involve movements along a given long-run cost schedule. For instance, a firm can effect an internal economy of scale by enlarging its rate of production if it is operating at any scale of plant smaller than the technically optimal scale of plant. In fact, competitive firms must enlarge output until all such internal sources of cost reductions vanish. In contrast, a single firm has no control over external economies which result from the entire industry expanding its rate of production. An industry's cost conditions are concerned with the impact of changes in industry output on the height of the cost schedules of individual firms in the industry. The distinction between internal effects and external effects is frequently confused, e.g., in discussions of public utilities. The electric power industry is often called a decreasing-cost industry when, in fact, the decrease in per-unit costs as output expands involves a movement along a given cost function.

Quasi and Virtual Supply Curves

We can make a distinction between *quasi* or *actual supply curves* that incorporate the external effects and *virtual* or *shadow supply curves* that do not include these effects. Both curves have their place in economics. Consider the two supply curves drawn in Figure 12–5. The curve labeled S_q is the quasi supply curve, reflecting external diseconomies that affect a MC curve; whereas ΣMC is the virtual supply curve, showing what firms think they would like to produce on the assumption there are no externalities.

Suppose a minimum price of $0P_2$ is legally imposed and actively enforced.[1] At this price, $0Q_1$ is sold, since $0P_2$ intersects demand at point A. With the use of both quasi and virtual supply curves, it is easy to demonstrate why the pressure on "rigged" nonequilibrium prices is generally greater than anticipated; and yet when these prices are abandoned, the actual change in output is less than one would expect, given the pressures. For instance, at the "rigged" price of $0P_2$, the rationing problem is only Q_1Q_2 (though it appears to be Q_1Q_3), since the quasi industry supply curve, S_q, intersects $0P_2$ at point B. However, the virtual supply curve, ΣMC, shows that the firms, neglecting externalities, would like to produce $0Q_3$ units of output at price $0P_2$—i.e., $0P_2$ intersects ΣMC at point C. Of course, the output points on the virtual supply curve would never be realized, except point E. That is, as firms expand output from, say, point E, they actually move along S_q because of the external diseconomies; although, when at point E, they think they would like to expand along the ΣMC curve. Since these firms are competitors, they do not presuppose externalities, but do adjust to them after they in fact occur.

FIGURE 12–5   Distinction between Quasi and Virtual Supply Curves

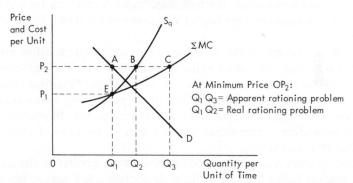

ECONOMIC EFFECTS OF PURE COMPETITION

One of the most important results of a basically competitive market system is that consumer sovereignty reigns. The process by which this occurs is as follows. Firms, in seeking to maximize profits, equate MR with MC. MR under competition equals price, and price is at the point which equates total demand and supply. If the public prefers a larger output of x than is being produced

---

[1] In addition to this example, Milton Friedman, *Price Theory; A Provisional Text* (Chicago: Aldine Publishing Co., 1962), pp. 88–93, also presents the effects of legal maximum and minimum prices when external economies affecting MC curves generate negatively sloping supply curves.

—i.e., if the quantity demanded exceeds the quantity supplied at the current price—the price of x will rise (law of demand and supply). At the new higher price of x, firms in the industry will find that MR exceeds MC and that therefore it will pay to increase output. If, at the output level at which MR and MC are brought back into equality, profits in the industry are above zero, additional firms will enter the industry and total supply will increase still further until profits are eliminated. (Whether the final long-run equilibrium price turns out to be higher, lower, or the same as the original price depends upon whether the industry is an increasing-, decreasing-, or constant-cost industry. Typically, external diseconomies of scale prevail, causing an increasing-cost situation and therefore an upsloping long-run industry supply curve.) Hence, the increased consumer demand for x automatically causes a reallocation of resources toward its production. The same analysis holds in reverse if the demand for a commodity decreases. Thus, in free and competitive markets, shifts in demand ordinarily in turn cause changes in supply in the same direction.

We can draw a parallel between the system in which individuals cast political votes to determine the society's political structure and the system in which individuals cast dollar votes to determine the society's economic structure. In both cases, whether it be in a large political or economic "constituency," an individual's influence is negligible. Only the combined influence of the hundreds, thousands, or even millions of individual choices is effective. The preferences of consumers as a group are therefore reflected in the prices they are willing to pay for various commodities. The general proposition is that, other things being equal, the higher the price consumers are willing to pay to purchase a commodity, the higher that commodity stands on their scale of preferences.

The big advantage of the economic over the political ballot box is that the individual is not committed to the popular decision. While everyone in the U.S., even those strongly opposed, is "stuck" with the President who won the election, a consumer may simply refrain from purchasing a commodity he or she dislikes even if the majority voted for its production. In general, the wide variety of substitute commodities allows a greater freedom of choice in economic than in political life.

In one respect the political ballot box offers greater individual choice than the market ballot box. In political democracy each person has the same number of votes as every other, whereas in economic democracy the number of votes available varies greatly among different individuals. The democratic political rule is, "one person, one vote"; whereas the economic rule is, "one dollar, one vote." Only in the case of perfect equality of income—i.e., if every individual had the same number of dollars to spend—would the two rules be equivalent. In fact, in the United States income is very unequally distributed. Of course, if the preference schedules of the wealthy were similar to those of the poor, this inequality would not affect the pattern of resource allocation. Generally, however, these preferences differ, with high-income households spending a relatively greater percentage of their budget on expensive luxury goods and services.

Society's Use of Its Scarce Means of Production

The second important economic result of the competitive market system concerns the optimal use of society's scarce means of production. A competitive society obtains the greatest social economic value possible from its given resource endowments.

The "social economic value" of a good or service has meaning only in terms of its ability to satisfy human wants compared to the ability of other goods and services to satisfy wants. The only objective method of measuring the relative want-satisfying power of a good or service is in terms of the price which consumers are willing to pay for it. The higher the price a consumer is willing to pay for a good, the greater the good's (marginal) utility compared to that of lower priced goods.

For the same reason, the social economic value of any productive service has meaning only in terms of its ability to contribute, directly or indirectly, to the satisfaction of wants. The only objective method of measuring the social economic value of a productive service, say, productive service a, is in terms of the amount of its marginal physical product (MPP_a) times the unit price of the commodity it helps produce, say, product x (P_x). The resulting figure is referred to as the *value of its marginal product* (VMP_a)—i.e., $VMP_a = MPP_a \cdot P_x$.

The importance of the VMP_a as a measure of social economic value can be illustrated with a simple example. Suppose with the use of a given amount of labor, equipment, fertilizer, seed, etc., an acre of land will yield, say, either 25 bushels of wheat or 50 bushels of oats. In which use the VMP of the land is greater depends upon the value consumers place on wheat and oats—i.e., the price of wheat and oats. If wheat has a free-market price of $3 per bushel and oats $1 per bushel, the VMP of land is greater in wheat output than in oats output. Hence, physical output alone has little economic significance.

Society will maximize the social economic value from its productive resources only if it is unable, by reallocating its resources, to add more value than it destroys. This maximization automatically happens in a perfectly functioning competitive economy in which consumption and production externalities are minimal.

Competitive Market Results

Free-market equilibrium consumer goods prices reflect consumer marginal evaluation of the goods. If $P_x = \$1$ and $P_y = \$2$, each consumer adjusts expenditures so that a unit of y is worth twice as much at the margin as one unit of x—i.e., $MU_y = 2MU_x$. However, resource allocation involves not only what consumers like to have, but also what it is possible for them to have— preference scales and production limitations. Just as subjective preferences are expressed in relative prices—in the prices buyers are willing to pay—so are objective production boundaries.

In equilibrium, $P_x = MC_x$ and $P_y = MC_y$; hence, in the above example, $MC_x = \$1$ and $MC_y = \$2$. But marginal money costs reflect marginal social economic costs. To produce one unit of y, society must give up, at the margin, two units of x. Since, in a free-enterprise economy, firms primarily produce to earn income for the resource owners, the more anything costs to produce, the higher the price. These costs of production in turn are a measure of the quantity of scarce productive resources used in producing the commodity and therefore of the sacrificed alternatives.

Marginal costs equal the sum of the firm's additional outlay on the extra productive services required to increase output by one unit—i.e., the sum of additional wages, interest, and rents required per extra unit of output. But the amount of wages, interest, etc., a firm must pay for productive services is the amount these services are worth in other uses.

A productive service's worth to a competitive firm is measured by its VMP. A market price of $10 per day for labor indicates that the VMP of the labor is $10 in its present employment. The transfer of a day's labor service out of a present employment means, then, the loss of $10 worth of output in the industry from which it is transferred. Hence, if $MC_x = \$1$ and $MC_y = \$2$, the resources required to produce one unit of y at the margin could instead produce two additional units of x. One might suppose, for instance, that x and y are commodities (perhaps personal services) that may be produced with labor alone. In our example, say, two hours of labor service are used to produce one unit of y. These same two hours of service could have produced two units of x. Thus, the opportunity cost of $y = 2x$. In short, if $P_x = \$1 = MC_x$, and $P_y = \$2 = MC_y$, society's relative evaluation of x and y is the same as the social opportunity costs of producing x and y. In this case, there is optimum allocation, for no reallocation would add more social value than it would destroy.

Allocative Efficiency: The Triple Equality

The desirable results discussed above are contained in the long-run optimum position of the competitive firm where "everything is equal" or where the *triple equality* reigns, $P = LAC = LMC$. The equality of price and minimum average cost indicates that the firm is using the most efficient known technology, is charging the lowest price, and is producing the greatest output consistent with its costs. Put differently, with competition the total value of the factors used to produce the optimal quantity of output is at an absolute minimum. In a competitive regime, firms not using the best available (least-cost) technology will not survive.

The equality of price and marginal cost indicates that resources are being allocated in accordance with consumer preferences. Efficiency in the production ($P = LAC$) of any collection of goods is desirable, but production must also entail the "right" goods or the goods consumers want the most. Since the money price of any commodity is society's measure of its value relative to the values of other commodities the productive services could have produced, the $P = LMC$ competitive result is also desirable. The competitive price system also reallocates resources in response to changes in consumer preferences, technology, resource supplies, etc., so as to maintain allocative efficiency over time.

In summary, a purely competitive price system organizes the private self-interest of consumers, resource owners, and business people along lines which usually promote the social good or welfare. No one strives to promote the interests of society as a whole. Actions based on private self-interest usually just happen to also benefit society in general. We include the qualifier "usually" because at least two more conditions are required for the long-run competitive model to provide an ideal output, namely: (1) the *LAC* must measure all the relevant costs, and (2) the distribution of income must not be too unequal. We will take up each of these in the following section.

LIMITATIONS IN A PERFECTLY FUNCTIONING COMPETITIVE ENVIRONMENT

The first objections that may be raised against an economy such as ours are those that would occur even in a perfectly functioning competitive milieu. Of course, a perfectly functioning competitive environment is a didactic device, not a description of reality. Nonetheless, it can serve as an ideal against which the operation of an actual economy can be compared. For instance, a broad group of commodities known as "collective" or "public" goods and services would be neglected because even a perfectly functioning price system responds only to those wants which individuals in the market can express.

Collective Commodities

Collective commodities, by their nature, cannot be consumed on an individual basis, yet benefit the collectivity of individuals. They generally are not bought and sold in markets, because their economic values are difficult to determine on an individual basis, or because society as a whole has a stake in their provision, or because transactions costs would be very large. Such things as national defense, police and fire protection, public health protection, education, and similar services are by their nature collective rather than individual and are frequently provided by government. Even perhaps the greatest promulgator of the doctrine of *laissez-faire*, Adam Smith, recognized and accepted the necessity of government intervention for this purpose. In some cases these goods or services could be produced and sold in a free market, although their precise value on an individual basis would be difficult to determine. For example, soldiers were originally mercenaries and, in professional armies, still are; private schools do exist and survive; "justice" is still bought and sold more than we care to think, etc.

Included in collective goods are those goods that have been labeled by some as "quasi-collective" goods. These are goods whose marginal social return or cost exceeds or falls short of the marginal private return or cost to the individual consumers (firms) directly consuming (producing) them. In such cases, there is said to be "third-party" effects, which are also referred to as "neighborhood effects" or "externalities." When these "third-party" effects are not taken into account, private unregulated market relations lead to over- or under-production and consumption of the commodity. When the marginal social return exceeds the marginal private return, such as in education and transportation, there is a below optimal assignment of resources to the commodity and more of the commodity should be added to the private market supply. Almost all members of a society benefit from a more educated citizenry and a developed system of transportation.

In addition to the benefits, economic and otherwise, an education bestows upon an individual, the entire society benefits from more enlightened citizens. One careful study has shown that a college education usually pays for itself in about ten years.[2] For every $100 spent on college, the average student increases his or her earning power by more than $100 a year. In addition, the national economy gains an estimated $2,000 a year for every $20,000 invested in the average four-year college education. Other commodities which yield *social revenues* — i.e., widespread satisfaction to third parties besides the direct consumer — include chest x-rays, polio shots, songs, etc.

Also important is the situation where the marginal social cost exceeds the marginal private cost, such as occurs from the unregulated production of narcotics or liquor. A. C. Pigou's classic example of marginal social costs being greater than the marginal private costs concerns the case of factories that belch smoke out of their chimneys, thereby imposing higher cleaning costs, medical costs, etc., on the whole community.[3] Because of the indirect harm caused to third parties, direct government involvement may be needed. Other commodities which impose *social costs* — i.e., widespread costs which the producer can avoid but society as a whole cannot — include polluted rivers, smog, and disabilities to workers caused by profit-seeking firms in an unbridled competitive environment. To the extent that these social costs are not included in the private costs depicted in our diagrams, the output of unregulated firms is too large. If the cost curves included these social costs, the equilibrium output would be smaller.

Once the collective goods have been identified, the general rule for determining the quantity of resources to allot to these goods is the following: Allocate resources to every collective commodity up to the point where the marginal social cost (plus any marginal private cost) equals the marginal social return (plus any private marginal return) yielded by it. Unfortunately, this principle is difficult to implement because no objective test of a commodity's social return exists. The social cost can be measured relatively easily in most cases by the market prices the government must pay for the productive services required for its production. The allotment of resources to any particular commodity is therefore decided at the political level. And many say that in our economy this has resulted in an underallocation of resources to collective commodities because of the exaggerated emphasis on the cost side to the neglect of the benefit side. Even when the returns can be measured with some

---

[2] Gary Becker, *Human Capital; A Theoretical and Empirical Analysis, with Special Reference to Education* (New York: Columbia University Press, 1964).

[3] Pigou's classic work, *The Economics of Welfare* (4th ed.; London: Macmillan & Co., 1932), remains an important landmark in the nonmathematical treatment of welfare economics.

degree of accuracy and are well in excess of costs, the potential net gain is not always exploited. An important example is the millions of dollars worth of property damage caused by floods year after year, despite the fact that adequate flood-control measures cost only a fraction of the cumulative property loss. Economically speaking, this is not a rational use of resources. However, the government has had success in varying degrees in correcting for divergencies between private and social costs and benefits in labor legislation, natural resource conservation, and zoning laws.

Static and Dynamic Considerations

While the competitive model is useful as a measure against which to examine the actual operation of an economy, it has some additional shortcomings. For instance, there is both a static ("right now") and a dynamic ("over time") criticism of the competitive system's use of productive techniques. The static criticism argues that in certain lines of production, existing technology may be such that the small-sized firms that prevail under pure competition may be too small to realize economies of mass production and distribution. The more efficient, but more expensive, capital equipment is simply out of the question for them.

The dynamic criticism states that the rate of technological advance is possibly slower under competitive conditions because firms lack both the means and the incentives to innovate. The absence of long-run profits in the past limits the means from which the competitive firm can undertake research. This argument is nullified, it would seem, if there is competition in the financial markets sphere, where banks and other financial intermediaries would be supplying the necessary capital wherever profit possibilities seem most promising. Secondly, the incentives are perhaps weaker because an innovating firm's profit rewards resulting from, say, a cost-reducing technical improvement quickly vanish or are competed away by rival firms. Under monopoly, however, there are long-run incentives to innovate.

It has also been suggested that under pure competition very sudden and violent fluctuations in prices can and do occur. This has been and continues to be the case in competitive industries such as farming, textiles, and raw materials.

Furthermore, a socially undesirable system of income distribution may result. An uneven distribution of income (dollar votes) leads to the production of trifles for the rich while denying the more basic needs of the poor. Members of a destitute family may starve. Both the mentally and physically weak or disabled may suffer under such a system. Of course, economic logic does not allow us to say anything definite about the ideal income distribution. The competitive model provides an efficient optimum, given the level of equity or income distribution in the society. While most economists favor more equity or less inequality, they shed their role as economists to draw this conclusion, basing it on noneconomic considerations.

Finally, some economists who would agree that price and output in a purely competitive market are: (1) "efficient" in the sense that no other division of output among the firms would produce the output as cheaply and (2) "correct" in the sense that $P = LMC$, do not think the system is "ideal" for the reasons given above. In addition, this model takes consumer desires for granted and assumes that they should be able to choose freely. Yet society is not always willing to accept this premise. We don't think children should be allowed to eat all the candy or poison that they want or that adults should be allowed to consume all the drugs or pornography that they want. On the other hand, we don't like a world where people are commanded what to consume.

SHORTCOMINGS AS A RESULT OF MARKET IMPERFECTIONS

More important than the limitations that result from a perfectly functioning competitive market economy are the limitations due to imperfections in the market. These market imperfections occur both on the consumers' side and more importantly on the producers' side.

Consumers' Side

On the consumers' side, the market system postulates that consumers attempt to get the most for their money and generally succeed in doing so. In fact, however, many consumers act impulsively with later regrets, make little effort to shop around, and pay little attention to the optimal use of the household budget. Moreover, to behave as they would like, consumers must have accurate information on prices and qualities of alternatives, which they often lack.

The extent to which the above elements destroy the economic basis for the free-market system is debatable. It should be noted, however, that the weaknesses mentioned are inherent in any system in which freedom of consumer choice prevails. Moreover, through better education, the spread of consumer goods testing services, etc., most of the apparent irrationality can be reduced.

Although state and local measures help protect consumers, they are limited in scope and effectiveness. Municipalities through ordinances and licensing have tried to maintain minimum standards of sanitation and safety. State governments have primarily helped in controlling weights and measures and labeling requirements. The federal government, with its greater resources and influence, has tried to help by at least reducing the cases where the consumer is positively misinformed. The two most important laws dealing with consumer protection are the Pure Food and Drug Act (1906)—extended and strengthened by the Food, Drug, and Cosmetic Act of 1938—and the Wheeler-Lea Act (1938). Since the late 1960s, the federal government has taken a much more active role in trying to help consumers protect their interests.

A federal agency, the Food and Drug Administration, part of the Department of Health, Education and Welfare, tests and inspects foods and drugs for their purity, safety, and conformity to minimum standards. The Wheeler-Lea Act empowered the Federal Trade Commission (FTC) to stop false or misleading advertising. Starting in the late 1950s, the FTC proceeded against hundreds of firms that used false and misleading advertising. For example, General Motors showed television advertisements and presumably demonstrated that GM's window glass was significantly clearer and more distortion-free than that of its competitors. However, FTC investigators discovered that the windows in the GM cars in the television ads were actually rolled down when the pictures that showed their "clear and distortion-free" glass were taken! The FTC looks as though it will take on a substantially expanded role in future years in this way.

Consumers have organized with the aim of protecting themselves. Two nonprofit consumer testing organizations, Consumers' Research (CR) and Consumers Union (CU), were formed. Although the former was organized first (in 1928), the second, organized a few years later, has become the dominant testing organization in the U.S. In their independent research laboratories, these organizations have objectively tested many products, free of special-interest pressure, and reported on them in their monthly publications, *Consumer Reports* (from CU) and *Consumers' Research Magazine* (from CR). The quantitative effect of these reports in the face of the mass media does not appear to have been great.

The most interesting and significant finding, based on the numerous tests conducted by these organizations, supports our earlier comments. Prices of branded products frequently lack much association with their quality ratings. This suggests some inefficient resource use and a malfunctioning of the price system. However, the growth of these private consumer testing organizations contributes to more efficient resource use through increasing consumer information. Unfortunately, this is only true to the extent that people in fact read the reports of these services. From all indications, the number of such people is quite small.

Producers' Side

No doubt, vastly more important in magnitude in our economy than the imperfections on the consumption side are those on the production side. Of course, a competitive market system postulates perfect competition in both the buying and selling of finished goods and services and of productive services. In fact, however, competition is never perfect. The absence of perfect competition means the presence of elements of monopoly. In this context, monopoly is broadly defined to refer to any situation in which a single buyer or seller, or group acting in concert, significantly influences total demand or supply and thus influences the market price. Such a situation sharply contrasts the position of an individual buyer and seller under perfect competition. The next several chapters will thoroughly analyze these monopoly positions.

QUESTIONS

1. How does the decision to produce or not produce differ for a firm in the short run and in the long run? Given this difference, describe the long run and the short run supply curves.

2. Give any reasons or examples you can think of for firms in pure competition to have lower costs than the other firms in the same industry. Would these firms earn profits while the other firms were earning zero profits, or would all of the firms earn zero profits? Explain.
3. After a permanent increase in the demand for a commodity produced by a purely competitive industry, the firms involved will temporarily earn profits. Describe the forces that will eliminate these profits in the long run.
4. The cost to society of producing a commodity is the value of the goods given up when resources are used in its production rather than elsewhere. How does the *MR = MC* optimality condition for the firm relate to society's goal of maximizing economic welfare?
5. "If there are no government regulations concerning pollution emissions, output in certain industries will be greater than it should be." Explain the meaning of this statement. Who bears the costs of pollution in these cases, and who do you think should bear these costs?
6. Zoning laws are a violation of the principle of private property rights. Using the concept of externalities, can you justify a zoning law which prohibits the keeping of livestock (pigs, chickens, cattle, etc.) on property in an otherwise residential area?

APPENDIX: MATHEMATICAL NOTES

Note 1. Long-Run Cost Functions and Competition

The text indicated that the profit-maximization analysis breaks down if constant returns to scale prevail. Such a production function, with a degree of homogeneity equal to one, yields a linear *LTC* function of the following form:

$$LTC = aq \tag{12.1}$$

This is associated with a linear expansion path and a constant value for a equal to both *LMC* and *LAC* (since $LMC = dLTC/dq = a$ and $LAC = LTC/q = aq/q = a$). Since *TR* equals *pq*, the profit function (π) can be expressed as:

$$\pi = pq - aq \tag{12.2}$$

The first-order conditions for a maximum require setting the first derivative of (12.2) equal to zero, or:

$$d\pi/dq = p - a = 0 \text{ or } p = a \tag{12.3}$$

Unless *P* and *LMC* happen to coincide, the entrepreneur has the impossible job of equating two constants, a and p. There are three possible outcomes:

1. $P > LMC$ (or $p > a$): The firm will expand its output indefinitely if it pays to produce at all.
2. $P < LMC$ (or $p < a$): The firm will leave the industry.
3. $P = LMC$ (or $p = a$): The firm's optimum output is indeterminate, with the first-order condition satisfied at all levels of production.

13 Pricing and Production under Pure Monopoly

This chapter will present a short- and long-run optimality analysis of monopolistic firms. All firms other than perfectly competitive ones have one common trait: they are price-makers facing downward-sloping demand curves for their product. The particular form of market organization that stands at the opposite end of the continuum of market structures from the purely competitive case is pure monopoly. Chapter 7 explained the general revenue conditions facing this and other monopolistic market firms. It stated that, in a purely monopolistic market, there is only one seller of a commodity which has no close substitutes, and barriers to entry prevent potential rivals from entering the industry.[1]

WHAT IS PURE MONOPOLY?

In its absolute form, pure monopoly—i.e., a sole seller with exclusive control of a commodity—is probably nonexistent. Almost any commodity has at least indirect and potential competition facing it. Put differently, the cross elasticity of demand for most commodities is positive and nonzero. For instance, given that consumers have limited budgets, all commodities are in a sense substitutes competing for a part of the budget. A dollar spent on, say, onions means a consumer has a dollar less to spend on, say, aspirins. In this broad sense, all commodities are substitutes.

However, a narrower definition of substitutability seems more relevant for most economic analyses. Thus, a monopoly is sometimes said to exist when there is a gap in the chain of substitutes. Therefore, the less stringent phrase "close substitutes" is used in the above definition of pure monopoly. However, most commodities have close but imperfect substitutes. A firm can have a monopolistic position in one market or segment of a market but not in another. For example, since candles, gaslights, and whale-oil lamps are poor substitutes

---

[1] It is commonplace to use a rather loose definition of barriers to entry in economics textbooks. Following George J. Stigler, *The Organization of Industry* (Homewood: Richard D. Irwin, 1968), p. 67, a barrier to entry should refer to "a cost of producing (at some or every rate of output) which must be borne by a firm which seeks to enter the industry but is not borne by firms already in the industry." This concept should be distinguished from economies of scale, which involve the relationship between the size of a firm (or plant) and its internal costs of production. Thus, entry can be free into an industry, i.e., involve no barriers to entry, even though capital requirements are high. Similarly, product differentiation is a barrier to entry only if the costs of differentiation are different for potential firms than they are for existing firms. This textbook will follow tradition and not maintain this distinction between barriers to entry, absolute capital requirements, and economies of scale.

for electric lighting, electric-power companies approximate pure monopolies in both commercial and residential markets. At the same time, these companies face stiff competition in the cooking and heating market. For example, in the commercial heating market, gas, oil, and steam heat compete with electricity; whereas in the residential heating market, fuel oil and natural gas are important competitors.

Since a monopolist's strength lies in the ability to raise price without losing many customers, a monopolist is sometimes described as a seller whose demand is not very elastic, say, $\eta < 10$. (For example, if $\eta = 50$, we know that $MR = MC = P[1 - 1/50]$ or $P - MC = P/50$. This means that price only exceeds MC and MR by 2 percent. Unless otherwise specified in this chapter, $\eta = |\eta|$.)

Finally, since barriers seldom prohibit entry absolutely over extended periods of time without government aid and sanction, the monopolist must be ever mindful of potential competition. For this reason the monopolist may choose not to fully exploit an advantageous position. The number of firms currently producing electronic computers, copying machines, and drugs suggests that it is difficult for monopolies and quasi-monopolies to remain intact if substantial profits are being earned. Perhaps the best short statement ever made on why a monopoly is usually fragile was by Nourse and Drury more than a quarter of a century ago:

> The man who today tries to fence in an industrial highway and exact an exorbitant toll from those who would travel this road to consumer satisfaction is in danger of defeating himself. Under modern conditions of technology, applied science is likely to find other means of progress. The chemist will build a detour around him, the physicist will drive a tunnel under him, or a biological overpass will be devised.[2]

These considerations also suggest that in most circumstances it is the number of potential rivals rather than the number of actual rivals that is important in market behavior. In fact, as will be discussed later, the theories of Bain, Bertrand, Clark, Cournot, Demsetz, and Modigliani revolve around the fact that the degree of competition is more closely associated with the number of potential rivals rather than with actual rivals.

Although monopoly is rare in its pure form, examples of near-absolute monopolies can be cited. For instance, the following industries have had in the past or have today conditions roughly approaching pure monopoly: public utilities (AT&T), aluminum (Alcoa), digital electronic computers and data processing equipment (IBM), shoe machinery (United Shoe Machinery Co.), molybdenum (Climax Molybdenum), nickel (U. S. Nickel Company of Canada), diamonds (DeBeers Company of South Africa), railroad cars (Pullman), locomotives (General Motors), telephone equipment (Western Electric), razor blades (Gillette), and magnesium (Dow Chemical Co.). Alcoa, DeBeers,

---

[2] As quoted, without further source, in Joel Dean, *Managerial Economics* (Englewood Cliffs: Prentice-Hall, 1951), p. 57, and repeated in Kristian S. Palda, *Pricing Decisions and Marketing Policy* (Englewood Cliffs: Prentice Hall, 1971), p. 48.

Dow, Gillette, and International Nickel each held about 90 percent of its principal markets; GM, Western Electric, and United Shoe Machinery each held about 85 percent; and IBM, Climax, Pullman, and AT&T each held about 70 percent.

Despite the empirical insignificance of pure or absolute monopoly, it is still important to examine it systematically. First of all, the model is useful in industries where one firm controls 80, 70, or even 60 percent of the market, although formally pure monopoly assumes a single seller with 100 percent of the market. Secondly, the more empirically relevant models of monopolistic competition and oligopoly are built upon this basic model of pure monopoly. In fact, once the polar models of pure competition and pure monopoly have been mastered, the other market forms are relatively easy.

Before turning our attention to an equilibrium analysis of pure monopoly, we should first ask two questions: How do monopoly positions arise in the first place? How are monopolists able to maintain these positions over time? In other words: What are the original sources of monopoly power? What are the barriers to entry that allow these firms to maintain these positions over time?

ATTAINING AND MAINTAINING MONOPOLY POSITIONS[3]

All sellers and buyers have an economic motive for wanting to acquire market power, for it gives them the ability to receive greater returns or pay lower prices (for reasons to be explained). Therefore, throughout our industrial history, firms have sought monopoly positions to either increase or secure their profit positions by reducing the vigor of competition. Though competition is usually desirable from a social point of view, it is most irksome to the individual producers subject to its rigor. In fact, it has been said that the greatest benefit from monopoly is a "quiet life." It seems inherent in a free, individualistic environment that the profit-seeking entrepreneur will attempt to break free of the restraining force of competition in trying to achieve a better position. The fact that our society has found it necessary to enact antitrust legislation attests to this.

The sources of monopoly power include the following nine general methods. This list is not meant to be exhaustive, only illustrative.

Natural Monopoly

In some sectors, the nature of the good or service or genuine economies of scale which are fully exploitable only by firms of large size relative to the total market demand preclude, on an economic basis, more than one producer (pure monopoly) or more than a few producers (oligopoly). While monopoly or oligopoly does not lead to optimal factor usage, it may be that no other unregulated market structure can perform as well.

---

[3] In this section monopoly is discussed in general terms and is not restricted to pure monopoly.

To take some simple examples of natural monopoly, consider the case of water mains or telephones. One water main can serve all the houses on a block. A more competitive market form with more firms would produce waste and would only add to costs. In the past there have been areas in the United States where two independent telephone companies operated. To be able to call everyone in town, a resident needed to have the phones of both companies. The homes of the more opulent families in these towns actually had two telephones hung side by side. In such cases, consolidation and elimination of such duplication would result in greater convenience and greater efficiency. This kind of situation has been most common in the so-called public utilities area: power, transportation, water, communications, etc.

In such situations where monopoly or oligopoly is the most efficient market structure, the economy usually selects one of two possibilities, public regulation or public ownership. Each approach, as will be described later, has its shortcomings. While in some cases the city, state, or federal government owns the utilities, most commonly they are privately owned and publicly regulated. The public utilities are permitted to operate as monopolies or oligopolies to gain the efficiencies, but their prices, services, costs, and profits are regulated typically by state commissions and in some cases by the federal government.

Efficiency through Economies of Large-Scale Production

In some industries for technical reasons, average (and marginal) costs of production can be lowered by enlarging the size of the firm. For example, assembly line techniques and the use of modern equipment in the automobile industry lower the cost of production per automobile, but only if the firm's output is large. The aluminum, automobile, and steel industries are three of the many heavy manufacturing industries which reflect these conditions. If in such industries a small number of firms of optimum size will satisfy the market, oligopoly will prevail. If only one firm can satisfy the market demand, pure monopoly will appear. Large-scale production sometimes brings lower costs; and the bigger the company, the more likely it is to have some degree of monopoly power in its market.

However, the efficiency excuse is often a rationalization for the existence of concentration. To equate size with efficiency is inaccurate in many industries. For instance, U. S. Steel illustrates the fact that sometimes bigness brings inefficiency. (One author has referred to it as a floundering phlegmatic, lackadaisical giant!)

How large a firm needs to be to attain maximum efficiency varies widely from industry to industry. George Romney, then president of American Motors, testified before a Senate investigating committee a number of years ago that an automobile factory capable of operating at the lowest possible cost had to be big enough to make about 200,000 cars a year. Forty-five automotive plants this size in the U. S. could produce our entire annual output of 9 million cars. But even 45 makers of equal size would not really be sufficient to permit pure competition. It is reasonable to believe that a large auto plant, even if operated at less than peak efficiency, would have significantly lower costs (and hence prices) than a small plant in pure competition would have, even if run at peak efficiency. Of course, even when a company has a plant of just the right size, there is no guarantee that it will not continue to expand by building or acquiring new plants to increase its power in the market, to diversify its production by adding new products, to increase its financial strength, or for some other reasons.

In the general computer business, General Electric wrote off a quarter of a billion dollars it had spent trying unsuccessfully to be competitive. RCA, despite enormous outlays, couldn't make it either. Even a large firm like Ford lost $250 million dollars on the ill-fated Edsel. General Dynamics, an early conglomerate, lost a similar amount trying unsuccessfully to compete in the aerospace field.

The computer and auto cases appear to be exceptional. (Even in autos General Motors has decentralized to secure the advantages of smaller operational units.) For one thing, relatively small firms persist in many industries dominated by a few very large firms. In fact, the available empirical evidence, while not entirely satisfactory, suggests that medium-size producers are the most efficient in many industries. Secondly, the advantages of a large plant are often different from the advantages of a large firm. Very often it is the larger plant, not the larger firm, which is efficient. Since most large firms have numerous plants, each of which is an efficient unit, the particular plants could be operated as single firms without losing the scale advantages.

Finally, some large firms achieve low average costs not so much because they have any real advantages over smaller producers in combining resources, but because they exert their superior bargaining power to depress resource prices. These pecuniary advantages, as distinct from real advantages, only lead to a redistribution of income to monopolists at the expense of the resource suppliers.

Research and Technological Progress

Another factor related to efficiency is the alleged institutionalization of research, which means that it is primarily the large, usually oligopolistic firms that have the financial means and incentive to undertake research. While this is true in some industries, in others – e.g., air transportation, electrical appliances, movies – the smaller firms, universities, governments, and even individuals do the innovating. A former vice-president of General Electric, Theodore K. Quinn, emphasizes in his book *Giant Business* that he knows of no electrical invention produced in the laboratories of any of the major corporations. He says that they were all produced and marketed by individual entrepreneurs. Similarly, Arthur Watson of IBM maintains that the random access memory was not developed in IBM's laboratories because the project was outlawed for overrunning its budget. It was developed on a bootleg basis at the risk of losing a job.

Differentiated Products

Perfect competition requires that all firms in a given industry produce a commodity that is homogeneous, one unit indistinguishable from another. However, in monopolistic competition and oligopoly, nonprice competition— product or quality competition, including advertising—predominates. Monopolistic competition is a market situation in which the products are differentiated, although they are close substitutes for each other, and each producer has a pure monopoly in its branded product but must compete with close substitutes. In oligopoly, there are fewer rivals and the nonprice competition is often even more vigorous. A useful, if only tolerably accurate, generalization of industrial organization is that the degree of nonprice competition in any market tends to vary inversely with the degree of pure competition.

Product competition includes all the nonprice devices firms use to attract customers—changes in the product's quality or its style of packaging, faster delivery, assured servicing and durability, guarantees, congenial sales help, convenient location, etc. The frantic efforts of the automobile, cigarette, and soap manufacturers to differentiate their products are sufficiently well-known that they need only be mentioned. The efforts involved in differentiating one's product are not free. They involve costs which we may label *product variation costs* and *sales costs*. (The second of these includes advertising expenditures.) In industries such as the clothing industry, especially women's dresses, and the automobile industry, these costs can be fantastic. One careful study estimated the costs of having different cars in the automobile industry over the years 1956–1960 (using the 1949 model as the base) at over $5 billion per year or about $700 per car.[4] These costs must always be weighed against the additional revenue they yield by making the product appear more desirable to existing and potential customers.

National advertising has been an especially effective source of monopoly and also a formidable deterrent to entry and perhaps innovation in many industries. The cigarette industry as a group, before the ban on television advertising, spent considerably in excess of $150 million per year on sales costs, especially advertising. More generally, the oligopolistic consumer goods industries, including cigarettes, take up the greatest portion of the national advertising and promotional expenditures budget in the U.S., which currently runs around $20 billion per year—roughly equivalent to the nation's annual outlay on primary and secondary public education!

Ownership of Essential Raw Materials

Another source of monopoly power or a barrier to entry once monopoly has been established is the ownership of essential raw material sources. The

---

[4] This cost includes not merely the cost of model changes, but the cost of the extra steel, gasoline, etc., needed for cars bigger than those of the 1949 line. See Franklin M. Fisher, Zvi Griliches, and Carl Kaysen, "The Costs of Automobile Model Changes Since 1949," *Journal of Political Economy*, Vol. LXX, No. 5 (October, 1962), pp. 433–451; reprinted in *Readings in Microeconomics*, edited by David R. Kamerschen (New York: John Wiley & Sons, 1969), pp. 579–604.

classic example of this is Alcoa, which was able to retain its virtual pure monopoly in the aluminum industry for a number of years through its control of all basic sources of bauxite, the major ore used in aluminum production.

The Investment Banker

Mergers have sometimes been the result of shrewd investment bankers. Mergers may be quite profitable to them because of the large promotion fees they receive from merely handling the sales of the new issues of stock, the overcapitalization that results, and the advantages that accrue from serving on the board of directors of companies doing business with one another. The formation of the U. S. Steel Corporation involved at least the first two of these sources of gain, with the Morgan banking syndicate securing a fee of over $62 million.[5]

The Established Firm Advantage

For a number of reasons an established firm with an entrenched market position has advantages over new or potential rivals. Consumer loyalty built up over the years to a "name" brand is difficult to change. In addition, going concerns have easy access on favorable terms to capital markets and an efficient administrative framework with experienced personnel.

The huge financial investment required in some cases make the original investment and its related barrier, economies of scale, quite formidable barriers to entry. The plant and equipment necessary for the establishment of an efficient firm in heavy industries may run into many millions of dollars.

Collusive Action or Anticompetitive Practices

Monopolistic positions may also be created or strengthened through the use of numerous devices designed deliberately to reduce competition. Some of these have already been discussed. The interested readers are invited to investigate other such devices for themselves. Some of the firms and industries involved make fascinating reading. Among these devices are: the formation of gentlemen's agreements, holding companies, trusts, mergers, cartels, basing-point systems, trade associations, bidding rings, interlocking directorates, and corporate interlocks; the buying up of competing firms; division of the market by territory or products; racketeering; facility preemption; exclusive dealing and tying contracts; "cut-throat" competition (predatory price cutting);

---

[5] The usual contention is that investment bankers sell the watered stock of the combined form to "untutored" investors at exorbitant prices, with the promoters reaping enormous fees in the process. In a classic case, the Morgan syndicate wrote up the book value of the constituents in the 1901 formation of the U.S. Steel Corporation from some $700 million to $1.4 billion. Yet, as the ever challenging George J. Stigler, *The Organization of Industry* (Homewood: Richard D. Irwin, 1968), emphasizes, the empirical evidence indicates that even with the $62 million of stock given to the Morgan syndicate, the investor was better off purchasing U.S. Steel than any other steel concern (except Bethleham Steel) for the years 1901-1925. The accumulated market value of the shares of "Big Steel" was twice that of the average of the other steel companies.

"squeezing"; reciprocal buying and malicious interference; product disparagement; control over sources of financing; the luring away of strategic personnel, etc.

It is worthwhile spending a moment on predatory price wars since the literature contains numerous references to a presumed "classic" case of this, Rockefeller's Standard Oil. Despite the fact that this example has been demonstrated to be false, it persists in textbooks. In general, cut-throat competition must be related to imperfections in the capital market. Some giant firm presumably slashes prices below costs and then forces its smaller rival into selling out at a substantially depressed price. Obviously this could work in an imperfect capital market where the smaller firm could not finance the predatory price war. Thus, the folklore of the business community is that the old Standard Oil Company, under John D. Rockefeller, engaged in such activity. In truth, the historical evidence shows that Standard Oil almost always bought oil rivals at attractive prices.[6] This was not done because the company was concerned with the social welfare. Buying up rivals at fair prices simply turns out to be almost always more economical than engaging in a costly price war.

The federal Sherman Antitrust Act (1890) is, of course, the prime source of the almost absolute prohibition (i.e., almost illegal *per se* status) of horizontal price-fixing agreements among firms. While this statute is only concerned with interstate commerce, there are numerous state laws and city ordinances patterned after the Sherman Act.

Probably the most famous, as well as one of the largest, recent price-fixing conspiracies involved the electrical equipment manufacturers; i.e., G.E., Westinghouse, Allis Chalmers, and a number of others.[7] In total, 29 firms were fined almost $12 million and 7 executives were sent to prison (in addition to paying personal fines) after pleading guilty to collusive price-fixing of heavy electrical machinery. [*City of Philadelphia* v. *Westinghouse Electric Corp.,* 210 F. Supp. 483 (E.D., Pa, 1962).] It has been estimated that the treble-damage suits and out-of-court settlements in the *Philadelphia* case approached a quarter of a billion dollars.

The electrical conspirators used a so-called "phase-of-the-moon" scheme to maintain market shares, whereby they rotated among themselves the opportunity to submit the lowest bid on public utility contracts. This scheme suggested enough quasi-randomness to avoid, for quite a long time, the suspicion aroused by identical bids.

A leading antitrust lawyer proposed the following optimization model for determining whether a firm should enter into a conspiracy.

---

[6] John S. McGee, "Predatory Price Cutting: The Standard Oil (N.J.) Case," *Journal of Law and Economics* (October, 1958), pp. 137–169. Predatory pricing is usually formally defined as "knowingly pricing below marginal cost in certain geographic markets for the purpose of disciplining or removing particular rivals, and, as an ancillary effect, discouraging new entrants." The theory and the existing empirical evidence on predation is surveyed in David R. Kamerschen, "Predatory Pricing, Vertical Integration, and Market Foreclosure: The Case of Ready Mix Concrete in Memphis," *Industrial Organization Review,* Vol. 2, No. 3 (1974), pp. 143–168.

[7] Richard Austin Smith, "The Incredible Electrical Conspiracy," *Fortune* (April and May, 1961).

$$r_c > C_o^f + C_o^p + aC_a^f + aC_a^p$$

Conspiracy should be entered if, and only if, the returns from conspiring (r_c) exceed the operating costs to the firm of conspiring (C_o^f), plus the personal operating costs to the conspirator (C_o^p) plus the anticipated costs to the firm of apprehension (C_a^f), discounted by a factor reflecting the likelihood of apprehension (a), plus the personal apprehension costs to the conspirator (C_a^p), similarly discounted.[8]

"Legal" Monopolies

Numerous sanctioned monopolistic practices can be delineated. A few of these practices are natural monopolies, licenses, taxes, patents, trademarks, and copyrights.

Natural Monopolies. Although the natural monopoly case was discussed above, it can also be considered a "legal" monopoly since certificates of public convenience and necessity are generally issued in a field considered to be a natural monopoly. Public utilities—water, gas, electricity, telephone service, transportation, sewage disposal systems, etc.—are the outstanding examples of this. In such fields, a single firm is usually granted an exclusive franchise or certificate of public convenience and necessity to serve consumers in a given geographical area, subject to the regulation of rates, services, profits, and other factors by the public utility commission or a similar agency. Although the federal government does some regulating, most public utilities are regulated by a state commission.

Licenses.[9] Although licensing was originally done to insure minimum standards of competency, they have often been used to restrict free competition, restrict entry, and protect private rather than public interests. Licensing is done at almost all political levels and includes almost every conceivable type of business, industry, occupation, profession, and trade. In all, there are some 1,200 occupational licensing laws covering all kinds of positions—airplane pilots, bakers, barbers, brokers, dry cleaners, food dealers, funeral directors and embalmers, milk dealers, nurses, plumbers, steam boiler maintainers, tailors, watchmakers, etc. The reader should be able to apply elementary supply and demand tools to show what happens to earnings (or prices) when supply is restricted through licensing.

Taxes. Taxes have encouraged mergers and restrained competition at both the federal and state levels. The Internal Revenue Act encourages mergers

---

[8] John Q. Lawyer, "How to Conspire to Fix Prices," *Harvard Business Review* (March–April, 1963), pp. 95–103. Our treatment of price-fixing conspiracies draws on the excellent summary in Kristian S. Palda, *Pricing Decisions and Marketing Policy* (Englewood Cliffs: Prentice-Hall, 1971), Chapter 7.

[9] An excellent discussion of licensing is contained in Simon Rottenberg, "The Economics of Occupational Licensing," *Aspects of Labor Economics,* edited by H. Gregg Lewis (Princeton: Princeton University Press, 1962).

by permitting firms to carry forward past losses as credits against future earnings. For instance, Kaiser-Frazer's $50 million in losses from 1949 to 1952 was important in Willys-Overland's decision to merge with it.

Patents, Trademarks, and Copyrights. The Constitution gave Congress the responsibility of protecting inventors from having their processes or products usurped by rivals that have not shared in the effort, money costs, and time that went into the innovations. Exclusive patent rights on inventions were granted not only to foster invention, but to encourage its development and commercial utilization and its disclosure to the public.

A common practice of cartels is to pool their members' patents and license their use as a means to control the industry. When one realizes that some corporate giants such as GE and AT&T have at times controlled nearly 10,000 patents, the system must at least be suspect.

The monopoly power achieved through patents can be cumulative in that the profits provided by one important patent can be used to finance research to develop new patentable processes and products. The importance of the patent as a monopolistic device is attested to by the following list of firms which have been accused of monopolistic practices based on patents: IBM, GE, RCA, Westinghouse, United Shoe Machinery, International Salt, Eastman Kodak, Univis Lens, Hartford Empire, National Lead, Standard Oil, Masonite, Western Electric, U. S. Gypsum, and a legion of lesser known firms.

Other Sanctioned Monopolistic Practices. Although we have neither the time nor the space to examine most of the other sanctioned monopolistic practices, the reader may wish to investigate the following exceptions to antitrust legislation. These acts have at various times exempted some firms from price-fixing laws: the Webb-Pomerene Act (1918), which allowed cartels to be formed for selling exports to foreign countries, and the Miller-Tydings Act (1936), which partially exempted retailers. In addition, there are various means through which unions, agriculture (Capper-Volstead Act), certain sectors of transportation such as railroads, insurance companies, professional sports, and oil (prorationing schemes) are exempted.

Some economists would argue that most barriers to entry cannot persist over time without the sanction or aid of government. Certain economists have argued at length that government has actually promoted monopoly in numerous cases. For instance, the sale of surplus steel facilities to U.S. Steel and other large steel concerns after the Second World War was hardly conducive to competition. However, in other instances—e.g., the aluminum industry—the government's disposal of surplus property did much to encourage competition in what was once a classic case of pure monopoly.

COST OF PRODUCTION AND SALES REVENUE UNDER MONOPOLY

The general principles of profit maximization developed for competition will also be applicable for monopoly. That is, if output n is a profit-maximizing level of output, then:

1. $MR_n = MC_n$ (13.1)
2. (a) $MC_{n-1} < MR_{n-1}$
   (b) $MC_{n+1} > MR_{n+1}$
3. (a) Short run: $TR_n \gtreqqless TVC_n$
   (b) Long run: $TR_n \gtreqqless TC_n$

Cost of Production

Both costs of production and revenue conditions are obviously crucial. On the cost side, we provisionally assume that although the firm is an unregulated monopolist in the product market, it hires resources competitively at constant factor prices. This also means that the same cost data employed for the purely competitive firm will be generally employed in the analysis for the monopolist. In other words, we assume that pure monopoly differs from pure competition only with respect to demand or revenue conditions and not with regard to costs. Later this assumption is relaxed. However, the basic analysis is unchanged.

Sales Revenue

The crucial distinction between an imperfectly and a perfectly competitive firm lies on the demand and revenue side of the market. The monopolist's market situation is such that the demand curve is downsloping and less than perfectly elastic. Since industry demand curves are invariably downsloping and since under pure monopoly the firm is identical to the industry, we assume a negatively sloped demand function for a pure monopolist. Competitors can do nothing about the market price. Their only decision regards output. On the other hand, monopolists have a price policy. They have two alternatives to consider in their decision: They can set the price and therefore let the demand curve at that price determine the output, or they can set the output and let the demand at that quantity determine the price.

To expand sales, (nondiscriminating) monopolists must lower the unit price. (Until specified otherwise, our analysis will only be concerned with monopolists who set one price and do not engage in price discrimination or a system of multiple prices.) This further means that MR must be less than P ($=AR$) for every level of output except the first, because the price cuts required to enlarge sales apply not only to the extra units sold, but also to the ones that could have been sold at a higher price. For instance, suppose at a price of $5, three units are sold; whereas to sell four units, the price must be $4. The extra unit sold brings in $4. However, each of the other three units now sells at $1 less than if only three units were sold. Therefore, the change in total revenue is not $4, but $4 − $3 or $1; total revenue goes from $15 to $16. Hence, although the price is $4, marginal revenue is only $1. More generally, we can derive the equation:

$$MR_2 = AR_2 + \frac{\Delta AR}{\Delta Q}Q_1 \qquad (13.2)$$

where MR_2 is the new marginal revenue, AR_2 the new price, and Q_1 is the original quantity. Since pure competitors cannot influence price by changing output (i.e., the slope of the demand curve is perfectly flat or zero), $\Delta AR/\Delta Q$ equals zero and (13.2) becomes: $MR_2 = AR_2 + 0 \cdot Q_1$ or $MR_2 = AR_2$. But monopolists negatively influence price as they try to increase sales, so that $\Delta AR/\Delta Q < 0$ and $(\Delta AR/\Delta Q)Q_1$ becomes negative, making $MR_2 < AR_2$ (i.e., $MR_2 = AR_2 - \epsilon$, where ϵ is some positive number).

The fact that MR is below AR and falling means that TR will be nonlinear. The slope of TR is MR; and since MR is not constant, TR is not linear. This can be seen in another important formula:

$$MR = P - P/\eta = P(1 - 1/\eta) \quad (\text{where } \eta = |\eta|) \tag{13.3}$$

Under competition as $\eta \to \infty$, $P/\eta \to 0$ and (at the limit) $MR \to P$. In other words, MR is treated as equal to P at all output levels. With monopoly, η is finite, so $0 < 1/\eta < \infty$ and $MR < P$ by the amount P/η.

(13.3) also indicates that:

$$\begin{aligned} &\text{if } \eta > 1, \text{ then } MR > 0 \\ &\text{if } \eta < 1, \text{ then } MR < 0 \\ &\text{if } \eta = 1, \text{ then } MR = 0 \end{aligned} \tag{13.4}$$

That is, when demand is elastic (inelastic), MR is positive (negative). For instance, if η is 2, substituting into (13.3) yields $MR = P - P/2$ and hence $MR = 1/2P$. If $\eta = \frac{1}{2}$, $MR = P - P/\frac{1}{2} = P - 2P = -P$. If demand is unitary, MR is zero, for $MR = P - P/1$ and hence $MR = P - P = 0$.

In addition to the fact that monopolists can influence the price of the product, there are at least three other important respects in which their demand curves differ from competitors' demand curves.[10] One already mentioned is that it may be possible under monopoly to discriminate or treat buyers differently. Under competitive conditions, this is impossible. The problem of price discrimination is taken up in Chapter 16. This chapter focuses on a nondiscriminating monopolist.

Another difference is that monopolists, in determining their optimal positions, must consider what the (discounted) effects on future cost and revenue will be from their current actions. In addition, they must estimate the possible effects their current decisions will have on the entry of rivals. In the first case, monopolists in the short run must consider their "corrected" MR and "corrected" MC, which take into account the impact of current P and Q on future P and Q. For example, a lower price may cause a larger demand in the future by making the product better known. Generally, the corrected MR curve tends to be greater than the crude MR curve for increases in output and vice versa. Since the long-run demand curve is more elastic than the short-run, lower prices are likely to have cumulative effects and hence raise the corrected MR.

---

[10] See George J. Stigler, *The Theory of Price* (rev. ed.; New York: Macmillan Co., 1952), pp. 204–207.

The threat of entry from potential rivals would also tend to increase the short-run corrected MR for increases in output since it increases the elasticity of the long-run demand curve. Since long-run input supply curves are more elastic than short-run, the corrected MC is less for increases in output.

The final difference is that monopolists may find it profitable to alter the demand curves facing them. Of the three most important determinants of demand—prices of other commodities, income, and consumer tastes—only consumer income cannot be affected significantly by monopolists' actions. Thus, monopolists can increase their product demand curves if they can decrease (increase) the availability of substitutes (complements). They can wholly or partially eliminate substitutes by: purchase or merger; tariffs; and "full-line forcing," i.e., making buyers who want items with poor substitutes also take the ones with good substitutes. Monopolists try to increase the output of complementary products by opposing tariffs on them and by producing the products themselves.

Monopolists try to influence consumer tastes by advertising. While part of these selling costs are necessary to disseminate information, efforts to persuade probably represent the better part of at least national advertising. Advertising in local newspapers seems to contain a much greater amount of useful information than does national advertising.

Under dynamic conditions, where prices, quantities, firms, etc., are changing, selling costs are necessary even under competition. It is persuasive, not informational advertising that is inconsistent with competition. Monopolists use persuasive advertising to establish or more firmly entrench their advantageous positions. Since advertising has a cumulative effect extending beyond the period in which the outlay is actually made, industries with enormous selling costs can provide a barrier to the entry of new firms.

MONOPOLY PRICING IN THE IMMEDIATE PERIOD

We can derive the optimum behavior of the monopolist in the immediate (very short-run) period, the short-run period, and the long-run period, assuming the monopolist has sufficient information about the relevant cost and revenue functions and the willingness to act on this information. The immediate period is one in which the maximum quantity that can be offered for sale has already been produced. In this period, $QS = QE - RD$, where QS is the quantity offered for sale, QE is the maximum quantity available for sale, and RD is the producer's reservation demand. In this case, the "bygones are bygones" principle is applicable, making the final pricing decision completely independent of costs of production.

Since costs of production are irrelevant in the immediate period, profit maximization—i.e., maximizing the objective function $\pi = TR - TC$—calls for selecting the price that maximizes total revenue. To illustrate this, Figure 13–1 demonstrates three separate quantities. If a monopolistic firm has produced $0A$ units of the commodity and faces the demand conditions illustrated by ED, the best it can do is sell all $0A$ units at a price of $0P_1$. It obviously cannot sell more than this by our assumption that $0A$ is the maximal amount available. Since demand is elastic in the range from zero to $0B$, the firm will not sell less than $0A$ since $MR > 0$ for decreases in quantity. As Figure 13–1 illustrates, TR increases as Q *increases* from zero to $0B$, and TR also increases as Q *decreases* from $0D$ to $0B$. At output $0B$, TR is at a maximum. In other words, demand is elastic from zero to $0B$ units of output, inelastic from $0B$ to $0D$ units of output, and unitary elastic at $0B$ units of output.

If the monopolistic firm happens to have produced $0B$ units, its best price is $0P_2$. At this point, total revenue is at a maximum since $MR = 0$ and $\eta = 1$.

Finally, if $0C$ units of output were produced, the firm would not sell all of it at price $0P_3$. Instead it would dispose of BC units, selling the remaining $0B$ units at the revenue-maximizing price of $0P_2$. Since demand is inelastic at $0C$, $MR < 0$; and hence decreasing the quantity sold results in higher TR. The monopolistic firm may destroy the quantity BC even if it is not perishable. When it is not perishable, the firm does have the option of storing it for the future when demand may be stronger.

This establishes a general principle: A profit-maximizing firm in the immediate run generally will not knowingly operate in the inelastic sector of its demand curve.[11] In fact, with nonnegative costs of production, this theorem may also be extended to the short-run and long-run periods. Even if total costs were negative, with larger output costing less than smaller output, the monopolist would probably still not operate in the inelastic sector. If the firm wanted the smaller quantity, it could always produce the larger quantity to realize the savings and dispose of the remainder.

MONOPOLY PRICING AND PRODUCTION IN THE SHORT RUN

Since the short-run pricing and production decision under monopoly follows the same general rules as illustrated for the pure competitor, the same three general outcomes are possible: profit maximization, loss minimization,

---

[11] Relatively minor exceptions can occur for the following reasons: (1) The disposal process may not be costless. (2) Long-run profit maximization may require short-run production in the inelastic stage—e.g., selling a quantity of, say, a new product in the short-run that produces less than the maximum TR, such as $0C$, in order to acquaint consumers with the product. (3) People may be ignorant as to demand, cost, service, etc. (4) The product selling in the inelastic sector, such as a so-called "loss leader," may have a strong complement that makes up for this apparent irrationality—e.g., selling a quantity of razors such as $0C$ in order to sell more razor blades which have such a high profit margin that they more than make up for the apparent overproduction of razors. The fact that the MC of the leader is greater than the MR of the leader is irrelevant; what is relevant is the MR from all products (prices remaining the same). The more a firm can sell of high-priced merchandise by manipulating the price of the loss leader, the less mark-up the loss leader should carry. In fact, the price of the loss leader can profitably be reduced below its acquisition cost if the consequent rise in sales and marginal profit from the sale of all other merchandise is sharp enough. (5) The product produced may be indivisible and the total profit may be higher from producing n units, which puts the firm in the inelastic sector, than it is from producing $n - 1$ units, which puts it in the elastic sector.

FIGURE 13–1   Elasticity and Monopoly Pricing

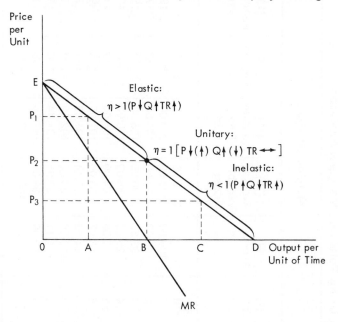

and close-down. To conserve space, we will cover only the profit-maximization case.

Using the "qualified" $MC = MR$ rule, the monopolist depicted in Table 13–1 produces six units of output selling at $141 per unit. At this point $MR \simeq MC \simeq 90$ (using the rule of selecting the last unit of output where $MR > MC$, if the figures are not exactly equal). At six units of output, column (7) indicates that the total profit of $236 is the highest obtainable under the given conditions of demand and cost. (Incidentally, the cost figures are exactly the same as those used in the purely competitive case.)

Since this is a short-run analysis, the presence of profits does not put the monopolist on any different footing than the pure competitor. The difference is that the competitive mechanism for eliminating profits — the entry of new firms — may be weak or nonexistent in the monopoly case.

Figure 13–2 graphically illustrates the general case of profit maximization as exemplified in Table 13–1. As in the case of pure competition, we can use both a total and a marginal analysis to determine the monopolist's equilibrium output. The only difference in this figure from the one given for the competitor is that the TR curve is nonlinear and MR and AR are downward sloping; the cost curves are assumed the same.

The short-run profit-maximizing rule for the monopolist is: Produce the quantity at which rising MC equals MR (provided $P \geqq AVC$); sell this quantity at the price permitted by the demand curve. Notice that while profits are maximized at output $0x_e$ in Figure 13–2, total sales revenue is maximized at $0x_m$. However, it is the former, not the latter, that is the objective sought by the firm.

TABLE 13–1   Short-Run Profit Maximization for a Monopolist, Using Total and Marginal Analyses

Total Analysis

(1) Total Product	(2) Price (Average Revenue)	(3) Total Revenue	(4) Total Fixed Cost	(5) Total Variable Cost	(6) Total Cost	(7) Profit(+) or Loss(−)
0	$201	$ 0	$100	$ 0	$ 100	$−100
1	191	191	100	100	200	−09
2	181	362	100	190	290	+72
3	171	513	100	270	370	+143
4	161	644	100	340	440	+204
5	151	755	100	420	520	+235
6	141	846	100	510	610	(+236)
7	131	917	100	610	710	+207
8	121	968	100	720	820	+148
9	111	999	100	840	940	+59
10	101	1,010	100	990	1,090	−80
11	91	1,001	100	1,190	1,290	−289

Marginal Analysis

(8) Total Product	(9) Average Fixed Cost	(10) Average Variable Cost	(11) Average Total Cost	(12) Marginal Cost	(13) Marginal Revenue
0	$ ∞	$ 0.00	$ ∞	$ 0	$ 0
1	100.00	100.00	200.00	100	191
2	50.00	95.00	145.00	90	171
3	33.33	90.00	123.33	80	151
4	25.00	85.00	110.00	70	131
5	20.00	84.00	104.00	80	111
6	16.67	85.00	101.67	(90)	(91)
7	14.29	87.14	101.43	100	71
8	12.50	90.00	102.50	110	51
9	11.11	93.33	104.44	120	31
10	10.00	99.00	109.00	150	11
11	9.09	108.18	117.27	200	−9

FIGURE 13-2 Short-Run Profit-Maximizing Equilibrium for a Monopolist

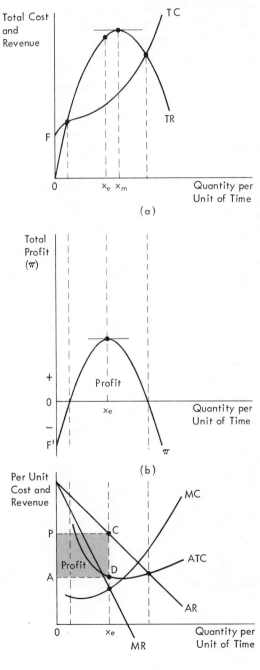

MONOPOLY PRICING AND PRODUCTION IN THE LONG RUN

To change the above short-run rule to a long-run rule, one merely has to shift from $SMC = SMR$ to $LMC = LMR$ and change the qualification $P \geqq AVC$ to $P \geqq LAC$, as was done in the competitive case. Since entry is blocked in the monopoly case, any expansion of output must come through scale of plant adjustments. These adjustments can lead to three possibilities. The monopolistic firm's revenue and cost conditions may cause it to build a scale of plant that is: (1) smaller, (2) exactly equal, or (3) larger than the technically optimum scale of plant. Figure 13–3 illustrates these three possibilities. The curves are labeled 1, 2, and 3 to correspond to the above numbering; e.g., $D_1 (MR_1)$ is the case of a monopolist using the less than technically optimum scale of plant and rate of output.

In general, monopoly power is much weaker in long-run periods than in short-run periods. If short-run profits are being made, new firms will try to enter the industry or try to produce a product that the consumers will regard as a substitute. Sometimes a monopolist may have to sacrifice possible short-run gains to maximize long-run profits. Or, depending on the interest rate, the present state of antitrust legislation, the immediate threat of potential entry, the closeness of substitutes, and other important economic variables, long-run

FIGURE 13–3   Long-Run Scale of Plant Adjustments by a Monopolist

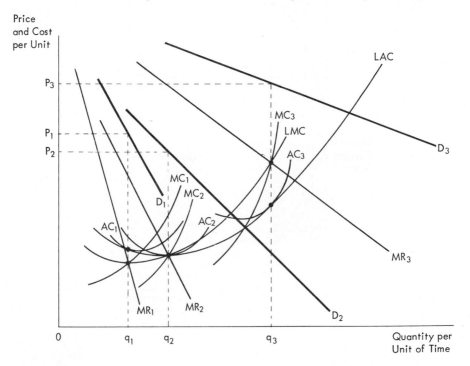

profit maximization may call for grabbing all the profits possible today. No truly profitable monopoly or oligopoly has ever lasted as long as 100 years.[12]

The ball-point pen industry in the U. S. is a classic case illustrating: (1) the ability of a monopolist to charge exorbitant prices and hence earn enormous short-run profits, (2) the likely entry of new firms in such cases, (3) the subsequent decline in prices and profits, and (4) a time lag that may be sufficiently long to keep firms innovating.[13] In October of 1945, Milton Reynolds started producing his patented pens in a firm with a capital value of $26,000. Gimbel's sold these pens, which cost $.80 to produce, at $12.50 (the maximum price allowed by the wartime agency, Office of Price Administration). With such a price policy, Reynolds was able to earn as much as $500,000 profits in a single month—20 times the original investment! Reynolds' early rivals introduced ball-point pens that sold at between $15 and $25. Reynolds' price held firm although average cost fell to $.60 per pen. However, by October, 1946, Reynolds was forced to drop the price to $3.85; average cost was then $.30. By Christmas, 1946, approximately 100 manufacturers were in production, some of them selling their pens for as low as $2.98. By February, 1947, Reynolds had to introduce a $.98 model. By mid-1948 prices had tumbled to $.39 and costs to $.10. In 1951, the typical price was $.25. Today the prices are fairly stable in the $.19 to $3.00 range. The era of fabulous profits is over. The market is now stable, orderly, and only moderately profitable. Of course, in contrast to the passing fads of hula hoops, skate boards, zoot suits, etc., the ball-point pen has remained on the U. S. business scene. But it is now a mature industry.

MULTIPLANT MONOPOLIST

A later chapter will take up the phenomenon of price discrimination or selling a given product in two or more distinct markets at different prices (not justified by cost differences). A related problem which we would now like to investigate is what the optimal strategy would be for a nondiscriminating monopolist selling in a single market but with two separate plants. The profit function for both plants a and b is: $\pi = TR_{ab} - (TC_a + TC_b)$. That is, total revenue depends on the quantity produced in plant a and plant b and on the total costs in both plants. Marginal analysis dictates that the MR for the output as a whole must equal the MC in each plant. If the MC were lower in one plant, additional production would take place in that plant until $MC_a = MC_b = MR_{ab}$, where MR_{ab} is the overall marginal revenue. In addition, the overall MR must be increasing less rapidly than the MC in each plant.

---

[12] "Of course, this does not call for excessive sympathy for the monopolist: if he can retain his position for nine years, earning $1 million of monopoly profits a year, the present value of this annuity (at 8 percent) is half of the value of a personal annuity of equal amount. Nine years in hand are worth nine hundred in a distant bush." George J. Stigler, *The Theory of Price* (3d ed.; New York: Macmillan Co., 1966), p. 227.

[13] Thomas Whiteside, "Where Are They Now?" *The New Yorker* (February 17, 1951); cited in Richard G. Lipsey and Peter O. Steiner, *Economics* (3d ed.; New York: Harper & Row, Publishers, 1972), pp. 287–288.

In Figure 13-4, MC_a and MC_b are the marginal cost schedules for the two plants which compose the monopolistic firm. Suppose the firm has decided to produce the quantity $0Q_1$, so that it must only determine how much each plant will supply of that total. It could have firm *b* produce the full amount, and the marginal cost would be MC_3. If it did so, it would become clear to the firm that by reducing the output of firm *b* by one unit, total cost would fall by the amount MC_3; and firm *a* could produce one unit and increase total cost by just MC_1. Since the decrease in total cost is greater than the increase in total cost, total cost decreased. The firm could continue to decrease the output of firm *b* and increase the output of firm *a* until the *MC* of *b* decreased and the *MC* of *a* increased enough to equal each other, at which point no further cost saving could be effected by altering relative outputs. The equality of *MC*s would occur when firm *a* produced $0Q_{a1}$ and firm *b* produced $0Q_{b1}$.

The curve labeled MC_{ab} is simply the horizontal summation of the individual *MC* curves. This sum is determined by adding the amount $0Q_{a1}$ to the amount $0Q_{b1}$ at MC_2 to get $0Q_1$. This is done for every *MC*. For example, at MC_3, length *A* equals length *A'*.

Figure 13–5 shows the optimum solution for a two-plant monopoly, and the technique is applicable for any number of plants in a given firm. In the case shown, the monopolist's output would be $0Q$, divided between plant *a*, producing $0Q_a$, and plant *b*, producing $0Q_b$. The firm can sell this output at price $0P$.

SIX COMMON MISCONCEPTIONS CONCERNING MONOPOLY

In this section, certain misconceptions that have grown up around monopoly will be exposed. Assuming for the moment that profit maximization is the goal of the firm, six common misconceptions may be isolated.

FIGURE 13–4   Marginal Cost for the Multiplant Monopolist

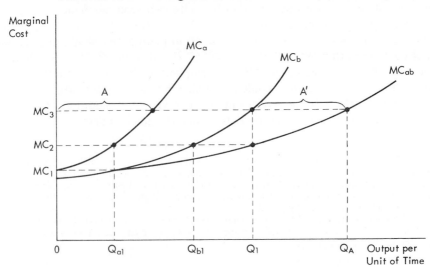

FIGURE 13-5   Optimum Solution for the
Multiplant Monopolist

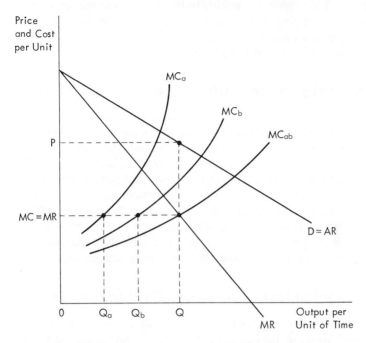

The Monopolist Charges the Highest Possible Price

Even the august Adam Smith perpetuated this misconception by making a similar pronouncement. On its face, this is a meaningless statement. But it may be interpreted as referring to the highest price at which the smallest quantity of the commodity can be sold. In fact, however, the monopolist selects the price that maximizes profits. In Figure 13-2 there are numerous prices above the one selected at which the monopolist can sell some positive amount of the commodity. However, these selections entail a smaller profit. In other words, since $\pi = TR - TC$ and since TR and TC each depend on the quantity sold (Q) as much as on P (and AC), the monopolist must be concerned with Q as well as P.

The Monopolist Tries to Maximize Per-Unit Profits

Generally, neither the competitor nor the monopolist tries to maximize per-unit profits. Both want to maximize *total* profits (π). Only in the special case where maximizing the profit margin is equivalent to maximizing π is the statement correct, but even then it is misleading.

The Monopolist Tries to Maximize Total Revenue

The idea that the monopolist tries to maximize total revenue is wrong or at best misleading. The goal of the firm involves π, not TR. Of course, since

$\pi = TR - TC$, in the rare instances where TC is constant at all output levels (i.e., $MC = 0$), maximizing TR is equivalent to maximizing π. In Figure 13–2, the maximum TR output, x_m, occurs to the right of the maximum π output, x_e. In general, maximizing TR involves a higher output level than the output level that maximizes profits. In fact, only when $MR = 0$ is TR at a maximum; hence, for the $MC = MR$ rule to hold, MC must equal 0.

The Monopolist Necessarily Makes "Excess" Profits

The association of monopoly with large profits is apparently quite common. However, there is no analytical or empirical foundation for this assertion. For instance, 28 of *Fortune*'s 500 largest U.S. industrial corporations in 1975 actually incurred losses, including such corporate giants as American Motors, Anaconda, Bell & Howell, Chrysler, Mattel, and Singer. Perhaps even more dramatic was the fact that such corporate leviathans as Lockheed Aircraft, the Penn Central Railroad, and Rolls-Royce (of Britain) recently had to declare bankruptcy. High cost and weak demand may prevent the monopolist from realizing any profit at all. However, to be sure, the probability of economic profits is greater for a monopolist than for a pure competitor.

The Monopolist Has an Inelastic Demand Curve

Only with "careless brevity" can one call a demand curve elastic or inelastic. Most demand curves have both elastic and inelastic ranges. Except for unusually shaped functions, most demand curves are elastic at high prices and inelastic at low prices. In practice, a demand curve for a monopolist cannot be inelastic through its entire length, because as long as the curve is inelastic, the monopolistic firm can raise its price, reduce the quantity sold, decrease its costs, and raise its revenue. Or, in short, the firm can raise profits by contracting output and increasing the price. Eventually its customers' entire incomes would be absorbed if the demand curve did not turn elastic at some price! Elastic demand curves lead to a fall in TR as prices increase. In other words, if demand were inelastic throughout the curve's length, one would arrive at the economic absurdity that a monopolist should produce an infinitesimal amount and sell it for an infinite price.

Since $MR = P - P/\eta$, when demand is inelastic ($\eta < 1$) MR is negative ($MR < 0$). No entrepreneur will ever persistently produce where MR is negative, since MC is never negative in the economically relevant area.

As already indicated, it is possible for a competitive industry to operate in the inelastic portion of its demand curve, even in long-run equilibrium, because demand is different for the firm and the industry. In a competitive market, MR can be positive for the firm and negative for the industry.

The Monopolist Has a Supply Curve

A monopolistic firm with its downsloping demand curve has no supply curve of the ordinary kind discussed earlier for a competitor. Since a supply schedule relates various amounts of output to various market prices, it is a valid concept only when a firm has no control over these market prices. However, the monopolistic firm is not *confronted* with a market price; it *determines* the price when it decides upon its rate of output. The output chosen, together with its associated price, constitutes a unique point. It is meaningful to ask a competitive "price-taker" how the firm will vary its rate of output in response to different prices. But it is not logical to ask a monopolistic "price-maker" how the firm will react to various prices if the firm itself determines these prices. In short, a supply curve — defined as showing the quantities the producer would offer for sale if *confronted* with various prices — is inapplicable to a monopolist who is not confronted with these prices but rather determines them.

The fact that a monopolist does not have a unique supply function will later be shown to have important implications for the predictive powers of the model. In particular, the competitive conclusion that, all else being equal, a rise in demand will always cause both price and output to rise will no longer be valid. For instance, in Figure 13–6 we show a case where a monopolist's demand increases from D_1 to D_2, becomes more elastic, and causes the equilibrium price to fall. If we reverse the situation and suppose demand falls from D_2 to D_1, it is interesting to note that this calls for a price increase. American steel firms have been called irrational for raising prices in the face of flagging domestic demand caused by intense foreign competition. Yet if demand becomes more inelastic, short-run profit maximization may require such an increase in price.

FIGURE 13–6   Increased (and More Elastic) Demand Lowers Equilibrium Price of the Monopolist

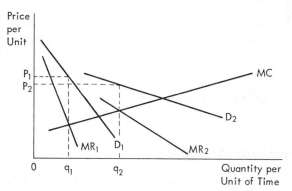

QUESTIONS

1. Analytically, what are the essential characteristics of monopoly as opposed to pure competition? Comment on the difficulties of comparing the economic or welfare implications of the two forms of market organization.
2. List the reasons for the existence of monopoly power. For each reason given, state whether you think the best public policy is to eliminate such monopoly by making monopoly illegal.

3. Draw a graph showing a feasible situation in which a monopolist would suffer losses and so would decide to go out of business.
4. Explain why a monopoly firm with three plants would probably operate the plants at different output levels.
5. Explain the fallacy (if there is one) in each of the following statements:
   (a) Monopolists always try to raise their prices.
   (b) Monopolists always try to make as much profit as they can on every unit sold.
   (c) The goal of monopolists is to sell as much of the product as possible.
   (d) Monopolists always face inelastic demand for their products.
   (e) The supply curve of a monopolist is less elastic than the supply curve of a competitive industry.
6. It is sometimes said that monopoly would be acceptable or even benevolent if the monopolist charged a "fair price." Do you have any idea what might be meant by a "fair price"?

APPENDIX: MATHEMATICAL NOTES

Note 1. *MR* < *P* Under Monopoly

Since the monopolist's total revenue (TR) function is:

$$TR = pq \tag{13.5}$$

marginal revenue (MR) is:

$$MR = \frac{dTR}{dq} = p + q\frac{dp}{dq} \tag{13.6}$$

Since a monopolist must lower the price for each unit to sell an additional unit, $dp/dg < 0$, so that (13.6) becomes $MR = p - (dp/dq)q$ or $MR < p$. Assuming the integration constant is zero (i.e., there is no TR if there is no output), TR equals the area under the MR curve:

$$\int_0^q \left(p + q\frac{dp}{dq}\right) dq = pq = TR \tag{13.7}$$

Note 2. Multiplant Monopolist

Previously it was demonstrated that a monopolist's profit (π)—where $\pi = TR - TC$ and both TR and TC are functions of output, $TR = f(q)$ and $TC = g(q)$—is maximized when:

$$d\pi/dq = f'(q) - g'(q) = 0 \text{ or } f'(q) = g'(q) \tag{13.8}$$

That is, MR must equal MC and:

$$d^2\pi/dq^2 = f''(q) - g''(q) < 0 \text{ or } f''(q) < g''(q) \tag{13.9}$$

That is, the second-order condition for a maximum requires that the algebraic value of the slope of MR must be less than that of the MC curve.

Now assume the monopolist can produce in two separate plants, while only selling in a single market. The only difference from the previous maximizing equation is that the total costs for both plants, not just one, is relevant:

$$\pi = f(q_1 + q_2) - g_1(q_1) - g_2(q_2) \qquad (13.10)$$

where the subscripts 1 and 2 refer to the two plants. Setting the partial derivative of (13.10) equal to zero yields:

$$d\pi/dq_1 = f'(q_1 + q_2) - g_1'(q_1) = 0 \qquad (13.11)$$

$$d\pi/dq_2 = f'(q_1 + q_2) - g_2'(q_2) = 0$$

$$f'(q_1 + q_2) = g_1'(q_1) = g_2'(q_2)$$

The economic interpretation of this is that overall MR must equal MC in each plant. The second-order conditions state that the principal minors of the relevant Hessian determinant:

$$\begin{vmatrix} f'' - g_1'' & f'' \\ f'' & f'' - g_2'' \end{vmatrix} \qquad (13.12)$$

must alternate in sign starting with a negative value. Economically, this means that overall MR must be increasing less rapidly than MC in each plant.

14 Pricing and Production under Monopolistic Competition

As the name suggests, monopolistic competition contains elements of both monopoly and competition. It is similar to the competitive model in that: (1) it contains a large number of independent sellers; (2) there is freedom of entry and exit; and (3) the costs of production are similar. On the other hand, it is like the monopolistic model in that the product of any particular firm is not identical to that of any other firm.

The first characteristic, that of many sellers, is not sufficient alone to distinguish monopolistic competition from the other market structures of pure competition or differentiated oligopoly (of the large-numbers, "fringe" variety). However, other criteria distinguish these markets. For instance, the fact that monopolistic competition involves differentiated products distinguishes it from pure competition, and the fact that there is no mutual interdependence separates it from differentiated oligopoly.

Typically, entry into monopolistically competitive industries is easy because the usual small size of the existing firms suggests that the usual entry-restricting forces, such as economies of scale, capital requirements, and advertising outlays, are weak. This leads to both a high birth and death rate for new firms. The entering costs are so small that people enter without much regard to their chances of success or failure.

High barriers to entry or blocked entry under monopolistic competition almost invariably result from artificial, not natural forces. Governmental regulations, such as licensing or zoning, are particularly important causes of artificial barriers. Licensing barbers and liquor stores in many states and requiring permits for many kinds of selling are examples of blocked entry in a model of monopolistic competition. However, blocked entry is exceptional.

Of the imperfectly competitive market models, monopolistic competition is the one most likely to have cost conditions similar to those of pure competition; yet these two market models will differ because of the product differentiation expenditures under monopolistic competition. Often product differentiation is a subjective state that exists in the mind of the consumer, who "thinks," say, brand A of aspirin is different from brand B. This belief may be founded on objective physical characteristics of the product, on services accompanying the sale, or on more subjective considerations derived from advertising or promotional outlays in general. In the case of aspirin, the last factor predominates, since it is well known that all five-grain aspirin tablets are made of a certain chemical compound that must conform to certain U.S.P. specifications, making all brands virtually identical. Yet some people are willing to pay two or three times as much for a heavily advertised, well-known brand of aspirin than for a relatively obscure brand.

While products can be differentiated on the basis of functional features such as materials, design, and workmanship, they may also be distinguished on the basis of advertising, packaging, trademarks, and brand names as well as by conditions surrounding the sale, such as convenience of location, congeniality of the sales help, and the reputation of the seller with regard to such things as servicing, credit terms, promptness of delivery, etc. In general, the goods sold by monopolistically competitive firms are close, but not perfect, substitutes for one another.

This means the demand curve facing a firm under monopolistic competition will be downsloping and less than perfectly elastic. The degree of elasticity will depend on the number of sellers and the extent of product differentiation. If the number of sellers is large, then the degree of market power depends exclusively on product differentiation. Generally, a firm under monopolistic competition will have a high, but not infinite, elasticity of demand for its product, since the degree of product differentiation is typically slight. Thus, the price under monopolistic competition will not be much higher than under pure competition.

The primary difference, then, between the model of pure competition and of monopolistic competition is that a firm under monopolistic competition must compete in four areas: quantity, price, product variation, and persuasive selling. A pure competitor need not engage in persuasive promotional activities or quality competition, but need only adjust the quantity of its homogeneous product to the market-determined price.

In most of this chapter the analysis of monopolistic competition will follow the presentation of Edward H. Chamberlin, the father of monopolistic competition.[1] However, the end of the chapter will touch upon a few of the objections that have been raised by Stigler and others regarding his formulation. We will also discuss the variables subject to manipulation by the firm under monopolistic competition.

PRICE POLICY

With product differentiation, the definition of an industry becomes blurred. Previously an industry was defined as a collection of firms producing an essentially standardized product. The coefficient of cross elasticity must be infinite between firms in pure competition in the same industry. But with product differentiation, the cross elasticity among the firms will be less than infinity. In graphical terms, we need a common denominator for the quantity axis; otherwise, we are trying to add apples and oranges. For example, there is no industry for soaps since the products are not homogeneous. While the

---

[1] Edward H. Chamberlin, *The Theory of Monopolistic Competition* (Cambridge: Harvard University Press, 1933).

concept of an industry is clear under pure competition or pure monopoly, it becomes fuzzy under monopolistic competition or oligopoly because of product differentiation.

Chamberlin's solution was to use the concept of a "group," which is defined as a collection of firms producing products which are close substitutes. In other words, a group consists of commodities with high positive cross elasticities of demand. While the determination of what is "high" is arbitrary, in practice the U. S. economy does have many readily recognized groups, such as shoes, automobiles, breakfast foods, cigarettes, etc. The theories of monopolistic competition and oligopoly are concerned with the analysis of such groups.

Another difficulty with a graphical analysis of an industry is that no single price prevails when the products are different. There is a cluster or group of prices for, say, soap. We will therefore confine our discussion of a group to verbal analysis, whereas we will present the firm in both verbal and graphical terms.

ASSUMPTIONS OF THE MODEL OF MONOPOLISTIC COMPETITION

The following equilibrium analysis will make several key assumptions. First, the analysis will be confined to Chamberlin's "large group" case in which a large number of firms are selling differentiated products. But perhaps the most stringent assumptions under which the Chamberlin model operates are what Stigler called the "uniformity" and "symmetry" assumptions.[2] That is, in his first approximation model, Chamberlin makes what he admits is a "heroic assumption" that each firm in the group has uniform or identical cost and demand curves. The "symmetry" assumption means that any change in price or output by any one producer in the group spreads its influence over so many competitors that the impact felt by any one is negligible. In short, the mutual interdependence characterizing oligopoly is assumed absent.

The uniformity assumption is said to be only a temporary expedient, although all of Chamberlin's comparisons with pure competition are made when this, and the symmetry assumption, are assumed to hold. Below, the effects of dropping the uniformity assumption are briefly discussed. The assumption of identical product cost curves rules out the possibility of firms producing commodities that are substantially different. The uniformity assumption only makes sense when the product differences and hence cost differentials are slight. Some would then argue that if the product differences must be so slight as to not entail any significant cost differences, in what important way does this analysis differ from that of pure competition? If the symmetry assumption fails, we are into the area of uncertainty about rivals' reactions

---

[2] George J. Stigler, *Five Lectures on Economic Problems* (New York: Macmillan Co., 1949), Chapter 2, pp. 12–24; reprinted in *Readings in Microeconomics*, edited by David R. Kamerschen (New York: John Wiley & Sons, 1969), Chapter 22, pp. 307–319.

and oligopoly analysis. While, on balance, most economists are willing to live with the assumptions of monopolistic competition, as uncomfortable as they may be at times, some of the minority views are expressed at the end of this chapter.

SHORT-RUN ANALYSIS

Figure 14–1 illustrates the three short-run equilibrium possibilities for a firm under monopolistic competition. In all cases the firm produces where marginal revenue (MR) = marginal cost (MC), and the price is set where that quantity can be sold according to the demand curve. In panel (a), this results in an economic profit; in panel (b), zero profit; and in panel (c), losses. Except perhaps for the higher elasticity, nothing here differs from the pure monopoly case; and except for the divergence of MR and AR, nothing differs from the purely competitive case.

LONG-RUN ANALYSIS

It is in the long run that the monopolistically competitive model takes on a distinctive flavor of its own. The long-run conclusion is the so-called "tangency solution," with each firm making zero economic profits and operating with some excess capacity. We will discuss shortly how we arrive at this result.

The long run is defined in exactly the same manner for monopolistic competition as for all the other forms of market organization. Since all resources are variable, two major types of adjustment are possible: (1) a firm can build any scale of plant that it desires, and (2) the number of firms in the group can change in the most typical case where entry and exit are easy.

Blocked Entry

If entry should be blocked, as occasionally happens, instead of a break-even long-run equilibrium solution, the result in either panel (a) or panel (b) in Figure 14–1 is possible. That is, either positive or zero profits can occur; but positive profits, depicted in panel (a), are far more likely because, as we will see in a moment, it is free entry (and exit) that pushes profits to zero in long-run monopolistic competition equilibrium. Since that force, by definition, is missing with blocked entry, we expect the results depicted in panel (a). Of course, the short-run position depicted in panel (c) is not a possible long-run situation since the firms will leave the group if they incur losses and there are no barriers to exit.

Open Entry

Since the case of open entry is far more likely, let us look at it in more detail. We will explore the likely repercussions of a large group earning profits in the short run. (The logic for the case where losses are being incurred

FIGURE 14–1 Three Short-Run Equilibrium Possibilities Under Monopolistic Competition

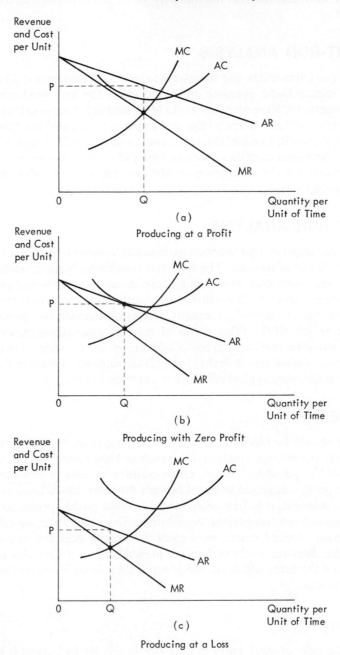

(a)

Producing at a Profit

(b)

Producing with Zero Profit

(c)

Producing at a Loss

is symmetrical.) The profits lure new firms into the group. As in pure competition, the entry can have two effects on the profit position of existing firms: (1) the individual firm's demand will shift, and (2) cost conditions may change. In the first instance, the commodity's increased supply as new firms enter tends to shift the *AR* and *MR* curves of existing firms downward. The same total consumer demand is now being shared by a larger number of suppliers.

Secondly, the entry may affect the cost curves facing the established firms. Once again there are three possible types of influences: the cost curve can shift upward, downward, or not at all, depending on whether the industry is one of increasing, decreasing, or constant cost. In the most likely case of rising factor prices and increasing cost curves as group expansion of output occurs, there would be the familiar two-way squeeze on profits for the firms — revenue falling and cost rising.

EXCESS CAPACITY

Figure 14–2 shows long-run equilibrium with free entry. The outstanding characteristic of the monopolistically competitive model is the phenomenon of excess capacity. The *excess capacity* theorem states that the optimum output of the "representative" firm occurs at an output less than that at which average total cost is at a minimum. This means that the monopolistically

FIGURE 14–2   Long-Run Equilibrium Under Monopolistic Competition with Excess Capacity

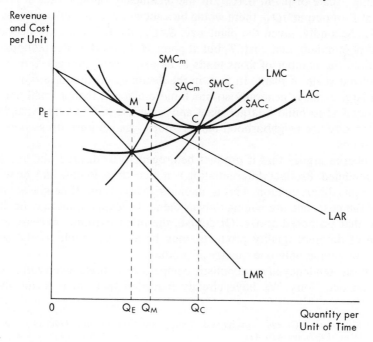

competitive firm will charge a price that exceeds both its (long-run) marginal cost and the purely competitive price. Excess capacity means that the individual firm builds a scale of plant, SAC_m, that is less than the technically optimum scale of plant, SAC_c in Figure 14-2; and it operates SAC_m at $0Q_E$, which is less than the technically optimum rate of output for that plant size of $0Q_M$.

Free entry forces the firm to produce where total revenue equals total cost, where $SAC_m = LAR = LAC =$ price, and where $SMC_m = LMC = LMR$. That is, free entry pushes each firm to the point where LAR is tangent to LAC. But since LAR is downward sloping, LAC must be also. Two tangential curves necessarily have the same slope at the point of tangency.

The ideal plant scale is thought to be the plant size with c subscripts, and the ideal scale of operation of that plant is at point C, where SAC_c is tangent to LAC. This is the output associated with the minimum LAC and SAC. Excess capacity is the difference between the ideal and the actual long-run equilibrium output.

Since John M. Cassels' study, most economists divide this excess capacity into two parts.[3] The economically optimal scale of plant for the firm in Figure 14-2 is SAC_m, given the revenue conditions and free entry. However, the optimal scale of plant from the point of view of the entire society is SAC_c. The resulting (negative) excess capacity is Q_EQ_C units of production.

This measure of excess capacity, Q_EQ_C, may be divided into two portions. First of all, the firm under monopolistic competition does not build the technically optimal scale of plant, SAC_c. This means that even if it operated the "wrong" scale of plant, SAC_m, at the technically optimal rate of production, point T, or output $0Q_M$, there would be a social waste or deficient capacity of Q_MQ_C. Secondly, given the plant size, SAC_m, the firm does not operate at the point of minimum unit cost, T, but at point M. In short, under monopolistic competition, the number of firms tends to be excessive, and each firm has an under-utilized scale of plant. In fact, in the declining portion of a firm's LAC curve, a large plant is generally so much more efficient than a small one that it is economical to build a larger plant and underuse it. Obvious examples of excess capacity are neighborhood barber shops, gas stations, drugstores, and grocery stores.

Chamberlin argues that if product heterogeneity is desired, the argument must be modified. Product differentiation is not costless. People may be willing to pay for this differentiation. This is an empirical question. If people are made aware of the costs and are willing to bear them, the ideal output may be different from that proposed above. Of course, the other extreme, excessive proliferation of different quality products, may be as undesirable as the boring sameness of having only one quality of product.

The firms' tendency in monopolistic competition to break even can be complicated on occasions. We have already indicated that entry is not always

---

[3] John M. Cassels, "Excess Capacity and Monopolistic Competition," *Quarterly Journal of Economics* (May, 1937), pp. 426–433.

completely unrestricted. There may be financial, legal, or technical barriers of a nontrivial magnitude. Product differentiation can sometimes provide formidable financial barriers. Firms may achieve a degree of "differentness" that rivals cannot duplicate even over a long period of time. For example, the monopolistic advantage gained from a favorable location or a patent may continue over a long span of time.

NONUNIFORM COST AND DEMAND FUNCTIONS

If the uniformity assumption is dropped, we can get a situation similar to that depicted in Figure 14–1, only now panels (a), (b), and (c) can represent different firms at the same time period. The different firms can be earning large, small, zero, or negative profits. In general, however, most members of a group are similar with respect to the sign of profits (plus or minus), although not the magnitude. If profits are positive for some firms, entry will take place, making existence difficult, if not impossible, for other firms such as those depicted in panels (b) and (c) in Figure 14–1.

NONPRICE COMPETITION

The feature that distinguishes the monopolistically competitive firm from the perfectly competitive firm is the amount of expenditure the firm can profitably devote to nonprice competition — i.e., expenditures on product variation and selling costs. The short-run profits of the firm under monopolistic competition can be raised if such expenditures cause total revenue to go up by more than the accompanying increase in the total costs.

The primary purpose of both selling costs and product variation to the firm is to shift the demand to the right and upward (thereby enlarging its share of the market). In addition, following the total spending test for elasticity, it would be to the firm's advantage to make the demand curve more inelastic above the existing price and more elastic below it. This means that total revenue would increase for either price increases or decreases. Since such control is seldom possible, it is the shift of the entire demand function to the right that is the fundamental strategy.

The analysis of quality adjustment as a feature of monopolistic competition is quite straightforward. Continuing to employ the uniformity assumption, the firm in Figure 14–3 is representative of all firms in the group. Each firm is at its optimum position at point A and the industry is in equilibrium. The firm's management can reason that if it can change the quality of the product in such a way as to attract enough new customers at the current price to offset the increased cost of producing the "better" product, profit will increase.

If the product improvement were to shift the demand curve to d_B at the same time that the long-run average cost curve shifted from LAC_A to LAC_B, the new optimum output for this firm would be at point B, where $LMC_B =$ price ($= MR$ because of the agreement to hold price constant for the analysis). Profit, in the amount P_1BFG, would be earned. Unfortunately for this firm, all

FIGURE 14-3   Quality Variation—Monopolistic Competition

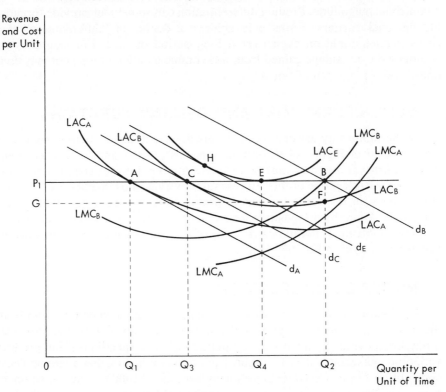

of its rivals are doing the same thing, which means that the demand curve will not shift all the way to d_B. It will move to d_C as rival firms improve their product quality. This is again a point of equilibrium (point C) where the profit has been driven off. This firm could again improve its product, increasing cost to a maximum of LAC_E. The final equilibrium would presumably not be exactly at point E but somewhat to the left of point E, which would require an increase in the price of the product (such as point H).

SELLING COSTS AND THE SELLING COST CURVE

"Selling costs" is a broad term used to cover all kinds of promotional activities—such as advertising expenditures and salespeople's expenses—designed to increase demand for the product. Chamberlin makes a theoretical distinction between selling and production costs that is sometimes difficult to apply in practice. He says that production costs are undertaken to adapt the product to the consumer, whereas selling costs are incurred to adapt the consumer to the product. In other words, with consumer tastes given, production costs are the costs of producing, transporting, and distributing the commodity. On the other hand, selling costs do not operate within given and static wants but rather are the costs incurred in trying to change consumer preferences. While this dichotomy is useful for a number of analytical purposes, it is difficult to classify something like, say, a more convenient and more colorful method of packaging as either a selling cost or a production cost.

One of the primary activities resulting in selling costs is advertising. We know that the purpose of advertising is to shift the demand curve outward. Of course, in certain situations if the media are saturated with the voice of "hucksters," the impact on demand may be slight or even negative. If advertising reaches a point at which it depresses rather than impresses the potential consumer, the firm would be better off not advertising since advertising would raise costs and reduce demand. While we expect that advertising will have diminishing marginal returns eventually, we generally expect that the stage of negative returns will not be reached. That is, we will assume that advertising does have a positive, although perhaps slight in some cases, influence on demand and sales.

Figure 14–4 depicts a U-shaped curve of selling costs along the lines suggested by Chamberlin in his seminal work on monopolistic competition. Interpret the curve in the following way. At a given price, with product quality and other firms' activities held constant, selling costs must increase to increase demand and therefore the quantity sold by the firm. Suppose a firm is selling at the rate of 1,000 units of its products per month and spending $100 per month for newspaper advertising. The average advertising cost is of course ten cents per unit. If it increases its advertising outlay to $150 per month and sales increase to 2,000 units, the advertising cost per unit of sales has decreased to seven and one half cents. The presumption, in drawing the curve as in Figure 14–4, is that there is a range in which the average cost of advertising decreases because any percentage increase in outlays results in more than that percentage increase in sales. This would happen if advertising exhibits increasing returns to scale such that the number of persons reached by the media increases more than proportionally to budget increases. For example, ads in a newspaper of 100,000 circulation may cost only 50 percent more than the same ad in a paper of only 10,000 circulation. Artists or ad writers who are twice as effective as others may charge only 50 percent more, and so on. Eventually,

FIGURE 14–4   Average Selling Cost Curve

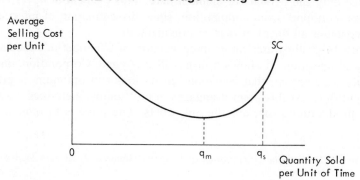

however, these economies are exhausted. Resistant buyers become more and more difficult to reach, and the curve turns upward.

The SC curve shifts upward if the price of the product is increased, meaning that to sell any given output, a larger selling expense would be necessary. We would also expect the curve to shift upward if the product's quality were reduced, or if rival firms decreased the prices of their products, improved the quality of their products, or increased their selling expenses. The curve would shift downward if any of the opposite events took place.

Equimarginal Principle

The entrepreneur will engage in advertising (or selling activity in general) on the same basis as any other productive activity; that is, until the expected marginal revenue of each medium — billboards, magazines, newspapers, radio, television, etc. — equals its marginal cost. In other words, the optimal advertising budget requires the profit-maximizing firm to produce where the combined marginal cost of production and selling activities is just equal to the marginal revenue of the product the firm is selling. Any other method of determining advertising expenditures — fixed percentage of sales, fixed dollar amount, etc. — is therefore not likely to be optimal.

To compute the socially optimal amount of information to be conveyed by advertising — or any other means of dispensing information — also invites a comparison of marginal benefits and costs. The provision of information is both a socially useful and socially costly process. As Stigler has said:

> Ignorance is like subzero weather: by a sufficient expenditure its effects upon people can be kept within tolerable or even comfortable bounds, but it would be wholly uneconomic entirely to eliminate all its effects. And, just as analysis of man's shelter and apparel would be somewhat incomplete if cold weather is ignored, so also our understanding of economic life will be incomplete if we do not systematically take account of the cold winds of ignorance.[4]

Any actual dollar amount of advertising contains a mixture of information — telling potential buyers about a firm's prices, quantities, and product qualities — and an element of emotional persuasion, pure and simple. We will emphasize only the persuasive element here. This element in advertising distinguishes monopoly from competition, since dissemination of information is necessary under all forms of market organization.

Figure 14–5 illustrates an adapted version of Chamberlin's model of advertising competition. It shows a firm, call it Myopic Corporation, under the uniformity assumption, that is initially in its long-run optimum at price $0P_1$ and output $0Q_1$. At this point it engages in no "selling" activities, so PC, the average production costs, are the only costs. The price is to remain at $0P_1$,

---

[4] George J. Stigler, *The Organization of Industry* (Homewood: Richard D. Irwin, 1968), p. 188.

FIGURE 14-5 **Competition in Advertising Under Monopolistic Competition**

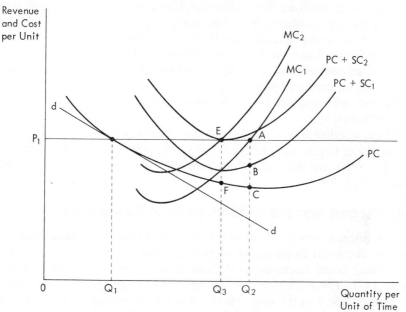

since any increase in quantities sold will come about through demand curve shifting activities represented by selling costs, not through price reductions. Since price is constant, marginal revenue is constant and equal to price. The firm, earning zero profits, might consider increasing sales by advertising. The average selling cost curve (SC) has been added to the average production cost curve (PC) to form the average total cost curve ($PC + SC_1$). The vertical distance between $PC + SC_1$ and PC at all quantities would form an SC curve like that of Figure 14-4. The MC_1 curve is marginal to the $PC + SC_1$ curve, so it is the change in the total cost of producing and selling one more or one less unit of output.

The optimum decision for this firm would seem to be to increase output to $0Q_2$ by engaging in advertising expenditures in the amount $BC \times 0Q_2$, where its costs of production are $Q_2C \times 0Q_2$, which leaves it the maximum profit of $AB \times 0Q_2$. (Total revenue is $Q_2A \times 0Q_2$.) This would appear to be a very happy result for Myopic Corporation; but the unhappy news is that if its sales increase from $0Q_1$ to $0Q_2$, the rival firms will suffer a sales loss and, furthermore, will observe the success of Myopic's advertising campaign and will probably emulate its activity.

If the other firms engage in a similar advertising program, the SC curve of our representative firm will shift upward (by a constant amount), because it will take a larger advertising outlay to effect a given sales volume than when the other firms were not advertising. The marginal cost curve associated with it will shift up by the same amount to MC_2.

This analysis started by observing that advertising provides a possibility of earning profit. However, every firm in the group will increase its advertising outlays. The more other firms advertise, the more the SC curve will shift upward for the representative firm. This competition in advertising will continue until all of the firms have exhausted the gains from such outlays. At the new optimum for all firms, the $PC + SC_2$ curve will be tangent to the price line, they will be maximizing profit by spending $EF \times 0Q_3$ on advertising and $FQ_3 \times 0Q_3$ on production, and profits will be zero. Actually, as pointed out in connection with Figure 14–3, the price would be slightly higher and the quantity a little less.

Thus, whether a firm in monopolistic competition tries to enlarge sales by cutting price, improving quality, or increasing advertising outlays, the results with free entry are the same. Each firm will be forced to a point at which it earns zero profits.

The Alleged Wastes of Monopolistic Competition

The alleged wastes of monopolistic competition associated with excess capacity discussed in an earlier section and the presumed wastes associated with selling costs discussed in the last section can now be combined as in Figure 14–6. There are two possible sources of higher prices under imperfect competition, even in the case where price equals average cost and no profits exist, as under long-run equilibrium under monopolistic competition. Not only do monopolistically competitive firms fail to produce at the lowest points on their average cost curves (i.e., they have excess capacity), but these curves themselves are apt to be higher than under pure competition.

In Figure 14–6 the curve labeled LAC_{pc} shows the long-run average cost curve on the assumption of no selling costs, whereas LAC_{mc} shows long-run

FIGURE 14–6   **The Alleged Wastes of Monopolistic Competition from Selling Costs and Excess Capacity**

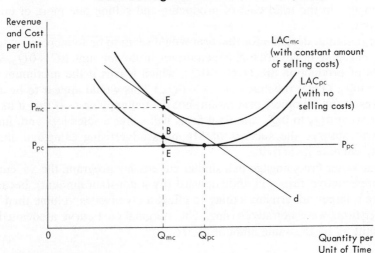

average cost including selling costs. Since LAC_{mc} represents monopolistic competition, assume that the selling costs are not of an informational variety, accurately describing commodity prices and qualities, but are of a persuasive, unsubstantiated "ours-is-better-than-theirs" type. As we indicated, informational advertising is not inherently inconsistent with pure competition.

The long-run equilibrium price under pure competition is $0P_{pc}$, which is equal to the lowest point on its LAC_{pc} curve; whereas the long-run equilibrium price under monopolistic competition is $0P_{mc}$, which is above the point of lowest average cost, LAC_{mc}. The difference between the two prices equals the (vertical) distance EF (composed of two segments, $EB + BF$). The segment EB represents that part of the higher price attributable to the higher costs of excess capacity—i.e., producing to the left of the point of minimum average costs. The segment BF represents that part of the higher price owing to the extra selling costs. Thus, consumers ultimately pay for the efforts to inform and persuade them.

Stigler's Position

George J. Stigler emphasizes that Chamberlin's theory of monopolistic competition has made a specific and a general contribution to the corpus of economic theory.[5] Its specific contribution was to provide an analysis of a many-firm group facing a falling demand curve, assuming uniformity and symmetry. He argues that Chamberlin's analysis was essentially correct and enriched the theory of the firm by including a market model different from that of pure competition, pure monopoly, or oligopoly. Stigler does not accept the contention that the model of monopolistic competition should be incorporated into the standard theory because it provides a more realistic description of real world industries. He feels that the proper test is whether it provides different or more accurate predictions than the model of pure competition. Stigler personally thinks the predictions of monopolistic competition are not very different, inasmuch as the firm is assumed to have a high demand elasticity. But he admits this is a question of fact and must ultimately be resolved by empirical testing. Yet after more than 40 years it is sad to admit that few predictions have been tested and confirmed.

The general contribution of monopolistic competition has been to make the models of pure monopoly and pure competition richer and more precise, which has led to the development of other important models. The definition and analysis of industries, commodities, advertising, trademarks, market structure, etc., were all enriched by the impetus given by monopolistic competition. The way economists think about monopoly has changed significantly.

---

[5] *Ibid.* For a much more sympathetic view of Chamberlin's contribution, see Robert L. Bishop, "The Theory of Monopolistic Competition After Thirty Years: The Impact on General Theory," *American Economic Review* (May, 1964), pp. 33–43; reprinted in *Readings in Microeconomics,* edited by David R. Kamerschen (New York: John Wiley & Sons, 1969), Chapter 23, pp. 320–331. We emphasize the critical instead of the sympathetic views in this section since our detailed presentation of the Chamberlin model as the generally accepted orthodox theory attests to the fact that it has supporters.

To be sure, there are still numerous instances of imprecise and cloudy thinking in this area. For instance, the distinction between a multiproduct firm and the multiproduct group of monopolistic competition is not always made clear. The fact that there are numerous well-known brands of soaps, cleansers, and detergents—Bold, Bonus, Biz, Camay, Cascade, Cheer, Cinch, Comet, Dash, Dreft, Duz, Ivory Soap, Ivory Flakes, Joy, Lava, Mr. Clean, Oxydol, Safeguard, Spic 'n' Span, Thrill, Tide, and Zest—does not mean this market is one of monopolistic competition. In fact, in this case, every one of the above brands is manufactured by one firm, Procter and Gamble, which alone has over half the national market in soaps, cleaners, cleansers, and detergents and which, with Lever Brothers, dominates the market.[6]

Overview of the Controversy

In summary, then, we have two conflicting views: one by Chamberlin, who argues that monopolistic competition is a more useful model, and one by Stigler and the "Chicago School," who say the same thing about pure competition. Unfortunately, we cannot resolve the debate between Chamberlin and the "Chicago School" in this book. The theories have simply not been sufficiently tested in a comparative way to permit this. Both monopolistic competition and pure competition may be useful for different problems. Although monopolistic competition does not have all the answers, it does have some. As such, most economists are willing to accept the Chamberlin analysis given in the early sections of this chapter as a useful addition to our corpus of economic theory. However, on the question of whether pure competition or monopolistic competition is more useful, there would be much less unanimity among economists. Fortunately, this controversy need not be resolved before the theory of the firm can be useful to us.

QUESTIONS

1. What essential characteristic distinguishes monopolistic competition from pure competition? Give several examples from your own experience.
2. Sponsors of Little League baseball teams and other amateur athletic activities are often firms which could be categorized as monopolistically competitive. Why would you think this might be true? Test this proposition in your own community.
3. Refer to point E on Figure 14–3. Why could this not be an optimum point? If H were the optimum point, compare this result with the result under pure competition.
4. It is said that one of the conclusions of monopolistic competition theory is that "excess capacity" will exist. How would you define "excess capacity"? Use service stations as typical examples of monopolistic competitors. Are there "too many" service stations in your community?

---

[6] The theory and illustration are from Jesse W. Markham, "Comment," *American Economic Review* (May, 1954), pp. 53–55. The top three firms produce over 80 percent of the industry's output.

5. In the monopolistic competition case, we saw that the value of advertising to a firm will in large part dissipate as the other firms in its group retaliate by increasing their own advertising expenditures. Why don't the firms recognize this process and all decline to engage in such countervailing activities?

APPENDIX: MATHEMATICAL NOTES

Note 1. Chamberlin's Monopolistic Competition and Long-Run Equilibrium[7]

The following variables and relations are important:

$$\text{Total Revenue} = TR = R(q,\ dic) \tag{14.1}$$
$$\text{Total Cost} = TC = C(q,\ dic)$$

where q is quantity and dic represents all demand-increasing costs, such as expenditures on promotional activities, location, and product quality.

$$\text{Average Revenue} = AR = TR/q \tag{14.2}$$
$$\text{Average Cost} = AC = TC/q$$

The marginal conditions for profit maximization are:

$$\frac{\delta TR}{\delta q} = \frac{\delta TC}{\delta q}, \quad \frac{\delta TR}{\delta dic} = \frac{\delta TC}{\delta dic} \tag{14.3}$$

and for the "group" to be in long-run zero-profit equilibrium, it is necessary that:

$$TR = TC \text{ or } AR = AC \tag{14.4}$$

Writing out the first part of (14.3) yields:

$$\frac{\delta TR}{\delta q} = AR + q\frac{\delta AR}{\delta q} = AC + q\frac{\delta AC}{\delta q} = \frac{\delta TC}{\delta q} \tag{14.5}$$

Using (14.4), (14.5) can be reduced to:

$$\frac{\delta AR}{\delta q} = \frac{\delta AC}{\delta q} < 0 \tag{14.6}$$

Since demand curves are negatively sloped (i.e., $\delta AR/\delta q < 0$), (14.6) gives us the excess capacity theorem since the AC curve must also be negatively sloped.

However, Harold Demsetz argues that this type of proof shows that AR and AC are downsloping only under the assumption that all the variables that influence AC and AR except q are held constant (at their profit-maximizing levels). Yet traditional production theory derives the AC curve by allowing the firm to change the quantities

---

[7] Harold Demsetz, "The Welfare and Empirical Implications of Monopolistic Competition," *The Economic Journal* (September, 1964), pp. 623–641.

of all inputs optimally. In other words, the above conditions are marginal and partial. Demsetz emphasizes that to prove the excess capacity theorem, one must actually show that at the optimum output the total derivative of AC with respect to q is negative. One cannot deduce the sign of this total derivative from Chamberlin's assumptions.

$$AR = A(q, dic), \quad AC = A(q, dic) \tag{14.7}$$

Indicating the total derivative by a prime, the total derivative with respect to q is: [8]

$$(AR)' = \frac{\delta AR}{\delta q} + \frac{\delta AR}{\delta dic}(dic)' \text{ and } (AC)' = \frac{\delta AC}{\delta q} + \frac{\delta AC}{\delta dic}(dic)' \tag{14.8}$$

The proof given earlier shows only that $\delta AR/\delta q$ and $\delta AC/\delta q < 0$. This deduction is insufficient to further deduce that $(AR)'$ and $(AC)' < 0$, since $\delta AR/\delta q$ and $\delta AC/\delta q$ are necessarily >0 (given that dic are both demand increasing and cost increasing!) and since $(dic)'$ is plausibly positive over some output ranges. A positive $(dic)'$ indicates that managers will find their most profitable course to be one that associates higher levels of dic with higher levels of output, a not unlikely association. To reject the excess capacity theorem does not require that $(dic)'$ be positive at all levels of output, but only that it not always be negative.

In summary, Chamberlin showed that $\delta AR/\delta q$ and $\delta AC/\delta q < 0$. But the seller, by changing dic, can shift the conventional demand curve so that the price need not fall

at larger rates of output. This will hold if $\left| \dfrac{\delta AR}{\delta q} \right| \leqq \dfrac{\delta AR}{\delta dic}(dic)'$.

---

[8] The definition of a total derivative for a function if $U = f(x,y)$ and $y = \phi(x)$ is: $U'\left(= \dfrac{du}{dx}\right) = \dfrac{\delta u}{\delta x} + \dfrac{\delta u}{\delta y} \cdot \dfrac{dy}{dx}$.

15 Pricing and Production under Oligopoly

As an empirical form of market structure, oligopoly is very important in the U.S. economy. In many of our manufacturing, mining, retailing, and wholesaling sectors, a few firms dominate. In particular, the aluminum, automobile, electrical equipment, steel, and tire industries are especially well-known examples of industries which seem to fit the theoretical description of oligopoly. Unfortunately, there is no one widely accepted theory of oligopoly which we can use to analyze the firms in these markets. There are a number of different theories, each of which makes different assumptions about the precise way oligopolistic sellers react to actions by a given seller.[1]

The wide range of theoretical predictions and actual behavior found in oligopoly make it an indeterminate market structure in that the mechanical links from cost and demand to price are not precise. But it is possible to develop theories which can predict with tolerable accuracy oligopolistic conduct and performance. However, to do so requires richer theories involving more variables than those in the two polar cases of pure competition and pure monopoly. This in large part explains why industrial organization is an applied branch of price theory which necessarily has to be concerned with institutional, descriptive, and empirical matters as well as theoretical issues. The best that can be hoped for in the quest for a realistic oligopoly theory is what Frederic Scherer calls "a kind of soft determinism: predictions correct on the average, but subject to occasionally substantial errors."

The mutual interdependence found under oligopoly is what distinguishes it from the other market models. Under oligopoly there are so few firms producing the bulk of the output that any firm must consider how its behavior will affect the decisions of its rivals. The oligopolist must not only consider the fairly predictable cost and demand data, but also the highly uncertain reaction of rivals. In other words, price and output are indeterminate under oligopoly since a firm needs more information on the strategies of rivals. In this sense, oligopoly has been likened to games of bridge, chess, or poker, in which a good player must consider the probable reactions of the opponents before taking any action.

---

[1] Different theories of oligopoly are inevitable. For example, the pure case of rational opponents with opposed interests facing each other is in a way not solvable in principle. It is only solvable given assumptions as to what one thinks of the other. A systematic and complete treatment of oligopoly can be found in Frederic M. Scherer, *Industrial Pricing: Theory and Evidence* (Chicago: Rand McNally & Co., 1973), which consists of five slightly revised chapters from his larger work, *Industrial Market Structure and Economic Performance* (Chicago: Rand McNally & Co., 1970).

This chapter will generally assume that the products are homogeneous (such as in the cement, copper, and steel industries) and are not differentiated (as in the automobile and cigarette industries). While this assumption is not always a good one for empirical reasons — most oligopolies, in fact, do have differentiated products — it is rather innocuous theoretically since the hallmark of oligopoly, mutual interdependence, prevails whether the products are homogeneous or not. Secondly, we will make the provisional assumption that pure competition holds with respect to the buying of factors. Thirdly, we will concentrate on the duopoly case of two sellers. Since the basic considerations for duopoly are the same as for the n-firm oligopoly model, this is a harmless simplification. Finally, we will examine both collusive and independent behavior. In all, following Fritz Machlup,[2] three general classes of models will be examined: class 1, unorganized noncollusion or independent action; class 2, perfect (organized) collusion; and class 3, imperfect (unorganized) collusion.

This three-fold classification is based on the degree of communication, coordination, and collusion among the firms and not upon the number and size distribution of firms, although indirectly the number of firms is relevant in that the difficulty of maintaining any collusive arrangement is positively related to the number of firms in the agreement. In particular, the difficulty of coordinating an informal, tacit collusion may rise exponentially with the number of firms. Without a central coordinating agency, each firm must tacitly or overtly communicate with each of its rivals about a feasible pricing system. Letting N be the number of firms in the relevant market, the number of two-way communication flows required is given by the combinatorial expression $C = N(N\text{-}1)/2$. Thus, in a market with 10 suppliers, $C = 10(9)/2 = 45$. In this example, 45 channels must be maintained to keep industry discipline. Thus, it should be apparent why some people consider collusion to be nothing but "communication par excellence." The number of sellers in a market is also relevant in that the larger the number of sellers, the greater the chances that at least one will adopt an independent and aggressive price policy, such as Henry Ford did in the automobile industry, Ernest P. Weir (president of National Steel during the 1930s) did in the steel industry, and Harvey Firestone did in the rubber tire industry.

Despite all the various forms that oligopoly theory can take, one element is common to almost all (except the Bertrand and Edgeworth models). That is, active price competition is almost never practiced. Oligopoly prices tend to be inflexible or sticky, especially in a downward direction. When changes do occur, all the firms usually change together. An excellent example of this is the automobile industry.

Any aberrations from the course of stable prices, such as price wars, are usually soon corrected. The typical rules of the game in oligopoly call for stable prices but vigorous nonprice competition. Usually the oligopolist is allowed

---

[2] Fritz Machlup, *The Economics of Sellers' Competition; Model Analysis of Sellers' Conduct* (Baltimore: The Johns Hopkins Press, 1952), especially pp. 363–365.

to advertise or change product quality to obtain and maintain customers, but is not supposed to chisel on price. In general, the tighter the control on price competition, the more intense the nonprice competition.

QUALIFIED JOINT PROFIT-MAXIMIZATION HYPOTHESIS

The distinction between perfect collusion and the other two oligopoly classes, imperfect collusion and independence, turns out to be a question of whether firms try to maximize their joint profits or not. A perfectly colluding cartel or group of firms whose goal is to foster monopoly conditions charges a monopoly price that maximizes the profit of the entire cartel. At the other extreme, the unorganized, noncollusive firms are concerned only with individual profit maximization. While the total possible profits are largest if the firms organize into a coalition and operate as would a pure monopolist, this does not mean the individual profits of any one oligopolist are maximized with such an arrangement. By shading price slightly from the cartel price, any one member can enlarge its share of a smaller total profit and possibly increase its individual profits. Some writers have advanced a qualified joint profit-maximization hypothesis to explain the two-way tug on an oligopolist by forces that move the firm both toward and away from joint profit maximization.[3]

> Among the factors that may predict a tendency toward joint profit-maximization are greater mutual recognition of interdependence, greater facility of tacit agreement, and greater barriers to entry.[4]

The more a firm recognizes that its policies on price, production, advertising outlays, product variation, etc., affect the behavior of its rivals and vice versa, the greater the possibility that a joint profit maximization will result. All else being equal, the individual firm will be more likely to recognize this interaction: (1) the fewer the number of sellers; and (2) the closer the firms' market shares, products, and production processes. In the limiting cases of pure competition and monopolistic competition, the number of sellers is so large that virtually no single firm recognizes the possible repercussions of any given policy. Also, the more nearly homogeneous the product, the more likely a firm is to realize that its actions lead to reactions by other firms. Similarly, if market shares are approximately the same, it is easier to agree on profit sharing under a joint profit-maximizing coalition.

The group will more nearly approximate joint profit maximization the easier it is to reach and abide by tacit, informal agreements. All else being

---

[3] Probably the first systematic development of this thesis appeared in the now classic work by William Fellner, *Competition Among the Few; Oligopoly and Similar Market Structures* (New York: Alfred A. Knopf, 1949), especially Chapters I, IV–VIII. (Chapters II and III also provide an excellent review of the literature.) However, this section follows the terser and more testable presentation of the hypothesis found in Richard G. Lipsey and Peter O. Steiner, *Economics* (New York: Harper & Row, Publishers, 1966), Chapter 29, pp. 321–328.

[4] Richard G. Lipsey and Peter O. Steiner, *Economics* (New York: Harper & Row, Publishers, 1966), pp. 327–328.

equal, it is easier to do this: (1) when the joint profit-maximizing price is stable or rising rather than falling, (2) the more certain and more similar the rival firms' expectations of future economic variables, and (3) when one firm dominates the group. It would obviously be harder to agree on each firm's share of the group's joint profits if they disagreed on what was likely to happen to their own and their rivals' costs, demands, etc., in the future. A firm that thinks its market share is likely to rise significantly in the future may not be willing to share profits according to its historical or present share of the market. Also, as will be shown in a moment, the existence of a dominant firm increases the likelihood of price leadership and hence of joint profit maximization.

Finally, the probability of a group's achieving joint profit maximization is greater, the greater the barriers to entry into its market. Of course, the higher these entry-deterring barriers, the greater the possibility of achieving maximum profits. All else being equal, these barriers to entry are greater: (1) the greater the economies of scale in production cost, selling cost, and product variation; (2) the greater the technical complexities involved in production; (3) the greater the amount of concentration of essential raw materials in the hands of one or a few producers; and (4) the greater the degree and effectiveness of past nonprice competition, and hence the greater the goodwill—through past advertising, product variation, etc.

We will first take up the class of oligopolies which is least likely to lead to joint profit maximization. It includes the unorganized, noncollusive models characterized by independent action on the part of individual firms. Included in this discussion are most of the classical models, which almost invariably assume independence. Next we will take up those theories that assume explicit or implicit collusion.

CLASS 1 OLIGOPOLIES: INDEPENDENCE, UNORGANIZED NONCOLLUSION

Formal analysis of oligopoly models goes back to at least the work of the French scholar A. Augustin Cournot (1801–1877), who published his duopoly theory in 1838.[5] While most of the models are crude and embrace some "heroic" assumptions, they do serve as a useful prelude to our more sophisticated contemporary theories. The three best-known classical theories of duopoly, Cournot's, Bertrand's, and Edgeworth's, all have one thing in common: each duopolist assumes the rival will do nothing in some particular important dimension, namely, price or quantity.

Cournot's Model

Cournot assumes two profit-maximizing duopolists, A and B, each of which produces an identical product. His example is mineral water from two adjacent springs which are assumed to produce mineral water at zero marginal cost. The

---

[5] Augustin Cournot, *Researches into the Mathematical Principles of Wealth,* translated by Nathaniel T. Bacon (New York: Macmillan Co., 1897).

model further assumes that each duopolist fully knows the linear demand curves. Each duopolist is presumed to act independently, without collusion, and to act under the assumption that the rival's output will remain exactly where it is now, even if the first firm changes its output (never its price). While this assumption is rather odd, it does give determinate results.

Figure 15-1 illustrates the simplified Cournot case described here for duopolists A and B. If pure competition prevailed, the equilibrium output would be $0Q_c$; and since $MC = 0$, price must also equal zero. The equilibrium price and quantity, if the two firms colluded, would be $0P_1$ and $0Q_1$. This is precisely where a pure monopolist would operate, since $MR = MC$ here. Or if A were the only seller in the market, this would be the solution. When B comes on the scene, B will, according to Cournot, assume that A will maintain its output at $0Q_1$. Since B regards AQ_c as the remaining demand, B's profit-maximization output would be one half of the remaining output or one fourth of the total demand. Thus, B equates the zero MC with MR, sells Q_1Q_2 units of output, and sets the price at $0P_2$. Both firms then sell at price $0P_2$, A selling $0Q_1$, B selling Q_1Q_2.

In turn, A now assumes B's output will remain fixed at $Q_1Q_2 = Q_2Q_c$. A's market is now three fourths of the total market, equal to $0Q_2$. Maximization again calls for selling one half of this or three eighths of the competitive output ($\frac{1}{2} \cdot \frac{3}{4} = \frac{3}{8}$).

This process continues on and on. But there is a limit or convergence point to this process. In equilibrium, Cournot's two duopolists will produce two thirds of the competitive output, charge two thirds of the monopoly price, and collect two thirds of the monopoly profit. The total duopoly output is between the larger competitive output $0Q_c$ and the smaller monopolistic output $0Q_1$. The general solution for the Cournot case is that the total oligopolistic equilibrium

**FIGURE 15-1   Cournot's Duopoly
Solution**

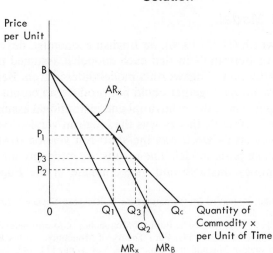

output of the industry will be Q_c $[n/(n + 1)]$, where Q_c is the competitive output and n is the number of oligopolists in the market. Each firm's output will be Q_c $[1/(1 + n)]$ and the price will be $[2(P_m - P_c)]/(1 + n)$, where P_m (P_c) is the monopoly (competitive) price. In the case of duopoly, $n = 2$, the industry output is Q_c $[2/(2 + 1)] = Q_c(2/3)$, and each firm's output is Q_c $(1/1 + 2) = Q_c(1/3)$. The price is $2 \cdot (P_m)/1 + 2 = (2/3)P_m$. As one would expect, the larger the number of firms, the closer are the price and quantity to the competitive output; formally, Q_c $[n/(n + 1)] \rightarrow 1$ as $n \rightarrow \infty$.

Bertrand's Model

A French mathematician, Joseph Bertrand, in reviewing Cournot's book in 1883, criticized the Cournot assumption of constant quantity for rivals and suggested that an assumption of constant price for rivals would be better, i.e., $\Delta P_D/\Delta P_C = 0$, where the C and D subscripts refer to the two rivals.[6] (Technically, this is referred to as zero conjectural price variation.) As did Cournot, Bertrand also assumed identical costs and identical products. He further assumed that any single duopolist was capable of satisfying the entire market demand at all prices.

Suppose firms C and D are the two duopolists. Further suppose, for the moment, firm C is alone in the market and sets the monopolist price of $0P_1$ in Figure 15–1. Firm D then comes into the market. Since D assumes that C's price is constant, D feels that it can take the entire market demand by shading the price slightly from $0P_1$. In turn, C lowers the price, causing D's rate of sales to fall to zero. This continues until price falls to the level of costs. Of course, the price cutting will stop here or losses would be incurred. This model demonstrates the point made earlier that competitive results can be reached with only a few firms, in this case only two, providing that each thinks it cannot influence the price of its rivals.

Edgeworth's Model

F. Y. Edgeworth (1845–1926), an English economist, developed a theory in 1897 similar to Bertrand's in that each duopolist assumed the rival's price was constant.[7] However, Edgeworth's model differed from Bertrand's in that it assumed the two firms together could not produce an output as large as the competitive output. Since the behavioral and institutional assumptions are the same, in a sense Bertrand's theory was the long-run version (variable level of output) and Edgeworth's work was the short-run version (restricted level of output) of the same basic model. The results are strikingly different, with the prices and quantities unstable and indeterminate in the Edgeworth model.

---

[6] Joseph Bertrand, "Theorie Mathematique de la Richesse Sociale," *Journal des Savants* (Paris, 1883), pp. 499–508.

[7] Francis Y. Edgeworth, "La Teoria Pura del Monopolio," *Giornale delgi Economisti* (1897), pp. 13–31; reprinted in English as "The Pure Theory of Monopoly," in his *Papers Relating to Political Economy* (London: Macmillan & Co., 1925), Vol. 1, pp. 111–142.

While price wars exist in both models, the Bertrand analysis predicts that price will eventually dampen to the competitive solution, whereas the Edgeworth theory postulates a perpetual oscillation of price between the competitive and monopoly position.

Figure 15–2, based on a diagram by Edgeworth himself, gives a satisfactory account of the model. Assume there are two duopolists, E and F, producing a homogeneous product for which the marginal costs are zero. The market is divided equally between them, with E's demand curve being DE and F's demand curve DF. The maximal amount that E can produce is $0N$ and the maximal amount F can produce is $0K$, and $0N = 0K$.

FIGURE 15–2   Edgeworth's Duopoly
Solution

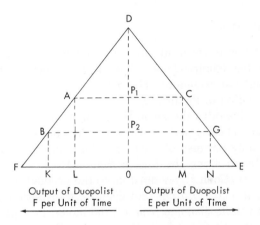

Output of Duopolist
F per Unit of Time

Output of Duopolist
E per Unit of Time

If the two firms were to collude, they would choose the monopoly price P_1, and the marginal revenue associated with the total demand curve would equal the zero marginal cost. Each oligopolist would supply one quarter of the total market demand (i.e., the quantity that would be demanded if the price were zero). That is, E would supply $0M$ and F would supply $0L$ ($LM = \frac{1}{2} FE$).

If collusion is ruled out, it would be to the advantage of either firm to lower the price below P_1. For example, if E lowered the price just slightly below P_1, all of F's customers (the amount $0L$) would shift to E; but E would be able to service only MN additional units, which would leave F with KL ($= NE$) amount of sales. Rather than accept this loss in revenue, firm F could lower price a little below the one set by E and recapture the lost sales plus the largest proportion of E's sales. In this manner, both oligopolists would lower prices until price P_2 is reached, where both firms would be selling all they are capable of producing.

Price P_2, however, is not a stable solution either since now one firm could raise the price and increase total revenue. As long as F keeps its price at P_2, its sales would be at its maximum output level, and E could raise the price without losing customers to F. Under this condition, demand curve DE is inelastic in the range CE, so E could raise price all the way back to P_1, at which point E's profit ($= TR$) is at a maximum. It would also be obvious to F that any price increase it initiated (up to P_1) would lose it no sales. Some of E's customers would move to seller F, and E would respond with a lower price.

There is no way to say where the price will be in this situation. If both firms refuse to learn how their rival will react, the price will fluctuate in the range P_1P_2 without end.

In summary, the Bertrand and Cournot models yield determinate solutions; Edgeworth's model is indeterminate. The reason for Edgeworth's different conclusion is that he assumed the two firms could not produce as much as the competitive output. The capacity limitation on each producer means that they cannot service the entire market but only some part of it, say, three fourths.

Hotelling's Model

Harold Hotelling devised an interesting model of oligopoly which can be reconciled with the empirical fact that oligopoly prices and quantities are usually stable and not oscillating. His model also introduces quality variance in the form of location of the firms.[8]

Figure 15–3 illustrates the basic Hotelling model. The two duopolists, G and H, have identical marginal costs of zero and a physically identical product that is different only because of location. The demanders are assumed to be uniformly distributed along the line in Figure 15–3, and the duopolists are located at G and H. Each buyer must go to the production site and transport purchases home at a cost of t per unit distance transported. If, for example, a buyer is located x units distance from G, the buyer must pay a transportation cost of tx for each unit of product. Thus, each seller has a partially sheltered or monopoly position over a certain range because of transportation costs. In particular, G has a competitive advantage regarding buyers to its left, H has one to its right, and each has an advantage halfway toward its rival's location. The prices and quantities are determinate and stable in such a model.

Now consider the problem of where G and H should locate in the long run when their plants are moveable. Each can expand its "monopoly" market by moving toward median point M. The final equilibrium for both sellers is stable and determinate at M.

FIGURE 15–3   Hotelling Spatial
                Equilibrium Solution

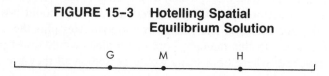

[8] Harold Hotelling, "Stability in Competition," *Economic Journal* (March, 1929), pp. 41–57; reprinted in *AEA Readings in Price Theory,* edited by George J. Stigler and Kenneth E. Boulding (Homewood: Richard D. Irwin, 1952), Chapter 23, pp. 467–484.

From a welfare point of view, this behavior would not give the consumers an ideal degree of product differentiation.[9] The principle demonstrated here is a very general one, applicable to all types of product differentiation, not just location. The general rule, which Kenneth Boulding calls the *principle of minimum differentiation,* states that any new firm coming into a group should make its product as similar to the existing products as it can without destroying the differences.[10] Thus, brand names are important in economic, political, social, and even religious life. A firm's best strategy is to make its product physically as much like its competitors' products as it can but call its product something different. The firm should then convince consumers through advertising of the superiority of its product. This principle explains spatial similarities: the usual close proximity of variety stores, the concentration of business districts and firms in given cities, etc. It also suggests why automobiles, ciders, political parties, religions, and economics textbooks are so similar! To attract members, the Baptists, Methodists, Presbyterians, and even Quakers tend to become more and more alike, keeping just enough distinction so as to be able to "advertise" their brand name. The similarity of the platforms of Democrats and Republicans, conservatives and liberals, etc., can also be explained by the same general principle.

To be sure, Hotelling's idea that two firms tend to get together in the center of the market does not necessarily hold for more than two firms. Professor Edward Chamberlin shows that the general tendency is for dispersion in quality competition in general, or location in particular, when there are more than two firms in the market.[11] Firms tend to scatter to avoid being caught between a pair of other firms, thus becoming restricted to a narrow "monopoly" range of buyers in which favorable transportation cost differentials prevail.

Chamberlin's Model

Edward Chamberlin developed a second model that emphasizes the relative price stability in oligopoly markets. His model assumes identical costs and products as in the Cournot solution, but replaces the naive Cournot assumption of fixed output with the assumption that firms recognize their interdependence and do something about it. Thus, Figure 15–1, used to describe the Cournot case, may be used here. Again duopolist A sets the monopoly price at $0P_1$ (the associated quantity is $0Q_1$) and duopolist B reacts optimally by producing Q_1Q_2 units at a price of $0P_2$. Now, however, Chamberlin assumes A will reflect on the stupidity of continuing to assume B's output is constant in the face of its changing. A knows the maximum (joint) profit occurs when a

---

[9] In the case of a linear market such as depicted in Figure 15–3, transportation costs are maximized at median point M, whereas they would be minimized at the quartile points, which would presumably be the collusive solution (not shown in Figure 15–3).

[10] Kenneth E. Boulding, *Economic Analysis* (3d ed.; New York: Harper & Row, Publishers, 1955), see pp. 631–634.

[11] Edward H. Chamberlin, *The Theory of Monopolistic Competition* (Cambridge: Harvard University Press, 1933), Appendix C.

price of $0P_1$ is set and $0Q_1$ units are sold. A therefore produces $\frac{1}{2}$ of $0Q_1$, leaving the other $\frac{1}{2}$ of $0Q_1$ to B. Since B is presently producing $Q_1Q_2 = \frac{1}{2}0Q_1$, a stable solution is obtained. This is collusion without communication. Thus, each duopolist not only has to be smart, but also has to believe that the other firm is smart and that the other firm believes the first is smart and so forth. If the cost curves or bargaining abilities are not exactly the same for each duopolist, some split other than 50-50 will result.

Sweezy's Kinked Demand Curve Model

A model of stable oligopoly prices that continues to be popular in economics textbooks is Paul Sweezy's "kinked" demand curve theory.[12] This is surprising in light of Stigler's devastating attack on both the theoretical and the empirical foundations of this theory.[13] The kinked demand curve model can be thought of as one demonstrating either independent action or tacit collusion. It explains how prices tend to remain rigid in a mature oligopolistic group. It assumes the current price (or cluster of prices if there is product differentiation) has already been determined. Once this conventional price is known, the theory indicates why it is not likely to change. This model does not, however, explain how this original price was arrived at, i.e., where the kink occurs.

The theory attempts to explain the pattern of business attitudes that would lead a firm to maintain fairly rigid prices. Suppose duopolists I and J are rivals in a given market. Firm I speculates on what the likely reaction of its rival will be to a change in price. One possibility is that rival J will match any price changes I initiates. This means I can only gain or lose sales from other industries, not from J, since I's and J's relative prices remain the same. This is illustrated in Figure 15–4(a), which depicts I's demand curve, which is relatively inelastic because I assumes that J will match all price changes initiated by I. Alternatively, if duopolist I assumes that J will ignore I's price setting, I's demand curve will be more elastic since changes in sales volume will be the result of J's changes in sales as well as from other industries. This is seen in Figure 15–4(b).

Now the question becomes: Which is the most likely possibility? Under certain assumptions, the answer is likely to be some combination of these two demand curves. The kinked demand theory assumes that each oligopolist expects rivals to choose the least favorable of the alternatives in response to a price change.

---

[12] Paul Sweezy, "Demand Under Conditions of Oligopoly," *Journal of Political Economy* (August, 1939), pp. 568–573; reprinted in *AEA Readings in Price Theory*, edited by George J. Stigler and Kenneth E. Boulding (Homewood: Richard D. Irwin, 1952), Chapter 20, pp. 404–409.

[13] George J. Stigler, "The Kinky Oligopoly Demand Curve and Rigid Prices," *Journal of Political Economy* (October, 1947), pp. 432–449; reprinted in Stigler and Boulding (eds.), *op. cit.*, Chapter 21, pp. 410–439. Stigler's view was reinforced in a later study by Julian Simon, "A Further Test of the Kinky Oligopoly Demand Curve," *American Economic Review* (December, 1969), pp. 971–975, in which data on business magazines gave no indication that oligopolists change prices less often than do monopolists, as the kinky-demand-curve hypothesis suggests they do.

FIGURE 15–4   Kinked Demand Curve Analysis

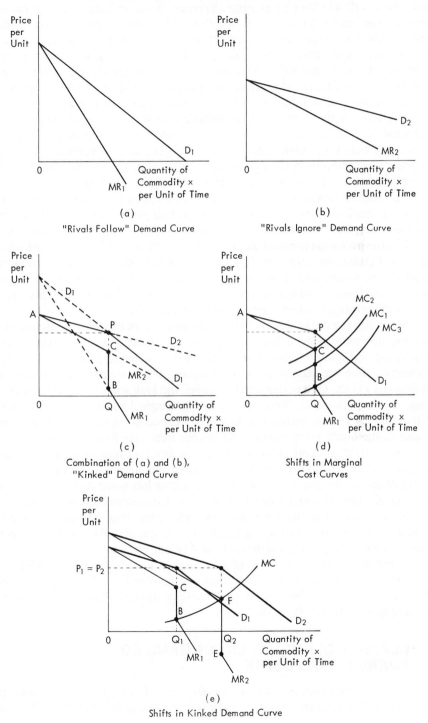

(a)

"Rivals Follow" Demand Curve

(b)

"Rivals Ignore" Demand Curve

(c)

Combination of (a) and (b),
"Kinked" Demand Curve

(d)

Shifts in Marginal
Cost Curves

(e)

Shifts in Kinked Demand Curve

Taking the going market price as PQ in Figure 15–4(c), firm I believes that firm J will: (1) match any price *decrease,* because keeping price constant would mean large sales losses, so that PD_1 and BMR_1 are the relevant demand and marginal revenue curves; and (2) not match any price *increase,* letting firm I price itself partially out of the market, so that AP and AC are the relevant demand and marginal revenue curves. In short, the kinked demand curve and its associated marginal revenue curve are APD_1 and $ACBMR_1$ respectively.

This kinked demand curve is highly elastic above the established price of PQ and less elastic, perhaps even inelastic, below PQ. The odd shape of the marginal revenue curve results from this sharp break in elasticity for prices above and below the going price of PQ. This produces a vertical break, gap, or finite discontinuity in the marginal revenue curve at an output of $0Q$. This is represented by the vertical segment CB in Figure 15–4(c).

The kinked demand curve analysis may explain the price rigidity in oligopolistic markets. The first reason for expecting price inflexibility stems from the cost side. This is illustrated in Figure 15–4(d). If the marginal cost curve is MC_1, the profit-maximizing point of $MC = MR$ would be associated with a price of PQ and an output of $0Q$. But the vertical strip of marginal revenue, labeled CB, means marginal cost can shift anywhere between MC_2 and MC_3 without eliciting a change in the optimum price and quantity. This means price rigidity reigns unless costs change substantially.

Secondly, the entire demand curve can increase or decrease without changing the optimum price if the kink remains near the old price level. This is illustrated in Figure 15–4(e) for an increase in demand from D_1 to D_2. (Alternatively, one can start from D_2 and consider the movement to D_1 a decrease in demand.) If the shift in demand is parallel, the kink will remain at the original price, so that $0P_1 = 0P_2$. Because the firm's marginal cost curve intersects the discontinuous vertical portion of both MR_1 between C and B and MR_2 between F and E, the firm's profit-maximizing output increases from $0Q_1$ to $0Q_2$.

The kinked demand curve's basic prediction that oligopoly price tends to be sticky even when cost and demand fluctuate moderately is consistent with some observed behavior. However, the analysis has some difficulties. It does not explain how the established price level was determined, nor does it tell us why the price is at that level and not some other. It can rationalize firm behavior once we are given some equilibrium price, but the big task of price theory is explaining the formation of equilibrium prices.

There are, in fact, a number of other ways to explain price rigidities. The most powerful is that transaction costs are involved in changing prices and that it is economically feasible to incur these costs only when the price change is large enough to justify them.

CLASS 2 OLIGOPOLIES: ORGANIZED, FORMAL COLLUSION

The classical solutions of Cournot, Bertrand, Edgeworth, etc., assume the firms act independently of one another in spite of the fact that their demands are interdependent. This section deals with explicit, formal, or perfect collusion among firms, and the next section takes up implicit, tacit, or imperfect collusion.

Centralized Cartel

Any collection of oligopolistic producers in a given group (or industry) always has strong incentives to join together into a formal organization to suppress the competitive forces in their particular market. Such a collection of firms, called a *cartel,* acts much like a purely monopolistic firm taking over an industry. Through such an organization, the firms can both increase and make more secure their profits. By reducing the uncertainties and thereby reducing price wars, the firms can have more secure profits. Most importantly, however, acting in concert instead of independently enlarges the firms' total profits.

For the most part, formal collusive arrangements are generally outlawed in the United States. However, tacit collusion has been found with some regularity in American industries, such as steel, paperboard, petroleum, and electrical equipment. The vehicles for promoting such conspiracies are often a trade association, meetings of a professional group, social meetings of all kinds, etc. Many countries outside the United States allow, and even encourage, overt cartels, and as a result the overall level of concentration in such countries is somewhat higher than in the United States.

The analysis of a perfect cartel that maximizes the joint profits of its member firms is identical to the problem of a multiplant monopolist in deciding how to allocate output. The control group in the cartel would want to allocate the group's output so as to minimize the cartel's total cost. This is done by having each firm produce the quantity of output for which its MC_i (marginal cost of the ith firm) equals MC_T and MR_T (where T refers to the total) for the entire group. That is, the cost-minimization and hence joint profit-maximization output calls for:

$$MC_1 = MC_2 = \ldots = MC_n = MC_T = MR_T \qquad \text{(15.1)}$$

The group's MC_T schedule is the horizontal summation of the member firms' MC schedules. In other words, once the joint profit-maximizing output has been determined, each firm's share of this designated production should be determined by the requirement that:

$$MC_1 = MC_2 = MC_3 = \ldots = MC_n \qquad \text{(15.2)}$$

If, e.g., firm 1's MC_1 is less than firm 2's MC_2 for any given level of output, then firm 1 (2) should produce more (less) of the output. Figure 15–5 illustrates the allocation of output among two firms to minimize costs. In this simple case, assume that there are only two duopolists, 1 and 2, and that setting $MR_T = MC_T$ indicates that output $0L$ should be produced. MC_1, which goes from left to right starting at 0, shows the marginal cost of duopolist 1. MC_2, which goes from right to left starting at L, is the marginal cost of duopolist 2. The two marginal cost curves intersect at point M where, if costs are rising (a necessary

**FIGURE 15–5   Cartel Output
Allocation**

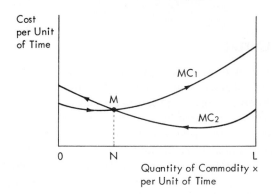

condition), costs are minimized. Duopolist 1 should produce output $0N$ and duopolist 2 output LN to achieve minimum costs. Since total variable cost is the area under the marginal cost curves, the combined output at point M minimizes TVC. Thus, even though duopolist 2 has a lower marginal cost for any given output than duopolist 1, the joint profit-maximizing solution still calls for some output from each.[14]

The centralized cartel makes all the decisions regarding the economic variables — prices, output, profit distribution, etc. But even in this perfect cartel, there are problems. The cartel price, output, and distribution of profits represents a compromise decision among different firms. The interests of these firms may not be identical. For example, some firms may be more interested in the security of profits than others. In addition, fulfillment of condition (15.1) may call for some firms to produce little or perhaps no output. Some firms may be reluctant to enter into any such "rationalization" scheme (i.e., integrated planning of production) with profit-pooling since someday the cartel group may decide the nonproducing group is no longer needed and the firm will be left out in the cold. The mutual distrust among most firms makes it unlikely that they would be willing to stop production entirely. Any firm loses its goodwill, experienced labor force, established marketing channels, etc., by not producing any output over some period of time. Yet in some cases if the highest cost firms do not reduce output substantially or shut down completely, the group's joint profit will be less. (Agreeing to do so has been likened to disarming.)

The difficulties of securing output and profit quotas are such that cartels are almost always imperfect. Any one cartel member has a tremendous incentive to shade its price from the joint profit-maximizing price if it is considered to be parametric and therefore not perceptibly affected by its output decisions.

---

[14] This solution has to be modified if one or more of the firms has falling marginal costs. See Don Patinkin, "Multiple-Plant Firms, Cartels, and Imperfect Competition," *Quarterly Journal of Economics* (February, 1947), pp. 173–205; and Wassily W. Leontief, "Comment," *Quarterly Journal of Economics* (August, 1947), pp. 650–651.

Since any one firm's demand may be quite elastic when all others hold their prices fixed, a cartel member will be strongly tempted to give secret price concessions. If price is above marginal cost, marginal revenue will be only slightly less than price for price cuts by any one member that can secretly violate the agreement. Furthermore, it is difficult to keep the meetings secret. Leaks inevitably develop. It is quite difficult to maintain joint profit-maximizing agreements in countries such as the United States where cartels are generally illegal.

If the precartel division of profits, say, $\frac{1}{3}$ share for each in a three-firm industry, forms the basis for the cartel agreement, all firms can be better off than before. Usually, however, cartel politics as well as economic considerations enter into the exact quota selected. If the pressures are too great for larger output quotas, a joint profit may result that is smaller than the maximizing one.

In general, cartels are more successful in preventing members from cheating: (1) the smaller the number of member firms, (2) the closer to being homogeneous the product, (3) the more geographically concentrated the firms, and (4) the better the business conditions generally. The larger the number of firms in the coalition, the harder it is to police the group for infractions. Since (2) and (3) leave little scope for product differentiation, the chances of cheating are substantially reduced. In prosperity, the incentives for chiseling are substantially reduced. In hard times, stockholder pressure may induce a member to look more to secret price concessions.

Market-Sharing Cartel

A *market-sharing cartel* is a collection of firms for which the centralized control does not determine all the important economic variables. The market-sharing cartel is a much looser grouping than a centralized cartel. In a market-sharing cartel, a joint profit-maximizing position is possible but improbable. Although restrictions are placed on member firms, some decision variables are left with them.

The two general methods of allocating production are by nonprice competition and by quota. In the first case, the cartel sets a minimum price and leaves the quantity sold to the ingenuity of each member firm. The generally similar prices that prevail on haircutting, legal services, medical services, theater tickets, etc., exemplify this. Competition is through nonprice channels entirely: sales promotions and product variation.

Fixing market shares by quotas is probably the most efficient of all methods of combating secret price reductions unless inspection of output is costly or ineffective. If the quota is exceeded, whether by accident or by design, a financial penalty is usually imposed. The financial strength and bargaining ability of member firms are crucial in determining the precise allocation of these shares. A firm's financial and bargaining strength is closely dependent on, among other things, its costs of production. The firm with the lower costs is given more weight lest a price war develop. Nonidentical costs of production

often make the profit-maximizing distribution of market shares harder to determine. If quotas are allocated on the basis of sales in some base period and
if costs change, costs may not be minimized if a shift of output from one firm
to another is necessary.

Instead of dividing the market on the basis of past sales, a cartel sometimes
divides the market geographically to establish a quota. For example, the
Supreme Court ruled in the 1951 *Timken Roller Bearing* case that there was
an allocation of market territories between the dominant American producer
of tapered roller bearings and English and French firms. The French firm was
jointly controlled by the United States (Timken) and British firms.

The above less formal types of colluding agreements are much more common in the United States than perfect cartels for obvious reasons. The rather
surprising thing about these verbal agreements—often called *gentlemen's
agreements*—is that they can lead to less desirable results than if a pure monopolist or perfect cartel were established in that industry. First, the costs may
be higher under a gentlemen's agreement. For instance, suppose there were
four firms, each producing in a separate plant; and these firms were located
as in Figure 15-6. Suppose consumer *A,* through substantial advertising, is
persuaded to buy from firm 2. With a multiplant pure monopoly situation, *A*
would be shipped the product from plant 4. However, if only informal colluding agreements bind these firms, firm 2 must ship the product to consumer *A.*
Thus, economies of scale are sacrificed through wasteful crosshauling. In
addition, considerable amounts are spent on persuasive (noninformational)
advertising and selling costs in general that would not be spent under pure
monopoly.

**FIGURE 15-6   Shipping Distance
Without Cartel**

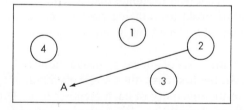

Also, substantial transactions costs are involved in policing and maintaining the industry pricing discipline, which would be done through legal channels
if cartels were permitted. For instance, policing a price agreement would involve an audit of "transaction" prices (which typically differ from "posted" or
"list" prices). Since securing these data is difficult and costly, the basic method
of detecting a price cutter is by observing that the cheating firm is getting business it would not otherwise be expected to obtain. With perfect collusion, no
buyer would change sellers voluntarily. Therefore, price cutting must be in-
ferred from buyer shifts. It is ironic that the government, in the case of sealed
bids, makes the cartel's job of detection easier by revealing the price the

government pays. The federal as well as most state and local governments require that most nonweapon supplies be purchased through sealed competitive bidding. These bids are opened publicly and normally contracts are awarded to the lowest qualified bidder. Any price cutter cannot escape the attention of its rivals. Moreover, any price cutter faces the threat that other buyers will demand similar reductions. As George Stigler once put it, "The system of sealed bids publicly opened with full identification of each bidder's price and specifications, is the ideal instrument for the detection of price cutting."[15] In this case no alternative method of secretly cutting prices exists except bribing purchasing agents. It is not coincidental that many of the antitrust cases in recent years have involved sealed bids to public bodies. In these cases prices have often been higher and less dispersed on public bids than in private negotiations.

Finally, the difficulty of negotiating a gentlemen's agreement may make prices less sensitive to structural changes in demand and supply than would be the case under a pure monopoly. For example, firms may be reluctant to lower prices in response to cost-reducing technological innovation for fear of not being able to reach another mutually satisfactory agreement.

CLASS 3 OLIGOPOLIES: INFORMAL, TACIT COLLUSION

The kinked demand curve and gentlemen's agreement models are also examples of tacit or imperfect collusion. Although we will not repeat the analysis here, we do wish to reemphasize the fragility of any nonbinding collusive agreements. Informal restrictive price-fixing and output-restricting agreements inevitably break down. First and foremost, a strong incentive is created to cut prices clandestinely from the rigged monopoly prices as long as the new price still exceeds marginal cost. As Stigler and others remind us, no one yet has devised a way to advertise price cuts to customers without revealing themselves to the other colluders. Second, the conspirators may have divergent ideas as to the appropriate price levels, market shares, geographical allocation of the markets, etc., and the resulting compromise may over time become increasingly more difficult to live with. The firm that becomes disgruntled over the compromise is often the one that cheats and cuts prices from the agreed level.

Price Leadership Models

Price leadership may arise when one (or several) firms typically initiate price changes and the rest of the firms in the industry follow the declared change. In some cases, e.g., the cigarette and oil industries, the price leader

---

[15] George J. Stigler, *The Organization of Industry* (Homewood: Richard D. Irwin, 1968), p. 44.

may change over time, whereas in other industries the same firm may persistently serve as the price leader. Price leadership may or may not be collusive. This is why it lies in the grey area of American antitrust law. (For example, there is no doubt that price leadership in the cigarette industry during the 1920s and 1930s established a collusive price structure.) In effect, price leadership eliminates any kink in the demand curve for any firm whose prices will be followed in both a downward and an upward direction.

Four separate types of price leadership may be delineated. The price leader may be: (1) the low-cost firm; (2) the dominant firm (in terms of assets, employment, or share of the market); (3) a "barometric" firm; or (4) the smallest firm.

Price Leadership by the Low-Cost Firm. The low-cost firm in a given industry is often allowed to set prices because the other firms know they could be severely hurt financially, if not bankrupted, should an all-out price war develop. Alcoa originally became the aluminum ingot price leader because of its low cost, although it was also the dominant firm in the industry. Figure 15–7 illustrates the case of the low-cost firm serving as the price leader.

Suppose there are two firms in the group producing a homogeneous product for which market demand is shown as *AR*. Further assume that an informal agreement has been made to split the market evenly so that each firm regards its demand curve as *ar* and its marginal revenue as *mr*. Figure 15–7 shows firm 2 as having significantly lower cost curves than firm 1. All else being equal, the high-cost firm 1 would charge price $0P_1$ and sell $0q_1$ units of output to maximize its profits. However, the low-cost firm 2 maximizes its profits by setting a lower price, $0P_2$, and selling $0q_2$ units of output. The high-cost firm follows

FIGURE 15–7 Price Leadership–
Low-Cost Firm

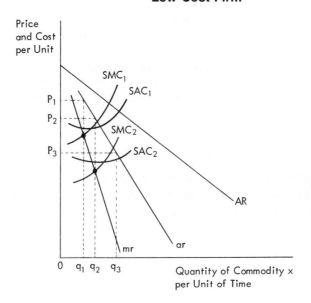

firm 2's price of $0P_2$ for fear that firm 2 might charge a prohibitive price such as $0P_3$.

While firm 2 could charge a price of $0P_3$, earn profits, and eventually eliminate firm 1, it is unlikely to do so. Fear of antitrust proceedings would dictate setting a price that is not prohibitive for a rival. However, the low-cost firm would generally not be willing to split the market evenly, given its substantial cost advantage.

Price Leadership by the Dominant Firm. Another type of tacit collusion that empirically seems to be more relevant than low-cost firm leadership is the so-called "umbrella price leadership" in which the dominant firm—controlling perhaps 25 percent or more of total industry output—sets a price that maximizes its profits and then allows the smaller firms in the industry to sell all they wish at that price. This dominant firm price leadership has been in evidence at one time or another in the virgin aluminum (Alcoa), cigarette (American and Reynolds), petroleum (Standard Oil), rayon (American Viscose), tin can (American Can and Continental Can), and farm tractor and cultivator (International Harvester) industries. The dominant firm's motive for such a leadership agreement is often fear of antitrust legislation. A large number of firms apparently make a group look more competitive to antitrust enforcers. On the other hand, the followers' prime motive for allowing the giant firm to set prices is usually fear of the big firm, although convenience is sometimes considered.

In the example of dominant firm price leadership depicted in Figure 15–8, the dominant firm is about the same size as the sum of all the small firms collectively. The small firms accept the price set by the dominant firm as given; hence, they behave as though they were competitors. Viewing their demand

**FIGURE 15–8   Price Leadership—
Dominant Firm**

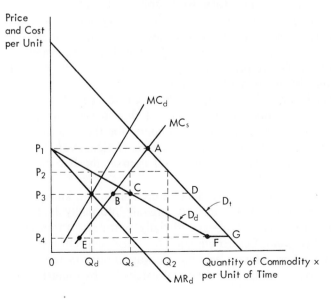

curves as horizontal lines at the price set by the dominant firm, the small firms produce that quantity at which $P = MC$. This means the MC curves of the small firms are thus supply curves and MC_s represents a horizontal summation of the MC curves of the small firms. The demand curve of the dominant firm, D_d, can be derived by taking the horizontal difference at any price between the total market demand, D_t, and the amount supplied by the small firms.

To show how D_d is derived, suppose the dominant firm sets the price at $0P_1$. At this price or higher, the small firms would fulfill the entire market demand; they would sell P_1A units at price $0P_1$. This gives us one point on D_d, namely at $0P_1$, where the quantity demanded for the output of the dominant firm is zero. If a price of $0P_3$ were set, the small firms would sell P_3B units, and the dominant firm would sell $BD = P_3C$ units of output. At a price of $0P_4$, small firms would sell P_4E units, whereas the dominant firm would sell $P_4G - P_4E = EG = P_4F$. This process can be repeated for all prices. If the small firms' MC_s curves cut the minimum point on the AVC curve at point E, the small firms would drop out of the market for a price below $0P_4$, leaving the total demand to the dominant firm. Thus, the dominant firm's demand curve, D_d, is P_1FGD_t and its marginal revenue is MR_d. To maximize profits, the firm sets a price of $0P_2$ and sells $0Q_d$ units of output where $MR_d = MC_d$. At this price the small firms sell $0Q_s$ units, and $0Q_d + 0Q_s = 0Q_2$.

This model, as well as the low-cost price leadership model, can take many different forms depending on the exact assumptions made. How many (dominant, small, total) firms are there? Is there product differentiation? Are there geographical differences between sellers? Are costs the same? While the results might change depending upon how each of the above questions is answered, the final solution would not differ significantly from that depicted in Figure 15–8.

Barometric Price Leadership. In some cases a firm is permitted to serve as a price leader because historically its pricing policy has been considered propitious. It is not a dominant or a low-cost firm, but merely one that it is customary or convenient to follow. Presumably a barometric price leader differs from a collusive price leader in that it does not set prices at the monopoly level, but this is not a watertight distinction.

Barometric price leadership works because in such markets, agreement among the firms is often more important than what they agree on. That is, firms will sacrifice their individual opinions for the sake of agreement. This makes the existence of some kind of customary signal very important; so once it gets started, it tends to continue. Of course, the barometric price leader is not always followed.

While barometric price leaders often only make known through formal price lists conditions which already prevail informally in the industry, this leadership pattern is not always socially harmless. Price leaders such as Standard Oil of Ohio, Bethlehem and U.S. Steel, and Du Pont have at various times influenced price levels, leading the way to price increases and discouraging further price cutting. The intent of ostensible barometric price leadership often is identical to that of collusive price leadership—maximization of joint industry profits. The copper, hard surface floor covering, paper, petroleum, rayon, and yarn industries have had barometric price leadership at certain times. In the copper, rayon, and hard surface floor covering industries, the identity of the barometric price leader has changed over time. Each of the "Big Three" in copper, Anaconda, Kennecott, and Phelps Dodge, have exercised price leadership at some time.

Small Firm Price Leadership. In some cases, one of the smaller firms can serve as the price leader. In particular, if all the firms have close to the same capacity, this form of price leadership may occur.[16] For example, the least fortunate or smallest firm may set the price for the retail gasoline group. The relative persistency of cut-rate gasoline in some centers suggests this type of behavior is not as uncommon as one might think. The larger firms follow price cuts by the small firm even though they prefer higher prices. The firms with the smallest share of the market would be hit hardest by a price increase. As a result, the small firms continue to charge lower prices than the large firms would like. Put differently, the large firms have the most to lose in a prolonged price war since their absolute share of the market is greatest. They therefore follow the small firms and shade prices below their profit-maximizing levels, but not below the small firms' price. The big firms do not want to precipitate a costly price war in which they either stand to lose some of their share of the market or force some smaller firms to leave the field and thus invite antitrust action.

Effective Price Leadership

Professor Jesse Markham compiled the following list of structural group characteristics that are most likely to provide quasi-monopoly results or what he calls "effective price leadership":[17] (1) There should be a few large firms that recognize their mutual interdependence. (2) There must be fairly substantial barriers to entry so a profitable price may be set. (3) The products must be sufficiently similar so that there is mutual interdependence. (4) The price elasticity of demand should not be highly elastic, or price cutting is too rewarding. (5) The cost curves should be similar, or the firms will find their respective profit-maximizing prices too divergent to permit a workable compromise.

Really successful price leaders have four time-tested tactics: (1) They minimize the size of price changes.[18] (2) They change price only if there is a significant change in cost and/or demand that is recognized throughout the industry.

---

[16] A good discussion of this case can be found in Kenneth E. Boulding, *Economic Analysis* (3d ed.; New York: Harper & Row, Publishers, 1955), pp. 644–645.

[17] Jesse W. Markham, "The Nature and Significance of Price Leadership," *American Economic Review* (December, 1951), pp. 891–905.

[18] It is worth repeating that price rigidity is not always socially harmful. There is a tradeoff between the information transmission costs of price changes and the malallocative costs of price stability. Anytime prices are changed, there are administrative costs, publication costs, and dissemination costs for the firm and there are assimilation costs for the marketers and customers.

(3) They direct public attention to any change in cost and to a lesser extent to any change in demand. (4) They are able to punish nonfollowers.

The U.S. Supreme Court considered the legality of price leadership in cases involving U.S. Steel and International Harvester, and in general it concluded that a well-established system of leadership is an important instrument facilitating tacitly collusive pricing behavior. In simple terms, the Court ruled that as long as all firms exercise their own independent judgment in choosing to follow or not follow a leader, they were not likely to be found guilty of an antitrust violation.

In the words of a leading authority in industrial organization, "the effect of both collusive and barometric price leadership in oligopoly tends to be the establishment of prices higher than they would otherwise be, other things being held equal."[19] This conclusion is drawn in full recognition of two important exceptions to this generalization. In some industries, such as primary aluminum, the leader may have lower costs and therefore may set a lower price than other firms desire. Secondly, strong price leaders may sometimes resist raising prices to the short-run maximization point during a boom to maximize long-run profits, avoid possible antitrust litigation, discourage entry, or simply display economic statesmanship. Still, price leadership tends to raise the level and reduce the dispersion of prices on the average.

QUESTIONS

1. What is (are) the major distinction(s) between oligopoly and monopolistic competition? Do you think a range could occur where you couldn't distinguish between the two forms of industrial organization?
2. Discuss the circumstances likely to upset a collusive or cartel arrangement by the firms of an oligopolistic industry.
3. The diagram for the Edgeworth duopoly case is shown on page 331. Describe the price-quantity adjustment process if duopolist F could produce the amount $0F$ (rather than just $0K$) and duopolist E could produce the amount $0E$ (rather than just $0N$). What would happen if F could only produce $0L$ and E could produce only $0M$?
4. In the Hotelling spatial model, the two-firm optimum condition is simple. Once the firms are located in the geographical center of the market, there is no incentive for either to relocate. But what would happen if a third firm decided to enter this market? Where would it locate? What would be the response of the existing firms? What do you think the *final* solution would be?
5. Show the construction of a kinked demand curve (and the associated MR curve) under the assumption that the oligopolist whose demand curve you are drawing thinks that if it raises its price its rivals will be sure to raise their prices as well, but if it lowers its price the rivals will not follow suit.
6. Draw the demand curve (and also the TR and MR curves) for the output of oligopolist B as a function of the relative price of B's product compared to A's price (where A is the firm of question 5). That is, there is some quantity of B's product demanded at the kink (current) price, and the quantity demanded will change as the ratio P_A/P_B

changes. Does this explain why the case presented in question 5 seems to be a very unlikely one?

7. (a) Explain why, if the cartel shown in Figure 15–5 (page 338) is producing at output $0N$, any change in the allocation of production will result in lower profits for the cartel.

   (b) Draw the two marginal cost curves such that all of the output would be allocated to one of the firms and none to the other.

8. (a) In Figure 15–8 (page 343), why does the demand curve for the dominant firm have its intercept at price $0P_1$?

   (b) What further information would be needed to be able to answer this question: What price would drive all small firms out of business?

APPENDIX: MATHEMATICAL NOTES

Note 1. Cournot Model

Let the industry's (inverse) demand function be $p = f(Q)$, where Q represents the industry's output, or $Q = q_i + q_j$ (where q_i and q_j are the outputs of duopolists i and j respectively). Also, let $C_i = C(q_i)$ be the cost function and $R_i = p \cdot q_i$ be the total revenue function of the ith duopolist. (Everything we say for i would be symmetrical for j.) Thus, the total revenue of the ith duopolist depends upon both its output and that of its rival:

$$R_i = f(Q) \cdot q_i \tag{15.3}$$

Since $\pi_i = TR_i - TC_i$, the profits of duopolist i are:

$$\pi_i = f(Q) \cdot q_i - C(q_i) \tag{15.4}$$

The first-order conditions for a maximum require that:

$$\frac{d\pi}{dq_i} = f(Q) + q_i f'(Q) + q_i f'(Q) \frac{dq_j}{dq_i} - C'(q_i) = 0 \tag{15.5}$$

Since Cournot assumed zero "conjectural" variation, $dq_j/dq_i = 0$. This means that since $p = f(Q)$, (15.5) becomes:

$$p + q_i \frac{dp}{dQ} = C'(q_i) \tag{15.6}$$

In economic terms, each duopolist must equate MR to MC. However, the marginal revenues of i and j are not necessarily identical. As (15.6) shows, the one with the larger rate of production will have the smaller marginal revenue.

The second-order conditions merely state that each duopolist's MC must not be decreasing more rapidly than its MR.

Note 2. The Market Shares Model

This duopoly model assumes that duopolist 2 always wants to maintain a fixed share of the market, irrespective of how this affects its short-run profits. This would make sense if the firm is primarily concerned with the long-run advantages of retaining a particular market share. If q_1 and q_2 refer to the quantities sold of duopolist 1 and 2 respectively, and if K is duopolist 2's desired market share, then:

$$\frac{q_2}{q_1 + q_2} = K \tag{15.7}$$

Solving this for q_2 yields the output produced by duopolist 2:

$$q_2 = \frac{Kq_1}{1 - K} \tag{15.8}$$

In determining q_2, firm 2 acts as if firm 1's output is invariant—i.e., $dq_1/dq_2 = 0$. On the other hand, firm 1's conjectural variation from (15.8) is $dq_2/dq_1 = K/(1 - K)$. As long as firm 2 attempts to retain its market share, firm 1's profits may be maximized with respect to only one variable, q_i. If firm 1's demand function is $P_1 = F_1(q_1, q_2)$, then its profit function is:

$$\pi_1 = q_1 F_1(q_1, q_2) - C_1(q_1) \tag{15.9}$$

We can substitute (15.8) into (15.9) to get:

$$\pi_1 = q_1 F_1\left(q_1, \frac{Kq_1}{1 - K}\right) - C_1(q_1) \tag{15.10}$$

This model has a stable equilibrium solution only if: (1) one firm allows the other firm to obtain its desired market share, or (2) both attempt to maintain fixed market shares such that the sum of these shares is unity.

Note 3. Cournot's Cost Theorem

In an interesting but neglected general theorem, Cournot showed that the difference in duopolists' outputs, when asymmetrical cost relations exist, is proportional to the difference in their marginal costs, the factor of proportionality being the reciprocal of the (negative) slope of the market demand curve. With positive costs, the firm equates marginal revenue to marginal cost to maximize profits. That is,

$$p + q_1 \frac{dp}{dq} = \frac{dc_1}{dq_1}, \qquad q_1 \frac{dp}{dq} = \frac{dc_1}{dq_1} - p \tag{15.11}$$

$$p + q_2 \frac{dp}{dq} = \frac{dc_2}{dq_2}, \qquad q_2 \frac{dp}{dq} = \frac{dc_2}{dq_2} - p \tag{15.12}$$

Subtracting (15.12) from (15.11) yields:

$$(q_1 - q_2) \frac{dp}{dq} = \frac{dc_1}{dq_1} - \frac{dc_2}{dq_2} \tag{15.13}$$

or

$$(q_1 - q_2) = \frac{dq}{dp}\left(\frac{dc_1}{dq_1} - \frac{dc_2}{dq_2}\right) \tag{15.14}$$

where p, q_1, and c_1 (p, q_2, and c_2) are the price, quantity, and total cost of the first (second) duopolist.

Since $dq/dp < 0$, the firm with the lower marginal costs will produce the largest output. This theorem is general for all possible shapes of demand and cost and is discussed in Robert L. Bishop's famous unpublished lecture notes.

16 More on Imperfect Markets

In the earlier chapters on pure competition, we concluded that, subject to certain provisos, pure competition results in an efficient allocation of resources. This means a number of things: consumers get the products they desire at the lowest average costs possible with zero profit; inefficient, high-cost firms are driven out of business, for the most efficient and cheapest combination of resources and technology must always be employed; and technological improvements and cost reductions are encouraged. This chapter will compare the results under imperfect competition with those under pure competition on these and other points.

The allocation of resources under monopoly is not optimal in that consumer satisfaction is not at a maximum. This is always true when price exceeds marginal cost. The price measures the marginal satisfaction consumers receive from commodity x; the cost measures the marginal sacrifice of other goods used in the production of x. The utility of commodity x to consumers exceeds the utility of the other goods that could be produced with these same resources. Since the additional production of x would result in greater satisfaction than is given up by reducing output elsewhere, the equimarginal principle indicates that more x should be produced. Too few resources are being devoted to the production of x. In fact, monopoly generally results in underproduction and overpricing of the monopolized commodity.

Competitive conditions, in contrast, offer the consumer greater production, a lower price, greater total utility, and more productive employment. Under competition, price is driven down to the level of costs. Under monopoly, output is lower, price is higher, employment in the x industry is lower, and price exceeds costs. Even if profits do not exist, the rest of the undesirable effects nonetheless hold. Monopoly results in a misallocation of resources even when no profits are earned! Of course, comparisons such as those made here can be made only if the costs of production in the monopoly firm are the same as for the competitive firm. To the extent that costs can be lower because of large scale, and large scale results in monopoly, no such conclusions can be reached.

RESULTS ASSUMING THE MONOPOLIST HAS LOWER COSTS

Figure 16-1 shows the comparison of the competitive and the monopolistic case, where monopoly costs are lower. The competitive costs are shown as the summation of the marginal cost curves (ΣMC_c) of the firms in the industry. In this circumstance the monopoly price is higher and the output lower

FIGURE 16-1 Monopoly vs. Competition

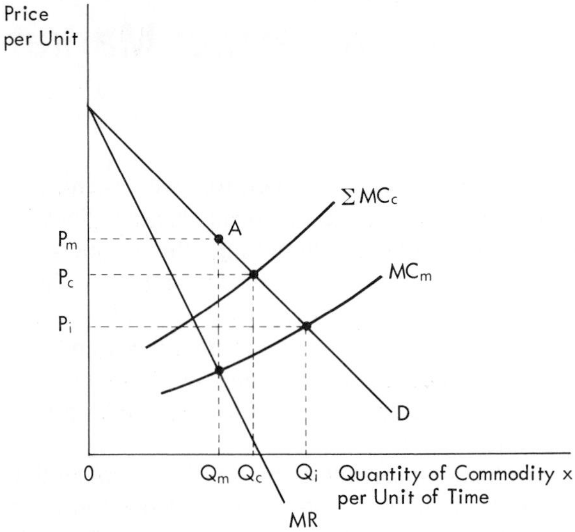

than for the significantly higher cost competitive firms. The ΣMC_c curve would have to be above point A for the competitive price to be higher and the quantity of x produced and sold to be lower under competition.

Suppose the cost difference is great enough that the monopolist's price is lower than the competitor's. Even though the consumer would be paying a lower price in that case, this would still not represent an optimal allocation of society's scarce resources. The consumer would still pay a price for commodity x that exceeds its marginal cost. The consumer's marginal satisfaction would still be greater than the marginal sacrifice. Clearly, the consumer would be better off if more units of x and fewer units of other commodities were produced by transferring resources from the production of other commodities to the production of x. We have thus established a general welfare principle. An optimal allocation of resources requires that the price of a commodity be equal to the marginal cost of producing that commodity. Whenever the price of a commodity exceeds marginal cost, too little of that commodity is being produced. The ideal solution in Figure 16-1 would be for price to be $0P_i$ and output $0Q_i$.

SUMMARY OF THE ECONOMIC EFFECTS OF IMPERFECT COMPETITION

The above description of the results achieved under monopoly as compared with pure competition is fairly accurate although incomplete. The reason we say "fairly" accurate is that, by necessity in such a terse treatment of a complex phenomenon, a number of the important qualifications must be left out. In the next several pages we attempt to remedy this by providing a more systematic development of the likely economic (and to a lesser extent the non-economic) effects of monopoly.

The Monopolist Has a Price Policy

Under pure competition, each price is determined or "set" by the free play of the impersonal market forces of supply and demand, with no one seller having any significant influence. Each seller accepts the price as given and decides how much to produce and sell. In contrast, the seller in imperfect competition sets the price, and buyers determine the quantity that will be sold.

Higher Prices and Lower Output Under Monopoly Conditions

To maximize profits, each firm equates its MR and MC. But under monopoly, $MR < P$ because of the downsloping demand curve for the monopolist's product; whereas under competition, $MR = P$. Hence, constant or rising MC becomes equal to MR at a smaller output under monopoly than under competition. One result of monopoly, then, is the tendency for output to be artificially restricted below the socially optimum level. In fact, regardless of the cost conditions, it will always pay monopolists to restrict output below and raise price above the competitive level if the industry demand curve is downsloping. By how much monopoly price exceeds and monopoly output falls short of competitive levels depends on the elasticity of demand (η). In general, the greater the η, the closer P is to MR and hence to MC, and vice versa.

A problem to enforcers of antitrust laws is reaching a balance between industrial concentration and productive efficiency. If up to a point bigness is necessary to attain low costs, and if, as bigness increases, the danger of lessened competition increases, an obvious social dilemma exists. If the goal is to obtain the lowest cost output, competition is excluded; if it is to realize the efficiency condition of equality between P and MC, monopoly is excluded. Happily, a number of empirical studies suggest that the minimum efficient size in most industries is sufficiently small that this dilemma is not a serious one.[1] Put differently, there is considerably more industrial concentration of sellers in our society than can be justified by scale economies.

Criticisms of Profit Maximization Assumption

There are three groups of criticisms that have been raised against economists' traditional assumption of profit maximization:[2] (1) Entrepreneurs do not know or do not use the information required in the marginal analysis. (2) A

---

[1] The seminal work is by Joe S. Bain, *Barriers to New Competition; Their Character and Consequences in Manufacturing Industries* (Cambridge: Harvard University Press, 1956). Also see Leonard W. Weiss, "The Survival Technique and the Extent of Suboptimal Capacity," *Journal of Political Economy* (June, 1964), pp. 246–261.

[2] See Richard G. Lipsey and Peter O. Steiner, *Economics* (New York: Harper & Row, Publishers, 1966), Chapter 30, pp. 329–337.

realistic model of the firm cannot assume that decision making is done independent of the particular individuals and type of organization making up the production unit. (3) Firms may not try to maximize profits.

Firms Lack Information. This group of critics maintains that firms could not behave the way theory says because of ignorance. For instance, they argue that most business people have never heard of *MC* or *MR;* but this objection is spurious on two counts. First, a model's usefulness does not depend on the realism of its assumptions in describing the "real world" accurately, but on its ability to predict the behavior of the individual or group under investigation. Secondly, the *MC = MR* rule is not purported to be an accurate description of how the firm goes about maximizing its profits. The business may approximately reach profit maximization by a number of different means – luck, experience, hunch, careful planning, etc. The *MC* and *MR* concepts are just tools economists use to explain this process.

Further, these critics argue that even if the decision maker is in fact familiar with the concepts of *MC* and *MR,* the imperfectness of the data available would make it virtually impossible to act as a profit maximizer. In short, data collecting is costly, time consuming, and usually done for accounting and not economic analysis.

A Firm's Organization Is Relevant. This group of critics argues that different kinds of organizations decide issues differently.[3] Some of the predictions of organization theory differ from those of profit-maximization theory. For example, organization theory predicts a positive correlation between firm size and conservatism in the sense of avoiding large risks. But once again, in all fairness, it must be stated that the evidence supporting the newer organization theory is scanty and desultory. It is better to regard organization theory as largely untested rather than wrong. Since it takes a reasonably well-tested theory to replace another reasonably well-tested theory, the older approach remains.[4]

Firms May Not Try To Maximize Profits. The group of critics that argue that firms do not, for various reasons, actively seek or even desire to maximize profits probably have made the most telling arguments that have been made against the traditional theory to date. Of course, the theories all recognize that some minimal level of profits is necessary for the firm to continue production indefinitely. But once that minimal goal has been attained, the firm may seek a number of other objectives.

---

[3] Probably the most publicized of the organization theories is that of R. M. Cyert and J. G. March, *A Behavioral Theory of the Firm* (Englewood Cliffs: Prentice-Hall, 1963).

[4] Of course, if the profit-maximization theory were largely untested, it would only take another largely untested theory to replace it.

Utility Maximization.[5] In place of profit maximization, it is possible to develop a more general theory of the firm — *utility maximization* — that recognizes nonprofit goals. The decision maker is assumed to act as if trying to maximize a multivariate preference function, given certain restraints. The analysis involves a constrained-maximization problem including many desirable aspects: high profits, large and expanding sales, growing market share, favorable price-earnings ratio of the stock, good liquidity position, job security, salary and stock options, good industrial relations, support of charities, acknowledged innovation leadership, leisure, control, etc. This utility index approach makes the theory of the firm analogous with the theory of consumer choice.

The utility-maximization approach recognizes that imperfect competition may have significant nonpecuniary advantages. It is entirely possible, for instance, that monopoly creates a calmer, less hectic life in the business world. And many feel that saving people's nerves by holding competition at arm's length may be more beneficial to society than an extra amount of goods and services "enjoyed" by the families of heart attack victims. Certainly, many people in the British economy — which has long tolerated and perhaps even encouraged a higher role of industrial concentration than in the United States — feel this way.

The various theories of the firm may be complementary rather than competing. If the firm has a number of important motives or priorities, a theory such as profit maximization that emphasizes only one may eventually be found to be inconsistent with the empirical evidence. As yet, however, no complex theory of the firm that can handle all or even a significant number of the motivating influences has been devised. Put differently, the utility-index theory is so general and flexible that to date no meaningful and testable hypotheses have come out of it. In addition, the organization theorists would question the notion of a well-ordered set of preferences for the large and complex firms of today. Therefore, it is still useful to examine the monistic theories.

Satisficing. Professor Herbert Simon has developed a theory which emphasizes that monopolists may prefer not to exert all the effort necessary to obtain the absolute maximum profits.[6] They may prefer the quiet life and may be happy *satisficing* — achieving a certain minimum level of profits, share of the market, or level of sales. Once the minimal rate of profit is achieved, any number of outcomes are possible. There is no unique optimum point as with the profit-maximizing model.

---

[5] See, e.g., Kenneth E. Boulding, *Economic Analysis* (3d ed.; New York: Harper & Row, Publishers, 1955), especially pp. 791–792. The analysis was first developed by Tibor Scitovsky, "A Note on Profit Maximization and Its Implications," *Review of Economic Studies*, No. 1 (1943), pp. 57–60; reprinted in *Readings in Price Theory*, edited by George J. Stigler and Kenneth E. Boulding (Homewood: Richard D. Irwin, 1952), Ch. 17, pp. 357–358. Also see Jose Encarnacion, Jr., "Constraints and the Firm's Utility Function," *Review of Economic Studies* (April, 1964), pp. 113–120.

[6] Herbert A. Simon, "Theories of Decision-Making in Economics," *American Economic Review* (June, 1949), pp. 253–283.

To become useful, the theory has to be testable. This requires a more careful specification of these minimum levels than has been attempted heretofore. The casual empiricism utilized by most proponents of this approach is not convincing. For instance, proponents argued that automobile manufacturers immediately after the Second World War were satisfied with their high profits and charged prices for new cars that were lower than those on used cars. However, the automobile manufacturers' behavior could be explained in a number of other ways, utilizing other theories: fear of attracting competitors, fear of public criticism, long-run profit maximization, etc.

Target Pricing. Quite similar to the satisficing theory is the *target pricing* theory associated with a study by Robert F. Lanzillotti.[7] While he concluded no single hypothesis was applicable to all 20 large firms examined, long-run goals seemed more important than short-run considerations. Although the pricing goals included such things as maintenance of a fixed share (American Can Company), the firms particularly stressed pricing according to a fixed or "target" return on investment (e.g., 20 percent for General Motors). Lanzillotti readily admitted the need for more definitive empirical research before the target theory could be considered more than an interesting speculation. However, the research has not yet been done.

Constrained Sales Revenue Maximization. Of all the newer theories of the firm, perhaps the most interesting — since it contains implications or predictions clearly different from those of profit-maximization theory and hence is testable — is William J. Baumol's constrained sales maximization (*CSM*) model.[8] This thesis rests on the separation of ownership and management in large firms. He claims that all the managers in certain monopolistic markets need do is earn some minimum level of profits to keep the stockholders satisfied; after that, they may pursue other goals.[9] While Baumol offers no precise, unambiguous definition of the minimum acceptable profit, clearly it would not be the same in all firms, in all industries, or in all phases of the business cycle. The theoretical presentation of his model only requires that this minimum level be less than maximal profits. Although sales maximization is sometimes consistent with (long-run) profit maximization — declining sales may mean more difficulty in bank financing, a loss of distributors and dealers, greater difficulty

---

[7] Robert F. Lanzillotti, "Pricing Objectives in Large Companies," *American Economic Review* (Dec., 1958), pp. 921–940. Also see A. D. H. Kaplan, Joel B. Dirlam, and Robert F. Lanzillotti, *Pricing in Big Business: A Case Approach* (Washington: The Brookings Institution, 1958). John M. Blair, *Economic Concentration; Structure, Behavior, and Public Policy* (New York: Harcourt, Brace & World, 1972), Ch. 18, pp. 467–497, attempts some crude testing of the target pricing thesis.

[8] The latest version of which is contained in William J. Baumol, *Business Behavior, Value and Growth* (rev. ed.; New York: Harcourt, Brace & World, 1967). In this edition his model is dynamicized to include the rate of growth of sales as the dominant motive. Since the other version of his theory has received considerably more attention, the text deals only with it.

[9] The Baumol thesis applies only to noncollusive, explicitly independent, imperfectly competitive firms, including all pure monopolies and monopolistic competitors (in the short run) and to minor firms in oligopoly.

in attracting and retaining key personnel, etc.—Baumol's thesis argues that firms view dollar sales as an end in itself. Since salary, power, and prestige all vary with the size of the firm as well as with profits, the manager prefers a large, normally profitable company to a small, highly profitable operation. Some empirical evidence supports Baumol's thesis. For example, it has been demonstrated that sales are more important than profits in determining executive salaries.[10]

Baumol's *CSM* thesis is graphically depicted in Figure 16–2. The vertical axis shows *TR*, *TC*, and profit (π), and the horizontal axis shows physical output. The curve labelled π is the profit function. If the firm were a strict profit maximizer, it would produce and sell an output of $0Q_1$, earning $0\pi_1$ profits. On the other hand, if the firm had no minimum profit constraint or if the constraint were not binding (i.e., $0\pi_2 < 0\pi_3$), it would maximize its *TR* by producing at $0Q_3$, earning a profit of $0\pi_3$. However, in the more interesting and

FIGURE 16–2   A Comparison of Constrained Sales Maximization with Unconstrained Profit Maximization

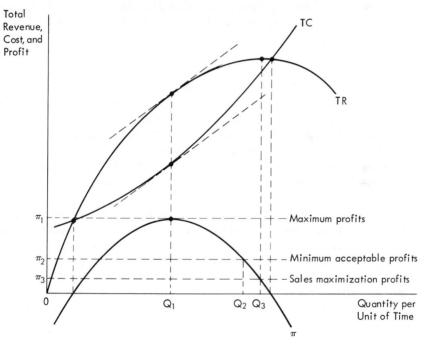

[10] David R. Roberts, *Executive Compensation* (New York: The Free Press of Glencoe, 1959); and Joseph W. McGuire, John S. Y. Chiu, and Alvar O. Elbing, "Executive Incomes, Sales and Profits," *American Economic Review* (September, 1962), pp. 753–761. On the other hand, William C. Pardridge, "Sales or Profit Maximization in Management Capitalism," *Western Economic Journal* (Spring, 1964), pp. 134–141, found no systematic difference between the profit/sales ratios in management controlled and closely held companies, which is not consistent with the *CSM* thesis. Unfortunately, almost all of the empirical studies which have been done to date are marred by statistical problems, e.g., multicollinearity.

no doubt more empirically relevant case where the profit restraint is binding, the CSM firm would sell $0Q_2$, the highest level of production and sales consistent with earning the minimum acceptable profit of $0\pi_2$.[11] In short, the CSM firm always sells more than the profit-maximizing level of output. It also differs from the full-cost pricing models since the decision maker is assumed to make marginal and not rule-of-thumb decisions. Finally, it also differs from most theories of oligopoly, which assume that mutual interdependence of prices is crucial.

The CSM is an interesting alternative theory of the firm since it has implications different from the profit-maximizing model and hence is testable. For instance: (1) An increase (decrease) in fixed costs — e.g., resulting from a lump-sum or profit tax — would cause a CSM firm to decrease (increase) output, whereas a profit maximizer's output would in general be unaffected. A rise in fixed costs reduces π and causes the minimal profit line to cut the π curve at a smaller optimum output and implies a higher price. (2) Sales costs (including advertising expenditures) or nonprice competition outlays in general would be greater for the CSM firm since they have the effect of enlarging sales. (3) MR for the CSM firms is generally less than MC, and price may be below MC if demand is sufficiently elastic. (4) The optimal output and optimal price for a CSM firm are closer to the socially desirable levels than are those of a profit-maximizing monopolist.[12]

Long-Run Profit Maximization.
Many of the problems that have puzzled critics of profit maximization may be resolved by arguing that firms do not maximize profits day-to-day, but on a long-run basis. For instance, the reluctance of some firms to raise prices and hence profits during short-run periods of excess demand may stem from their desire to maximize long-run profits. This may entail restraining short-run profits in the hope of not attracting rivals into the industry or avoiding public criticism, which could include antitrust action.

The difficulty with this approach is that it is tempting to make it tautological and consistent with any sort of behavior. Anytime a firm is not maximizing profits for some time period, one can argue that the relevant time span is some other, longer time period. Until the theory is able to provide a concrete and testable definition of "long-run profits," it will not be a very useful approach. The most promising approach is to postulate the firm's objective function to be the maximization of the value of the firm's ownership. Thus, the time frame is infinity.

---

[11] Although, for simplicity, we have made no distinction here, it can make a difference whether the firm is a constrained sales maximizer or a constrained output maximizer. See Milton Z. Kafoglis, "Output of the Restrained Firm," *American Economic Review* (September, 1969), pp. 583–589.

[12] In fact, both constrained-revenue and constrained-output maximizers will have lower prices and larger outputs than profit-maximizing firms. The output of the latter will be smaller than (the same as) that of the former if $\eta < 1$ ($\eta > 1$) in the range of the constraint. However, both the constrained-revenue and constrained-output maximizers can attain non-Pareto optimal prices and output whether costs are constant, decreasing, or increasing. See Kafoglis, *op. cit.*

Separation of Ownership and Control. It is noteworthy that the non-profit-maximization theories of the firm center on the fact that in today's corporate world, ownership and control are separate. The managers or decision makers in the firm are not generally the owners. Control is in the hands of professional managers. While in rare instances stockholders can force out the managers by vote and perhaps even bring suit against them, in general stockholders can discipline managers only by their decision to invest or not to invest in the firm. If the aggregate decision is negative, the price of the stock will fall. The fact that ownership is divorced from control would not change anything if the desires of owners and managers were identical. But some claim that managers pursue goals that are not consistent with profit maximization. However, the empirical evidence that has been accumulated on the performance—particularly with respect to profits and dividends—of owner-controlled versus manager-controlled firms over the last few years has not provided support for this allegation.[13] For instance, some studies have found that the type of control—i.e., owner versus manager—was not a statistically significant variable in the determination of profit rates among the larger firms in our economy.[14]

Some Additional Theories of the Firm. While the above alternative theories of the firm cover most of the more prominent hypotheses, there are others. Some are merely variants of the profit-maximizing theory; others are more hostile to the traditional approach. For instance, one writer stresses that profit maximization takes different forms depending on who really runs the company: a management-controlled firm tries to maximize retained earnings, whereas the stockholder-controlled firm tries to maximize dividends.[15] Gerhard Tintner, *et al.*, recognized that other features of the probability distribution of profits besides the mathematical expectation—such as dispersion, kurtosis, and skewness—are important.[16] Still others, such as K. W. Rothschild, emphasize the firm's desire for security or secure profits.[17]

Other writers drop the notion of profit maximization altogether. Kenneth E. Boulding, for example, advocates a "balance-sheet homeostasis" theory of the firm in which management attempts to maintain some desired set of accounting ratios.[18] Finally, there are the "managerial discretion" theories

---

[13] The studies are surveyed in David R. Kamerschen. "Further Thoughts on Separation of Ownership and Control." *Rivistia Internazionale di Scienze Economiche e Commerciali* (February, 1973), pp. 179–183.

[14] See, for example. David R. Kamerschen. "The Influence of Ownership and Control on Profit Rates," *American Economic Review* (June, 1968), pp. 432–447, and *idem*, "Correction," *ibid.* (December, 1968), p. 1376. Also see *idem*, "A Theory of Conglomerate Mergers: Comment," *Quarterly Journal of Economics* (September, 1970), pp. 608–674.

[15] J. R. Wilson, "Maximization and Business Behavior," *Economic Record*, Vol. 28, No. 54 (May, 1952), pp. 29–39.

[16] For example, see Gerhard Tintner, "The Theory of Production Under Non-Static Conditions," *Journal of Political Economy* (October, 1942), pp. 646–667.

[17] K. W. Rothschild, "Price Theory and Oligopoly," *Economic Journal*, Vol. LVII (1947), pp. 299–320, reprinted in *Readings in Price Theory*, edited by George J. Stigler and Kenneth E. Boulding (Homewood: Richard D. Irwin, 1952), Ch. 22, pp. 440–464.

[18] Kenneth E. Boulding, *Reconstruction of Economics* (New York: John Wiley & Sons, 1950).

of oligopoly—e.g., Williamson and others emphasize management expense preferences and emoluments, especially staff expenditures of various kinds.[19]

Despite the attractiveness of some of the non-profit-maximization theories, the assumption of profit maximization or more generally maximization of the present value of the firm is taken as valid in this text.[20]

> No economist would deny that all entrepreneurs are subject also to other desires that may conflict with profit maximization, nor even that some of these other forces may be widespread and important. Rather, the position is that profit maximization is the strongest, the most universal, and the most persistent of the forces governing entrepreneurial behavior. This is a judgment based upon wide observation of entrepreneurs under innumerable sets of conditions: of the need for profit incentives to obtain maximum output even in war; of the enormous risks and the monotonous toil that are incurred because of the prospects of profits; and especially, from the success of predictions based on this assumption. . . . If, for example, an undefined and unmeasured "sense of fairness" is put into the theory of the firm, we can no longer predict anything the firm will do. With a rise in wage rates, for example, the firm may restrict output at the ruling price to maximize profits, or it may leave output unchanged to avoid discharging workers, or it may increase output because buyers suffer even more from the wage increase. There is no objection in principle to these alternative goals, but in their presently underdeveloped state they are seldom useful in general analysis. And I would support the controversial position that persistent patterns of entrepreneurial behavior can usually be explained on profit maximizing grounds.[21]

Perhaps the best "proof" that profits are still the major concern of the modern corporation is a statement by Alfred Sloan, former head of General Motors—a firm often cited as the example *par excellence* of a business entity vitally concerned with things other than profits. Sloan stated that: "The fundamental concern of a business is to earn a return on its capital."[22] Thus, throughout this textbook we have used maximum profit as the objective function.

The Monopolist Can Earn Profits Even in the Long Run

Profits over and above the amount required to induce firms to stay in business are eliminated in the long run under competition through the entry of new

---

[19] Oliver E. Williamson, *Corporate Control and Business Behavior* (Englewood Cliffs: Prentice-Hall, 1970). See his extensive "Bibliography," pp. 182–190, for further citations on many of the non-profit-maximization theories.

[20] The present value of the firm is the discounted value of it's future income stream. We need to know the interest rate to evaluate these streams. For instance, a three-year profit stream returning $100, $200, and $50 has a discounted value that is larger, smaller, or equal to one of $100, $50, and $220, depending on the interest rate. The first profit stream is more valuable at higher interest rates, e.g., rates of 15, 20, and 25 percent; the second stream, at low interest rates, e.g., 1, 5, and 10 percent; and they have the same present value at an interest rate of 13.3 percent.

[21] George J. Stigler, *Theory of Price* (rev. ed.; New York: Macmillan Co., 1952), p. 149. He hastens to add, however, that the broad tautological definition of profits which includes every conceivable motive is not useful.

[22] Alfred Sloan, *My Years with General Motors,* edited by John McDonald and Catharine Stevens (New York: Doubleday & Co., 1964), p. 61.

firms into any industries enjoying profits. But under monopoly, entry is restricted, and thus the competitive mechanism for eliminating profits is weak or nonexistent. As pointed out earlier, however, such returns to monopoly power would be capitalized, and the rate of return on the value of the monopoly position would be just equivalent to the rates available in other alternatives.

Monopoly Has More Nonprice Competition [23]

There are channels other than price through which the winds of competition can blow: advertising, credit, service, etc. Monopolists try to enlarge sales by changing promotional outlays and product quality. Nonprice competition is emphasized in monopoly because: (1) advertising and quality variations are harder for rivals to match and less likely to get out of hand than price changes; and (2) only monopolists have the financial resources necessary to support large-scale advertising and product development. The majority of American industries seem to be more independent (and less collusive) in their product than in their price policies.

Nonprice competition is not necessarily inferior or less efficient than price competition. Whether price or nonprice competition is more effective rests upon empirical judgment. That is, the rather common belief that price competition is more efficient than nonprice competition is based upon the plausible assumption that marginal production costs rise less rapidly than marginal nonproduction costs, where the latter includes outlays on advertising, product differentiation, and other nonprice variables.

In some cases, product or service standardization is impossible. This is especially true for service industries. Convenience of location is a "built-in" mark of differentiation for establishments in the retail drug, food, gasoline, and laundry lines. Homogeneity would require the same location for all establishments in a given industry. Nor can the differences in ability, personality, and training of, say, brokers, dentists, physicians, and lawyers be eliminated. In other cases, the extra benefits from differentiation exceed the extra costs. So whenever homogeneity and hence pure competition is not feasible because of the impossibility of commodity standardization — or where, even if standardization were possible, the extra advantages of differentiation exceed the extra costs involved — only commodity differentiation and hence monopoly can obtain the ideal resource use.

Monopoly May Reduce the Macroeconomic Flexibility and Stability of the Economy [24]

In a fully competitive market, adjustment to changes in aggregate demand or supply conditions is effected primarily through price changes. But under

---

[23] This and other sections of this chapter draw heavily on David R. Kamerschen, "Recurrent Objections to the Theory of Imperfect Competition," *Zeitschrift für Die Gesamte Staatswissenschaft* (October, 1969), pp. 688–694, which in part is a review article of George J. Stigler's omnibus *The Organization of Industry* (Homewood: Richard D. Irwin, 1968).

[24] Our entire discussion of macroeconomic stability follows the convincing comments of Frederic M. Scherer, "Rigid Prices and Macroeconomic Stability," *Industrial Market Structure and Economic Performance* (Chicago: Rand-McNally & Co., 1970), pp. 304–323.

monopoly, prices tend to become rigid and inflexible in a *downward* direction, with the result that adjustment to change often occurs in output and employment rather than through relative prices.

Suppose, for example, that aggregate demand falls. Regardless of the market structure, output will decline in most industries.[25] But the *degree* of output responses is likely to be greater if the market is monopolistic. In a purely competitive industry, as demand decreases, price responds in the same direction, thereby moderating the decline in the quantity of the good purchased. In a monopolistic industry, to the extent that price is rigid as demand declines, the full impact of the decline in demand is absorbed by the contraction of output.

The alleged rigidity of monopolistic prices also supposedly damages an economy's macroeconomic stability, including aggregate employment, aggregate consumption, and aggregate investment. In its crudest form, this argument is specious. The most common fallacy is the idea that monopoly always causes macroeconomic unemployment because it restricts output. The fallacy is in the implicit assumption that the freed resources are unemployed. It is entirely possible through the intelligent application of monetary and fiscal policy correctives that an economy could have full employment even if the entire economy was monopolistic. Aggregate unemployment need not result from the restriction of output and employment by individual monopolists. We know of no empirical evidence that concentration has a systematic impact on the cyclical behavior of employment stability.[26]

The Monopolist's Response to a Change in Demand

Because a monopolist does not have a supply curve in the conventional sense, the purely competitive conclusions with respect to a shift in demand do not necessarily hold for a monopolist. Take the case of an increase in demand in response to enhanced taste for the commodity. The normal short-run response in pure competition and the most likely response in monopoly is for price and quantity to increase. Even in the long run with constant- or decreasing-cost industries, quantity will rise although price may not. For a monopolist, we can make only the trivial prediction that both price and quantity cannot fall as demand increases. From the very definition of an increase in demand, it is impossible for both the new price and quantity to be lower than the old price and quantity. In short, on logical considerations, when demand shifts we can predict virtually nothing under monopoly. As an empirical matter, it is perhaps not unreasonable to expect that in a large number of cases the general direction of the monopolist's reaction in price and quantity will be similar to the pure competitor's reaction.

---

[25] The exceptional cases are noted in the following section.
[26] Richard Selden and Horace de Podwin, "Business Pricing Policies and Inflation," *Journal of Political Economy* (April, 1963), pp. 309–314.

Monopoly Prices and Quantities Relative to a Change in Costs

Under any type of market structure, with normal elasticities of demand and supply, a decline in costs will lead to an increase in output and a fall in price. This means any technological innovation or decrease in some kinds of taxes that lowers MC will, to some extent at least, be passed on to the consumers in the form of a lower price. However, for any given decrease in MC, the monopolist's price (quantity) will fall (rise) less than will a competitor's. This is illustrated in Figure 16–3. The decrease in costs from MC_1 to MC_2 produces a decrease in price from P_{c1} to P_{c2} and an increase in quantity of $Q_{c1}Q_{c2}$ for the competitor since these marginal cost curves are the firm's supply curves. In contrast, the identical shift from MC_1 to MC_2 for the monopolist only produces a decline in price of $P_{m1}P_{m2}$ and a rise in quantity of $Q_{m1}Q_{m2}$. Clearly $Q_{c1}Q_{c2} > Q_{m1}Q_{m2}$ and $P_{c1}P_{c2} > P_{m1}P_{m2}$. The competitor moves from point C to point E, whereas the monopolist only moves from point A to point B.

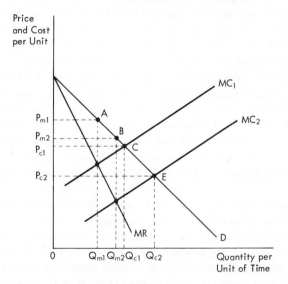

FIGURE 16–3   Comparison of the Responses
of Pure Competitors and
Monopolists to a Change in *MC*

Monopoly May or May Not Be Conducive to Technological Advance and Innovation

Whether monopoly promotes technological progress more than does competition is a hotly debated controversy in economics. Actually, this argument has at least three variants. Various scholars have claimed that: (1) large firms,

(2) more diversified firms, and (3) more monopolistic firms are conditions conducive to technological progress. The evidence suggests that no firm size is uniquely conducive to technological progress. There is apparently room for firms of all sizes. Similarly, there is little empirical support for the belief that diversification spawns successful innovation. In a nutshell, this hypothesis suggests that highly diversified firms are both better able to profit from the unexpected inventions that often flow from R&D expenditures and are more effective in hedging uncertainty and risks.

Some economists believe, and some evidence partially supports their thesis, that monopoly fosters technological improvements—new products, new processes, new production functions. Other economists dispute this conclusion, and some of the evidence partially supports their position. They charge that the research claims are often exaggerated and that trivial or excessive product variation is the result. However, this much is clear: Both the monopolist and the competitor have a short-run incentive to cut costs and therefore increase profits. In contrast, only the monopolist can continue to reap profits in the long run.

Monopoly Prevents the Optimal Allocation of Resources

It should be noted that all discussions of economic efficiency assume that, given the values of our society, the fundamental welfare criterion is maximization of individuals' satisfaction. Given this premise, the argument that monopoly is likely to lead to a misallocation of resources may be easily demonstrated.

Marginal costs are less than price under monopoly. Since prices reflect consumer evaluation of goods and services and marginal costs reflect the social costs of production, it follows that resources are not yielding maximum satisfaction. For example, if $P_x = \$1$ and $MC_x = \$.75$, an additional unit of output of x would socially cost the reduction in output of other goods worth $\$.75$ while adding a dollar's worth of output in the x industry. Total satisfaction would be increased by producing more of x. This again conforms to the earlier conclusion that monopoly artificially restricts output below the socially optimum level.

The general implication is that any form of monopoly would cause a nonoptimum allocation of resources.[27] For a monopolistic firm, MR is less than the price of the commodity it produces. Therefore, in equating MR with MC to maximize profits, an output is produced which has MC less than P. Since individual consumers purchase the good in such quantities as to make the marginal utility (MU) of the good equal to the MU of that amount of money (price) spent on other goods, it follows that the MU of the commodity is greater than the MU of the amount of its MC.

Figure 16–4 provides a graphical illustration of monopoly's malallocative effects. Suppose that the costs of production would be the same regardless of

---

[27] Which, given the values of our society, is measured by the fundamental welfare criterion of the maximization of individuals' satisfaction.

**FIGURE 16–4 Dead-Weight or Welfare Loss
from Monopoly**

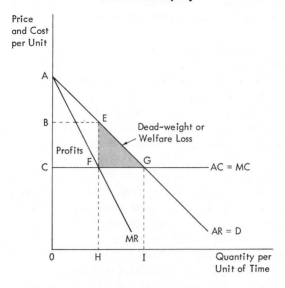

whether the industry were organized as a monopoly or as a competitive group of firms. Further suppose, for simplicity, that marginal and average costs are constant. In the long-run competitive equilibrium, the (Marshallian) consumer surplus is given by the area of triangle ACG (which represents the total utility received from consuming $0I$ units of x minus the total expenditure necessary to acquire $0I$ units of x). The competitive price is $0C$ and the quantity sold is $0I$.

If this industry were to be monopolized, the profit-maximizing price, where $MC = MR$, is $0B$ and the equilibrium quantity is $0H$. The price is now higher and the output lower than under purely competitive conditions.

At the new higher prices and lower quantities, consumers lose to the monopolist part of their consumer surplus, namely, rectangle $BCFE$. Consumers are still left with a surplus equal to triangle ABE. But note that triangle EFG has not been claimed by anyone; indeed it cannot be appropriated since it no longer exists. This is the so-called *dead-weight* or *welfare loss* that results from allocative inefficiency under monopoly. Even if the government were to deprive the monopolist of the entire profit rectangle $BCFE$ through, say, a fixed or lump-sum tax, the inefficiency loss of triangle EFG still remains. This should clearly demonstrate that it is not so much the profits under monopoly that the economist objects to, but the undesirable effects on resource allocation from overpricing and underproducing the product.

Alternatively, it is possible to think of the "welfare" loss in the following way. The MC, measured in terms of alternative outputs sacrificed at output $0H$, is FH. However, the monopolist produces a commodity that consumers value at EH. A one-unit expansion of output would thus increase the community's net income by FE. Additional production would also raise the aggregate income, but by an ever-declining amount up to point G, where $P = MC$. In short, the area of triangle EFG gives an approximate measure of the increase in real income that would result if production were pushed to the competitive level.

Elimination of the underproduction (overpricing) of HI (BC) displayed in Figure 16-4 would take a shift of resources of the magnitude suggested by the area labeled $HFGI$. A shift in resources from competitive to monopolistic industries would enlarge the total monetary value of the output produced with the same given quantity of resources. A logical question then becomes: What is the approximate size of this shift in resources that would be required to do this in our economy? Or better yet, what is the approximate size of the triangle labeled "welfare" losses in the U.S. economy?

Obviously, any attempt to measure the magnitude of the resource misallocation and the consequent loss of "welfare" [28] due to monopoly must serve as only a rough approximation. Some quite stringent, even heroic, assumptions are sometimes necessary to elicit the desired economic information out of the accountant's data. Arnold Harberger made an imaginative attempt to determine the orders of magnitude involved for the U.S. economy, using data on profit rates for 1924–1928.[29] He concluded that the total welfare loss (in 1953 prices) was less than $\frac{1}{10}$ of 1 percent of national income or less than $1.50 per person in the U.S.! In fact, George Stigler remarked that: "If this estimate is correct, economists might serve a more useful purpose if they fought fires or termites instead of monopoly." [30] However, he went on to add that there were a number of reasons for believing the estimate was too low. A more recent study that took account of Stigler's and other objections placed the most likely estimate at roughly 6 percent of national income in the late 1950s–early 1960s.[31] This is a substantially larger figure and accords more with the importance placed on the monopoly problem in our economy. And more recent and refined estimates have put the figure even higher.[32] To be sure, even if the figure were

---

[28] The word "welfare" is in quotation marks since really only the allocative efficiency losses are taken into account.

[29] Arnold C. Harberger, "Monopoly and Resource Allocation," *American Economic Review* (May, 1956), pp. 77–87. His methodology was based on the theoretical ideas of Harold Hotelling.

[30] George J. Stigler, "The Statistics of Monopoly and Merger," *Journal of Political Economy* (February, 1956), pp. 33–40; reprinted in *Readings in Microeconomics*, edited by David R. Kamerschen (New York: John Wiley & Sons, 1969), Ch. 24, pp. 332–343.

[31] David R. Kamerschen, "An Estimation of the 'Welfare' Losses from Monopoly in the American Economy," *Western Economic Journal* (Summer, 1966), pp. 221–237. While Senator Philip Hart and Ralph Nader have made reference to this 6 percent figure, it should only be viewed as a general order of magnitude and not as anything precise. A number of more recent findings or criticisms of these Hotelling-type welfare loss models can be found in David R. Kamerschen, "Monopoly and Welfare," *Zeitschrift fur Nationalokonomie* (December, 1971), pp. 507–510, and David R. Kamerschen and Richard L. Wallace, "The Costs of Monopoly," *Antitrust Bulletin* (Summer, 1972), pp. 485–496.

[32] For example, Thomas R. Saving, "Concentration Ratios, the Degree of Monopoly Power and the Share of the 250 Largest Manufacturing Firms," (unpublished manuscript). A portion of the theoretical part of this paper is published as "Concentration Ratios and the Degree of Monopoly Power," *International Economic Review* (February, 1970), pp. 139–146. This paper is also interesting in that it demonstrates that the traditional measure of monopoly power, the concentration ratio, has a clear relationship to the most acceptable theoretical measure of the degree of monopoly power, the Lerner index.

quite low, it might still be wise to devote substantial attention and resources to monopoly. The loss may be small because of the diligence currently devoted to combating monopoly. Without this, the losses might be considerably larger.

Monopoly Tends To Redistribute Income

If incomes are not fairly evenly divided, the persistent economic profits which monopolistic firms can realize may contribute to greater inequality in income distribution. Since these monopoly profits accrue to the corporate shareholders and corporate executives who largely come from the upper income group, income inequality is increased. Of course, the fact that these gains are not widely distributed cannot necessarily be deemed undesirable. The desirability of a certain distribution depends upon the values of the community as a whole. However, our society generally considers undesirable the extreme degrees of inequality to which at least pure monopoly and oligopoly are likely to contribute. This means the case against monopoly is based on both equity and efficiency grounds. One student of industrial organization put the general issue this way:

> In short, the link between income distribution and concentration is both weak and complex. Economists prefer to leave policy toward income distribution to the field of taxation, which is much better equipped to deal with it directly. This exclusion seems wise.[33]

Monopoly May Be More Discriminatory in Employment

Since Gary Becker's seminal study, *The Economics of Discrimination*,[34] economists have known that there are theoretical reasons for expecting that monopolies have a greater margin for satisfying their tastes for discrimination. Purely competitive firms cannot afford the added costs of such indulgences and survive. Of course, most employers discriminate in employment in that, *ceteris paribus,* they prefer cordial colleagues to curmudgeons, punctual workers to tardy ones, etc. But such discrimination reflects differential productivity. Monopolists may be able to afford the more reprehensible discrimination based on extraneous ethnic, racial, or sexual characteristics in evaluating job applicants and considering promotions. In a recent study, William G. Shepherd, using data compiled by the U. S. Equal Employment Opportunity Commission, found that discrimination in white-collar employment was positively and substantially related to market power.[35] In general, competitive and nonprofit agencies tended to be relatively nondiscriminatory.

---

[33] Richard Caves, *American Industry: Structure, Conduct, Performance* (3d ed.; Englewood Cliffs: Prentice-Hall, 1972), p. 96.

[34] Gary Becker, *The Economics of Discrimination* (Chicago: University of Chicago Press, 1957).

[35] William G. Shepherd, "Market Power and Racial Discrimination in White-Collar Employment," *Antitrust Bulletin* (Spring, 1969), pp. 141–161. Also see his *Market Power and Economic Welfare; An Introduction* (New York: Random House, 1970), Ch. 14, especially pp. 208–222.

Miscellaneous Effects of Monopoly [36]

There are several other possible harmful effects of monopoly. (1) Monopoly may provide social and political power all the way from the local to the international level. Important issues of the day concerning the military-industrial complex, alienation, imperialism, etc., may be linked with market power. Unfortunately, while they may be ultimately the most important effects of monopoly, they are the least provable by statistics. (2) There may be other inefficiencies directly traceable to monopoly, such as: (a) X-inefficiency or organizational slack [37] – the internal inefficiencies resulting from the fact that monopolists have a greater tendency to pay themselves excessive salaries, hire too large a staff, provide lavish office accommodations, engage in empire building by adding unprofitable satellite firms, or support worthwhile community and philanthropic causes – all of which come out of shareholders dividends or consumers pockets in the form of higher prices; (b) malallocative expenditures resulting from excessive transportation charges from wasteful cross hauling as a result of basing point or other price schemes; (c) unneeded excess capacity growing out of such quasi-monopolistic practices as the restriction of petroleum output through production quotas in the prorationing scheme set in the big oil-producing states; (d) operating plants, and perhaps the entire firm, at suboptimal levels below the point where all economies of scale can be realized; and (e) promulgating tariffs and quotas on foreign-made products to protect inefficient domestic firms from the chilling winds of competition. (3) Finally, the loss of resources attendant to the present imperfect system of public regulation is easily visable and quite substantial. Frederic Scherer's eloquent protest regarding the interface between competition and regulation bears repeating.

> The Supreme Power who conceived gravity, supply and demand, and the double helix must have been absorbed elsewhere when public utility regulation was invented. The system is cumbersome, vulnerable to incompetence, and prone toward becoming ingrown and co-opted. In some respects it is directly conducive to inefficiency; in others, it may be merely ineffective in altering the behavior of the companies regulated . . . In the classic public utility sectors it is difficult or impossible to achieve fully competitive market structures without unacceptable scale economy sacrifices. Yet the instruments of direct public regulation evolved to compensate for the absence of workable competition have created so many new problems that we are drawn once again toward relying upon competitive forces, perhaps in attenuated or hybrid forms, whenever it is at all feasible.[38]

---

[36] A more detailed treatment of some of these factors is contained in Frederic M. Scherer, *Industrial Market Structure and Performance* (Chicago: Rand-McNally & Co., 1970), Ch. 2.

[37] The pioneering piece is by Harvey Leibenstein, "Allocative Efficiency vs. 'X-Efficiency,'" *American Economic Review* (June, 1966), pp. 392–415.

[38] Frederic M. Scherer, *op. cit.*, pp. 537, 542.

PUBLIC POLICIES TOWARD MONOPOLY

In those cases where the economies of scale result in so few optimum-sized firms as to preclude pure competition, there is a conflict between the social objectives of combining productive resources in a given use in the most economical manner and allocating resources among alternative uses in an optimal pattern. For example, in the automobile industry, if we are to have the advantages of pure competition, each firm would have to be so small that its costs of production would be higher than if each firm were very large. To obtain the benefits of mass production, only a few firms can survive; but with only a few firms in the industry, the potentiality of producing at minimum average costs is unrealized.

We want not only efficiency in allocation, but also dynamic growth of our economy. To the extent that large-scale enterprise encourages more rapid growth by facilitating research, by more easily mobilizing required capital, and by providing the necessary protection against inherent risks of innovation, monopolistic business organizations may have advantages over purely competitive ones.

Finally, to the extent that consumers prefer a wide variety of a given type of commodity, with one variety only slightly differentiated from another, imperfect competition—especially monopolistic competition—is more appropriate than pure competition. However, consumers should know the economic cost of such a preference.

Economically Unjustifiable Monopolies and Monopolistic Practices

Of course, in many cases there is no social dilemma because of a conflict of objectives. In these cases the verdict is fairly clear-cut. The monopolist is guilty of misallocating society's scarce productive resources. However, whether the existing situation should be attacked by increasing public regulation, increasing public ownership, or trying to restore effective, vigorous competition is subject to debate.

Monopolies that would fall under the category of "unjustifiable" are those which result from collusive action, not from the economies of large-scale production, product technology, or innovation. The alleged benefits or economies of bigness are often exaggerated. It would be a serious error to conclude that large-scale operations are always more efficient than smaller scale operations. Probably the most unbiased conclusion that can be reached is that in some monopolistic industries, real economies of scale exist, partially justifying the market structure; whereas in other monopolistic industries, the uneconomically large scale adds to the other social wastes of monopoly. Finally, such monopolistic practices as "sleeping" patents, suppression of technological improvements, product disparagement, discriminatory pricing, restrictive patent-licensing, "cut-throat" competition, etc., are obviously unjustified.

Social Objections to Monopolies

In addition to economic considerations, there are several sociopolitical or, for short, social implications of monopoly. Many people are as concerned about the social and political consequences of bigness as they are of considerations of economic efficiency.

The most significant noneconomic implications of monopoly derive from the heavy concentration of economic power in giant corporate businesses. For instance, it is estimated that the largest 100 manufacturing firms own roughly 50 percent of all manufacturing assets in the U.S. And through interlocking directorates and holding companies, the actual decision making is even more concentrated.[39] Not only are power and wealth concentrated in large firms, but also power within these firms is concentrated in the hands of a relatively small number of executives and large stockholders.

Economic power has a habit of spilling over into the sphere of political and social relations, raising, especially for democratic societies, important problems of social policy. Concentration of economic power can lead to concentration of political power. The growth of concentrated power or monopoly (while these terms are not quite synonymous, the identity does not lead to a significant error) leads to either the monopoly exerting improper political power and therefore influencing the government and public policy or the government being forced to regulate the monopoly. In short, government must control monopoly or be controlled by it. Of course, big business may not abuse its power if endowed with "social consciousness," a "corporate soul," or a sense of "social responsibility" as some allege. Nonetheless, the potential threat of concentrated economic power to democratic institutions is a proper subject for concern. The experience in Nazi Germany and Japan in the 1930s attests to this.

Monopoly also may seriously restrict economic freedom, especially of small enterprises. Top executives in big business have extensive power over those who work for them and over their customers, though this power is limited by rivalry with other monopolies for both customers and productive services and by the power of workers organized into large labor unions. In turn, in recent years some observers have feared the potential improper economic and political power of trade unions.

U.S. Policies to Promote Competition and Control Monopoly

Our theoretical apparatus shows that if pure competition exists, then the kind of economic performance most people desire will generally result. Pure competition in this context refers to a set of structural conditions, such as many

---

[39] Peter C. Dooley, "The Interlocking Directorate," *American Economic Review* (June, 1969), pp. 314–323.

sellers and easy entry. This kind of reasoning suggests a direct link between structure on the one hand and performance on the other, and it follows from this that laws which can maintain or produce a competitive structure would be desirable laws. It is also possible to seek good behavior or performance from firms by regulating their conduct. The conduct approach would make illegal certain kinds of acts, such as price-fixing, uniform delivered prices, or misleading advertising.

The federal laws designed to promote competition incorporate both the structural and the conduct aspects of competition. Although the laws which strive to maintain competition have their basis in economic theory, the prime cause for their adoption is a set of historical facts rather than the arguments of economic theorists. The Sherman, Federal Trade Commission, and Clayton Acts are the main antitrust laws. However, there is a complex web of various federal statutes, state laws, and city ordinances which restrict pricing freedom for the avowed purpose of fostering vigorous competition.

REGULATING MONOPOLIES

In cases where natural monopoly is thought to prevail because of substantial scale economies, the government frequently sets up and regulates public utilities. Of the alternative methods available to the government to control monopolistic utilities, two are particularly important: (1) direct control through regulation of price, cost, service performance, profit, etc.; and (2) indirect control through taxation. Other possible methods of monopoly control will not be considered here, such as the yardstick approach, in which the government builds a pilot plant to use for comparative purposes, and the actual operation and ownership of the entire industry by the government.

Controlling Price

The two general cases when prices are regulated differ because of contrasting assumptions about the average cost curve. The first involves the usual U-shaped long-run average cost curve (LAC), whereas the second deals with the natural monopoly case of a continuously falling (in the relevant range) LAC curve. The first case is illustrated in Figure 16–5. The regulatory agency, usually a state commission authorized to regulate the utilities, is interested in inducing a more optimal rate of production and price than would be forthcoming from an unregulated monopolist. In general, the regulatory commission would like the monopolist to produce a larger output and sell it at a lower price than would be the case if unconstrained.

"Normal" Cost Case. Before any kind of regulation, the utility depicted in Figure 16–5 would maximize profit by producing $0q_1$ and selling at price $0P_1$. The regulatory commission can impose a maximum price below $0P_1$, say,

FIGURE 16–5   Direct Regulation of Monopoly by Price Control

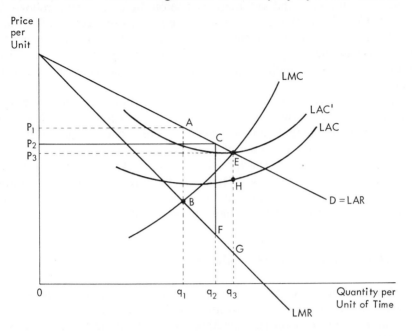

$0P_2$, so that the demand curve facing the firm can be described as P_2CD, meaning that the firm can sell any amount it wishes up to $0q_2$ (i.e., P_2C), but sales greater than $0q_2$ will require lower prices. The regulated price means that $LMR = LAR$ in the range P_2C, and LMR is discontinuous from point C to point F and then follows the original LMR curve. So $LMR = P_2CFLMR$. The optimum position for the firm is to produce output $0q_2$, where $LMR = LMC$.

The regulator has been able to lower price and increase the monopolist's output. But this successful policy can only be pushed so far — namely, to price $0P_3$. If the regulated price is set below $0P_3$, the intersection of LMC and LMR will be at a level of output less than the output level at price $0P_3$, and any further decreases in the controlled price will reduce output still further. Thus, $0P_3$ is the best price the regulator can set. Production will be at $0q_3$. The demand curve (= LAR) will be P_3ED. The LMR curve will be P_3EGLMR. Profit will be $(EH)(0q_3)$, but since this is viewed as the return to "the right to do business as a monopolist," the value of the firm will be recapitalized upward and the LAC curve will shift up to LAC', so that nothing called profit will exist. Thus, the competitive solution will be reached where $LMR = LMC = LAR = LAC$.

Natural Monopoly Case. The second possibility concerns the natural monopoly case, where the LAC slopes downward continuously in the feasible range as in Figure 16–6. If the regulator sets a price where LAR equals LMC

FIGURE 16-6 Price Regulation in the Natural Monopoly (Falling Cost) Case

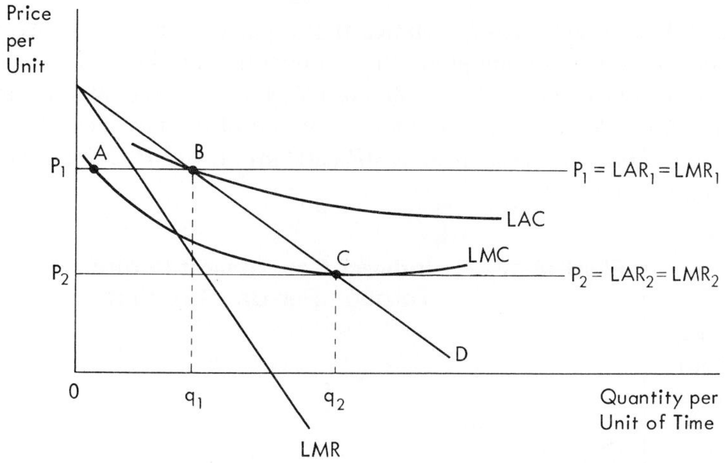

(as was done in the previous case), the firm loses money since the price $0P_2$ at point C is less than LAC. Since in general the government is not willing to subsidize firms, and without a subsidy the firm would quit business at regulated price $0P_2$, the economically ideal solution is not available.

The commission can set the price at $0P_1$, determined by the intersection at point B where $LAR_1 = LMR_1$ (since LMR with control price is horizontal) $= LAC$. The optimum output for the firm is $0q_1$, given control price $0P_1$. Notice that this is not where marginal revenue equals marginal cost. $MR = MC$ at point $A;$ but in this unusual instance, LMC intersects LMR_1 from above since LMR with control price is horizontal. The firm can reduce losses by continuing to increase output until it reaches point B. At this point the firm again earns zero profit.

Controlling Monopoly Through Taxation

The other general method of regulating monopolies is through the indirect method of taxation. In showing how the monopolist would react to various kinds of taxes, we shall also indicate the corresponding responses if competition were present. Basically, there are two types of taxes which we can consider: (1) A *specific*, or *variable tax* of so much per unit, e.g., a tax of $1 per unit of output, is analogous to variable cost. Similar effects result if instead a tax is levied as a fixed percentage of the sales revenue or output price, e.g., a tax of 10 percent of sales or price. This is called an *ad valorem tax* and is quite common in international trade. (2) A *lump-sum* or *fixed tax* of so much regardless of output, e.g., a $100 franchise fee, is analogous to fixed cost. Similar results occur if a profits tax of a certain fixed percentage of profits is levied, e.g., 20 percent of profits. All of these conclusions regarding taxation hold, *mutatis mutandis,* for a subsidy, which is merely a negative tax.

Per-Unit Tax. Figure 16–7 assumes that a per-unit tax of t is levied on the monopolist. When uninhibited, the monopolist produces $0q_1$ units of output at a price of $0P_1$ and makes profits of CP_1AB. Since the tax is a variable cost, it shifts STC, SMC, and SAC by the amount of the tax. Therefore, output is reduced to $0q_2$ and price raised to $0P_2$, and profits of EP_2GH are received to regain equilibrium.

FIGURE 16–7   Indirect Government Control Through Per-Unit Taxation

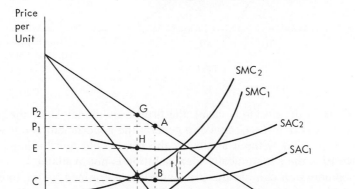

In short, part of the tax is passed to the consumer via higher prices (and lower output). Similarly, the producer pays part of it in the form of lower profits. We know that profits are lower since they were maximized at output $0q_1$; so that even without taxes, profit at $0q_2$ is less than at $0q_1$.

The proportion of the tax that falls on the consumer depends upon the relative slopes or elasticities of the demand and marginal cost curves. In fact, the percentage of the tax borne by the consumer is $a/(a + b) = \phi/(\eta + \phi)$, where a is the slope of the demand curve in absolute terms and b is the slope of the marginal cost curve. Also, η is the price elasticity of demand and ϕ is the elasticity of the marginal cost curve. The higher is ϕ or the lower is η, the greater the burden borne by consumers. If the demand for the monopolist's product is relatively inelastic, consumers will bear the brunt of the tax burden. In short, the general result is for the change in price (ΔP) to be less than the amount of the tax t ($\Delta P < t$), with part of the tax being passed on to consumers. This is always true for a horizontal MC curve and generally true if the MC curve is not horizontal.[40]

Competitive Case. In the competitive case, the short-run results are the same as the short-run (and long-run) results under monopoly, with $\Delta P < t$ and part of the burden shifted to the consumer. This occurs because costs are rising in the short run. The previous section demonstrated why this necessarily results in $\Delta P < t$.

However, in the long run things may be quite different. Whether $\Delta P \gtreqless t$ depends upon the slope of the MC or supply curve. Figure 16–8 demonstrates the three cases of a rising, constant, and falling supply curve. In all three panels, the tax of $\$t$ per unit shifts the supply curve vertically upward from S_1 to S_2 and leads to an increase in price from $0P_1$ to $0P_2$ or ΔP. If the industry is one of increasing (decreasing) cost, $\Delta P < t\ (\Delta P > t)$; whereas in the constant cost case, $\Delta P = t$.

Lump-Sum Tax. A lump-sum tax is like a fixed cost in that it shifts the AC (and AFC) curve upward, but not the MC curve. However, in one respect it is not like a fixed cost: the tax can sometimes be avoided by going out of business, whereas a fixed cost cannot be. Since MC is not affected by the tax and of course MR is not related to the tax, the $MC = MR$ rule tells us that the equilibrium price and quantity will not change in the great majority of cases. The short-run effects on both the competitor and the monopolist are the same: the change in fixed costs affects neither price nor quantity, but only profits. The producer bears all of the tax. The one exception to this is if the after-tax TR is less than the TVC, in which case the firm — whether it be a competitor or a monopolist — will abandon production. In the long run, the identical conclusion of no effect is reached for the monopolist, with the qualification changing to TR must be greater than TC ($= TVC + TFC$) or production will cease. Of course the tax change influences only costs, not revenue. In either the short run or long run, the monopolist's profits are reduced; but they cannot be reduced to less than zero or production would stop.

The long-run competitive result is again different since the competitor has no "fat," so to speak, from which to absorb the tax increase. Since the previous competitive long-run equilibrium involved zero profits, the representative firm will now be losing money if price and quantity do not shift. Although the firm is stuck with its equipment in the short run, it will not replace it as it depreciates in the long run. The end result is that the industry contracts its output to the scale at which the price rise exactly absorbs the entire tax and LTR once again equals LTC. As in the specific tax case, the long-run competitive equilibrium results in all of the tax being passed on to the consumer.

---

[40] While it is possible for $\Delta P > t$ for a monopolist, the condition is so complex and unlikely that it will not be discussed here.

FIGURE 16–8   Effects of a Per-Unit Tax Under
Various Cost Conditions

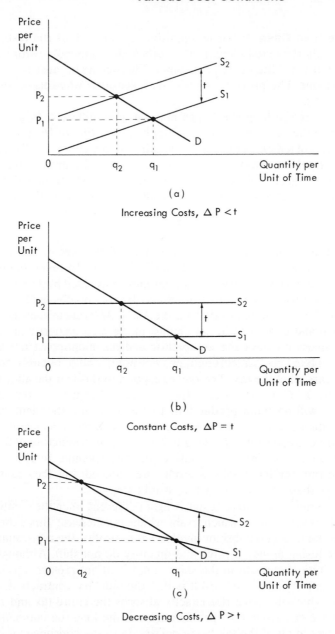

(a)

Increasing Costs, $\Delta P < t$

(b)

Constant Costs, $\Delta P = t$

(c)

Decreasing Costs, $\Delta P > t$

Profits Tax. In general, a (constant-percentage) profits tax has no effect on either the competitor's or the monopolist's short-run or long-run prices and quantities. This is because a tax that is a certain fixed percentage of profits, say, t, does not affect MC (or MR). Therefore, it has no effect on equilibrium price or quantity. What does change is the *AC* and hence profits, making the producer absorb all of the tax. Of course, a profits tax has no long-run effect on the competitive firm since it has no profits. This is illustrated in Figure 16–9. If output $0q_m$ was the profit-maximizing output before the tax, it must still be after the tax.

FIGURE 16–9   Constant Percentage Profits Tax

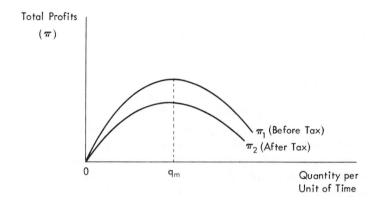

In practice, the U.S. corporate profits tax and most so-called profits taxes are not true profits taxes. Imputed costs of various sorts – imputed wages, interest, dividends, etc. – are included in the accounting profits used for taxation. Whenever the tax is not on "pure" profits but on some hybrid involving some opportunity costs, the general effects are in the same direction, although not of the same magnitude, as a variable or per-unit tax. That is, since factor payments (or variable costs from the firm's viewpoint) are affected, so are the equilibrium price and quantity.

PRICE DISCRIMINATION [41]

All of us are aware of the phenomenon of price discrimination, although we may not have used that title to describe it. *Price discrimination* occurs

---

[41] Some of the better treatments of this phenomenon are found in R. G. Lipsey and P. O. Steiner, *Economics* (New York: Harper & Row, Publishers, 1966), Ch. 24, pp. 273–279; Joe S. Bain, *Industrial Organization* (2d ed.; New York: John Wiley & Sons, 1968), Ch. 9, pp. 400–436; Donald S. Watson, *Price Theory and Its Uses* (3d ed.; Boston: Houghton Mifflin Co., 1972), Ch. 17, pp. 371–389; Frederic M. Scherer, *Industrial Market Structure and Economic Performance* (Chicago: Rand-McNally & Co., 1970), Chapter 10, pp. 253–272; and Josef Hadar, *Mathematical Theory of Economic Behavior* (Reading: Addison-Wesley Publishing Co., 1971), Chapter 6, especially pp. 79–88. An interesting twist can be found in Walter Y. Oi, "A Disneyland Dilemma: Two-Part Tariffs for a Mickey Mouse Monopoly," *Quarterly Journal of Economics* (February, 1971), pp. 77–96. He shows that a discriminatory two-part tariff, in which $P = MC$ and all consumer surpluses are appropriated by a lump-sum tax, is the best of all pricing strategies for a profit-maximizing monopolist. His analysis of two-part tariffs also provides an illuminating rationale for the IBM pricing policy and for volume discounts.

when different units of a *homogeneous* product are sold at different delivered prices in the same time period, for reasons not associated with differences in costs, with due allowance for risk and uncertainty. Of course, the usual reason for engaging in price discrimination, when feasible, is the desire to enhance profits.

Some cases of price discrimination with which the reader may be familiar are different prices for: (1) commercial and residential purchases of electrical power; (2) motels for tourists and traveling salespeople; (3) adults and children at theaters, ballgames, and other recreational activities; (4) out-of-state students at state universities, etc. Price discrimination may also refer to situations in which two similar goods, say the ith and jth commodities, have the following relationship: $P_i/MC_i \neq P_j/MC_j$ or $(P_i - MC_i) \neq (P_j - MC_j)$. That is, price discrimination is said to exist if two or more similar goods are sold at prices which are either in different ratios to marginal cost or not accounted for by the difference in marginal cost. Either approach is satisfactory.

From a positive economics viewpoint, price discrimination is considered neither favorable nor unfavorable. We can say only that it is a phenomenon often observed in monopolistic markets. It has some features which, according to most Western standards of equity and efficiency, would be considered desirable and some that would be considered undesirable.

For price discrimination to be successfully practiced, the following conditions must hold: (1) The seller must have sufficient monopoly power to control the supply of the commodity offered to particular buyers. (2) There must be at least two classes of buyers whose elasticities of demand at each price differ appreciably. (3) The seller must be able to segment or separate the market at a reasonable cost in that the resale of the product from one buyer to another can be prevented. For instance, time of the day, season of the year, and slight product modification are often costless or inexpensive ways to obtain effective segregation.

Control Over Supply

The fact that price discrimination requires some control over supply means it is a phenomenon that is unique to monopoly. However, it must be recognized that not all monopolists are able to discriminate.

Elasticities Differ

If there were not significant differences in the willingness of different classes of buyers to purchase the commodity — i.e., if the elasticities did not differ for any given price — price discrimination could not be profitably undertaken. To illustrate this in the simplest case, suppose a monopolist selling in two distinct and separable markets has already produced a certain quantity of output so that costs are now irrelevant. Total revenue will be maximized by equating the MR's in the two markets. If the MR_A in market A were \$10 and the MR_B in market B were \$5, the discriminating monopolist should obviously sell more units in market A and less in market B. The general principle for a profit-maximizing optimal allocation of a given amount of output is:

$$MR_A = MR_B = MR_C = \ldots = MR_N \tag{16.1}$$

where $A, B, C, \ldots, N$ refer to different markets or individuals.

When (16.1) holds, the prices differ for markets with unequal price elasticities.[42] This can be seen by the previously derived relationship that $MR = P - P/\eta$. If $MR_A = MR_B$, then $(P_A - P_A/\eta_A) = (P_B - P_B/\eta_B)$ and hence $P_A(1 - 1/\eta_A) = P_B(1 - 1/\eta_B)$. As one might expect, the price will be higher in the market with the more inelastic demand.

The optimal solution for a discriminating monopolist is illustrated graphically in Figure 16–10. The two distinct markets are A and B, with B having a smaller or more inelastic point elasticity of demand. (For example, market B might be the domestic U.S. market for wheat and market A the foreign market.) The quantity of x is increasing from left to right in market A and from right to left in market B. If the quantity available for sale is less than $0Q_0$, the entire amount will be sold in market B since MR_A is everywhere below MR_B until this point. Therefore, the TR from selling all the output in market B will exceed any division of the given product between markets A and B. If the total output is $0Q_T = 0Q_A + 0Q_B$, the discriminating monopolist should set a price of $0P_A$ and $0P_B$ respectively, since $MR_A = MR_B$ at these prices and quantities.

Market Segmentation

Market segmentation is necessary to prevent speculators from arbitraging and equalizing the price by buying in a low-price market and selling in a high-price market. The nature of the product is an important determinant of the ability to prevent its resale. For instance, personal services are generally not transferable and hence provide an excellent opportunity for price discrimination. Goods requiring a physical connection between the facilities of the monopolist and the consumer or requiring installation by the producer are more difficult to resell. Geographical factors such as tariffs, quotas, transportation costs, language, etc., also make it possible to segment the market for discrimination. Similarly, price discrimination may conceivably take place when the monopolist's product is highly perishable or when the existence of the price differentials can be kept secret. Also, maintaining market segmentation

---

[42] If $\eta_A = \eta_B$, then $P_A = P_B$ and there would be no price discrimination. Terutomo Ozawa, "Intermarket Price Discrimination Under Pure Monopoly: A Supplementary Note," *Nebraska Journal of Economics and Business* (Winter, 1971), pp. 55–59, emphasizes that the concept of demand price elasticity relevant for price discrimination is not the overall elasticity condition of the entire market but a specific point elasticity on the market's demand curve.

FIGURE 16–10   Distribution of a Given Output
Among Markets with Price Discrimination

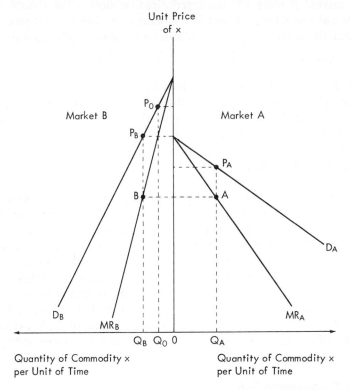

often involves costs, so the increase in profit from discriminating must be greater than the costs of keeping the markets separate.

The classic case of price discrimination involved an international chemical cartel agreement involving the sale of acrylic products, including the plastic molding powder methyl methacrylate. Duopolists Röhm and Haas and Du Pont charged 85¢ a pound to general industrial users or commercial moulders, but sold special mixtures to dental laboratories and dentists for use in denture manufacturing for between $22 and $45 a pound. However, profitable arbitrage by firms buying in the industrial market and selling in the dental market threatened to undercut this agreement. To stop this, Röhm and Haas considered lacing the industrial powder with arsenic to prevent oral usage! While the firm ultimately rejected the idea, it did encourage rumors that the industrial powder had been adulterated.[43]

[43] This classic is discussed in Frederic M. Scherer, *Industrial Market Structure and Performance* (Chicago: Rand-McNally & Co., 1970), pp. 253–254; George W. Stocking, Myron W. Watkins, *et al, Cartels in Action; Case Studies in International Diplomacy* (New York: Twentieth Century Fund, 1946), pp. 402–404; and H. H. Liebhafsky, *The Nature of Price Theory* (rev. ed.; Homewood: The Dorsey Press, 1968), pp. 374–375.

PERFECT OR FIRST-DEGREE PRICE DISCRIMINATION

It is possible to distinguish between two degrees of discrimination: "perfect" ("first-degree," "take-it-or-leave-it," or "all-or-nothing") discrimination and "imperfect" discrimination.[44] The perfectly discriminating monopolist is assumed to know the demand curve of each buyer and to charge a different price for each unit bought. This procedure allows the monopolist to exact the full amount of consumer surplus from the buyer. Thus, in Figure 16–11, the price of the first unit is $0P_1$, the price for the second unit is $0P_2$, and so on. Notice that in this pricing rule, $MR = P = AR = D_x$.

An equivalent and probably more feasible pricing practice is to set the price and the quantity which the buyer is permitted. In Figure 16–11, setting the price at $0P_3$ and quantity at six yields the same revenue to the seller as

FIGURE 16–11   Ordinary vs. "All-or-Nothing" Demand Curve

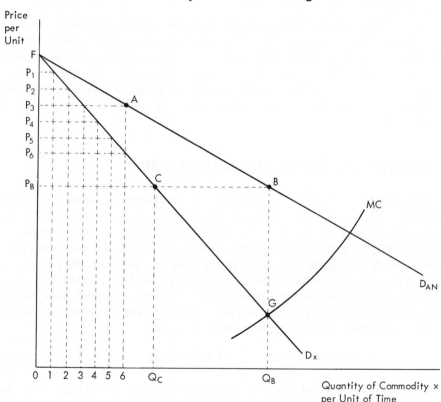

---

[44] A. C. Pigou, the great English economist, made a tripartite division into first-, second-, and third-degree discrimination. In our analysis, the last two are combined into the category "imperfect price discrimination," and the first-degree price discrimination is referred to as "perfect" price discrimination.

selling the six units at the six different prices. This is known as "all-or-nothing" pricing. Point A can be viewed as a point on the perfectly discriminating monopolist's demand curve in that this buyer will take the quantity of six at price $0P_3$. The buyer would prefer to buy only three units at price $0P_3$ but doesn't have that option, and will be willing to buy six at $0P_3$ rather than not have any of the commodity. The total utility in dollar value equals the total outlay, which again says that there is no consumer surplus.

A second point, point B on the "all-or-nothing" demand curve D_{AN}, is also shown on Figure 16–11 to illustrate some additional observations. First, observe that the total revenue (or total consumer outlay) is rectangle $0P_BBQ_B$, which equals area $0FCQ_C$; so the areas of triangles P_BFC and CBG are also equal. The MR curve for the discriminating monopolist is the D_x curve, which has the usual relationship to the demand curve D_{AN}. Thus, if the marginal cost curve intersects D_x at point G as shown, the profit-maximizing strategy for the firm dealing with this buyer is to set the price at $0P_B$ and the all-or-nothing quantity at $0Q_B$.

It is fairly obvious that, given the stringent conditions required, perfect price discrimination is quite unusual. Rarely is the monopolist able to capture the entire consumer surplus. However, it is fairly common for a monopolist to capture part of the available consumer surplus—e.g., by discriminatory electricity, gas, and telephone rates. The phenomenon of capturing only part of the consumer surplus is called imperfect (or second- and third-degree) price discrimination.

IMPERFECT PRICE DISCRIMINATION

Condition (16.1) demonstrated that a discriminating monopolist, once the output has been produced, can maximize profits by equating the MR's in the two separate markets, A and B. Now we are interested in looking at how a discriminating monopolist plans future production with costs taken into consideration. Assuming the MC of supplying a unit of output in either market is the same—that is, assuming there is a common total MC, labeled MC_T—the MR's in the two markets must be equal ($MR_A = MR_B$) as in the given output case; but in addition they must equal MC_T. In other words, a profit-maximizing optimal allocation of future production requires that:

$$MR_A = MR_B = MR_C = \ldots = MR_N = MC_T \qquad \textbf{(16.2)}$$

In Figure 16–12, the demand curves and marginal revenue curves in the two separable markets are D_A, D_B, and MR_A, MR_B respectively. MR_T (total MR) is obtained by summing horizontally the two MR curves, and it illustrates the total quantity that can be sold at various marginal revenues. The optimal output is $0Q_T$, where $MR_T = MC_T$. Furthermore, condition (16.2) states that the discriminating monopolist can obtain the greatest possible total revenue

FIGURE 16-12   Optimal Rate of Production with Price Discrimination

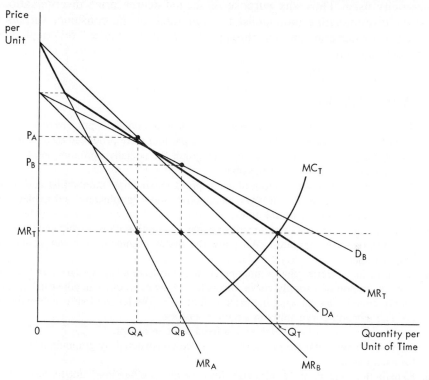

(TR) for a given volume of sales by allocating $0Q_T$ between markets A and B such that the marginal revenues are equal—i.e., $MR_A = MR_B = MR_T = MC_T$. Obviously, if the $MR_A > MR_B$, transferring sales from market B to market A would increase the monopolist's total receipts.

In Figure 16–12 it turns out that $0Q_A$ units should be sold in market A at a price of $0P_A$ and $0Q_B$ units should be sold in market B at a price of $0P_B$, where $0Q_A + 0Q_B = 0Q_T$.[45] Of course, the market with the more elastic demand has a lower price, $P_A > P_B$.

The practice of charging different prices in different markets for a standardized product is called "third-degree" price discrimination. While it is the most common form of price discrimination, "second-degree" price discrimination is also widely practiced, particularly in the public utility field. With second-degree price discrimination, one rate applies to all buyers, but this rate changes as the volume consumed changes. For instance, a local electric utility might charge a given rate for the first 100 units of electricity used per

---

[45] Although this analysis is only strictly valued in the highly improbable case that the two markets are independent, with the demand curve in either market completely divorced from the price set in the other, it provides essentially correct results in all but the most extreme cases.

time period, a lower rate for the next 100, and still a lower rate for all additional electricity used. Thus, the purpose of second-degree price discrimination is for the discriminating monopolist to skim some of the consumer surplus by inducing greater consumption through the quantity, "block," or "stepladder" discounts offered.

QUESTIONS

1. Show graphically the conditions necessary for a monopolist's price to be lower and quantity larger than would be the case if the product were produced by a large number of competitive firms. Show on your graph the socially optimum point. Under what conditions is this point possible?
2. If a lump-sum tax were imposed on a profit-maximizing monopolist and a constrained sales-maximizing (*CSM*) monopolist, show graphically and explain how their output responses would differ.
3. Profit maximization may not be a reasonable assumption if ownership and control of an enterprise are separated. What are the major arguments for and against this proposition?
4. It is invariably argued that a monopolist does not have a supply curve. In the traditional definition of a supply curve, this is true. However, one can construct "pseudo supply curves" by showing the price-output points under the following conditions:
   (a) The demand curve shifts in a parallel fashion.
   (b) The demand curve rotates with a fixed price intercept.
   Show how these two supply curves could be constructed by graphing three points for each curve.
5. Explain the concept of "dead-weight loss" or the "welfare loss" due to the existence of monopolistic firms.
6. Consider the situation of an unfettered pure monopolist. Explain why a government regulator could set a lower price (than the monopolist's optimum price) and the monopolist would increase output. How low can the regulator set the price and still have this result?
7. Show that if a monopolist has two separable markets, but demand curves for both markets are the same, that price discrimination will not take place.
8. Prove that a perfectly discriminating monopolist's total revenue (or the buyer's total outlay) is the same whether the monopolist charges the maximum price the buyer is willing to pay or uses the all-or-nothing single-price technique. Use Figure 16–11, page 379, as your reference.

APPENDIX: MATHEMATICAL NOTES

Note 1. Baumol's Constrained Sales Maximization (CSM) Model

Given total revenue, $R = r(q,a)$, where q is the rate of output and a is the level of advertising expenditures, and total cost, $C = c(q)$, then profit, $\Pi = \pi(q,a) = r(q,a) -$

$c(q) - a$. Letting the minimum profit constraint, however defined, be equal to K, a constant, the *CSM* model emphasizes that the firm should maximize $r(q,a)$ subject to:

$$\pi(q,a) \geq K \qquad (16.3)$$

Since (16.3) is assumed effective, the *CSM* model calls for maximizing:

$$Z = r(q,a) + \lambda\pi(q,a) \qquad (16.4)$$

where λ is a LaGrangian multiplier, which is equivalent to maximizing:

$$Z = R + \lambda \ (R - C - a - K) \qquad (16.5)$$

The first-order conditions for a maximum require that:

$$\frac{\delta R}{\delta q} + \lambda\frac{\delta\Pi}{\delta q} = 0; \qquad \frac{\delta R}{\delta a} + \lambda\frac{\delta\Pi}{\delta a} = 0; \qquad \pi(q,a) = K \qquad (16.6)$$

The first two conditions in (16.6) become:

$$\frac{\delta R}{\delta q} = \frac{\lambda}{1+\lambda} C'(q); \qquad \frac{\delta R}{\delta a} = \frac{\lambda}{1+\lambda} \qquad (16.7)$$

or

$$\frac{\delta R}{\delta q} \div \left[\frac{\delta R}{\delta q} - C'(q)\right] = -\lambda; \qquad \frac{\delta R}{\delta q} = \frac{\delta R}{\delta a} C'(q) \qquad (16.8)$$

Thus, equations (16.7) and (16.8) tell us that, at the optimum, marginal revenue $(\delta R/\delta q)$ is less than marginal cost $C'(q)$, since $|\lambda|$ must be greater than one to be feasible. That is, marginal profits must be negative and less than marginal revenue. In addition, these equations tell us that the marginal return from advertising is less than one or that marginal revenue equals the marginal return from advertising times marginal cost.

The general form of the constraint is:

$$R - VC - Wa \geq K \qquad (16.9)$$

where V, W, and K are constants, and $V > 1$, $W > 1$, and $K \geq 0$. For example, if profits are to equal or exceed a given proportion of dollar sales, (16.9) becomes:

$$\frac{R - C - a}{R} \geq K \qquad (16.10)$$

then $R - \dfrac{C + a}{1 - K} \geq 0$ and $V = W = 1/(1 - K)$, and $K = 0$.

Note 2. Form of Taxation and Monopoly Output

In the text, we demonstrated that a lump-sum or profit tax does not affect the optimum price-quantity combination unless post-tax $TR < TVC$. Producers must bear the decline in profits. In contrast, a specific tax (given in terms of the number of dollars per unit sold) or an *ad valorem* tax (given in terms of a percentage of the sales price or revenue) does reduce (increase) the quantity (price) level. And again the profit level falls.

Since $\pi = TR - TC$, where revenue and cost are both a function of output, the profit function can be written:

$$\pi = R(q) - C(q) \tag{16.11}$$

where R is total revenue, C is total cost, and q is the quantity sold. If an available lump-sum tax is levied, (16.11) becomes:

$$\pi = R(q) - C(q) - F \tag{16.12}$$

where F is the amount of the lump-sum tax which is independent of the level of output. The first-order condition is therefore identical with that when no F is levied since a constant vanishes upon differentiation.

$$d\pi/dq = R'(q) - C'(q) = 0 \qquad R'(q) = C'(q) \tag{16.13}$$

That is, MR must again equal MC. (The second-order conditions are not repeated here since they are identical with those derived earlier when no tax is levied.)

A profit tax which: (1) is levied on the economist's definition of profit; and (2) has a marginal rate less than 100 percent, i.e., $0 < t < 1$, also does not affect price or quantity. Equation (16.11) now becomes:

$$\pi = R(q) - C(q) - t[R(q) - C(q)] = (1 - t)[R(q) - C(q)] \tag{16.14}$$

That is, $\pi = TR - TC - t(\pi)$. The first-order condition setting (16.14) equal to zero yields:

$$d\pi/dq = (1 - t)[R'(q) - C'(q)] = 0 \tag{16.15}$$

Since $(1 - t) > 0$, if $[R'(q) - C'(q)] = 0$, we will fulfill (16.15). This can be done by setting:

$$R'(q) = C'(q) = 0 \qquad R'(q) = C'(q) \tag{16.16}$$

In other words, the first-order condition is the same as for an untaxed monopolist, namely $MR = MC$.

If a specific tax of, say, β is levied, (16.11) becomes:

$$\pi = R(q) - C(q) - \beta q \tag{16.17}$$

and the first-order condition is:

$$d\pi/dq = R'(q) - C'(q) - \beta = 0 \qquad R'(q) = C'(q) + \beta \tag{16.18}$$

Thus, the monopolist now reaches the optimum by equating MR with MC plus the tax. The net result is a smaller quantity sold and a higher price.

Finally, if an *ad valorem* tax is levied as a proportion $0 < \alpha < 1$ of total revenue, (16.11) becomes:

$$\pi = R(q) - C(q) - \alpha R(q) = (1 - \alpha)R(q) - C(q) \tag{16.19}$$

Setting the derivative of (16.19) equal to zero produces:

$$d\pi/dq = (1 - \alpha)R'(q) - C'(q) = 0 \qquad (1 - \alpha)R'(q) = C'(q) \qquad \text{(16.20)}$$

Since the new profit-maximization condition requires that MC be equal to the portion of MR the monopolist is allowed to keep, the optimum output (price) level has fallen (increased).

Note 3. Price Discrimination

A discriminating monopolist's profits from the sale of the product in two distinct markets, subscripted by 1 and 2, are equal to the difference between total revenue from both markets and total costs.

$$\pi = R_1(q_2) + R_2(q_2) - C(q_1 + q_2) \qquad \text{(16.21)}$$

To achieve maximum profits, the partial derivatives of (16.21) must be set equal to zero.

$$\frac{\delta\pi}{\delta q_1} = R'_1(q_1) - C'(q_1 + q_2) = 0 \qquad \text{(16.22)}$$

$$\frac{\delta\pi}{\delta q_2} = R'_2(q_2) - C'(q_1 + q_2) = 0$$

or

$$R'_1(q_1) = R'_2(q_2) = C'(q_1 + q_2)$$

In economic terms, this means the marginal revenue in each market must be equal to the other and to the marginal cost of the output as a whole.

The second-order conditions require that the principal minors of the relevant Hessian determinant:

$$\begin{vmatrix} R''_1 - C'' & -C'' \\ -C'' & R''_2 - C'' \end{vmatrix} \qquad \text{(16.23)}$$

alternate in sign starting with a negative sign. Expansion of the principal minors implies that $(R''_2 - C'') < 0$ or in economic terms that the MC for the entire output must be increasing more rapidly than the MR in each market.

Of course, the equality of MR in the two markets does not mean the prices are equal. In fact, from the fundamental equation $MR = p(1 - 1/\eta)$, where η refers to point elasticity of demand, we know that when $MR_1 = MR_2$:

$$P_1(1 - 1/\eta_1) = P_2(1 - 1/\eta_2) \qquad \text{(16.24)}$$

This means if the MC is the same for both markets (i.e., $MC_1 = MC_2$), then:

$$\frac{P_1}{P_2} = \frac{1 - 1/\eta_2}{1 - 1/\eta_1} = \frac{(\eta_2 - 1)/\eta_2}{(\eta_1 - 1)/\eta_1} \qquad \text{(16.25)}$$

More generally, if no assumption is made about costs, we know that the firm will equate MR to MC in each market so that:

$$MC_1 = MR_1 = P_1[(\eta_1 - 1)/\eta_1] \tag{16.26}$$
$$MC_2 = MR_2 = P_2[(\eta_2 - 1)/\eta_2]$$

or

$$\frac{P_1}{P_2} = \frac{MC_2[\eta_2/(\eta_2 - 1)]}{MC_1[\eta_1/(\eta_1 - 1)]} \tag{16.27}$$

Equation (16.27) reduces to (16.25) when $MC_1 = MC_2$.

Either approach tells us that the price will be lower in the market with the greater point demand elasticity. In addition, only if $\eta_1 = \eta_2$ will $P_1 = P_2$ in the $MC_1 = MC_2$ case. More generally, if $\eta_1 = \eta_2$, we get from (16.27) that:

$$\frac{P_1}{P_2} = \frac{MC_1}{MC_2} \tag{16.28}$$

This equality means there is no price discrimination.

5 DISTRIBUTION THEORY

17 Short-Run Factor Pricing and Employment

The preceding chapters have been concerned with the price and quantity of commodities in the product market. In producing any commodity, a firm must hire factors of production which, directly or indirectly, are owned and supplied by resource owners in the household sector. Therefore, the next two chapters will turn from the pricing and employment of output to the pricing and employment of the inputs needed in accomplishing this output. If from the output side the firm's optimum behavior involves producing, say, 100 units of output, the best position from the input side would likewise involve hiring the quantity of inputs that could produce this 100 units of output in the most efficient (least costly) method possible.

This and the next chapter will develop the general theory underlying equilibrium factor service prices and quantities. This analysis will always emphasize the price of the flow of factor *services,* not the price of the factors themselves. Thus, the price of capital and labor refers to the cost of using the factor for a period of time, not the price of buying the factor. In Chapter 19 the general principles developed in Chapters 12 and 13 will be applied to particular factor returns—wages, rent, interest, and profits.

ESSENTIALS OF INCOME DISTRIBUTION

The study of factor pricing and employment is of more than technical interest as a part of the theory of the firm since this is precisely what determines the income distribution of the people living in the economy. Almost all of the criticism of market-directed economies boils down to criticism of the income distribution which results in such an economy. Intelligent evaluation of such criticism requires an understanding of the reasons the distribution is what it is and the implications of changing the system. An important distinction in this connection is between *functional* income distribution and *personal* income distribution. *Functional income distribution* refers to the payments made to factors of production for the contribution of those factors to the output. *Personal distribution* refers to the income received by the individuals in the society. In a free market system, an individual's income is the price of the factor service times the quantity of that service the person makes available to a producing entity. The quantity of productive services (which somehow includes quality) the individual can command depends upon the individual's wealth (including human wealth), which in turn depends upon a host of historical factors — inheritance, past saving, education, portfolio decisions, etc.

It is, of course, the personal income (and/or wealth) distribution which disturbs the critics of capitalist economies. The issues involved are humanistic, often egalitarian or focusing on value judgements about equity. The problem is to arrive at a "fair" distribution with as little distortion as possible on the efficiency of production, which depends on the functional distribution. The more efficient the economy, the larger the total income to be distributed, which introduces the question of whether individuals' welfare depends upon their absolute income or on their income relative to the income of others.

It is very tempting to discuss some of the approaches that have been taken and the successes and failures; but for such a discussion to be fruitful, one must understand the theory of functional distribution. This is what we now turn to.

The Law of Supply and Demand in the Resource Market[1]

In a free market economy, the price of a productive service is determined in the factor service markets like any other price — by the forces of demand and supply. The basic principles of price determination are no different for productive services — including both material resources such as capital equipment or land and personal services of human beings — than for final commodities.

Assuming approximately competitive conditions in the factor service markets, the law of supply and demand tells us the equilibrium price of any productive service is such that the total quantity supplied equals the total quantity demanded. Other things being equal, the greater the demand for a service or the less its supply, the higher its free market price. Although this law strictly holds only for a purely competitive factor market, the principles determining competitive factor prices are essential for understanding imperfectly competitive models.

The application of the law of supply and demand to a competitive resource market in determining factor service prices can be illustrated graphically. Let us analyze the determination of the price of labor services, assumed to be the only variable input, in producing gadgets. In Figure 17–1 we show a "representative" gadget firm in panel (a) and the industry in panel (b). This illustration makes the reasonable assumption that industry and firm demand curves for productive services are downsloping and that industry supply curves are upsloping; the precise explanation for this relationship is left for later. The commonsense explanation on the supply side is that high factor prices in a particular industry or occupation encourage households to supply more of the services of their human and property resources. On the demand side, businesses find it profitable to substitute low for high priced resources to minimize production costs. These two factors result in an upsloping industry supply curve and downsloping industry demand curve.

---

[1] The analysis in this chapter depends heavily on the material presented in Chapters 8 and 9 on production theory. The reader who is not thoroughly familiar with these principles should review these chapters.

FIGURE 17-1   Wages and Employment, Firm and Industry

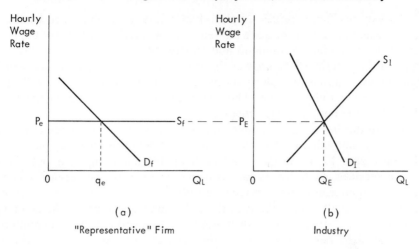

(a)
"Representative" Firm

(b)
Industry

In panel (b) the two industry curves intersect at an hourly wage rate of $0P_E$ and quantity of $0Q_E$. (More properly, this quantity is the quantity of an input in terms of its services per unit of time. However, for convenience, we will often refer to the quantity of, say, labor instead of hours of labor service.) These equilibrium values are analogous to those found in the product market. An above-equilibrium wage rate would result in fewer labor services being demanded than supplied. Some workers would be unemployed, leading them to offer to work at lower wages. This would continue until the wage rate fell to $0P_E$. At below-equilibrium wage rates, firms could not hire all the labor they desired. Thus, they would compete for labor services by bidding up wages. Only at $0P_E$ are all workers employed and all employers fully satisfied with the number of employees.

This market-determined wage set by the impersonal forces of supply and demand is a given for the single firm. To any single employee or employer, it is a "take-it-or-leave-it" wage rate over which the individual has no control. Therefore, the supply curve facing a single firm in a purely competitive factor market is horizontal, as depicted in panel (a). The firm is free to hire all the labor it desires at the going market wage rate of $0P_e$. In this case it elects to hire $0q_e$ units of labor. If it tries to pay less than the going rate, under conditions of perfect mobility, it will have no employees. By the same token, there is no point in the single firm offering more than $0P_e$. Note the firm does not determine this factor's marginal productivity and then pay it accordingly. Instead, the firm takes the market-determined price as given and adjusts the quantity of the input it hires.

As in the product market, shifts in demand, supply, or both cause new equilibrium values to be determined. The *magnitude* of the change in the equilibrium wage and quantity hired in response to a given shift in demand or supply depends upon the elasticity of the schedules.

A Terse Outline of the Marginal Productivity Theory

To say that factor prices, like product prices, are determined by the law of supply and demand is of quite limited value without knowledge of the fundamental underpinnings of demand and supply. What determines the level and shape of the functions? To answer this question, we first examine demand and then supply. The basic underlying principle on the demand side will be the marginal productivity theory. The basic underlying principle on the supply side will be the net advantage theory.

Before turning to these fundamental determinants of factor prices and employment, a simplified view of the rudiments of factor pricing may be obtained utilizing Figure 17–1. As the result of competitive bidding for a factor's productive services, each firm is forced to pay a price for the service which reflects, in equilibrium, the service's *marginal contribution to the economy's output*. This result comes about in the following way. Suppose the given type of labor service, such as our gadget worker in Figure 17–1, has an equilibrium wage rate of $2 per hour or $0P_E$ in the diagram. At this wage rate, the total quantity of the service demanded equals the total quantity offered (definition of "equilibrium" price of the service). Each firm hiring the labor must pay the prevailing wage. The aggregate quantity of the labor service demanded equals the sum of the quantities demanded by all the firms employing the labor. But each of these firms employs the labor only up to the point where the *extra cost* of an additional hour of labor equals the *extra revenue* derived from the sale of the *extra output* produced by the additional hour of labor. (Otherwise the firm is not maximizing its profits.) But the extra cost of an additional hour's labor service equals, under competition in the factor market, the hourly wage rate; whereas the resulting extra revenue equals the value of the service's marginal product (its VMP) under competition in the product market or equals the marginal revenue product (its MRP) more generally. Hence, if labor's marginal contribution to output (or revenue) is not as great as the wage rate, the total quantity employed would be reduced. The unemployed workers would offer to work at lower wages, and the wage rate would fall. If labor's marginal contribution to output is greater than the wage rate, the total quantity of labor demanded would be increased, employers would seek to attract more workers, and the wage rate would rise. Therefore, anything that increases the value of a service's marginal product and hence the demand for that service will tend to cause its free market price to rise. The quantities, qualities, and prices of other productive services; the level of output demand; the state of technology; and the degree of managerial and labor efficiency all help to determine the marginal productivity and hence the demand for any particular input service.

The owners of factor services will seek to employ their services such as to produce their greatest net advantage — including both pecuniary and nonpecuniary factors, where the latter includes such factors as working conditions, geographical location, risk, and convenience. Since the nonpecuniary elements are relatively stable over time, the pecuniary factors dominate in determining factor supply schedules. In general, paying more for factor services in a given employment results in a greater quantity of that service being made available.

Optimum Factor Proportions and Absolute Factor Amounts

Chapters 8 and 9 gave the conditions necessary for a firm to produce any given level of output at the lowest possible costs, given pure competition in the factor market, i.e., fixed factor prices. According to Alfred Marshall's principle of substitution, a firm should substitute cheap inputs for dear inputs so as to always combine factors in the optimum proportions:

$$MPP_a/P_a = MPP_b/P_b = MPP_c/P_c = \cdots = MPP_n/P_n \qquad (17.1)$$

That is, the least-cost combination for producing any output requires that inputs be combined so that the marginal physical product (MPP) per dollar's worth of any one factor equals the MPP of each of the other factors. However, (17.1) gives only the optimal factor *proportions,* not the optimal *absolute* amounts of the factors that should be used.

Of course, the correct absolute amounts of the factors from the point of view of a profit-maximizing firm are those associated with the $MR_x = MC_x$ output. In other words, in all our cost diagrams and analyses, we have assumed that the firm is using the least-cost combination at any output level. But the firm is not interested in just any output, but only in the best profit level of production. To see this best, put equation (17.1) in its equivalent form in terms of MC_x. Suppose there are two inputs, a and b. Further suppose there is competition in the input market so that the firm hires at constant factor prices. Under these conditions, the marginal factor expense of a (MFE_a) equals the price of the factor, where MFE_a is defined as showing the change in the firm's total cost resulting from a one-unit change in the purchase of the factor per unit of time (i.e., $MFE_a = \Delta TC/\Delta Q_a$). Under these conditions, an extra unit of factor a: (1) increases a firm's total cost by an amount equal to P_a, and (2) increases the firm's total product by an amount equal to MPP_a. Since P_a is the change in total cost and MPP is the change in total output per unit change in input a, P_a/MPP_a shows the change in the firm's TC per unit change in output or $\Delta TC/\Delta Q_x$. But this is precisely what we defined as marginal cost previously. Hence, $MC_x = P_a/MPP_a$ (or P_b/MPP_b, from [17.1]).[2] This means the least-cost combination given in equation (17.1) can be written as:

$$MPP_a/P_a = MPP_b/P_b = 1/MC_x \qquad (17.2)$$

Assuming that $MPP_a > 0$ and $MPP_b > 0$ in the relevant range, we can take the reciprocals of (17.2) and write it as:

$$P_a/MPP_a = P_b/MPP_b = MC_x \qquad (17.3)$$

Either expression (17.2) or (17.3) may be interpreted as showing that all factors are equally efficient at the margin when the least-cost combination of factors is used. The MPP per dollar spent on all factors is the same. When the firm is at its optimum, the increase in cost for·any small increase in output is the same regardless of which factor is augmented.

---

[2] The more general definition of marginal cost, covering both competition and monopsony in the factor market, is $MC_x = MFE_a/MPP_a$.

Once again expressions (17.2) and (17.3) show us only the correct proportions, not the correct absolute amounts. To achieve both the proper proportions and absolute amounts, a firm must produce that output at which $MR_x = MC_x$.[3] If $MR_x > MC_x$ ($MR_x < MC_x$) and equation (17.1) holds, the inputs are being used in the correct proportions for that output, but not enough (too much) output is being produced and hence not enough (too many) units of either input is being used. Therefore, to obtain both the proper combination and absolute amounts of its variable resources, the firm should hire n inputs such that:

$$MPP_a/P_a = MPP_b/P_b = \cdots = MPP_n/P_n = 1/MC_x = 1/MR_x \quad \text{(17.4)}$$

or again, taking reciprocals,

$$P_a/MPP_a = P_b/MPP_b = \cdots = P_n/MPP_n = MC_x = MR_x \qquad \text{(17.5)}$$

This equation states that a firm both minimizes costs and maximizes profits when it hires factors such that the value of the marginal physical product (defined as $VMP_a \equiv P_x \cdot MPP_a$) of that factor just equals its factor price. For example, since under pure competition $MR_x = P_x$ and since $P_a/MPP_a = MR_x$ (at the optimum point), $P_a = MPP_a \cdot P_x = VMP_a$. The VMP_a shows the market value of a firm's increase in output when it increases the quantity of any input by one unit per unit of time.

DEMAND FOR A PRODUCTIVE SERVICE

A firm is basically not interested in the physical output an extra worker will produce, say, two bushels of wheat, but rather in the extra revenue it will receive from selling those two bushels of wheat, say $8. Under competitive conditions in the factor market, each profit-maximizing firm will try to hire factors such that the value of that factor's marginal product equals its price. The more general condition that allows for monopsony in the factor market is that a profit-maximizing entrepreneur should adjust the employment of each variable factor such that its marginal revenue product equals its marginal factor expense. Before examining the derivation of factor demand curves for the cases of one-variable factor and several-variable factors, we should first discuss the meaning and significance of the concept that the demand for factors is a "derived" demand.

Factor Demand as a Derived Demand

While finished or final commodities *directly* satisfy consumer wants, factor services—with the exception of certain personal services such as barbers, lawyers, and physicians—contribute *indirectly* to satisfying human wants. No one wants to directly consume a wheat combine, a plot of farmland, or a farmer's labor services, but people do demand these services indirectly by demanding the farm products which these factors help produce. Similarly, the

---

[3] Of course, in the case of competition this can be expressed as $P_x = MC_x$. However, the $MR_x = MC_x$ form is used so that the analysis in this section will hold for both competition and monopoly in the output market.

demand for computer programmers, college professors, and carpenters is *derived* from the demand for computer services, educational services, and housing respectively.

The derived nature of factor demand implies that the strength of the demand for any factor will depend upon: (1) the (marginal) physical productivity of the factor; and (2) the market price of the commodity it is producing, or more generally the revenue which can be obtained from the sale of the product. The worth of a factor will be great if it has high physical productivity in turning out a commodity highly sought by the economy.

Table 17-1 presents the demand for economic resources, assuming first pure competition and then monopoly in the output market. First examine columns (1) through (3), which show the physical production relations for both cases. Assume there is one variable input, labor, which along with given amounts of other factors produces the total physical output shown in column (2). The marginal physical product (MPP_L) is the *change* in total output associated with a small change in the variable input (here taken to be one input of labor), all other inputs held constant.

The Marginal Revenue Product

The marginal revenue product (MRP) is more important to the business decision maker than is the marginal physical product. MRP is the increase in total revenue (TR) resulting from the use of each additional input of a factor. Since under purely competitive conditions in the output market, a firm's marginal revenue is the same as the price of its product, the value of the marginal product—defined as $VMP_L = MPP_L \cdot P_x$—is identical to $MRP_L = MPP_L \cdot MR_x$. Under any form of imperfect competition, the downsloping firm product demand curve means $P_x > MR_x$ and therefore $VMP_L > MRP_L$. However, it is always the MRP_L curve that is crucial in the firm's hiring of inputs, regardless of whether it is the same or less than the VMP_L curve.

Shape of the Marginal Revenue Product Curve

The general shape of the MRP_L curve under competitive conditions is the same as that of its MPP_L curve. Under pure competition, MR_x is a constant, so the MRP_L curve is merely the MPP_L multiplied by a constant. In short, after the law of diminishing marginal returns becomes operative, the MRP_L curve is a downsloping function. Under noncompetitive conditions, the negative slope of the MRP_L curve results from both the decline in the MPP_L and the decline in the MR_x.

Table 17-1 verifies that factor demand curves are downsloping. Under pure competition in the output market, $P_x = MR_x$ and therefore $VMP_L = MRP_L$, and both are downsloping after the law of diminishing marginal returns sets in. Under monopoly, $P_x > MR_x$ and therefore $VMP_L > MRP_L$. Both are downsloping because of both diminishing MPP and diminishing MR_x. Columns (6) and (7) in Table 17-1 show that $VMP_L = MRP_L$ under competition.

In section (B) of Table 17-1, the monopoly values are calculated in exactly the same manner as those in section (A). The MRP_L is less than the VMP_L

TABLE 17–1   The Demand for a Factor Under Pure Competition and Monopoly in the Product Market

(1) Units of Factor Q_L	(2) Total Physical Product TPP	(3) Marginal Physical Product $\Delta(2)$ MPP_L	(4) Product Price = Marginal Revenue $P_x = MR_x$	(5) Total Revenue $(2)\times(4)$ TR_x	(6) Value of the Marginal Product $(3)\times(4)$ VMP_L	(7) Marginal Revenue Product $\Delta(5)/\Delta(1) =$ $(3)\times(4)$ MRP_L	(8) Product Price (Greater than the Marginal Revenue) $P_x > MR_x$	(9) Total Revenue $(2)\times(8)$ TR_x	(10) Value of Marginal Product $(3)\times(8)$ VMP_L	(11) Marginal Revenue Product $\Delta(9)/\Delta(1)$ MRP_L
	Common Values		Purely Competitive Values (A)				Monopoly Values (B)			
1	5	5	$1.00	$ 5.00	$ 5.00	$ 5.00	$1.70	$ 8.50	$ 8.50	$ 8.50
2	13	8	1.00	13.00	8.00	8.00	1.50	19.50	12.00	11.00
3	22	9	1.00	22.00	9.00	9.00	1.35	29.70	12.15	10.20
4	33	11	1.00	33.00	11.00	11.00	1.20	39.60	13.20	9.90
5	41	8	1.00	41.00	8.00	8.00	1.14	46.74	9.12	7.14
6	46	5	1.00	46.00	5.00	5.00	1.07	49.22	5.35	2.48
7	49	3	1.00	49.00	3.00	3.00	1.00	49.00	3.00	–.22
8	51	2	1.00	51.00	2.00	2.00	.95	48.45	1.90	–.55
9	51	0	1.00	51.00	0.00	0.00	.95	48.45	0.00	0.00
10	48	–3	1.00	48.00	–3.00	–3.00	1.02	48.96	–3.06	.51

because of the decrease in sales price which must be taken on all units of output sold in order to sell additional units. For example, 22 units can be sold at $1.35 each, yielding a TR of $29.70. To sell 33 units, however, price must be lowered to $1.20 per unit, and total revenue becomes $39.60. The change in total revenue (ΔTR_x) is thus $9.90. The VMP_L of $13.20 exceeds the MRP_L of $9.90.

Figure 17–2 shows how the MRP_L curve varies in each of the four market situations: (a) pure competition, (b) monopolistic competition, (c) oligopoly (of the kinked demand curve variety), and (d) pure monopoly.[4] In each case the marginal physical product curves are assumed identical in shape. The MPP_L curves, when multiplied by the appropriate MR_x curves in the upper row of diagrams, will result in the MRP_L curves of different slopes and elasticities shown in the lower row of diagrams. (For convenience, the VMP_L has been suppressed in Figure 17–2. In panel (a), $VMP_L = MRP_L$; whereas in all other cases, $VMP_L > MRP_L$.) In every case, the MRP_L is downsloping. It is interesting to note that if the factor price were to increase, the largest resulting reduction in employment would occur in the most competitive market, panel (a),

FIGURE 17–2 Marginal Revenue Product Curves in Different Market Situations

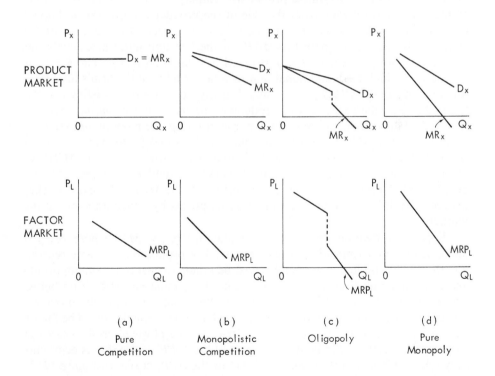

(a) Pure Competition

(b) Monopolistic Competition

(c) Oligopoly

(d) Pure Monopoly

---

[4] This section draws on Alan M. Cartter, *Theory of Wages and Employment* (Homewood: Richard D. Irwin, 1959), Ch. 5.

and the next largest in panel (b). If the factor price increase were to lie within the gap between discontinuous sections of the MRP_L curve in panel (c), there would be no short-run change in employment, although there would be for the pure monopoly case in panel (d).

FACTOR EQUILIBRIUM ANALYSIS

The declining portion of the firm's MRP_a schedule for any factor constitutes the firm's demand schedule for that factor, provided that it is the only variable factor. When a firm hires several variable factors, the MRP_a curve is generally no longer its demand curve. To explain this, we must first establish the principle or rule which guides a profit-seeking firm in hiring any factor.

The Equimarginal Principle for Hiring Factors

The *equimarginal principle* in general states that the optimal or most preferred position is reached when the marginal return equals the marginal cost. The marginal productivity theory of factor prices applies the general marginal analysis of pricing and quantity determination to factor employment. In its application to factor employment, the theory may be stated as follows: A producer desiring to maximize profits will employ units of the factor as long as the additional revenue from the sale of the product exceeds the additional cost of employing the factor. That is, it is advantageous to hire units of the factor up to the point where the MRP_a of the last unit hired just equals the *marginal factor expense* (MFE_a) incurred in hiring that factor. The MFE_a is the amount which each additional unit of a factor adds to the firm's total (factor) expense or $\Delta TC/\Delta Q_a$. One should always be careful to distinguish between MC_x or the extra cost of producing one more unit of *output* ($MC_x = \Delta TC/\Delta Q_x$) and MFE_a or the extra expense of hiring one more *input* ($MFE_a = \Delta TC/\Delta Q_a$). The $MRP_a = MFE_a$ rule may be illustrated for the variable factor labor. If the producer is hiring such a number of workers that the MRP_L of the last workers as well as additional workers would exceed their MFE_L, clearly profit increases by hiring more workers. If the MFE_L of the last worker exceeds the MRP_L, the firm can increase its profits by laying off some of the workers.

Earlier we demonstrated that the equation $MC_x = MR_x$ where MC_x is falling leads to maximization of losses instead of profits. By the same reasoning, the MPP_a and hence the MRP_a must be falling to ensure maximum profits and not maximum losses. (More generally, MC_x must cut MR_x from below and MFE_a must cut MRP_a from below for maximization of profits to occur.) The output market requires that price exceed average variable cost. The factor market analogue to this requirement is that average physical product (APP_a) must exceed MPP_a. That is, the only part of the MPP_a curve that is economically relevant is that portion which lies below the APP_a curve. In Figure 17–3, only the rising portion of the MC_x curve above AVC_x (segment AB) is economically relevant in determining the firm's output supply curve, and only

FIGURE 17-3 **Relevant Portions of** *MC* **and** *MPP* **Curves**

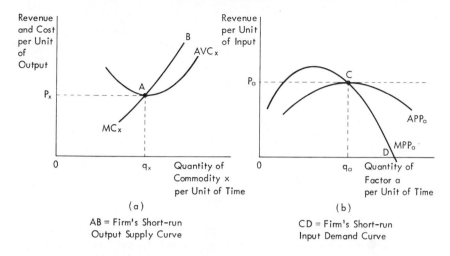

(a)

(b)

AB = Firm's Short-run
Output Supply Curve

CD = Firm's Short-run
Input Demand Curve

the falling portion of the MPP_a curve below the APP_a curve (segment CD) is economically relevant in determining the firm's input demand curve.

We can define average revenue product (ARP_a) as APP_a times the price of the output ($ARP_a = AR_x \cdot APP_a$) and MRP_a as $MR_x \cdot MPP_a$. If competition is assumed in the output market, $AR_x = MR_x$, and the ARP_a and MRP_a curves obtain their general shapes from the APP_a and MPP_a curves respectively.

As illustrated in Figure 17-4, both the ARP_a and MRP_a curves can be derived from the TRP_a curve—defined as the total revenue from hiring Q_a units of input a. In this diagram, only the portion of the MRP_a curve labeled FG constitutes the firm's factor demand function in the case of a single variable factor. To demonstrate that the MRP_a curve above the ARP_a curve is not included in the demand for the factor curve, suppose that this firm hires factors competitively and therefore can hire all the factors it wishes at the constant price of $0A$. If the firm's MRP_a curve were its demand curve in this range, it would dictate that the firm hire $0D$ units at this price to reach the desired $MRP_a = MFE_a$ point, or in this case the $MRP_a = P_a$ point. The firm's total variable costs ($P_a \cdot Q_a$) would equal the area of rectangle $0ABD$ (which equals the price of the variable factor $P_a = 0A$) times the quantity of the variable input $Q_a = 0D$. On the other hand, the firm's total revenue ($P_x \cdot Q_x$ or $AR_x \cdot Q_x = ARP_a \cdot Q_a$) equals $0CED$. Clearly, $0ABD > 0CED$ or $TVC > TRP$, and the firm will close down rather than produce any output and hence will not hire any inputs at factor prices higher than $0F'$.

Summary of Factor Market Equilibrium Conditions

As in the output market, the basic decision-making algorithm for the firm in the factor market can be summarized in three conditions. The factor employment level n is optimal if:

FIGURE 17–4 **Derivation of *ARP* and *MRP* Curves**

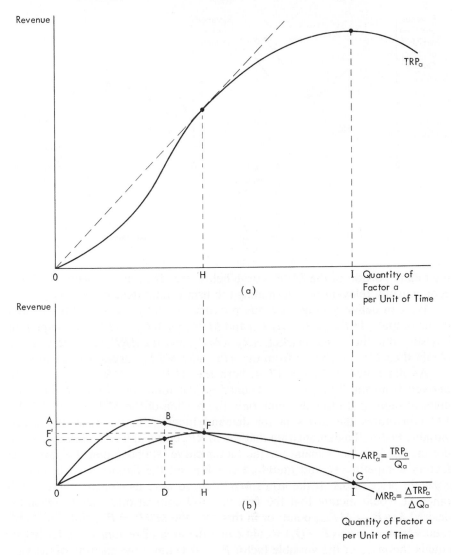

$$MRP_n = MFE_n \qquad \text{marginal equality} \qquad \textbf{(17.6)}$$

$$\left.\begin{array}{l} \text{(a) } MRP_{n-1} > MFE_{n-1} \\ \text{(b) } MRP_{n+1} < MFE_{n+1} \end{array}\right\} \quad \text{marginal inequality} \qquad \textbf{(17.7)}$$

$$\begin{array}{l} \text{(a) } TRP_n \gtreqless TFE_n \qquad \text{short run} \qquad\qquad \textbf{(17.8)} \\ \text{(b) } TRP_n \gtreqless TC_n \qquad \text{long run} \end{array}$$

where $n-1$ ($n+1$) represents in general smaller (greater) levels of factor usage than level n, TFE_n represents all variable factor outlays, and TC_n represents all factor outlays.

As in the output market, the marginal inequality is a more powerful and general approach to finding an optimal value than the marginal equality. In geometric terms, the marginal inequality (or second-order condition) states that the slope of the MFE_a should be greater than the slope of the MRP_a.

Total Analysis and Marginal Analysis

Just as the firm's optimum output position was formulated in total and in marginal terms, so can a firm's equilibrium input position be formulated. The analogue to a firm's output total analysis comparing TR_x and TC_x is its input total analysis comparing TRP_a and TFE_a (total factor expenses). The analogue to the marginal output condition that $MR_x = MC_x$ is that $MRP_a = MFE_a$. In addition, as will be shown algebraically below, the input conditions do not provide an additional task for the firm that has solved the output problem. One solution implies the other. They are merely another way of looking at the same thing.

Figure 17–5 illustrates the total input analysis. The market demand and supply for factor a are assumed given so that the price of a is a constant. The

**FIGURE 17–5   Optimal Input Employment:
Competitive Factor Market**

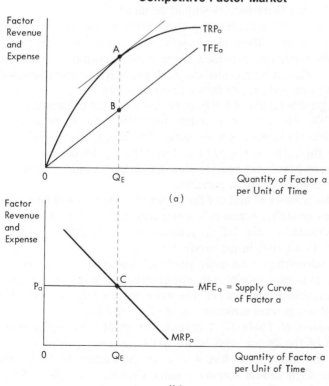

firm's production process involves fixed inputs and fixed costs, but for the moment only one variable factor; hence, the total factor expense is determined entirely by factor a. The quantity of the factor at which the vertical distance between TRP_a and TFE_a is maximized is shown by AB at $0Q_E$ units of the factor in panel (a). This corresponds to point C in panel (b), where the $MRP_a = MFE_a$ at $0Q_E$ units of factor a.

MRP Curve as the Firm's Short-Run Demand Curve

We can summarize this section by repeating that the firm's short-run factor demand curve is that portion of its declining MRP_a curve that lies below the maximum point on its ARP_a curve. This holds whether monopoly or competition exists. "Short run," in the context of factor demand curves, means that there is only one variable factor. (In the long run, when all factors are variable, the firm's MRP curve no longer has to be its demand curve.)

The MRP_a curve shows the various quantities of the resource that would be demanded at various factor prices, and that is in fact what a demand curve is supposed to show. If in Figure 17–5(b) the input price were greater than $0P_a$, the firm would hire that quantity indicated by the intersection of this higher price line with the MRP_a curve (provided $MRP_a \leqq ARP_a$). This means less of factor a would be hired. For prices lower than $0P_a$, the intersection would signify that more factors should be hired.

As Figure 17–6 indicates, the conclusions in the above paragraphs hold regardless of whether there is competition, panel (a), or monopoly, panel (b), in the product market, provided there is competition in the factor market (i.e., $MFE_a = P_a$). In both cases, the declining MRP_a curve (provided $MRP_a \leqq ARP_a$) is the firm's short-run factor demand curve.

In both panels (a) and (b), $0P_a$ is both the market price and marginal factor expense of the resource since under competition the P_a remains constant at the firm's different levels of employment. The supply curve of the factor to the firm is thus the same as the MFE_a. The MRP_a reflects diminishing marginal productivity in panels (a) and (b) plus declining marginal revenue in the noncompetitive case depicted in panel (b).

$0q_a$ is the number of units of the factor that the firm will hire since $MRP_a = MFE_a$ at this quantity. When pure competition exists on the input side, the P_a may be substituted for the MFE_a, yielding the rule that $MRP_a = P_a$. Further, if pure competition exists in the product market, $P_x = MR_x$, so $VMP_a = MRP_a$; and this substitution may be made yielding the profit-maximum rule of $VMP_a = P_a$. But this is a very special rule, applicable only when pure competition appears on both sides of the market. The more general rule, and the one that holds regardless of the market structure, is $MRP_a = MFE_a$.

Examination of Table 17–1 reveals the profit-maximizing rule in action. If the price of the factor (and hence MFE_a) were equal to \$11, column (7) shows that the firm should hire 4 units of the factor. At \$8 it should hire 5 units, and at \$3 it should employ 7 units. Column (7) is the MRP_a schedule; and since it shows the various quantities of the factors the firm will hire at various resource prices, it is also the factor demand schedule.

FIGURE 17-6 Optimal Factor Use in a Competitive Factor Market: Competition and Monopoly in the Product Market

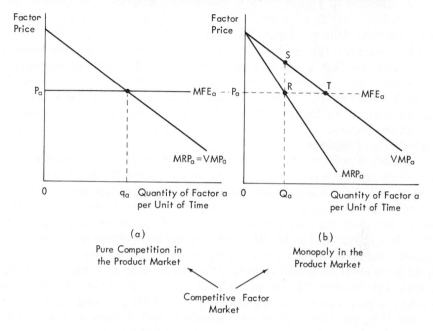

(a)
Pure Competition in
the Product Market

(b)
Monopoly in the
Product Market

Competitive Factor
Market

MARKET IMPERFECTIONS: MONOPOLY AND MONOPSONY

Market imperfections in the form of some degree of market power by the sellers of commodities have been discussed at length in earlier chapters. Firms may also have some market power over the factor market in which they buy factor services. The possibilities for a firm are the following:

	Product Market	Factor Market
(a)	competition	competition
(b)	competition	monopsony
(c)	monopoly	competition
(d)	monopoly	monopsony

The number of "cases" could be increased substantially (even without getting into degrees of noncompetitiveness) by noting that both the product and the factor markets have other sides. For example, under (a) we have competition in the product market, but the buyer or buyers could be either a monopsonist or competitors; and on the factor-market side the sellers could be in competition or monopoly. We will not bother the reader with all of these cases since the principles of price and quantity determination are applicable in all cases. The important point to be stressed is that there is no necessary connection between the nature of the market on the product side and the nature of the market on the factor side. In other words, the product and factor markets are essentially independent of each other.

Monopoly

In panel (b) of Figure 17–6, a monopolist, as does a competitor, hires where $MRP_a = MFE_a (P_a)$. But since $MR_x < P_x$ and hence $MRP_a < VMP_a$, noncompetitive firms pay inputs less than the VMP_a of that input. The fact that a factor is paid less than its VMP_a does not mean that a monopolistic firm pays each factor less than it can earn in alternative employments or less than do competitive firms. Rather the monopolist hires inputs such that $P_a = MRP_a$, but at this point the $P_a < VMP_a$. Thus, even though inputs are paid the same amount, they have a higher VMP_a when employed by a monopolist than by a competitor because of the monopolist's restricted production and hence employment of inputs.

In other words, the general effect of any monopoly is to restrict *output* below competitive levels, and hence we would expect the demand for *inputs* to be restricted also. Since inputs are desired only to produce output, a restriction of output curtails input demand. Figure 17–6(b) shows that the MRP_a curve – the short-run factor demand curve – of the imperfectly competitive firm is less elastic than if the firm were a purely competitive one. Under competitive conditions, the input price of P_a would result in a larger output, associated with point T instead of $0Q_a$. This can be seen in Table 17–1, where column (11) shows that 2 units of the input would be hired at a price of $11.00; whereas a pure competitor, equating P_a with VMP_a, would, according to column (10), produce somewhere between 4 and 5 units or between the VMP's of $13.20 and $9.12 at an input price of $11.00.

Monopsony

The other general case of imperfection concerns monopsony (one buyer) in the factor market. Under competitive conditions in the factor market, the MFE_a equals the price of the factor. There are too many firms hiring the factor for any one of them to be able to influence the price. The "company town" or "factory town" in which one firm is the primary source of employment, or the government's purchases of, say, some defense materials would fit into the pure monopsony category. In general, improvements in communication and transportation facilities have increased the mobility of labor and reduced the likelihood of monopsony or oligopsony.

In the pure monopsony case, the firm's supply schedule for a factor is the total supply schedule. If the supply schedule has the upward shape normally assumed, the monopsonist must pay higher wages to secure more workers. This means that with monopsony the MFE of labor exceeds the price of the labor or the wage rate.

The distinction between the supply conditions in competitive and monopsony markets is illustrated in Figure 17–7. Basically, the $MFE_a > P_a$ under monopsony because the hiring of an additional unit of a factor increases total (factor) expense by more than the P_a, since all units employed receive the new higher price. This is illustrated in Table 17–2.

FIGURE 17-7   Supply of Factors in Competitive and Monopsonistic Factor Markets

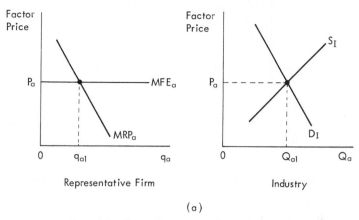

Representative Firm

Industry

(a)

Pure Competition in the Factor Market

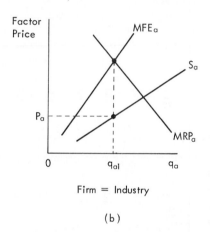

Firm = Industry

(b)

Pure Monopsony in the Factor Market

If there is competition in the factor market so that the factor price is given to the individual firm, the MFE_a will be constant and equal to P_a as shown in columns (2) and (4). In contrast, under monopsony the hiring of additional factors requires a higher factor price. For instance, one factor can be hired at a price of $11. But the hiring of a second factor forces the firm to pay a higher price of $12. Therefore, the MFE_a is $13 – the $12 paid to the second factor plus a $1 raise for the first factor. The higher factor price involved in attracting additional factors will have to be paid to all factors currently employed at the lower price. This means that the marginal cost of hiring an additional worker is the wage of this worker plus the necessary wage increments that must be paid to existing employees. Thus, to the monopsonist, the MFE_a of hiring any input is greater than the P_a.

TABLE 17–2   Supply of a Factor Under Pure Competition (PC) and Monopsony (M) in the Factor Market

(1) Units of Factor	(2) Price of Factor (PC)	(2)' Price of Factor (M)	(3) Total Factor Expense (PC): (1) × (2)	(3)' Total Factor Expense (M): (1) × (2)'	(4) Marginal Factor Expense (PC): Δ3	(4)' Marginal Factor Expense (M): Δ3'
1	$11	$11	$11	$11	$11	$11
2	11	12	22	24	11	13
3	11	13	33	39	11	15
4	11	14	44	56	11	17
5	11	15	55	75	11	19
6	11	16	66	96	11	21
7	11	17	77	119	11	23
8	11	18	88	144	11	25
9	11	19	99	171	11	27
10	11	20	110	200	11	29

The monopsony model with first competition and then monopoly in the output market can be seen in Figure 17–8. In panel (a), pure competition in the output market (that is, $P_x = MR_x$ so that $VMP_a = MRP_a$) is coupled with monopsony (that is, $MFE_a > P_a$) in the input market. To maximize profits, the firm will hire that quantity of inputs such that $MFE_a = MRP_a$. This is labeled point a in the diagram. This means the firm will hire $0Q_m$ units of the factor and will pay the factor price of $0P_m$ indicated by the factor supply curve. The profit-maximizing rule on the input side is always the following: Hire the quantity of factors at which MFE_a equals a declining MRP_a (provided $MRP_a \leq ARP_a$) and pay this quantity of factors the price called for by the factor's supply curve. This is similar to the rule on the output side: Under monopoly, a firm produces where $MR = $ rising MC (provided $P \geq AVC$) but charges the price permitted by the demand curve.

These results may be compared to those which the competitive input market would have yielded at point c in Figure 17–8, panel (a). Under competition, $0Q_c$ units of the factor would have been hired and the factor price would have been $0P_c$. That is, monopsonistic conditions in the factor market will result in a lower level of employment and a lower factor price than would occur when the factor is purchased under competitive conditions. Other things

FIGURE 17-8   Factor Price and Quantity in Monopsony Firms

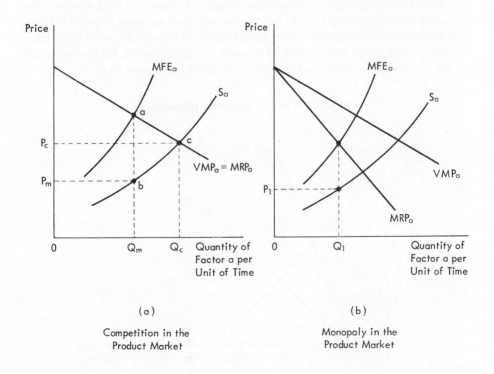

(a)

Competition in the
Product Market

(b)

Monopoly in the
Product Market

being equal, the monopsonistic firm hires fewer inputs and pays them lower factor prices, and society gets a smaller output. Just as a monopolistic seller restricts output to obtain above-competitive commodity prices, so does the monopsonistic employer restrict employment so as to realize below-competitive factor prices (and therefore costs).

When a firm is both a monopolistic seller and a monopsonistic buyer, it has things its own way on both sides of the market. The price of the factor and the quantity of the factor demanded are both less than in the pure competition (in the output market) case. Figure 17–8(b) shows this case.

Bilateral Monopoly

A case of some theoretical interest is the situation where a monopsonistic buyer employs a factor of production from another firm which has monopoly control over the supply of that factor service. This is called *bilateral monopoly,* and the graphic analysis is shown in Figure 17–9.

The monopolist's marginal cost of producing the factor is MC. The demand for the factor by the monopsonistic firm is its marginal revenue product ($MRP = D$), and the associated marginal revenue of the monopolist is labeled MR. We would ordinarily (that is, when the number of buyers is large) expect the monopolist to choose the optimal position of producing the quantity at which $MR = MC$ (i.e., $0Q_S$), setting the price at $0P_S$. But since there is only one buyer, that buyer may not accept those conditions.

The buyer's optimal position is to employ the quantity $0Q_B$ at which the marginal factor expense (MFE) equals the marginal revenue product (MRP). The buyer would pay the price $0P_B$ if the suppliers of the factor were numerous. Under conditions of competition in the sale of the factor the MC curve would be the supply curve and the MFE curve would be marginal to it.

FIGURE 17–9   Bilateral Monopoly

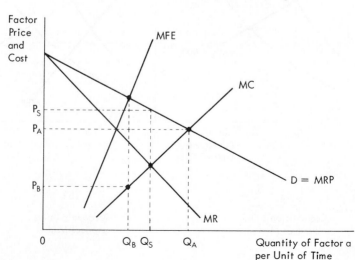

There is a stalemate here, or an indeterminacy, since the single buyer and single seller have different optimal prices and quantities, and no economic forces exist to reconcile them. The relative bargaining power of the two parties will then determine whether the price will be close to $0P_S$ or $0P_B$.

Notice that if a third party (such as in compulsory arbitration) sets the price, that price would become the supply curve to the buyer (so $P = MFE$ to the MC curve) and the demand curve for the seller (so $P = MR$ to the MRP curve). In that event, the price that would "clear the market" would be $0P_A$, and the seller would wish to sell $0Q_A$ and the buyer would wish to buy $0Q_A$.

A Summary of the Effects of Monopoly on Income Distribution

We may now summarize the effects of monopoly and monopsony on income distribution. Since monopoly tends to restrict output, it also restricts the demand for factor service inputs and therefore keeps the employment of the factor services below competitive levels; and if some degree of monopsony power exists, factor prices will also be lower. Put in other terms, monopolistic or monopsonistic firms pay factor service prices which are lower than the value of the services' marginal product. And factors are being inefficiently allocated whenever the VMP_a for any factor is not equal in all of the factors' alternative employments. For monopolies, the extra revenue derived from the sale of the marginal output of a factor is less than the VMP_a of the input. This is because, for monopolies, marginal revenue is less than price. But it is through equating the marginal revenue with the marginal expense of the factor that the firm maximizes profits. For monopsonists, the marginal expense of a factor is greater than the price of the factor, because each added factor has to be paid a higher price which then applies to all other units of the factor. But in maximizing profits, it is the marginal factor expense rather than the price of the factor that is relevant.

Monopoly-Monopsony Exploitation

We can contrast the above situations with pure competition, where the marginal revenue product of a factor equals its VMP_a and the marginal factor expense equals the factor's price. In other words, departures from competitive conditions in the product and/or the input market result in a lower volume of employment and a divergence between the factor price and the value of the marginal product. The smaller volume of employment correlates with the accepted idea that monopoly restricts the volume of production. The gap between VMP_a and MRP_a in input terms (or $P_x - MC_x$ in output terms) due to monopoly power is sometimes called *monopolistic exploitation* of the factor. The gap between the MRP_a and P_a due to monopsony power is sometimes called *monopsonistic exploitation* of the factor.

According to exploitationists, labor (or any factor) is exploited in monopolistic but not in competitive industries. Yet wages may be lower in competitive industries than in the exploited monopolistic industries, even though the workers in the latter case receive a wage that is less than their VMP. Secondly, all factors, including both labor and capital, are exploited in the sense that their price is less than their VMP. However, people tend to emphasize the exploitation of labor and neglect capital. Thirdly, raising the price of a factor does not solve the problem since monopolistic firms would simply reduce their level of employment of the factor until the MRP_a again equaled the higher P_a. The problem is that these monopolistic firms do not produce the socially desirable level of output and hence do not hire the socially desirable quantity of factors. Fourthly, any type of product differentiation results in $P_x > MR_x$, $VMP_a > MRP_a$, and $VMP_a > P_a$, and hence exploitation. Even if all product differentiation were of a socially desirable type, exploitation would still exist. Finally, the removal of exploitation could be quite costly in terms of some people's notion of a good society. For example, it would most likely require more government involvement, either in the form of state ownership and operation or in stringent price controls.

The picture with regard to removing monopsonistic exploitation is much brighter. The basic causes of monopsony—specialized factors and immobility—can be counteracted in several ways.

A specialized factor is one which has a productivity in its present employment that is significantly higher than in its next best alternative employment. The monopsony due to specialized factors can be attacked by setting fixed minimum prices above the monopsony price. However, the difficulty of determining and enforcing the proper minimum price is considerable.

Immobility of factors also causes monopsony. Anything which holds factors to a particular geographical area or firm can cause an upsloping MFE_a curve. A lack of information, inadequate transportation facilities, security and pension plans, emotional ties, etc., can all cause immobility.

DETERMINANTS OF SHORT-RUN FACTOR DEMAND

Having determined that the MRP_a curve is the firm's short-run factor demand curve if only one factor is variable, it is important to summarize the factors that influence short-run factor demand. Our derivation of short-run factor demand suggested two determinants: the factor's physical productivity and the value of that productivity to the firm. The latter element depends on the demand and hence the market price and marginal revenue of the commodity the factor is helping to produce. In addition, the previous analysis of product demand indicated that another element, the prices of "other" factors, is also important.

The Factor's Physical Productivity

Other things remaining equal—in particular, given the product price of the commodity the factor produces—the greater the physical productivity of any resource, the greater the factor demand. Any given factor's productivity depends not only on the quantity and quality of that factor's productivity, but also on the quantities and qualities of the other factors with which it works, as well as on the general state of technology and the level of efficiency of the entire national economic organization. The marginal productivity and the income earned of any given factor will be greater, the greater the quantity and the higher the quality of other cooperating productive services, the higher the quality of the factor in question, the more advanced the state of technology, and the higher the level of efficiency of the national economic organization.

Diminishing returns can be offset through improvements in technology and economic organization or increases in the quantity and quality of other factors. These improvements would shift upward the entire MPP_a curve and, *ceteris paribus,* the demand for the factor. In the United States and some other advanced countries, this has, in fact, happened to the labor factor. Rising real wages have been associated with rising population (and work force) levels because of advancing technology, improved economic organization, increased quantity of capital, and improved quality of labor. Of course, this is not a repeal of the $LDMR$, but merely a violation of its "other things being equal" proviso. The law of diminishing returns applies under a given state of technology. But if there are technological advances and productivity increases, most of the factors of production will have a higher marginal productivity, and returns will tend to rise. Similarly, if the quality of other factors improves, the productivity of, say, the labor factor will increase. One of the other factors which may vary in quality is managerial efficiency. Since production is not merely a physical process but a social process involving the employment of different factors, the quality of these factors is important in any such cooperative venture. Clearly, with given supplies of productive factors and a given state of technology, a more efficient management will increase labor productivity. In a like manner, with a given amount and quality of factors, state of technology, and managerial efficiency, one form of social and economic organization will lead to greater production than another. The system of land tenure, the soundness of financial institutions and the monetary system, the degree to which the advantages of specialization are exploited, the general governmental attitude toward business, etc., are all relevant considerations.

A final element determining the position of the marginal product of labor curve is the quality of labor itself—i.e., productivity per hour of work, with the supplies of all factors, the state of technology and economic organization, and the level of managerial efficiency being given. Productivity per worker-hour depends upon: (1) the physical and mental health of workers, (2) the level of education and skills, and (3) the institutional and social environment—attitudes, incentives, etc.

Demand for the Commodities that the Factor Produces

Since factor demand is a derived demand, the demand and hence product price and marginal revenue influence the "value" productivity or MRP_a curve of any resource. Given the marginal physical product, the greater the commodity price, the greater the "value" productivity. Thus, anything that increases the demand for the product being produced increases the MRP curves of the factors utilized in its production.

The Prices of Other Factors

Just as the prices of other goods affect commodity demand, the prices of other factors are a determinant of factor demand. Factors may have a substitute, complement, or independent relationship with one another, depending on whether $\Delta MRP_a/\Delta Q_b \lessgtr 0$. If the quotient is less than zero, the factors are substitutes, since an increase in the quantity of factor b leads to a decrease in the *MRP* of factor a and hence its demand curve.[5] Typically factors are substitutes. For instance, the rise in labor costs in the United States has historically led to the development of labor-saving machinery. In turn, generally when the price of labor drops, the firm can reach its least-cost point by increasing its use of labor and decreasing the quantity of capital demanded. However, this substitution effect may be offset wholly or in part by an accompanying output, scale, or expansion effect. A lower price of labor means lower (marginal) costs and higher equilibrium levels of output. A larger output necessitates more inputs and a greater demand for all (superior) factors. The net effect of the decline in the price of labor upon the demand for capital depends upon the relative magnitude of these two effects. As in the commodity market, the substitution effect normally is considerably larger than the output effect.

FIVE PRINCIPLES REGULATING THE ELASTICITY OF FACTOR DEMAND

The elasticity concept developed in the product market also applies to the factor market. Alfred Marshall developed four principles — he did not develop rule (2) — regulating factor demand elasticity. The elasticity of demand for a factor will be smaller (i.e., more inelastic): (1) the more essential the factor or the fewer the good substitutes it has, (2) the shorter the time period involved, (3) the more inelastic the supply of other factors, (4) the smaller the elasticity of demand for the final product, and (5) the smaller the proportion of total costs for the final good accounted for by the expenditure on the factor.

The first and second of these principles are closely related. The larger the number of substitutes and the closer the substitutes, the more elastic the factor demand. The longer the time period, the more variable the factors and hence the more likely the firm will be to achieve the most economical combination of resources. In addition, the longer time period allows buyers of the commodity to make a fuller adjustment to a change in price. We cannot emphasize enough that substitution is possible on a much wider scale than most people think. To take an extreme case, glass and brick can be good substitutes in building houses by merely varying the size of the windows. The fewer the number of substitute factors and the less readily other services can be substituted for the factor in question, the more inelastic the factor demand.

---

[5] As in the product market, a precise definition of substitutability requires that the output or income effect be removed. Basically, the relationship among inputs (outputs) involves a movement along a given isoquant (indifference curve) as relative prices change, not a movement from one curve to another.

If factors a and b are substitutes, a rise in the P_a will lead to an increase in the demand for factor b. The more inelastic the supply of factor b, the greater its rise in price as its demand increases. This will tend to mitigate the advantages from using factor b in place of factor a. Thus, the more factor b rises in price, the less factor a will be replaced, i.e., the more inelastic will be the demand for factor a.

If factors a and b are complements, a fall in P_a will lead to an increased usage of factor a and hence an increase in the MRP_b and an increase in the demand for factor b. This in turn will increase the firms' desire to use factor a. The firms will want to use more of both factor a and factor b and less of other factors. However, the more inelastic the supply curve of factor b facing the industry, the more the P_b rises, which tends to reduce the attractiveness of using this complementary set. That is, the more inelastic the supply of factor b, the more difficult it is to substitute the set of factors a and b for other factors, and therefore the less elastic the demand for factor a.

The direct logic of rule (3) is obvious. This rule can be stated as follows: The larger the price elasticity of demand (η) for any commodity, the higher the elasticity of derived demand for all factors specialized in its production.

Since factor demand is a derived demand, the elasticity of final demand (rule 4) is obviously important in determining factor demand elasticity. As the (noninferior) factor price rises, marginal cost rises, the price of the commodity rises, quantity demanded falls, and hence fewer factors are needed. How many less factors are needed depends on how much quantity demanded falls as the price of the commodity increases — i.e., it depends on commodity demand elasticity.

All of the first four rules are unambiguous. Rule (5), however, is not so clear-cut, despite its strong intuitive appeal. The notion that the smaller the cost of a given factor, as a portion of the total cost of the final commodity, the smaller the elasticity has been called the "importance of being unimportant." A tailor's demand for thread or buttons is supposed to be quite inelastic since the expenditures on them represent a small part of the total cost of a suit. Building trade workers in general, such as plumbers, reputedly have been successful in raising their wages without seriously diminishing the quantity of their services demanded because their wages are only a small fraction of the total cost of a new house and there are few if any possibilities of substitution.

One line of argument that may be taken against arguments like the above is that they amount to saying that entrepreneurs do not economize. Such arguments seem to suggest that the quantity of an input used per unit of output is independent of the price of the factors. In other words, the rule is necessarily true only under the assumption of fixed proportions between the factors. Finally, the rule is fallacious because elasticity measures *proportionate* changes and this rule deals with the *absolute* size of the cost outlays. For example, an "all-important" factor accounting for 100 percent of the total costs would not have a large elasticity, but rather it would be exactly -1.[6]

---

[6] This same criticism applies to the corresponding rule for commodity demand elasticity. See Jack Hirshleifer, *Price Theory and Applications* (Englewood Cliffs: Prentice-Hall, 1976), p. 129.

In any actual case, the net factor elasticity in either competition or monopoly will depend on the relative importance of all the different elements specified in the rules. They need not all work in the same direction. For instance, the demand for aluminum may be highly inelastic for use in conducting electricity because users might be relatively price insensitive with respect to the purchase of electricity as opposed to alternative energy sources such as natural gas. On the other hand, the demand for aluminum might be highly elastic because of the high substitutability between, say, copper and aluminum in conducting electricity.

QUESTIONS

1. Discuss the importance of the distinction between functional and personal income distribution. Do you think the two are inseparable?
2. Assuming a condition of pure competition in both the product and the factor markets, tell whether the wage, as well as the quantity employed, of a particular category of labor would increase, decrease, or not change from the following circumstances:
   (a) The demand for the product increases.
   (b) Immigration of this class of labor increases.
   (c) A new law requires that this type of labor be given a 15 minute (paid) break every hour. (None was given before the law.)
   (d) The price of the product falls.
   (e) New, more efficient machines with which this labor works are installed.
   (f) New requirements of longer apprenticeship periods are imposed.
3. An important point made in this chapter is that when a firm has made the "correct" decision on the quantity of the various factors to use, it has implicitly made the "correct" decision on how much of its commodity to produce. Prove it.
4. Study Table 17–1, page 394, in particular column (11), where MRP is seen to decline from the second to the eighth unit of the variable factor, but then rises for the ninth and tenth units. While this seems unusual, it is correct. Can you explain why it happens?
5. Explain why any firm wishing to maximize profits would employ a factor of production at the point where the marginal factor expense equals the marginal revenue product of that factor.
6. (a) Explain, without the use of graphs or equations, why the MRP of a noncompetitive firm is less than the VMP for a factor.
   (b) Explain, without the use of graphs or equations, why the MFE of a monopsonist is greater than the price of the factor.
7. Consider the bilateral monopoly case shown in Figure 17–9, page 406.
   (a) Suppose a government agency decreed that the price should be half way between P_S and P_A. Which party would petition to have the price lowered, and why?
   (b) Suppose the agency set the price between P_A and P_B. Which party would petition for an increase in price, and why?
8. Describe a condition you believe would constitute exploitation of (say) labor. What would be a remedy for that situation? Would any undesirable consequences flow from the remedy?
9. List a group of occupations that you would expect to have an inelastic demand and explain the reason you put that occupation in the group.

APPENDIX: MATHEMATICAL NOTES

Note 1. Profit Maximization with Monopsony

With competition in the factor market, the proof that equilibrium is achieved when $MRP_a = P_a$ and the slope of the MRP_a curve is less than the slope of the factor supply curve is the same as the short-run output analysis given previously, with TRP_a, TFE_a, and Q_a substituted for TR_x, TC_x, and Q_x. It is therefore not repeated here. What is to be included, however, is a summary of the analysis under monopsony.

The simplest case we can consider is the monopsonistic firm which hires a single input, labor, to produce a commodity which it sells in a competitive market. The production function shows output (q_x) as a function of the amount of labor services (L) employed.

$$q_x = g(L) \tag{17.9}$$

The total revenue (TR_x) and total cost (TC_x) functions are $TR_x = p_x \cdot q_x = p_x h(L)$ and $TC_x = W \cdot L$, where W is the price (wages) of labor. With monopsony, W is an increasing function of the quantity of labor employed (L).

$$W = g(L) \tag{17.10}$$

where $\frac{\delta W}{\delta L} = g'(L) > 0$. The MFE of labor can be written:

$$\delta TFE/\delta L = W + Lg'(L) \tag{17.11}$$

Since $g'(L) > 0$, the $MFE_L > W$ for $L > 0$. The monopsonist's profits are:

$$\pi = TR - TC = p_x h(L) - WL \tag{17.12}$$

The first-order conditions for a maximum require that the derivative of (17.12) with respect to L be set equal to zero.

$$\delta \pi/\delta L = p_x h'(L) - W - Lg'(L) = 0 \tag{17.13}$$
$$p_x h'(L) = W + Lg'(L)$$
$$VMP_L = MFE_L$$

Thus, the necessary conditions are that labor be employed up to the point where $VMP_L = MFE_L$. The second-order conditions are:

$$\frac{\delta^2 \pi}{\delta L^2} = p_x h''(L) - 2g'(L) - Lg''(L) < 0 \tag{17.14}$$
$$p_x h''(L) < 2g'(L) + Lg''(1)$$
$$\text{Slope } VMP_L < \text{Slope } MFE_L$$

This states that if there is pure competition in the output market, the rate of change of the VMP_L must be less than the rate of change of the MFE_L.

If there is monopoly in the output market, price then becomes a function of the commodity produced instead of a constant. The first-order condition then becomes $MRP_L = MFE_L$ and the second-order condition indicates that the MFE_L must be increasing more rapidly than the MRP_L at the point of equilibrium.

18 Long-Run Factor Pricing and Employment

In this chapter our primary aim is to: (1) develop what the factor demand curve would look like in the long run or when there are several variable resources, and (2) develop some idea of the elements determining factor supply conditions in both the short run and the long run. The elements affecting factor demand are usually discussed under the heading marginal productivity analysis, whereas the forces influencing factor supply are usually taken up under the rubric of net advantage analysis.

LONG-RUN FACTOR DEMAND CURVES: THE CASE OF SEVERAL VARIABLE RESOURCES

When a firm uses several variable productive services, the demand curve for any one of them is no longer the MRP_a for that input. The reason is that in the short-run analysis in which the short-run factor demand curve is equal to the MRP_a curve, it is assumed that the quantity of all other factors is held constant—i.e., $\bar{Q}_b$, where b represents all other factors. In the long-run analysis, where there are several variable factors, the long-run factor demand curve assumes that other factor prices are held constant—i.e., $\bar{P}_b$.

From the definition of elasticity, it should be expected that the long-run factor demand curve would be more elastic than the short-run factor demand curve. Since the greater the elasticity of any function, the greater the change in quantity relative to price, it is reasonable to expect the long-run demand curve for factor a (with the price of b fixed) to be more elastic than the short-run demand curve (where the quantity of b is assumed constant).

Factors are defined as complements, substitutes, or unrelated on the basis of how the marginal productivity of any factor, say, factor a, changes in response to a change in the quantity utilized of some other factor, b.

$$\frac{\Delta MPP_a}{\Delta Q_b} \begin{array}{l} > 0 \quad \text{complements} \\ = 0 \quad \text{unrelated} \\ < 0 \quad \text{substitutes} \end{array} \qquad (18.1)$$

In either the case of complements or substitutes, the elasticity of the long-run factor demand curve is greater than that of the short-run (MRP_a) curve. The fact that factors are interdependent causes the quantities of some other factor to change as the price and quantity of one factor shifts. This change in quantity of other factors in turn shifts the MRP curve of the original factor whose price has fallen. These changes can be referred to as *firm* or *internal* changes. In deriving the firm's long-run factor demand curve, we must consider these internal effects. The final result is shown in Figure 18–1.

FIGURE 18-1 Long-Run Factor Demand Curve

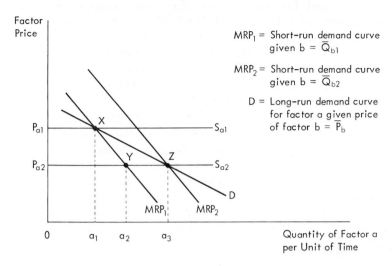

MRP_1 = Short-run demand curve given $b = \bar{Q}_{b1}$

MRP_2 = Short-run demand curve given $b = \bar{Q}_{b2}$

D = Long-run demand curve for factor a given price of factor $b = \bar{P}_b$

Quantity of Factor a per Unit of Time

Assume there are only two factors, a and b, and the price of factor a falls. Further imagine that factor a is either a complementary or substitute input to factor b. Originally the firm is at its optimum at point X, where the factor supply curve S_{a1} represents an input price of $0P_{a1}$. The firm adjusts its quantity hired to $0a_1$ so that the MRP equals the factor price. The MRP_1 curve assumes that the quantity of factor b is held constant at some level, call it $\bar{Q}_{b1}$.

Now let the perfectly elastic factor supply to the firm shift to S_{a2}, associated with the lower factor price of $0P_{a2}$. Since at $0a_1$ the MRP is now greater than the new factor price, the firm will tend to increase its rate of utilization of factor a to point Y (involving $0a_2$ units of factor a) along the original MRP_1 curve. The increase in the quantity of factor a used changes the MRPs of the related factors. If factor b is a substitute factor, its MRP curve is shifted leftward and inward. Since the prices of other factors remain constant $(\bar{P}_b)$ the firm will hire less of these substitute factors. This will shift the MRP_a curve outward and rightward, perhaps even twisting it as well.

Although there may be many related factors—some substitutes and some complements—the sum of all the direct and indirect internal effects must result in a shift to the right of the MRP_1 curve to, say, MRP_2 in Figure 18-1. This means the new optimum will be reached at point Z, where the firm is now hiring $0a_3$ units of factor a.[1] The reason that the decreased utilization of factor b shifts the MRP curve for factor a outward is that the relationship between factors is assumed symmetrical: if $\Delta MRP_b/\Delta Q_a < 0$, then $\Delta MRP_a/\Delta Q_b < 0$. Therefore, if the initial increase in the quantity hired of factor a, as its price falls, leads to

---

[1] The final result is necessarily one in which the quantity hired after the price decrease is associated with a lower MRP_a. Even though the increase in the rate of utilization of other variable factors increases the MRP_a curve of factor a to the right, the fact that factor a is increasing relative to the fixed factors causes the MPP_a and hence the MRP_a to fall.

a decrease in the MRP_b because they are substitutes, this will lead to less of factor b being used. But a decrease in the Q_b leads to an increase in the MRP_a since the factors are substitutes. Similarly, the increase in the Q_a causes the MRP_b to rise for substitutes and hence causes more of factor b to be used, i.e., $\Delta MPP_b/\Delta Q_a > 0$. But from the symmetry, we know that the MPP_a increases as the Q_b increases since $\Delta MRP_a/\Delta Q_b > 0$. Thus, whether the factors are complements or substitutes, the long-run factor demand curve is more elastic than the short-run factor demand curve.[2]

This conclusion also holds even if there is monopoly in the output market.[3] (However, in the case of monopoly, the factor demand curve is generated by connecting points obtained from the successive changes in the market factor price and the MRP_a curves.) Note, however, that if the factors are unrelated, there are no secondary effects so that $MRP_1 = MRP_2$ and hence the short-run factor demand curve equals the long-run factor demand curve. In general, however, factors are related. Finally, whether the inputs are inferior or superior, the final optimum quantity employed of factor a will increase as its price falls.[4]

---

[2] In general, there is some presumption that the complementary effects are likely to dominate. It has been proved that the greater the product demand elasticity, the greater the chance that the factors will be complements. See Thomas R. Saving, "Note on Factor Demand Elasticity: The Competitive Case," *Econometrica* (July, 1963), pp. 555–557.

[3] However, the long-run factor demand curve will be less elastic than in the competitive case, because the increase in the MPP_a as more of factor b is used and output is expanded must be compared with the fall in MR_x as output rises. Thus, while the fall in MR_x counterbalances the increase in MPP_a, it cannot completely overcome it, and the MRP_a must shift outward and rightward. See Charles E. Ferguson, "Inferior Factors and Theories of Production and Input Demand," *Economica* (May, 1968), pp. 140–150, for a proof of this. For a contrary view, without proof, see Milton Friedman, *Price Theory; A Provisional Text* (Chicago: Aldine Publishing Co., 1962), p. 178.

[4] The above analysis assumes that all the factors are superior. If factor a were inferior, the results would appear as follows.

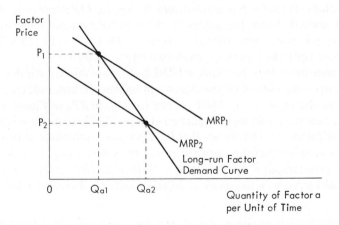

Note that even though the MRP curve shifts backward and leftward from MRP_1 to MRP_2, the final quantity consumed of factor a is higher at the new lower price.

Figure 18–2 presents, in more detail, exactly how the long-run factor demand curve is derived from the various shifts in the MRP_a curves. You will note that each separate MRP_a curve assumes that factor b is held constant at a different level. Further note that as the MRP_a curves increase or move to the right from MRP_1 all the way to MRP_5, each successive curve is associated with higher quantities of factor b in the case of complements and lower values of factor b in the case of substitutes. For example, MRP_2 assumes that factor b is held constant ($\bar{b}_2$) at four units for substitutes, whereas at MRP_1 the quantity of factor b is held fixed at five units. Of course, the better the substitutes or complements that factor a has, the more elastic the long-run factor demand curve will be.

The above analysis could also be derived in terms of the substitution and output effects. The fact that a change in relative factor prices leads to a change in the quantities of factors used can be attributed to these effects. Since this derivation was done in the earlier chapter on isoquants, it is not repeated here.

FIGURE 18–2   Substitutes and Complements in Long-Run Factor Demand Curve Derivation

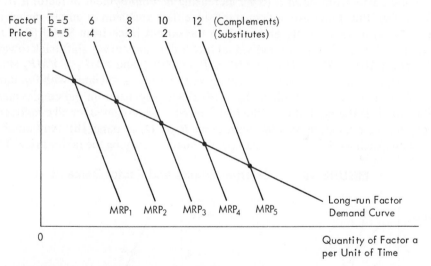

MARKET DEMAND CURVE

The aggregate, industry, or market demand curve for a variable factor is a horizontal summation of the demand curves of the individual firms in the industry. To be sure, this summation is not a simple one for a competitive industry since adjustment has to be made for *market* or *external* effects arising from the fact that the simultaneous expansion or contraction of all firms lowers or raises the output price and therefore lowers or raises each firm's factor demand curve. On the other hand, if a group of pure monopolists are the sole purchasers of the factors, the market demand curve is a simple horizontal summation of the individual demands of each firm. No market or external effects would result from a decrease in the output price as expansion occurs since these have already been taken into account in drawing up each monopolist's factor demand curve. However, for market demand curves under monopolistic competition or oligopoly, one must make adjustments just as in the competitive case, except that the individual demand curves under monopoly markets are derived from the MRP_a instead of the VMP_a curves.

The external effects of factor price changes on the industry demand curve are illustrated in Figure 18–3. A "representative" competitive firm is depicted in panel (a) and the entire industry in panel (b). Suppose that at the going market factor price of $0P_1$ the representative firm shown in Figure 18–3 moves along its factor demand curve, hiring $0q_1$ units of the (superior) factor a. If we sum the quantities hired by all firms employing this factor, we find that $0Q_1$ units are hired, and one point, point A, is established on the industry demand curve D_1. Also suppose that this equilibrium is associated with an output price of $3. The variable input is labor services. If the price of labor falls to $0P_2$ from, say, an increase in the supply of labor, each firm will expand its quantity of factor a (labor) hired[5] since it will want to expand output in response to a fall in its (marginal) costs. *Ceteris paribus,* the firm would move along its factor demand curve from point a to a', increasing its employment of factor a from $0q_1$ to $0q_2$. But things are not constant since the expansion of output means an increase in market supply and a fall in the output price from $3.00 ($P_{x1}$) to, say, $2.50 ($P_{x2}$). Therefore, individual factor demand curves shift back toward d_2 since $VMP_1 = P_{x1} \cdot MPP_1$, $VMP_2 = P_{x2} \cdot MPP_2$, and $VMP_1 > VMP_2$ since $P_{x1} > P_{x2}$. As a result, each firm will move to point b associated with $0q_3$ units of factor $a;$ the external effects have restricted expansion in the employment of factor a. If the quantities of the factor hired are aggregated for all employers, $0Q_2$ units are used, associated with point B on D_1 in panel (b). Any number of points such as $A, B, \ldots, N$ can be obtained by varying the factor price. The

FIGURE 18–3   External Effects and Factor Demand

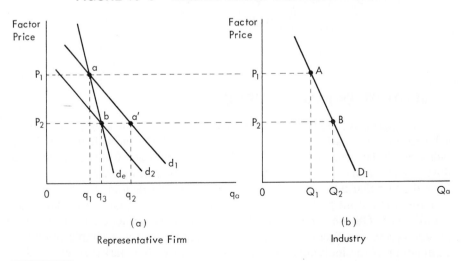

(a)
Representative Firm

(b)
Industry

[5] Assuming it is not an inferior good in terms of the factor market. In fact, unless otherwise specified, it will be implicitly assumed that all factors are "superior."

line connecting all these points forms the industry demand curve for factor a. In the most typical case of external diseconomies such as described above, the D_I curve is steeper (more inelastic) than it would be without taking into account these adjustments.[6] If external economies prevailed, the D_I would tend to be more elastic.

The curve labeled d_e in panel (a) is constructed by allowing for external effects, just as the long-run factor demand curve in Figure 18–2 was constructed by allowing for internal effects. The industry demand curve D_I is thus composed of the sum total of the d_e curves for each firm in the industry.

THE SUPPLY OF PRODUCTIVE SERVICES[7]

While no classification of variable productive services is satisfactory for all purposes, the following broad classification into four groups is useful in discussing factor supplies: land (including natural resources), labor (including managerial ability), capital, and intermediate goods. The latter category mostly consists of those products produced and sold by one firm to another firm which uses them in producing its output. If we assume commodity supply curves are generally upsloping, the supply of intermediate goods would be upsloping since they represent the output of some producer. By the same token, since natural resources and capital typically form the commodity outputs of mining and capital goods companies respectively, they are positively sloping (supply) curves. The factor supply schedule that is most difficult to pin down is labor; hence we will spend more time on it than on the other factors. Most likely, nonspecialized labor in any time period, and specialized labor in the long run, have upsloping supply curves.

---

[6] Along the D_I curve, the output demand curve is assumed constant, $\bar{F}(x)$, whereas along the ΣD_f curve, which simply sums the firm's demand curves without allowing for adjustments, the output price is assumed constant, $\bar{P}_x$. As can be seen in the accompanying diagram, the ΣD_f curve is necessarily more elastic than the D_I curve. Similarly, the factor demand curve for the economy as a whole would also tend to be more inelastic than the sum of the demand curves for all the firms. See Thomas R. Saving, *op. cit.*, for a discussion of several types of possible factor relationships. His findings are corroborated in Milton Friedman, *Price Theory; A Provisional Text* (Chicago: Aldine Publishing Co., 1962); and Charles E. Ferguson and Thomas R. Saving, "Long-Run Scale Adjustments of a Perfectly Competitive Firm and Industry," *American Economic Review* (December, 1969), pp. 774–783; and the Ferguson textbook, *Microeconomic Theory* (3d ed.; Homewood: Richard D. Irwin, 1972).

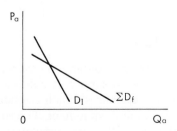

[7] An excellent discussion of the factor supply conditions is found in R. G. Lipsey and P. O. Steiner, *Economics* (3d ed.; New York: Harper & Row, Publishers, 1972), Chapters 19–22.

The factors determining the supply of labor are more dependent upon non-economic considerations than are the factors influencing the demands for other factors. This is particularly true of the factors determining the *total* supply of inputs. It is much less true of the supply of factors for *particular uses* — i.e., particular industries, firms, occupations, geographical areas, etc. The economic or market forces tend to be significantly more influential in determining the supply of particular kinds of labor services than in determining the total quantity of all labor services supplied in the country. In fact, almost all of the analyses to date have assumed that the supply of factors to a particular industry, firm, or occupation depends on the price paid by that industry, firm, or occupation relative to the price paid by other industries, firms, or occupations that operate in the same factor market. In discussing the product market, we assumed that factors would move between industries, firms, and occupations, leaving those offering lower earnings and moving to those offering higher earnings. While some spatial movement might also be expected between geographical areas in response to better opportunities, labor is expected to be considerably more immobile between geographic areas than between jobs in a given geographical area.

The assumption that the quantity of factors supplied will be an increasing function of the price of the factor (which was used in the previous analysis of the product market) is now to be treated as a hypothesis to be defended. The previous behavior postulate that an upsloping factor supply curve is simply the result of the economic motive to maximize one's income will be qualified in what will be called the *hypothesis of equal net advantage*. But before investigating that, we will examine the factors influencing the total supply of factors.

The Total Supply of Factors

In general, the total supply of factors is less rigidly limited, especially land and natural resources, than many people think. It is useful to distinguish between human and material resources because nonmonetary considerations are much more important in the mobility of labor than any other factor because the factor involved and the owner of it are inseparable. Thus, for instance, the desire for leisure is very important in determining labor supplies. People often desire to work fewer hours, sacrificing higher earnings to obtain leisure. In contrast, whether land or capital equipment would "desire" leisure is obviously not considered.

Supply of Human Effort

The total labor supply of an economy, measured by the total number of hours the population is willing to supply, is culturally and sociologically determined as well as market determined. Such considerations are perhaps less evident in the case of, say, capital equipment. The supply of human effort primarily depends on: (1) the size of the total population, (2) the proportion of the population willing and able to work in the labor force, and (3) the number of hours worked per year by the members of the labor force.

Although economic forces affect these factors somewhat, the essentially noneconomic elements predominate. While there is some evidence that the birth rate is positively related to the general level of economic activity, not all of the variation in population is explainable in economic terms.[8] The number of people in the labor force is much more responsive to economic conditions — rising in good times and falling in bad times — than is the total population. The dramatic increase in married women and people over 65 who joined the labor force during the labor-scarce Second World War provides an excellent example of this.

The supply curve of human effort by an individual was developed as an exercise in the use of indifference curves in Chapter 6 (Figure 6–9). There, the uninhibited market situation was portrayed. In fact, a number of circumstances alter that simpler analysis, most of which can also be shown with the aid of the indifference curve technique. An example of one of these is that workers may have a choice between income from labor effort and some given amount of transfer payments from government or nongovernment agencies. Figure 18–4(a) shows the decision process of workers faced with a choice between given wage rates and a fixed amount of income (I_t) that they would receive per day if they chose not to work.

With a wage rate reflected by the slope of line $0y_1$, this person could work $0L_1$ hours and receive an income of $0I_t$, which is the amount receivable as a transfer payment with no work and 24 hours of leisure per day. Since to this individual leisure is a good thing, the choice would be not to offer any labor service at all. In fact, the wage rate would have to rise until $0y_2$ is the wage line before this worker would offer any labor. At this wage the number of hours of work offered would be $0L_2$, and income would be $0I_A$. The reason the wage would have to be this high is that the utility from zero hours of work and income I_t is the same (is on the same indifference curve) as the utility from L_2 hours of work and income I_A. As wage rates rise above that reflected by line $0y_2$, this individual would increase the hours of labor effort offered to employers.

This person's labor supply curve, then, would be no work when wages are less than $0y_2/24$, and would be an increasing function at all wages above that one, as in Figure 18–4(b). The aggregate labor supply curve would look like AS_L in Figure 18–4(c), where a demand curve has been added to show that the equilibrium condition would include unemployment in the amount $0N_1 - 0N_2 = U$. If the transfer payment level were increased, the elastic segment would shift upward and the new supply curve would be BS_L, and unemployment would increase to U'.

An important observation about the worker's decision process is the amount of income tax to be paid on each possible level of income. If that tax is a proportional one, the *disposable* income is simply some proportion of the gross income. Graphically, the effect is to make the relevant wage constraint

---

[8] An excellent survey and extension of the important work done on the influence of economic factors on fertility is contained in the complete issue of the *Journal of Political Economy* (March/April, 1973), entitled "New Economic Approaches to Fertility," and in the March/April, 1974 issue entitled "Marriage, Family, Human Capital, and Fertility," edited by Theodore W. Schultz. These issues include the work of a number of specialists in the area.

FIGURE 18-4 Labor Supply with Guaranteed Minimum Income

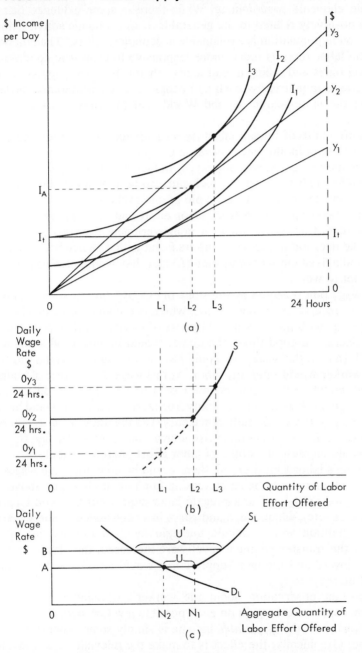

a straight line with a lesser slope than the $0y$ lines of Figure 18-4. A progressive tax establishes a curvilinear constraint such that the curve is increasing at a decreasing rate. With traditionally drawn indifference curves, the implication would be that more labor services would be offered with no tax than with taxes, and more labor would be offered with a proportional tax than with a progressive tax system for any given wage rate.

Another consideration which makes this analysis seem irrelevant to many is the widespread condition of employment that the worker will work eight hours per day. That is, the worker cannot choose the number of hours to work, but is given an all-or-nothing alternative by the employer. As an empirical matter, however, workers do have some room for adjusting their hours of labor, even in this case, by increasing or decreasing the number of "sick days," taking longer or shorter vacations, "moonlighting," quitting one employer and accepting a position with another after the desired leisure time has been accomplished, and so on.

Land, Natural Resources, and the Nonhuman Capital Stock

Land and natural resources can both respond in part to economic forces. Certainly the total amount of cultivable land — depending on drainage, irrigation, and fertilization schemes or, in general, the quality of the land — may be varied in response to varying economic conditions, although the total land area is virtually fixed in supply and has no degree of elasticity. (In rare cases, such as the Netherlands, even the total land area as opposed to sea areas can be extended.) Similarly, natural resources are augmented by new discoveries, new processes, and new technology. For example, each year in the United States we discover about as much coal annually as we use. In addition, through new processes we can now use low-grade iron ores once thought worthless. Finally, new technology has allowed us to exploit atomic energy and produce synthetic rubber.

The nonhuman capital stock is probably the most flexible of all the factors *in total*. The supply of capital has increased dramatically over time in the so-called advanced modern countries. The only thing limiting growth in the capital stock, given a nation's production possibilities, is the willingness of the population to divert resources from present consumption to future consumption (investment). In addition to the steady long-run increase in capital, investment expenditures seem to respond to shorter run cyclical variations in economic activity, rising in good times, falling in bad. A detailed discussion of the theoretical niceties of such an interaction can be found in almost any intermediate macroeconomics textbook.

Supply of Factors in Particular Uses

Turning now to the supply of factors in *particular uses* instead of in total, we find that economic forces become considerably more important. Our working hypothesis is that the factor owners try to maximize their incomes, subject to certain nonmonetary considerations. Since nonpecuniary things such as working conditions, degree of risk, convenience, geographical location and climate, social status of the profession, etc., are important, it is not true that factors will continue to move until their earnings are equalized in each possible case; instead factors will move until no *net* advantage, including both pecuniary and nonpecuniary advantages, can be gained by further movement. That is, the hypothesis of equal net advantage predicts that factor owners will choose that use for their factor services that provides the maximum net advantage, where net advantage includes both monetary and nonmonetary elements.

Since this hypothesis is as important in distribution theory as maximizing profits is in allocation theory, it is necessary that we be clear on what it does and does not say. To make this truly a testable hypothesis and not an irrefutable tautology, we must make some assumption about the relative stability of pecuniary and nonpecuniary advantages. The alternative of defining nonpecuniary benefits so that they can be measured in monetary terms is virtually impossible.

How does one make measurable the nonmonetary advantage of a good climate, favorable working conditions, a cordial employer, etc.? It is tautological and not very useful to argue that if, *ceteris paribus,* (including such things as equal utility, education, etc.) a beginning bank clerk makes $1,000 less than a ditchdigger in a certain geographical area, then the nonmonetary advantages of banking must equal $1,000. Such a statement could never be refuted and would not be very useful.

Instead, by assuming that the nonmonetary advantages are roughly constant or at least change more slowly than the monetary ones, we obtain the expected upsloping supply curve. For example, if we assume that whatever the nonmonetary advantages banking has today relative to the working conditions of the ditchdigger—say, air conditioned offices, music by Muzak, prestige, etc. —were probably the same, say, 15 years ago and will probably change independently of monetary considerations in the near future, then we can predict that if, say, banking salaries go up by $1,000, more people will enter banking and leave other employments. Obviously, if at the same time the nonmonetary factors were also changing—say, banks decide to do without air conditioning and the piped-in-music—we could not make such a prediction. However, we can predict that any change in *relative* factor prices will cause factors to flow where returns have increased and vice versa. Such a prediction gives us a rising factor supply curve in particular uses.

Factor Mobility and Factor Supply Elasticity

Of course, not all factors and not even different units of the same factor are equally responsive to changes in their prices. Factor mobility varies widely both between and within factor groups. Land, in the sense of location, a physically immobile factor, is one of the more economically mobile factors. The supply of land for any one particular use may be easily changed through switching from other employments. The supply of land used for wheat, corn, housing developments, office buildings, etc., can easily rise in response to a higher rental price, although the total quantity of land may not. Of course, once land is built upon, it is considerably more immobile; hence agricultural land is generally more mobile than urban land. In contrast, most capital equipment is economically though not physically immobile. Since most machinery is quite specific, it is not very mobile. For example, a machine that stamps out right rear fenders for Ford Pintos is almost without alternative uses. This capital immobility means that declining industries die slowly. The long-run liquidation of plant and equipment must be accomplished by not replacing it as it wears out or becomes obsolete.

Labor is, for obvious reasons, the most important factor—for everyone owns at least one unit of it; this cannot be said of any other factor. Nonmonetary considerations are more important in the case of labor than any other factor due to the inseparability of the factor owner and the factor services.

If all workers were *homogeneous* (equally educated or trained, equally able, equally motivated, etc.), all jobs were *equally attractive,* and (labor) markets were in *long-run competitive equilibrium,* all workers would receive about the same wages. Actually, substituting the word "factors" for "workers" would yield the more general proposition that all factor prices tend toward the same level, under the stipulated condition. While the factor labor will be used in most of the subsequent analysis, the reader is urged to keep in mind that these comments apply to all factors. In fact, the whole theory of factor prices is quite general. If one is concerned with labor, one should read wages when factor prices are discussed; if land, read rentals; if capital, read interest, etc.

Dynamic Disequilibrium vs. Static Equilibrium Differentials

Each of the italicized phrases in the above conditions for wage equality are important. The causes of factor price differentials in a nonhomogeneous world are of two kinds: (1) *dynamic* ones that exist only in disequilibrium situations, and (2) *static* ones that persist even in equilibrium situations.

In the first case, these differences are called *transitional differences,* caused by an incomplete adjustment of supply and demand. Shifts in demand or supply lead to factor price differentials. While this may be a slow process, in long-run equilibrium these differentials will disappear. An example of transitional differences is the high (low) returns earned by engineers (farmers) after the Second World War. Similarly, the relatively high returns currently earned by computer programmers and long-haired singing groups will no doubt prove to be transitory. In a free market, the entry (exit) of factors would eventually eliminate these differentials. The qualifier "equilibrium" was thus inserted to eliminate the ephemeral element.

The qualifying term "long run" was inserted into the requirements for identical wages to recognize the fact that labor or any other factor is much more mobile in the long run than in the short run. For labor services requiring extensive training or experience, the short-run labor supply will be relatively inelastic. It is very difficult for people to change occupations in the short run. Over long periods, the possibility of new workers entering the field and to a lesser degree the possibility of retraining other workers for new occupations increases factor supply elasticity considerably. Our educational system allows us to make great increases in the supply of virtually any desired labor skill within as short a period as ten years. In addition, it is also possible for retrained workers to go into a lucrative field rather quickly.

Static or equilibrium price differentials differ from the above in that they would persist even in long-run competitive equilibrium. They are due to differences in the factors themselves or to nonhomogeneous nonmonetary conditions in alternative factor employments. For instance, the qualifying word "competitive" was inserted in the required conditions for identical wages to take into account the geographical, artificial, and sociological immobilities that exist due to market imperfections. People are often unwilling to absorb the nonmonetary costs and inconveniences of moving—new job, new friends, new schools, new community, new homes, etc. In other cases, they may simply be ignorant of job opportunities and the pay scales in other geographical areas. Of course, all that is really necessary for effective mobility are adjustments at the margin, not a "drifting" labor force. While the mobility in the United States is higher than in most European countries, it is still true that more mobility is needed—e.g., out of "sick" industries, such as soft coal mining, ice manufacturing, railroading, some branches of agriculture, and cotton textile manufacturing. Unfortunately, it usually turns out that when the mobility is needed the most—in times of a severe depression—labor is most reluctant to move. In fact, there seems to be a direct relationship between general economic activity and labor's willingness to move from low-wage to high-wage areas. In general, labor seems more concerned with the probability of obtaining a job than with wage scales when considering a move.

The sociological immobilities refer to the sexual, religious, racial, age, ethnic, and political discrimination that exists in our society and other societies. It is well known that people of the same skill receive different wages for the same job, depending on such things as whether they are male or female, white or black, young or old, Christian or Jewish, etc.[9] In recent years, such discrimination has been declining, though at a slow pace.

The artificial immobilities refer to the man-made barriers to labor mobility, such as the "closed shop," which requires all members of a plant or trade to be a member of the union; eligibility requirements for unemployment compensation; job seniority; licensing; and private pension plans. The discrimination included in sociological immobilities could have been listed here as well.

To be sure, many of the above man-made barriers have beneficial aspects. Licensing, for example, is done to insure a minimum degree of competency; job seniority is meant to protect older employees from layoffs; medical schools severely limit enrollments to maintain "high standards"; and so on. However,

---

[9] William G. Shepherd, *Market Power and Economic Welfare* (New York: Random House, 1970), Chapter 14. Defining discrimination in employment as the inclusion of otherwise extraneous ethnic, racial, or religious characteristics as elements in the evaluation of job applicants and as criteria for promotions, he found a positive and substantial relationship between discrimination in white-collar employment and market power. Generally speaking, competitive firms and nonprofit agencies tended to be nondiscriminatory.

in each case the effect is to limit the factor supply and raise the returns to the incumbent practitioners.

The qualifying phrase *equally attractive* in the statement describing the necessary conditions for equal pay for all people allows for *equalizing differences* that must be paid to compensate for the nonmonetary differences in various jobs. Workers have different preferences for occupations, ranking some higher than others. Other things being equal, the job with attractive nonmonetary conditions will have a lower equilibrium wage than one with low nonmonetary rewards, since the factor supply prices in the more attractive jobs are lower. Personal satisfaction (e.g., teaching) or prestige (e.g., bank vice-presidents) often partially substitutes for higher pay. In other words, unequal wage rates tend to equalize the net advantages in different occupations.

Finally, the *homogeneous* qualification was inserted to take into account the fact that capacities and training differ for different groups of workers. In particular, the labor force is said to consist of a number of *noncompeting groups*, each of which may be composed of several or possibly just one occupation for which the members of this group qualify. This concept can partially account for the persistent differences in returns both between people in different occupations and between people within a given occupation. These noncompeting groups can be the result of natural or artificial factors. For instance, only a relatively small group of workers have both the ability and opportunity to be brain surgeons, concert pianists, nuclear physicists, all-star baseball players, or "Philadelphia" lawyers. The concept of noncompeting groups can explain differentials within as well as between occupations. O. J. Simpson and Raquel Welch are able to obtain fabulous salaries because of their superior talents. Very few people can produce services that are similar to theirs. In short, even in long-run competitive equilibrium with no nonmonetary differentials, a "skilled" worker earns more than an "unskilled" worker.

In most cases, all of these factors will play a role in the explanation of actual factor price differentials. When it is said that "dirty" jobs pay more than "clean" jobs, this statement implies that other things are equal. Foundry work is dirtier work than that of a physician. Yet medical doctors have average incomes considerably higher than the earnings of foundry workers. This does not mean that equalizing differences are not operating. Rather, what has happened is that the physicians fall into a noncompeting group because of the educational and financial prerequisites to enter the profession. If it were not for the unpleasantness of the foundry laborer's job, the differentials would have been even greater.

Another argument in the explanation of factor price differentials is differential risk. The risk can be physical harm to a worker or to real capital (fire, etc.), or it can be the risk of very low returns or extremely variable incomes in the future. Construction workers, for example, are paid higher hourly wages than comparable workers, it is said, because of the great risk of unemployment, both seasonal and cyclical. The same may be true of actors, lawyers, and others. On the other hand, until recently government civil service employees' relatively low wages were justified by the argument that the degree of job security and certainty was so great.

SUMMARY OF FIVE POSSIBLE FACTOR SUPPLY CONDITIONS

Figure 18–5 illustrates five possible supply functions. Panel (a) represents the supply conditions, S_1, that would be facing a firm that buys factors in a competitive market. It can hire as many units of the input factor as it wishes without perceptibly affecting the factor price. A horizontal factor supply curve

FIGURE 18–5   Possible Factor Supply Curves

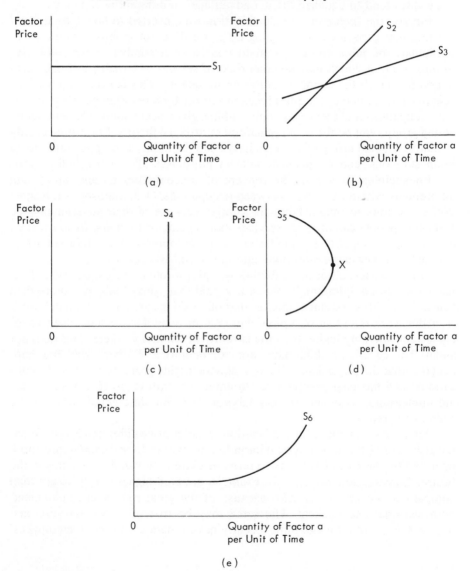

could also occur if an entire industry or even a group of industries hired only a tiny portion of the flow of services of the factor. In general, the smaller the share of an industry in the market for a factor, the more elastic the supply curve of that factor at the industry level. For example, the hairpin industry may hire such an insignificant share of the total steel consumed annually that it may face a perfectly elastic supply curve for steel.

The most likely shape of the supply function of at least nonspecialized resources at the industry level is that depicted in panel (b) by either S_2 or S_3. Increases in the quantity of factors hired call for increases in factor prices. For an entire open economy in which factors are allowed to move freely, the supply curve could also be upsloping. As discussed below, even if all individuals have backward-bending supply curves, such as S_5, the aggregate supply curve can still be upward sloping if the points at which the bends occur are different.

It is also possible for an industry to have first a horizontal supply curve when it is small and then an upsloping one as it gets larger. This is shown in panel (e) for supply function S_6.

Panel (c) is representative of the short-run supply curve of an entire economy or group of large industries. In addition, a highly specialized factor could have a supply curve of this shape. When the supply curve is vertical, as is S_4, increases in demand bring only increases in factor prices and no additional quantities of the factor. This type of curve could also represent a dedicated worker such as the late Albert Schweitzer, with the fixed quantity at the level of maximum capacity.

Finally, panel (d) shows a backward-bending supply curve S_5, which turns backward after point X. The shape of this curve was previously explained in Chapter 6 in terms of the substitution and income effect. An increase in demand would cause an increase in the real wage rate, and an increase in the real wage rate has two effects: (1) the substitution effect makes a worker want to work more hours since the opportunity cost of leisure has gone up; and (2) the income effect makes a worker want to work less hours since if the same number of hours are worked, real income goes up. This means more of all (superior) goods will be demanded, including leisure. The backward-bending segment therefore occurs when the income effect dominates the substitution effect, such as beyond point X on the S_5 curve. It should be noted that even if each individual worker had a backward-bending supply curve, the aggregate supply curve could still be upsloping since a higher wage rate might attract more people into the labor force.

CRITICISMS OF THE MARGINAL PRODUCTIVITY THEORY[10]

The marginal productivity theory has been criticized on many counts. Yet when most of the criticisms are examined in detail, they often turn out to be

---

[10] Some of these are discussed in R. G. Lipsey and P. O. Steiner, *Economics* (3d ed.; New York: Harper & Row, Publishers, 1972); and Alan M. Cartter, *Theory of Wages and Employment* (Homewood: Richard D. Irwin, 1959).

based on misconceptions of the theory.[11] First of all, some people will not accept it because they feel it is merely a defense of the existing distribution of income. Given reasonably competitive conditions, the theory argues that, following the Western ethical philosophy of private property, people "deserve" the "fruits of their labor."[12] Furthermore, some people argue that the theory makes the factor returns incapable of change, being determined by nature. Of course, even if this were true, which it is not, it would not be sensible to reject the theory. It would be foolish for us to reject the theory of supply and demand or Newton's theory of gravity as a fact because we do not like its implications. At any rate, we have seen that any action that raises a factor's marginal productivity raises its rate of remuneration.

On the other hand, it may be argued that whereas a factor is paid according to its private product, the social product is what is relevant for social welfare. For instance, dope peddlers may be getting paid according to their "marginal private product." While this argument does point out one of the questionable aspects of the market price system, it does not state that individuals should not get their marginal product if appropriately computed.

In the end, the question of whether payment by marginal productivity produces distributive justice involves an ethical, normative proposition. A positive proposition that can be made regarding factor payments according to the marginal productivity theory is that it achieves allocative efficiency by producing society's maximal output with a given stock of resources. Returning to the distributive question, many people feel the verdict of the market is too harsh on people with unequal opportunities—the aged, the blind, the mentally and physically handicapped, etc. In other cases, people feel that what the market metes out is "fair."

A detailed analysis of these complex ethical considerations is beyond the scope of this book. What should emerge from the above discussion, however, is that acceptance of the theory of factor price determination does not commit one to any necessary ethical position—e.g., that the prevailing income distribution is "proper." A more important question, for the purposes of a positive approach to price theory, than the question of whether the existing theory is "just" is whether the present theory explains the distribution of income in our society with a reasonable degree of accuracy. A criticism that says the marginal productivity theory does not provide a good explanation of distribution is a much more telling blow than those involving normative value judgments. That is, if it can be demonstrated that factor payments and value productivities are unrelated, the theory is useless. Such an empirical refutation of the existing

---

[11] For an example of a successful defense of the marginal productivity theory against an alleged alternative formulation, see E. E. Liebhafsky, "A 'New' Concept in Wage Determination: Disguised Productivity Analysis," *Southern Economic Journal* (October, 1959), pp. 141–146; reprinted in *Readings in Microeconomics*, edited by David R. Kamerschen (New York: John Wiley & Sons, 1969), Chapter 30, pp. 443–452.

[12] Regarding the belief that the imputation of marginal productivity under competition to factors is a "natural law" which is "morally justifiable," see, e.g., J. B. Clark, *The Distribution of Wealth* (New York, 1899). A famous economist once remarked something to the effect that this is the first time that anyone had made idols out of partial derivatives!

theory has not been convincing. Indeed, the theory seems to stand up to empirical testing quite impressively.

Much of the evidence that has been forthcoming, generally using the Cobb-Douglas production function[13] and Kendrick's technique,[14] has been consistent with the marginal productivity theory. In recent years economists have made some useful attempts to provide a testable aggregate theory of distribution. Probably the most famous of these are by M. Kalecki[15] and N. Kaldor.[16] Kalecki's mark-up theory uses the degree of monopoly power to explain the distribution of wages and profits. While his theory denies that the marginal productivity theory is useful in explaining labor's share, his own theory is so broad that it does not explain precisely what does determine it. For example, anything and everything—advertising, union pressure, etc.—can and does affect the "degree of monopoly power" and hence relative factor shares in his model.

Kaldor's "widow's cruse" theory attempts to explain wages and profits with a macro theory of national income instead of a micro theory of relative prices. His model hinges on the fact that the saving coefficients of profits and wages received are assumed constant and different, with wage earners having a lower propensity to save. Although his theory has been subject to some testing, much more careful work is necessary. It may even turn out that the Kaldor and marginal productivity theories are not inconsistent with one another. Some of the most important and interesting work to be done in economics in the near future is likely to come in the area of income distribution.

A second misconception involves the criticism that business firms' frequent failure to adjust factor employment in response to a change in factor prices is inconsistent with the theory. This is not necessarily accurate. First of all, over very short periods of time, factor demand is quite inelastic since output demand is relatively inelastic in the short run. Secondly, price and employment changes of any kind are not costless. A firm will therefore want to make sure these price changes are likely to persist before acting. Finally, there are cases, such as the kinked demand theory of oligopoly, where shifts in factor prices change marginal cost, but marginal cost still intersects marginal revenue in the latter's vertical range. Hence, no change in output or inputs may take place.

---

[13] For two excellent surveys including references, see Nicholas Kaldor, "Alternative Theories of Distribution," *Review of Economic Studies*, No. 2 (1956), pp. 83–100, reprinted in *Readings in Microeconomics*, edited by David R. Kamerschen (New York: John Wiley & Sons, 1969), Chapter 27, pp. 381–406; and Melvin W. Reder, "Alternative Theories of Labor's Share," *The Allocation of Economic Resources: Essay in Honor of Bernard Francis Haley*, edited by Moses Abramovitz and others (Palo Alto: Stanford University Press, 1959), pp. 180–206, reprinted in David R. Kamerschen (ed.), *op. cit.*, Chapter 29, pp. 414–442. A more recent survey of empirical work supporting the marginal productivity theory can be found in David R. Kamerschen, "A Reaffirmation of the Marginal Productivity Theory," *Rivistia Internazionale Di Scienze Economiche E Commerciali* (March, 1973), pp. 286–290.

[14] John W. Kendrick and M. R. Pech, *Productivity Trends in the United States* (Princeton: Princeton University Press, 1961).

[15] M. Kalecki, *Theory of Economic Dynamics* (New York: Monthly Review Press, 1968).

[16] Kaldor, *loc. cit.*

The rest of the misconceptions involve the fact that some people forget that the marginal productivity theory attempts only to explain the demand for factors. The other half of orthodox distribution theory involving the supply of factors argues that factors tend to move to maximize their net advantage. This concept is also necessary to determine factor prices.

The third of the misconceptions is that the theory assumes pure competition in all markets. This is wrong. The factor demand curve in the short run is the *MRP* curve, regardless of whether there is competition or monopoly in the output market. However, before a factor is paid a price equal to its *MRP*, there must be competition in the factor market.

A fourth misconception is that factor prices will equalize in all employments. This is incorrect. In fact, the theory predicts that factors will move until net advantage, not factor payments, equalize. Such things as disequilibrium, nonpecuniary factors, noncompeting groups, etc., all prevent factor prices from equalizing.

EULER'S THEOREM

Swiss mathematician Leonhard Euler proposed the following important economic concept:

$$\text{Total output} = L \cdot MPP_L + K \cdot MPP_K \tag{18.2}$$

where L (K) refers to the quantity of labor (capital) employed and MPP_L (MPP_K) refers to the marginal physical product of labor (capital). The total product equals the sum of all inputs multiplied by their respective marginal physical products (or total revenue equals the sum of all the inputs multiplied by their VMP's if both sides of the above equation are multiplied by the price of the output).[17] This theorem is really an identity, holding for all values of the variables if the production function is homogeneous of degree one—i.e., if constant returns to scale prevail everywhere. It was left to J. B. Clark, Philip Wicksteed, and other founders of the marginal productivity theory to show that in long-run competitive equilibrium, payment in accordance with marginal productivity will precisely exhaust the total product.

But one may argue about the realism of the assumption of constant returns to scale. If constant returns prevail everywhere, the total product will be exhausted regardless of factor proportions, and factor returns will be independent of the size of the firm. A determinate competitive equilibrium is impossible if returns are everywhere constant. If $P_x > AC$, the firm will expand indefinitely until it becomes a monopoly; if $P_x < AC$, the firm will shut down; and if $P_x = AC$, the firm size is indeterminate. In addition, if there is monopoly, rewarding each factor according to its *MPP* will not exactly exhaust the total product.

---

[17] To be precise, the most general formulation on the left-hand side of the expression should be total output multiplied by the degree of homogeneity.

The solution is that the exhausting of total product is an equilibrium condition. In long-run competitive equilibrium, the firm's cost curve is horizontal at its minimum point. This momentary constancy of AC means constant returns to scale at that point. Thus, only at the point of long-run competitive equilibrium do constant returns and the Euler-Clark-Wicksteed ideas become relevant.

QUESTIONS

1. Explain why the short-run MRP curve is not the demand curve for a factor of production in the long run. Compare the impact on the elasticity of demand of internal vs. external effects.
2. In discussing the supply of factors of production, why is it useful to distinguish between human and nonhuman factors of production?
3. An important issue in macroeconomics is the effect on employment of changing price levels. To consider one aspect of this problem, suppose the vertical axis of Figure 18–4 is in real terms (i.e., money amounts divided by the price level), so that the workers' indifference curves reflect comparative valuations of real income and leisure. Now suppose the price level rises. This results in a flatter $0y$ curve for any given money wage rate; but if the wage rate and the price level change proportionally, nothing happens to the $0y$ curves. The question to answer here is: What happens to the supply curve of labor in Figure 18–4(b) and 18–4(c) if wages and prices rise proportionally but the guaranteed minimum income remains the same in dollar terms? What happens to employment?
4. Suppose a (silly) law was passed that everyone graduating from a college or university next year would have to be paid the same salary. Which specific labor supply curves would you expect to be most significantly affected? Suppose another segment of the same law specified that in ten years the salary differentials of all graduates must be eliminated. What kind of results would you expect? (A less interesting way to ask this same question is: What is the economic role of wage differentials?)

19 Wages, Rent, Interest, and Profit

In the previous chapter we analyzed the strategic factors underlying factor demand and supply in general. In this chapter, we try to apply these general theoretical principles to the particular supply conditions to see how wages, rent, interest, and profit are determined.[1] Once again we emphasize that it is the prices of productive factor services, not the prices of the factors themselves, that concern us at this point. We want to explain, say, the rental per year from a given plot of land, not the value of this land. Any factor which yields a flow of income over a long period of time requires an interest rate, since future flows are not as valuable as present ones and thus must be appropriately discounted.

WAGE DETERMINATION

We first turn to labor and its associated factor return, wages, for both theoretical and empirical reasons. In the first place, the general marginal productivity theory of distribution is perhaps more applicable to the case of labor services and wage rates than to other factor shares. Secondly, from a statistical point of view, wages are the most important factor share, typically comprising roughly three fourths of the national income. To be precise, in 1975 compensation of employees (basically wages and salary) was 76.3 percent of national income. While many people do not own property resources such as land and capital, we all at least own our own labor services.

Real Wages, Money Wages, and Productivity

Real wages basically depend on labor productivity, given the supply of labor. In particular, the high level of wages in the United States rests fundamentally on the high productivity of the average U.S. laborer. Although many factors can influence particular wages at different times, employers cannot pay wages that exceed productivity for any sustained length of time. Under competitive conditions, if wages exceed the value of the marginal product, profits will be negative and private enterprise businesses must cease production. On

---

[1] A masterful summary of what economists know about income distribution is contained in Martin Bronfenbrenner, *Income Distribution Theory* (Chicago: Aldine-Atherton, 1971). For instance, his Chapters 6–9 on the demand and supply of inputs are excellent. However, the reader should recognize at the outset that: "The present state of distribution theory is most unsatisfactory." See Melvin W. Reder, "Alternative Theories of Labor's Share," *The Allocation of Economic Resources; Essays in Honor of Bernard Francis Haley,* edited by Moses Abramovitz *et al.* (Stanford: Stanford University Press, 1959), p. 180; reprinted in *Readings in Microeconomics,* edited by David R. Kamerschen (New York: John Wiley & Sons, 1969), Chapter 29, pp. 414–442.

the other hand, competitive producers cannot persistently pay substandard wages, because the competition among businesses for workers will tend to bid wages up to the level justified by labor's productivity. While these tendencies are broad and inexact, it is true that productivity is the major force establishing wages in the U.S. economy.

In the analysis of labor as a factor of production, real wages are crucial, because *real* wages, not *money* wages, determine the workers' well-being. Before discussing the difference between real and money wages, we can make several other distinctions. For instance, "wages" or the wage rate differ from "earnings" in that earnings depend on both the wage rate and the number of time periods (e.g., hours) that labor is supplied in the market. If a worker's wage rate is $2 an hour, that person's "earnings" would be $16 for an eight hour working day.

Money wage rates are the amounts of money received per hour or other time unit. *Real wages,* on the other hand, are the amounts of commodities that money wages can purchase. Since real wage rates are the purchasing power of money wages, they depend upon both money wages and the prices of commodities—i.e., real wages = money wages/price level. In general, money wages represent smaller (larger) real wages when prices are higher (lower). If money wages double and the price of consumer goods and services also doubles, real wages remain the same; on the other hand, if the price level more (less) than doubles when money wages double, real wages fall (rise).

Real wages in the United States are roughly five times as high as they were 60 years ago. Although the U.S. population and the labor force have grown significantly over the decades, these increases in the supply of labor have been more than offset by the rapid increase in the demand for labor caused by dramatic increases in labor productivity. The real wage rate has risen at a rate of 1 to 2 percent per annum. If this long-run, or secular, increase in wage rates is going to continue, labor productivity must also continue to increase. Thus, if labor unions really raise real wages, as some claim, they must do it by raising labor productivity (either by the *TPP* curve shifting upward or by movements to the left along the curve). Yet unions are usually able to immediately and directly influence only money wages. Unions in the aggregate cannot artificially increase real wages by forcing money wages higher without an accompanying increase in labor productivity. An increase in labor productivity tends to raise real wage rates, regardless of union activity.

Supply and demand analysis explains the general level of wages among countries and regions of a given country as well as the specific wage levels for particular types of labor in different markets. Wage rates and earnings in the United States are considerably higher than those in, say, India and China for the same reason that they are generally higher in the East and North of the U.S. than in the South: because of productivity differentials based on the interaction of supply and demand.

The supply of labor in the United States has been restricted because of the past stringent immigration laws, the relatively low natural increases in population, the relatively small percentage of the population in the labor force, and the relatively large amount of leisure time enjoyed by U.S. workers. In contrast, the high and increasing productivity of labor has led to a strong and rising demand for labor. This productivity, in turn, is due to such things as our economy's great supply of capital (e.g., the average manufacturing worker has something like $35,000 worth of plant, machinery, and equipment with which to work), our great supply of land and natural resources, and our advanced state of technology and management, in addition to the contribution made by labor itself through superior education, accumulated skills, and favorable work habits. In short, the large quantity and high quality of other factors with which U.S. labor has had to work is at least as important in explaining its high productivity as the relatively high quality of labor itself.

Specific Wages and Market Structure

Demand and supply analysis is also the key to understanding wages received by specific workers rather than workers in general. There are several basic market models that might be investigated. For instance, competition or monopsony in the input market may be coupled with either competition or monopoly in the output market. Since these four models were thoroughly examined in the last two chapters, only a summary analysis is presented here. In addition, some union models are investigated that were not previously discussed. Figure 19–1 illustrates the first four models.

In panel (a) the firm is buying factors (we will be using labor for the example) in a purely competitive market; hence, the supply curve of labor, the price of labor ($0\bar{P}$), and the marginal factor expense (MFE) curve are identical, constant, and perfectly elastic. If the output market is competitive, the firm's demand curve for labor (D_C) is the value of the marginal product curve for labor (VMP). Under monopoly in the output market, the firm's demand curve for labor (D_M) is the marginal revenue product curve for labor (MRP).

By these diagrams we can show that a monopolist can be thought of as hiring fewer factors than would a competitor. At wage rate $0\bar{P}$ the monopolist would hire only $0Q_M$ units of labor compared to the $0Q_C$ units hired by the competitor. We may conclude, therefore, that even when there is competition in the factor market, total employment and hence factor incomes are less when the hiring firm is an output monopolist than when it is an output competitor.

Panel (b) depicts monopsony in the factor market; hence, MFE is above the supply curve. The output competitor pays a higher wage rate, $0P_C$ compared to $0P_M$, and hires a larger number of workers, $0Q_C$ compared to $0Q_M$, than does the output monopolist. We may conclude that, given a monopsony labor market, greater labor employment at higher wage rates and hence a greater total income to distribute occurs when a competitive output market exists. (Alternatively, if a monopsony firm receives "quantity" discounts for hiring a larger volume of factors, the S ($=AFE$) curve can be downsloping, and therefore $MFE < S$. But this is not considered typical.) To summarize, in general total income is lower, factor employment is lower, and/or factor prices are lower whenever there are market imperfections, either in the output market, the input market, or both markets.

FIGURE 19–1   Factor Markets

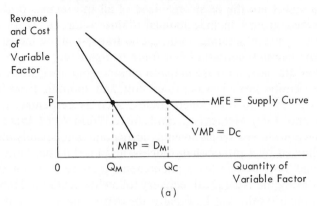

(a)

Competitive Factor Market

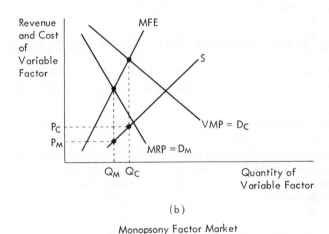

(b)

Monopsony Factor Market

THE GROWTH OF UNIONS

Over the past century, and especially since the 1930s, workers have increasingly organized themselves into labor unions to strengthen their bargaining position with employers. In the collective bargaining process, wage rates, hours of work, working conditions, seniority rights, etc., are settled and formalized in a contract binding both labor and management for a specific period. However, only since the 1930s has federal law in the United States supported the right of workers to organize into unions of their own choosing. While there is general agreement that since the 1930s unions have improved the general position and strength of the U.S. worker, there is considerable disagreement as to what extent the unions have actually raised wages.

In the United States today approximately 20 million workers or roughly one fourth of the total labor force (approximately 29 percent of the nonfarm labor force) are union members. Still unorganized for the most part are important groups such as some "white-collar" workers; professional people; and managerial, supervisory, farm, and service industry personnel. Geographically, the southern states are the least organized of all the regions in the U.S. The highly organized groups include manual, "blue-collar" workers in building, communications, manufacturing, mining, and transportation industries. About one half of the manual, nonfarm labor force is organized.

The rather dramatic increase in union membership over the years has been most uneven. Union growth was rather slow and sporadic from its early beginning in the 1790s in the skilled trades, such as carpentry, printing, and shoemaking, until 1900. However, from 1900 to World War I, there was a slow, steady advance, followed by an upsurge during and immediately after the war. This was followed by a rather sharp decline and leveling off during the 1920s. The 1930s and 1940s exhibited a phenomenal increase in union membership that started during the New Deal recovery following the Great Depression and continued through World War II. Finally, the period since 1947 has been one of increasing government regulation of, and intervention in, labor-management relations and stagnation in union growth.

BASIC WAYS UNIONS TRY TO RAISE WAGES

Unions use four basic approaches in trying to increase wages and/or protect existing wages in particular industries:

1. Decrease the supply of labor.
2. Increase the derived demand for labor and/or lower the elasticity of demand.
3. Raise standard wage rates directly through collective bargaining.
4. Reduce or remove monopsonistic (but not monopolistic) exploitation by the employer. (This countering of monopsony hiring power by monopoly bargaining power is taken up later in the chapter.)

Decrease the Supply of Labor

A union may employ various devices to restrict the supply of labor and hence raise the wage rate: immigration barriers, shorter working hours, high initiation fees, long and restrictive apprenticeships or training periods, compulsory early retirements, child labor laws, and longer vacations. In addition, there are other more subtle methods of decreasing the labor services available to an industry: jurisdictional and other "unjustified" strikes; sit-downs; slow-downs; and "featherbedding" practices, such as artificial limits put on the number of bricks that can be laid per day, the width of union members' paint brushes, and the employment of firemen on diesel locomotives, etc.

Increase the Demand for Labor

The union may try to shift the whole demand curve and/or lower the elasticity of the demand curve to reduce the possible undesirable employment effects of a wage increase. In the case in which either the entire demand function shifts upward or the union counteracts the monopsony exploitation by employers, increases in both wages and employment are possible.

The unions may influence derived demand by supporting employers in their demands for governmental tariffs for their products (as with china and pottery), by helping the industry advertise its products and "union labels" in general, or by encouraging employees to increase their efficiency or productivity. This last result can be accomplished in two ways: (1) The higher money wages paid to union members may have a "shock effect" of inducing greater managerial efficiency or technological improvements. For those who argue that the stick of adversity is as powerful as the carrot of incentive, this argument is especially appealing. (2) The higher wages paid to union members may raise worker productivity through improving the mental and physical conditions of workers. That is, the physiological and psychological effects from raising wages of making ill-fed workers stronger and disgruntled ones more energetic can be important. Of course, in modern advanced nations the physiologically under-nourished argument has little support, except in impoverished subsections such as the Appalachian region in the United States, though it might be im-portant in the underdeveloped lands of the world. However, the favorable mental effects on a worker's morale from raising wages—making the workers feel the employer is a "good" or "fair" person that deserves a good day's work—can be important in our economy. In other words, this last analysis reverses the usual line of causality that emphasizes $W_L = f(MRP_L)$ and argues $MRP_L = g(W_L)$. This means that a higher wage rate can shift the entire MRP_L rightward and outward.

Increase Standard Wages Through Collective Bargaining

Wage determination through collective bargaining alters the supply curve of labor facing employers. Suppose the current equilibrium wage rate in a given industry is $0W_E$, where the demand for labor (D_L) intersects the supply of labor (S_L) at $0Q_E$, as in Figure 19–2. Through a collective bargaining agree-ment a new standard wage of $0W_2$ is set.

Forcing wages above the equilibrium level leads to unemployment. The labor supply at the new standard wage becomes W_2ABS_L. The amount of labor demanded, and therefore employment, falls from $0Q_E$ to $0Q_D$. At the new higher wage rate, $0Q_S$ workers are seeking employment. So, not only is there a decrease in the number of workers the firms wish to employ, but the number of workers seeking employment increases. How much employment will ac-company the wage hike is basically determined by the elasticity of demand for labor services. The more inelastic the demand for the union's labor services, the smaller the decrease in employment.

You will recall that the primary factors that determine factor demand elas-ticity are the elasticity of demand for the products the factor is helping to pro-duce, the proportion of the total cost accounted for by the factor, and the degree of substitutability between that factor and other inputs. Since this last de-terminant varies directly with time, labor is expected to be better able to raise

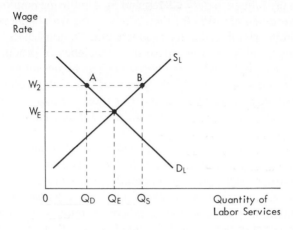

FIGURE 19–2   Increase Standard Wage
Through Collective Bargaining

wage rates with less adverse effect on employment in the short run than in the
long run. The mining and railroad industries provide illustrations of how a
powerful union can achieve high wages in the short run at the expense of substantial unemployment in the long run. For example, employment in bituminous
coal mining fell from its peak of about 700,000 workers in 1923 to only 400,000
in 1947 to around 100,000 workers in 1975. Employment on the railroads fell
from 1.7 million to 1.3 million to about 500,000 over the same periods. More
particularly, the Brotherhood of Locomotive Firemen and Engineers dwindled
from 130,000 members in 1920 to 50,000 in 1970. While the higher wages may
not be the complete explanation for these reductions in employment, they certainly contributed.

Monopsony and the Economic Effect of Unions

Clearly, any gains achieved by forcing an above-equilibrium pay scale
generally results in some amount of unemployment, the precise figure depending upon the elasticity of labor demand and supply. However, a union
that counteracts monopsony or oligopsony power has beneficial effects on both
the wage rate and employment. This is illustrated in Figure 19–3. Suppose
initially that the monopsonistic firm hires $0L_1$ units of labor at the price of
$0W_1$. If the union establishes a contract wage of $0W_2$, the supply curve becomes W_2AS_L and the MFE_L is identical to the supply curve over the range
W_2A. The MFE_L then is discontinuous at A and finally becomes BC. That is,
with an enforced wage of $0W_2$, the supply curve of labor (S_L) is W_2AS_L and
MFE_L is W_2ABC. Under these conditions the profit-maximizing quantity of
labor for this firm to hire is $0L_2$, since $MRP_L = MFE_L$ at this point.[2]

_____

[2] This can be verified as a maximum by the fact that $MRP_L > (<) MFE_L$ for outputs smaller
(larger) than $0L_2$. Of course, if the firm was also maximizing initially, the new level of profits at
$0L_2$ must be smaller than before (at $0L_1$).

FIGURE 19-3   The Effect of Unions in Counteracting Monopsony Power

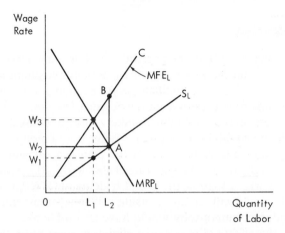

This is not the only option available to the union. Precisely what it does depends on its objectives. At the wage rate of $0W_2$, employment is maximized. On the other hand, if the union has as a goal the maintenance of the original employment level $0L_1$, it can secure a maximum wage of $0W_3$. Finally, if this union seeks to maximize the workers' total money income, the precise wage selected will depend upon the firm's elasticity of demand for labor. However, anywhere between a wage of $0W_1$ and $0W_3$ the union can secure both increases in employment and the wage rate compared to the preunion condition. Notice, however, that once a union wage has been set at or above $0W_2$, any increases in the wage will reduce employment. Thus, as a general principle, labor unions can secure simultaneously an increase in wages and employment only when they eliminate monopsonistic exploitation. The precise area between $0W_1$ and $0W_3$ constitutes the monopsony "bargaining range" over which the union can negotiate. However, the union has no influence over any "monopolistic exploitation" that may exist, where this would be measured by the difference between the VMP_L (not shown in Figure 19–3) and MRP_L curves.

Effect of Wage Changes on Employment

In general, we have seen that wage increases tend to lower employment. The exceptions are few and for the most part have already been alluded to in the preceding discussion. But let us summarize the conditions under which wage rates can be increased without unemployment: (1) If, as a direct result of the wage increase, worker productivity increases through greater managerial efficiency (the "shock effect") or through the improved mental and/or physical condition of the workers, unemployment need not result. (2) If previously existing monopsonistic exploitation is reduced or eliminated, higher wages can be achieved with the same or higher employment. (3) If the oligopoly employer was still operating in the kinked portion of the demand curve after labor costs and therefore marginal costs of output were increased by the wage increase, unemployment need not result.

Minimum Wages

The conclusion regarding the possibility of imposing a fixed price to counteract monopsony and therefore increasing both employment and factor price has sometimes been used as a justification for economy-wide minimum wages. However, the numerous variations in the degree of monopsony power in different labor markets makes it highly unlikely that a blanket, economy-wide minimum wage would fall into the precise range for all monopsonists such that they would simultaneously increase factor employment and price. In terms of Figure 19-3, if the wage rate were raised above $0W_2$, the monopsonist would employ fewer workers than at $0W_2$; and if demand (MRP_L) were elastic, the total wage bill would fall. In short, using a blanket minimum wage law as a device to counteract monopsony would have its problems.

What about the effects of imposing a minimum wage when there is competition in the factor market? For this analysis, it is not crucial whether the output market is competitive or monopolistic. In equilibrium, each firm is hiring workers such that the wage equals the MRP_L. An increase in the wage rate that is not the result of a rise in productivity must lead to unemployment as the employers move back up labor's MRP_L curve until the new higher wage rate equals the MRP_L. In other words, if the employers are forced to pay a minimum of $3 an hour, they will get rid of all workers whose MRP_L is below $3. The net result is that the "poor" workers, who were presumably the reason the minimum wages were imposed, are left unemployed! Even worse, as these people go into other unregulated areas where the wage equals their MRP_L, say, $2.50 an hour, the supply of labor increases and thus the MRP_L and hence price of labor falls. This may lead to a reduction in the MRP_L and wage to some lower figure, say, $2.25 an hour! As is usually the case, interfering with the price system and competitive supply-and-demand mechanism to correct income distribution is inefficient. In this case it hurts those who were supposed to be helped. It is of little consolation to low-paid and unskilled persons to know that the employer must pay them $3 per hour when the fact that they must be paid that amount is what keeps them from being employed. The available empirical evidence shows that low-productivity workers have suffered unemployment as a direct result of higher minimum wage rates.[3]

The irony is that the workers who already receive wages above the legal minimum will benefit from the minimum wages because they will face less

---

[3] A summary of some of the empirical studies examining the effect on employment of minimum wages is contained in Bevars Mabry, *Economics of Manpower and the Labor Market* (New York: Intext Educational Publishers, 1973), pp. 322–325. Also see Yale Brozen, "The Effect of Statutory Minimum Wage Increases on Teenage Unemployment," *Journal of Law and Economics* (April, 1969), pp. 109–122; and Finis Welch and Marvin Kosters, "The Effects of Minimum Wages on the Distribution of Changes in Aggregate Employment," *American Economic Review* (June, 1972), pp. 323–332.

low-wage competition from unskilled workers. That is why many unions support higher minimum wage legislation. Any employers (or employees) in places where wages are already high will benefit from less competition from businesses that might build factories where the large pools of unskilled workers are located. On these grounds, it is not surprising that northern manufacturers and unions, especially in New England, support higher legal minimum wage rates vigorously. And the losers in our society are those with low productivity. Women, teenagers, and blacks (any combinations of these three are even harder hit) are the biggest losers. It is *income,* not wage *rates,* that needs governmental support. Milton Friedman has said: "The use of the legal minimum-wage rate is a monument to the power of superficial thinking." [4]

Similarly, the "equal pay for equal work" legislation that has been enacted in some states and countries to protect various minorities, especially working women, from receiving discriminatory wages can have an opposite effect of that intended.[5] The only way a group being discriminated against can offset this prejudice is by offering compensating advantages; in particular, by working for a lower wage rate. But this "equal pay for equal work" legislation prevents the disadvantaged group from offsetting the prejudice against them, and more, not less, discrimination will result. In exactly the same manner, the fact that unions have reduced the dispersion in wages among union members works against the discriminated group. This can be generalized by stating that reducing the cost of discrimination, as in these cases, encourages discrimination. On the other hand, laws of the type administered by the Fair Employment Practices Commission, such as litigation, fines, imprisonment, unfavorable publicity, etc., for discriminators, increase the cost of not hiring disadvantaged groups, discourage discrimination against the disadvantaged, and promote discrimination against those in the previously advantaged group.

It is also possible to analyze minimum wages in terms of the long-run factor demand curve involving more than one variable factor. If all labor could be divided into skilled and unskilled, and the two were substitutable, then a minimum wage law would generally cause the representative firm to hire fewer unskilled workers. By the definition of substitutes, $\Delta MRP_a/\Delta Q_b < 0$, the employment of fewer unskilled workers shifts the MRP_L (or VMP_L) curve for skilled workers rightward and outward and more skilled labor is hired. Once again the avowed purpose of the legislation—helping the unskilled, inefficient workers—is not fulfilled. Given competitive factor markets and profit-maximizing firms, all that will result is the substitution of skilled for unskilled labor.

HAVE UNIONS RAISED REAL WAGES?

While the answer to the question, "Have unions raised real wages?" might seem to the casual observer to be obviously yes, careful studies of this

---

[4] Milton Friedman, "Minimum Wage Rates," *Newsweek* (September 16, 1966).

[5] An excellent discussion of these and related matters is found in Armen A. Alchian and Reuben A. Kessel, "Competition, Monopoly, and the Pursuit of Money," and the comments by Gary S. Becker and Martin Bronfenbrenner in *Aspects of Labor Economics,* edited by H. Gregg Lewis (Princeton: Princeton University Press, 1962), pp. 3–20.

question have cast significant doubts about union abilities in this capacity. Although wage increases almost always follow collective bargaining negotiations, beware of the "after this, therefore because of this" fallacy. The careful studies all indicate that the most important determinant, over the long run, of wages and labor's market income is labor's productivity. The answer to the above question, therefore, in competitive factor markets reduces to, "Do unions raise labor productivity?"

In other words, unions generally cannot, in competitive factor markets, artificially raise real wage rates without an accompanying increase in labor productivity, and an increase in labor productivity tends to raise real wage rates, regardless of the degree of union activity. This is confirmed by the historical experience in the United States, where average real wage rates and output per worker-hour have been very closely correlated.

Although the statistical evidence is not unambiguous, the following things have been fairly well agreed upon: (1) Unions appear to gain the largest wage increases at the time the firm or industry is first organized. Later wage increases generally follow gains in productivity. (2) There is no historical evidence that real wage rates have risen more in unionized industries than elsewhere in the economy. In fact, since 1933 workers in many low-pay, nonunionized trades have achieved larger percentage increases in pay than union members. While the absolute differentials have remained constant, the percentage pay differentials between union and nonunion wages have narrowed. (3) It is true that the level of average union wages is higher than that of nonunion wages. However, even before they were unionized, these same industries paid higher-than-average wages. Obviously the industries most likely to capture the eye of the union organizers are the profitable, growing, high-skill, high-productivity, concentrated, large industries that already pay above-normal wages. Thus, it is not clear which is cause and which effect. The high wages may have been what caused the unionization rather than vice versa. On the other hand, the union gets no credit for its influence when firms and industries raise wages to keep the union out.[6] (4) Finally, and perhaps most importantly, there is no historical evidence that labor's slice of the total income pie is related to the strength of unionization. One of the remarkable facts about functional income distribution is that wages (or labor's relative share) have represented between 60 to 75 percent of national income over the last 100 years, regardless of ebbs and flows in union strength. The remarkable stability over time of labor's share is hard to reconcile with the thesis that labor as a whole has gained relative to other groups through unionization. Union supporters claim labor's share of national income does not necessarily have to grow to show the influence of unionization.

---

[6] One must be careful with arguments of this type. For example, the argument that the differentials between union and nonunion workers is not larger because unions "hold up or support" the wage scale of nonunion workers is dangerous. If labor markets are reasonably competitive, a union that forces an above-equilibrium wage rate causes unemployment. For wages in other nonunion industries to rise also, given the increase in supply of labor into that industry as a result of the unemployment in the unionized industry, factor demand curves would have to be upward sloping in these industries!

They feel that both wage rates and labor's share would have been much lower without unions.

In summary, the evidence so far is inconclusive as to the effect of unions on labor's absolute and relative wage rates and their return as a whole. A synthesis of the existing data by H. Gregg Lewis suggests that unions have probably achieved a 10 to 15 percent wage advantage for members as compared with nonunion members.[7] Of course some unions have been able to do better than this—e.g., coal miners' wages may be 50 percent higher. It is also true that the impact of unions has varied over the years; with unionization less ubiquitous in the 1920s, wages may have been pushed up as much as 20 percent; whereas after World War II, the effect has almost surely declined.

The fact that unions may have had only a modest effect on wages does not indicate they have failed in their basic mission. In what many regard as the most important areas of union activity—better fringe benefits; greater job security and job tenure; improved work speeds and working conditions; and most particularly enhanced civil rights, political power, and dignity—the unions have been eminently successful.

On the other hand, Cartter and Marshall, after surveying the statistical studies, concluded that: (1) Unions did raise the money wages of union members, but not more than 10 percent above that of nonunion members. (2) The unions did not increase real wages since there were disadvantageous effects (from labor's point of view) that probably cancelled out the modest increase in money wages. (3) They found no clear evidence that unions had causally affected the share of the national income going to labor.[8]

RENT [9]

Rent may be thought of as consisting of two types. First, there is *contract rent* or rental income, which refers to the price of the services of rented or leased land, buildings, and equipment. Rather than buy, a business may prefer to rent needed land or capital equipment. Contract rent is determined by the supply and demand of rentable services.

---

[7] H. Gregg Lewis, *Unionism and Relative Wages in the United States* (Chicago: University of Chicago Press, 1963). Also see Albert Rees, "The Effects of Unions on Resource Allocation," *Journal of Law and Economics* (October, 1963), pp. 69–78, who concludes that perhaps a third of the trade unions have raised their members' wages by 15 to 20 percent above what they might have been if there were no union, another third by 5 to 10 percent, and the remaining third, not at all.

[8] Alan M. Cartter and F. Ray Marshall, *Labor Economics; Wages, Employment, and Trade Unionism* (Homewood: Richard D. Irwin, 1967), pp. 357–359. For a corroborating view, see Clark Kerr, "Labor's Income Share and the Labor Movement," *New Concepts of Wage Determination,* edited by George W. Taylor and Frank C. Pierson (New York: McGraw-Hill Book Co., 1957), p. 287; and for a dissenting view see Harold Levinson, "Collective Bargaining and Income Distribution," *American Economic Review* (May, 1954), pp. 308–316.

[9] The literature on rent theory is reviewed in Dean A. Worcester, Jr., "A Reconsideration of the Theory of Rent," *American Economic Review* (June, 1946), pp. 258–277; reprinted in *Readings in Microeconomics,* edited by David R. Kamerschen (New York: John Wiley & Sons, 1969), Chapter 32, pp. 480–500. Two more recent contributions are Robert H. Wessel, "A Note on Economic Rent," *American Economic Review* (December, 1967), pp. 1221-1226; and Martin Bronfenbrenner, *Income Distribution Theory* (Chicago: Aldine-Atherton, 1971), Chapter 14.

Economic rent is the second type of rent and is the most important concept of the two to the economist. *Economic rent* is any persistent earning or return to any factor of production that exceeds its opportunity cost or the minimal amount required to retain the services of that factor. This payment is in the form of a residual, excess, or surplus that exceeds what the factor could earn in its next best alternative use. Put differently, economic rent is a persistent return to a factor whose quantity is fixed and nonaugmentable—i.e., a factor that is inelastic in supply. We emphasize the word "persistent" to distinguish the long-run concept of economic rent from the short-run concept of quasi-rent. A *quasi-rent* is any earning in excess of opportunity cost that exists because of a temporary or short-run shortage and thus will not persist indefinitely as will an economic rent.[10] It is the existence of these quasi-rents that entices resource owners to shift their resources into the industries earning them. Thus, a quasi-rent is a payment that has no effect on the current or present quantity of the good in existence now, but which does affect the current rate of production and therefore the amount that will exist in the future.

Both the long-run concept of economic rent and the short-run concept of quasi-rent are measured by the difference between a factor's value in its current use and its value in its next best use. In each case, rent or quasi-rent, the payment is economically (as distinguished from legally or morally) unnecessary to retain the services of the factor. To achieve social optimality, rents and quasi-rents must be *paid,* but they need not be *received* by anyone. In other words, rent serves a rationing but not an incentive function. In recognition of the fact that the sum paid to a factor that is inelastic in supply need not be paid to call forth the supply, it has been suggested that this sum be called "non-supply-regulating income" instead of rent.[11]

Figure 19–4 illustrates the necessarily nonnegative return called quasi-rent. This figure shows the conventional short-run curves for an individual firm. As usual, *SMC, ATC,* and *AVC* refer to short-run marginal cost, average total cost, and average variable cost, respectively. Assuming the market price is $0A$ and output is $0N$, the total outlay necessary to maintain the employment of the variable (mobile) resources is $0DJN$. Since these payments just equal the alternative employment opportunities for these factors, these payments cannot be reduced without causing the factors to move. Since the total revenue in this case is $0ALN$, the amount left for paying fixed factors after paying variable factors is $DALJ$. This is the quasi-rent. If the price were $0D$, quasi-rent would be $EDHG$. Similarly, if the price were $0F$, there would be no quasi-rent, since $TR = 0FRP$, $TVC = 0FRP$, and $TR = TVC$. The difference between TR and

---

[10] This modern definition of quasi-rent differs from Marshall's original treatment in that in the modern version, quasi-rents cannot be negative. See Alfred Marshall, *Principles of Economics* (8th ed.; London: Macmillan & Co., 1920). The footnote on pages 426–427 of Marshall's text defined quasi-rents as the total returns to temporarily specialized (fixed) productive services minus the cost of maintenance and replacement. As such, Marshall's quasi-rents: (1) can be negative, and (2) cannot be illustrated in the firm's conventional cost diagrams. See Charles E. Ferguson, *Microeconomic Theory* (3d ed.; Homewood: Richard D. Irwin, 1972), pp. 409–411.

[11] Vivian Charles Walsh, *Introduction to Contemporary Microeconomics* (New York: McGraw-Hill Book Co., 1970), pp. 272–275.

FIGURE 19-4   Quasi-Rent for a Firm

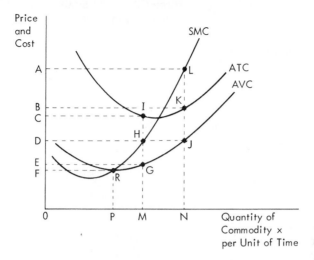

TVC is therefore one measure of quasi-rent. Now it should be apparent why quasi-rent can never be negative—i.e., why *TR* cannot be less than *TVC.* If price fell below 0*F, TR* would be less than *TVC* and the firm would shut down, in which case *TR* = *TVC* = 0. Clearly, by definition the sum of *TVC* and quasi-rent must equal the total value of output.

Transfer Earnings and Economic Rent Contrasted

The total payments to any factor may thus be thought of as consisting of two parts: opportunity cost, which is just enough to keep the factor from transferring to another use, and the economic rent, which makes up the remainder of the total payment. The general principle is that the more inelastic the factor supply curve, the greater the amount of the total factor payment that is a rent and the less that is a required payment. Figure 19–5 illustrates the two extreme cases and the more moderate case. The return to a factor with a perfectly or infinitely elastic supply curve contains no economic rent, since the going price is required to obtain any of its services. At the other extreme, all of the return to a factor with a zero-elastic (perfectly inelastic) supply curve consists of economic rent, since no payment would be required to obtain its services. Between these two extreme cases is the case of a rising supply curve with an elasticity between zero and infinity, which involves economic rents to all units of the factor except the last unit to be employed. In all cases shown in the figure, the shaded areas indicate economic rents.

Quasi-Rent

Economic rents can accrue to any factor of production that meets the inelasticity of supply criterion. In the short run, the payment to a piece of capital equipment, once installed, that is highly specialized with no alternative uses

FIGURE 19–5   Economic Rent Under
                Three Different Factor
                Supply Conditions

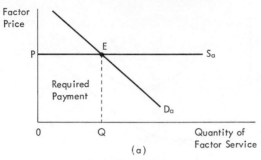

(a)

Perfectly Elastic Factor Supply:
No Economic Rent

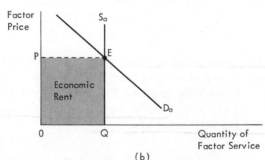

(b)

Perfectly Inelastic Factor Supply:
Pure Economic Rent

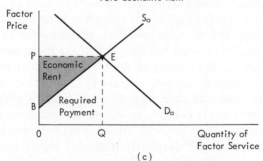

(c)

Normal Factor Supply Elasticity:
Part Economic Rent and Part Required Payment

would be a quasi-rent, since the payment is not necessary to keep it in its present use. However, in the long run, as the machine wears out, it will not be replaced unless it provides an adequate return to its owner. If the payment is not forthcoming, the machine will not continue to be allocated to that employment in the long run.

General Concept of Surplus

The concept of a surplus payment, which traditionally has been called a rent, is very general. It is applicable both on the consumption and the production side of the market. An economic surplus or rent is said to exist whenever a buyer (seller) makes a purchase (sale) for a sum less (greater) than the greatest (least) sum for which the buyer (seller) would have been willing to make the purchase (sale). Thus, what we earlier called consumer surplus and producer surplus are obviously in the "rent" family.

Henry George and the Single-Tax Movement

One American economist, Henry George (1839–1897), became so obsessed with the idea of economic rent that he wrote one of the few best selling books ever written on an economic issue, *Progress and Poverty* (1879). In this volume he advocated a "single-tax movement" to fall entirely on land rents. His notion so won the day that he very nearly was elected Mayor of New York City in 1886 on a platform that included the "single-tax movement" and not much else. Since the surplus returns to land could be taxed without reducing the quantity of land services supplied or changing their allocation, the only effect of such a tax would be a transfer of the rent from the landowners to the government; the market rental price of land would be unaffected. In short, the distribution of income could be changed by a tax on factors receiving rents without distorting resource allocation; for unlike nonland resource prices, land prices do not perform an incentive function—i.e., they do not call for an increased flow of services as price rises. Unfortunately, the virtual impossibility of determining rents and the inadequacy of the revenues from rents if they could be determined for a modern economy have left this interesting proposal with but a handful of supporters today.[12]

In addition to these practical objections, the proposal has some logical shortcomings. The tax should also be levied on the value of inherited nonland property, such as a piece of capital. Furthermore, even if this were taken into account, the tax would unjustly penalize those people who paid the capitalized value for the property and did not expropriate a free gift of nature. Finally, a confiscatory tax of this type would undermine the rationing function of rent as a mechanism for allocating property optimally. Under competition, the landowner has an incentive to let the most productive user—the highest bidder—employ the land. But if the entire amount is to be taxed, the owner is indifferent as to who gets the land. On balance, the single-tax movement has been defeated (but not destroyed) on pragmatic rather than theoretical grounds.

---

[12] The University of Missouri is one of the last bastions of the single tax, having a rich heritage of disciples starting with H. J. Davenport, the father of the opportunity cost doctrine, and extending down to the late Professor Emeritus Harry Gunnison Brown and former FPC Commissioner Pinkney C. Walker.

INTEREST

Older economics texts divided the factors of production into four categories: land, labor, capital, and entrepreneurship. Rent was said to be the payment for the services of land, wages the payment for labor services, interest the payment for the use of capital, and profit the residual appropriated by the entrepreneur. This way of organizing the discussion of income distribution served its purpose, and even today we use these concepts as a rough shorthand in place of the more rigorous ideas when precision is not required.

One should recognize, however, that there is no way to define these categories of factors of production such that a meaningful distinction among them is possible. What part of a machine is capital and what part land (nature)? What part of a particular parcel of land is capital and what part land? Even the services of a human being are in part capital, in part labor. A firm's decision maker does not decide to use so much land, so much capital, and so much labor, but decides which land, what kind of equipment, and what qualities of human effort to employ. A particular kind of labor may be a closer substitute for a particular machine than is another kind of machine.

On the demand side, the firm wishes to employ productive services. It is interested in the productivity of those services and will pay what it must for those services it chooses to employ. Whether it owns the wealth which provides the services or pays the owner the market price for them is a question of secondary importance and is itself a profit-maximizing decision. A firm could conceivably own nothing of substance and buy all of the services from others.

The payments made for productive services (explicit or implicit) are the income earned by the owners of the wealth providing the services. The value of the wealth, given its productive capabilities, depends on the expected future income to be derived from it. What these expected future returns are worth today depends on the interest rate and on expected future interest rates. Present value calculations can be very complex, so for our example we adopt the simplest possible case, which will suffice for the general purpose needed here.

Present value may be illustrated with a piece of land that has a market price of $100 per year based on its *MRP*, and this return will continue from now to eternity. (We assume that the return is forever to simplify the arithmetic.) How much would you be willing to pay for this land that yields $100 of perpetual income? Answer: It is worth exactly the same to you as the amount of money you would need to invest in the market in an equally risky venture to yield the same expected income.

If 4 percent is the market rate of interest on investments with the same degree of risk as investment in the land, it would take a $2,500 investment to get an annual income of $100. The *present discounted capitalized value* (or present worth of future income) of any factor may be computed in this way.

The present value of any asset is found by dividing the expected annual return by the appropriate market rate of interest. The rule is:

$$PV = \$R/i \qquad\qquad (19.1)$$

where PV = present value of an asset

$\$R$ = permanent annual return

i = interest rate expressed as a decimal

In our example, $2,500 = $100/.04. If the market rate rose to .05 or fell to .02, PV would equal $2,000 and $5,000, respectively. If the interest rate is 5, 4, or 2 percent, any perpetual income will sell for exactly 20, 25, or 50 times its annual income (for $20 = 1/.05$, $25 = 1/.04$, and $50 = 1/.02$). In short, PV varies *inversely* with the interest rate. If the return is not perpetual but is for some limited period, a more complicated formula would be necessary.[13] The general result of this would be as expected: an asset whose returns lasted, say, ten years would have a lower PV than one whose returns lasted forever.

If the marginal revenue product of the services of a particular asset were to increase, the present value of that asset would increase. This means that the demand for the services has increased, and the demand for the asset itself increases because its worth (PV) is greater than its current price. The market price of the asset would then increase (unless the supply is infinitely elastic) until the price was equal to its PV. The quantity of the factor (asset) would then increase, the amount of the increase depending upon the elasticity of supply. But as the quantity of the asset and hence the supply of its services increase, the MRP and the price of the service decline, causing the PV to fall. Equilibrium occurs when the present value of the asset equals its price and the marginal cost of producing the asset equals the marginal revenue to the pro- ducing firm. The marginal revenue product of the service of the asset would still equal the price of the service, but these would both be driven down to the point where the rate of return per dollar on this asset was the same as the rate of return on all other assets.

This conclusion is completely general—it holds for dollars spent for edu- cation, buildings, or equipment, or for improving the fertility of a plot of earth. Thus, the interest rate plays this focal role in relating the stock of wealth to the flow of income expected from assets. In other words, interest is the payment for all productive services over time of all durable wealth, whether that wealth is called land, capital, or human capital. The one exception to this statement is that labor must also be rewarded for the exertion of effort or, alternatively, for giving up leisure. This effort pay would be most of the wage for unskilled workers, but only a small portion of the wage of, say, a neurosurgeon or a recording star.

The rate of interest is a way of expressing the productivity of real assets per dollar, per year. Where, then, does the notion that interest is the payment received by bond holders or lenders come in? We have a loanable funds theory

---

[13] The standard formula is:

$$PV = \frac{R_1}{(1+i)} + \frac{R_2}{(1+i)^2} + \frac{R_3}{(1+i)^3} + \cdots + \frac{R_n}{(1+i)^n} + \frac{S}{(1+i)^n}$$

where the R_i are the net returns to be received in the designated year, and S is the expected value of the asset in the nth year.

which concludes that the interest rate is determined by the supply of lending and demand for borrowing. The liquidity preference theory of interest rate determination asserts that the rate of interest is determined by the supply and demand for the stock of money, where bonds are the alternative asset to holding money.

The relationship between borrowing and capital creation is straightforward. If anyone sees profitable prospects from owning a particular form of wealth, the purchase funds can be borrowed. If the yield on the real asset is expected to be greater than the interest payment obligation, the transaction is expected to be advantageous. This kind of borrowing can take place through bond issuance, stock flotation, direct borrowing, or self finance. Thus, the distinction made in the business world between dividends, retained earnings, and interest is not made in economic theory.

The lender represents the other side of the coin. For new wealth to come into existence (investment is defined as the act of adding to the stock of wealth), saving must take place (saving is defined as the process of consuming less than current income or production). The act of saving frees resources to be used in the production of wealth (capital), but savers must be compensated for foregoing current consumption. The reward for saving is the rate of return earned on the assets created by the investment.

The individual income recipient must decide how much to consume and how much to save. This decision will depend on the interest rate, given the individual's preferences between current and future consumption. The higher the interest rate, the greater the future consumption (saving). At low rates of interest, the individual may have a negative amount of saving and thus may borrow from himself/herself or from someone else.

The interest rate is probably stock dominated. That is to say, the rate of interest is determined by the supply of and demand for the outstanding stock of instruments of indebtedness. The additions to this stock (borrowing) per week or per month (or even per year) are relatively small compared to the outstanding stock.

PROFIT

In earlier chapters of this text we have shown profit to be the difference between a firm's total revenue and total cost in some time period. We have stressed that both revenue and cost must include explicit and implicit elements. We have shown that if nothing impedes entry to or exit from the industry, the profit will be eliminated and competitive firms will earn zero profit. This probably seemed somewhat unrealistic, but at this stage of understanding it should seem very plausible in that everyone who contributes to the production of the product earns an income equal to the value of that contribution. In particular, the entrepreneur earns income for any managerial or other labor inputs and receives the value of the contribution of the services of any property owned by the entrepreneur and used by the firm.

Since entry is restricted in the monopoly case, the profit is not driven out by new firms entering the market. In that case the profit is capitalized. The value of the firm increases until the profit rate just equals the rate of return on all other assets. What was profit becomes a cost of production — interest on the value of the ownership of the complex called the corporation.

Profit occurs only as a result of uncertainty. If revenues and costs in the future are known with certainty, all returns would be capitalized accurately and there would be no residual return to anyone. Thus it is that profit is sometimes described as the payment for accepting risk. Consider this simple example. A firm receives a large contract from the government to produce a new weapons system. The price is fixed in the contract. All costs and production relations are known with certainty. If the difference between the revenues and the costs is large, the stock market will bid the price of the shares of the firm up until the additional returns yield only the same rate as the shares of all other stock. Notice that the recipients of the gain in this case are the owners of the stock at the moment the information about the contract becomes known. Afterwards, the only return to the stockholders is the normal return equal to that on other assets. In a world of uncertainty the process works the same way, but of course there are time lags for information to become known, and different situations are subject to different degrees of uncertainty.

The Function of Natural Scarcity Profits

The *possibility* of making profits is necessary to motivate people to accept the risk of losses in an enterprise, to organize and direct production, and hence to guide resource allocation. As with prices in general, profits provide information efficiently and effectively and provide an incentive for factor owners and factor users who are guided by and follow this information. Individuals must have sufficient incentive to engage in entrepreneurship; i.e., to bear uncertainty and risk innovation to combine factors into a going concern.

Because risk and uncertainty exist, these entrepreneurs do not know if these ventures will prove successful. Some writers, following Frank Knight, draw a sharp distinction between risk and uncertainty.[14] The term "risk" is used to describe situations in which the probabilities of the various outcomes are known and therefore insurable, whereas "uncertainty" is used to describe situations in which the probabilities are unknown and therefore uninsurable. Among the uninsurable uncertainties are future governmental policies, population changes, and innovations by others.

Profits accrue to entrepreneurs for assuming *uninsurable* uncertainty. Some types of risk, such as deaths, fires, accidents, and theft, can be estimated fairly closely by the celebrated "law of large numbers." Firms can avoid these risks by paying a small (certain) cost in the form of an insurance premium; e.g., on key employees. It is the uninsurable uncertainties stemming from uncontrollable and unpredictable fluctuations in demand and/or supply which form the basis for potential economic profits.

Although the insecurity of not knowing what the future may bring to a business can never be completely eliminated, business people try to reduce it

---

[14] Frank H. Knight, *Risk, Uncertainty, and Profit* (Boston: Houghton Mifflin, 1921).

in at least two other ways besides buying insurance. They seek additional information and diversify their activities.[15] Efficient managers continually search for more complete and reliable information on business conditions which will narrow the gap between anticipation and realization. Since information is not free, optimal behavior calls for the equation of the marginal cost of information search with the marginal returns from search. The reduction of uncertainty through diversification takes many forms: producing several different and statistically unrelated products, putting plants in different geographical locations, borrowing from different financial sources, etc. The better able a firm is to control uncertainty, the better its performance in general.

Some scholars, following Joseph Schumpeter, emphasize that profits result solely from the successful application of innovations (as distinct from inventions which may not be carried into practice).[16] These innovations would include the introduction of a new product, a new quality of a product, or a new method of production; the opening of a new market or source of supply, whether or not it existed before; or the reorganization of an industry by creating or destroying a monopoly. For Schumpeter, profits were natural, implacable, and beneficial concomitants of the growth process in a credit economy. Those who get there the "firstest with the mostest" share in the bounty.

The Significance of Profits

While in the case of risk, uncertainty, and innovation, profits are desirable in the proper functioning of the allocative mechanism, profits due to *artificial* or *contrived* scarcities as compared with natural scarcities are not. The profits due to a monopolistic position do not represent a return for socially productive services. They are economic rent or interest in a static analysis, although they are functional in the Schumpeter dynamic economy. Thus, to some economists profits are the result of either disequilibrium and/or monopoly.[17]

Under competition, profits and losses serve as a signaling device to inform firms which products the consumers prefer to have produced. Firms that produce too much of a product, charge too high a price, or produce a product of low quality may incur losses. The signal of "negative profits" or losses means produce less, become more economical and efficient, and hence lower costs of production and price, or improve the quality of the product. Similarly, competitive short-run profits are essential in signaling for expansion in that firm or industry. Thus, the difference between rents and profits is that rents cannot be

---

[15] See, e.g., Gerald L. Nordquist, *The Behavior of Competitive Enterprise* (Morristown, N.J.: General Learning Press, 1972).

[16] Joseph A. Schumpeter, *The Theory of Economic Development* (Cambridge: Harvard University Press, 1934).

[17] This is the orthodox position. Professor Demsetz and some other members of the "Chicago School" maintain that without barriers to entry, profits are more likely due to low costs than high prices and are therefore an indicator of "efficiency," "superior ability," or "competitive superiority" rather than "monopolism." See Harold Demsetz, "Industry Structure, Market Rivalry, and Public Policy," *Journal of Law and Economics* (April, 1973), pp. 1–9. Also see John McGee, *In Defense of Industrial Concentration* (New York: Frederick A. Praeger, Inc., Publishers, 1971).

competed away in long-run equilibrium as can profits. Economic profits must be zero in long-run competitive equilibrium, but economic rents need not be zero.

In contrast, under monopoly there are by definition certain barriers hindering the entry of new firms. This allows firms to charge high prices and/or produce shabby products or poor service and still reap profits. As opposed to the other sources of profits, monopoly profits often serve no socially useful purpose and as such are socially undesirable.

In summary, competitive profits serve a useful purpose in solving the allocation, stability, distribution, and economic growth problems. The expectation of profits induces innovation and investment and thus influences the level of employment and income and the future growth rate of the economy. Investment spending is one of the three main sources of total spending (along with consumer and governmental spending) in our economy, and it is the level of total spending that determines the volume of employment and income in a society. Similarly, how much goes into investment or capital goods as opposed to consumer goods is an important determinant of the future level of economic growth of a country.

Despite these important contributions on the macro side, the basic function of profits (and losses) is on the micro side in solving the allocation and distribution problems. Profits and losses provide the "carrot" and "stick" in motivating firms to assign resources in accordance with consumer preferences.[18]

QUESTIONS

1. Being as specific as you can be with respect to both the theory of wages and the historical evidence, how do you account for the great growth in real wages in the U.S.? What does your crystal ball indicate about the prospects of this rapid growth continuing?
2. A popular expression with which most people seem to agree is "equal pay for equal work," and regulations seem to measure conformance to "affirmative action" requirements by the proportions of workers compared to proportions in the population. Suppose that (1) the law rigidly requires equal pay for all workers in an occupation, (2) the law requires an equal number of men and women to be employed, and (3) while productivity is the same for men and women, (4) the supply curves are different. Compare wages in a competitive industry before and after these laws go into effect. (Examples you might think of would be kindergarten teachers or steelworkers.)
3. Imagine an economy in which all of the firms are monopolies and all workers are unionized. What would be the result if the unions forced the money wage to increase at a time when no increase in labor productivity occurred?
4. How is "economic rent" or "quasi-rent" supposed to differ between land and machines?

---

[18] It should be noted that wages and profits are not necessarily "competitive" with one another. Paul A. Meyer, "A Paradox on Profits and Factor Prices," *American Economic Review* (June, 1967), pp. 535–541, demonstrates that an increase in the price of a factor of production may increase short-run profits in a competitive industry.

5. "Interest is a component of all incomes." Explain this assertion. Why do lenders demand a return called interest? Why are borrowers willing to pay this thing called interest?

6. Since our basic conclusion is that the forces at work in an economy act in the direction of eliminating profit, and that even in a world of uncertainty expected profits may be zero, how can we account for the fact that firms continue to exist, new firms continue to enter markets, and people still want to buy ownership in firms?

7. Explain the role of profits in an economic system. In the course of your answer, distinguish between actual profits and the possibility of profits.

AUTHOR INDEX

A

Abramovitz, Moses, 431 n.13, 434 n
Alchian, Armen A., 88 n, 443 n.5
Allen, R. G. D., 96
Allen, William R., 88 n

B

Bailey, Martin J., 135 n
Bain, Joe S., 351 n.1, 375 n
Baumol, William J., 10 n, 354–355, 382–383
Becker, Gary S., 25 n.4, 278 n.2, 365, 443 n.5
Bertrand, Joseph, 328, 330
Bilas, Richard A., 84 n
Bishop, Robert L., 321 n, 348
Blair, John M., 354 n.7
Boulding, Kenneth E., 15 n, 53, 131 n, 332 n, 333, 334 n. 12-n.13, 345 n.16, 353 n.5, 357
Bronfenbrenner, Martin, 4, 166, 434 n, 443 n.5, 445 n.9
Brown, Harry Gunnison, 449 n
Brozen, Yale, 442 n
Brumberg, Richard E., 28 n

C

Cartter, Alan M., 395 n, 429 n, 445
Cassels, John M., 314
Caves, Richard, 365 n.33
Chamberlin, Edward H., 309–310, 314, 316–317, 321–324, 333–334
Chiu, John S. Y., 355 n
Clark, J. B., 430 n.12, 432–433
Cobb, Charles W., 166
Cournot, A. Augustin, 328–330, 347–348
Cyert, R. M., 352 n.3

D

Davenport, H. J., 449 n
Dean, Joel, 284 n

D

Demsetz, Harold, 323–324, 454 n.17
Dirlam, Joel B., 354 n.7
Dooley, Peter C., 368 n
Douglas, Paul H., 166

E

Edgeworth, Francis Y., 96, 328, 330–332
Elbing, Alvar O., 355 n
Encarnacion, Jose, Jr., 353 n.5
Engel, Christian, 57
Euler, Leonhard, 432–433

F

Fellner, William, 327 n.3
Ferguson, Charles E., 7 n.3, 142 n, 195 n.4, 211, 256 n, 416 n.3, 419 n.6, 446 n.10
Fisher, Franklin M., 288 n
Friedman, Milton, 7, 135 n, 273 n, 416 n.3, 419 n.6, 443

G

Gayer, Arthur D., 99 n.6
George, Henry, 449
Griliches, Zvi, 288 n

H

Hadar, Josef, 375 n
Harberger, Arnold, 364
Harriss, C. Lowell, 99 n.6
Henderson, J. M., 258 n.4
Hicks, John R., 58, 96, 121 n, 131 n, 136 n, 208
Hirshleifer, Jack, 411 n
Hotelling, Harold, 332–333, 364 n.29, n.31
Houck, James P., 59 n, 65 n
Houthakker, H. S., 57 n.10
Hutchison, T. W., 7

J

Jevons, W. S., 90
Jung, Allen F., 89 n.10
Jureen, Lars, 56 n.7

K

Kafoglis, Milton Z., 356 n.11-n.12
Kaldor, N., 431
Kalecki, M., 431
Kamerschen, David R., 28 n, 99 n.6,
  117 n, 135 n, 154 n, 288 n, 290 n.6,
  310 n, 321 n, 357 n.13-n.14, 359 n.23,
  364 n.30-n.31, 430 n.11, 431 n.13,
  434 n, 445 n.9
Kaplan, A. D. H., 354 n.7
Kaysen, Carl, 288 n
Kendrick, J. W., 195 n.3
Kerr, Clark, 445 n.8
Kessel, Reuben A., 443 n.5
Knight, Frank H., 7 n.4, 453
Koo, A. C. Y., 143 n.9
Kosters, Marvin, 442 n

L

Lanzillotti, Robert F., 354
Lawyer, John Q., 291 n.8
Leftwich, Richard H., 80 n.5
Leibenstein, Harvey, 366 n.37
Leontief, Wassily W., 338 n
Leser, C. E. V., 57
Levinson, Harold, 445 n.8
Lewis, H. Gregg, 291 n.9, 443 n.5, 445
Liebhafsky, E. E., 430 n.11
Liebhafsky, H. H., 378 n
Lipsey, Richard G., 301 n.13, 327
  n.3-n.4, 351 n.2, 375 n, 419 n.7, 429 n

M

Mabry, Bevars, 442 n
McDonald, John, 358 n.22
McGee, John S., 290 n.6, 454 n.17
McGuire, Joseph W., 355 n
Machlup, Fritz, 7 n.3, 326
Malanos, George, 80 n.4
March, J. G., 352 n.3
Markham, Jesse W., 154 n, 322 n, 345
Marshall, Alfred, 80, 85–86, 164, 179,
  391, 410, 446 n.10

Marshall, F. Ray, 445
Menger, Carl, 90
Meyer, Paul A., 455 n
Mill, John Stuart, 7 n.4
Mishan, Edward J., 25 n.3
Mitchell, Wesley C., 7 n.5

N

Nordquist, Gerald L., 454 n.15

O

Oi, Walter Y., 375 n
Ozawa, Terutomo, 371 n

P

Palda, Kristian S., 284 n, 291 n.8
Pardridge, William C., 355 n
Pareto, Vilfredo, 196
Patinkin, Don, 338 n
Pech, M. R., 431 n.14
Pierson, Frank C., 445 n.8
Pigou, A. C., 278, 379 n
Podwin, Horace de, 360 n.26
Pontney, Jack A., 121 n
Prais, S. J., 57 n.10

Q

Quandt, R. E., 258 n.4
Quinn, Theodore K., 287

R

Rader, Trout, 121 n
Reder, Melvin W., 431 n.13, 434 n
Rees, Albert, 445 n.7
Reynolds, Milton, 301
Robbins, Lionel, 7
Roberts, David R., 355 n
Rothschild, K. W., 357
Rottenberg, Simon, 291 n.9

S

Samuelson, Paul A., 7 n.6, 96, 143
Sato, Ryuzo, 195 n.3
Saving, Thomas R., 364 n.32, 416 n.2,
  419 n.6

Scherer, Frederic M., 325, 346 n, 359 n.24, 366, 375 n, 378 n
Schultz, Theodore W., 421 n
Schumpeter, Joseph A., 154, 454
Scitovsky, Tibor, 353 n.5
Selden, Richard, 360 n.26
Shepherd, William G., 365, 426 n
Shih-yen Wu, 121 n
Simon, Herbert, 353
Simon, Julian, 334 n.13
Sloan, Alfred, 358
Slutsky, Eugene, 131 n
Smith, Adam, 185, 277, 303
Smith, Richard Austin, 290 n.7
Spencer, Milton H., 99 n.6
Steiner, Peter O., 301 n.13, 327 n.3-n.4, 351 n.2, 375 n, 419 n.7, 429 n
Stevens, Catharine, 358 n.22
Stigler, George J., 15 n, 57 n.10, 89, 99 n.5, 131 n, 136 n, 196 n, 283 n, 289 n, 294 n, 301 n.12, 310, 318, 321–322, 332 n, 334, 341, 353 n.5, 357 n.17, 358 n.21, 359 n.23, 364
Stocking, George W., 378 n
Stone, Richard, 57
Sweezy, Paul, 334–336

T

Taylor, George W., 445 n.8
Tintner, Gerhard, 357

V

von Mises, Ludwig, 7 n.4

W

Wallace, Richard L., 364 n.31
Walras, Léon, 80, 82, 90
Walsh, Vivian Charles, 143 n.8, 446 n.11
Watkins, Myron, 378 n
Watson, Arthur, 287
Watson, Donald S., 141 n, 375 n
Weiss, Leonard W., 351 n.1
Welsh, Finis, 442 n
Wessel, Robert H., 445 n.9
Whiteside, Thomas, 301 n.13
Wicksteed, Philip H., 15 n, 432–433
Williamson, Oliver E., 358
Wilson, J. R., 357 n.15
Wold, Herman, 56–57
Worcester, Dean A., Jr., 445 n.9

SUBJECT INDEX

A

Actual supply curve, 272–273
Ad valorem tax, 371
Alternative cost doctrine, 214
Arc elasticity, 59–60
Average fixed costs, 222–223
Average physical product, 169
Average product, 169
Average revenue, 45
Average total costs, 225
Average variable costs, 223–225
Axiomatic choice theory, 96

B

Balance-sheet homeostasis theory, 357
Barometric price leadership, 344–345
Barter, 13
Bertrand's oligopoly model, 330
Bilateral monopoly, 406–407
Blocked entry, 311
Bond market, 14
Budget line, 112–115
Budget space, 112

C

Capitalization of returns to fixed factors, 267–268
Capitalized value, present discounted, 450
Capital stock, nonhuman, 423
Cardinal utility, 69–70; applications of, 85–91; ordinal utility approach relative to, 117–119
Cartel, 158; centralized, 337–339; market-sharing, 339–341
Centralized cartel, 337–339
Ceteris paribus, 9
Chicago School, 322
Cobb-Douglas production function, 166–167, 431
Collective bargaining, increases in wages through, 439–440
Collective commodities, 277–279
Collusion, 289–291
Commodity market, 13–14

Commodity space, 107
Compensated demand function: Hicksian method, 132–133; ordinary demand function vs., 134–135; Slutsky method, 133
Competition: characteristics of, 151; economic effects of imperfect, 350–366; imperfect, 157; interproduct or interindustry, 153; long-run cost functions and, 282; monopolistic. *See* Monopolistic competition; monopoly compared with, 349–350; nonprice, 315–316, 359; perfect, 155–157; promoting, 368–369; pure, 150–151, 273–277; taxation under, 373
Competitive environment, limitations in a perfectly functioning, 277–280
Complements, 111; gross, 55, 64
Completeness assumption, 97–98
Conflict curve, 138
Consistency assumption, 98
Constant costs, 271–272
Constant returns to scale, 233
Constant-returns-to-scale production function, 172
Constrained sales maximization, 354–356, 382–383
Consumer behavior, 72–79; objectives, limitations, and problems affecting, 68–69
Consumer equilibrium, 91–92
Consumer surplus, 85–87, 94–95, 136–137
Consumption, nonnormal indifference curves and, 121–123
Contract curve, 138
Contract rent, 445
Cost and demand functions, nonuniform, 315
Cost conditions, normal, 238–239
Cost curves: per-unit, 221–230; selling, 316–322; total, 218–221
Cost functions: competition and long-run, 282; derivation of, 239–240; long-run, 231–233, 238; short-run, 217–230, 237–238

Costs: average fixed, 222–223; average total, 225; average variable, 223–225; constant, 271–272; decreasing, 272; increasing, 269–271; incremental, 226; marginal, 225–230; meaning of, 214–215; normal, 369–370; product variation, 288; sales, 288; selling, 316–322; social, 278; supply and, 217; total, 220–221; total fixed, 218–219; total variable, 219–220
Costs of production: importance of, 28–29; under monopoly, 293
Cost theorem, Cournot's, 348
Cross elasticity of demand, 64
Cross price elasticity of demand, 54–56

D

Dead-weight loss, 363
Decreasing costs, 272
Decreasing returns to scale, 233
Demand, 20; change in, 20; cross elasticity of, 64; cross price elasticity of, 54–56; derivation of firm's elasticity of, 263–264; derived, 392–393; determinants of price elasticity of, 51–53; effective, 15; elasticity of, 37; factor, 392–393, 410–412; formulas for price elasticity of, 38–39; income elasticity of, 56–58, 63–64; labor, 438–439; law of, 23–25; mathematical notes on elasticity of, 63–64; monopolist's response to change in, 360; other determinants of, 22–23; own price elasticity of, 63; price elasticity of, 38, 126–127; for productive service, 392–396; short-run factor, 408–410; side of the market, 14–23; stock, 15
Demand and cost functions, nonuniform, 315
Demand and supply. *See* Supply and demand
Demand curve: derived from indifference curve, 123–125; firm's, 21; industry, 261; kinked, 158–159; linear, 41; long-run factor, 414–417; marginal revenue product curve as firm's short-run, 400; market, 20, 417–419; normal, 23; proof of down-sloping factor, 209–210; stock, 16; time and the, 22

Demand functions: compensated, 132–135; ordinary vs. compensated, 134–135
Demand schedule, derivation of down-sloping, 80–84
Derived demand, 392–393
Diamond-water paradox, 89–91
Differentiated products, 288
Differentiation, principle of minimum, 333
Diminishing marginal rate of substitution, law of, 101
Diminishing marginal rate of technical substitution between factors *a* and *b*, 192–193
Diminishing marginal utility, law of, 70–72
Diminishing returns: law of, 30, 167; point of, 168
Discommodity, 77
Discounted capitalized value, present, 450
Discrimination: employment, 365; imperfect price, 380–382; perfect or first-degree price, 379–380; price, 375–378, 385–386
Disequilibrium differentials, dynamic, 425–428
Dominant firm price leadership, 343–344
Duopoly, 152
Dynamic disequilibrium differentials, static equilibrium vs., 425–428

E

Economic efficiency, 163–164
Economic rent, 446; transfer earnings contrasted with, 447
Economics, definition of, 1
Economic theory, characteristics of, 8–11
Economies of large-scale production, 286–287
Economies of scale: external pecuniary, 234–235; external technical, 234; internal vs. external, 233–236
Edgeworth-Bowley box diagram, 137
Edgeworth's oligopoly model, 330–332
Effective demand, 15
Efficiency: economic, 163–164; engineering, 163–164; technical, 163–164

Elasticity, 37–45; arc, 59–60; graphical representation of, 41–45; income, 129–130; other types of, 53–58; output, 197; revenue and, 45–51; total spending test of, 39–41; unit, 38, 41; unitary, 38, 41

Elasticity of demand, 37; cross, 64; cross price, 54–56; derivation of firm's, 263–264; income, 56–58, 63–64; mathematical notes on, 63–64; own price, 63; price, 38–39, 51–53, 126–127

Elasticity of expectations, 58

Elasticity of factor demand, 410–412

Elasticity of factor supply, 424–425

Elasticity of substitution, 194–195

Elasticity of supply, 37, 59; graphic demonstration of, 60–61; linear, 65; mathematical notes on, 65–66; price, 59–61; proof of linear, 61

Employment: effect of wage changes on, 441–442; under monopoly, 365

Engel curves, 57; income-consumption curve and derivation of, 128–129; income elasticity and, 129–130

Engineering efficiency, 163–164

Entry: blocked, 311; open, 311, 313

Equality method, 76

Equal net advantage, hypothesis of, 420

Equilibrium: consumer, 91–92; factor, 396–400; factor market, 397–399; firm and industry short-run, 259–260

Equilibrium differentials, static, 425–428

Equilibrium price, 31

Equimarginal principle, 73–74, 214, 318–320; for hiring factors, 396–397

Established firm advantage, 289

Euler's theorem, 432–433

Ex ante utility, 67

Excess capacity, 313–315

Exchange, 88, 137–139

Expansion effect, 179

Expansion path, 205, 211

Expected utility, 67

Expense, marginal factor, 396

Exploitation: monopolistic, 407–408; monopsonistic, 407–408

Ex post utility, 67

External economies of scale, internal vs., 233–236

External effect, 417

External pecuniary economies of scale, 234–235

External technical economies of scale, 234

Extreme apriorism, 7

F

Factor-cost curve, 202

Factor-cost equation, 202–204

Factor demand, 392–393; determinants of short-run, 408–410; elasticity of, 410–412

Factor demand curves: long-run, 414–417; proof of downsloping, 209–210

Factor equilibrium analysis, 396–400

Factor expense, marginal, 396

Factor market, conditions for equilibrium in, 397–399

Factor mobility, 424–425

Factor optimum, 209

Factors: equimarginal principle in hiring, 396–397; fixed, 163, 181–185; interrelationships among, 179–181; total supply of, 420; variable, 163

Factor's physical productivity, 408–409

Factor supply, in particular uses, 423–424

Factor supply conditions, 428–429

Factor supply elasticity, 424–425

Factor symmetry, 176–178

Firm, decision-making by, 213–217

Firm and industry short-run equilibria, 259–260

Firm's demand curves, 21; market organization and, 155–159

Firm's elasticity of demand, derivation of, 263–264

Firm's short-run supply curve, competitive, 254–255

Fixed costs: average, 222–223; total, 218–219

Fixed factor, 163; varying the, 181–185

Fixed tax, 371

Flow-dominated market, 14, 20–22

Functional income distribution, 387

G

Giffen good, 85; inferior good vs., 135–136

Good: collective, 277–279; Giffen, 85; Giffen vs. inferior, 135–136; inferior, 24, 57, 64; neutral, 129; normal, 24, 57; quasi-collective, 277; superior, 24, 57, 64

H

Hicksian method, 131–133
Homogeneous functions, 95, 210–211
Homogeneous production function, 184; of degree *n,* 212; of degree one, 211–212
Hotelling's oligopoly model, 332–333

I

Immediate period, monopoly pricing in, 295–296
Imperfect competition, 157; economic effects of, 350–366
Income-consumption curve, derivation of Engel curves and, 128–129
Income distribution: effects of monopoly on, 407; essentials of, 387–392; functional, 387; personal, 387; under monopoly, 365
Income effect, 84–85, 130–136
Income elasticity, Engle curves and, 129–130
Income elasticity of demand, 56–58, 63–64
Increasing costs, 269–271
Increasing returns to scale, 233
Incremental cost, 226
Indifference curve, 103; characteristics of, 107–111; consumption determination with nonnormal, 121–123; derivation of demand curve from, 123–125; from indifference schedule, 102–107; summary of optimality with normal, 121; utility maximization with, 115–116
Indifference curve approach, 96. *See also* Ordinal utility approach
Indifference map, 102
Indifference relationships, nature of, 97–102
Indifference schedule, 99–102; indifference curves from, 102–107

Industry effect, 53
Industry short-run supply curve, competitive, 257–259
Industry supply and demand curves, 261
Industry supply curves, 28; long-run, 268–273
Inferior boundary, 144; constructing the, 145–147
Inferior good, 24, 57, 64; Giffen good vs., 135–136
Interest, 450–452
Internal economies of scale, external vs., 233–236
Internal Revenue Act, 291–292
Intuitive approach, 80
Investment banker, 289
Isocline, 199–202
Isocost curve, 202
Isocost equation, 202–204
Isocost function, 202
Isocosts, optimum combination of inputs and, 202–208
Iso-product curve, 189
Isoquant, 189–202; characteristics of, 192–194; graphic illustration of, 191; slope of, 192
Iso-utility curve, 103

J

Joint profit-maximization hypothesis, qualified, 327–328
Joint supply, 29–30

K

Kendrick's technique, 431
Kinked demand curve, 158–159
Kinked demand curve model, Sweezy's, 334–336

L

Labor, increase in demand for, 438–439
Labor market, 14
Labor supply, 139–141; decrease in, 438
LaGrangian multiplier technique, 92, 94
Land, 423
Large-scale production, economies of, 286–287
Law of demand, 23–25

Law of diminishing marginal rate of substitution, 101

Law of diminishing marginal rate of technical substitution of factor *a* for *b*, 193

Law of diminishing marginal utility, 70–72

Law of diminishing returns, 30, 167

Law of proportionality, 167–168; importance of, 218; qualifications of, 168

Law of supply, 30–31

Law of supply and demand, 31; in resource market, 388–389

Leadership, price, 341–346

Legal monopoly, 291–292

Licenses, 291

Linear demand curve, 41

Linear production function, 184

Linear supply curves, 65–66

Linear supply elasticities, 65; proof of, 61

Logical positivism, 7

Long run, 230–231; monopolistic competition in, 311, 313; monopoly pricing and production in, 300–301; monopoly profits in, 358–359; profit maximization in, 356

Long-run cost functions, 231–233, 238; competition and, 282

Long-run factor demand curves, 414–417

Long-run industry supply curves, 268–273

Long-run relations, short-run relations and, 196–199

Long-run supply curve, 265–267

Loss minimization, 253

Low-cost firm price leadership, 342–343

Lump-sum tax, 371, 373

M

Managerial discretion theory, 357

Marginal costs, 225–230

Marginal equality, 244

Marginal factor expense, 396

Marginal inequality, 244

Marginalists, 90

Marginal physical product, 169

Marginal product, value of, 275

Marginal productivity theory, 390; criticisms of, 429–432

Marginal profit, 244

Marginal rate of substitution, law of diminishing, 101

Marginal rate of technical (or factor) substitution of factor *a* for *b*, 192

Marginal revenue, 46

Marginal revenue product, 393

Marginal revenue product curve: as firm's short-run demand curve, 400; shape of, 393, 395–396

Marginal utility, 70; law of diminishing, 70–72

Marginal utility schedule, derivation of downsloping demand schedule from, 80–84

Market, 149; bond, 14; characteristics of competitive, 151; commodity, 13–14; definition of, 13; demand side of, 14–23; factor, 397–399; firm demand curves and organization of, 155–159; flow-dominated, 14, 20–22; four basic models of, 149–150; imperfections in, 401–408; labor, 14; money, 14; nature of, 13–14; resource, 388–389; results of competitive, 275–276; stock-dominated, 14–20; structural characteristics of, 153–154; supply side of the, 26–30

Market demand curve, 20, 417–419

Market effect, 417

Market imperfections, shortcomings as result of, 280–281

Market segmentation, 377–378

Market shares model of oligopoly, 347–348

Market-sharing cartel, 339–341

Market structure, specific wages and, 436

Market supply curve, 28–39

Marshallian approach, 80–82

Maximization: constrained sales, 354–356, 382–383; long-run profit, 356; profit, 175–176, 351–358, 413; utility, 74–79, 115–116, 353

Methodology, 6–8

Microeconomic theory, 1–2

Minimum wages, 442–443

Mobility, factor, 424–425

Modern axiomatic choice theory, 143

Money market, 14

Money wages, 434–436

Monopolistic competition, 152, 308–309; alleged wastes of, 320, 321; assumptions of model of, 310–311; Chamberlin's, 323–324; long-run analysis of, 311, 313; short-run analysis of, 311

Monopoly, 401–402; attaining and maintaining positions of, 285–292; bilateral, 406–407; change in demand under, 360; competition compared with, 349–350; controlling through taxation, 371–375; costs of production and sales revenue under, 292–295; economically unjustifiable, 367; economic effects of, 350–366; employment discrimination under, 365; income distribution under, 407; income redistribution under, 365; legal, 291–292; long-run profits under, 358–359; miscellaneous effects of, 366; misconceptions concerning, 302–305; $MR < P$ under, 306; multiplant, 301–302, 306–307; natural, 285–286, 291, 370–371; nonprice competition under, 359; output under, 383–385; price policy under, 351; prices and output under, 351; prices and quantities under, 361; public policies toward, 367–369; pure, 151–152, 283–285; regulating, 368–375; resource allocation and, 362–365; social objections to, 368; taxation under, 383–385; technological advance under, 361–362

Monopoly pricing and production in the long run, 300–301

Monopoly pricing and production in the short run, 296–299

Monopoly pricing in the immediate period, 295–296

Monopsonistic exploitation, 407–408

Monopsony, 401–406; economic effect of unions and, 440–441; profit maximization under, 413

Multiplant monopolist, 301–302, 306–307

Negative slope, 23

Neutral good, 129

Noncompeting groups, 427

Nonprice competition, 315–316; under monopoly, 359

Nonsatiation assumption, 98

O

Occam's Razor, 69

Oligopoly, 152–153, 158–159, 325–327; Bertrand's model of, 330; class 1, 328–336; class 2, 336–341; class 3, 341–346; Cournot's cost theorem of, 348; Cournot's model of, 328–330, 347; Edgeworth's model of, 330–332; Hotelling's model of, 332–333; market shares model of, 347–348; Sweezy's kinked demand curve model of, 334–336

Open entry, 311, 313

Optimality, 121

Optimality assumption, 99

Optimality conditions, 187–188, 261–262; algebraic solution of, 79

Optimum, factor, 209

Optimum combination of inputs, isocosts and, 202–208

Optimum rate of output, technical, 230

Ordinal utility, 69–70

Ordinal utility approach, 96; cardinal utility approach relative to, 117–119. *See also* Indifference curve

Ordinal utility theory, applications of, 136–142

Ordinary demand function, compensated demand function vs., 134–135

Output: least-cost or maximum, 178–179; technical optimum rate of, 230; under monopoly, 351, 361, 383–385

Output effect, 179, 207–208

Output elasticity, 197

Own price elasticity of demand, 63

P

Perfect competition, 155–157

Personal income distribution, 387

Per-unit cost curves, 221–230

Per-unit tax, 372–373

N

Natural monopoly, 285–286, 291

Natural resources, 423

Planning curve, 233
Positive slope, 30
Present discounted capitalized value, 450
Price: controlling, 369–371; equilibrium, 31; reservation, 15
Price-consumption curve, 125; derivation of demand curve from indifference curve and, 123–125; deriving price elasticity of demand from, 126–127
Price discrimination, 375–378, 385–386; imperfect, 380–382; perfect or first-degree, 379–380; second-degree, 381; third-degree, 381
Price elasticity of demand, 38; cross, 54–56; derived from price-consumption curve, 126–127; determinants of, 51–53; formulas for, 38–39; own, 63
Price elasticity of supply, 59–61
Price leadership: barometric, 344–345; dominant firm, 343–344; effective, 345–346; low-cost firm, 342–343; models of, 341–345; small firm, 345; umbrella, 343
Price-maker, 150
Price policy, 309–310; under monopoly, 351
Price-taker, 150
Price theory, 2
Pricing: monopoly, 296–299, 300–301, 351, 361; target, 354
Producer surplus, 87
Product: average, 169; average physical, 169; marginal physical, 169; marginal revenue, 393, 395–396
Product differentiation, 288
Production: costs of, 28–29, 293; economies of large-scale, 286–287; monopoly, 296–301; society's use of scarce means of, 275
Production functions, 162–167, 186–187; Cobb-Douglas, 166–167, 431; constant-returns-to-scale, 172; homogeneous, 184; homogeneous of degree n, 212; homogeneous of degree one, 211–212; linear, 184; short-run, 167–181
Production possibility curve, 4–6
Productive services: demand for, 392–396; supply of, 419–428

Productivity: factor's physical, 408–409; real wages, money wages, and, 434–436
Productivity theory: criticisms of marginal, 429–432; marginal, 390
Product variation costs, 288
Profit maximization, 175–176, 252–253; illustration of short-run, 245–253; long-run, 356; under monopsony, 413; short-run, 242–245
Profit maximization assumption, criticisms of, 351–358
Profit-maximization hypothesis, qualified joint, 327–328
Profit-maximizing algorithm, proof of, 243–245
Profits, 452–455; artificial, 454; function of natural scarcity, 453–454; marginal, 244; meaning of, 214–215; significance of, 454–455; supply and, 217
Profits tax, 374–375
Proportionality: law of, 167–168, 218; qualifications of law of, 168
Proportions, variable, 167–175
Pure competition, 150–151; economic effects of, 273–277
Pure monopoly, 151–152, 283–285

Q

Qualified joint profit-maximization hypothesis, 327–328
Quantity demanded, 20; change in, 20
Quantity supplied, 20; change in, 27
Quasi-collective goods, 277
Quasi-rent, 446–448
Quasi supply curve, 272–273

R

Rank ordering, 97
Raw materials, ownership of, 288–289
Real wages, 434–436; unions and, 443–445
Rent, 445–449; contract, 445; economic, 446; quasi-, 446–448; transfer earnings contrasted with economic, 447
Research and technological progress, 287. *See also* Technological progress
Reservation price, 15

Resources, 169; law of supply and demand in market for, 388–389; managing scarce, 3–4; monopoly and allocation of, 362–365; natural, 423

Returns to fixed factors, capitalization of, 267–268

Returns to scale: algebraic formulation of, 184–185; causes of, 185; constant, 172; decreasing, 233; increasing, 233

Revealed preference approach, 96

Revealed preference theory, 143–147

Revenue: average, 45; elasticity and, 45–51; marginal, 46; sales, 293; social, 278; total, 45, 65–66

Ridge line, 199–202

S

Sales costs, 288

Sales maximization, constrained, 354–356, 382–383

Sales revenue, under monopoly, 293–295

Satisficing, 353–354

Scale line, 205

Scarcity, 1; function of profits from natural, 453–454

Search, economics of, 88–89

Selling cost curve, 316–322

Selling costs, 316–322

Seriatim method, 75

Shadow supply curve, 272–273

Sherman Antitrust Act, 290

Short-run: monopolistic competition in, 311; monopoly pricing and production in, 296–299

Short-run competitive industry's supply curve, 257–259

Short-run cost functions, 217–230, 237–238

Short-run equilibria, firm and industry, 259–260

Short-run production functions, 167–181

Short-run profit maximization: illustration of three possible outcomes of, 245–253; rules for, 242–245; three possible outcomes of, 242–243

Short-run relations, long-run relations and, 196–199

Short-run supply curve, competitive firm's, 254–255

Single-tax movement, 449

Slope: negative, 23; positive, 30

Slutsky method, 131–133

Small firm price leadership, 345

Social costs, 278

Social revenue, 278

Specific tax, 371

Static equilibrium differentials, dynamic disequilibrium vs., 425–428

Stock demand, 15

Stock demand curve, 16

Stock-dominated market, 14–20

Stock supply, 15

Substitutability, 98–99

Substitutes, 111; gross, 55, 64

Substitution: elasticity of, 194–195; law of diminishing marginal rate of, 101; principle of, 164–165, 179

Substitution approach, 92–93

Substitution effect, 84–85, 130–136, 179, 207–208

Superior boundary, 144; constructing the, 144–145

Superior good, 24, 57, 64

Supply, 20; change in, 27; conditions for factor, 428–429; control over, 376; costs, profits and, 217; determinants of, 27–28; elasticity of, 37; joint, 29–30; law of, 30–31; linear elasticity of, 65; mathematical notes on elasticity of, 65–66; price elasticity of, 59–61; proof of linear elasticity of, 61; stock, 15

Supply and demand: analysis of, 31–35; law of, 31; in resource market, 388–389

Supply curve, 26; competitive firm's short-run, 254–255; competitive industry's short-run, 257–259; industry, 28, 261; linear, 65–66; long-run, 265–267; long-run industry, 268–273; market, 28–29; normal, 30; quasi, 272–273; shifts in, 255–256; virtual, 272–273

Supply elasticity, 59; graphic demonstration of, 60–61

Supply of factors: in particular uses, 423–424; total, 420

Supply of human effort, 420–423

Supply of labor, decrease in, 438
Supply of labor services, 139–141
Supply of productive services, 417–428
Supply side of the market, 26–30
Surplus: concept of, 449; consumer, 85–87, 94–95, 136–137; producer, 87
Sweezy's kinked demand curve model, 334–336
Symmetry, factor, 176–178
Symmetry assumption, 310

T

Tangency solution, 311
Target pricing, 354
Taxation: under competition, 373; under monopoly, 383–385; as monopoly control, 371–375
Taxes, 291; ad valorem, 371; fixed, 371; lump-sum, 371, 373; per-unit, 372–373; profits, 374–375; single, 449; specific, 371; variable, 371
Technical efficiency, 163–164
Technical optimum rate of output, 230
Technological progress, 154, 208–209; importance of, 165; monopoly and, 361–362; research and, 287
Theory, economic, 8–11
Third-party effects, 277
Time, production function and, 165–166
Total cost curves, 218–221
Total costs, 220–221; average, 225
Total fixed costs, 218–219
Total revenue, 45, 65–66
Total spending test of elasticity, 39–41
Total utility, 70
Total variable costs, 219–220
Trademarks, 292
Transfer earnings, economic rent contrasted with, 447
Transitional differences, 425
Triple equality, 268–272, 276–277

U

Ultraempiricism, 7

Umbrella price leadership, 343
Uniformity assumption, 310
Unions: growth of, 437–438; monopsony and economic effect of, 440–441; real wages and, 443–445; wage raises and, 438–443
Unitary elasticity, 38, 41
Utility: cardinal, 69–70, 85–91, 117–119; concept of, 67–70; ex ante, 67; expected, 67; ex post, 67; interpersonal comparisons of, 87–88; law of diminishing marginal, 70–72; marginal, 70; ordinal, 69–70, 117–119, 136–142; total, 70
Utility maximization, 74–79, 353; with indifference curves, 115–116
Utils, 69

V

Value, present discounted capitalized, 450
Value of marginal product, 275
Variable costs: average, 223–225; total, 219–220
Variable factor, 163
Variable proportions, 167–175
Variable tax, 371
Virtual supply curve, 272–273
Von Neumann-Morgenstern measurement technique, 96

W

Wage determination, 434–436
Wages: collective bargaining and raises in, 439–440; effect on employment of changes in, 441–442; market structure and specific, 436; minimum, 442–443; money, 434–436; real, 434-436; unions and real, 443–445; ways unions try to raise, 438–443
Wage-work curve, 139
Walrasian approach, 82–84
Welfare loss, 363